Lecture Notes in Computer Science　　　10274

Commenced Publication in 1973
Founding and Former Series Editors:
Gerhard Goos, Juris Hartmanis, and Jan van Leeuwen

Editorial Board

David Hutchison
　Lancaster University, Lancaster, UK
Takeo Kanade
　Carnegie Mellon University, Pittsburgh, PA, USA
Josef Kittler
　University of Surrey, Guildford, UK
Jon M. Kleinberg
　Cornell University, Ithaca, NY, USA
Friedemann Mattern
　ETH Zurich, Zurich, Switzerland
John C. Mitchell
　Stanford University, Stanford, CA, USA
Moni Naor
　Weizmann Institute of Science, Rehovot, Israel
C. Pandu Rangan
　Indian Institute of Technology, Madras, India
Bernhard Steffen
　TU Dortmund University, Dortmund, Germany
Demetri Terzopoulos
　University of California, Los Angeles, CA, USA
Doug Tygar
　University of California, Berkeley, CA, USA
Gerhard Weikum
　Max Planck Institute for Informatics, Saarbrücken, Germany

More information about this series at http://www.springer.com/series/7409

Sakae Yamamoto (Ed.)

Human Interface and the Management of Information

Supporting Learning, Decision-Making and Collaboration

19th International Conference, HCI International 2017
Vancouver, BC, Canada, July 9–14, 2017
Proceedings, Part II

 Springer

Editor
Sakae Yamamoto
Tokyo University of Science
Tokyo
Japan

ISSN 0302-9743 ISSN 1611-3349 (electronic)
Lecture Notes in Computer Science
ISBN 978-3-319-58523-9 ISBN 978-3-319-58524-6 (eBook)
DOI 10.1007/978-3-319-58524-6

Library of Congress Control Number: 2017939721

LNCS Sublibrary: SL3 – Information Systems and Applications, incl. Internet/Web, and HCI

Printed on acid-free paper

This Springer imprint is published by Springer Nature
The registered company is Springer International Publishing AG
The registered company address is: Gewerbestrasse 11, 6330 Cham, Switzerland

Foreword

The 19th International Conference on Human–Computer Interaction, HCI International 2017, was held in Vancouver, Canada, during July 9–14, 2017. The event incorporated the 15 conferences/thematic areas listed on the following page.

A total of 4,340 individuals from academia, research institutes, industry, and governmental agencies from 70 countries submitted contributions, and 1,228 papers have been included in the proceedings. These papers address the latest research and development efforts and highlight the human aspects of design and use of computing systems. The papers thoroughly cover the entire field of human–computer interaction, addressing major advances in knowledge and effective use of computers in a variety of application areas. The volumes constituting the full set of the conference proceedings are listed on the following pages.

I would like to thank the program board chairs and the members of the program boards of all thematic areas and affiliated conferences for their contribution to the highest scientific quality and the overall success of the HCI International 2017 conference.

This conference would not have been possible without the continuous and unwavering support and advice of the founder, Conference General Chair Emeritus and Conference Scientific Advisor Prof. Gavriel Salvendy. For his outstanding efforts, I would like to express my appreciation to the communications chair and editor of *HCI International News*, Dr. Abbas Moallem.

April 2017   Constantine Stephanidis

HCI International 2017 Thematic Areas and Affiliated Conferences

Thematic areas:

- Human–Computer Interaction (HCI 2017)
- Human Interface and the Management of Information (HIMI 2017)

Affiliated conferences:

- 17th International Conference on Engineering Psychology and Cognitive Ergonomics (EPCE 2017)
- 11th International Conference on Universal Access in Human–Computer Interaction (UAHCI 2017)
- 9th International Conference on Virtual, Augmented and Mixed Reality (VAMR 2017)
- 9th International Conference on Cross-Cultural Design (CCD 2017)
- 9th International Conference on Social Computing and Social Media (SCSM 2017)
- 11th International Conference on Augmented Cognition (AC 2017)
- 8th International Conference on Digital Human Modeling and Applications in Health, Safety, Ergonomics and Risk Management (DHM 2017)
- 6th International Conference on Design, User Experience and Usability (DUXU 2017)
- 5th International Conference on Distributed, Ambient and Pervasive Interactions (DAPI 2017)
- 5th International Conference on Human Aspects of Information Security, Privacy and Trust (HAS 2017)
- 4th International Conference on HCI in Business, Government and Organizations (HCIBGO 2017)
- 4th International Conference on Learning and Collaboration Technologies (LCT 2017)
- Third International Conference on Human Aspects of IT for the Aged Population (ITAP 2017)

Conference Proceedings Volumes Full List

Human Interface and the Management of Information

Program Board Chair(s): **Sakae Yamamoto, Japan**

- Takako Akakura, Japan
- Yumi Asahi, Japan
- Linda R. Elliott, USA
- Shin'ichi Fukuzumi, Japan
- Michitaka Hirose, Japan
- Yasushi Ikei, Japan
- Yen-Yu Kang, Taiwan
- Keiko Kasamatsu, Japan
- Daiji Kobayashi, Japan
- Kentaro Kotani, Japan
- Hiroyuki Miki, Japan
- Hirohiko Mori, Japan
- Shogo Nishida, Japan
- Robert Proctor, USA
- Ryosuke Saga, Japan
- Katsunori Shimohara, Japan
- Jiro Tanaka, Japan
- Takahito Tomoto, Japan
- Kim-Phuong Vu, USA
- Tomio Watanabe, Japan

The full list with the Program Board Chairs and the members of the Program Boards of all thematic areas and affiliated conferences is available online at:

http://www.hci.international/board-members-2017.php

HCI International 2018

The 20th International Conference on Human–Computer Interaction, HCI International 2018, will be held jointly with the affiliated conferences in Las Vegas, NV, USA, at Caesars Palace, July 15–20, 2018. It will cover a broad spectrum of themes related to human–computer interaction, including theoretical issues, methods, tools, processes, and case studies in HCI design, as well as novel interaction techniques, interfaces, and applications. The proceedings will be published by Springer. More information is available on the conference website: http://2018.hci.international/.

General Chair
Prof. Constantine Stephanidis
University of Crete and ICS-FORTH
Heraklion, Crete, Greece
E-mail: general_chair@hcii2018.org

http://2018.hci.international/

Contents – Part II

Recommender and Decision Support Systems

Supporting Collaboration and User Communities

Case Studies

Contents – Part I

Information and Interaction Design

Knowledge and Service Management

Multimodal and Embodied Interaction

Information and Learning

A Problem-Solving Process Model
for Learning Intellectual Property Law Using
Logic Expression: Application
from a Proposition to a Predicate Logic

Takako Akakura[1(✉)], Takahito Tomoto[2], and Koichiro Kato[3]

[1] Faculty of Engineering, Tokyo University of Science,
6-3-1 Niijuku, Katsushika-ku, Tokyo 125-8585, Japan
akakura@rs.tus.ac.jp
[2] Faculty of Engineering, Tokyo Polytechnic University,
11583 Iiyama, Atsugi-Shi 243-0297, Japan
t.tomoto@cs.t-kougei.ac.jp
[3] Graduate School of Innovation Management, Kanazawa Institute
of Technology, 1-3-4 Atago, Minato-Ku, Tokyo 105-0002, Japan
kkato@neptune.kanazawa-it.ac.jp

Abstract. We have previously proposed a problem-solving process model using logical expressions, based on the observation that legal statements can be described using logical expressions when considering the problem-solving process model used by engineering students in the study of law. However, propositional logic alone has a limited range of application to practice problems, and so here we examine the description of practice problems using predicate logic by extending propositional logic to first-order predicate logic, and consider the effectiveness of this approach.

Keywords: Problem-solving process · Learning of intellectual property law · Predicate logic

1 Introduction

More than a decade has passed since the establishment of the Intellectual Property Basic Act in Japan. During this time, the pace of globalization has intensified and there are increasing opportunities for foreign companies to operate in Japan. In this context, industry has expressed a desire that students acquire basic knowledge of intellectual property while at university, but the adoption of education in intellectual property law is still far from adequate [1]. Although engineering departments recognize the importance of intellectual property training, it has been difficult to establish many lectures on intellectual property because of its relationship with other courses. In a survey that we conducted looking at the syllabi of engineering departments in universities around Japan, we found that about two academic units (30 h of class time) is the best that can be managed, and there were also cases where several hours were allocated to teaching intellectual property as part of ethics courses [2–4]. Thus, an

© Springer International Publishing AG 2017
S. Yamamoto (Ed.): HIMI 2017, Part II, LNCS 10274, pp. 3–14, 2017.
DOI: 10.1007/978-3-319-58524-6_1

important question is whether it is possible to prepare teaching materials to enable students to efficiently learn intellectual property law while also raising their motivation to learn. Against this background, we have developed an e-learning system for intellectual property law as a study support system to enable students to study on their own outside of regular teaching hours for the two academic credits (30 h) of intellectual property law coursework offered by engineering departments.

In this paper, we first analyze the relationship between the frequency with which students use our developed system and their motivation to learn. We then propose a problem-solving process model for engineering students learning intellectual property law. The learning system utilizing this model is still under development but involves the use of logical expressions to represent legal articles in intellectual property law so that solutions can be derived automatically by a computer and feedback on errors can be provided to the students by comparing the logical expression for their entered solutions with the logical expression generated computationally and looking at the difference [2–5]. The aim of this paper is to consider how this system can be further developed to make it more suitable as a learning system for engineering students.

2 Example of Intellectual Property Law Training in an Engineering Department

2.1 Training System Used so Far

In a major offered by the engineering department of a certain university, two academic units (30 h) of classes were allocated to intellectual property law. The subject is optional and students can freely choose whether to take it. Almost none of the students have any prior knowledge of law, and so the subject matter consists of 6 h of lectures on basic law in general, followed by lectures on industrial property law (the Patent Act, the Utility Model Act, the Design Act and the Trademark Act) and copyright law over the remaining 24 h of classes. Every year, all lectures are recorded on video and made available to course participants outside class hours as an e-learning system. The lecture notes handed out in class can also be downloaded via the e-Learning System. The e-learning system is for self-study and supplementary lessons, and its use is optional.

2.2 Course Evaluation by Students

We conducted a survey (n = 53) about the 2013 intellectual property law course [6]. The survey content relevant to this section are as follows. All items were scored on a four-point scale.

(1) Motivation to learn prior to the course (1 = "none" 4 = "high")
(2) Sense of value after 30 h of lectures (1 = "none" to 4 = "high")
(3) Satisfaction after 30 h of lectures (1 = "none" to 4 = "high")
(4) Desire to continue learning after 30 h of lectures (1 = "none" to 4 = "high")
(5) How often did you use the e-learning system? (1 = "not at all" to 4 = "very often" as well as an option for "only to print out lecture notes")

(6) Evaluation of using the e-learning system (1 = "not at all useful" to 4 = "extremely useful"; only assessed for students who answered either "fairly often" or "very often" in question (5))

In relation to motivation to learn, Fig. 1 shows a comparison of the results of questions (1) and (4). Five students answered "none" before the lectures started but no student answered "none" afterward.

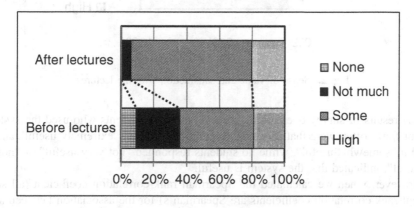

Fig. 1. Change in motivation to learn before and after lectures

As shown in Table 1, 23 students increased their motivation to learn after the lectures (the shaded cells), while 1 student remained at a low level (2→2), 25 students remained at a high level (3→3 or 4→4) and 4 students had lower motivation after the lectures (3→2 or 4→3). Overall, most students showed increased motivation to learn after the lectures.

Figure 2 shows the results for "sense of value" (2) and "satisfaction" (3).

Turning to survey question (5), we found that 43 of the 52 respondents used the system "some", "fairly often", and "very often".

Table 1. Comparison of motivation to learn before and after lectures

		Motivation after lectures				
		1	2	3	4	Total
	1	0	1	2	2	5
	2	0	1	12	1	14
Motivation before lectures	3	0	3	16	5	24
	4	0	0	1	9	10
	Total	0	5	32	17	54

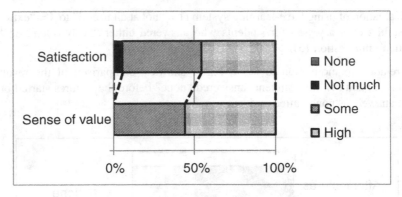

Fig. 2. Sense of value and satisfaction with the lectures

The results of survey question (6) directed at those students who used the system very or fairly often were that 20 students found the system "extremely useful" and 6 found it "somewhat useful", while no students responded "not very useful" or "not at all useful", indicated that the system is useful.

However, when we calculated the Spearman rank-correlation coefficient (all subsequent rank-correlation coefficients are Spearman's) for the association between survey questions (1) to (4) and question (5) on usage frequency (Table 2), none of the correlations were significant, meaning that students who use the system often do not necessarily have high satisfaction or motivation to learn.

Table 2. Correlations between frequency of system usage and other assessments

	Rank-correlation coefficient
Motivation to learn before lectures	0.144
Sense of value	0.159
Satisfaction	0.168
Motivation to learn after lectures	0.212

Table 3 shows the rank-correlation coefficients for survey questions other than questions on usage frequency, namely, questions (1) to (4). Given that both "sense of value" and "satisfaction" are assessments made after the course completed it is perhaps not surprising that these are significantly correlated with motivation to learn after the course.

2.3 System Issues

We conducted the same survey in 2014 and 2015, obtaining very similar results [2, 3]. Summarizing these results, we found that overall the sense of the value and satisfaction with the course was high, with most students finishing the course with higher

Table 3. Rank-correlation coefficients for each pair of assessments

	Motivation before lectures	Sense of value	Satisfaction	Motivation after lectures
Motivation before lectures	1	0.401**	0.205	0.386**
Sense of value	0.401**	1	0.616**	0.599**
Satisfaction	0.205	0.616**	1	0.443**
Motivation after lectures	0.386**	0.599**	0.443**	1

*Test of no correlation *p<0.05,**p<0.01*

motivation to learn than when they began. The e-learning system that we have been operating was assessed as useful, but students who used the system often did not necessarily have high satisfaction or sense of value. As discussed above, despite the importance with which intellectual property training is regarded in engineering departments, not much time can be allocated to teaching it, and so it would be desirable to develop a system that can increase students' motivation to learn. With his in mind, we hoped to develop a system that takes into account the cognitive and problem-solving processes of engineering students.

3 Problem-Solving Process Model in Intellectual Property Law

3.1 Comparison with the Problem-Solving Process in Physics

Hirashima et al. [7] have modeled the problem-solving process in physics in three stages:

1. the process of generating a surface structure from the problem text;
2. the formalization process of generating a formal structure from the surface structure; and
3. the solution-derivation process of generating the target structure (including the solution) from the formal structure using quantitative functions.

However, problem questions in intellectual property law do not have quantitative relationships. This prompted us to define and propose a problem-solving process whereby logical expressions are used to derive solutions from formal structures [2, 5], taking advantage of the fact that legal statements can be represented using logical expressions [8].

3.2 Problem-Solving Process Model for Patent Law

The constraint structure here differs from the one in physics. Problem questions in physics have quantitative relationships. However, these kinds of relationships cannot be established for quiz problems in patent law. This means that it is necessary to define a constraint structure for deriving new information based on relationships.

There have been many studies (e.g., [8] to [11]) looking at converting legal statements into logical expressions that can be subjected to logical operations. Tanaka et al [9] found that legal statements are made up of a topic, conditions, object, content, and stipulations with the following structure:

$$\text{Topic} \wedge \text{Conditions} \Rightarrow \text{Object} \wedge \text{Content} \wedge \text{Stipulations}$$

These studies are based on the concept that legal statements have a prototypical structure and assume that legal statements can be converted into a particular structure because "Legal clauses are a form of natural language but can also be regarded as a controlled language that is employed intentionally" [10]. The goal of these studies is to use these structures in search systems for legal clauses and the like. Referring to these earlier studies, we considered that the conversion of legal statements to logical expressions could be utilized to support learning. That is, we believed that the relationships between properties in patent law can be represented using logical expressions, thereby enabling the same kind of learning support as for physics.

3.3 Example of a Logical Structure from Patent Law

Figure 3 shows the requirements for issuing a patent. The right-hand side of Fig. 3 lists clauses ① through ⑦ on which these requirements are based. Figure 4 shows how the details of how the logical expressions for clauses ①, ②, and ③ have been put together, resulting in Expression (1). Similarly Fig. 5 shows how Expression (2) is derived. Clauses ④ through ⑦ produce expressions (3) through (6), which are then combined to produce the final constraint structure in the same way as shown for expressions (1) and (2) in Figs. 4 and 5.

Clauses ④ to ⑦ can be annotated as follows:

④ Not obvious	$I \rightarrow \bar{I}$	(3)
⑤ Earliest application filed	$J \rightarrow \bar{J}$	(4)
⑥ Does not harm the public interest	$K \rightarrow \bar{K}$	(5)
⑦ Description filed according to regulations	$L \rightarrow L$	(6)

and so Figure 3 can be summarized as

$$(1) \wedge (2) \wedge (3) \wedge (4) \wedge (5) \wedge (6) \Rightarrow \textbf{Patented invention} \qquad (7)$$

Consider the practice question given in Sect. 3.1, namely, "John has created a special method for treating cancer patients. (The rest is omitted)" In the practice problem, a method for diagnosing, treating, or operating on human beings should be

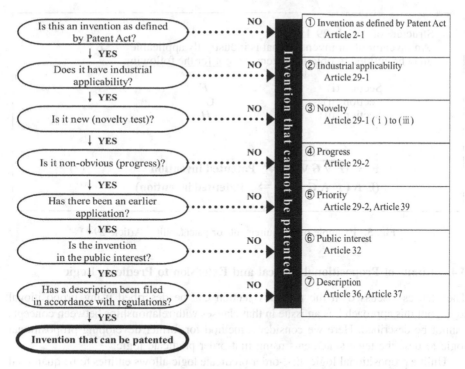

Fig. 3. Requirements for patentability

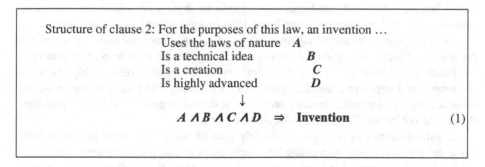

Fig. 4. Requirements for invention

made widely available on humanitarian grounds and thus "has no industrial applicability", so we can state that the invention is not patentable (due to insufficient properties).

When answering a question on intellectual property law, a student assembles a logical expression. If the student's answer is incorrect, it is possible to work out where the mistakes are made by looking at the difference between the correct logical expression and the logical expression assembled by the student. It should be possible to create a learning support system that systematizes this approach.

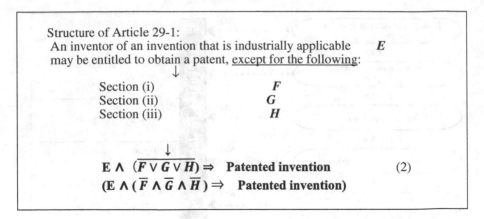

Fig. 5. Example of a requirement for patentability (Article 29-1)

3.4 Limits of Propositional Logical and Extension to Predicate Logic

The clauses discussed in the previous section can be described using propositional logic, but this approach has an issue in that clauses with relationships between concepts cannot be described. Here we consider a method for further developing propositional logic to describe legal statements using first-order predicate logic.

Unlike propositional logic, first-order predicate logic allows entities to be quantified using existence quantifiers ($\exists$), universal quantifiers ($\forall$), and so on. Predicate logic that allows quantification of predicates and functions in addition to entity quantification is called second-order predicate logic, while predicate logic with additional generalizations is called higher-order predicate logic. First-order predicate logic can express such things as the properties and inclusion relations of various concepts, and—in contrast to propositional logic—is capable of expressions that go inside their respective concepts.

Practice problems on legal topics often involve describing relationships between the subject and object in a way that goes inside the concept, and so by using first-order predicate logic to formalize practice problems, it should be possible to handle problems that could not be handled using propositional logic.

Legal statements have been extensively studied using first-order predicate logic since the 1980s [11]. By expressing legal statements in computer-readable code, these studies have been applied to legal expert systems, enabling legal inferences and making it to possible to check legal systems for consistency. When concepts are meticulously defined as in these studies, it seems likely that the concepts thus defined can be reused in formalizations for other problems.

However, to date there has been no research on the possibility of first representing law using first-order predicate logic (representing combinations of the legal articles to be studied) before having students studying law express their understanding using first-order predicate logic (entering this into the system) and then providing learners with feedback based on the difference between the two expressions. Moreover, the research on legal statements using first-order predicate logic that has been conducted to date does not consider the concepts and expressions used in the text of practice

in(Patent Act) ∧ def(invention, x) ⇒
def(x, technical idea) ∧ do(x, uses, laws of nature) ∧ def(x, creation) ∧ def(x, advanced
)

Fig. 6. Formalizing a clause (Article 2-1 of the Patent Act)

problems, and it will therefore be necessary to reconsider the formalizations and expression formats used in order to apply first-order predicate logic in a learning system.

Accordingly, in this study we formalize legal statements using the relationship expressions used in problem text. In this study, we refer to the functions representing the relationships between multiple concepts as "predicates" and prescribe the formalization of legal statements for the learning support system in this study as follows.

For example, Article 2-1 of the Patent Act states "'Invention' in this Act means the highly advanced creation of technical ideas utilizing the laws of nature". In this study, this formula is formalized as shown in Fig. 6.

Here x is the target creation, while in(x) indicates that this statement has full force and effect in the articles of act x. Similarly, define(x,y) indicates the relationship "x is y" and d(x,y,z) represents a predicate of the form "x does y to z." These predicates correspond to problems such as "What is ...?" and "What does ... do?"

We perform the same kind of formalization for problems. For example, a practice problem such as

In the Patent Act, inventions use (   )

is formalized as shown in Fig. 7.

Moreover, in response to a question such as "In the Patent Act, inventions use ( )," by simultaneously inferring the statement "An inventor of an invention that is industrially applicable may be entitled to obtain a patent for the said invention, except for the following [inventions]," we can infer that patents are for inventions and inventions use the laws of nature.

For similar practice problems based on the same pattern, we can also express the predicate using a similar format. For example, in relation to the duration of patent rights, various laws make prescriptions as follows.

- Article 67-1 of the Patent Act:
  The duration of a patent right shall expire after a period of 20 years from the filing date of the patent application.

in(Patent Act) ∧ def(invention, x) ⇒ do(x, uses, y)

Fig. 7. Formalizing a practice problem

- Article 15 of the Utility Model Act:
  The duration of a utility model right shall expire after a period of 10 years from the filing date of the application for utility model registration.
- Article 21-1 of the Design Act:
  The duration of a design right (excluding design right of a Related Design) shall expire after a period of 20 years from the date of registration of its establishment.
- Article 19-1 of the Trademark Act:
  The duration of a trademark right shall expire after 10 years from the date of registration of establishment of such right.

Suppose that here we establish a function called "Term", for example, and that this function is a predicate indicating that x (the duration of patent rights) is the period starting from *start* (the date when the patent was filed) and until *end* (a period of 20 years), then such a predicate expression can be represented as shown in Fig. 8.

$$\text{Term}(x, \quad start, \quad end)$$

Fig. 8. Predicate expressing the term of duration

By extending propositional logic to first-order predicate logic in this way we can expect to be able to handle a greater number of different types of problems using various formalizations or combinations of formalizations.

3.5 Potential for Improving Understand Through Logical Representations

These kinds of logical expression relationships seem likely to come naturally to engineering students, and when we asked 17 students taking classes in intellectual

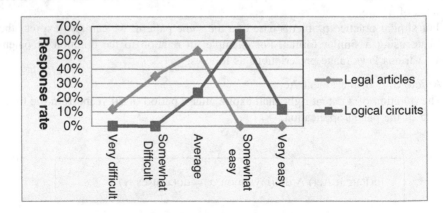

Fig. 9. Clauses versus logical circuits

property law to compare logical expressions (logical circuits) against a collection of legal texts in terms of which were easier to understand, we obtained the results in Fig. 9. From this, it is clear that, for engineering students (who tend to be good at logical thinking), the methodology of representing legal statements using logical expressions and logical circuits is easier to understand than simply reading legal articles. Thus, we can expect that a learning support system that uses this kind of logical structure to be very effective for enhancing students' understanding.

4 Discussion

In this paper, we have considered the effectiveness of a learning support system that uses a problem-solving process model to model the way that engineering students solve problems in the process of learning intellectual property law. The result was that describing intellectual property law using logical expressions is easy for engineering students to understand, and so the next step required is to continue to develop the learning support system by increasing the number predicate expressions.

Acknowledgments. This research was partially supported by a Grant-in-Aid for Scientific Research (B) (#16H03086) from Japan Society for the Promotion of Science (JSPS), and also by Service Science, Solutions and Foundation Integrated Research Program (S3FIRE), Research Institute of Science and Technology for Society (RISTEX), Japan Science and Technology Agency (JST).

References

1. Iguchi, Y., Sera, K., Matsuoka, M.,Muramatsu, H.,Kagohara, H., et al.: Present status and future trends of intellectual property education. Patent, vol. 64, no. 14, pp. 8–18 (2011). (in Japanese)
2. Akakura, T., Ishii, T.: Development and evaluation of a self-learning support system for patent act suited to the current state of intellectual property education in engineering departments. In: Proceedings of 2016 IEEE International Conference on Teaching, Assessment, and Learning for Engineering (TALE 2016), pp. 128–133 (2016)
3. Akakura, T., Ishii, T., Kato, K.: The current state of intellectual property education in engineering departments of universities and development of learning support system. IEICE Technical report, vol. 116, no. 351, pp. 55–60 (2016). (in Japanese)
4. Akakura, T., Ishii, T., Kato, K.: Proposal of a problem-solving process model for learning intellectual property law using forst-order predicate logic and development of a model-based learning support system. In: 11th Annual International Technology, Education and Development Conference(INTED 2017)(2017)
5. Akakura, T., Eshita, K., Tomoto, T.: A computation-process model and system for the study of intellectual property law. IEICE Technical report, vol. 115, no. 50, pp. 21–26 (2015). (in Japanese)
6. Akakura, T., Tomoto, T.: Change in motivation of engineering students to learn about intellectual property law. IEICE Technical report, Education Technology, vol. 114, no. 121, pp. 27–32 (2014). (in Japanese)

7. Hirashima, T., Azuma, S., Kashihara, A., Toyoda, J.: A formulation of auxiliary problems. J. Japan. Soc. Artif. Intell. **10**(3), 413–420 (1995). (in Japanese)
8. Nobuoka, S., Nakamura, M., Shimazu, A.: Translating legal sentences into logical forms. In: Proceedings of the 13th Annual Meeting of the Association for Natural Language Processing, pp. 254–257 (2007). (in Japanese)
9. Tanaka, K., Kawazoe, I., Narita, H.: Standard structure of legal provisions. IPSJ SIG Technical reports, vol. 93, no. 79, pp. 79–86 (1993)
10. Kawazoe, I., Maki, T., Tanaka, K.: Standard structure of legal provisions (2) legal knowledge processing by standard structure. IPSJ SIG Notes **95**(52), 97–104 (1995). (in Japanese)
11. Shimazu, A.: Language analysis of legal documents: research on legal engineering. IEICE Technical report, vol. 110, no. 245, pp. 1–6 (2010). (in Japanese)

Predictive Algorithm for Converting Linear Strings to General Mathematical Formulae

Tetsuo Fukui[✉] and Shizuka Shirai

Mukogawa Women's University, Nishinomiya, Japan
fukui@mukogawa-u.ac.jp

Abstract. Standard input methods for entering mathematical expressions on digital devices are cumbersome. Our goal is to develop an intelligent mathematical input method that allows users to input mathematical expressions using colloquial linear strings. This paper presents the evaluation of an improved predictive algorithm for converting linear strings into general mathematical formulae. The results of our evaluation show that the prediction accuracy of the top ten ranking for our method is 85.2%.

1 Introduction

In recent years, computer-aided assessment (CAA) systems have been used in mathematics education. However, current mathematical input methods for digital devices are cumbersome for novice learners [1,2].

To reduce the effort required to input mathematical expressions, we propose an interactive conversion input method that uses linear strings in a colloquial style [3,4]. In this method, a list of candidates for the desired mathematical expression is shown in a "what you see is what you get" (WYSIWYG) editor. After all the elements are interactively chosen, the desired expression is formed. We have previously shown that an interface implementing this method is 1.2 to 1.6 times faster than standard interfaces [5]. However, users must convert each element into the appropriate colloquial-style mathematical strings in the correct order from left to right [6].

We have previously addressed this shortcoming and proposed a predictive algorithm [7–9] for converting linear strings into complete mathematical expressions using a perceptron [10]. The results of an evaluation that involved the entry of quadratic polynomials achieved a prediction accuracy of 96.2% for the top-ten ranking. The mean CPU time for predicting each mathematical expression was 0.44 s.

However, it is not clear whether this algorithm results in the same high level of prediction accuracy for more general mathematical formulae. In fact, the results of our previous investigation showed that the prediction accuracy for complicated mathematical formulae decreased to approximately 70% and the prediction time increased remarkably, to more than 6 min in some cases.

This study aims to address these shortcomings by extending the previous algorithm to a wider field of mathematics. We present the improved algorithm

© Springer International Publishing AG 2017
S. Yamamoto (Ed.): HIMI 2017, Part II, LNCS 10274, pp. 15–28, 2017.
DOI: 10.1007/978-3-319-58524-6_2

and the results of its evaluation using a dataset containing 4,000 mathematical formulae. The prediction accuracy of the top-ten ranking for this improved method is 85.2%.

2 Predictive Conversion

In this section, we review our previously proposed predictive conversion system [7–9]. First, we define the linear string of a mathematical expression to be input by the user. We describe an intelligent predictive conversion system of such linear strings in Sect. 2.2. In Sect. 2.3, we formulate a predictive algorithm using machine learning.

2.1 Linear String Rules

The rules for a linear mathematical string for a mathematical expression are as follows:

Definition 1 (Linear String Rules). *Set the key letters (or words) corresponding to the elements of a mathematical expression linearly in the order of the colloquial (read or spoken) style, without considering two-dimensional placement and delimiters.*

In other words, a key letter (or word) consists of the ASCII code(s) corresponding to the initial or clipped form (such as the LaTeX form) of the objective mathematical symbol; a single key often supports many mathematical symbols. For example, when a user wants to input θ^2, the linear string is denoted by "t2," where "t" represents the "theta" symbol. It is unnecessary to include the power sign (i.e., the caret letter (^)). The linear string denoting $\frac{3}{x^2-1}$ is "3/x2−1," where it is not necessary to include the denominator (which is generally the operand of an operator) in parentheses, because they are not printed.

Other representative cases are shown in Table 1. For example, the linear string for $e^{\pi x}$ is denoted by "epx." However, the linear string of the expressions $e_p x$, e^{px}, and $e^{\pi} x$ are also denoted by "epx." Hence, there are some ambiguities when representing mathematical expressions as linear strings using these rules.

2.2 A Predictive Conversion System

In 2015, we proposed a predictive algorithm [7,8] to convert linear string s into the most suitable mathematical expression y_p. For prediction purposes, we devised a method in which each candidate to be selected is ranked by its suitability. Our method uses the function $\text{Score}(y)$ to assign a score proportional to the occurrence probability of mathematical expression y, which enables us to predict candidate y_p, using (1), as the most suitable expression with the maximum score. Here, $Y(s)$ in (1) represents all possible mathematical expressions converted from s.

$$y_p \text{ s.t. } \text{Score}(y_p) = \max\{\text{Score}(y)|y \in Y(s)\} \tag{1}$$

Table 1. Examples of mathematical expressions using linear string rules.

Category	Linear strings	Math formulae
Variable	t	t or θ
Polynomial	x2 + 2x + 1	$x^2 + 2x + 1$
Fraction	3/4	$\frac{3}{4}$
Equation	(x−3)2 = 0	$(x-3)^2 = 0$
Square root	root2	$\sqrt{2}$
Trigonometric	cos2t	$\cos^2 \theta$
Logarithm	log10x	$\log_{10} x$
Exponent	epx	$e^{\pi x}$
Summation	sumk = 1nak	$\sum_{k=1}^{n} a_k$
Integral	intabf(x)dx	$\int_a^b f(x)dx$

Generally, any mathematical expression is represented by a tree structure consisting of nodes and edges, which correspond to the symbols and operating relations, respectively. In other words, any mathematical expression y is characterized by all the nodes and edges included in y. We identify each node or edge as a mathematical element in the formula.

First, all node elements of the mathematical expressions are classified into the nine categories listed in Table 2. Thus, a node element is characterized by (k, e, t), where k is the key letter (or word) of the mathematical symbol e that belongs to type $t(= N, V, P, A, B_L, B_R, C, Q, R,$ or $T)$ in Table 2. For example, the number 12 is characterized as ("12",12, N), the variable a as ("a", a, V), and the Greek letter π can either be characterized as ("pi", π, V) or ("p", π, V). As an example of an operator, ("/", $\frac{\triangle_1}{\triangle_2}, C$) represents a fraction symbol with input character "/", where $\triangle_1$ and $\triangle_2$ represent arbitrary operands.

An edge element, i.e. an operating relation, is characterized by (e_p, i, e_c), where the parent operator e_p operates the i-th operand whose top element is e_c. For example, expression $\frac{\pi}{12}$ consists of three nodes,

$$\{e_1, e_2, e_3\} := \{(\text{``}p\text{''}, \pi, V), (\text{``}/\text{''}, \frac{\triangle_1}{\triangle_2}, C), (\text{``}12\text{''}, 12, N)\}, \tag{2}$$

and the following two edges:

$$\{(e_2, 1, e_1), (e_2, 2, e_3)\}. \tag{3}$$

In this study, our prototype system implements a total of 509 mathematical symbols and 599 operators in node element table $\mathcal{D}$.

The totality $Y(s)$ of the mathematical expressions converted from s is calculated using Procedures 1–3 (cf. [4,7]), referring to node element table $\mathcal{D}$.

Table 2. Nine types of mathematical expressive structures

Math element type	Type codes	Examples
Number	N	3, 256
Variable, Symbol	V	a, x, α, θ, π
Prefix unary operator	P	$\sqrt{\triangle_1}$, $\sin \triangle_1$
Postfix unary operator	A	$\triangle_1'$, $\triangle_1^\circ$
Bracket	B_L, B_R	$(\triangle_1)$, $\{\triangle_1\}$, $\lvert\triangle_1\rvert$
Infix binary operator	C	$\triangle_1 + \triangle_2$, $\triangle_1 \times \triangle_2$, $\frac{\triangle_1}{\triangle_2}$
Prefix binary operator	Q	$\log_{\triangle_1} \triangle_2$
Prefix ternary operator	R	$\int_{\triangle_1}^{\triangle_2} \triangle_3$
Infix ternary operator	T	$\triangle_1 \overset{\triangle_2}{\to} \triangle_3$

$\triangle_1, \triangle_2$, and $\triangle_3$ represent operands.

Procedure 1. A linear string s is separated in the group of keywords defined in (4) using the parser in this system. All possible key separation vectors $(k_1, k_2, \cdots, k_K)$ are obtained by matching every part of s with a key in $\mathcal{D}$.

$$s = k_1 \uplus k_2 \uplus \cdots k_K \text{ where } (k_i, v_i, t_i) \in \mathcal{D}, i = 1, ..., K \qquad (4)$$

Procedure 2. Predictive expressive structures are fixed by analyzing all the key separation vectors of s and comparing the nine types of structures in Table 2.

Procedure 3. From the fixed structures corresponding to the operating relations between the nodes, we obtain $Y(s)$ by applying all possible combinations of mathematical elements belonging to each keyword in $\mathcal{D}$.

2.3 Predictive Algorithm

Let us assume that the occurrence probability of a certain mathematical element is proportional to its frequency of use. Then, the occurrence probability of mathematical expression y, which is a possible conversion from string s, is estimated from the total score of all the mathematical elements included in y. Given the numbering of each element from 1 to the total number of elements F_{total}, let θ_f be the score of the $f(= 1, \cdots, F_{total})$-th element, and let $x_f(y)$ be the number of times the f-th element is included in y. Then, Score(y) in (1) is estimated by (5), where $\boldsymbol{\theta}^T = (\theta_1, \cdots, \theta_{F_{total}})$ denotes the score vector and $\boldsymbol{X} = (x_f(y))$, $f = 1, \cdots, F_{total}$ is an F_{total}-dimensional vector.

$$h_\theta\left(\boldsymbol{X}(y)\right) = \boldsymbol{\theta}^T \cdot \boldsymbol{X}(y) = \sum_{f=1}^{F_{total}} \theta_f x_f(y) \qquad (5)$$

Equation (5) is in agreement with the hypothesis function of linear regression and $\boldsymbol{X}(y)$ is referred to as the characteristic vector of y. To solve our linear regression problem and predict the occurrence probability of a mathematical expression, we conduct supervised machine learning on the m elements of training dataset $\{(s_1, y_1), (s_2, y_2), \cdots, (s_m, y_m)\}$. To obtain the optimized score vector, our learning algorithm utilizes the following four-step procedure:

Step 1. Initialization $\boldsymbol{\theta} = \boldsymbol{0}$, $i = 1$
Step 2. Decision regarding a candidate.

$$y_p \text{ s.t. } h_\theta \left(\boldsymbol{X}(y_p) \right) = \max\{h_\theta \left(\boldsymbol{X}(y) \right) | y \in Y(s_i)\} \tag{6}$$

Step 3. Training parameter.
  if$(y_p \neq y_i)$ {

$$\begin{aligned} &\text{if}(\theta_f < S_{\max})\{\theta_f := \theta_f + 2 \quad \text{for} \quad \{f \leq F_{total} | x_f(y_i) > 0\}\} \\ &\qquad\qquad \theta_{\bar{f}} := \theta_{\bar{f}} - 1 \quad \text{for} \quad \{\bar{f} \leq F_{total} | x_{\bar{f}}(y_p) > 0\} \end{aligned} \tag{7}$$

  }

Step 4. if$(i < m)$\{ $i = i + 1$; repeat from **Step 2**}
       else { Output $\boldsymbol{\theta}$ and end}

This learning algorithm is simple and is similar to a structured perceptron used for natural language processing (NLP) [10]. However, in our previous study [7], we revised the increase weight from one to two in (7) to avoid negative score learning. When two different candidates belonging to the same key appear in the training dataset, e.g., the pair a and α, their scores change into a positive value from a negative value or vice versa; even if a candidate with a negative score has occurred many times, it has lower priority than one with a score of zero. Here, $S_{\max}$ in (7) is a suitable upper bound for any mathematical element score, preventing the score parameter from continuing to increase as the algorithm runs.

3   Main Algorithm

In previous investigations [7–9] of the learning algorithm in Sect. 2.3, limiting the entered expressions to quadratic polynomials resulted in a prediction accuracy of 96.2% for the top-ten ranking. The mean CPU time for predicting each mathematical expression was 0.44 s.

However, the algorithm in Sect. 2.3 did not provide the same high performance given more general mathematical formulae. In fact, the results of our investigation using a dataset of 4000 math formulae from broader fields of mathematics (cf. Sect. 4.1) showed that prediction accuracy decreased to approximately 70% and prediction time increased considerably; for a complicated mathematical formula, prediction took more than 6 min.

As the reason for the decrease in prediction accuracy and increase in prediction time, we found the following three challenges in predicting general mathematical expressions.

1. Scores can increase based on the number of elements, instead of their priority.
2. If $Y(s)$ includes the same mathematical expressions, but has different internal tree structures, machine learning does not work well.
3. The number of complicated mathematical expressions, which lead to long prediction times, increases when general mathematics fields are considered.

To overcome these shortcomings, we have revised the weight calculations of the score in Sect. 3.1, introduce a normal form for mathematical tree expressions in Sect. 3.2, and improved the search routine, breaking it off after ten seconds that is described in Sect. 3.3.

3.1 Balancing Scores with the Key Character Length

An expression' score can increase based on the number of its elements, instead of their priority. For example, the score of $sinx(= s \otimes i \otimes n \otimes x)$ is higher than the score of $\sin x$ because $sinx$ includes 7 nodes and 6 edges, compared to the 3 elements in $\sin x$. (Here, in this paper, the symbol $\otimes$ is used for recollection of an invisible multiplication that is also treated as an operator or node element.)

Generally, when $Y(s)$ from linear string s with character length n is obtained by Procedures 1–3, s can be decomposed into a key separation vector with n elements, per (4), because the character keys of almost all ASCII codes are registered in our system's key dictionary $\mathcal{D}$.

For example, if $s = $ "pi", there exist two key separation vectors ("pi") and ("p", "i") from s, and the totality of candidates $Y(\text{"pi"})$ is estimated to be

$$Y(\text{"pi"}) = \{\pi, pi, p^i, p_i, \cdots\}. \tag{8}$$

The score of the first candidate in (8) is estimated only by parameter θ_π, whereas the score of the second candidate $pi(= p \otimes i)$ is summed among the five parameters as

$$h_\theta\left(\boldsymbol{X}(pi)\right) = \theta_p + \theta_\otimes + \theta_i + \theta_{(\otimes,1,p)} + \theta_{(\otimes,2,i)}. \tag{9}$$

Therefore, h_θ does not become proportional to the occurrence probability of such a mathematical expression, because its score can increase according to its number of elements if the value of each score parameter has the same degree. This shortcoming also occurs for multidigit figures (e.g., 123) and some operators (e.g., sin).

To overcome this issue, we revise the score's weight calculations by adding a suitable weight to the score parameters depending on the length of key characters. Let K be the length of linear string s when a candidate expression $y_p(s)$ is formed from s. The tree structure of a product of K variables consists of $2K - 1$ nodes and $2(K - 1)$ edges. In this study, we have adopted the following score functions (10–12) for numbers N, variables/symbols V, and operators $\mathcal{O}$ onto $m(= 1, 2, 3)$ numbers of operands as a weight balance, respectively.

$$\text{Score}(N) = \text{Len}(N) + 3S_{\max}\{\text{Len}(N) - 1\} \tag{10}$$

$$\text{Score}(V) = \theta_V \times \text{Len}(V) + 3S_{\max}\{\text{Len}(V) - 1\} \tag{11}$$

$$\text{Score}(\mathcal{O}) = \theta_{\mathcal{O}} \times \text{Len}(\mathcal{O}) + 3S_{\max}\{\text{Len}(\mathcal{O}) - 1\} + 2mS_{\max} \tag{12}$$

Here, $\text{Len}(e)$ stands the length of the key string of element e, and θ_V and $\theta_{\mathcal{O}}$ are the score parameters for nodes V and $\mathcal{O}$, respectively. Any score parameter $\theta_f \leq S_{\max}$, as described in (7). Using (8), $\text{Score}(\pi) = 2\theta_\pi + 3S_{\max}$, per (11), and if $\theta_\pi \approx \theta_p \approx \theta_i$, then $\text{Score}(\pi) \geq h_\theta(\boldsymbol{X}(pi))$.

Therefore, we propose to revise the algorithm in **Steps 1–4**, by altering **Step 2** to

$$y_p \text{ s.t. Score}(y_p) = \max\{\text{Score}(y)|y \in Y(s_i)\}. \tag{13}$$

3.2 Unique Normal Form for Mathematical Expressions

There exist innumerable tree representations of mathematical expression with the same notation but different internal structures. For example, $a + b + c$ is denoted without any parentheses, given the associativity of addition (14). However, it can be represented by two different tree structures, shown in Fig. 1.

$$(a + b) + c = a + (b + c) \tag{14}$$

This becomes a challenge in the machine learning stage; in **Step 3** in Sect. 2.3, candidate y_p is judged to be different from the correct formula y_i, despite the same notation in both expressions. Thus, our system cannot definitively predict the desired mathematical expression.

To overcome this shortcoming, we define a normal form for mathematical notation.

Definition 2 (Normal form for mathematical notation). *A normal form for a mathematical notation ensures that all trees based on a mathematical expression with the same notation are recorded uniquely.*

Normal form was discussed using "term rewriting system" by Knuth and Bendix [11] in 1967 and a unique normal form in computer algebra systems was discussed in [12], in particular, that there exists a unique normal form for polynomial systems. We proposed a normal form for mathematical notation to use

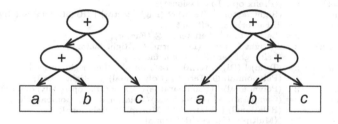

Fig. 1. The different tree structures of $a + b + c$

in a math input interface in [4], in which we concretely define the normal form for mathematical notation to implement into our prediction system for general mathematical formulae.

First, we define the order for all formulae per algebraic rules in Table 3 to prescribe the unique normal form for mathematical notation. The definition for all elements that constitute a formula using Buchus' normal form (BNF) in Table 3 stands for a recursive definition from a elements of low rank to those of high rank. The order of operators are conducted as in (15), per algebraic rules.

$$\otimes < \oplus < \text{Comparison op.} < \text{Relational op.} < \text{Multiple op.} \qquad (15)$$

Namely, any formula can be a high-rank multiple form ⟨Multiple⟩. Here, $\otimes$ stands for an invisible multiplication, $\oplus$ for an addition-type binary operator ($+$ or $-$) and $\pm$ for a prefix unary sign operator ($+,-$ or $\pm$). Let ⟨Term⟩ and ⟨Factor⟩ be an algebraic term (e.g., xy^2z) and a factor (e.g., x, y^2, z), respectively. As prescribed by Table 3, the right-hand side of an invisible multiplication $\otimes$ can be a ⟨Factor⟩ and a factor ⟨Right factor⟩ prefixed by sin, lim, log, $\sum$, $\int$, etc., can be arranged on the right side of $\otimes$ but is forbidden on the left side of $\otimes$. For example, $\int f(x)dx$ is a ⟨Right factor⟩ because if the factor y was arranged on the right side of such an integral, y could not be distinguished from an integral calculus variable. Similarly, a ⟨Left factor⟩ like a signed factor (e.g., $-x$) is forbidden on the right-hand side of $\otimes$.

For example, the tree structure on the right in Fig. 1, which is formed as ⟨Factor⟩ $\otimes$ ⟨Term⟩, is excluded because such a form is not included in the definition equation for ⟨Term⟩ in Table 3.

Therefore, we treat only the normal form defined by Table 3 for mathematical tree expressions in this study. We converted the 4000 math formulae in the training dataset to the normal form and use only the normal form to predict

Table 3. The definition equation for the normal form of mathematical formulae using BNF

⟨Number⟩	::= ⟨Value⟩ | ⟨Value⟩.⟨Value⟩;
⟨Non number symbol⟩	::= ⟨Symbol⟩ | ⟨Text⟩ | ⟨Sym͡bol⟩ | ⟨Symbol⟩ | ⟨Symbol⟩ | ⟨Sym͢bol⟩;
⟨Factor⟩	::= ⟨Non number symbol⟩ | (⟨Factor⟩⟨Postfix unary op.⟩) |
	(⟨Bracket⟩⟨Multiple⟩) | $\sqrt{⟨\text{Polynomial}⟩}$ | ⟨Factor⟩$^{⟨\text{Polynomial}⟩}$ |
	⟨Factor⟩$_{⟨\text{Polynomial}⟩}$ | $\frac{⟨\text{Polynomial}⟩}{⟨\text{Polynomial}⟩}$;
⟨Term⟩	::= ⟨Number⟩ | ⟨Factor⟩ | ⟨Term⟩ $\otimes$ ⟨Factor⟩;
⟨Right factor⟩	::= (⟨Prefix op.⟩⟨Expressions⟩);
⟨Right term⟩	::= ⟨Right factor⟩ | ⟨Term⟩ $\otimes$ ⟨Right factor⟩ | ⟨Right term⟩ $\otimes$ ⟨Right factor⟩;
⟨Left factor⟩	::= $\pm$⟨Factor⟩ | $\pm$⟨Left factor⟩;
⟨Left term⟩	::= ⟨Left factor⟩ | ⟨Left term⟩ $\otimes$ ⟨Factor⟩;
⟨Left-right term⟩	::= $\pm$⟨Right factor⟩ | ⟨Left term⟩ $\otimes$ ⟨Right factor⟩ |
	⟨Left-right term⟩ $\otimes$ ⟨Right factor⟩;
⟨Polynomial⟩	::= ⟨Term⟩ | ⟨Right term⟩ | ⟨Left term⟩ | ⟨Left-right term⟩ |
	⟨Polynomial⟩ $\oplus$ ⟨Term⟩ | ⟨Polynomial⟩ $\oplus$ ⟨Right term⟩;
⟨Comparable⟩	::= ⟨Polynomial⟩ | (⟨Comparable⟩⟨Comparable op.⟩⟨Polynomial⟩);
⟨Relational⟩	::= ⟨Comparable⟩ | (⟨Relational⟩⟨Relational op.⟩⟨Comparable⟩);
⟨Multiple⟩	::= ⟨Relational⟩ | ⟨Matrix⟩ | (⟨Multiple⟩, ⟨Relational⟩) |
	(⟨Multiple⟩⟨Space⟩⟨Relational⟩);

the N-best candidates from a linear string using the algorithm proposed in this section.

3.3 Complexity of Candidate Math Expressions and Calculation Time

Generally, the number of elements in $Y(s)$, denoted by $n(Y(s))$, increases rapidly corresponding to the increase in the length of s. For example, because the key character "a" corresponds to seven symbols ($Y("a") = \{a, \alpha, \mathsf{a}, \mathbf{a}, \boldsymbol{a}, \mathtt{a}, \aleph\}$) and the invisible multiplication between a and b corresponds to $Y("ab") = \{ab, a^b, a_b, {}^ab, {}_ab\}$, then $n(Y("abc")) = 7^3 \times 5^2 = 8575$. However, for a mathematical input interface, it is sufficient to calculate the N-best high score candidates in $Y(s)$ as shown in (1).

Therefore, we improve the search routine, breaking it off after ten seconds, because the mean runtime for cases in which the length of s was less than 16 required less than 10 s (cf. Sect. 4.3). To improve the efficiency of calculation, we obtain the N-best candidates in $Y(s)$ as follows:

1. In Procedure 1, all the key separation vectors $(k_1, k_2, \cdots, k_K)$ of s are sorted in ascending order of K in (4), i.e., in order starting from higher probability.
2. In Procedure 2, we set an upper limit $T = 10$ s for breaking down all possible calculations of the predictive expressive structures.
3. In Procedure 3, to obtain the N-best candidates in $Y(s)$, we apply only the N-best mathematical elements for operand expressions related to an operator, instead of all possible combinations.

4 Experimental Evaluation

In this section, we experimentally investigate the prediction accuracy of the algorithm described in the previous section. Then, we present the results of this evaluation in Sect. 4.2 and discuss the results of this study in Sect. 4.3.

4.1 Method

We examined prediction accuracy using a dataset of 4000 mathematical formulae $\mathcal{E} = \{(s_i, y_i) | i = 0, \cdots, 3999\}$ from a five-volume mathematics textbook [13], organized into the following categories: algebra, geometry, vector algebra, sets/logic, numbers, probability/statistics, trigonometry, exponents/logarithms, sequences, limits, and calculus, which are studied in the tenth through twelfth grades in Japan. Dataset $\mathcal{E}$ was generated manually with our previous system [14] in the order of appearance in the textbook by choosing individual expressions y with the corresponding linear string s, the length of which is less than 16.

In the experimental evaluation, we measured the proportion of correct predictions for 500 test datasets after learning the parameters using the predictive algorithm described in Sect. 3 on a training dataset consisting of 3500 formulae by 8-fold cross-validation.

4.2 Results

The machine learning results for our predictive algorithm are given in Table 4 for various training set sizes. Figure 2 illustrates this result and shows that 3500 training data are sufficient for performing our machine learning algorithm.

The accuracy of "Best 1" with our predictive algorithm was approximately 51.5% after being trained 3500 times and that of "Best 3" was 72.4%. However, for its top-ten ranking, this algorithm achieved an accuracy of 85.2%.

The mean CPU time for predicting each mathematical expression with corresponding linear string of length less than 16 was 2.85 s ($SD = 0.16$).

The search ratio omitting the best score was only 0.6%; nevertheless, the calculation break ratio was 16.5%, which indicates that the improvements described in Sect. 3.3 worked well for finding the N-best candidates.

Table 4. Prediction accuracy using our predictive algorithm (%)

Training no.	Best 1	Best 3	Best 10
0	16.0 (0.7)	20.2 (0.9)	23.8 (1.5)
500	36.4 (2.9)	49.9 (5.2)	61.3 (7.9)
1000	45.3 (2.6)	63.6 (1.8)	77.2 (1.9)
1500	47.5 (4.2)	67.4 (2.6)	80.7 (1.6)
2000	49.9 (3.3)	69.7 (2.2)	82.7 (1.6)
2500	51.6 (4.5)	71.2 (3.6)	84.0 (1.7)
3000	50.9 (3.9)	71.5 (3.3)	84.0 (1.7)
3500	51.5 (3.1)	72.4 (2.2)	85.2 (1.8)

Numbers in parentheses denote *SD*.

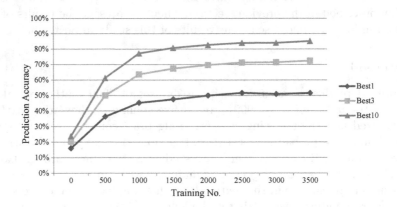

Fig. 2. Prediction results for varying numbers of training examples

4.3   Discussion

Analysis on Length of s. The 4000 test data consist of approximately 66% of the mathematical expressions included in a five-volume textbook [13]. There is a negative association ($R^2 = 0.83$) between the length of s and prediction accuracy for top-ten rankings (Fig. 3). The mean CPU time to obtain y_p from various lengths of string s is illustrated in Fig. 4. The mean runtime when the length of s is less than 16 required less than 10 s, although when the length is greater than 10, the mean runtime increases rapidly, because the complexity of candidate math expression increases with the length of string s (c.f. Sect. 3.3). Therefore, this algorithm is insufficient for predicting the N-best candidates from strings whose length is greater than 16. In this case, we need another strategy, like a predictive conversion limited from a part of s.

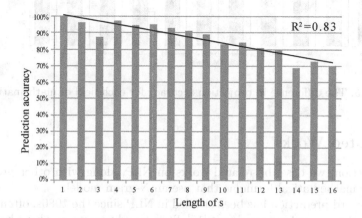

Fig. 3. Length of s effects prediction accuracy

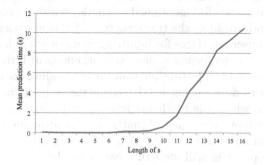

Fig. 4. CPU time for varying lengths of s

Differences Across Mathematics Fields. Figure 5 shows the difference in projection accuracy for each field of mathematics after learning with 3500 training data. The line indicates the data distribution of each field. The prediction accuracies for vector algebra and trigonometry are greater than 90% for the top-ten ranking, but are low for exponents and sequences because mathematical expressions, such as recursive formulae can be complex.

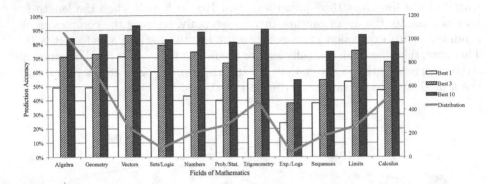

Fig. 5. The difference in projection accuracy for each field of mathematics

5   Related Works

In this section, we describe related works on NLP, along with other predictive inputs for mathematical formulae that use an N-gram model.

Input-word prediction has been studied in NLP since the 1980s, often to predict input characters for a word unit [15]. Structured perceptrons have been used in NLP to input Japanese characters since the 1990s. As explained in Sect. 2, our predictive algorithm uses a structured perceptron; however, mathematical formulae have tree structures, rather than the sentential chain structures of natural language. Indeed, none of the aforementioned methods consider sentence structures, although our method considers the tree structure of mathematical formulae.

Structure-based user interfaces for inputting mathematical formulae are popular. They enable users to format a desired mathematical formula on a PC in a WYSIWYG manner by selecting an icon corresponding to the structure of the expression. Users do so using a GUI template, e.g., a fraction bar or an exponent form, into which the mathematical elements can be entered. Hijikata et al. improved the input efficiency of mathematical formulae by proposing an algorithm for predicting mathematical elements using an N-gram model [16]. However, their proposal is still structure-based in the sense that users must understand the entire structure of a desired mathematical formula before selecting the corresponding icons.

In contrast, our predictive conversion method predicts mathematical structures from a linear string in a colloquial style, separating it from structure-based input methods.

6 Conclusion and Future Work

In this study, we proposed a predictive algorithm for linear string conversion to the N-best candidate mathematical formulae, with an accuracy of 85.2% for the top-ten ranking, by improving upon a previously proposed structured perceptron algorithm to apply to general categories of mathematics. The mean CPU time for predicting each mathematical expression with a corresponding linear string of length less than 16 (obtained from a five-volume mathematics textbook) was 2.84 s.

The most important avenues for future research are to reduce prediction time and to develop an intelligent mathematical input interface by implementing our proposed predictive algorithm.

This work was supported by JSPS KAKENHI Grant Number 26330413.

References

1. Pollanen, M., Wisniewski, T., Yu, X.: Xpress: a novice interface for the real-time communication of mathematical expressions. In: Proceedings of the Workshop on Mathematical User Interfaces (2007)
2. Sangwin, C.: Computer aided assessment of mathematics using STACK. In: Cho, S.J. (ed.) Selected Regular Lectures from the 12th International Congress on Mathematical Education, pp. 695–713. Springer, Cham (2015). doi:10.1007/978-3-319-17187-6_39
3. Fukui, T.: An intelligent method of interactive user interface for digitalized mathematical expressions. RIMS Kokyuroku **1780**, 160–171 (2012). (in Japanese)
4. Fukui, T.: The performance of interactive user interface for digitalized mathematical expressions using an intelligent formatting from linear strings. RIMS Kokyuroku **1785**, 32–44 (2012). (in Japanese)
5. Shirai, S., Nakamura, Y., Fukui, T.: An interactive math input method for computer aided assessment systems in mathematics. IPSJ Trans. Comput. Educ. **1**(3), 11–21 (2015). (in Japanese)
6. Shirai, S., Fukui, T.: Improvement in the input of mathematical formulae into STACK using interactive methodology. Comput. Educ. **37**, 85–90 (2014). (in Japanese)
7. Fukui, T.: Prediction for converting linear strings to mathematical formulae using machine learning. In: Proceedings of ARG WI2, vol. 6, pp. 67–72 (2015). (in Japanese)
8. Fukui, T., Shirai, S.: Predictive algorithm from linear string to mathematical formulae for math input method. In: Proceedings of the 21st Conference on Applications of Computer Algebra, pp. 17–22 (2015)
9. Shirai, S., Fukui, T.: Evaluation of a predictive algorithm for converting linear strings to mathematical formulae for an input method. In: Kotsireas, I.S., Rump, S.M., Yap, C.K. (eds.) MACIS 2015. LNCS, vol. 9582, pp. 421–425. Springer, Cham (2016). doi:10.1007/978-3-319-32859-1_36
10. Manning, C.D., Scheutze, H.: Foundations of Statistical Natural Language Processing. The MIT Press, London (2012)
11. Knuth, D.E., Bendix, P.B.: Simple word problems in universal algebra. In: Proceedings of Oxford, vol. 67, pp. 263–298 (1967)

12. Sasaki, T., Motoyoshi, F., Watanabe, S.: Computer Algebra System, vol. 36, Shoukoudo (1986). (in Japanese)
13. Matano, H., et al.: Vols. I301, A301, II301, B301, and III301 of Mathematics, Japan. Tokyo Shoseki (2014). (in Japanese)
14. Shirai, S., Fukui, T.: MathTOUCH: mathematical input interface for e-assessment systems. MSOR Connections **15**(2), 70–75 (2016)
15. Garay-Vitoria, N., Abascal, J.: Text prediction systems: a survey. Univers. Access Inf. Soc. **4**(3), 188–203 (2006)
16. Hijikata, Y., Horie, K., Nishida, S.: Predictive input interface of mathematical formulas. In: Kotzé, P., Marsden, G., Lindgaard, G., Wesson, J., Winckler, M. (eds.) INTERACT 2013. LNCS, vol. 8117, pp. 383–400. Springer, Heidelberg (2013). doi:10.1007/978-3-642-40483-2_27

Development and a Practical Use of Monitoring Tool of Understanding of Learners in Class Exercise

Yusuke Hayashi[✉], Mitsutaka Murotsu, Sho Yamamoto, and Tsukasa Hirashima

The Department of Information, Hiroshima University, Higashihiroshima, Japan
hayashi@lel.hiroshima-u.ac.jp

Abstract. In mass teaching, the learning goal is often set focused on the average students. The advantage of this is that learning outcome can become homogenized and be reached a certain level. On the other hand, students above or below the level cannot get enough support. Information communication technology enable teachers look over the progress of learners. Learning management systems and classroom management systems collect learners' answers to exercises, learners' behavior on the systems and so on. These data are expected to lead information that teachers keep track of progress of learners and identify which learner need support. In addition to this, this study aims at develop a monitoring tool of understanding of learners in class exercise. The result of practical use of this shows teachers accept this tool and actually they have given individual guidance not depending on their usual understanding of students.

Keywords: Learning by problem-posing · Monitoring tool · Teacher support

1 Introduction

Teachers diagnose the learners' cognitive and affective state from students' facial expressions, attitude, responses to teacher's questions and so on. Especially, they focus on the students who have low academic abilities or are not-good attitude and manage classes. In this study, understanding of learners refer to that teachers diagnose learners' cognitive and affective states. A popular way for teachers to understand learners is to walk around the class and check how students are doing while the class exercise. It is called "Kikan-shido", another name of it is "between desk instruction", that is a method of monitoring and guiding student activity in class [1, 2, 7]. This study aims at developing a system help teachers to find students need instruction based on their understanding free from teachers' preconception.

This study developed a system to support teachers' understanding of leaners in the class exercise with Monsakun that is an environment of learning by problem-posing as sentence integration [4, 5]. This system provides teachers not only learners' answer and summary of correctness but also types of mistakes happened in their exercise. This system has been practically used for 64 h by five teachers in three elemental schools.

© Springer International Publishing AG 2017
S. Yamamoto (Ed.): HIMI 2017, Part II, LNCS 10274, pp. 29–39, 2017.
DOI: 10.1007/978-3-319-58524-6_3

2 Teachers' Activity in Class Exercise

2.1 Individual Guidance in Class Exercise

Instruction in class has two types: mass instruction and individual instruction. In classroom, teachers can conduct individual instruction in class exercise by walk around the class and check how students are doing. Mass instruction usually focus on students have middle academic abilities. Such instruction make students have high academic abilities bored and make students have low academic abilities feel too much difficulty. Especially, individual instruction in class exercise gives teachers chance to understand students more and to compensate for lost learning of low ability students in mass instruction. However, it is difficult for teachers to find students need instruction while walking around the class. What teachers can usually do is to estimate their understanding from students' facial expressions, attitude and description on notebook or worksheet. It is difficult for teachers to check all the students and instruction might be biased. In addition to that, teachers' estimation not always same as students' understanding.

2.2 Teacher Support for Learner Understanding

There are many systems supporting teachers' learner understanding: audience response system (clicker), learning management system (LMS), display sharing. These systems make teachers possible to total and look over learners' answer as well as to provide feedback to learners immediately [3, 6]. This increases the interactivity between teachers and learners in classroom, however, this is just overview of learners and it is difficult for teachers to check learners individually or point by point. This enable teachers to understand students without walking around. How to deal with this information is lay in the hands of teachers and it depends on the teachers' ability. It is very difficult for teachers to gather information of students within a class period in conventional classroom because it takes much time and energy. These systems make it convenient for them to do so as much as possible within a class period. On the other hand, the information provided these systems is a kind of raw data that teachers need to process for understanding learners.

This study aims at providing teachers with information about learners' thought in addition to concrete answers in an exercise. This means that the system tells teachers not only concrete learners' answer and the correctness but also the cause of error and the history. These information helps teachers to understand learners more deeply and more quickly within a class period. This is expected to facilitate teachers to find students that teachers would guide and to be helpful for good guidance to the students.

3 Support of Learner Understanding for Individual Guidance in a Class

3.1 Necessary Information for Individual Guidance in a Class Exercise

What teachers do in the class exercise are to find the impasse in students by the observation of them, to guide students individually, and to understand students in the class as the whole and make a future plan. This study lists necessary information for individual guidance in a class as the following information about (1) learning progress to find the impasse in students, (2) learners' thinking for adaptive feedback, (3) the state of class as the accumulation of each student's state. While the first one is available in the conventional systems, the second on is the characteristic of this study. The second one also contribute to differentiate the proposed system from the conventional ones in the third point.

3.2 Requirements of Monitoring Tools for Individual Guidance in a Class Exercise

This study develops a monitoring tool of learning state of learners in a class exercise that also provides the information about learners thinking. The purpose of the tool is the facilitation of teachers to understand students within a class exercise and to find students that teachers would guide in the exercise. Concretely speaking, the following three functions are the requirement of the monitoring tool for individual guidance in a class exercise:

1. to provide each student's progress on the seat configuration for finding students need guidance,
2. to provide the trends of errors in addition to the numbers of trial and correct answer for facilitating teachers' adaptive guidance, and
3. to provide the summary of state of students as the whole class for future planning.

4 Development of a Monitoring Tool for Individual Guidance in a Class Exercise

This study develops a monitoring tool for individual guidance in a class exercise with the learning environment of arithmetic word problems for elementary school students by problem-posing as sentence-integration, called Monsakun Touch. In conventional class exercise, teachers estimate learners' understanding from students' facial expressions, attitude and description on notebook or worksheet. However, through the practical use of Monsakun, it is difficult for teachers to estimate learners' understanding in class exercise with tablet computers because teachers are not familiar with the such situation and difficult to put their experience. Through the interviews with teachers have used Monsakun in their class, they feel difficulty in guiding students in the class exercises with it. In Monsakun Touch, students pose problems by piece together sentences provided by the system as stated below. In this exercise learners continue to pose problems until they can pose a problem meet the requirement. This style of exercise can record all the learners' answers and enable to analyze the trend of errors and estimate students' understanding as the cause of errors. The monitoring tool provides the information about learning progress and the analysis of it for the better guidance of teachers to students within class exercises.

4.1 Monsakun Touch

Monsakun Touch is a learning environment of arithmetic word problem for elementary school students by problem-posing. This is based on Triplet structure model [5] that defines problem posing of arithmetic word problem with only one arithmetic operation as a structure of three sentences composed of objects, numerical quantities and a predicate. With this definition Monsakun can diagnose posed problems automatically and give feedback about the correctness to the learners. This resolve the bottleneck of learning by problem-posing in which teachers have difficulty in diagnosis of posed problems by learners because learners pose a wide variety of problems in free problem-posing. This also provides learners with many more opportunities for conducting learning by problem posing. Figure 1 shows the screenshot of Monsakun.

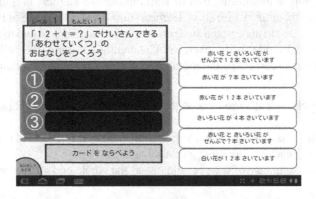

Fig. 1. Monsakun touch

In Monsakun, learners pose problems meet the requirement on the left top with three sentences from six sentences on the right. For example, in this exercise, the required problem is the combination of "There are 12 red flowers", "There are 4 yellow flowers" and "There are ? red and yellow flowers altogether". If learners can pose a problem with "There are 12 <u>white</u> flowers" instead of "There are 12 <u>red</u> flowers", it does not consist with "There are ? <u>red</u> and <u>yellow</u> flowers altogether" about the objects. Triplet-structure model defines the requisite conditions of an arithmetic word problem with only one arithmetic operation as calculation structure, story structure, object structure, numerical quantities relation and sentence structure and problem posing is defined the task to compose sentences meet all the conditions [7, 9]. Based on the definitions of arithmetic word problems and problem-posing task, Monsakun can diagnose the correctness of posed problems by learners and identify the reason of errors in posed problems.

4.2 Development of Monsakun Analyzer for Teachers

One form of practical use of Monsakun in class is individual use of it as class exercise. The role of teacher in this use is to find learners who need help and provide adaptive guidance fit to the students' impasse. Monsaku Analyzer is the tool to support teachers in such situation. This overlays an overview of learners' state on the seat configuration of students. Students are distinguished with colors by the correct rate with a threshold set by teachers. The screenshot of this is shown in Fig. 2.

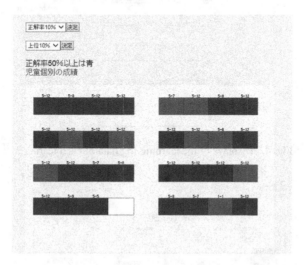

Fig. 2. Display of associate the correct rate and the seat of the student

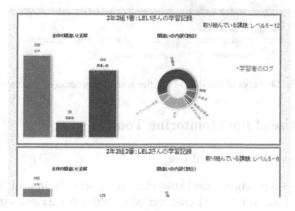

Fig. 3. Displays of the data about the learning processof each learner

From here teacher also check the state of each student. Figure 3 shows the screenshot of the summary of a learner's state including the number of assignments the learner has tackled, the numbers of correct and incorrect answers, and the trend of errors. Figure 4 shows the screenshot of the history of answers with the diagnosis of each error. In addition to the individual student data, this also shows the data of whole class for the help of teacher's future planning of classes. Figure 5 shows the screenshot of the summary of whole class.

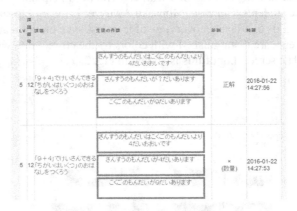

Fig. 4. Displays of the learning log data of each learner

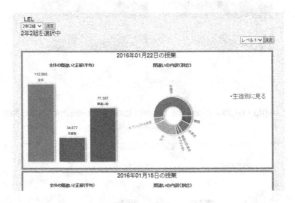

Fig. 5. Displays of the data about the learning process of each class

5   Practical Use of the Monitoring Tool

5.1   An Overview of the Practical Use

The monitoring tool is practically use in two elementary schools. In an elementary school (school A) the tool was used for 11 class periods in third grade class with 39 students. We interviewed the teacher about the usability of it after the classes. In the other school (school B) the tool was used for 2 class periods in each of second and third grade class with 31 and 26 students respectively. We also interviewed the teachers and analyzed the relationship between individual guidance and the learners' performance in school B.

5.2 The Result of Interviews

In the interview with the teacher in school A, he said the monitoring tool was useful in class exercise. He actually used the tool check each learner's progress and gave guidance to students made many mistakes. He said class exercise with monitoring tool makes him easier to find students need guidance and to make future plan based on the state of whole class. In the interview with the teacher in school B, teachers said the information from the monitoring tool is useful so that teachers can find the unexpected impasse of learners that they have considered high ability students as well as learning state of each and whole of students. They also said that it is also useful to analyze the exercise after class. From these results, the subjective impression of teachers on the monitoring tool is positive.

5.3 Analysis of Teachers' S Activity

From a subjective inquiry with the interviews to teachers, it is found that they have given individual guidance to students based on the information from the monitoring tool. To confirm the effectiveness of the monitoring tool, we investigate the relation among the teachers' guidance, their usual understanding of students and the performance in Monsakun at the data of school B. The teachers' guidance is counted with the video-recording of the classes. Teachers' usual understanding of students is checked by the score of a test about the problem-solving in arithmetic word problems done before the use of Monsakun. The performance in Monsakun is measured by the percentage of correct answers. The assumption in this study is that teachers choose students to give guidance depending on the performance on Monsakun if they use the monitoring tool. If teachers gave guidance depending on their usual understanding of student, for example, the past achievement, attitudes and behavior of students in everyday school life and so on, they give guidance to students scored low in pre-test more than one scored high.

Firstly, we investigate the relation between the teachers' guidance and the result of pre-test. Especially, we check whether the guidance depends on the pre-test. That is, we test the following two assumptions:

- The Lower group of students in pre-test got individual guidance at the same rate of higher group students in the pre-test.
- Lower group of students in Monsakun got individual guidance more than higher group students in Monsakun.

In the analysis between the pre-test and the individual guidance, students are distinguished into higher and lower students by the average od the score of the pre-test.

Table 1 shows the average and the standard deviation of pre-test in second grade students in school B. Table 2 shows the presence or absence of individual guidance distinguished by the result of pre-test. With two-sided Fisher's exact test using a level of significance of 0.05, there is no significant difference between the higher and lower group in the pre-test.

Table 1. Average and standard deviation about the second grade

Average in the pretest	Standard deviation in the pretest
6.87	2.012328

Table 2. A result of teaching about the second grade (based on pretest)

	w/teaching	w/o teaching	Total	
Higher group in the pretest	9 (42.9%)	12 (57.1%)	21	p = 1.0000
Lower group in the pretest	4 (40.0%)	6 (60.0%)	10	
Total	13 (41.9%)	18 (58.1%)	31	

Table 3 shows the average and the standard deviation of pre-test in second grade students in school B. Table 4 shows the presence or absence of individual guidance distinguished by the result of pre-test. With two-sided Fisher's exact test using a level of significance of 0.05, there is no significant difference between the higher and lower group in the pre-test.

Table 3. Average and standard deviation about the third grade

Averagein the pretest	Standard deviation in the pretest
8.61	1.856382

Table 4. A result of teaching about the third grade (based on pretest)

	w/teaching	w/o teaching	Total	
Higher group in the pretest	11 (64.7%)	6 (35.3%)	17	p = 0.4185
Lower group in the pretest	4 (44.4%)	5 (55.6%)	19	
Total	15 (57.7%)	11 (42.3%)	26	

There are no significant differences in both case. This shows teachers gave individual guidance to students not depending on teachers usual understanding of students in both case.

In the analysis between the individual guidance and the percentage of correct answers in Monsakun, we use the decision tree analysis with CART (Classification and Regression Trees) algorithm to decide the threshold to distinguish the higher and lower students in the percentage of correct answers. The target variable is the presence or absence of individual guidance and the categorical variables are the result of pre-test and the percentage of correct answers in Monsakun. Figures 6 and 7 show the results of decision tree analysis of second and third grade students, respectively. In the nodes, "yes" and "no" show the presence and absence of individual guidance and the left numbers are the number of students not given guidance and the right numbers are the number of ones given. "rate" refer to the percentage of correct answers in Monsakun and "pre1" refer to the result of pre-test.

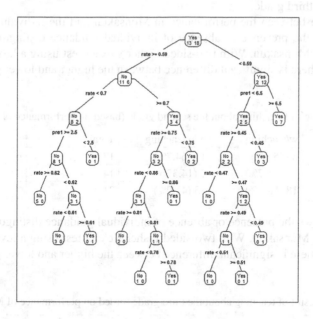

Fig. 6. A result of the decision tree analysis in the second grade

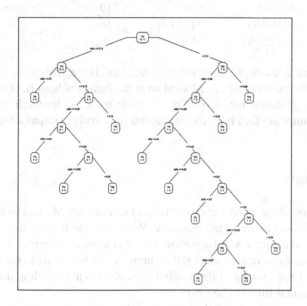

Fig. 7. A result of the decision tree analysis in the third grade

Bothe decision tree of second grade students primary categorizes students by the percentage of correct answers in Monsakun. The percentage is 59% in the second grade and 74% in the third grade.

The relation between the performance in Monsakun and the individual guidance. Table 5 shows the presence or absence of individual guidance distinguished by the performance in Monsakun. With two-sided Fisher's exact test using a level of significance of 0.05, there is significant difference between the higher and lower group on the performance.

Table 5. A result of teaching about the second grade (based on performance of Monsakun)

	w/teaching	w/o teaching	Total	
Higher group	6 (35.3%)	11 (64.7%)	17	p = 0.0094
Lower group	12 (85.7%)	2 (14.3%)	14	
Total	18 (58.1%)	13 (41.9%)	31	

Table 6 shows the presence or absence of individual guidance distinguished by the performance in Monsakun. With two-sided Fisher's exact test using a level of significance of 0.05, there is significant difference between the higher and lower group on the performance.

Table 6. A result of teaching about the third grade (based on performance of Monsakun)

	w/teaching	w/o teaching	Total	
Higher group	2 (20.0%)	8 (80.0%)	10	p = 0.1092
Lower group	9 (56.3%)	7 (43.7%)	16	
Total	11 (42.3%)	15 (57.7%)	26	

From the results of analysis among the teachers' guidance, their usual understanding of students and the performance in Monsakun at the data of school B, at least, teachers gave individual guidance not depending on their usual understanding of students. However, we cannot say they have found students have had the impasses in the exercise with Monsakun.

6   Conclusions

This study developed the monitoring tool of class exercise with Monsakun for supporting teachers to find students need their guidance. We define the information necessary for instruction in class exercise as information about (1) learning progress of each student, (2) learners' attempts and errors, and (3) the summary of whole class as the accumulation of students. The development of the monitoring tool aims at providing the information to the teachers in real-time in class exercise.

In this paper, we report the analysis result of the practical use of the tool in terms of (1) and (2). The results show teachers accept this tool and actually they have given individual guidance not depending on their usual understanding of students. However, the effectiveness of the tool is partially shown in the statistical test, only in the second grade.

The future works of this study are the following. Firstly, it requires further investigation of the effectiveness of this system. We need more data to show the evidence that teacher can find students require teachers' guidance. Secondary, we develop functions to support (3) the summary of whole class as the accumulation of students. The reflection after class is also important for teachers. Combination of information about learners' activity with teachers' individual guidance activity is useful for teachers to make future plan of classes.

References

1. Banky, G.P.: Looking for Kikan-Shido: are elements of it detectable in tertiary engineering pedagogy? In: Paper Presented at the Australasian Association for Engineering Education 2007 Conference, Melbourne, Australia (2007)
2. Clarke, D.J.: Kikan-Shido - between desks instruction. Annual Meeting of the American Mathematical Research Association (2004). http://extranet.edfac.unimelb.edu.au/DSME/lps/assets/Clarke_Kikan-shido.pdf
3. Davis, R.C., Lin, J., Brotherton, J.A., Landay, J.A., Price, M.N., Schilit, B.N.: A frame- work for sharing handwritten notes. In: Proceedings of the 11th Annual ACM Symposium on User Interface Software and Technology (UIST 1998), pp. 119–120 (1998)
4. Hirashima, T., Yokoyama, T., Okamoto, M., Takeuchi, A.: Learning by problem-posing as sentence-integration and experimental use. In: AIED 2007, 254–261 (2007)
5. Hirashima, T., Yamamoto, S., Hayashi, Y.: Triplet structure model of arithmetical word problems for learning by problem-posing. In: Yamamoto, S. (ed.) HCI 2014. LNCS, vol. 8522, pp. 42–50. Springer, Cham (2014). doi:10.1007/978-3-319-07863-2_5
6. Landay, J.A.: Using note-taking appliances for student to student collaboration. In: Proceedings of the 29th ASEE/IEEE Frontiers in Education Conference, pp. 12c4–15–20 (1999)
7. Hasanah, N., Hayashi, Y., Hirashima, T.: Investigation of students' performance in monsakun problem posing activity based on the triplet structure model of arithmetical word problems. In: Proceedings of ICCE 2015, pp. 27–36 (2015)
8. O'Keefe, K., Xu, L.H., Clarke, D.J.: Chapter four: kikan-shido: between desks instruction. In: Clarke, D.J., Emanuellson, J., Jablonka, E., Mok, I.A.C. (eds.) Making Connections: Comparing Mathematics Classrooms Around the World. Sense Publishers, Rotterdam (2006)
9. Supianto, A.A., Hayashi, Y., Hirashima, T.: Visualizations of problem-posing activity sequences toward modeling the thinking process. Res. Pract. Technol. Enhanced Learn. 11, 14 (2016). doi:10.1186/s41039-016-0042-4

Evaluation of the Function that Detects the Difference of Learner's Model from the Correct Model in a Model-Building Learning Environment

Tomoya Horiguchi[✉] and Tetsuhiro Masuda

Graduate School of Maritime Sciences, Kobe University,
5-1-1, Fukaeminami, Higashinada, Kobe, Hyogo, Japan
horiguti@maritime.kobe-u.ac.jp, tetsu9988@gmail.com

Abstract. In science education, the model-building learning environment is one of the promising methods for promoting learners' ability to make appropriate models of various phenomena with scientific concepts. However, it isn't an easy task for most learners and some assistance is necessary. We have developed the function that detects difference between learners' models and the correct models and gives feedback about errors to learners. We conducted an experiment for evaluating the function which revealed that: (1) the degree of model completion increased by using the function, (2) the degree of final model completion was correlated with the frequency of using the function, and the correlation was clearer for easier tasks, and (3) the learners who preferred mathematical explanation of errors thought more deeply about why their models were erroneous.

Keywords: Science education · Model-building learning environment · Feedback to learners' errors · Difference between learners' models and the current models

1 Introduction

In science education, it is one of the most important purposes for learners to acquire the ability to make appropriate models of various phenomena based on scientific concepts. Learning with model-building learning environments (MBEs) [1, 2] is a promising method for promoting the ability. In MBE, learners are usually given a set of components of models and build their model by combining them. They can also simulate their model to see whether it behaves as they expected. If it doesn't, they modify the model and try simulation again. Through such process, learners become to be able to make models with which they can explain and predict various phenomena based on scientific concepts.

However, it isn't an easy task for most learners to make correct models in MBEs. In order for composed models to be calculable, the components usually correspond to some scientific/mathematical concepts and they must be combined in scientifically/mathematically right way. Learners who aren't familiar to such concepts and formulation often have difficulties. Therefore, some assistance is necessary.

© Springer International Publishing AG 2017
S. Yamamoto (Ed.): HIMI 2017, Part II, LNCS 10274, pp. 40–49, 2017.
DOI: 10.1007/978-3-319-58524-6_4

In previous MBEs, various kinds of functions for assistance have been implemented such as *online help* (that provides general explanation of the usage of model components) and *syntax checker* (that detects and indicates formally illegal usage of model components) [3]. However, experiments revealed few learners initiatively used these functions when making models, and the effect of the functions significantly varied depending on the difficulty of tasks and learners' prior knowledge [4].

In this research, we evaluate the effect of the function that detects and explains the difference between learners' models and the correct models. The function was implemented as a module of a MBE we have developed [5]. We report about the experiment and its result that was conducted for investigating whether the function assists learners, what type of learners/tasks it helps for, and what type of explanation promotes learners' understanding.

2 Model-Building Learning Environment

2.1 Previous Model-Building Learning Environments

In order to facilitating learners' modeling activity, several model-building learning environments (MBE) have been developed [1–3, 6, 7]. In early MBEs, mathematical expressions were used as the modeling language and numeric results were derived [8]. However, the abstract concepts represented by mathematical expressions are relatively inaccessible to learners in elementary education. It is also difficult for them to interpret the results of numeric calculation. Additionally, mathematical expressions can't capture many crucial aspects of models, such as the conditions under which a model is applicable.

In contrast, in recent MBEs, ontological primitives of qualitative reasoning are used as the modeling language, which makes it possible to capture conceptual aspects of models' behavior, such as causality [2, 3]. These environments allow young learners to articulate knowledge using intuitive concepts.

The usefulness of MBEs has been verified through experiments in elementary and science/engineering education.

2.2 Evans: A MBE of Qualitative Modeling and Simulation

We have developed a MBE called *Evans* [5]. In Evans, learners can make qualitative models of dynamical systems by using components designed according to the vocabulary of qualitative reasoning. Learners can also see the qualitative behavior of their model by qualitative simulation.

Figure 1 shows an example of a model made with Evans that represents the relation among a species' population, birth rate and death rate. It consists of the constraints such as *C1: the change rate is the difference between the birth rate and death rate, C2: the population is the integration (I+) of the change rate, C3/C4: the birth/death rate is proportional to the population* etc. Figure 2 shows the simulated behavior of this model. *QS0(0)* represents the initial state in which the population, birth rate and death rate are decreasing while the change rate is negative but increasing. This state instantly transfers to the state *QS1(1)* in which all variables are approaching to zero. Since their numerical values change every moment but their qualitative values don't in *QS1(1)*, their behaviors are aggregated into a qualitative state. Thus, qualitative modeling and simulation enables learners to focus on the important features of the system and its behavior.

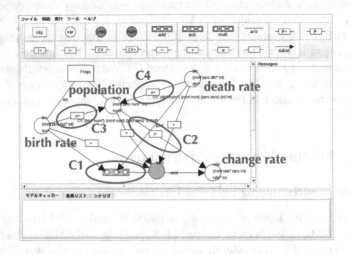

Fig. 1. Model of the change of a species' population

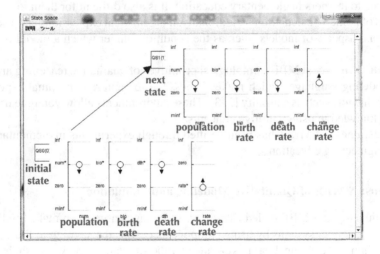

Fig. 2. Behavior of the model of the change of a species' population

2.3 Difficulty and Assistance in Modeling

Though qualitative terms are more intuitive and easier to use for learners than quantitative (i.e., mathematical) ones, it isn't still easy task for them to build qualitative models because components must be combined according to the formalism of qualitative reasoning language. In spite of visual and intuitive GUI, learners often make erroneous models. When a model made by learners includes syntactic errors, it can't be simulated.

Therefore, we previously implemented a *model checker* in Evans that detects formally illegal usage and combination of model components. Figure 3 shows an example of the assistance by the model checker. In Evans, *subst* link (substitution) should be used between an *amount* node (variable or constant) and *operation* node (addition, subtraction or multiplication), but used between two amounts in this example. Such syntactic errors are detected and indicated by the model checker.

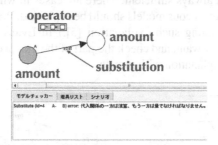

Fig. 3. Model checker's message about a syntax error

Preliminary experiment revealed the model checker promoted learners' carefulness and correction of syntactic errors, and was effective in decreasing the number of such errors. However, the degree of completion of their model (correspondence to the correct model) wasn't necessarily high. Though the model checker was helpful in making models calculable, learners couldn't interpret the unexpected behavior of models and modify them appropriately. We, therefore, designed the function that detects and explains the difference between learners' models and the correct models.

3 Difference List

We have implemented a module of Evans that detects difference of learners' models and correct ones and gives feedback about errors to learners. This module is called *difference list*. It compares learners' model to the correct model made by a teacher and detects the following differences: (1) components that are in the correct model but aren't in learners' model (*lacking part*), (2) components that aren't in the correct model but are in learners' model (*extra part*) and (3) components that are in both correct model and learners' one but erroneously described in the latter (*erroneous part*). Difference list shows and explains each detected part as learners' error. There are two types of explanation: *structural explanation* and *mathematical explanation*. The former explains merely that some components are lacking/extra/erroneous. The latter explains the mathematical role of the components. For example, suppose the model shown in Fig. 4 is correct while the model shown in Fig. 5 is erroneous. In these models, the parts marked with red circles are the difference between them. In this case, structural explanation is as follows: *In your model, amounts num and dth are connected with integral link, but they aren't in the correct model. A necessary integral link isn't in your model. The direction of the greater-than link between amounts dth and zero is reversed.* (Fig. 6) Mathematical explanation is as follows: *In your model, when amount dth is greater/less than zero, amount num increases/decreases, but num doesn't in the correct model. A necessary integral link isn't in your model. Amount dth is less than zero.* (Fig. 7) Thus, both explanations clearly indicate how the erroneous model should be modified. On the other hand, the former explanation doesn't explain why erroneous parts are inappropriate, while the latter explanation suggests the reason by explaining the mathematical role of the components. (It isn't always sufficient. There are cases in which physical unnaturalness of the behavior of erroneous models should be explained. We previously proposed the framework for generating such explanation [5].) In Evans, learners can invoke difference list anytime they want, and check the part of the model correspondent to each error by pointing each explanation with mouse.

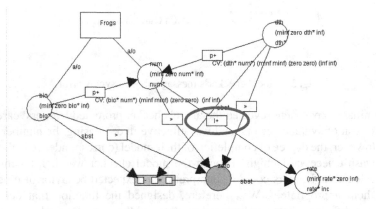

Fig. 4. An example of correct model (Color figure online)

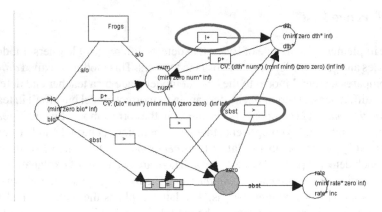

Fig. 5. An example of erroneous model (Color figure online)

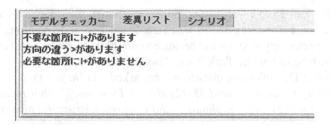

Fig. 6. An example of structural explanation

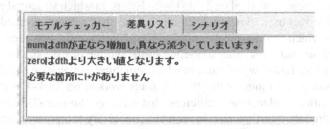

Fig. 7. An example of mathematical explanation

4 Experiment

We conducted an experiment for evaluating the effectiveness of difference list in making models in Evans.

4.1 Design

Purpose. The purpose of this experiment is to clarify (1) whether the degree of model completion is increased by using difference list during making models, (2) whether there is a correlation between the frequency of using difference list and the degree of final model completion, and (3) whether the type of explanation by difference list influences learners' model making.

Subjects. Six students whose major was engineering participated.
Instruments. The following materials were prepared and used.

- *Evans:* The model-building learning environment described in the previous sections. Difference list module was embedded.
- *A booklet for tutorial:* Basic usage of Evans to make models was explained with some examples.
- *Modeling tasks:* Task-1 dealt with a model of the water level of a bathtub with an inflow and an outflow. Task-2 dealt with a model of the population of frogs in a forest that increased by birth rate and decreased by death rate. Task-3 dealt with a model of the water flow between two tanks of which bottoms were connected with a pipe. Task-4 dealt with a model of the heat flow between two objects which touched each

other. Task-1 and Task-3 were isomorphic (i.e., though their domain was different, they had the same structure), and so was Task-2 and Task-4. In addition, Task-1 and Task-2 were relatively easy tasks (because some parts of their models were introduced in the tutorial), while Task-3 and Task-4 were advanced tasks.

- *Questionnaire:* The following questions were asked. (1) *Do you think the difference list was useful for making a model?*, (2) *How did you modify your model based on the feedback?* and (3) *Which explanation did you prefer, structural or mathematical?*

Procedure. In the first week, after a briefing of the outline of the experiment (5 min), the experimenter demonstrated the modeling with Evans by using the booklet for tutorial (10 min). Then, subjects worked on Task-1 with Evans, in which structural explanation of difference list was used (Session-1, 25 min). After that, subjects worked on Task-2 with Evans, in which mathematical explanation of difference list was used (Session-2, 25 min). In the second week, after a briefing of the outline of the experiment (5 min), subjects worked on Task-3 with Evans, in which structural explanation of difference list was used (Session-3, 30 min). After that, subjects worked on Task-4 with Evans, in which mathematical explanation of difference list was used (Session-2, 30 min). At last, subjects answered the questionnaire. In each task, necessary components were prepared by the system, so subjects combined them and inputted necessary values of parameters. During each session, subjects were instructed to save their model every five minutes. All operations by subjects during each session (i.e., the usage of difference list) were automatically recorded as operation logs.

4.2   Results

As for each session, every saved model was scored based on the criteria for the degree of completion. That is, the score of a model by subjects was the number of correctly connected links (in this experiment, the correct model was uniquely defined). Figure 8 shows an example of the transition of scores of a model by a subject in Session-3 (polygonal line graph). In each interval (i.e., 5 min between two saves), the frequency of using difference list counted with operation log is also indicated (bar graph).

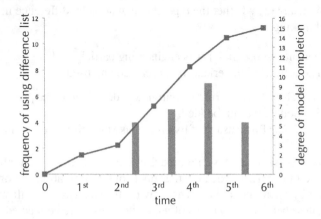

Fig. 8. An example of the transition of model completion and frequency of using diff list

Table 1 shows (1) the total number of intervals in which difference list was/wasn't used (called *dl-interval* and *non-dl-interval*, respectively), (2) the total increase of scores in dl-intervals and non-dl-intervals, (3) the average total increase of scores in dl-intervals and non-dl-intervals, that is, the total increase of scores divided by the total number of dl-intervals and non-dl-intervals, respectively (here, 'total' means the sum of data of all subjects). As for the total of all sessions, the average total increase of scores in dl-intervals is significantly greater than that in non-dl-intervals. This fact suggests using difference list was effective in the increase of model completion. In addition, in Session-1 and Session-2, the average total increase of scores in dl-intervals is equal or less than that in non-dl-intervals, while in Session-3 and Session-4, the average total increase of scores in dl-intervals is greater than that in non-dl-intervals. This fact suggests difference list was more effective in more difficult tasks. That is, since task-1 and task-2 were similar to the examples in the tutorial, subjects could work on them without difference list to a certain degree. On the other hand, task-3 and task-4 were unfamiliar to the subjects, and more complicated with more components than task-1 and task-2.

Table 1. Increase of scores in dl-intervals and non-dl-intervals

Diff list	Number of intervals		Total increase of scores		Average total increase of scores	
	Used	Not used	Used	Not used	Used	Not used
Session-1	10	20	10	27	1.00	1.35
Session-2	19	11	31	17	1.63	1.55
Session-3	20	16	43	28	2.15	1.75
Session-4	24	12	67	14	2.79	1.17
Total	73	59	151	86	2.07	1.46

Figure 9 shows the relation between the frequency of using difference list and the final model completion in Session-1. ANOVA, excluding the outliers (i.e., the data of subjects who rarely used difference list), revealed that these factors were significantly

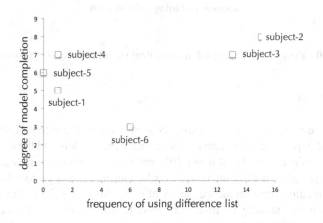

Fig. 9. Frequency of using diff list and final model completion (Session-1)

correlated $(F(1, 1) = 1875, p < .05)$. As for Session-2 and Session-3, there was no significant correlation but the data tended to lie on a straight line that suggests positive correlation. As for Session-4, however, there was no significant correlation and any tendency of correlation wasn't suggested. This is because most subjects' final model completion indicated full marks (i.e., ceiling effect). The reason is supposed that task-4 was isomorphic with task-3 and that the subjects got experienced after the preceding three tasks.

In the questionnaire, three subjects who answered to question (2) *'I modified my model after considering why it was incorrect'* preferred mathematical explanation in question (3), while other three subjects who answered to question (2) *'I modified my model merely according to the message by difference list'* preferred structural explanation in question (3). As for the model completion, there was no significant difference between these two groups. That is, the learner who considered her/his model deeply preferred mathematical explanation while those whose purpose was merely to complete her/his model preferred structural explanation. This fact suggests though using difference list was effective in learners' model completion, it didn't necessarily promote their understanding (Fig. 10).

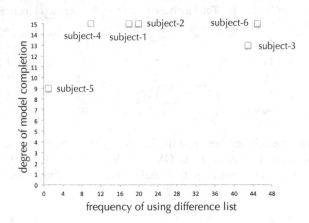

Fig. 10. Frequency of using diff list and final model completion (Session-4)

5   Conclusion

In this paper, we reported about the experiment to evaluate the effect of difference list that detects and explains the difference between learners' models and the correct models in MBE. The results revealed that using difference list was effective in learners' model completion, especially in difficult tasks. In addition, it was suggested that there was significant correlation between the frequency of using difference list and model completion, and that learners' strategy for modifying model correlates their preference of explanation by difference list. These results suggest the usefulness of difference list in MBE.

However, the following problem was also revealed. That is, in this experiment, the frequency of executing simulation of models was much less than that in the preceding preliminary experiment in which difference list wasn't implemented. This fact suggests using difference list makes learners focus on the elimination of listed differences, rather than the refinement of models by observing their behavior through simulation. Therefore, it is our important future work to find the method for appropriately combining the difference list and simulation to promote learners' activity and understanding in modeling.

References

1. Biswas, G., Schwartz, D., Bransford, J.: Technology support for complex problem solving-from SAD environment to AI. In: Forbus, K.D., Feltovich, P.J. (eds.) Smart Machines in Education, pp. 72–97. AAAI Press (2001)
2. Bredeweg, B., Linnebank, F., Bouwer, A., Liem, J.: Grap3 – workbench for qualitative modeling and simulation. Ecol. Inform. **4**(5–6), 263–281 (2009)
3. Forbus, K.D., Carney, K., Sherin, B., Ureel, L.: Qualitative modeling for middle-school students. In: Proceedings of QR 2004 (2004)
4. Bravo, C., van Joolingen, W.R., de Jong, T.: Modeling and simulation in inquiry learning: checking solutions and giving intelligent advice. Simulation **82**(11), 769–784 (2006)
5. Horiguchi, T., Hirashima, T., Forbus, K.D.: A model-building learning environment with error-based simulation. In: Proceedings of QR 2012 (2012)
6. (1985–2017). http://www.iseesystems.com
7. Jackson, S.L., Stratford, S.J., Krajcik, J., Soloway, E.: A learner-centered tool for students building models. Commun. ACM **39**(4), 48–49 (1996)
8. Costanza, R., Voinov, A.: Modeling ecological and economic systems with stella: part iii. Ecol. Model. **143**(1–2), 1–7 (2001)

Development of a Seminar Management System: Evaluation of Support Functions for Improvement of Presentation Skills

Yusuke Kometani[✉] and Keizo Nagaoka

School of Human Sciences, Waseda University, 2-579-15 Mikajima,
Tokorozawa, Saitama 359-1192, Japan
kometani@aoni.waseda.jp, k.nagaoka@waseda.jp

Abstract. We propose that seminar activities should be a focus of university education in the future. Under this principle, we have been developing a seminar management system and a learning management system for traditional classroom instruction and e-learning environments for university education. The main point of seminar activities is not only acquiring knowledge and skills, but also the ability to mutually assess growth with appropriate instructor support and foster student self-learning. Recognizing the importance of seminar activities in university education, we discuss seminar activities that should be the center of university education five to ten years from now to consider policies and support methods now.

Keywords: Seminar activity · Seminar management system · University education · Communication skills · Fundamental competencies for working persons · Presentation skills

1 Introduction

Since the early 2000s, different methods for providing universal access via distance education, such as the OpenCourseWare program and massively open online courses, have rapidly gained prominence, and universities worldwide have been pressed to change with the times. Although it seems that in the near future most lecture-type classes will likely be offered through distance education to off-campus locations, discussion- and participatory-type lessons continue to be performed mainly at university campuses, and even at Japanese universities still require in-person attendance.

The transformation of Japanese universities advances along with the dynamics of Japanese society. The significance of the existence of the university is about to change. As an example of this, corporate society requests that universities cultivate the Fundamental Competencies for Working Persons, which consist of three competencies (Action, Thinking, Teamwork) and 12 capacity elements (Ministry of Economy, Trade and Industry 2006). Face-to-face communication is essential in nurturing these abilities. From the above, expert knowledge education will shift to distance education, and the center of competency education will shift to university face-to-face education respectively.

S. Yamamoto (Ed.): HIMI 2017, Part II, LNCS 10274, pp. 50–61, 2017.
DOI: 10.1007/978-3-319-58524-6_5

Professor Keizo Nagaoka of Waseda University suggests that the core role of competency education in face-to-face education is "seminar activities" (Nagaoka and Kometani 2016). There are some peculiarities in Japanese seminar activities. In most Japanese universities, seminars are institutionalized in the curriculum. Seminars and laboratory classes taken by undergraduates at science and engineering universities emphasize training similar to that of traditional craftsmen, in which tacit knowledge, rather than intellectual knowledge, is emphasized.

Such family-like seminar activities have worked well for human-resource training of engineers from science and engineering universities and departments, especially during Japan's period of high economic growth from the 1960s to the 1970s (McGuire 1996). They were perhaps consistent with the goal of fostering capable talent who could work in an industrialized society. However, a more rational sophistication that is compatible with the mature post-industrialization society of Japan and the present knowledge society is necessary.

Learning management systems (LMS) that facilitate the operation and management of lectures have been introduced in 74.8% of national universities in Japan (Ministry of Education, Culture, Sports, Science and Technology 2013). If we consider seminar activities as the center of university education, a similar seminar management system (SMS) is necessary. We are currently developing a SMS and using it in actual situations. In this paper, we report on the development state. First, we organize and structure seminar activities and introduce learning management functions for competency education in seminar activities. We then evaluate the developed SMS's effectiveness at developing presentation skills, a required competency, through usage results and a questionnaire survey of the perspectives of seminar students using the developed SMS.

2 Structure of Seminar Activity

2.1 The Process of Skill Improvement

As a measure of competency training, it is effective to repeat instruction until students become accustomed to the process of goal setting, behavior, evaluation, and reviewing. Instructors are required to reflect on seminars and form educational philosophies and facilitation methods that build a better learning community. In this research, we applied triple-loop learning (e.g., Romme and Van Witteloostuijn 1999) to seminar activities for organizational learning (Fig. 1), and we developed supporting functions on the premise of this learning process. Mouri (2007) states that instructor encouragement to enhance the group's positive entrainment in seminar activities is indispensable, and Fushikida et al. (2014) stated that instructor encouragement led to a sense of growth in generic skills (competencies) and was effective toward student satisfaction with seminar activities. The "community improvement" process shown in Fig. 1 is thus important for effective learning in seminar activities.

Fig. 1. Improvement cycle of seminar activities

2.2 The Curriculum of Standard "Seminar Activity"

The expertise to be acquired varies among seminars, so it is difficult to realize faculty development through seminar activities (Mouri 2007). In contrast, the goals of activities and their required communication skills are common to many seminars, so support is possible. We therefore categorized representative seminar activities (Table 1). The classifications are based on the seminar activity studies of Mouri (2007) and Fushikida et al. (2014).

Table 1. Classification of seminar activities based on educational goals (competencies) and activity goals

Goal	Presentation	Speech	Discussion	Document production
Learn from previous studies	Prior research introduction		Prior research discussion	Literature review writing
Developing students' own research	Presentation of research progress		Graduation research meeting	Research activity report
Job hunting	Job hunting lecture	Adlib speech	Current topics discussion	Entry sheet mutual check
Seminar camp	Sharing camp experience	Training while traveling by bus	Workshop in camp	Camp study report
Seminar selection	Seminar briefing session			Seminar advertisement competition

Both affirmed the benefit of incorporating group activities, and additionally Fushikida et al. (2014) suggests the effectiveness of incorporating situational aspects, such as job hunting. Mouri (2007) affirmed the technical reading conventionally implemented in seminar activities as a means of knowledge composition through communication.

To incorporate the merits of science and engineering seminars pointed out by McGuire (1996), in this research document production (text communication) is positioned as a competency, and "developing student-initiated research" as an activity goal. We have already developed functions aimed at supporting document production in seminar activities, and our SMS has been expanded to integrate the results (Kometani and Nagaoka 2015, 2016).

3 Functions for Skill Improvement in Seminar Activities

3.1 System Targets and Difficulties During Action Improvement

In previous research, many methodologies have been used to improve students' presentation skills. However, this has not yielded sufficient research for supporting students through seminar activities on a daily basis. Therefore, our system used the action improvement cycle in Fig. 1 to specifically target support for daily improvement.

To improve presentation skills, students must objectively know their own presentation behavior, and change this behavior based on the specific needs of the presentation. Without support, it is difficult for novice presenters to improve their reflections and planning skills in the action improvement process.

3.2 Functions

To address these difficulties, we developed presentation summary functions. Figures 2, 3, 4, and 5 show the system's user interface (UI).

The UI consists of 6 parts:

  i. Presentation slide-sharing function
 ii. Presentation video-sharing function
iii. Presentation evaluation and comments function
 iv. Self-evaluation, peer evaluation, and instructor evaluation overlay radar-chart
  v. Real-time comments function
 vi. General comment-sharing function
vii. Presentation comparison function

Figure 2 shows the UI for learning outcomes in the developed SMS (Nagaoka and Kometani 2016). Figure 2 shows the presentation "mode", which can be combined with presentation files, videos, and colored radar charts for self and peer assessments, along with peer comments. It is designed for feedback regarding the activities listed in Table 1 by associating multiple students. In the case of a speech, the presentation file is hidden. During discussions, 360° video can be shown, and then, and hidden during document production.

Fig. 2. Presentation summary UI (elements i, ii, iv, v)

Fig. 3. Evaluation and comment UI (element iii)

スライドの光りやさ	木田雄川		
スライドの見やすさ	長谷川利治	○（できていた）	図とコメントのバランスがとてもいいです
スライドの見やすさ	吉井秀平	♡（素晴らしい）	
スライドの見やすさ	奈良緑	○（できていた）	
スライドの見やすさ	保坂明子	♡（素晴らしい）	
スライドの見やすさ	佐々木遼太	○（できていた）	
スライドの見やすさ	妻鹿宏紀	○（できていた）	
スライドの見やすさ	半澤春奈	○（できていた）	
スライドの見やすさ	森下瑞季	○（できていた）	見やすい！
スライドの見やすさ	柏瀬理沙	○（できていた）	シンプルで見やすかったです！

閉じる

Fig. 4. Overall comment function (Popup UI; element vi)

Fig. 5. Two presentations being compared for reflection (element vii)

4　Practice

4.1　Methodology

The students are third-year undergraduate students (7 males and 3 females), and are novice presenters enrolled in a seminar taught by the authors. Each student gave five presentations throughout the period, during 120-minute seminar classes that introduce previous research (Table 1). The feedback methods varied. Paper assessment sheets were used in the first presentations. In the second and third presentations, students used a prototype SMS that provides raw assessment data. In the fourth and fifth presentations, the functions described above were used. Before using the proposed functions, the students assessed a senior student's presentation as an exercise. The data was obtained in 2015.

In each seminar activity, two to four students made presentations of about ten to fifteen minutes per person, and received peer assessments using the assessment items in Table 2. The assessment scores were 3 ("excellent"), 2 ("good"), or 1 ("not good").

Table 2. List of assessment items

Category	Assessment item
Contents	Did you understand the content of the presentation?
	Was the presentation concisely summarized?
	Was the presenter interested in the content?
	Did the presenter go beyond just reading slides?
	Was the presenter sufficiently prepared?
Delivery	Were the slides legible?
	Were the slides interesting?
	Was the presenter's voice volume appropriate?
	Was the presenter's speaking speed appropriate?
	Did the presenter pause appropriately?
	Did the presenter make eye contact with viewers?
	Was the presenter relaxed?
	Did the presenter use good body language?
Others	Was the presentation of an appropriate length?
	Did the presenter provide concise answers to questions?

4.2 Change in Peer Assessments

As Table 3 shows, mean peer assessments improved after each presentation. Improvements between the third and fourth presentations are particularly notable. This may be a result of assessing presentations by fourth-year students following introduction of the new system, through which the novice presenters gained various insights.

Table 3. Changes in peer assessment scores

	1st	2nd	3rd	4th	5th
Mean score of all students and items	1.70	1.80	1.85	1.96	1.98
Score growth over previous presentation (absolute)		0.10	0.05	0.11	0.03
Score growth over previous presentation (percentage)		5.68%	2.54%	6.11%	1.29%
Final growth from initial presentation					16%

5 Questionnaire Survey

5.1 Overview

We developed these functions and implemented them over the 2015 and 2016 school years. The presentation theme was a literature survey for third-year students enrolled in the seminar. A total of 18 students (8 in 2015, 10 in 2016) answered the questionnaire. The question items inquired into the following:

(1) Usefulness of the functions for preparation
(2) Usefulness for increasing awareness of areas for improvement
(3) Usefulness for deciding which presentation behaviors must be changed.

Each question was evaluated on a 6-point Likert scale, along with a free description section for describing the reasons for the evaluation or situation where students could use the functions effectively to improve their presentation skills. Function (vii) is planned to be offered in future development, so this is excluded from the evaluations considered in this paper.

5.2 Results

5.2.1 Usefulness of Functions for Preparation

Figure 6 shows student responses regarding usefulness of the developed system for preparation of presentations. Many students responded that the functions were useful. Figure 7 shows which functions were reported to be useful for preparation. Presentation slides were most useful for students. Student comments stated that "seeing the good points of other students' slides were useful when making my own slides", that "good slides provide good examples", and that "beautiful slides made by more experienced students are useful". During preparation, presentation slides with assessment data are effective.

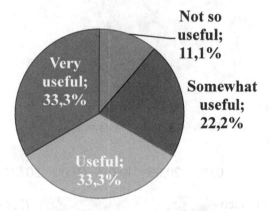

Fig. 6. Usefulness for preparation

5.2.2 Effects on Awareness

Figure 8 shows the usefulness for awareness. Many students reported that the functions were useful when reviewing their presentations. Figure 9 shows which functions were useful for awareness. The presentation video and radar chart functions were especially useful, with students making comments such as "I can check results of the evaluation, comments, and the presentation video, so I can clearly determine where I need to improve", and "I can check my own presentation objectively". The presentation video with assessment data and comments were effective for improving awareness.

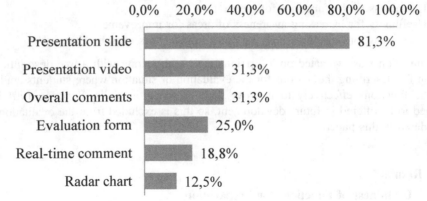

Fig. 7. Useful functions for preparation

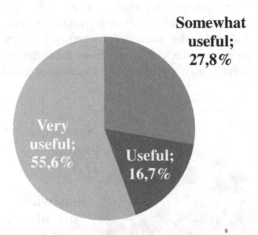

Fig. 8. Usefulness for awareness

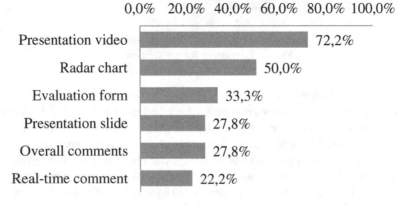

Fig. 9. Useful functions for awareness

5.2.3 Effect for Behavioral Change

Figure 10 shows the usefulness for preparation. Many students reported that the functions were useful for effecting behavioral changes in their presentation. Figure 11 shows which functions were useful for behavioral change. As in the results for awareness, the presentation video was most useful and the presentation slides, radar chart, and overall comments were useful as supplementary resources. Students made comments such as "I can imitate the good behavior of other students", and "I can objectively observe the volume of my voice and my body movement, so I can check if my behaviors are improved".

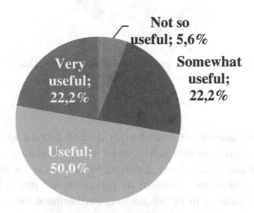

Fig. 10. Usefulness for behavioral change

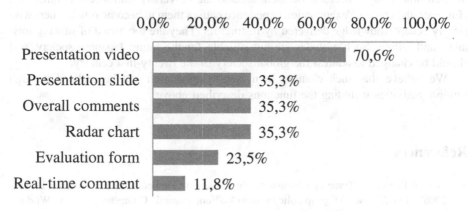

Fig. 11. Useful functions for behavioral change

5.2.4 Overall Evaluation

Figure 12 shows overall student evaluations of the functions. All students reported that the functions were useful overall, indicating that there is a need for these functions. Therefore, the functions can be used in daily seminar activities.

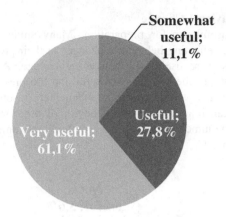

Fig. 12. Overall evaluation of usefulness for presentation skill improvement

6 Conclusion

The results of the peer assessment described in Sect. 4 and the questionnaire survey revealed that students have positive opinions of the presentation skill improvement functions of the developed SMS, showing that its functions can be introduced in actual situations. To increase the convenience of its functions, we intend to develop a data analysis and feedback method in future studies. Furthermore, functions for improvement of overall communication skills will be developed.

Undergraduate students who are new to the seminar community have self-confidence in their knowledge, because of their success at university entrance examinations. However, the entrance examination experience causes them to become rote learners who simply accept knowledge delivered by instructors. They are too afraid of making mistakes and failing. Such attitudes are not suitable for the future Japanese society, and should be changed to address the global society of the twenty-first century.

We believe that such changes in university education can be realized through seminar activities including the functions described above.

References

Ministry of Economy, Trade and Industory: Fundamental Competencies for Working Persons (2006). http://www.meti.go.jp/policy/kisoryoku/Fundamental Competencies for Working Persons.ppt. Accessed 6 Feb 2017

Nagaoka, K., Kometani, Y.: Seminar Activity as Center of University Education - SMS: Seminar Management System, Proposal and State of Development - Research Report, pp. 307–314. Japan Society for Educational Technology, JSET16–1 (2016). (in Japanese)

McGuire, J.R.: Engineering education in Japan: my experience. In: Proceedings of Frontiers in Education Conference, pp. 368–371 (1996)

Ministry of Education, Culture, Sports, Science and Technology: Research on utilization of ICT in higher education institutions (2013). http://www.mext.go.jp/a_menu/koutou/itaku/1347642. htm. Accessed 6 Feb 2017. (in Japanese)

Romme, A.G.L., Van Witteloostuijn, A.: Circular organizing and triple loop learning. J. Organ. Change Manage **12**(5), 439–454 (1999)

Mouri, M.: Possibility and necessity of FD concerning class of seminar style. Kagawa Univ. Jpn. **15**, 1–6 (2007). (in Japanese)

Fushikida, W., Kitamura, S., Yamauchi, Y.: The effects of lesson structures in undergraduate seminars on growth in generic skills. J. Jpn. Soc. Educ. Technol. **37**(4), 419–433 (2014). (in Japanese)

Kometani, Y., Nagaoka, K.: Development of a seminar management system. In: Yamamoto, S. (ed.) HCI 2015. LNCS, vol. 9173, pp. 350–361. Springer, Cham (2015). doi:10.1007/978-3-319-20618-9_35

Kometani, Y., Nagaoka, K.: Construction of a literature review support system using latent dirichlet allocation. In: Yamamoto, S. (ed.) HIMI 2016. LNCS, vol. 9735, pp. 159–167. Springer, Cham (2016). doi:10.1007/978-3-319-40397-7_16

Designing the Learning Goal Space for Human Toward Acquiring a Creative Learning Skill

Takato Okudo[1(✉)], Keiki Takadama[2], and Tomohiro Yamaguchi[1]

[1] National Institute of Technology, Nara College, Nara, Japan
{okudo,yamaguch}@info.nara-k.ac.jp
[2] The University of Electro-Communications, Tokyo, Japan
keiki@inf.uec.ac.jp

Abstract. This paper presents the way to design the learning support system toward acquiring a creative skill on learning. The objective of this research is designing the learning goal space for a creative learner. There are two research goals. One is to establish designing the creative learning task. The other is to make clear the human sense of creativity. As the background of this research, the jobs having the difficulty for both AI and computer will remain in the future. Both AI and computer need high creativity or social skills. However, it is too difficult for computer to acquire human's creativity. To solve this problem, we focus on the way to utilize higher creativity of human than that of computers. We proposed three kinds of the methods. First, it is the visualization of learning traces to support awareness of creativity on the learning. Second is the discovery support for unknown solutions by generating the derived achievement based on negation of his/her found solution. Third is generating the derived achievement by the justification of the found solution. We conducted the preliminary learning experiment by three human subjects. In addition, to evaluate the meaning of these results, we conducted the questionnaire and the hearing investigation. By the preliminary experimental results, we make the hypothesis that the proposed methods are effective to the motivation on creative learning.

Keywords: Creative learning · The learning goal space · Derived achievement · Learning support

1 Introduction

This paper presents the way to design the learning support system toward acquiring a creative skill on learning. The objective of this research is designing the learning goal space for a creative learner. There are two research goals. One is to establish designing the creative learning task of the learning support system. The other is to make clear the human sense of creativity. In the background of this research, the progress of information technology will make that about half of human jobs are replaced by computers in near future. The remained jobs having technical difficulty for both AI and computers need high creativity or social skills.

This paper describes the creativity for both human and the system. Previous research on human creativity suggests that "creativity is the ability to come up with

S. Yamamoto (Ed.): HIMI 2017, Part II, LNCS 10274, pp. 62–73, 2017.
DOI: 10.1007/978-3-319-58524-6_6

ideas or artifacts that are novel and valuable" [1]. In addition, "one process of creating ideas involves making unfamiliar combinations of familiar ideas, requiring a rich store of knowledge" [1]. However, it is too difficult for computer to acquire human's creativity. The reason is that it is not clear to combine familiar ideas by unfamiliar ways.

To solve this problem, we focus on the way to utilize higher creativity of human than that of computers. We propose the mechanism based on the framework of our continuous learning support system for a human learner to see the creativity on his/her own learning. In the proposed mechanism, the support system generates a derived learning achievement by combining the original achievement and the solution found by the learner. Then the learner can reflect his/her own learning trace on the learning goal space. Owing to them, the support system suggests the awareness toward both unclear learning results and the sense of values for the learner.

There are three kinds of the proposed support methods. First, it is the visualization of learning traces to support awareness of creativity on the learning. We design the learning goal space to visualize learning traces. They are the distribution of the learning goals found by the learner who learns the original achievement and the derived one generated by the support system. It makes easier to reflect the learning orientation by means of showing the relative positioning of the learning goal to the learning trace.

Second is the discovery support for unknown solutions by generating the derived achievement based on negation of his/her found shortest solution. It encourages the learner to perceive his/her unclear solutions. Third is the generating the derived achievement by the justification of the found redundant solution. It encourages the learner to perceive his/her unclear sense of values.

2   Background

This section describes the theoretical background of this research. After the research on the creativity is described, we summarize an overview of continuous learning because it is the basic framework of our creative learning process, and then we describe the creative learning skill.

2.1   The Research on the Creativity

We consider creativity at the base of J.P. Guilford's approach. Guilford says creativity has primary characteristics, *sensitivity to problems, fluency in generating ideas, flexibility* and *novelty of ideas*, and *the ability to synthesize and reorganize information* [2]. *Sensibility to problems* is the skill to find the problem. We consider that it is the skill to comprehend the learning task. *Fluency in generating ideas* shows how many ideas a human create. *Flexibility* is the skill to create various ideas. *Novelty of ideas* is the skill to create unusual ideas. *The ability to synthesize and reorganize information* is the skill to utilize a thing for the divergent purposes. We consider it needs to focus on the interpretation of the meta-learning process.

Then we describe several characteristics which are concerned in our research. As *sensibility to problems* in the task, the learner can comprehend the structure of the learning environment through the trial and errors. As *fluency in generating ideas* in the task, the learner can find many solutions since the task gives the achievement to him/her. As *flexibility* in the task, the learner can find the various solutions by seeing his/her learning trace in the learning goal space.

2.2 The Creative Learning

We define *the creative learning* as continuous learning with discoveries of unusual solutions from achievements in the learner's own. In our previous research [6], the human designed the achievements for a learner as the sequence of mazes. However, creative learner needs a new achievement continuously. In other words, it is necessary for the creative learner to discover the new achievements by himself/herself, but it is not easy. So we propose the interactive mechanism between a human learner and the learning support system in which the system derives the achievements from his/her found solutions with two kinds of heuristics. Once the learner found an unusual solution, the system can derive the new achievements from the unusual one.

2.3 The Creative Learning Process

An overview of continuous learning

Our creative learning process is based on the individual continuous learning process [5]. The concept of continuous learning comes from Industrial and organizational psychology [4]. One of conceptual definitions of individual continuous learning is follows; "Continuous learning at the individual level is regularly changing behavior based on a deepening and broadening of one's skills, knowledge, and worldview" [3]. In detail, please refer [6].

The flow of the creative learning process

Figure 1 shows the flow of the creative learning process based on the continuous learning process. This process consists of triple cycle. Innermost cycle is called *a trial*. A *trial* is defined as a transition sequence from start state to encountering either a goal state or a wall. In this cycle, a learner repeats an action and his/her mental process including awareness until he/she results in either success or fail of the task. Second cycle is called *an achievement*. An *achievement* is defined as a unit of the main task which is the learning of a maze with the start and the invisible goal. In this cycle, when the trial terminates by the encounter with a goal, the learner finds the solution of the achievement. Then, the learner reflects the trial by the reflection of viewing his/her learning traces on the learning goal space. This process is described at Sect. 3.4. If current trial is not accomplished, he/she restarts the trial from the start state. Outmost cycle is the creative learning cycle. When the learner accomplished current achievement, the system generates a derived achievement according to the learner's solution, and then, He/she can challenge next new achievement. Section 3.3 describes this process.

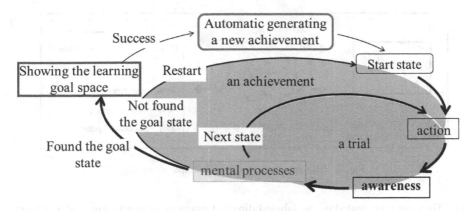

Fig. 1. The flow of the creative learning process

2.4 The Creative Learning Skill

We define *the creative learning skill* as the learning skill to try to find more creative solutions on the given tasks or problems having optimal or entrenched solution. We propose the interactive mechanism consisting of two parts. The human part is to find a new solution from the achievement. The support system's part is to generate a new achievement derived from the human learner's solution by adding the sub-reward on it randomly to support the learner to find more creative solutions.

3 Designing the Creative Learning Support System

3.1 The Learning Environment by an Maze Model

As the learning environment for a human learner, we adopt a grid maze from start to goal since it is a familiar example to find the path through a trial and error process. First, we define *a maze*, *a path* in the maze, and *a solution* in the maze. A *maze* is the shape of 2D maze defined by three kinds of states (start, goal and normal state) and the walls surrounding the states. In detail, it is described later as the maze model. A *path* consists of states and action transition sequence from the start state to the goal state. A *solution* is a path of the achievement of the maze.

A maze model for creative learning version consists of five elements, state set, transitions and walls, action set, and rewards. Figure 2 shows the structure of a 2D grid maze. The n × m grid maze with four neighbors consists of the n × m n number of 1 × 1 squares. It is called a *simple maze* which is surrounded by walls in a rectangle shape. Figure 2(a) shows a 3 × 2 simple maze with a start and a goal. In a grid maze, every square touches one of their edges except for a wall. Each square in a maze model is called *a state*. A state can be visited at once.

Transitions between states in a maze model is defined whether corresponding square with four neighbors, {up, down, left, right} is connected or not connected by a

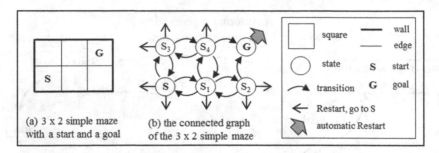

Fig. 2. The structure of a 3 × 2 simple maze [5]

wall. They are represented as the labeled directed graph as shown in Fig. 2 (b). Action set is defined as a set of labels to distinguish the possible transitions of a state. In a grid maze, the learner can take four kinds of actions: up, right, down, left.

Note that a trial is a transition sequence from the start state to encountering either a goal state or a wall, and the action toward a wall results in the transition to the start state to restart the trial. Transition to the goal state results in the success of the achievement, then the learner finds a solution and obtains a main reward (+1).

3.2 Designing the Creative Learning Support System

This section describes the way to automatically generate a new achievement as shown in Fig. 1. First we describe a stage, an achievement and a stage in the creative learning task. A stage is a set of achievements of the same maze shape. An achievement of the creative learning task is defined as the learning of a maze to find a path from the start state to the goal state. An achievement consists of a maze shape and generated sub-rewards if any. It is a unit of the learning which is either an original achievement which consists of only maze shape or a derived achievement which contains generated sub-rewards.

Figure 3 shows the flow of generating a new achievement by the system. The inner loop in Fig. 3 shows the interactive process of generating a new achievement by the system from the solution the learner searched. After a solution is found by the learner, if it is a new one, it is displayed on the learning goal space as the found learning goal for the reflection of the learner, and then the system derives the achievement by adding a reward according to the type of the solution. The system resets the achievement and the learner tries it. The outer loop in Fig. 3 shows the progress of the learning stage. It is two ways. One is when the learner decides to leave a current stage. Another is the decision of the system when the learner finds same solution in series. In this paper, the sequence of the rectangle-shaped maze shape of the stage is predefined as 2 × 3, 3 × 3, 3 × 4, 4 × 4, and so on.

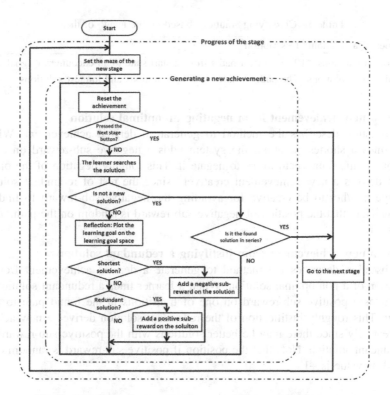

Fig. 3. The flow of generating a new achievement by the system

3.3 Designing Automatically Generating the Derived Achievement

Classification of the solutions for creative learning

This section describes the classification of the solutions for creative learning. First, we mention the size of solution. Table 1 shows the classifying solutions based on the length of them. We classify them whether it is shortest or not. Note that to make a redundant solution into the learning goal, it is necessary to introduce some optimality.

Second, we introduce the optimality of a solution to define the quality of solution. This paper adopts average reward reinforcement learning framework. In it, optimal solution is defined as a solution with the maximum average reward. Note that average reward of it is the sum of the acquired rewards divided by the solution length. Therefore, the shortest solution with acquiring rewards has a tendency to be optimal.

In the field of reinforce learning, the way to find an optimal solution has been investigated in recent years. However, it is not the end of learning on creative learning. So we focus on the learning after an optimal solution found, and also focus on redundant, i.e. non-optimal solutions to utilize them since they have not been drawn attention as learning goals. Next subsection describes how to derive the learning goal from a shortest solution and from a redundant solution.

Table 1. Classifying solutions based on the length of them

The types of a solution	Description
The shortest solutions	The shortest paths from a start state to an encountering goal state
The redundant solutions	The paths besides shortest solutions and longest solutions

Deriving a new achievement from negating an optimal solution

This subsection describes the method to generate a derived achievement. When a learner finds a shortest solution, the system adds a negative sub-reward on one of transitions in the found path to try to negate it. This roughly negation of the optimal solution derives a new achievement creatively since the rest of redundant solutions encourage him/her to be creative for avoiding the negative sub-reward to find new solutions. Note that the position of negative sub-reward is random on the path, and its value is −1.

Deriving a new achievement from justifying a redundant solution

This subsection describes the method to generate a derived achievement from the justification of a non-optimal solution. When a learner finds a redundant solution, the system adds a positive sub-reward on one of transitions in the found path to try to justify it. This roughly justification of the redundant solution derives a new achievement creatively since there may be better solutions with the positive sub-reward than this redundant solution. Note that the position if positive sub-reward is random on the path and its value is +1.

3.4   Designing the Learning Goal Space

An overview of the learning goal space

The learning goal space is the space in which learning goals are positioned to display. The learning goal space has the vertical axis as the solution quality and the horizontal axis as the solution size. *A learning goal* is a set of solutions which both the solution quality and the solution size are the same in solutions found at achievements by the learner. It is positioned as a point on the learning goal space. In this paper, the vertical axis is defined as the total self-entropy based on the acquired rewards, and the horizontal axis is defined as the length of the solution. Note that these definitions are not presented to a human learner. Figure 4 shows the illustrated example of the learning goal space. LGi is the ith learning goal found by the learner. The number of LG expresses the order in which the learner finds them. The transition from LG1 to LG2 shows that the direction of learning is right, and it means the learning only increases the solution size towards the horizontal learning goal. LG3 is transited from LG2 towards the vertical direction in which the solution quality only grows. LG4 is transited from LG3 towards the direction simultaneously to increase both the solution size and the solution quality.

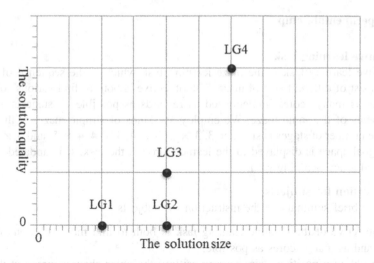

Fig. 4. The illustrated example of the learning goal space

The total self-entropy based on the acquired reward

In this research, we employ the difficulty to obtain positive sub-rewards in solutions as the index expressing the solution quality. Based on the self-entropy in the field of information theory, the self-entropy is proportional to the reciprocal of the occurrence probability of an acquired reward. In this paper, the self-entropy based on the acquired reward equation is as follows:

$$I(r) = -\log_{10} P(r)$$

where r is acquiring the positive sub-reward as the event and $P(r)$ is the occurrence probability of the event per a step. Here, the occurrence probability of the positive sub-rewards is as follows:

$$P(r) = n(r)/L$$

where $n(r)$ is the total positive sub-reward sizes and L is the expected length of the cycle. The total self-entropy based on the acquired reward is as follows:

$$S = \sum_{r \in \mathbb{R}} I(r)$$

where S is the total self-entropy based on the acquired reward and $\mathbb{R} = \{r_1, r_2, \ldots\}$ is the set of the positive sub-reward.

4   Preliminary Experiment

To examine the effects of our creative learning support system, we conducted the preliminary experiment by three subjects.

4.1 Experimental Setup

The creative learning task

The creative learning task is the maze learning task which is the sequence of stages which consist of different size of maze. The objective is both to find various solutions and to get as many scores implemented as rewards as possible. A stage is a set of achievements of the same maze. We employ six kinds of simple mazes with visible walls. The number of stages is six, $2 \times 3, 3 \times 3, 3 \times 4, 4 \times 4, 4 \times 5,$ and $5 \times 5.$ The learning goal space is displayed to the learner through the task. It is updated when a subject find a new learning goal.

The instruction for subjects

We show a brief summary of the instruction for subjects.

- The objective of the creative learning task is both to find more solutions in each maze and as many scores as possible.
- If you obtain a positive score on a transition, the color changes green at the corresponding rectangle grid between the neighboring square grids.
- If you obtain a negative score on a transition, the color changes purple at the corresponding rectangle grid between the neighboring square grids.
- If you find a same solution in series, the stage progresses.

The measurement items

The major measurement items of the experiment are as follows:

(a) the number of the trials
(b) the number of the found solutions
(c) the number of the learning goals
(d) the total number of the acquired positive sub-rewards
(e) the total number of the acquired negative sub-rewards
(f) Score
(g) The experiment duration

Note that (g) = (c) + (d) − (e).

4.2 Experimental Results

The experimental results suggest that the subjects learned continuously because the average experiment duration of three subjects is twenty five minutes (one thousand five hundred seconds), and the average number of the found solutions of the subject is one hundred twenty two. Table 2 shows the experimental results. Especially, the number of the stages in which three subjects found more than ten solutions is three. This is the same as the half of the all six stages.

Next, we report the detail of the results. Table 3 shows the average learning results of three subjects per stage in which they found more than ten solutions.

In these stages, the average number of the found solutions per stage is 36.7 and the total number of the found solutions in the three stages accounted for ninety percent

Table 2. Experimental results

measurement items subjects	(a) The number of trials	(b) The number of the found solution	(c) The number of the learning goals	(d) The total number of the acquired positive sub-rewards	(e) The total number of the acquired negative sub-rewards	(f) Score	(g) The experiment duration (sec)
subject1	202	169	79	1061	183	1000	1628
subject2	140	96	67	395	78	415	1425
subject3	122	102	51	328	91	370	1447
Average	154.7	122.3	65.7	594.7	117.3	595.0	1500.0
Standard deviation	42.0	40.5	14.0	405.2	57.2	351.5	111.4

Table 3. The average learning results per stage in which three subjects found more than ten solutions

measurement items subjects	(b) The number of the found solution	(c) The number of the learning goals	(d) The total number of the acquired positive sub-rewards	(e) The total number of the acquired negative sub-rewards	(g) The experiment duration (sec)
subject1	52.3	40.3	349.3	60.7	561.0
subject2	27.0	42.0	128.0	23.7	402.0
subject3	30.7	32.3	105.7	29.0	387.3
Average	36.7	38.2	194.3	37.8	450.1
Standard deviation	13.7	5.2	134.7	20.0	96.3

(330/367) of the total number in all the stages. From above, it is suggested that the subjects found an average of more than one hundred solutions in the learning experiment, and they could continuously conduct the task.

Then, we describe the effect of the support toward finding creative solutions by automatically generating the derived achievement. As shown in Table 3, the number of the acquired positive sub-rewards by automatically generating the derived achievement accounted for ninety eight percent (1048/1061, 384/395, 317/328) in the stages in which the subjects found more than ten solutions. These suggest that the support by automatically generating the derived achievement motivated the three subjects creatively to find new solutions.

Table 4. The factors which motivate the subject

questionnaires / subjects	What are the factors motivate you to continue the experimental task in the whole experimental task and each stage?	
	In the whole experiment task	In each stage
subject1	Searching solutions and Score	Searching solutions, Score, and Appearances of the sub-rewards
subject2	Searching solutions, Score, and The number of solutions	Score and The number of the found solutions
subject3	Searching solutions, Appearances of a new maze task, Finding solutions	Searching solutions, Finding a goal state, and The learning goal space

4.3 Discussions

First, we analyze how effect our proposed creative learning support methods gave to the subject's creative learning from the questionnaires. Table 4 shows the factors which motivate the subject to continue the task. In the questionnaire, all subjects answered searching the solutions motivated them to continue the task. In the hearing investigation, two subjects answered that the learning goal space motivated them to continue the task and they do not pay attention the sub-rewards. By contrast, the other subject answered that he don't see the learning goal space and he find out how to add a sub-reward.

Second, we discuss the effect of the reflection of learning by presenting the learning goal space. Figures 5, 6, and 7 show the results of the learning goal space of each subject. Figure 5 shows the experimental result of the learning goal space of the subject who obtains the maximum sum of the positive score (the sum of the positive rewards) within three. The learning goals on it are narrowly distributed toward upper as the solution grows in comparison with that of other subjects shown in Figs. 6 and 7. Note that the number of learning goals on the learning goal space equals the number of the

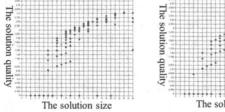

Fig. 5. The learning goal space of 1st subject

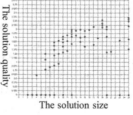

Fig. 6. The learning goal space of 2nd subject

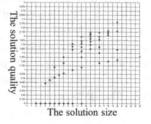

Fig. 7. The learning goal space of 3rd subject

points on the learning goal space, and the points on the horizontal axis are the solutions without positive sub-rewards.

Third, we discuss the meaning of our creative learning support which is directing the creative learning by adding two kinds of sub-rewards. Automatically generating the derived achievement supports both convergent thinking and divergent thinking on creative thinking. Adding a positive sub-reward to the found path supports convergent thinking because the learner tries to approach the similar solution to the found one to obtain the positive sub-reward. In contrast, adding a negative sub-reward to the found path supports divergent thinking because the learner tries to find different solution against the found one to avoid the negative sub-reward. So the learning diverges.

5 Conclusions

This paper presented the interactive method for the human to creatively learn under the learning support system. We described the way to design the learning support system towards acquiring the creative skill on learning. We proposed automatically generating the derived achievement from the found solution and the learning goal space to the learner as the reflection of learning. As the future work, we are planning to conduct the update version of the experiment.

Acknowledgements. The authors would like to thank Prof. Habib and Prof. Shimohara for offering a good opportunity to present this research. This work was supported by JSPS KAKENHI (Grant-in-Aid for Scientific Research ©) Grant Number 16K00317.

References

1. Frey, C.B., Osborne, M.A.: The future of employment: how susceptible are jobs to computerisation? Oxford Martin School Working Paper No. 7 (2013)
2. Finke, R.A., Ward, T.B., Smith, S.M.: Creative Cognition. Institute of Technology, Massachusetts (1992)
3. Sessa, V.I., London, M.: Continuous Learning in Organizations: Individual, Group, and Organizational Perspectives, pp. 17–36. Psychology Press, New York (2006)
4. Smita, J., Trey, M.: Facilitating continuous learning: review of research on individual learning capabilities and organizational learning environments. In: The Annual Meeting of the AECT International Convention, Louisville (2012). http://www.memphis.edu/icl/idt/clrc/clrc-smita-research.pdf
5. Yamaguchi, T., Takemori, K., Tamai, Y., Takadama, K.: Analyzing human's continuous learning processes with the reflection sub task. J. Commun. Comput. **12**(1), 20–27 (2015). David Publishing
6. Yamaguchi, T., Tamai, Y., Takadama, K.: Analyzing human's continuous learning ability with the reflection cost. In: Proceedings of 41st Annual Conference of the IEEE Industrial Electronics Society (IECON 2015), pp. 2920–2925 (2015)

Proposal of Educational Curriculum of Creating Hazard Map with Tablet-Type Device for Schoolchildren

Daisuke Shirai[1(✉)], Makoto Oka[1], Sakae Yamamoto[2], and Hirohiko Mori[1]

[1] Tokyo City University, Tokyo, Japan
g1681806@tcu.ac.jp
[2] Tokyo University of Science, Tokyo, Japan

Abstract. In this paper, we propose a new educational curriculum of creating hazard map with tablet-type device for disaster prevention especially for school-children and a application software as the educational tool. To create educational curriculum and application, we interviewed the elementary school teachers and found features schoolchildren. In addition, we experimented in order to evaluate the educational curriculum and the application, and reveal new features of school-children. As a result, schoolchildren could learn about disaster prevention by an our educational curriculum. In addition, we revealed new two features of the schoolchildren. First, recognition of landmark is different from between school-children and adults. In addition, schoolchildren frequently used landmarks that are familiar to them life such as related to the city and public facility. Second, schoolchildren can do operation of electronic map such as changing map scale and slide according to the purpose.

Keywords: Education for disaster prevention · Hazard map · Tablet-type device · Disaster and schoolchildren

1 Introduction

1.1 Current Situation of Education for Disaster Prevention

In Japan, large-scale seismic disasters occur frequently. In suffering from the disaster, it is important to ensure ourselves from the ricks, and to do so, the education for disaster prevention at elementary schools is considered significant. It is often said that creating the hazard map of the town they live in is one of the good ways to learn the disaster prevention for the schoolchildren. A hazard map is a map where the necessary information in the disaster are appeared, such as the place of the evacuation centers, what kinds of risks will happen at the place where now we are [1] (Fig. 1). Schoolchildren can know the necessary information of the town when a disaster occurs by creating a hazard map by themselves and can learn about the evacuation route and how to decrease the risks using it.

In Japan, we do not have a specific subject of "disaster prevention education" and the education has been done within the framework of the school curriculum guideline issued by the Ministry of Education. As the new subject of the "Period of Integrated Study" was

© Springer International Publishing AG 2017
S. Yamamoto (Ed.): HIMI 2017, Part II, LNCS 10274, pp. 74–84, 2017.
DOI: 10.1007/978-3-319-58524-6_7

established in 1998 and the education for disaster prevention is sometimes set as one of the themes in the "Period of Integrated Study" among a variety of fields such as financial education and law education and so on, the time to be able to assign for the education for the disaster prevention has been limited. Though The Central Council for Education is discussing to set the education for the disaster prevention as a new subject, the policy has not been completed yet at this moment.

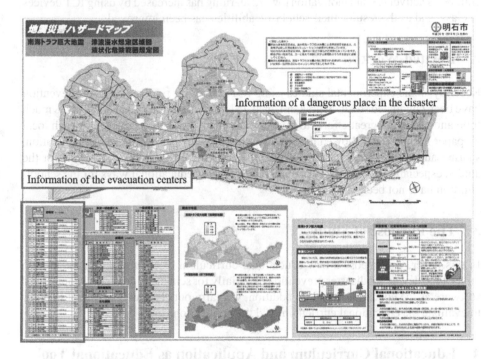

Fig. 1. The hazard map of seismic disaster in Akashi, Hyogo

1.2 Current Situation of Education Using ICT Device

The tablet-typed devices are widely been introduced to the educational field, and The Ministry of Education in Japan reported in "Survey results on actual situation of digitization of education" that the number of the tablet-type devices is 156,018 units in 2015 while 72,678 in 2014, and the use of tablet-type device in elementary school classes has been increased [3]. The advantages of applying ICT device in class are as follows:

- We can use the animations and sounds easily
- We can use various functions such as camera function
- It is easy to update and share the data.

However, the disparity are caused among schools because the capability of the teachers about the ICT and the financial condition of each school.

1.3 Effects by Utilizing ICT Device in Class

Previous researches showed effects of utilizing ICT devices in class. The report of The Ministry of Education in Japan showed that 98.0% of the teachers who carried out the classes utilizing ICT evaluated the effects of increasing interests of the students in learn by providing some fun. The survey on schoolchildren [4] also reported that the schoolchildren's activeness and motivation toward learning has increased by using ICT devices in class, and as the results, their scholastic abilities has been improved.

2 Related Work

Recently, some experimental studies using ICT device for regional disaster prevention have been conducted so far. Murakami, et al. [5] pointed out the issues that it takes much time and needs the great efforts to integrate the many local maps created in each local by paper into one, and showed the effects of the ICT devices of easiness in integration, sharing and updating in real time of map data. As these researches were done for the adults, especially for the elderly people, the effects the educational ways for the schoolchildren have not been known.

3 The Purpose of Study

In this paper, we propose a new educational curriculum of creating hazard map with tablet-type device for disaster prevention especially for schoolchildren and a application software as the educational tool. In addition, we carry out class as experiment in order to evaluate the educational curriculum and the application.

4 Educational Curriculum and Application as Educational Tool

Based on the interview with the elementary school teachers, we developed an educational curriculum and application.

4.1 Educational Curriculum

The classes proposed in this curriculum proceed in following order:

1. The schoolchildren learn how to use the tablet-type devices and our application,
2. The schoolchildren walk around the school for the fieldwork dividing several small groups,
3. The schoolchildren complete the hazard map and discuss about the dangerous place they found using the complete hazard map.

Class of Learning How to Use Tablet-Type Devices and the Application. The teachers stated that some schoolchildren inexperienced the operation of the tablet-type devices. Therefore, we teach schoolchildren how to use the tablet-type devices. It includes the basic operations of tablet-type device, such as how to turn on the tablet, and how to use our application.

The Fieldwork. In this class, the schoolchildren go outside of the school to find seemingly dangerous places in the disaster, and create the hazard map aiming to grasp how to prevent the risks of disaster.

Here, in Japan, public elementary schools are located close to schoolchildren's houses and they can go to school by walk every day. Therefore, the areas for the fieldworks were set about 20–30 min walking around elementary school.

In the fieldwork, the schoolchildren input the location information of objects on the electronic map. In addition, they input comment and type about the object, and take a picture of the object in order to keep memory.

The teachers stated that schoolchildren apt to become their sights narrow when they concentrate on one task. Therefore, if the elementary school student concentrates on the operation of the tablet-type device during the fieldworks, the risk of "walking while using the tablet-type device" increase. Therefore, we decided to instruct not to input information on the map outside but to do it in the classroom.

Class of Completing the Hazard Map and Consideration About the Dangerous Places in Their Town. In this class, schoolchildren complete the hazard map reviewing the fieldwork in each group. After that, each map is integrated into one map, and using it, they discuss with the other groups about where the dangerous places, why they are dangerous, and the useful items they found in their town when a disaster occurs.

4.2 Application as Educational Tool

We developed a creating hazard map application as the educational tool. We show the overview in section.

Basic Function. By turning on application, the map is appeared on screen of tablet. In addition, by operations that pinch in and pinch out, we can change map scale. In addition, by long tapping on map screen, we can put marker which represents the useful items or the dangerous place on the map (Fig. 2).

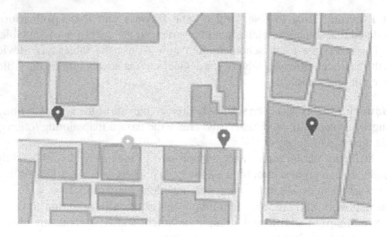

Fig. 2. Map screen and marker

After putting a marker, we can write the comment and select what the type of the object the marker is, and take picture of object (Figs. 3, 4, 5).

Fig. 3. Screen of inputting comment

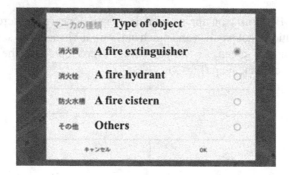

Fig. 4. Screen of inputting type of object

By tapping marker, information it was inputted is showed (Fig. 5).
We can integrate maps which is created by each group to one map (Figs. 6, 7).

Fig. 5. Screen of taking picture object

Function for Schoolchildren. In Japan, the fourth grade children does not have learned the meanings of the map symbols. Instead of the map symbols, therefore, we adopted to display the landmarks, such as shop names, parks and so on in the form of character on the map as a store name or a building name. In applying this curriculum for the higher-grade children who have learned the map symbols, the landmarks can replace the map symbols in our application.

Fig. 6. Screen of marker's information

Fig. 7. The map it was integrated

We walked around the elementary school in order to collect the landmarks such as the name and type of the building. As a result, we got information of about 400 buildings and we added information on buildings that seemed to be familiar to schoolchildren on the map.

5 The Experiment

The fourth grade children in the elementary school were involved in this experiment.

5.1 The Purpose of the Experiment

We experiment in order to evaluate the educational curriculum and the application, and reveal new features of schoolchildren in the fieldwork.

5.2 The Method of the Experiment

In this experiment, divided 43 children into 10 groups according to the areas they live in in order to find the dangerous places in their well-known areas. To maintain their safety, one experimenter joined each group. They made the round trip of the routes they always walk to go to school (Fig. 8).

As the searching objects, we set "a fire extinguisher", "a fire hydrant", "a fire cistern" and "others," supposing fires after earthquakes.

The experimenter attached a wearable video camera in order to record the children's behaviors.

Fig. 8. Scene of the fieldwork

6 Results and Consideration

We got the video about 90 min of the fieldwork. By analyzing these data, we investigated the new features of schoolchildren.

6.1 Distinctive Landmark of Schoolchildren

From the analysis of the video in the fieldworks, we found what landmarks children use. They frequent used landmarks are shown in Table 1.

Table 1. Landmarks and their grouping

Landmarks	Grouping
Okubo street	Group of city
Tyuo street	
crosswalk	
Minami city	
Saiku city	
Naka city	
Nakamati park	Group of public facility
Yamabushi park	
Ushigome police station	
Miyagi Michio's memorial house	
Aizitsu child institution	
Aizitsu elementary school	
Schoolchidren's house	Group of house
Grandmother's house	
Lawson (convenience store)	Group of shop
Butazanmai (beef barbecue restaurant)	
Yasaikeikaku (greengrocer)	
NTT Ushigome building	Group of high building

Table 1 indicates that the landmarks for the children are classified into five types: the names of the main streets and the towns, the public facility (such as the parks and the schools), their own and their relatives' houses, the name of the shops, and the high buildings. The former three results showed that children use the places deeply concerned with their lives as their landmarks, such as the schools, the parks and the friends' houses. This means that the recognition of the landmarks is different from the adults because their living areas and their lifestyle are different from adults. For example, while, from the observation of the adults, they tended to use the name of shops such as Starbucks as a landmark, the children grasp it simply the restaurant. Furthermore, the adults did not tend to use big buildings as landmarks.

This means that, even among the schoolchildren, the landmarks must be different as they develop. As, in our applications, we can easily change landmarks according to the users, we can apply it on the every class of every grades.

6.2 Operation of Electronic Map

Hearing the interviews before conducting the experiment, we had worried whether the fourth grade children would be able to understand maps and they would be able to connect the physical views of the town with the abstract representation of the maps.

However, they could understand the map due to the features of the electronic maps. The electronic maps allows the users to change the scales by zooming in and out. From the analysis of the video in the fieldworks, we observed that they changed the scales of the map according to situation. Schoolchildren used the following two types of map scales.

1. Overall scale where they can grasp the entire school district (Type i).
2. Detail scale where they can confirm just around landmarks (Type ii).

When schoolchildren are walking and putting the marker on the map, they used "Type ii" by zooming in. After putting the maker, they zoomed out the map of "Type i" and confirmed their current position on the map and, confirming it, they went back to "Type ii." In addition, when they can grasp their current position on map but current position was out of the map, they did not zoom our but just moved the displayed area in the same scale. These results means that the electronic map helps the children to comprehend the map and to connect the physical view of the town with the abstract representation of the map.

On the other hand, we could observed some difficulties in operating the tablet. From the video about search scenery, we discovered that when schoolchildren operate electronic map, often the operation result was different from the operation result he was imagining. For example, when schoolchildren slide a map screen, map screen was slid than they had imagined. And then, schoolchildren were confused. They also accidentally touched the screen of the tablet and eventually a displayed area or the scale of the map was changed and moved to the different area from their current position. In occurring such accident, they lost their position on the map. These results indicate that we need to improve the applications as to limit the scale-range of the map, in particular, we should limit the scale range to the above two types. In addition, we should reduce the function of zooming by pinch in and the button for zoom in and out should be implemented.

7 Conclusion

We interviewed the elementary school teachers in order to find features of the schoolchildren. In addition, based on the found feature, we created and propose a new educational curriculum of creating hazard map with tablet-type device for disaster prevention especially for schoolchildren and an application software as the educational tool. Schoolchildren could learn about disaster prevention by our educational curriculum. In addition, we revealed new features of the schoolchildren in following:

- We revealed that recognition of landmark is different from between schoolchildren and adults. In addition, schoolchildren frequently used landmarks that are familiar to them life such as related to the city and public facility. By using tablet-type device, we can prepare landmarks that suitable for elementary school students and show these landmarks to map. In addition, we can do these works to easy.
- We revealed that elementary school students can do operation of electronic map such as changing map scale and slide according to the purpose. This result means that the electronic map helps the children to comprehend the map and to connect the physical view of the town with the abstract representation of the map, electronic map is suitable for a class of creating hazard map.
- In addition, we revealed that elementary school students are not used to operation of tablet-type device or they are difficult to operate tablet-type device accurately. Therefore, we need to improve development applications such as limit the range scale of the map and slide range to and make application operation easier.

8 Prospects for the Future

In experiment, we revealed that distinction of schoolchildren. By developing application based on revealed distinction, we can provide application that simple to use for schoolchildren to operate as an educational tool.

We revealed features of schoolchildren in a fieldwork. Next, we need to reveal features schoolchildren in a deskwork. It makes possible us to provide educational curriculum and application as the educational tool that more suitable for schoolchildren.

References

1. Katada, T., Kimura, S., Kodama, M.: Desirable utilization of flood hazard maps for risk communication. Jpn Soc. Civ. Eng. D, **63**(4), 498–508 (2007)
2. Cabinet Office, Government of Japan: Special Topic of Education for Disaster Prevention, The Page about Information of Disaster Prevention. http://www.bousai.go.jp/kohou/kouhoubousai/h21/01/special_01.html

3. Center for Education Computing: Bulletin About Investigation of the Effect of a Class with Information Communication Technology. http://www.cec.or.jp/cecre/monbu/report/H19ICTkatsuyoureport.pdf
4. Ministry of Education, Culture, Sports, Science and Technology: The Companion About the Information in Education, Chapter 3 Utilizing ICT for Coaching of Education. http://www.mext.go.jp/a_menu/shotou/zyouhou/1259413.htm
5. Murakami, M., Ichi, T., Shibayama, A., Hisada, Y., Endo, M., Hu, Z., Zama, S., Ozawa, Y.: Study on a workshop for disaster miting using WebGIS. In: The 12th Japan Association for Earthquake Engineering, March 2006

Report on Practice of a Learning Support System for Reading Program Code Exercise

Takahito Tomoto[1(✉)] and Takako Akakura[2]

[1] Faculty of Engineering, Tokyo Polytechnic University, Tokyo, Japan
t.tomoto@cs.t-kougei.ac.jp
[2] Faculty of Engineering, Tokyo University of Science, Tokyo, Japan

Abstract. Reading the source code of software programs is an effective way of learning, but novice programmers need (1) exercises that involve reading programs by tracing execution manually, and (2) feedback when they interpret the program incorrectly. In this paper, we propose exercises in which students read programs, and we report on the development of a system that provides feedback on mistakes. Furthermore, we also report the results of a comparison, conducted in a laboratory environment, between the approach proposed here and the conventional approach of learning via creating programs, as well as the results of two teaching trials.

Keywords: Learning programming · Learning by reading · Code reading · Tracing

1 Introduction

In courses on computer programming, a common pattern is for the lecturer to first explain syntax or the approach to programming and then present example programs before asking students to create programs in a series of exercises. However, in our experience, reading and understanding other people's programs is just as important as creating programs. The process of reading the source code of a program in this way is known as "code reading", and is regarded as very important.

However, books on the subject typically do little more than describe tips for deciphering programming code. Likewise, most explanations of example code in university courses are conveyed by a one-way flow of information, from teacher to students. This means that students are not explicitly given tasks that involve reading code. In this study, we propose program trace exercises as one type of exercise for reading programs. We also develop and evaluate a learning support system to support these exercises.

2 Program Trace Exercises

2.1 Exercise for Reading Programs

The importance of reading programs is widely recognized, but there are few systems that explicitly require students to read a program and provide feedback on their activities.

© Springer International Publishing AG 2017
S. Yamamoto (Ed.): HIMI 2017, Part II, LNCS 10274, pp. 85–98, 2017.
DOI: 10.1007/978-3-319-58524-6_8

Kanamori et al. [1] and Arai et al. [2] advocate exercises involving reading programs with the goal of understanding the content of the program. Some earlier studies [3] divide the process of creating a program into "algorithm design" (thinking about the flow of processing) and "coding" (converting the flow of processing into the specific expressions of the programming language), but Kanamori et al. propose a reading process that reverses this order. That is, reading can be divided into the process of "decoding" (deciphering the processing flow based on the language-specific expressions) and "meaning deduction" (understanding the goal, or meaning, of the program based on the processing flow). Deconstruction is the inverse of construction above, while comprehension is the inverse of algorithm design (Fig. 1). However, these studies do not present exercises for actually tracing the flow of processing in a program in detail.

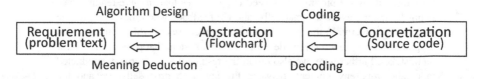

Fig. 1. Program reading process (Kanamori et al.)

To read a program, it is important to learn how to trace "program behavior". This entails working out which line (location) of the program is currently executing, which line will be executed next, and what will happen as a result. Students who cannot accurately trace program behavior in this way will not be able to debug their own programs properly and will end up creating programs with a half-formed understanding. Accordingly, in this study we propose exercises that require students to trace program behavior line-by-line and to think about what kind of instructions are being performed at each line.

2.2   Proposed Program Tracing Exercises

In this section, we explain the program trace exercises proposed by this study, using Fig. 2 for illustration.

To make students think about program behavior, program trace exercises are of two types: (A) exercises asking which line will be executed, and (B) exercises asking about the details of the instructions executed by each line. In these exercises, students are first given some source code. Students are then asked to (A) select which line in the source code will be executed first. Next, students are asked to (B) describe changes in the values of variables or the details of the output. The intent is to have them think about the instructions executed by that line. For loop processing and conditional branching, the flow of program processing changes depending on the outcome of the conditions, and so students are asked to describe the outcome of conditions as well. Thereafter, students are asked to describe the behavior of the program until the program terminates, by selecting which line will be executed next, and so on in the same manner. For programs with a sequential structure, the execution order will be almost the same as the

| | (A) | | (B) | | | | |

ソースコード	実行する行	変数の値			出力	判定
		i	j	a		
void main(){	void main(){					
int i , j , a = 0 ;	int i , j , a = 0 ;			0		
for(i = 1 ; i < 3 ; i++){	for(i = 1 ; i < 3 ; i++){	1				満たす
for(j = 1 ; i < 3 ; j++)	for(j = 1 ; i < 3 ; j++)		1			満たす
a = a + j ;	a = a + j ;			1		
printf(" %d¥n", a);	for(j = 1 ; i < 3 ; j++)		2			満たす
}	a = a + j ;			3		
}	for(j = 1 ; i < 3 ; j++)		3			満たさない
	printf(" %d¥n", a);				3	
	⋮					

Fig. 2. An example program trace exercise

order in which the lines appear in the source code, but for loops, conditional branching and functions, the processing flow jumps from one line to another, and so these exercises test whether students can trace this processing flow properly. This kind of task is a daily activity for an experienced programmer, but there are beginners who either do not know about this kind of task or who know about it but cannot do it properly and require guidance. For this reason, we believe that it is important to explicitly provide learners with such tasks, and to also provide them with feed-back.

2.3   Previous Research

Yamaguchi et al. [4] developed a system that visualizes which line in the source code is currently executing and changes in the execution environment for that line. Similarly, Yamaguchi et al. [5] visualize differences between the correct program behavior and the program entered by the user as changes in the execution environment. However, these studies go no further than observing behavior, and do not require the learner to generate the behavior themselves. Sugiura et al. [6] and Noguchi et al. [7] require learners to generate behavior consistent with an algorithm in order to develop their ability to create algorithms. However, the goal of these studies is to understand algorithms, and, unlike in this study, they do not ask users to trace behavior based on the source code. Egi et al. [8] have developed a support system that instructs novices in the process of tracing. This system provides support by prompting novices to trace their program when they get stuck creating a program, as well as guidance using trace instructions for diagnosing the state of the system or identifying the location for the solution. However, this system does not conduct traces in the sense of understanding program behavior itself.

3   Learning Support System

3.1   System Overview

As part of this study, we have developed a learning support system with the goal of helping students understand program behavior [9]. The goal of this system is to present learners with program trace exercises, ask them to enter information about program behavior, and then provide them with feed-back. Learners are given source code and asked to (A) select which line will be executed (the execution point) and (B) enter information about the details of the processing executed by that line (such as the values of variables, input and output, and the details of condition evaluations). If the learner's input is incorrect, the system provides feedback designed to prompt them to find the error themselves. Within the range of constraints (A) and (B), this system is not affected by language specifications, but language features outside of this range (such as event-driven programming, pointers and reference passing, objected-oriented programming) are out of scope for this system. We have prepared eight exercises in the C programming language for this system. When users select a problem number, the selected problem is displayed.

3.2   Interface

Figure 3 shows the interface for the system. The system first provides learners with source code (the left-hand side of the screen). Next, learners are asked to click lines in

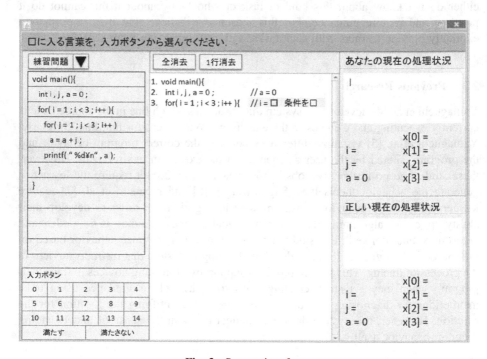

Fig. 3. System interface

the source code in the order in which they are executed (center of the screen). In addition, when processing of constructs such as variable assignments or conditional branching is performed, learners use the input buttons at the bottom left of the screen to enter the details of the corresponding processing.

3.3 Feedback Function

We anticipate that beginners will have errors in understanding of the order of execution and with entering processing details. The program trace exercises themselves can be completed using pen and paper, but when learning independently with pen and paper, or by methods such as looking at reference books, learners may proceed to the next step without realizing that they have made a mistake. When this happens, they will not notice their mistake until they look at the answer at the end of the exercise, if they notice at all. However, they then realize their mistake because they have seen the answer, and so they lose the opportunity to fix the mistake by themselves. Even in cases where exercises are conducted by a teacher in an educational setting, the one-to-many nature of the classroom makes it difficult to expect adequate support. For normal debugging, there is often a trace function, and this can also be used for learning. Many of these debugging functions allow the user to trace program execution by stepping through the program one line at a time, and many also allow users to check the values of variables or the screen output at each line. However, when learning using a debugger, users still find out the correct answer straightaway, and so this approach is still inadequate in terms of learners realizing their mistakes.

In this study, we visualize information input by the user (such as screen output or changes to internal variables that occur in accordance with the program behavior) as "Your current processing state". At the same time, we also visualize the correct screen output and variable values that match the program behavior as "Correct current processing state" (right-hand side of the screen in Fig. 2). If a learner has made a mistake regarding the execution order or the processing for a particular line, then the visualization will show a discrepancy between these two parts of the screen. The learner is asked to check the discrepancy and then identify and fix the error own their own.

Figure 4 shows an example of the visualization content for a learner error. This error is a common mistake that learners make regarding "for" statements. In "for" statements, the processing for the third clause is executed every time the loop repeats but before the continuation condition in the second clause is evaluated as true or false. If the condition is not met, then the loop ends. This means that in the example where the continuation condition is "j < 3", then the loop will end when the value of j becomes 3. However, some learners will see this "for" statement and interpret it vaguely as "repeat with j ranging from 1 to 2". In this case, they will not understand that j is equal to 3 when the loop ends. In this kind of example, a discrepancy will occur in terms of whether the processing for the third clause is performed at the end of the loop or in the part where the condition in the second clause is evaluated. This discrepancy is then visualized as a gap in the timing of the screen output, or a difference in the value of j. Because learners are asked to constantly check these discrepancies in output results or internal variables, they are able to review their answer at the point when the discrepancy occurs.

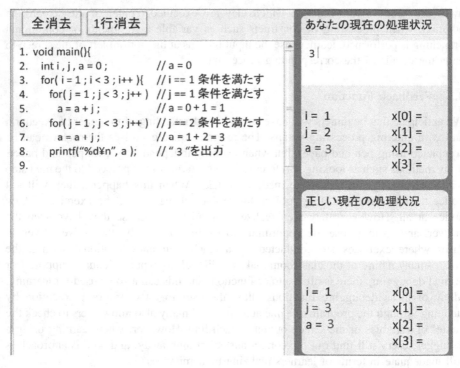

Fig. 4. Feedback from the system

4 Comparison Test

4.1 Test Overview

Objective

We conducted an experiment to assess whether learning with this system promoted better understanding of program behavior than the normal approach of learning by creating programs. In this experiment, we conduct three types of test before and after students used the support system in order to assess whether the system is able to promote more effective program comprehension than normal study. We also assessed whether the proposed program trace exercises and support system were in alignment with the goals of this study, based on subjective assessments by the students (questionnaires).

Test procedure

The test participants were 18 engineering students who had learned the C programing language at university, divided randomly into a test group and a control group with 9 subjects in each group. Both groups took a 30-minute pre-test, followed by 60 min of learning and then a 30-minute post-test and questionnaire. The test group learned via the support system, whereas the control group learned in the conventional manner by creating programs.

Test types

We conducted three types of test for the pre- and post-tests: (1) an output result test, where subjects are asked to write down the output results for given source code, (2) a trace test, where subjects are asked to describe the execution order and variable changes for given source code, and (3) a coding test, where subjects are given output results and source code with blank spaces and asked to write a program by filling in the blanks.

Each test consisted of five problems, with each problem worth one point, for a total of five points. The problems were as follows: (1) source code including nested structures of "for" and "if" statements, (2) source code including double "for" statements, (3) source code including a "for" statement where the control variable is involved in the condition expression, (4) source code including substitutions to the values of arrays and functions, and (5) source including recursive functions.

4.2   Experiment Results

Test results

Table 1 shows the test results, and Table 2 shows the ANOVA results with one between-subjects factor (A: test group versus control group) and two within-subject factors (B: pre-test versus post-test; C: test type). Interactions between A and B were apparent in the ANOVA results, and so we assessed the simple main effects. The results are listed in Table 3, which shows a significant difference between groups for the post-test results ($p < 0.05$). From this, we see that by using the system the test group achieved better results in all three types of test. In particular, there is a clear difference in the post-test results for the trace test and the output result test, implying that learning via the system fosters the ability to trace program behavior. Furthermore, although the control group learned via creating programs, the test group was still able to achieve

Table 1. Results of tests

	Output test			Trace test			Coding test		
	Pre	Post	Difference	Pre	Post	Difference	Pre	Post	Difference
Test group	0.67	2.44	1.77	0.44	2.11	1.67	0.78	2.33	1.56
Control group	0.67	1.22	0.55	0.44	0.78	0.34	0.78	1.44	0.66

Table 2. Results of ANOVA

	Sum of squares	Degrees of freedom	F value	Significance
A: Group	8.90	1	1.76	n.s.
B: Test timing	32.2	1	90.4	<0.01
AB	8.90	1	25.0	<0.01
C: Test type	3.02	2	2.45	n.s.
AC	0.24	2	0.20	n.s.
BC	0.13	2	0.22	n.s.
ABC	0.24	2	0.41	n.s.

Table 3. Results of means for AB interaction

	Sum of squares	Degrees of freedom	F value	Significance
Group (pre)	0.00	1	0.00	n.s.
Group (post)	17.8	1	6.55	<0.05
Test timing (test group)	37.5	1	105.2	<0.01
Test timing (control group)	3.63	1	10.2	<0.01

better results than the control group in the coding test. These results indicate the possibility that students can improve their ability to create proper programs via learning that focuses on tracing program behavior.

Questionnaire result

Table 4 shows the results of the questionnaire given to the test group after they had used the system (four-level multiple choice: 1 Not at all; 2 Not really; 3 A bit; 4 Quite a lot). From these results, we found that participants felt that the visualization of the execution process improved their understanding of the program, and that they reviewed their answers by comparing the visualizations of their own processing state with the correct state. We also found that students felt that their activities using the system led to an understanding of the program. From these results, we found that subjects felt the system and feedback were valuable.

Table 4. Mean answers on questions ($N = 9$)

Do you think that visualization of the execution process and output state makes the program easier to understand?	3.2
If there was a difference between your processing state and the correct processing state, did you think about where you went wrong?	3.3
Do you think your understanding of the program was improved by the system?	3.1

5   Teaching Trial

5.1   Experiment Overview

Objective

In Sect. 4, we found that learning via using the system promoted understanding of program behavior more than normal learning via creating programs. However, only nine participants used the system, the limited assessment took place in a test lab environment, and the entire process from pre-test through to post-test took a bit more than two hours without interruptions. University courses consist of 90-minute time slots, so that conducting an assessment over a similar amount of time would require two time slots, and students may lose concentration. Accordingly, we conducted further experiments to assess whether the system can be used in the context of two normal 90-minute university time slots in an environment where teaching staff cannot thoroughly monitor student activities. We also assessed whether we can expect learning benefits from using the system.

Experimental procedure

Two courses conducted by the Department of Industrial Management and Engineering of the Faculty of Engineering at the Tokyo University of Science were selected as the targets for this experiment: Information Technology Lab 1 (IT1; first semester of second year, 80 students), which is the course where students first study programming and master syntax and elementary coding technology; and Information Technology Lab 3 (IT3; second semester of third year, 66 students), where students with a certain amount of experience studying programming learn about algorithms in greater detail. The timing of the tests was the latter half of each course, namely, July for IT1 and December for IT3. Both of these courses are compulsory for students in the department and are taken by all students, not just those who are particularly good at programming. 73 of the participants in IT1 and all of the participants in IT3 are focusing on the C programming language. In normal classes for these courses, the procedure is for students to learn by creating programs through a series of exercises after first hearing an explanation from the teacher.

For the test procedure, we used a shortened form of the same procedure as was used in the comparison test. However, for the comparison test, we conducted assessments using a 30-minute pre-test, 60 min of learning, and a 30-minute post-test. However, the time slots for the course are 90 min long, meaning that two time slots are required. Accordingly, we decided to conduct the trial by spending the first 30 min of the first time slot on the pre-test, followed by 20 min explaining the system and the lecture content, with the remaining 40 min spent learning via the system. The first 20 min of the second time slot was spent on learning via the system (for a total of 60 min of system usage over the two time slots), followed by a 30-minute post-test and questionnaire. Note that the four teaching assistants in each course were instructed to allow students to work out how to solve problems on their own, only answering questions on how to use the system and responding to technical issues.

Test types

Three types of test were conducted for the pre- and post-tests, in the same manner as for the comparison test: (1) an output result test, where participants are asked to write down the output results for given source code; (2) a trace test, where participants are asked to describe the execution order and variable changes for given source code; and (3) a coding test, where participants are given output results and source code with blank spaces and asked to write a program by filling in the blanks. The problems and marking methods were also the same as for the comparison test.

5.2 Experimental Results for Information Technology Lab 1

Test results for Information Technology Lab 1

Table 5 shows the test results for when the system was used in IT1 (first semester of second year), consisting mainly of students with no programming experience. Table 6 shows the ANOVA results with two within-subject factors (A: pre-test versus post-test; B: test type [output result, tracing or coding]). As seen in Tables 5 and 6, we found a significant difference in test timing (pre-test vs. post-test), showing that using the system promotes students' understanding. Moreover, Table 7 shows the results for the simple main effects in the interaction between factors A and B. In Tables 5 and 7, significant differences are apparent between test types (output results, tracing and coding) in the pre-tests, and so we conducted multiple comparisons for test type in the pre-test results. The results, summarized in Table 8, show significant differences between the tracing test and the other tests. From this, we found that the novice programmers taking IT1 could, as a result of learning via the system, improve their ability to predict output based on given source code, as well as their ability to create appropriate source code based on required output and their ability to understand program behavior based on source code. In particular, we found that the ability to properly understand program flow improved as a result of the system, despite being weaker than the other skills at the time of the pre-test.

Table 5. Results of tests for IT1

	Output test			Trace test			Coding test		
N = 80	Pre	Post	Difference	Pre	Post	Difference	Pre	Post	Difference
IT1	0.95	1.35	0.40	0.33	1.23	0.90	0.76	1.34	0.58

Table 6. Results of ANOVA for IT1

	Sum of squares	Degrees of freedom	F value	Significance
A: Test timing	46.9	1	1.76	<0.01
B: Test type	12.1	2	90.4	<0.01
AB	5.15	2	25.0	<0.01

Table 7. Results of means for A*B interaction for IT1

	Sum of squares	Degrees of freedom	F value	Significance
Test timing (output)	6.40	1	15.8	<0.01
Test timing (trace)	32.4	1	80.0	<0.01
Test timing (coding)	12.2	1	32.7	<0.01
Test type (pre)	16.5	2	14.9	<0.01
Test type (post)	0.76	2	0.69	n.s

Table 8. Means on factor B (a1) for IT1

	Nominal significance level	t value	Significance
Output-trace	0.017	5.32	<0.01
Output-coding	0.033	1.60	n.s.
Coding-trace	0.033	3.72	<0.01

Questionnaire results for Information Technology Lab 1

Table 9 shows the results of the questionnaire given to the students taking IT1 (four-level multiple choice, as before). The results obtained are positive, as was the case for the comparison test. The students taking IT1 are programming novices, but we

Table 9. Mean answers on questions for IT1 ($N = 80$)

Do you think that visualization of the execution process and output state makes the program easier to understand?	3.3
If there was a difference between your processing state and the correct processing state, did you think about where you went wrong?	3.3
Do you think your understanding of the program was improved by the system?	3.0

found that they believe that their understanding of programming has improved as a result of their learning activities using the system, and that they feel that their understanding of the programs has improved as a result of the visualization of the execution process. We also found that they reviewed their answers by comparing their own processing state with the correct state. From these results, we found that learning via system and the feedback provided by the system were received as valuable, even by novices with no programming experience.

5.3   Experimental Results for Information Technology Lab 3

Test results for Information Technology Lab 3

Table 10 shows the test results for when the system was used in IT3 (second semester of third year), which is a course for students who have already studied a certain amount of programming to develop a deeper understanding of more advanced algorithms. Table 10 shows the ANOVA results with two within-subject factors (A: pre-test versus post-test; B: test type [output result, tracing or coding]). As seen in Tables 10 and 11, we found a significant difference in test timing (pre-test versus post-test), just as for IT1. From these results, we infer that the system has learning benefits for students who have already studied some programming and algorithms. Moreover, Table 12 shows the results for the simple main effects in the interaction between factors A and B. In Tables 10 and 12, significant differences are apparent in the test timing (pre-test versus post-test) for all test types. In addition, significant differences are also apparent between test types (output results, tracing and coding) in the pre-tests, and so we conducted multiple comparisons for test type in the pre-test results. The results, summarized in Table 13, show significant differences between the coding test and the other tests. One possible reason that the scores for the coding test were lower than for the other tests is that the goal of IT3 is for students to understand algorithms, rather than to learn coding as such. A certain amount of study on tracing programs and predicting output results may have already been covered in the course.

Table 10. Results for IT3

	Output test			Trace test			Coding test		
N = 66	Pre	Post	Difference	Pre	Post	Difference	Pre	Post	Difference
IT3	1.02	1.85	0.83	1.05	1.77	0.73	0.65	1.95	1.30

Table 11. Results of ANOVA for IT3

	Sum of squares	Degrees of freedom	F value	Significance
A: Test timing	90.2	1	104.2	<0.01
B: Test type	1.25	2	0.58	n.s.
AB	6.20	2	5.94	<0.01

Table 12. Results of means test for A*B interaction

	Sum of squares	Degrees of freedom	F value	Significance
Test timing (output)	22.9	1	36.0	<0.01
Test timing (trace)	17.5	1	27.4	<0.01
Test timing (coding)	56.0	1	88.0	<0.01
Test type (Pre)	6.34	2	3.98	<0.05
Test type (Post)	1.10	2	0.69	n.s

Table 13. Means on factor B (a1)

	Nominal significance level	t value	Significance
Output-trace	0.033	0.195	n.s.
Output-coding	0.033	2.34	<0.05
Coding-trace	0.017	2.54	<0.05

Table 14 summarizes the test results for IT1 and IT3. In this study, we used the same tests for both courses, and so the pre-test results for the more advanced IT3 students tend to be better. Moreover, we also found that the improvement in scores was more apparent for IT3. This result seems to indicate that the system may be more effective for students who are more advanced and who have a better understanding of algorithms.

Table 14. Comparison of results of tests for IT1 and IT3

	Output test			Trace test			Coding test		
	Pre	Post	Difference	Pre	Post	Difference	Pre	Post	Difference
IT1	0.95	1.35	0.40	0.33	1.23	0.90	0.76	1.34	0.58
IT3	1.02	1.85	0.83	1.05	1.77	0.73	0.65	1.95	1.30

Questionnaire results for Information Technology Lab 1

Table 15 shows the results of the questionnaire given to the students taking IT3 (four-level multiple choice, as before). The results obtained are positive, as high or higher than the questionnaire results for IT1. From these results, we see that the participants in IT3, who are somewhat more advanced in their study of programming and algorithms, have a greater recognition of the value of the system, feedback and learning method than the novice programmers in IT1.

Table 15. Mean answers on questions for IT3 ($N = 66$)

Do you think that visualization of the execution process and output state makes the program easier to understand?	3.6
If there was a difference between your processing state and the correct processing state, did you think about where you went wrong?	3.6
Do you think your understanding of the program was improved by the system?	3.5

6 Conclusion

In this study, we proposed exercises for learning programming that require students to actually trace the behavior of program processing. Using this system appears to be beneficial for learning programming, and the questionnaire results show positive responses, indicating that students accept the system.

Here, for the sake of input simplicity, we have asked students to trace behavior one line at a time. However, a "for" statement, for instance, includes multiple expressions in a single line, and it is important that students properly understand the order of execution of these expressions. In future, we aim to support program tracing at the level of individual expressions.

Acknowledgment. Part of this study was funded by a Grant-in-Aid for Scientific Research, Basic Research (C) (10508435).

References

1. Kanamori, H., Tomoto, T., Kometani, Y., Takako, A.: Proposal for 'Learning via Reading Programs' in the programming process and development of a learning support system for the 'Comprehension' process. Trans. Inst. Electron. Inf. Commun. Eng. Jpn. **J97-D**(12), 1843–1846 (2014)
2. Arai, T., Kanamori, H., Tomoto, T., Kometani, Y., Akakura, T.: Development of a learning support system for source code reading comprehension. In: Yamamoto, S. (ed.) HIMI 2014. LNCS, vol. 8522, pp. 12–19. Springer, Cham (2014). doi:10.1007/978-3-319-07863-2_2
3. Shinkai, J., Sumitani, S.: Development of programming learning support system emphasizing process. Jpn. Soc. Educ. Technol. **31**(Suppl.), 45–48 (2007). (in Japanese)
4. Yamashita, K., Nagao, T., Kogure, S., Noguchi, Y., Konishi, T., Ito, Y.: An educational practice using a code reading support environment for understanding nested loop. IEICE Tech. Rep. **114**(82), 7–12 (2014). (in Japanese)
5. Yamoto, R., Noguchi, Y., Kogure, S., Yamashia, K., Konishi, T., Ito, Y.: A learning environment for teaching students how to debug systematically. In: Proceedings of the 39th National Convention, Japanese Society for Information and Systems in Education, pp. 453–454 (2014). (in Japanese)
6. Sugiura, M., Matsuzawa, Y., Okuda, K., Ohiwa, H.: Introductory education for algorithm construction: understanding concepts of algorithm through unplugged work and its effects. J. Inf. Process. **49**(10), 3409–3427 (2008). (in Japanese)

7. Noguchi, Y., Nakahara, T., Konishi, T., Kogure, S., Itoh, Y.: Construction of a learning environment for algorithm and programming where learners operate objects in a domain world. Int. J. Knowl. Web Intell. 1(3–4), 273–288 (2010)
8. Egi, T., Takeuchi, A.: Development and evaluation of debugging support system of guide tracing for beginners. Jpn. J. Educ. Technol. 32(4), 369–381 (2009). (in Japanese)
9. Tomoto, T., Asai, K., Tamura, Y., Akakura, T.: Development and evaluation of learning support system for programming reading exercise. IEICE Tech. Rep. 115(50), 7–10 (2015). (in Japanese)

Information in Virtual and Augmented Reality

Basic Study on Connecting AR and VR for Digital Exhibition with Mobile Devices

Taiju Aoki[1(✉)], Takuji Narumi[2], Tomohiro Tanikawa[2], and Michitaka Hirose[2]

[1] Graduate School of Interdisciplinary Information Studies,
The University of Tokyo, 7-3-1 Hongo, Bunkyoku, Tokyo 113-8656, Japan
aoki@cyber.t.u-tokyo.ac.jp
[2] Graduate School of Information Science and Technology,
The University of Tokyo, 7-3-1 Hongo, Bunkyoku, Tokyo 113-8656, Japan
{narumi,tani,hirose}@cyber.t.u-tokyo.ac.jp

Abstract. In this paper, we propose a prototype of an AR–VR (Augmented Reality-Virtual Reality) connected system in which users can enter a space in which they cannot go physically while emphasizing spatial consistency between the real and VR space. Museums have important collections that cannot be displayed, such as crumbling buildings, lost sceneries, and fragile trains. To display them, museums have used AR or VR systems. In AR systems, the visitors can appreciate the collections with their context because AR systems emphasize spatial consistency, and users can compare the current and past scenery around the collections. In VR systems, the visitors can interact with the collections with a high degree of freedom because VR systems have spatial extensibility and the users can ignore the physical limitations. Therefore, we connect the AR and VR systems to take advantage of the technology in appreciating collections with high comprehension of their context and degree of freedom. We implemented a prototype AR–VR connected system in which users can transition from the real space to the VR space seamlessly. In our system, they first superimpose mobile tablets onto the museums' collections, such as a crumbling building. Then, the current scenery in the tablet will gradually change to a VR scenery where they cannot enter physically. Finally, they can move around the VR space using their own body. Through our experiments, we found that the concept of connecting the AR and VR systems could be acceptable, and the system could work well in actual exhibitions.

Keywords: Mobile AR · Mobile VR · Digital museum

1 Introduction

Museums have attempted to convey their exhibits effectively in many ways. The exhibits, as well as its background information, are important to be conveyed to their visitors [1]. However, museums cannot convey the background information of their collections, such as crumbling buildings, lost sceneries or too fragile trains because of their great value and their physical constraints. To solve this problem, we focused on AR and VR exhibition systems with respect to its spatial consistency and spatial extensibility.

© Springer International Publishing AG 2017
S. Yamamoto (Ed.): HIMI 2017, Part II, LNCS 10274, pp. 101–112, 2017.
DOI: 10.1007/978-3-319-58524-6_9

The AR system can emphasize a spatial consistency and have an effect of conveying a correspondent positional relationship between the real scenery and the superimposed scenery [2]. As a result, users can easily notice what is changed and unchanged in the place, which leads users to understand the background information of the place more deeply [3]. On the other hand, the VR system can provide experiences beyond the real space constraints by showing elaborate CG images. When users wear an HMD and sit on the chair, they can go anywhere they want to go. In addition, given the rising the technique to distort users' perception of space, such as Redirected Walking [4], the VR system can emphasize a spatial extensibility. For example, when users wear an HMD and walk around the room, they can feel as if they could go to a prohibited or even a lost place, and move a lot larger than it actually is. Therefore, if the AR and the VR systems are integrated into an AR–VR connected system with respect to its spatial consistency and spatial extensibility, the AR–VR connected system can lead users to understand the background information beyond the real space constraints. For example, when users visit the site of a building where another building is already standing, by using the system, it is possible for visitors to enter inside and appreciate the past building where they cannot physically enter.

Therefore, we implemented a prototype AR–VR connected system that can connect the real space and VR by offering both AR and VR system's advantages, namely, spatial consistency and spatial extensibility.

2   Related Work

2.1   Conveying Background Information by Using AR Exhibition System

On-site virtual time machine [2] is an on-site AR exhibition system that superimposes past-scene photographs onto a current scene through a PC display using Bundler and PTAM. This study suggests that compared to simply viewing printed images on-site, seeing superimposed images on a PC display can allow users to understand the background information of the contents more deeply. Reliving Past Scene Experience System by Inducing a Video-camera Operator's Motion with Overlaying a Video-sequence onto Real Environment [5] is also an on-site AR exhibition system. In this system, users search for the photographed position. Upon reaching the ideal location to view an AR content, the system starts to overlay a past scene in video materials onto the real environment and gives users the experience on how the camera operator captured the scene by inducing them to move similar to the operator. The Westwood Experience [3] is also a mobile on-site AR system in which users can view some contents associated with the real landscape and appreciate a 360-degree spherical image. Users can look at a 360-degree spherical image, while the system can detect the gyro sensor value in their tablet.

These studies show that the on-site AR system can convey the background information of the content, and active appreciation methods, such as searching for the photographed position, can induce the interest of the users in the content itself. However, in the AR exhibition system, instead of its spatial consistency, users have to be in the exact location as the photographed location and cannot appreciate the content from various view points.

2.2 Providing Expanded Experience in the Constrained Real Space by Using VR Exhibition System

The digital display case [6] enables users to interact with an intangible object in real space, such as clay figures and train trucks, through the exhibition case. In this system, users can use a controller and control the intangible object in the VR space and understand the mechanism that cannot usually be seen. In addition, VR applications, which can enable a walkthrough in the image-based VR space, are becoming popular [7, 8]. These applications can enable users to experience image-based VR spaces by allowing them to explore larger spaces despite not moving around the real space. These system and applications can enable users to experience larger and not constrained spaces even in small real spaces, but they actively restrict the users' activity to appreciate the contents themselves because these systems can be used without moving their own body. However, Redirected Walking [4] can be mentioned as a method of walking in a large VR space by using the users' body. By showing a distorted motion of the users in the real space to users in the VR space, the system can make users change their real walking direction without noticing it, and the system can allow the users to move around a larger virtual environment. The important point is that using this system, the users can move around a larger VR space despite being in a small real space.

To take advantage of the AR system, the AR–VR connected system should run on a mobile tablet, and the system should detect the users' movement, such as translation and rotation, to apply the concept of Redirected Walking. To detect the movement of users, the Mobility Change-of-State Detection Using a Smartphone-based Approach [9] can be applied. The system can detect the users walking motion by using mobile devices, such as smartphone and other tablets. In this system, the user wears the smartphone on the waist belt and presume the user's state, namely, walk, stop, stand, and sit, according to the value of its acceleration sensor. Especially, to detect the walking state, the system monitors a sudden change in acceleration in the vertical direction.

Therefore, by adding appropriate gain for the movement of users and using the acceleration sensor in mobile tablets, the system can allow the users to move around a VR space despite being under the real space constraints, and the system can take advantage of both the AR and VR systems.

3 Design of the Prototype AR–VR Connected System

3.1 Concept of AR–VR Connected System

In this chapter, we introduce our implementation of the prototype AR–VR connected system, which can emphasize a spatial consistency as an AR system, as well as emphasize a spatial extensibility and provide experiences beyond the real space as VR system. To take advantage of the AR–VR system, the proposed system should run on a mobile device because users have to move around the real space. As a result, the main required functions of our proposed system are as follows:

1. AR mode for emphasizing a spatial consistency.
2. Seamless connection between AR–VR mode.
3. VR mode for providing experiences beyond the real world constraints.

3.2   AR Mode for Emphasizing a Spatial Consistency

The main function of AR mode is to convey an accurate correspondent relation between the real scenery and the scenery that appears later by superimposing the user's mobile tablet onto the target object.

First, the users are instructed by the proposed system to superimpose their own tablet onto the real object that has some correspondence with the place, such as a sign of demolished building or a building itself, or an ornament involved in the place. Second, the users walk around to find the scenery shown on the screen. Third, the users superimpose their tablet onto the real object (Fig. 1). As a result, the system can detect the relative position and angle of the real object and users using the image recognition function.

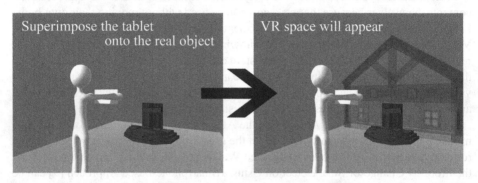

Fig. 1. Concept of the AR mode in the system

Through these procedures, the users can instinctively understand that what they will see next on their tablet is related to the superimposed real object because of its characteristics as on-site AR system. For example, when they superimpose their tablet onto a sign of demolished building, they will see a past image of the building with the same sign as they are superimposed. Finally, they can easily understand the sign of the building.

3.3   Seamless Connection Between AR–VR Mode

The main function of Seamless connection between AR–VR mode is to transit to the VR mode from the AR mode while taking advantage of the AR system.

To transition to the VR mode while taking advantage of the AR system, the users must understand the positional relationship between the real space and the VR space. Therefore, the system gradually transits the appearance on the tablet from the scenery of the real space to the landscape of the VR space. The system recognizes three-dimensional relative positional relationship and relative angle with the gyro sensor and the camera on their tablet to reflect appropriately the movement of the user in the real space to the movement of the user in the VR space. For example, when they superimpose their tablet onto a site of a building, the users' view will gradually invade the inside of the building (Fig. 2), and the system keeps the relative position and angle between the users and the building to reflect them in the VR space.

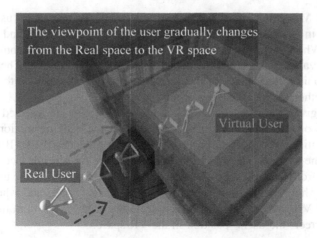

Fig. 2. Concept of the seamless connection between the AR–VR mode in the system

3.4 VR Mode for Providing Expanded Experience in the Constrained Real Space

The main function of the VR mode is to allow users to move around the VR space according to the movement of the users' body. Specifically, when users move in the real space, the viewpoint in the VR space moves according to the two types of users' movements (Fig. 3). To expand the range that the users can move in the VR space, the system can apply a certain degree of gain to the movement of users in the real space. For example, when the users in the real space walk 1 m, the viewpoint in the VR space can move 3 m.

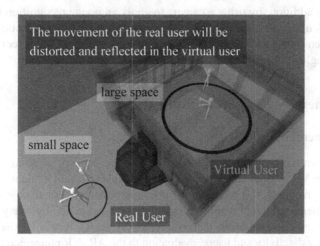

Fig. 3. Concept of the VR mode and expanding the VR space

Translational Movement in VR space: The system can detect the users' walking movement by monitoring the changes in acceleration of their tablet and value of the gyro sensor. When users walk, the waveform of the acceleration becomes a specific shape, but the value of the gyro sensor does not change significantly. Therefore, while the system monitors the values of the acceleration and gyro sensors, the system can determine whether they are walking or not.

However, given the users' rotational movement or other unexpected motion, this walking detection function sometimes fails to detect the walking motion. To correct this misrecognition, we use iBeacon [10], which can broadcast BLE (Bluetooth Low Energy) that the system can catch from each iBeacon. As a result, according to the value of RSSI from each iBeacon, the system can roughly recognize the users' position in real space. Therefore, we set some beacons in the real space and when the users' position in the VR space is greatly different from the users' position in the real space, the system corrects the users' position in the VR space.

Rotational Motion in VR space: The system can detect the users' rotational motion by using the gyro sensor on their tablet.

Specifically, when users look around in the real space, the value of the gyro sensor changes and the system detects the degree of the user's rotation. Therefore, when users look around in the real space to look around in the VR space, the system can rotate the line of sight of the users in the VR space.

However, given that the gyro sensor drifts after using the system for a long time, the direction of the users' line of sight will turn to the wrong direction in the VR space compared to the users' line of sight in the real space. To correct this drifted value, we use a compass and a camera on the tablet. Using a compass, the system can roughly detect which direction the users are facing and the system monitors the changes in the value of the compass and gyro sensor for every five seconds. Then, the system can correct the value of the drifted gyro sensor by comparing the values of the compass and gyro sensor. In addition, by using a camera to apply an image recognition function, the system can calculate the relative angle between the superimposed object and the users. Therefore, when the system detects the superimposed object on the screen, the system corrects the angle in the VR space according to the relative angle.

4 Experiments at Actual Exhibitions

4.1 Experimental Purposes

These experiments are aimed to evaluate whether the concept of connecting the AR system and the VR system can be acceptable for the users, and evaluate the system's possibility of providing the background information of historical objects. We conducted experiments in actual exhibitions, which were evaluated by many users.

In the first experiment, using the prototype system, we measured the relationship between the users' activity and users' evaluation to the AR–VR connected system itself. In the second experiment, we exhibited an application with the system, which can show users a VR space twice as large as the real space. We compared the AR–VR system and a conventional VR system in which users can appreciate the VR content without any spatial consistency and with virtual joystick with respect to the users' interest in the content.

4.2   Experiment 1: Evaluation on the Indicators to Measure the Performance of the System

Detailed Procedure: We exhibited an iPad application with a system under prototype "Walking in the Memories" to evaluate the indicators to measure the performance of the system. Using the application, users can move around the exhibition room in the real space (about 10 m × 4 m). We archived a past 360° scenery of the exhibition and made VR space in which users could move around similar to ordinary image-based VR contents. Therefore, when users move around the room, they can see and compare both the past scenery and the current scenery. In addition, we had two VR spaces, namely, the exhibition one year ago and the exhibition half a year ago (Fig. 4, left). Then, the users could see the current exhibition and two previous exhibitions on the iPad.

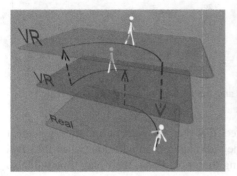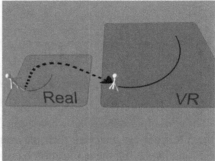

Fig. 4. Concept of the VR space in the experimental application. Left: similar sizes of multiple VR spaces. Right: incompatible size of the VR space.

When users touch the iPad and start the application, they can see a tutorial of the system. After the tutorial, the users superimpose the iPad onto a small sign of the exhibition as AR mode. In a few seconds, the scenery on the screen transitions to next exhibition, and in a next few more seconds through the screen, the users can see the current scenery of the exhibition. Then, on the iPad, the users can see the previous exhibition and move around. After the screen transitions to the VR screen, the users in the VR space can move around according to their movement. Since we install some iBeacons in the exhibition, when the system catches the value of iBeacons, it can correct the position of the users. Finally, when the users tap the quit button on the application or return the iPad to its original location on an exhibition stand, the screen transitions to a questionnaire view, and users can answer the questionnaires. We had 359 users who participated in this experiment.

Results and Discussion: Figure 5(a) shows the relationship between the average play time and the answer users provided after finishing the application. For the question "Did the movement between you in real space and in VR space match?" the users answered with a Likert scale. For example, if a user thought his movement matched greatly, he answered as 7 points. The correlation coefficient is 0.97, and the degree of coincidence of the users' action has a strong correlation with the play time. Figure 5(b) also shows the relationship between the average play time and the answer. For the question "Did you feel interesting in experiencing application by moving your body?", the users responded with Likert scale. The correlation coefficient is 0.99, and the degree of interest in playing the application by moving the body has a strong correlation with the play time.

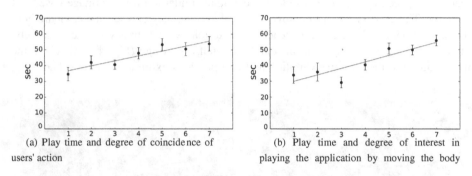

(a) Play time and degree of coincidence of users' action

(b) Play time and degree of interest in playing the application by moving the body

Fig. 5. Relationship between play time and the answer values with Likert scale

These results suggest that when users feel that their movement and the movement in the VR space are matched, their play time will increase. In addition, when they feel interesting in playing the application by using their own body, their play time will also increase. Therefore, we thought that to evaluate the system's accuracy of the movement detection capability and the users' interest in the content with the AR–VR connected system, the play time of an application with the system can be one of the main indicators.

4.3   Experiment 2: The Evaluation of the System for Spatial Consistency and Spatial Extensibility

Following the previous experimental results, the concept of the AR–VR connected system could be substantially acceptable and be practically used by ordinary users. Therefore, in this experiment at an actual exhibition, we evaluate whether the spatial consistency could lead to the increase in the users' interest in the content, and whether the spatial extensibility could be acceptable by using the users' own body.

In the exhibition, similar to Experiment 1, the users can touch the iPad with the system and see the tutorial. After the tutorial, the users superimpose a small sign of the application near the exhibition stand. Then, the system transitions the users to the VR space where there is a similar sign as on the exhibition (Fig. 6). As a result, when the

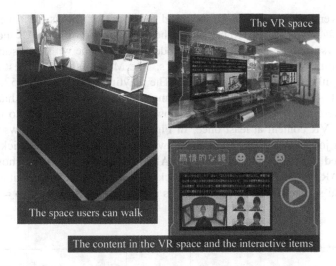

Fig. 6. The screen of the application with the system and the exhibition space

users move to the VR space, they can see and compare the sign on the exhibition and on the VR space. The VR space is about 1.5 times as large as the real space (the real space: 3.0 m × 3.0 m; the VR space: 5.5 m × 2.3 m). The system increases the amount of walking movement in the VR space relative to the user's real step (Fig. 4, right). In the VR space, users can see some contents they can interact with, such as gazing at some content for a while and starting a movie that explains the VR space. We exhibited the application with the system under different conditions as follows.

The system with/without a virtual joystick: In this system, we compared which method could attract the users' interest: the proposed VR input method, walking and rotation by using the users' body, and an ordinary VR input method such as virtual joypad. In the VR mode, the system can randomly choose which input method should be applied for each user. After the AR mode, the users can move around the VR space with/without a joystick. We had 494 users (253 users with Joystick condition, 241 users without Joystick condition) who participated under the condition with/without Joystick.

The system with/without AR mode: In this system, we evaluated whether the AR mode could provide the spatial consistency and help users to have an interest in the content. Then, the system can randomly choose with/without the AR mode. With the AR mode, after the tutorial, the users have to superimpose the iPad onto the target, and the view of the iPad gradually changes into the VR view. In addition, the relative angle between the users and the target is detected and reflected to the VR view. However, without the AR mode, after the tutorial, the screen transitions to the VR mode immediately. We had 344 users (169 users with AR condition, 175 users without AR condition) who participated under the condition with/without the AR mode.

Results and Discussion: Figure 7 shows the average playtime under the two conditions: with/without Joystick and with/without the AR mode. In Fig. 7 (left), the red bar shows the average time with a joystick and the blue bar shows the time without a joystick. In Fig. 7 (right), the red bar shows the average time with the AR mode and the blue bar shows the time without the AR mode. The playtime with a joystick is 48.4 s and the playtime without a joystick is 51.1 s. The Mann–Whitney U test shows that there is no significant difference ($p = 0.12$). The playtime with the AR is 52.3 s and the playtime without the AR is 49.7 s. The Mann–Whitney U test shows that there is a marginal difference ($p = 0.02$). Figure 8 shows the rate of the users who made interaction in the VR content at least once. In Fig. 8 (left), the red bar shows the rate of users with a joystick and the blue bar shows the rate without a joystick. In Fig. 8 (right), the red bar shows the rate with the AR mode and the blue bar shows the rate without the AR mode. The rate with a joystick is 0.29 and the rate without a joystick is 0.32. The Chi-square test shows that there is no significant difference (p = 0.60). The

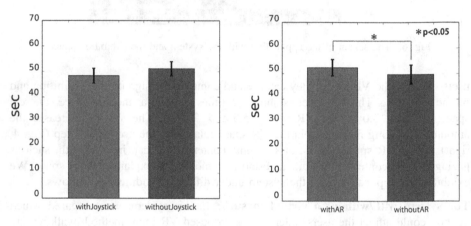

Fig. 7. Play time of the application under the two conditions. Left: with/without Joystick as input method. Right: with/without the AR mode.

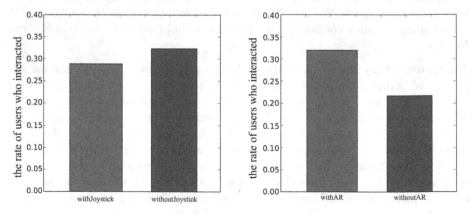

Fig. 8. Rate of users who interacted with the item in the content at least once. Left: with/without Joystick as an input method. Right: with/without the AR mode.

rate with AR is 0.32 and the rate without AR is 0.22. The Chi-square test shows that there is no significant difference (p = 0.13).

In terms of spatial consistency, we thought that since the playtime was longer and the rate was higher than not applying the AR mode, the application of the AR mode could be effective for providing the relationship between the actual location of the users and the VR space, and for increasing the users' interest in the content. This scenario could be attributed to the view of the current scenery that could transition to the view of the VR scenery with warp-like effect under the condition with the AR mode. Therefore, the users could have a sense of spatial continuity: a sense that the object in the real space and the object in the VR space are the same object. The sense of spatial continuity could help the users in comparing the real space and the VR space. Therefore, the users could easily have an interest in the VR space itself. These results suggest that the users' interest in the content could be increased by the spatial consistency. In terms of the input method, using users' own body could be acceptable for users similar to the use of a virtual joystick. This finding could be caused by the accurate system detection of the user's motion and the user's natural understanding of the system. In addition, despite the larger VR space than the real space, the users could play the application naturally. Therefore, these results suggest that using their own body and expanding the users' experience space have good compatibility.

5 Conclusion

In this paper, we proposed a prototype of an AR–VR connected system, which runs on personal mobile devices. The system can enable users enter a space in which they cannot go physically while emphasizing spatial consistency between the real space and the VR space. The AR system can emphasize spatial consistency and have an effect of conveying a correspondent positional relationship between the real scenery and the superimposed scenery. On the other hand, the VR system can emphasize a spatial extensibility and provide experiences beyond the real space constraints. Therefore, integrating the AR system and the VR system into an AR–VR connected system while respecting its spatial consistency and its spatial extensibility can lead users to understand the background information beyond the real space constraints.

We implemented a prototype AR–VR connected system, which can connect the real and VR space by offering both AR and VR system's advantages, namely, spatially consistency and spatial extensibility. After the users superimpose their tablet onto the real object, the system gradually transits the appearance on the tablet from the scenery of the real space to the scenery of the VR space. Then, users can move around the VR space according to the movement of the users' body. For example, when they superimpose the tablet onto a site of a building, the view on the tablet will gradually enter the inside of the building where they cannot physically enter. Next, the users in the VR space can move around and appreciate the inside of the building by using their body.

Through our experiments, we found that the AR mode in the system could induce users to have interest in the content. We also found that using the users' own body and expanding the VR space could have good compatibility. These results suggest that the concept of connecting the AR system and the VR system could be acceptable, and the system could work well in actual exhibitions to provide background information of their collections.

References

1. Narumi, T., Hayashi, O., Kasada, K., Yamazaki, M., Tanikawa, T., Hirose, M.: Digital diorama: AR exhibition system to convey background information for museums. In: Shumaker, R. (ed.) VMR 2011. LNCS, vol. 6773, pp. 76–86. Springer, Heidelberg (2011). doi:10.1007/978-3-642-22021-0_10
2. Nakano, J., Narumi, T., Tanikawa, T., Hirose, M.: Implementation of on-site virtual time machine for mobile devices. In: 2015 IEEE Virtual Reality (VR), pp. 245–246 (2015)
3. Wither, J., Allen, R., Samanta, V., Hemanus, J., Tsai, Y.T., Azuma, R., Carter, W., Hinman, R., Korah, T.: The westwood experience: connecting story to locations via mixed reality. In: 2010, IEEE International Symposium on Mixed and Augmented Reality-Arts, Media, and Humanities (ISMAR-AMH) (2010)
4. Razzaque, S., Kohn, Z., Whitton, M.C.: Redirected walking. In: Proceedings of EUROGRAPHICS, vol. 9, pp. 105–106 (2001)
5. Arakawa, T., Kasada, K., Narumi, T., Tanikawa, T., Hirose, M.: Reliving video experiences with mobile devices. In: 2012 18th International Conference on Virtual Systems and Multimedia (VSMM), pp. 581–584. IEEE (2012)
6. Kajinami, T., Hayashi, O., Narumi, T., Tanikawa, T., Hirose, M.: Digital display case: museum exhibition system to convey background information about exhibits. In: 2010 16th International Conference on Virtual Systems and Multimedia (VSMM), pp. 230–233. IEEE (2010)
7. Uyttendaele, M., Criminisi, A., Kang, S.B., Winder, S., Szeliski, R., Hartley, R.: Image-based interactive exploration of real-world environments. IEEE Comput. Graph. Appl. 24(3), 52–63 (2004)
8. Tanaka, R., Narumi, T., Tanikawa, T., Hirose, M.: Navigation interface for virtual environments constructed with spherical images. In: 2016 IEEE Virtual Reality (VR), pp. 291–292. IEEE (2016)
9. Hache, G., Lemaire, E.D., Baddour, N.: Mobility change-of-state detection using a smartphone-based approach. In: 2010 IEEE International Workshop on Medical Measurements and Applications Proceedings (MeMeA), pp. 43–46. IEEE (2010)
10. Apple iBeacon. https://developer.apple.com/ibeacon/

Using Virtual Reality to Assess the Elderly: The Impact of Human-Computer Interfaces on Cognition

Frédéric Banville[1(✉)], Jean-François Couture[2], Eulalie Verhulst[3], Jeremy Besnard[3], Paul Richard[3], and Philippe Allain[3]

[1] Université de Montréal, Montréal, Canada
frederic.banville@umontreal.ca
[2] Centre de développement et de recherche en imagerie numérique, Matane, Canada
[3] Université d'Angers, Angers, France

Abstract. Prospective memory (PM) is defined be the capacity to remember to realize an intended action in the future. This is a very important cognitive function that permit to maximize autonomy in everyday life. Unfortunately, few assessment tool, valid, reliable and ecological is accessible for clinicians. To obtain a verisimilar and ecologically prospective memory assessment tool, virtual reality seems to be a promising way. A specific and sensible tool could help the clinician to detect subtle changes in the cognition of the elderly and, ideally detect pathological aging soon before the beginning of decline. Because older adults are not really at ease with technology, these (dis)abilities could be confounded with cognitive inefficacy and lead to false positives diagnostics. To avoid this, the psychometrician must consider the impact of human-computer interfaces (HMI) on cognition. This paper present three experiments that show the impact of HMI on stress, capacity to achieve a task and on cognitive load. The first pilot study shown that a "heavy to use" HMI generated stress and difficulty to achieve the task with healthy adults. The second pilot study revealed that VMT-2 is judged moderately challenging cognitively and it seems to be more for older participants. The third pilot study shown that a complex virtual environment (in terms of navigation and interaction) is more cognitively challenging than a simple virtual environment for older peoples compared to young participants. These results indicated the importance of considering HMI as a potential variable that could create bias in the cognitive measurement.

Keywords: Virtual reality · Human-computer interface elderly · Assessment · Prospective memory · Cognition

1 Introduction

Prospective memory (PM) is a set of cognitive functions responsible for our ability to remember to carry out an intended action at a specific time in the future [1]. It is now recognized that proper functioning of the prospective memory is essential in everyday life because it gives people a maximum of independence in carrying out normal activities. By providing a certain degree of personal safety in everyday life, prospective memory also has a direct effect on people's quality of life and on their social

© Springer International Publishing AG 2017
S. Yamamoto (Ed.): HIMI 2017, Part II, LNCS 10274, pp. 113–123, 2017.
DOI: 10.1007/978-3-319-58524-6_10

participation. Some activities governed by prospective memory include remembering to take medication, arriving at an appointment on time and turning off the stove after using it [2]. PM is a major set of cognitive function to allow an independent life. Indeed, three types of remembering based on the nature of prospective cues have been described: Event-based, Activity-based and Time-based [3]. Event-based PM tasks are facilitated when a cue is present in the environment. The best example is the person who wishes to buy orange juice on the way home: here prospective remembering "pops up" with the appearance of a grocery store. Activity-based prospective memory consists of achieving a specific action (for example, taking a medication) in association with the realization of another action (for example, when the person is going to the work). Finally, Time-based prospective memory tasks consist of remembering an intention at a specific time (e.g. 10 o'clock) or after a specific delay (e.g. in a 20-minute delay). A good example of a Time-based prospective memory event is meeting a colleague at a specific time and day or removing a cake from the oven after 30 min.

Assessing PM is primary to understand patient's difficulties in everyday life. For instance, aging population reports frequently PM problems as evaluate by some laboratory tasks [4] but PM problems seem to be difficult to observe in the everyday life. This particularly the case when patients are performing during natural tasks (a) realized in a familiar context, (b) interfolded in everyday life and (c) executed on several days. This contrast into the results could be explained by anxiety generate in a laboratory setting or by the fact that the elderly could use compensatory strategies in the everyday life such as a calendar, Post-it, etc. Here, virtual reality (VR) could be a good means to assess prospective memory in a verisimilar ecological manner with standardized procedures. VR is a computerize simulation of the real world. It allows to propose virtual environment (VE) designed fully to assess cognitive function in everyday life without unwanted distractors or possibilities for the patient to use his familiar compensatory strategies.

Authors have proposed an interesting model of PM (The Multiprocess Model) [5]. This model argues it has 2 main modes of remembering: automatic and strategic. More specifically, when people achieve a prospective task under automatic processes, the contact with the cue in the environment is sufficient to remember the attended action. In fact, this remembering could depend more on environmental cues, thus soliciting more memory and attention than executive functions. Strategic remembering implies bigger cognitive resources because it supposes a strategic and voluntary monitoring between ongoing and prospective tasks [5]. This process might be supported by the Supervisory Attention System (SAS), an attention-executive process [6]. The SAS facilitates encoding an association between an external event and the intended action. After, the SAS monitors the environment and searches the targeted cue to indicate the right time to perform the action [1, 7]. When the target is identified, the SAS interrupts the ongoing task, turns the attention toward the prospective task and lets the person realize the intended action. In summary, the role of the SAS in the Multiprocess model is to support the realization of the action plan by the activation of the intended scripts and by diminishing the non-pertinent scripts; this process could be implied also when the individual performs in attention mode. The SAS implies that attention resources are limited in "energy". Actually, when attention is focused on one element of the entire task, it is difficult to pay attention to the other part of the task. In VR, we could think that when participant is concentrated on the navigation with an external device (e.g. joysticks, mice) into the virtual environment (VE), his/her cognitive readiness for the task are reduced. That could create a bias in the measurement obtained into the VE.

Because PM is a cognitive function weakened in pathological aging such as mild cognitive impairment [8], it is very important to consider the best way to assess it efficacy. Several authors said the PM must be systematically assessed by neuropsychologist when a diagnostic of dementia is suspected [9]. Unfortunately, very few assessment and clinically useful tool for PM exist because some of them lack reliability. VR could be a better alternative to assess PM but with these tools it is essential to be able to understand which part of the cognitive load is solicited by the Human-Machine interface (HCI).

1.1 Assessing Prospective Memory

The ecological validity of measures of cognitive function is contingent on the functional and predictive relationship between an individual's performance on a set of neuropsychological tests and their real-life behaviour at home, at work, at school or in the community [11]. In other words, a test is ecologically valid if it is able to predict an individual's level of function or detect potential problems in his/her daily life. The major challenge concerning a new paradigm in neuropsychological assessment is to develop tools with a good face-and-content validity (i.e. tasks should more closely resemble those of daily life) and with predictive validity (i.e. test must be correlated with the individual's real-life functioning). From a psychometric perspective, ecological validity is represented by the link between the results observed in a test and the capacities of the subject as it is seen in everyday life [12]. Two dimensions of ecological tests have been reported [13]; that is useful in the understanding of a cognitive assessment from an ecological perspective. To sum up, the test can be constructed or reviewed from a "veridicality" or "verisimilitude" perspective.

Veridicality concerns all existing traditional tests and the way which they are linked empirically with everyday life [12]. Originally, the test had not been created to simulate daily-living activity. On the other hand, it can be predictive on how cognitive functions will help or not in the realization of an activity. The Trail Making Test (TMT), attention and executive functions test, is a good example of this kind of assessment. The theoretical construct of the TMT is not ecological, but it can be useful in terms of prediction. Here, it is important to remember that a test having good diagnosis capacities is not necessary ecologically valid. Moreover, [13] have found some contradictions concerning correlations obtained between some traditional tests (e.g. WCST, TMT, Controlled Oral Word Association Test) and everyday performance in naturalistic tasks that imply executive functions. In brief, veridicality is a field of ecological assessment which claims that it is possible to use a traditional neuropsychological test in order to predict everyday performance; in the end, further research in this field as far as current literature is concerned must be conducted.

Verisimilitude represents the capacities of a test to have the same cognitive demands as those found in everyday life from a theoretical perspective [12]. This approach required reinventing neuropsychological assessment in order to create a new assessment protocol, nearer to the reality of the person [24]. In this way, the expectation was to have a test with better content and criterion validity compared to a traditional one. Efforts such as those mentioned above, which set out to create every day-like tests, make better the distinction between verisimilitude and veridicality of the neuropsychological assessment.

A very good verisimilar neuropsychological test is the Multiple Errands Test (MET), which was initially developed by [14]. In this task, participants are asked to carry out tasks in a real environment. For example, the subject has to purchase some items and spend less money as possible, to avoid buying non-asked items, to respect some arbitrary rules (e.g. "Don't talk to the evaluator during the task;" "Don't exit a definite perimeter," etc.). Although the MET has been shown to detect subtle problems of day-to-day living, it lacks reliability from a psychometric point of view [15]. Because the test is naturalistic, results obtained from the test in real-life settings are difficult to reproduce from individual to individual and from situation to situation [16]. But some authors have argued these psychometric considerations are contoured by a good inter-rater reliability [16, 17]. The main advantages of the MET are its sensitivity to specific neuropsychological deficits and its ecological validity [15].

From a neuropsychological perspective, the main challenge to developing new assessment tools is the standardization of assessment procedures that contain naturalistic and plausible tasks regarding day-to-day life. The development of ecological neuropsychological tests leads to the review of test structure [18]. However, if the task implies real activity and interactivity with daily-living activities, then it could lack reliability in the way of repetition of measure. Therefore, some authors have tried to create new assessments performed in the office of the neuropsychologist with an ecological construct.

Several situations in the everyday life demand good prospective memory capacities [19]. It seems to be difficult to have ecological and "verisimilar" measures of PM. To reproduce day-to-day living in a more realistic way and to assure standardized, reliable, and valid measures, several researchers have explored the potential of VR technology. In VR, the user navigates in a computer-simulated environment and interacts with objects in real time, 'like in real life' [20]. This technology offers researchers the best of both worlds [18]: it allows them to observe real-life situations in a laboratory setting [21]. There are several advantages that make it attractive to those in the field of neuropsychological assessment. Firstly, it allows access to the construct of prospective memory in a systematic, rigorous, and standardized manner [21–23] while at the same time providing a degree of ecological realism [24]. Also, because the effects of extraneous variables commonly encountered in real life can be controlled, VR researchers can assess the effects of standardized 'unexpected situations' in these environments [21].

VR is therefore considered as an ecologically valid tool to assess cognitive functions involved in everyday life. Studies in our group have shown the capacities of VR to detect cognitive dysfunction after traumatic brain injury or dementia [25, 26]. We have also demonstrated significant correlations between performance on virtual tasks and neuropsychological measures [27, 28]. However, our works have also demonstrated that HCI can generate a cognitive overload which affects cognitive functioning and creates a measurement bias. In accordance with our finding, some authors have demonstrated that VE can generate cognitive overload, mainly for people who are not familiar with video games, which is the case for the elderly [29]. Others have also found a significant cognitive overload in students performing tasks in a VE experienced [30]. These students reported having difficulty to direct their attention, to keep in mind several sources of information when exploring the virtual world. Therefore, there would be several active cognitive processes in the foreground and in the background when it comes to using a VE to evaluate the cognitive skills of an individual [31], particularly in the mobilization of cognitive resources by HCI.

1.2 Objectives

To investigate the effect of HCI on cognition during a neuropsychological assessment with VR, we have conducted three complementary pilot studies. All these studies implicated participants without brain lesions or psychiatric history. The purpose of these studies was to assess the normal functioning of an adult doing tasks in a VE; a magnifying glass will be focused on older participants. All these studies were conducted with the Virtual Multitasking Test (VMT) [32].

2   Method

2.1   Pilot Study 1

The aim of the first pilot study was to assess the effect of a technology known as "heavy use" (i.e. disturbs the navigation and interactions with the VE) on tasks realization during immersion in the VMT.

Participants. Five healthy adult participants (2 women & 3 men) were recruited into the general population. The mean age was 34, 5 (SD: 12,07) and mean years of education was 15 (SD: 1,55).

Virtual environment. The Virtual Multitasking Test (VMT) aims, at the beginning of its development, to assess PM and executive functions using a multitasking paradigm [33]. Different scenarios are implanted into a 6 ½ rooms virtual apartment, each room including at least one task except the bathroom. At the beginning of the test, participants are told that they are visiting their best friend. During the day, he is at work and they must live in his apartment. In the evening, they will go to a show with their best friend. However, during the day, they must perform several tasks alone based on daily life. For instance, they must store the groceries on the counter as quickly as possible (even if they are told there is no time limit to complete the activities), answer the phone, and perform other tasks such as faxing a document, search for show tickets, dry a shirt, feed a fish. PM tasks require, among other things, to close a door just when exiting the master bedroom to prevent a dog from climbing on the bed. Unforeseen events occur during the execution of the tasks. For instance, the occurrence of a storm which overthrow objects in the guest room and let water seep into the dining room. For example, storms that reverse objects in the guest room and that let water seep into the dining room. Every time a person is exposed to the VMT, they start a training phase of the environment. Afterwards, the experimental phase began and the person had to carry out the tasks proposed by the scenarios planned by researchers.

Materiel. A Head Mounted Display (eMagin z800) was used in this experimental setting that got the head movements and allowed immersion. Participants wore a 6DOF sensor on the dominant hand (Ascention's Flock of Bird) to manipulate objects in the VE. They had in their other hand a mouse that guaranteed their movements and they had to manipulate the right, left and centre buttons to perform certain actions in the VE. The experiment was realized standing to find consistency and keep the realism of the proposed scenario. Blood pressure and heart rate measurements were also taken every 5 min through an Ambulatory Blood Pressure Monitor (ABPM) (Whelsh Allyn) to evaluate the biological variations, i.e. probable stress indicators or measurement of the workload during the task completion.

Results. In the first experimental setting, participants felt a little stressed or anxious in relation to the upcoming experimentation (2.33 ± 2.7 on a scale of 10), and blood pressure was in the limit of normal at the time of starting the experimental protocol. After immersion, they reported that the interaction with the VMT was difficult and frustrating (8.40 ± 2.07 on a scale of 10). The analysis of individual performance demonstrated that no participant came to efficiently complete the task and that there was a great variation in the immersion time (total time of immersion: 19.45 ± 17.55 min), indicating a rise of workload during the immersion. Moreover, many mistakes were made and tasks were performed in a none-efficient way. Concerning the reported biological measures, three out of five (60%) participants showed a higher level of blood pressure during the immersion thus achieving prehypertension thresholds (120/80 mmHg) compared to initial measure. Heart rate was also affected, rising above 80 beats per minute for two participants (40%; while the normal threshold at rest was 70 beats per minute). However, despite these observations and changes of the participant's internal state, the average sense of presence has remained satisfactory (7.67 ± 0.816/10).

2.2 Pilot Study 2

The aim of this study was to explore the effects of mental workload generated by the VMT second version.

Participants. Thirteen healthy adults were recruited into the general population to participate in this study. Six were aged between 18 and 45 years old (mean: 30; SD: 8,83) and 7 were aged over 65 years old (mean: 67,25; SD: 2,87). The experiment took place on two non-consecutive half days: the first one to take neuropsychological assessment to evaluate the executive functions, which involves "traditional" tests such as Delis-Kaplan Executive Function – System (D-KEFS) and the California Verbal Learning Test (CVLT) and "ecological" tests such as the Behavioural Assessment of the Dysexecutive Syndrome (BADS) and the Rivermead Behavioural Memory Test (RBMT) and the second to realize several tasks in the VMT.

Virtual environment. Based on the results obtained in the first pilot study, to conduct this second study, VMT was migrated from VIRTOOL towards UNITY 3D to simplify HCI and to make the task in the VE more fluid. Several modifications were brought to the original scenario to complexity and made it more valid on a theoretical point of view the assessment.

Procedure. The experimental procedure was divided in two phases (learning and test) of the new VMT-2, which was used in a non-immersive mode. The necessary equipment for the study was a computer with a multimedia projector, a keyboard for movement and mouse for gripping objects. At the end of the experiment, eight participants completed the entirety of the experimental protocol. Attrition was mainly explained by the length of the experiment (duration when including the two phases: 6 h under two days). The latter fact could possibly explain the dropout from the study.

Results. At the end of the experiment, the participants didn't experience cybersickness (sum = 4.43 ± 3.78/64). The feeling of presence was, for its part, in the average (mean = 2.47 ± 0.45/4). On the basis of the NASA-TLX questionnaire, VMT-2 appeared to induce a relatively modest cognitive load (i.e. 46% of estimated cognitive load). However, considering the standard deviation obtained, it seemed that some people are more likely to judge the environment as rather demanding. Indeed, it seemed that it was mainly the case for those aged over 65 years old.

2.3 Pilot Study 3

This third and final pilot study want to explore, while simplifying the HCI, if there was an age-related difference between young and elderly adults: (a) when the requested tasks in a VE were more complex and (b) on the user's experience with the interactive system design (UX) based on the VE used. In sum, the experimental design consisted of age-related comparison of the cognitive load caused by two different VEs.

Participants. Nine young adult (18–45 years; mean = 30.44 years ± 4.98 years) and 8 elderly participants (55 years and up; 68.38 ± 9.13 years) were recruited from the general population. Hence, to be eligible for this study, participants must not have a neurological or psychiatric history; for the elderly, the Montreal Cognitive Assessment (MoCA) should be fewer than 26. Neither group differed significantly on the education plan [$F(1,15) = 3.07$; $p = 0.1$]. When asked to give a percentage (/100%) on the level of comfort use with computers, young adults (80 ± 17.79) expressed more comfort compared to elderly adults (55.63% ± 36.79); [$F(1,15) = 3.36$; $p = 0.09$].

Procedure. Participants had to perform scripted tasks in the VMT-2 as described previously, environmental named "complex". They must also in a "simple" environment make coffee with milk and two sugars. Therefore, we used the Non-Immersive Coffee Task from [27]. In this VE, participants were projected in a kitchen in which they did not have to move themselves. To achieve the task, objects must have been manipulated on the table - with computer mouse - in a logical order. The two tasks are carried out consecutively in a counterbalanced order. Following the completion of each task, participants were asked to complete two questionnaires. At first, the NASA-TLX was administered. The latter has the advantage to easily allow comparison of tasks while assessing the fluctuation of mental load according to the changing environment. The second questionnaire was AttrakDiff 2 [34]. The latter is a subjective measure of the ease of using technology by characterizing the experience in contact with VR. Three subscale are included: (a) the pragmatic qualities of the VR (usability utility); (b) hedonic qualities characterized by pleasure and satisfaction in contact with the VR; (c) the attractiveness or overall quality of the interaction with the VR.

Results. The results showed a significant age-related difference for the cognitive load requested by the VE. The VMT-2 generated a greater cognitive load in the elderly compared to the young adults [$F(1,12) = 8.30$; $p = 0.017$]. Cognitive load generated by the Non-Immersive Coffee Task was similar in both groups [$F (1,12) = 3.40$; $p = 0.617$]. A subsequent analysis of the subscales revealed that the main age-related difference in the VMT-2 was in the load time, effort and performance. As for the Non-Immersive Virtual Coffee Task, they differed on the physical demands requested. Moreover, no significant difference between groups and between environments on the UX was found. That was good news because the pragmatic & hedonic aspects of our environment don't raise the cognitive workload. Indeed, all participants described their experience as pleasant thus satisfying the two VE to which they were exposed. Finally, despite the small sample, some preliminary results have shown that the elderly spend more time in the VMT, they were less efficient in terms of movements, they are more disoriented and they need more time in the training phase compared to the younger adults. In summary, in this pilot study, both environments were considered equal in terms of UX and means of interaction were similar and simplified. The study has demonstrated that the accumulation of tasks to perform in a VE and their associated complexities bring a greater challenge for older adults in terms of requested cognitive resources.

3   Discussion

This paper wants to show how important is the impact of technology on cognition in the elderly. In the beginning, we suppose that VR is a good and reliable/valid means to assess cognitive functions. In the same way, we think that PM is a cognitive function particularly useful to detect pathological decline in aging. But, when we claim that VR is ecologically valid, it is possible to be wrong or to have difficulties to show it, if the cognitive load of the HCI is not considered. To begin this reflection, we conducted 3 very small pilot study with different experimental designs.

After the first pilot study, it was possible to see that the level of stress increased during the immersion in most participants due to navigational and manipulation difficulties in the VE. The limits of this pre-experimental study, in addition to the small number of participants, are seen in the type of measurement selected to observe the cognitive overload (i.e., time to complete the task, blood pressure and heart rate). Other measures would have allowed us to better reflect on cognitive demands of the experimental protocol; thus explaining - at least partially - the fact that the participants did not properly complete the task.

At the end of the second pilot study, we observed, when using a smaller sample that was comparable on multiple variables (i.e. cybersickness, sense of presence, anxiety, executive functions), that: while simplifying the HCI, the more a person must complete tasks in each space, the higher the cognitive load could possibly raise on several dimensions. Finally, the results showed an age effect in the HCI and in the achievement of the VMT-2 tasks.

Concerning the third pilot study, results have shown that the elderly spend more time in the VMT, they were less efficient in terms of movements, they are more disoriented and they need more time in the training phase compared to the younger adults. In summary, in this pilot study, both environments were considered equal in terms of UX and means of interaction were similar and simplified. The study has demonstrated that the accumulation of tasks to perform in a VE and their associated complexities bring a greater challenge for older adults in terms of requested cognitive resources.

To conclude, despite small sample sizes, these 3 pilot studies demonstrated that similar factors increased the solicitation of cognitive resources during task performance. These factors included the means of interaction, the nature of the required tasks and the characteristics of the participants and the VE. These factors were of importance when reinventing the neuropsychological assessment, to make it more ecological by using VR. Hence, the first study suggested that inefficient and complex interfaces could interfere significantly with the neuropsychological assessment thus affecting the validity of the measure. The second study illustrated that not all tasks were equivalent in VE. Indeed, those that required more interaction with the control devices were those that are effortful and were consequently the most frustrating. Lastly, the third study suggested that a larger virtual apartment, in which they are more movements, also influenced the cognitive load - probably through the solicitation of navigation, orientation and memory processes. These components must always be integrated with the neuropsychological measures taken in the VE. Finally, elderly adults appeared to be less skilled with technology. They were consequently more at risk of performing less efficiently in VR than in daily life actions since the measure is taken by a computer. This impacts negatively the sensitivity of the tool for the detection of mild cognitive impairment or for the early identification of neurocognitive disorders such as dementia. Although these age-related changes may fade with the aging of the current young population since they are more familiar with computers and gaming interfaces, it is still essential to consider the current age effects when evaluating in the VR a normal aging population or a clinic population.

References

1. Ellis, J.: Prospective memory or the realization of delayed intentions: a conceptual framework for research. In: Brandimonte, M., Einstein, G.O., McDaniels, M.A. (eds.) Prospective Memory: Theory and Applications, pp. 1–22. Lawrence Erlbaum Associates, Mahwah (1996)
2. Shum, D., Fleming, J.M., Neulinger, K.: Prospective memory and traumatic brain injury: a review. Brain Impairment 3(1), 1–16 (2002)
3. Kvavilashvili, L., Ellis, J.: Varieties of intention: some distinctions and classifications. In: Brandimonte, M., Einstein, G.O., McDaniel, M.A. (eds.) Prospective Memory: Theory and Applications, pp. 23–51. Lawrence Erlbaum Associates Publishers, Mahwah (1996)

4. Azzopardi, B., Auffray, C., Juhel, J.: L'effet paradoxal du vieillissement sur la mémoire prospective: hypothèses explicatives. Gériatrie et Psychologie Neuropsychiatrie du Vieillissement **13**(1), 64–72 (2015)
5. McDaniel, M.A., Einstein, O.G.: Strategic and automatic processes in prospective memory retrieval: a multiprocess framework. Appl. Cogn. Psychol. **14**, S127–S144 (2000)
6. Norman, D.A., Shallice, T.: Attention to action: willed and automatic control of behaviour. In: Davidson, R.J., Schwartz, G.E., Shapiro, D. (eds.) Consciousness and Self-regulation: Advances in Research and Theory. Plenum Press, New York (1986)
7. Burgess, P.W., Shallice, T.: The relationship between prospective and retrospective memory: Neuropsychological evidence. In: Conway, M.A. (ed.) Cognitive Models of Memory, pp. 247–272. The MIT Press, Cambridge (1997)
8. Thompson, C., Henry, J.D., Rendell, P.G., Withall, A., Brodaty, H.: Prospective memory function in mild cognitive impairment and early dementia. J. Int. Neuropsychol. Soc. **16**(2), 318–325 (2010)
9. Van den Berg, E., Kant, N., Postma, A.: Remember to buy milk on the way home! A meta-analytic review of prospective memory in mild cognitive impairment and dementia. J. Int. Neuropsychol. Soc. **18**(4), 706–716 (2012)
10. Lewis, M.W., Babbage, D.R., Leathem, J.M.: Assessing executive performance during cognitive rehabilitation. Neuropsychol. Rehabil. **21**(2), 145–163 (2011)
11. Sbordone, R.J.: Ecological validity: some critical issues for neuropsychologist. In: Sbordone, R.J., Long, C.J. (eds.) Ecological Validity of Neuropsychological Testing, pp. 15–42. St-Lucie Press, New York (1996)
12. Franzen, M.D., Wilhelm, K.L.: Conceptual foundations of ecological validity in neuropsychology. In: Sbordone, D.R.J., Long, C.J. (eds.) Ecological Validity of Neuropsychological Testing, pp. 91–112. St. Lucie Press, Delray Beach (1996)
13. Chaytor, N., Schmitter-Edgecombe, M.: The ecological validity of neuropsychological tests: a review of the literature on everyday cognitive skills. Neuropsychol. Rev. **13**, 181–197 (2003)
14. Shallice, T., Burgess, P.W.: Deficits in strategy application following frontal lobe damage in man. Brain **114**, 727–741 (1991)
15. Cuberos-Urban, G., Caracuel, A., Vilar-López, Ré, Valls-Serran, C., Bateman, A., Verdejo-García, A.: Ecological validity of the Multiple Errands Test using predictive models of dysexecutive problems in everyday life. J. Clin. Exp. Neuropsychol. **35**(3), 329–336 (2013)
16. Dawson, D.R., Anderson, N.D., Burgess, P., Cooper, E., Krpan, K.M., Stuss, D.: Further development of the multiple errands test: standardized scoring, reliability, and ecological validity for the baycrest version. Arch. Phys. Med. Rehabil. **90**(1), S41–S51 (2009)
17. Knight, C., Alderman, N., Burgess, P.W.: Development of a simplified version of the multiple errands test for use in hospital settings. Neuropsychol. Rehabil. **12**(3), 231–255 (2002)
18. Morris, R.G., Kotitsa, M., Bramham, J., Brooks, B., Rose, F.D.: Virtual reality investigation of strategy formation, rule breaking and prospective memory in patients with focal prefrontal neurosurgical lesions. In: Proceedings of 4th International Conference on Disability, Virtual Reality and Associated Technologies, Hungary, pp. 101–108 (2002)
19. Burgess, P.W., Gonen-Yaacovi, G., Volle, E.: Functional neuroimaging studies of prospective memory: what have we learnt so far? Neuropsychologia **49**(8), 2246–2257 (2011)
20. Pratt, D.R., Zyda, M., Kelleher, K.: Virtual reality: in the mind of the beholder. IEEE Comput. **28**(7), 17–19 (1995)
21. Schutheis, M.T., Rizzo, A.A.: The application of virtual reality technology in rehabilitation. Rehabil. Psychol. **46**, 296–311 (2001)
22. Wilson, P.N., Foreman, N., Stanton, D.: Virtual reality, disability and rehabilitation. Disabil. Rehabil. **19**(6), 213–220 (1997)

23. Tarr, M.J., Warren, W.H.: Virtual reality in behavioral neurosciences and beyond. Nat. Neurosci. **5**, 1089–1092 (2002)
24. Zhang, L., Abreu, B.C., Masel, B., Scheibel, R.S., Christiansen, C.H., Huddleston, N., Ottenbacher, K.J.: Virtual reality in the assessment of selective cognitive function after brain injury. Am. J. Phys. Med. Rehabil. **80**(8), 597–604 (2001)
25. Zalla, T., Plassiart, C., Pillon, B., Grafman, J., Sirigu, A.: Action planning in a virtual context after prefrontal cortex damage. Neuropsychologia **39**, 759–770 (2001)
26. Banville, F., Nolin, P., Lalonde, S., Henry, M., Dery, M.P., Villemure, R.: Multitasking and prospective memory: can virtual reality be useful for diagnosis? Behav. Neurol. **23**(4), 209 (2010)
27. Banville, F., Nolin, P.: Using virtual reality to assess prospective memory and executive functions after traumatic brain injury. J. CyberTherapy Rehabil. **5**(1), 45–55 (2012)
28. Allain, P., Etcharry-Bouyx, F., Verny, C.: Executive functions in clinical and preclinical Alzheimer's disease. Revue Neurologique **169**(10), 695–708 (2013)
29. Besnard, J., Richard, P., Banville, F., Nolin, P., Aubin, G., Le Gall, D., Richard, I., Allain, P.: Virtual reality and neuropsychological assessment: The reliability of a virtual kitchen to assess the daily-life activities in victims of traumatic brain injury. Appl. Neuropsychol. Adult **23**(3), 223–235 (2016)
30. Ang, C.S., Zaphiris, P., Mahmood, S.: A model of cognitive loads in massively multiplayer online role playing games. Interact. Comput. **19**, 167–179 (2007)
31. Nelson, B.C., Erlandson, B.: Managing cognitive load in educational multi-user virtual environments: reflection on design practice. Educ. Tech. Res. Dev. **56**, 619–641 (2008)
32. Cicourel, A.V.: Cognitive overload and communication in two healthcare settings. Commun. Med. **1**(1), 35–43 (2004)
33. Banville, F., Nolin, P., Cloutier, J., Bouchard, S.: Description of the Virtual Multitasking Test (V-MT). In: Conference Présenté at the Virtual Rehabilitation Conference: From Vision to Reality, Edmonton (2007)
34. Burgess, P.W.: Strategy application disorder: the role of the frontal lobe in human multitasking research. Psychol. Res. **63**, 279–288 (2000)
35. Hassenzahl, M., Burmester, M., Koller, F.: AttrakDiff: Ein Frage-bogen zur Messung wahrgenommener hedonischer und pragmatischerQualität. In: Ziegler, J., Szwillus, G. (eds.) Mensch & Computer 2003. Interaktion in Bewegung, pp. 187–196. B.G. Teubner, Stuttgart (2003)

An AR Application for Wheat Breeders

Kaitlyn Becker, Frederic Parke, and Bruce Gooch[✉]

Texas A&M University, College Station, USA
kaitlyn.c.becker@gmail.com,
parke@viz.tamu.edu,
gooch@tamu.edu

Abstract. We report on an Augmented Reality interface to speed the workflow of food crop breeders. The goals of the interface are to make data collection in the field more efficient to accelerate the breeding cycle. For hardware combine the Recon Jet sports computer sunglasses and a Neutab N7 Android tablet. For software, we augment the Kansas State University open source Fieldbook application with barcode reading capability, a speech recognition interface, and information displays. We design and evaluate the application using a cohort of wheat breeders.

Keywords: Augmented reality · Agriculture · UIUX · Speech based interface · Plant breeders

1 Introduction

As the world's population continues to increase, food production works to keep up. The Food and Agricultural Organization of the United Nations (FOA) defines wheat as a staple food. The FAO also states that wheat along with rice and maize make up 60% of the world's food intake. However, we lose over half of the world's wheat to disease and pests. We need new varieties that are more resistant to disease and pests, which are tolerant of poor growing conditions, and that have higher germination rates and produce more grain per stalk. This ongoing research is imperative to keep up with the world's growing demand for food.

Many researchers today still rely on traditional log books for data collection. In scientific fields like chemistry and archeology, entomology and anthropology, the tried and true pen and paper method of note-taking is common. Accuracy and neatness are emphasized because the research is only as accurate as the data collected. As mobile technology becomes more widely available, developers are offering more efficient alternatives to traditional data collecting methods. On a computer, keeping notes organized is simple, and with a mobile computing device, this technology is as portable as a paper notebook.

Field Book is an open source application intended as a digital note-taking tool for wheat researchers. The goal is to provide researchers and growers with technology that is more efficient and accurate than traditional log books. A key goal of the initiative is to make information technology accessible by making tools inexpensive and intuitive.

© Springer International Publishing AG 2017
S. Yamamoto (Ed.): HIMI 2017, Part II, LNCS 10274, pp. 124–133, 2017.
DOI: 10.1007/978-3-319-58524-6_11

In the field, crop scientists work in teams of three. One person visually identifies the plant to be measured. They visually grade the plant then speak aloud in a wheat grading markup language. The second person writes the plants condition in the Field Book. The third person navigates the group and tells the grader which plant to grade.

While Field Book supports digital data collection, it requires manual input. Researchers are forced to juggle between manipulating plants and recording data, slowing the process and requiring multiple people. We implemented hands-free field data collection without the need for an assistant. We assume that users do not have internet access while recording data in remote areas. As such, the data collection capabilities of the software have no internet dependency. We export data from the Android tablet in the lab.

Field Book currently allows users to record speech for later transcription. This feature is not commonly used by researchers because of the time it takes to later transcribe these notes (Trevor Rife, personal communication, May 19, 2015). With speech recognition, the user would have a written record that could be transmitted to colleagues immediately without the transcription time.

By utilizing speech-based software developed for multiple languages, the interface could also be made available to non-English speaking researchers. With the addition of speech synthesis, the app could read aloud (in the native language) instructions or descriptions to the user, making this app accessible to those with limited literacy. Since the system is most often used in bright sunlight (Trevor Rife, personal communication, May 19, 2015), read aloud functionality could be useful when screen readability is poor. Spoken text could also be added to the in-built tutorial.

The system augments the current Field Book application. It contains three components. The first is barcode recognition software to aid in visually identify the particular plant in a greenhouse or test plot. The second system is speech recognition software. It is important that the user not feels the need to check the accuracy of each entry. Therefore the third component is feedback in the form of an information display.

Since the advent of modern agriculture, field researchers have used paper to record their data. Survey books with waterproof pages made to fit in a pocket are often used. There are conventions as to how these pages are laid out and how the data is recorded.

Figure 1 shows an example of data layout. Traditionally, data in columns are on the left, and figures and sketches are on the right. The necessity for precision makes recording in a survey book a time consuming endeavor. Researchers have the option of designing and reproducing a form that is custom tailored to their specific project. This requires the researcher to know ahead of time what data they will be collecting and offers little flexibility.

Crop Scientists currently mark test plots with barcode markers that identify the gene line. Following barcode recognition, the display illustrates the name of the gene line. The grader then speaks aloud as usual. We used PocketSphinx application and recordings of Scientists speaking all the phrases in the plant grading markup language. We used PoketSphinx because it is free and can operate without internet access. The application records and recognizes speech and displays an icon based information display of the plant's grade. The grader can then move to the next position.

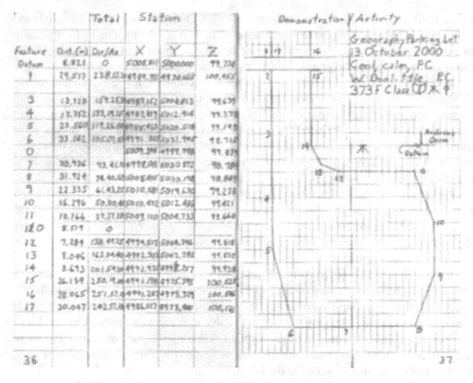

Fig. 1. An example of a paper journal currently used in field scouting.

2 Background

2.1 Mobile Applications for Data Collection

Users are becoming more comfortable using technology for tasks previously done on paper. According to a survey conducted by Princeton Survey Research Associates International, 50% of American adults own and use either a tablet or e-reading device (Zickuhr and Rainie). In recent years, researchers have begun adopting new technology in an attempt to make the process of data collection easier and more streamlined. With advances in mobile technology, digital tablets are becoming more useful as data recording media. They offer the portability of a logbook with the computational power of a computer. With a well written application, a user can edit, reorganize and customize their recorded data, as well as disseminate the gathered information efficiently.

Of the researchers who use a tablet as part of their data collection, many rely on Microsoft Excel. Excel offers a customizable grid and powerful mathematical functionality. Averages, totals and other survey data can be calculated and updated on the fly and can be translated into graphical format to help visualize information.

Excel is useful for data visualization and organization, but when it comes to mobile data collection, it proves unwieldy. Data cells and input keys are small and can be difficult to press accurately. The display is nearly impossible to see in bright lighting conditions on tablets with inadequate glare reduction. The grid format for information is inefficient on large plots due to the standard serpentine order of collecting. It can also be difficult to maintain the correct position in a spreadsheet when it is necessary to skip cells that do not have data to be input.

Many applications have been developed in the past decade to ameliorate these limitations. Some focus on global data management, allowing collaborators to pool their collective knowledge. Applications like Magpi (DataDyne Group) and Epicollect (EpiCollect.net) provide tools for creating mobile data collection forms and include functionality like GPS location and photo uploads. While they support data collection, their primary goal is organized dissemination of data.

Reference guides are particularly well-suited to mobile application development. Some, like Plant-o-matic (Ocotea Technologies, LLC) and the iBird Guide (Mitch Waite Group), present the user with a powerful search tool with which they can identify a specimen. Other references, like Project Noah (Networked Organisms), rely on the contributions of 'citizen scientists' to report and identify sightings of fauna across the globe. The application serves as a hub for a community of users to share their findings or seek help from fellow researchers.

2.2 Speech Recognition

Speech interfaces have been successfully incorporated into video games, office applications, art pieces and vehicle consoles. In these diverse settings, speech interfaces are beneficial for different reasons. For vehicle consoles, having hands free operation that doesn't take the driver's eyes off the road improves safety. In office applications, the most commonly used feature is dictation. The computer can transcribe the user's thoughts as they speak them, thus allowing users who think faster than they type to capture their message more quickly and efficiently. The main benefit of a speech interface for a video game is a wider command base. On console games in particular, there are sometimes not enough buttons to encompass the commands. As such, most games that utilize a diverse number of commands (for example, World of Warcraft) have to use the computer keyboard. The addition of a speech interface allows for the use of far more commands without needing extra buttons or button combinations.

The process of speech recognition involves three main steps. The first is to sample an incoming analog waveform to a digital representation. Next, this digital data is divided into distinct units of sound called phonemes and pauses. Finally, the resulting phonemes are run through an algorithm to determine the resulting text. The algorithm used differs between various speech recognition software, and can have varying levels of complexity depending upon the needs of the system.

All speech recognizers use a dictionary. A dictionary consists of a list of all the words a recognizer can distinguish alongside the combination of phonemes that make up that word. It is possible for a single word to have multiple phoneme combinations just as it is possible for words in a language dictionary to have several definitions. Figure 1 shows an excerpt from one such dictionary.

A speech recognizer might also consult a grammar when parsing a phrase. A grammar tells the recognizer the context in which a word can be used. For example,

Fig. 2 shows the grammar written for the Field Book augmentation. Much like a simplified version of a language grammar, it lays out the rules for when and how certain words are used. From this, the recognizer can better detect what words are being spoken by comparing them within the context of the phrase.

```
public <basicCmd> = <command>;
<command> = go forward | go back | <relocate> |<setTrait>| <query> | undo last | cancel;
<relocate> = <move> <location>;
<move> = go to | move to | i am at;
<location> = plot <number> | next plot | last plot;
<setTrait> = set <trait> to <number> <atLoc>*;
<trait> = flower|height;
<atLoc> = at <location>;
<number> = <digits> <digits>* <digits>*;
<tens> = ten|twenty|thirty|forty|fifty|sixty|seventy|eighty|ninety;
<teens> = eleven|twelve|thirteen|fourteen|fifteen|sixteen|seventeen|eighteen|nineteen;
<digits> = one|two|three|four|five|six|seven|eight|nine;
<query> = where am i | what row * | what column * | what plot * | what is <trait> set to;
```

Fig. 2. The grammar written for the *Field Book* augmentation. Much like a simplified version of a language grammar, it lays out the rules for when and how certain words are used. From this, the recognizer can better detect what words are being spoken by comparing them within the context of the phrase.

There are two main types of speech recognition: local and remote. In a local system, there is a dictionary file stored on the device that is referenced by the recognition algorithm. All computations are processed locally. These systems tend to be more accurate when dealing with a small dictionary and often have less sophisticated algorithms than remote systems. Our application only requires local speech recognition due to the small dictionary.

2.3 Field Book

Field Book is engineered specifically for field data collection. The application was developed with the needs of wheat researchers in mind. Users create a grid in Microsoft Excel, or other spreadsheet software, detailing the title or id (usually a number), row and column of each plot and import it to the tablet. Field Book then generates a map of the field. When creating a new data set, users specify the data points, referred to as 'traits', they will be collecting (i.e. flowering date, height, exertion), and the name of the researcher inputting the data. Field Book then allows the user to input the data per plot. Traditionally, researchers follow a serpentine pattern when collecting data; completing one row in ascending order, then following the next row in descending order. An example of this path is shown in Fig. 3. Field Book assumes this layout when progressing through a data set. Field Book's visual design is high contrast with large text and large buttons to facilitate its intended use in bright sunlight. Inputting data is streamlined, making data collection faster and easier than traditional paper methods. Users can export their collected data in spreadsheet format, allowing them to make use of Excel's mathematical capabilities.

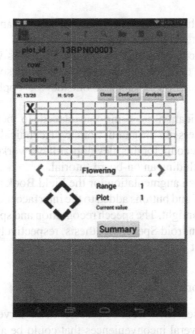

Fig. 3. An example of a screen in the Field Book application.

Field Book maintains flexibility for users by allowing them to define the traits they wish to record for a specific crop. The user can create data points of many different types including numeric, date, text, photo and audio. This allows the user to fine-tune the process to suit the needs of different research projects.

3 Implementation

3.1 Design Considerations

In designing an augmentation for Field Book, it was important to take into consideration the current implementation of the software. The application was designed for 7 inch tablets to maximize available screen space while keeping the device small enough to be easily portable. It was first developed for Android systems because the cost of these devices is lower and distributing the application is free and easy. This is in keeping with the goal of the "One handheld per breeder" movement. By keeping costs low, the application is available to more researchers. Android offers tablet models that are constructed to be durable, making them practical for field work.

A potential challenge faced by an outdoor speech recognition application is input sound quality. In practice, there will likely be environmental noise from wind, nearby roads or other interference. Distance of the user from the microphone (for speech recognition) or the speakers (for audio feedback) can reduce the user's ability to properly communicate with the system. The user could hold the tablet closer to their head, but this defeats the purpose of hands-free functionality. We used an inexpensive headset to provide quality audio input and output.

We assume that researchers will not have internet access while recording data in remote fields. As such, the data collection capabilities of the software have no internet dependency. Data dissemination is handled outside the application following data export.

The Field Book application is being introduced to both new and seasoned researchers. Prospective users run the gamut from avid technical gurus to traditional pen and paper enthusiasts. To account for this, developers have worked to make the interface as intuitive as possible, including an on-board tutorial.

We developed the speech augmentation for the Field Book application on a Neutab N7 Android tablet. The text and buttons added to the interface are large and high contrast to be seen easily in bright sunlight. The speech recognition and speech synthesis software used (PocketSphinx and Android Speech Synthesis, respectively) are available for free and operate locally without access to the internet.

3.2 Workflow Evaluation

We accompanied wheat researchers from Texas A&M on a survey of their project fields. On the trip, we noticed several inconveniences that could be ameliorated by a speech interface. First, the tablets require two hands to input data. This can be inconvenient for users who must also handle the plants or other equipment (like a measuring pole). The researcher also mentioned that the tablet touch screens tended to be less responsive in rain or mist, making data difficult to input. Inputting data also requires the user to look at the screen. It can be difficult to see the screen when the sun is very bright. With a speech system, input is handled via a microphone, minimizing the need to handle the device or view the screen.

We used this experience to lay out my concept for the interface. To ascertain the most intuitive setup, we framed the system as a kind of digital secretary. We asked the researchers to go over how they would relay their information if they had an assistant. Having one researcher call out information and one record it is common practice for large fields, as it speeds up the process. We made note of when the speaker would announce information, and when the recorder would ask for confirmation. In the case of a speech recognition system, particularly the less accurate local variety, it was necessary to assume this digital secretary was rather hard of hearing and would have to ask for confirmation more frequently than a human counterpart.

Researchers first state out loud plot number they are recording information. They then announce the trait to record and value of that trait. For example, in Texas there are five types of Wheat fungus. Plants are scored in six categories, no fungus or fungus type one through five. Plants with fungus are next scored with a percentage of disease from 2% to 100% in 20 point increments.

Researchers sometimes have to overwrite previous data as more information becomes available. For example, a researcher says that a particular plot must have flowered a day ago based on the appearance of the panicle (the loose, branching cluster of flowers found at the top of the plant) and the amount of pollen it has released. If the researcher then scores a plant a few rows down that has released less pollen but clearly did not begin flowering today. The researcher records that the current plot flowered yesterday and edits the previous plot to say it flowered two days ago. Collecting data that requires estimation, like flowering date, is subjective and users must be able to go back and modify the data if they change their minds.

3.3 Audio Feedback

Since the user should not feel the need to look at the screen when using this interface, audio feedback becomes the primary way of communicating information. It is necessary for the user to know when the system is listening, when the system recognizes or fails to recognize a command, and when it requests confirmation. To accomplish this, the system provides audio feedback for each case. This system makes use of both speech and tonal feedback, depending on the situation.

The system is always listening, but only activates command detection when it is specifically addressed using the keyphrase "Field Book". This prevents the system from trying to interpret everything it hears as commands. When the application detects the keyphrase, the system issues a notification sound to alert the user. Here, sound was employed rather than a spoken phrase to minimize the time between the user activating the system and speaking their command.

When the system recognizes a command, it issues a unique notification tone, then repeats the command it heard. For example, if the system recognizes the command 'move forward', plays the command recognized sound (a synthesized chime), then says "Moving forward to plot [next plot]". In the case of any error, the system will first play an error notification sound (a descending pair of tones). If it fails to recognize a given command, it says "[command issued] is an invalid command". If the command has a problem, for instance if the user attempts to move to a plot outside the map's bounds, the system will speak to the specific problem, in this case "The maximum plot is [# of plots], cannot access plot [the plot the user attempted]".

It is necessary for the researcher to receive audio feedback to ensure accuracy of data collected. For the trait command, the system announces the trait and value it is going to record, as well as the plot it is recording in. The system awaits feedback in the form of a 'yes' or a 'no' from the user prior to making changes in case the data is incorrect. The same occurs for the move command. Unlike other commands, the move forward and move backward commands do not await confirmation as they are used to move quickly between plots. The potential risk of falsely triggering these commands are combatted by their dissimilarity to other command phrases.

The user can request data such as the current row, column, plot, and trait values of the current plot using the commands detailed in the previous section.

3.4 What We Learned

In exploring this speech-based system, we worked out a series of do's and do not's for those considering the use of a similar system.

Do expect a good speech-based control system to feel like a conversation. Because this type of system requires the user to talk to it, and for the system to talk back, it inherits many of the characteristics of a traditional conversation. It can be more engaging to users than a passive point and click system. With a large enough command base, this type of system is also intuitive. The user can request a specific action, and the system will return the expected result.

Do expect a hands-free experience. Given the appropriate command base and audio feedback, the user does not have to physically interact with the system at all except for listening and speaking. This leaves the user free to use their hands and eyes elsewhere.

Do the research for what type of recognizer your system will need. Be aware of the requirements of the proposed system. Does it need a free or opensource software, or will it need a proprietary package? Know the priorities of speed, accuracy and flexibility. Will the developer define the grammar or use an open ended phonetic interpreter? A wider command base can mean less overall accuracy. Does the system require access to the internet? Internet dependent systems have access to more processing power and can handle larger dictionaries, but they can also be slower or less reliable depending on your connection.

Do expect to have to update your system. The first iteration (and likely the fifteenth) will not be perfect. Be prepared to make changes to the command base, the grammar, and the command interpreter many times to get it to a useable state.

Don't expect the recognizer to be completely accurate. Even the best recognizers have some degree of error. Always prepare your system for that eventuality and make sure it can handle miscommunications. It is far better to prepare for failures that never happen than to not be prepared for the one that does.

Don't expect the recognizer to be instant. Speech recognition takes time. The fastest systems still require a second or so to process. Speech controls are therefore not appropriate for situations requiring twitch controls such as in first person shooter games.

Don't get discouraged. Speech recognition is a conversation. It doesn't always go the way you'd expect. Be prepared to deal with the frustration of fine tuning the system to get it to a point where it is useable.

Overall, this system does what it was expected to do. It facilitates the use of the *Field Book* application as a hands-free tool. The user can move, set traits and "view" information without having to handle or look at the device.

4   Future Work

For future improvements of the system, I would like to continue to refine the accuracy of the recognizer. The incorporation of a remote recognizer could provide better translation while adding the requirement of continuous internet access. The system could also potentially incorporate user profiles, which would improve accuracy by training the system to a specific user's speech traits. I would also like to expand the commands the system is capable of handling, including the ability to navigate the main menu, load maps, and create new traits. More expansion possibilities include translation to other languages, and dictation for notes. In an ideal setup, users could add customized commands through an intuitive interface rather than having to modify the code.

5   Conclusion

We introduced the AR Field Book application to both new and seasoned researchers. Prospective users run the gamut from avid technical gurus to traditional pen and paper enthusiasts. The AR application reduced the time needed to navigate menus and submenus. For example, to access a non-adjacent plot using the current version of Field Book, the user must expand a drop-down menu, open the map, wait for it to initialize, and then count the unlabeled cells to find the next test plot to grade. With the implementation of speech-based commands, the user can just say 'Go to plot 285'.

Field Book currently allows users to record speech for later transcription. This feature is not used due to the costs in time or currency of transcription. With speech recognition, users have a written record to transmit to colleagues immediately.

References

1. Allen, J., Hunnicutt, S., Carlson, R., Granstrom, B.: MITalk-79: the 1979 MIT Text-to-speech system. Acoustical Society of America 65.51 (1979): n. pag. AIPScitation. AIP Publishing LLC, 11 August 2005. Web. 29 September 2015
2. Davis, K.H.: Automatic recognition of spoken digits. J. Acoust. Soc. Am. **24**(6), 627–642 (1952)
3. Doolittle, W.E.: Recording Data. Field Techniques, 23 June 2015
4. Dudley, H., Riesz, R.R., Watkins, S.A.: A synthetic speaker. J. Franklin Inst. **227**(6), 739–764 (1939). Effective, Affordable, Reusable Speech-to-Text (EARS)
5. Flanagan, J.L.: Speech Analysis Synthesis and Perception, pp. 166–167. Springer, Heidelberg (1965). Speech-to-Text (EARS). Electronic Frontier Foundation, n.d. Web, 05 November 2015. EpiCollect. Computer software. EpiCollect.net. Wellcome Trust, n.d. Web, 30 June 2015
6. Global Autonomous Language Exploitation. The Idiap Research Institute, 05 November 2015
7. GOOG-411 Team: Goodbye to an Old Friend: 1-800-GOOG-411. Web log post. Official
8. One Handheld Per Breeder. McKnight Foundation, n.d., 04 November 2015

A New Experience Presentation in VR2.0

Yasushi Ikei[1]([✉]), Tomohiro Amemiya[2], Koichi Hirota[3],
and Michiteru Kitazaki[4]

[1] Tokyo Metropolitan University, Tokyo 1910065, Japan
ikei@computer.org
[2] NTT Corporation, Kanagawa 2430198, Japan
amemiya.tomohiro@lab.ntt.co.jp
[3] The University of Electro-Communications, Tokyo 1828585, Japan
hirota@vogue.is.uec.ac.jp
[4] Toyohashi University of Technology, Aichi 4418580, Japan
mich@tut.jp

Abstract. The present paper proposes a new virtual reality presentation of bodily re-living experience that is focused on reproduction of the experience of other person including his/her body sensation. The characteristics of the re-living experience are discussed in three aspects of visual, bodily and subjective (agency) presentation problems. Four kinds of duality in implementation of the re-living experience are explained as a basic condition of an intrinsic hybrid structure of a presentation system. A preliminary implementation was built to provide the re-living experience of walking in a virtual space. Avatar rendering was also evaluated in terms of bodily sensation.

Keywords: Virtual experience · Bodily sensation · First-personness · Avatar · Passivity/Activity · Ultra reality

1 Introduction

The virtual reality technology can provide various experiences by reproducing the space. In the generation of experiences, it is usually necessary first to reproduce the space of the external 3D space as an environment. By acting on its own in the reproduced environment, the user can gain experience in a specific environment. Such an experience enables the user to know the past three-dimensional environment (space) through its own actions, and it is extremely effective in giving practically close knowledge as obtained by a person experienced at that time.

However, it is the current user who senses the environment and acquires those knowledge, and the experience is not the same sensory experience as what the past people felt when acting. In order to pass on the actual past actions of other people and the sensation they received at that time, the past experiences themselves must be handed down. There are various levels of experiences, from physical motion in space to those with deep thought, however it is a very difficult goal at any level to pass on such experiences themselves [1]. Especially, it

© Springer International Publishing AG 2017
S. Yamamoto (Ed.): HIMI 2017, Part II, LNCS 10274, pp. 134–143, 2017.
DOI: 10.1007/978-3-319-58524-6_12

is a difficult task to transfer high presence experiences involving physical activity and experiences based on dexterous physical skills including sport motion. Physical motion is the base of all human activity, and if we can share that experience, exchanging the exclusive value that an excellent person possesses will increase the average activity level of human beings. It is expected to accelerate the development of human society.

2   Re-living Experience

Conventionally, linguistic expressions in books etc. or images such as movies have been used as media for transferring general experiences (see Table 1). Both of them can cover a wide range of activities as an expression of the events of experience, however they can not include the sense of bodily motion itself through the audiovisual channels. They are distinctive in psychological depictions and in depicting the world of the first person or third person viewpoint. In books etc., experiences are created internally by interpretation and imagination based on memory. In recent years, movies extended to multiple senses have emerged [2]. This includes presentation of vestibular stimulation, airflow, scent, mist, tactile sensation to the back and feet, in addition to stereoscopic images and stereophonic sounds. By the extended movie, it is possible to greatly enhance the presence of the space. In addition, the sensation of riding on the same vehicle in the movie is typically rendered. In such a movie, the tactile sensation of the viewer is stimulated by the device that applies pressure and vibration implemented in the seat. The tactile sensation received by an arbitrary person in the movie is also reproduced. Such a multisensory presentation contrihoweveres to raising the sensation of presence as a part of the story production, however it lacks essential parts as a re-living experience. An ordinary movie is not composed mainly of depiction from a first person viewpoint which is a unique characteristic as a re-living experience.

To reproduce the actual physical experience of someone, it is necessary to present the changing visual field as the result of the viewpoint motion during his/her action. In addition, the sensation of the body motion executed at the time of the past action must be presented. In particular, if advanced motor skills are to be re-lived, it is necessary to present the sensation of the position and posture of the body in action and the muscular strength control for each part of the body when performing it. These features stem from the fact that it is a reproduction of the first person's perspective. Strictly speaking, it will be a reproduction based on all cognitive events during the life of an individual, however this is impossible to realize. The important element is the sensation of the body due to the action and the visual perception according to the change of the view point. This is the conclusion from that the fundamental policy is to reproduce the body sensation that always existed in the actual experience.

As described above, there is a difficulty in the physical re-living experience which regenerates after others on the basis of the body. It is a different way of perception from ordinary external perception. The difference is that the perception during the action is modified corresponding to the control input of the

Table 1. Media and contents providing re-living experience

Presentation Media	Record Format	Channel of User Input	Method of Cognition of Experience	User's Body Motion	Essential Components of Experience
Books, Documents	Text data	Visual (reading)	Imagination, interpretation based on memory	No	Psychological description, narrativity, 1st and 3rd person experience
Radio, TV, Movie	Audio, video data	Auditory, visual	Auditory, visual experience (perceptually real)	No	Environmental reality, narrativity, 3rd person experience
Extended Movie (4D)	Movie format (3D) plus additional device format	3D auditory, visual plus vestibular, olfactory, wind, mist, tactile	3D movie experience plus multisensory experience (rendition)	Yes (vestibular)	Realistic environment experience, narrativity, 3rd person experience
VR display (Multi-sensory)	4D movie plus omnidirectional 8K video data, multisensory sensor data	Extended movie channel plus body motion (proprioception)	4D movie plus immersive multisensory experience (perceptually real)	Yes (multi-sensory)	Realistic immersive experience, body motion (proprioception), 1st person experience

physical motion. For example, in visual perception, there is a saccade suppression in which the input is modified during the motion of the eyeball [3]. There is a fundamental difficulty that it is required to regenerate the situation of such embodied perception [4,5] by others, performed in different physical conditions. This introduces implementation difficulties from several viewpoints.

First, there is difficulty in visual expression. Showing high-quality images at remote places imparts the sensation of presence of the environment, especially if resolution and viewing angle are large, however it is insufficient for the body-dependent first person's sight. It is difficult to make the image perceived by the user (the reliving person) precisely identical to the one seen by others at the level of scan path. To control the motion of eyeballs is harder than to measure the scan path of the past observer. However, it is possible to acquire a specific task skill of the visual processing by tracking the gaze point of the other person, although the scan path is inaccurate where the movements of the eyeballs do not match between the user and the past person. In that case, the scope of application is considered limited. By recording and playing back the video, the re-living visual experience can be provided where the user perceives what was going on in the outside world at the actions of others. However, in order to render it closer to the first person's experiences, its characteristics must be introduced. Specifically, it is necessary to introduce the vection that is invoked in the first person activity such as walking in addition to the physical property from which the motion of visual field is created. As a method to visually introduce such physical feature in walking, perturbation of visual field was investigated [6]. More directly, rendering the image of one's own body is considered effective. However, the effect of the body image has not been clarified sufficiently when it is observed from the first person viewpoint.

Second, there is a difficulty in presentation of the body sensation. Actual physical motion is the basis of human activity, however the degrees of freedom of movement and the amount of space are so large that its measurement and reproduction are difficult to implement. A motion capture system of a fixed measurement space is required to obtain accurate body motion data of others. Although a wearable motion sensor is convenient to measure a free body motion, it is still difficult to achieve sufficient accuracy so that the outdoor behavior for a long duration is a difficult problem at present. Furthermore, in order to reproduce the sensation during physical motion, it is necessary to evoke sensations of limbs, hands, trunk, head similar to others. For this purpose, the re-living user should do the same motion as others, however it is almost impossible to execute the same motion in the real space. What virtual reality technology has mainly developed up to now is the virtual expression of the outside world to the user, however in the next second stage (2.0), the virtual expression of self body sensation is considered to make its feature. The sensation of physical motion is represented by proprioception and skin sensation, however vestibular, visual and auditory sensations also play an important role. It is necessary to synthesize and provide integrated stimuli to these sensory organs, which is a difficult technical problem, especially in terms of high degrees of freedom of motion and its speed.

Thirdly, there is a problem of representation of agency that is the subjective sense of body movement. Re-living other person's behavior is to receive the whole sensation perceived including body sensation. However, general actions are originated by oneself, and the resultant sensations are utilized in the actions. In other words, there is a loop of active movement in which active motion produces the sensation and the next motion is generated based on the sensation. This is incompatible with the fact that the re-living is a projection of replicated sensation. In order for the re-living to be equivalent to the experience of oneself including his/her physical motion, the same sensation as others must be received as, at the same time, the result of active motion of the user. In other words, causality must be reversed as that from the sensation to the agency. Consequently, the information obtained in the re-living experience should approach to that from his own experience, otherwise it is considered that the user is not able to reproduce that motion by oneself (especially in the case of advanced motor skills). Although this is a mere re-examination as a third party, it is necessary to become your own experience, however the problem of the active movement loop remains.

3   Hybrid Re-living: A New Experience Presentation

There is the difficulty mentioned above for the re-living experience involving physicality. For this reason, we decided to extend its scope as follows. Although the brain process in which the first person experience related to physical motion is created is not elucidated to a sufficient level, this is the process where a consistent memory of subjective actions is created. The extent of matching to the other's experiential data can take up to a level of theoretically perfect identity from that is only perceived as being in the same environment. Among them, except for the ideal state that can fully be recognized as one's own experience, the both of the perception of other person's experience and the perception of one's own experience coexist at the same time. Thus, it is a re-living experience in a hybrid state. Furthermore, in terms of rendering of the visual avatar introduced to realize the re-living experience, duality of physical body perception is also recognized. It is duality of an avatar's body and the self body, and duality of first person drawing and third person drawing. In addition, there is duality of passivity and activity in the re-living process.

Thus, following four hybrid properties, or duality is an issue of design.

- Self and the other person
- Self body and the avatar's body
- First person and third person viewpoints
- Activeness and passiveness

3.1 Reproduction of First-Person Experience from Third-Person Data

Experience is a consistent representation of the outside world and the self body depending on a physical body. It is thought that the perception of the other person's state is performed by using the perception mechanism of own body [7]. However, at the same time it is clear that it is not their own physical body state, as there is a gap in perceptual identity. Therefore, it is a problem of virtual reality 2.0 to make equivalent perceived state even if its own body perception is not exactly the same as the other's. In the beginning, the goal of the virtual reality was to make the perception of the external virtual world equivalent to the actual one, and the accuracy of the drawing of the outside world was sought for that. In the perception of the re-living experience, since the goal is to make the perception equivalent to that perceived by the other person of the outside world and the body, it is a hybrid perception state assuming the existence of others. On that premise, it is necessary to draw constructively the outside world information and the bodily information corresponding to the behavior of the other at an appropriate level.

The Table 2 represents experiential elements at each concept level of vision, body, and agency. In order for a series of actions to have meaning, a structure of *High* level is necessary, however since the VR technology operates at a perception level, the *Low, Mid* levels are the targets of rendering. For these, the VR system gives the user the properly operated input for the experience reconstruction.

Regarding visual perception, we record and present the audiovisual information of the outside world, however as shown in the above discussion, the Low level is difficult to intervene, so we provide information recorded in the *Mid* level. The image of the remote place from the viewpoint of a person flows along with the walking that is the basis of the person's action. If the image in the direction of the head only was recorded, the user see simply the playback of the image. On the other hand, if an omni-directional image is recorded, the active head rotation is allowed to the user in the viewing experience. In both cases, the optic

Table 2. Action and result in three levels (Act: activation, Rst: result)

		Low	Mid	High
Vision	Act	Scan paths	Head motion paths	Thought paths
	Rst	Object recognition	Scene recognition	Situation recognition
Body	Act	Muscle activity paths	Postural paths	Task interaction paths
	Rst	Somatic sensation	Unit motion/posture	Task execution
Agency	Act	Muscle drive	Intention of motion	Intention of task
		coupling	coupling	coupling
	Rst	Force sensation	Desired motion	Task achievement

flow by walking provides an important part of the sensation of motion, and it has a great effect on the transmission of behavior.

As for the body, by adding movement stimuli to the vestibular sensation and the limbs, the sensation of a moving body can be created. Although the degrees of freedom of the motion are considerably restricted in the implementation technology, the sensation of walking and running which are the basis of a human spatial motion, can be generated to a considerable extent. Because walking and running are of high importance in human motion, automation (rhythm generation, standardization of motion pattern) of the execution control of the body movement is implemented in the CNS. Therefore, it is considered that the perception of body movement may be easily replaced by that from an external force input. Motion of the hand based on a visual feedback control requires a good design for the device that reproduces the movement sensation of the hand which is thought to be more difficult to be automated than walking and running.

Avatar expression of the body is a powerful clue that connects visual and body sensations. When rendering an avatar, it is possible to choose whether it is a model of yourself or a model of another person, and whether to render from first person viewpoint or third person viewpoint. In the case of rendering from the first person viewpoint, by placing the virtual camera near the eyeball of the head of the avatar, the body of the avatar can be observed by looking downward. In the case of rendering from the third person viewpoint, although it is free where to place the viewpoint, it is appropriate to set a field of view from which the avatar's body can be observed from the back of the avatar. In the case of the third person viewpoint, the motion state such as walking is clearly understood, and the impression of the walking experience in the recorded environment becomes clear under the condition that the entire body of the person or another person is in the field of view. In the case of the first person viewpoint, the view is almost the environment of the outside world, however if you swing hands largely during walking you can see the hand. If you look down, you can see your feet, however while walking you are looking at the front almost so the visual impression of the body is not great.

Agency of physical motion is obtained by driving your own body by yourself and getting matched change of the result. It is almost always established in a normal experience. Although, we do not have to be conscious of it, in the case of experiences driven by your own body, it is obviously a necessary relationship. In a re-living experience, this agency poses a problem. The goal is that the user's body motion is the same as the other's motion, however the user himself can not perform it. By externally driving the user's body motion, it may be possible to bring the motion trajectory closer, however it is no longer a self-driving experience. As with other duality, a meaning can be added to this agency problem by introducing the continuity of the level of the agency in the spectrum of the re-living experience. Partially introducing active selection into passively transmitted environment and body data is considered to contribute to the activity of the experience. Under the multiple duality described above, the quality of the re-living experience is considered to be determined.

3.2   Implementation and Evaluation

Multisensory Passive Stimulation. By giving passive body motion of walking as well as images of the environment, it is possible to present the sense of walking and driving to a considerable extent. The presentation of body sensation is based on external stimulation to the body. If no activity is given, the user on the seat simply receives multi-sensory presentation. Under this condition, the movement stimulation to the body is captured by the vestibular sensation, the proprioception, and the skin sensation. This provides the whole bodily sensation considerably similar to the normal body motion (walking etc.). Audiovisual information is presented in monocular omni-directional images recorded at remote locations, and the user was allowed the head rotation. Figure 1 is a multi-sensory presentation system (FiveStar) operating at the exhibition of a conference. This system provided a physical re-living experience whose data was recorded by the omni-directional camera during walking in a remote place (Toronto and Niagara fall, Canada).

It was revealed in the stimulus presentation experiment that these multiple sensory stimuli each have an effect of enhancing walking sensation. The vestibular stimulation by the motion seat can present lifting and driving sensation of the left and right legs with pitching/rolling and lifting to the front, back, left and right. Foot motion display represents the sensation of locomotion with alternating up/down and back/forth movements of the legs. One of the characteristics of these motion expressions is that very small amount of motion is appropriate as compared with the actual motion during walking motion. This is related to the problem of the activity. The sensation of passive motion is felt greater than the motion sensation evoked as result of active motion.

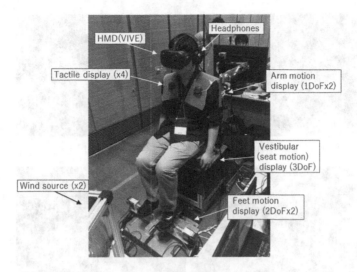

Fig. 1. Multisensory presentation system (minimized system) at a conference exhibit.

Avatar Rendition. Presenting a visual body, an avatar, as shown in Fig. 2 makes the perception of motion state in the remote environment clearer. This is the image of a scene where the avatar based on the 3D measurement of the experiment participant is walking in the city of Toronto. We constructed a virtual tour that walks Toronto and Niagara for about 3 min with a screen composition that the view point follows just behind this avatar. The realism of the experience of this virtual tour was evaluated by 80 participants of the virtual reality academic conference. As a questionnaire of presence, a visual analogue scale that spans from the conference venue (0.0) to the Niagara falls (1.0) was used. The result of presence evaluation was at a value of 0.738 (standard error 0.016) which means that the sensation evaluated was closer to the sensation of being in Niagara.

Furthermore, using these individualized avatars, we presented the city view with a walking avatar from the viewpoint as first person and third person shown in Fig. 3. The stimulus was only visual information (not multisensory) with a

Fig. 2. Participant's avatars walking virtually in Toronto.

Participant A (first/third person views)

Participant B (first/third person views)

Fig. 3. Avatars walking in Toronto.

duration of 60 s. The participant was sitting on a stationary seat. We added a condition with active commitment of the participant who was allowed to stop the movie by aborting the arm swing. Using these avatars, we evaluated walking sensation and body ownership when the viewpoint was changed as first person and third person like Fig. 3. As a result, it is suggested that the first person's avatar rendering was more effective in improving the walking sensation of the participant. Body ownership rating was almost the same as the rating of walking sensation. There was no significant difference as to whether the avatar was self or another person. On the other hand, the active condition where the movie was stopped by aborting the arm swing had higher walking sensation and body ownership than the condition that the movie was played without arm swing.

4   Conclusion

In this paper, we presented a new structure and implementation examples to reproduce the body sensation of others as a next generation (ver. 2.0) virtual reality experience, When presenting the sensation of motion of others to pass on bodily experience, it is necessary to consider duality in several respects. The duality was found in the virtual experience where both self and others are present at the same time, and where there is a difference between your true body and the avatar's body posture and movement, and where both viewpoints of the first person viewpoint playback and the third person view playback are useful. It is also the problem of activeness of real experience and passivity of re-living experience. Because of these aspects of duality, the re-living experience is required to have hybrid properties as its basic characteristics. It is a challenge to optimize this hybridity in the design. An implementation by a multi-sensory display including an omni-directional movie and bodily stimulus revealed preliminary knowledge about body presentation by an avatar and placement of viewpoint. As activeness of physical motion and agency are important characteristics of the bodily experience, resolution of incompatibility with the passivity of re-living experience is one of the future tasks.

Acknowledgments. This work was supported by MIC SCOPE Project (#141203019) and a Grant-in-Aid for Scientific Research (A) 26240029, MEXT.

References

1. Polanyi, M.: The Tacit Dimension, Reissue edition. University of Chicago Press, Chicago (2009)
2. Media Mation MX4D. http://www.mediamation.com/products_x4d.html
3. Bridgeman, B., Van der Heijden, A.H.C., Velichkovsky, B.M.: A theory of visual stability across saccadic eye movements. Behav. Brain Sci. **17**, 247–258 (1994)
4. Rosch, E., Thompson, E., Varela, F.J.: The Embodied Mind: Cognitive Science and Human Experience. MIT Press, Cambridge (1991)
5. Gazzaniga, M., Mangun, G.R.: The Cognitive Neurosciences. MIT Press, Cambridge (2014)
6. Lecuyer, A., Terziman, L., Lecuyer, A., Hillaire, S., Wiener, J.M.: Can camera motions improve the perception of traveled distance in virtual environments? In: 2009 IEEE Virtual Reality Conference, pp. 131–134 (2009)
7. Rizzolatti, G., Fadiga, L., Gallese, V., Fogassi, L.: Premotor cortex and the recognition of motor actions. Brain Res. Cogn. Brain Res. **3**, 131–141 (1996)

Characterization of Mild Cognitive Impairment Focusing on Screen Contact Data in Virtual Reality-Based IADL

Yuki Kubota[1]([✉]), Takehiko Yamaguchi[2], Tetsuya Harada[2], and Tania Giovannetti[3]

[1] Graduate School of Tokyo University of Science, Tokyo, Japan
yuki.kubota.hrlb@gmail.com
[2] Tokyo University of Science, Tokyo, Japan
tk-ymgch@te.noda.tus.ac.jp
[3] Temple University, Philadelphia, USA
tgio@temple.edu

Abstract. The aim of this study was to explore the feature pattern of Mild Cognitive Impairment (MCI) in a Virtual Reality based Instrumental Activities of Daily Living (VR-IADL) that runs on a tablet PC and requires touch interaction to complete the task. Twelve participants (MCI: 4, history of MCI: 2, healthy elderly: 6) were recruited from the region of Philadelphia in the USA to perform a VR-IADL task. We found that touch interaction in toast task and coffee task are more difficult than that of MCI patients with having history of MCI as well as healthy older adults. Also, we found that behavioral features using autoregressive model with finger velocity data calculated from finger position data measuring in VR-IADL. Several types of feature patterns were extracted from touch interaction and finger position data. Based on the feature pattern, Support Vector Machine (SVM) was performed to calculate the accuracy of the feature patter for characterization of MCI. As the result, the sensitivity and specificity were 83%.

Keywords: Virtual reality · IADL · VR-IADL · Touch interaction · Behavioral feature

1 Introduction

According to the World Alzheimer's Report (2016), the number of dementia patients will continue to increase in the future. The prevalence of dementia patients is expected to demonstrate a three-fold increase from 47 million in 2015 to about 13 million people in 2050. The increase in dementia patients may lead to a range of social problems; consequently, it is urgent to improve the screening and intervention for older adults at risk of and with dementia. Dementia is a disorder that in cognitive function is markedly deduced in comparison to healthy elderly people. There is currently no clear treatment for dementia; it is impossible to recover from dementia to a healthy state once it develops. However, if early detection can be made at the stage of mild cognitive impairment (MCI), which is the precursor state of dementia, recovery or prevention of dementia may be possible. Therefore, in the present situation where no clear treatment for dementia has been established, early screening for MCI can be optimal method as a prevention of

© Springer International Publishing AG 2017
S. Yamamoto (Ed.): HIMI 2017, Part II, LNCS 10274, pp. 144–153, 2017.
DOI: 10.1007/978-3-319-58524-6_13

dementia. Regarding the screening for MCI, proposals and research are advanced from various viewpoints. Currently, the mainstream in the screening for MCI is the Mini-Mental State Examination (MMSE) that is 30 points questionnaire that is used extensively in clinical and research settings to measure cognitive impairment, such as date of examination execution date. And the cognitive decline is evaluated based on the score. However, problems of this method include low accuracy and length of test time. Previous studies have shown that the accuracy of MMSE is 45–60% sensitivity and 65–90% specificity [1]. Recently, there has also been reported a screening method for MCI using a biomarker. Uchida et. al. published a method to discriminate by means of regression analysis with a multi-marker, which is a combination of the three serum proteins of complement protein, apolipoprotein, and transthyretin among the sequester proteins contained in the blood [2]. This study has shown that by using this method, it is possible to identify whether the cognitive function is normal or MCI with an accuracy of about 80%. However, the problem of this method is invasive and it is necessary to request medical institutions. Thus, screening methods that can be performed easily and with high accuracy is required. Therefore, we focused on the behavioral function which has attracted attention in recent years. It is recently known that the decline in cognitive function appears in behavioral functions, and it is a method that is drawing attention among neuropsychology [3]. In particular, it is reported that MCI patients have obstacles to behavioral functions in instrumental activities of daily living (IADL), which is a complicated behavior accompanied by cognitive activities, among the activities of daily living (ADL), which is an action that we normally do casually [4, 5]. Then, Naturalistic Action Test, which is a screening method for MCI focused on behavioral dysfunction, was represented [6]. This method is evaluating by using human error (HE) occurrence frequency and type of HE during IADL task. We take the video of the experiment condition in which the subject actually performs the IADL task. By using the video, neuropsychologists specify HE. On the other hands, recently, some studies have shown that information technology introduce to improve the method focusing on behavioral dysfunction such as NAT, especially, by introducing Virtual Reality (VR) technology [7]. The IADL task built in this VR environment (VR-IADL) is represented for rehabilitation with dementia and screening for MCI [8, 9]. This system made identifying HE automatically. Martono et al. suggested the algorithm identifying the tendency of HE occurrence using the norm of acceleration data calculated from the finger position data at the time of VR-IADL. Thus, these previous studies are progressing to create a discriminative model of MCI and healthy elderly focusing on error occurrence. However, as a problem of this method, it is necessary to take two steps of defining an error and creating a discriminative model. Also, previous studies focused on the HE occurrence simply, if the nature of behaviors hidden behind the error becomes clear, clinical application is difficult. Therefore, the purpose of this research is to create a discriminative model of MCI and healthy elderly in VR-IADL environment, focusing on action indicators other than HE occurrence. In particular, since the VR-IADL environment can operate with only one tablet terminal, it will be expected to spread in the future. In this report, we generate some feature of MCI with relation between touch interaction, which is a characteristic index unique to the VR-IADL environment, and the composition of IADL tasks and finger position data during VR-IADL task. And we constructed an identification model of MCI and healthy elderly people.

2　Previous Study

In our previous research, we conclude that screen non-contact time, which is the time when finger doesn't touch on the screen, is longer for MCI patients at the time of VR-IADL. VR-IADL installed in the tablet device outputs the value of 1 and 0, which represent screen contact. If someone touch the screen with his finger, the time interval is defined as Touch Time (TT), and if someone doesn't touch the screen, the time interval is defined as Non Touch Time (NTT) as shown Fig. 1.

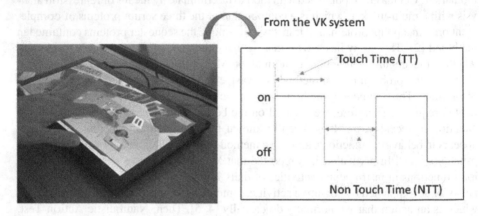

Fig. 1. Definition of touch time and non touch time

As a result of the previous study, there was a significant difference between the MCI patients and the healthy elderly people at the 5% level in the sum of the NTT. From this result, it was suggested that the characterization of MCI focusing on touch interaction may be effective. In the previous study, the value of RNTT obtained by normalizing the sum of the NTT with the task achievement time (the sum of the contact time TT of the screen and the finger and the NTT) shown in the expression (1).

$$RNTT = \frac{\sum_{n=1}^{N} NTT_n}{\sum_{n=1}^{N} TT_n + \sum_{m=1}^{M} NTT_m} \tag{1}$$

Then, our previous study has shown that declining cognitive function may be represented by behavioral dysfunction. In this report, we focused on Touch Interaction including this RNTT and analyzed it. Especially, MCI was characterized from the relationship between touch interaction and IADL structure. And we try to analyze finger position data measured in VR-IADL. Lastly, we create a discriminative model of MCI and healthy elderly.

3   Method

In this experiment, various behavior data were measured to characterize MCI in VR-IADL. Touch Interaction data which can be seen from the output data of VR-IADL, finger position data were measured to find behavioral features.

3.1   Participants

Subjects requested cooperation from 14 men and women aged 60 or older living in the state of Pennsylvania, USA. Subjects were asked to undergo various neuropsychological tests shown in Table 1 and MMSE and other subjects on condition that they lived alone, not depression, MCI and healthy subjects were identified [10, 11].

Table 1. Test

Domain	Test
Language	Category fluency; Boston Naming Test
Executive function	WAIS-R digit span backward; Trail Making Test version B
Memory-Immediate	Rey Figure in recall; WMS-R: logical memory II Story A
Episodic memory ability	Rey Figure copy; WAIS-R: picture completion
Attention	TMT part A, WAIS-R: digit span forward
Processing speed	TMT part A, crossing-off test

3.2   Experimental Setup

In this experiment, a tablet device installed VR-IADL application, a web camera for recording the state during the experiment, and a reflection marker and a leap motion sensor for measuring the finger position data are used as shown Fig. 2. The subject sat in front of the tablet device placed on the desk. Reflective marker was attached to the index finger of the subject. The interaction technic is a touch screen, when you touch an object in the VR-IADL environment with your finger, you can have an object. Also, moving a finger while touching the tablet allows you to move objects in the VR-IADL environment. When you release your finger from the screen, you can release the object in the VR-IADL environment. Before doing the task, I explained the operation practice of the VR-IADL, the purpose of the task and points to be noted until the subject understands. In this experiment, Virtual Kitchen System (VK) was used as VR-IADL environment. VK is a non-immersive type VR-IADL application and has two IADL tasks (i) Toast & Coffee Task, (ii) Lunchbox Task. Screen shots of these tasks are shown in Fig. 3. First, Toast & Coffee Task has two tasks of making a cup of instant coffee with sugar and milk and a piece of toast with jam and butter. In order to achieve the task completely, it is necessary to perform a total of 13 steps of operations in combination of the two tasks. Below is the process of Toast and Coffee Task.

(1) place a slice of bread into the toaster;
(2) turn on the switch to toast;
(3) remove toast and place on the plate;
(4) take butter;
(5) spread butter on the toast;
(6) open the jelly jar;
(7) place jelly on the toast with knife;
(8) open the coffee jar;
(9) take a spoonful of coffee powder with spoon and into the cup;
(10) open the sugar pot jar;
(11) place sugar into cup with spoon;
(12) pour milk into the cup;
(13) stir cup of coffee with spoon.

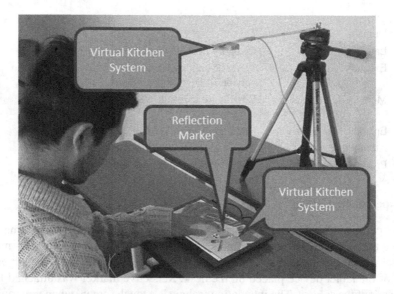

Fig. 2. Experimental setup

(a) Toast & Coffee Task   (b) Lunchbox Task

Fig. 3. screen shots the VR-IADL

Next, the Lunchbox Task is a task of packing a sandwich with peanut butter and jam with aluminum foil, a juice filled water bottle, and a sweet wrapped in aluminum foil into a lunch box. In order to achieve these tasks completely, it is necessary to carry out a total of 16 steps. The details are shown below.

(1) take bread;
(2) open the jelly jar;
(3) place jelly on the bread with knife;
(4) open the peanut butter jar;
(5) place peanut butter on bread with knife;
(6) take another piece of bread to close sandwich;
(7) take a sheet of foil to wrap the sandwich;
(8) pack the wrapped sandwich into the lunchbox;
(9) take cookies (one by one);
(10) take a sheet of foil then wrap the cookies;
(11) pack the wrapped cookies into the lunchbox;
(12) pour the juice into the thermos;
(13) seal the thermos with lid;
(14) seal the thermos with cap;
(15) pack thermos into the lunch box;
(16) close the lunch box

4   Result

4.1   Characterization of MCI Using Touch Interaction

We analyzed touch interaction data at each subtask. The calculated parameters are the sum of Touch Time (TT), the sum of Non-Touch Time (NTT), the number of times of contact with the screen, and time to completion of each task. First, from the measured screen contact/non-contact data, the sum of NTT and RNTT were calculated using the data of the entire task. A Wilcoxon rank sum test showed there was a significant difference ($p < .05$) in the sum of NTT and RNTT between the healthy participants and MCI participants for both tasks. The data showed that participants with MCI spent more time not making contact with the screen.

Next, touch interaction data were analyzed at each subtask. First, we built an algorithm to show whether the task was achieved and the separate subtasks that comprised each task (breakfast & lunch). The graphs are shown in Fig. 4. The time during which the participant performed the toast task is shown in blue and the time during which the coffee task was performed is shown in green in Fig. 4(a). For these five subtasks (toast, coffee, sandwich, snack and thermos task), the time to completion, the sum of TT, NTT and the number of touch interactions on screen were calculated were analyzed. A Wilcoxon's rank sum test, showed that there was a significant difference ($p < .05$) between MCI and healthy elderly in the time to completion, the sum of TT, and NTT for the toast task. There was a trend for a difference ($p = .10$) between MCI and healthy elderly in the number of the screen contact times on screen in toast task and the sum of

TT, NTT in coffee task, the number of the screen contact times on screen and time to completion. The results show that MCI patients showed meaningful differences in toast tasks and coffee tasks compared with healthy elderly people.

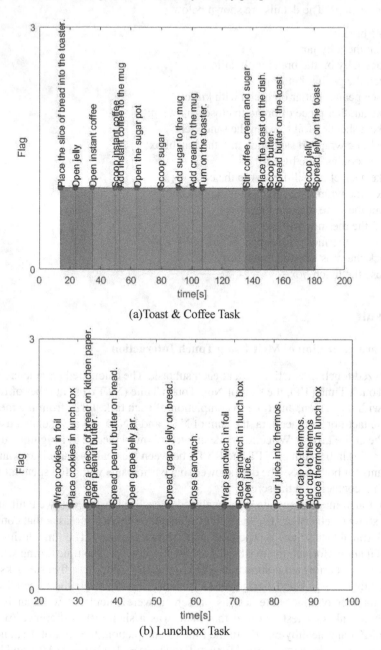

(a)Toast & Coffee Task

(b) Lunchbox Task

Fig. 4. Graph showing the time at which each subtask was performed and the total time required to achieve each task

4.2 Characterization Using Autoregressive Model

Finally, the characterization of MCI was carried out by using the norm data of the velocity calculated from finger position data acquired in the VR-IADL environment. For this time, the autoregressive coefficient (m = 10) which autoregressive model generated as shown in (2).

$$x(l) = \sum_{i=1}^{m} a^m(i)x(l-i) + \epsilon(l) \tag{2}$$

An autoregressive model is a type of stochastic process expression that predicts time varying data. The reason for introducing this model is the difference in behaviors between MCI patients and healthy elderly. Previous studies have reported that MCI patients have more HE occurrences than healthy elderly people [4].

As a result, this 10-dimensional autoregressive coefficient was calculated and subjected to principal component analysis. As the result of the principal component analysis, the first principal component whose contribution ratio was 90% or more was taken as the feature quantity. From this feature quantity, we identified MCI with healthy elderly people using a linear support vector machine. As a result, both sensitivity and specificity were 0.83 and AUC was 0.94. From this result, it can be said that in the VR-IADL environment, there is a difference in movement of fingers in healthy subjects and MCI patients. The result indicated that MCI patients are constructed as models that include errors occurrence as predictions when modeling changes in the velocity of fingers when performing tasks, and the autoregressive coefficients to be determined are based on healthy elderly and MCI patients. It is predicted that a difference will appear.

5 Create Discriminative Model

We standardized the 20-dimensional feature quantities of the 10-dimensional feature quantity extracted from the relationship between Touch Interaction and subtask and the 20-dimensional feature quantity extracted from the position data of the finger to obtain the Z score, we constructed a discrimination model of healthy elderly and MCI using support vector machine. This ROC analysis is shown in Fig. 5. From this result, the sensitivity was 83% and the specificity was 83%. It is higher than the sensitivity of 45–60% and the specificity 65–90% of MMSE, which is conventionally used in the mainstream. From this, it can be said that even in the VR-IADL environment, the decline in cognitive function affects everyday function.

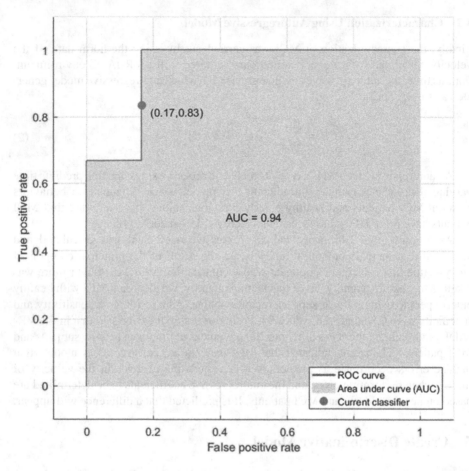

Fig. 5. ROC analysis

6 Conclusion

In this report, we have characterized MCI from touch interaction data measured for each subtask in the VR-IADL environment. Based on the features, we created a discriminative model of MCI or healthy elderly, and confirmed its usefulness. From the data of touch interaction, it was suggested that the toast task and the coffee task performed this time are effective for extracting the characteristics of MCI. In the characterization by autoregressive model using the finger position data, cognitive function affects everyday function. We created a discriminative model of MCI or healthy elderly people using these behavioral features and confirmed its usefulness. As a future prospect, I would like to quantify subtasks and clarify the causal relationship with behavior.

References

1. Saxton, J., et al.: Computer assessment of mild cognitive impairment. Postgrad. Med. **121**, 177–185 (2009). doi:10.3810/pgm.2009.03.1990
2. Uchida, K., Shan, L., Suzuki, H., Tabuse, Y., Nishimura, Y., Hirokawa, Y., Asada, T.: Amyloid-β sequester proteins as blood-based biomarkers of cognitive decline. Alzheimer's Dement. Diagn. Assess. Dis. Monit. **1**(2), 270–280 (2015)
3. Belchior, P.D.C., Holmes, M., Bier, N., Bottari, C., Mazer, B., Robert, A., Kaur, N.: Performance-based tools for assessing functional performance in individuals with mild cognitive impairment. Open J. Occup. Ther. **3**, 1–21 (2015)
4. Giovannetti, T., Bettcher, B.M., Brennan, L., Libon, D.J., Burke, M., Duey, K., Nieves, C., Wambach, D.: Characterization of everyday functioning in mild cognitive impairment: a direct assessment approach. Dement. Geriatr. Cogn. Disord. **25**, 359–365 (2008)
5. Seligman, S.C., Giovannetti, T., Sestito, J., Libon, D.J.: A new approach to the characterization of subtle errors in everyday action: implications for mild cognitive impairment. Clin. Neuropsychologist **28**, 97–115 (2013)
6. Schmitter-Edgecombe, M., McAlister, C., Weakley, A.: Naturalistic assessment of everyday functioning in individuals with mild cognitive impairment: the day-out task. Neuropsychology **26**, 631–641 (2012)
7. Richard, P., Massenot, L., Besnard, J., Richard, E., Le Gall, D., Allain, P.: A virtual kitchen to assess the activities of daily life in Alzheimer's disease. In: Proceedings of the International Conference on Computer Graphics Theory and Applications, pp. 378–383 (2010)
8. Yamaguchi, T., Foloppe, D.A., Richard, P., Richard, E., Allain, P.: A dual-modal virtual reality kitchen for (re) learning of everyday cooking activities in Alzheimer's disease. Presence Teleoperators Virtual Environ. **21**(1), 43–57 (2012)
9. Allain, P., Foloppe, D.A., Besnard, J., Yamaguchi, T., Etcharry-Bouyx, F., Le Gall, D., Richard, P.: Detecting everyday action deficits in Alzheimer's disease using a nonimmersive virtual reality kitchen. J. Int. Neuropsychological Soc. **20**(05), 468–477 (2014)
10. Seelye, A., Hagler, S., Mattek, N., Howieson, D.B., Wild, K., Dodge, H.H., Kaye, J.A.: Computer mouse movement patterns: a potential marker of mild cognitive impairment. Alzheimer's Dement. Diagn. Assess. Dis. Monit. **1**, 472–480 (2015)
11. Kaye, J.A., Maxwell, S.A., Mattek, N., Hayes, T.L., Dodge, H., Pavel, M., Zitzelberger, T.A.: Intelligent systems for assessing aging changes: home-based, unobtrusive, and continuous assessment of aging. J. Gerontol. Ser. B Psychol. Sci. Soc. Sci. **66**(suppl. 1), i180–i10–i190 (2011)

Attention Sharing in a Virtual Environment Attracts Others

Takuji Narumi[✉], Yuta Sakakibara, Tomohiro Tanikawa, and Michitaka Hirose

Graduate School of Information Science and Technology, The University of Tokyo,
7-3-1 Hongo, Bunkyo-Ku, Tokyo 113-8656, Japan
{narumi,sakakibara,tani,hirose}@cyber.t.u-tokyo.ac.jp

Abstract. Virtual reality offers a highly interactive and flexible experience. It has the advantage of enhancing users' understanding and interest as well as the disadvantage of overlooking the main features in a virtual environment. The excessive amount of information and interactive options in most virtual reality settings may cause users to quit exploring before experiencing the entire content of the virtual environment. In this paper, we propose a new method of inherently encouraging users to continue their experience in virtual environments while permitting free exploration through social interactions. The proposed method generates a joint attention by displaying the movement of the position and gaze direction of other concurrent/previous users. We introduced the proposed method into a virtual museum exploring system and demonstrated it in a real museum to evaluate the effectiveness of our method when used by a large number of people. The results showed that the proposed method enhances users' interest and prolongs the experience time of virtual museum exploring.

Keywords: Attention · Social interaction · Digital museum · Virtual reality

1 Introduction

Virtual reality offers a highly interactive and flexible experience. It is widely recognized that it enhances users' understanding and interest in virtual objects/environments more effectively than learning through passive media. This is because their active selections of interactive objects that attracts their interest makes their experience more subjective and unforgettable [1–3]. For example, when users want to experience a virtual environment, it is more effective for users to explore and understand it through their own navigation than to passively watch instructional videos.

Recently, museums have high expectations for this effect and have introduced interactive technologies, including virtual reality into their exhibition methods to effectively provide supplementary background information regarding their exhibits [1, 4, 5]. Notably, photorealistic virtual content based on spherical image capturing have been a focus of attention to preserve and transmit cultural heritage. Spherical images are suitable for easy construction and use in immersive and realistic virtual environments [6]. A spherical image contains the entire information of the landscape of all angles from a location. The popularization of omnidirectional cameras, which can capture spherical

© Springer International Publishing AG 2017
S. Yamamoto (Ed.): HIMI 2017, Part II, LNCS 10274, pp. 154–165, 2017.
DOI: 10.1007/978-3-319-58524-6_14

images instantaneously, has facilitated the archival of a real space. Additionally, the usage of experiential devices such as tablet devices and head-mounted displays has become widespread. The experience of spherical images by using a hand-held device, such as a tablet device, is known to be immersive and effective in the understanding of geometric space [6–9].

However, virtual reality has these merits as well as the disadvantage of overlooking the main features in a virtual environment. In most virtual reality settings, there is so much information and interactive options that users may quit exploring prior to experiencing the entire content in the world.

Particularly, users should be discouraged from quitting a virtual experience without interacting with items the designers of the virtual world consider important. For example, in a photorealistic virtual museum, the most important objects are the exhibits but less important objects or information such as lighting, room arrangements, and spatial orientation should not be ignored because these are usually part of the exhibition design. Furthermore, it is possible to induce the psychological phenomenon that an increase of gazing time by an appropriate amount enhances the preference for the object (the mere exposure effect) [10, 11]. Therefore, it is necessary to make users aware of the important exhibits while they are exploring.

Guidance methods to guide users to pre-defined locations in the virtual environment have been suggested. One of these methods focused on steering users along a pre-defined path while at the same time allowing some extent of free exploring [12–14]. Another method uses an explicit arrow pointing at the target locations [15]. However, these methods are so intrusive that users cannot enjoy free exploration in the environment, and they hardly achieve a sense of accomplishment to find the target, which may decrease the quality of the experiment.

To inherently guide users to pre-defined locations in the virtual environment, while continuing to permit free explorations, Tanaka et al. proposed a method of inducing users to look at a pre-defined point in the spherical image by redirecting the virtual camera [8]. The user's virtual camera direction is shifted to look at a point closer to a target point. Moreover, Tanaka et al. also proposed the guidance method "Guidance field" [16], which slightly alters user's input for locomotion and rotation based on a potential field, which represents the drawing force to a target location. They showed that these modifications successfully guided users to pre-defined locations and made users aware of the target objects in the virtual environment. However, this method did not extend the experience time of users. This result suggested that this method would enable us to draw users' attention, but not enhance their interest to search virtual environments.

Then, as an alternative approach, we focused on the influence of others. Joint attention refers to a social-communicative skill used by humans to share attention directed at interesting objects or events with others via implicit and explicit indications such as gestures and gaze. Because of joint attention, we tend to be attracted to objects or events that others are looking at. Behavioral contagion is a type of social influence and refers to the propensity for certain behaviors exhibited by one person to be copied by others who are in the vicinity of the original actor. Milgram et al. reported that the larger the size of a stimulus crowd standing on a busy city street looking up at a building, the more frequently passersby adopt the behavior of the crowd [17]. These influences on others can be used for attracting people's attention and enhancing interest to particular objects or events [18].

This phenomenon is already utilized for supporting navigation in virtual environments using virtual agents. For example, virtual humans can give directions or transport users to locations [19]. Other research proposed the use of a flock of virtual animals to indicate interesting places in a virtual environment and confirmed this method's effectiveness [20]. Additionally, to instruct users on how to interact with an exhibit in a museum, a system that records and three-dimensionally superimposes past visitor interactions around the exhibit was proposed [21]. In this system, visitors see the behaviors of previous visitors, and thereby, obtain a better understanding of the exhibit.

In this study, we propose a new method of encouraging users to continue their experience in a virtual environment while permitting free exploration by using the effect of social interactions. As mentioned above, people tend to more frequently direct their attention to the objects/events that someone is directing. Therefore, we employed a method that generates a joint attention by displaying the movement of the position and gaze direction of other users.

2   Attention Sharing in a Virtual Environment by Sharing the Position and Gaze Direction of Others

In this chapter, we first describe the premises of the virtual environment used in the following experiment. Next, we explain the proposed method that displays the movement of the position and gaze direction of concurrent users or previous users.

2.1   Photorealistic Virtual Environment Used in this Study

As described above, the construction of virtual environments with a sequence of spherical images is becoming popular because the virtual spaces constructed with spherical images are more realistic, immersive, and easy to construct compared to virtual spaces constructed with computer graphic models [7, 22–24].

We then developed an application that enables virtual environments to be explored and named it "Window to the Past" [16]. This application depicts a virtual museum space constructed with a large sequence of spherical images. The application uses images of the Modern Transportation Museum in Osaka, Japan, with an area of 10,000 m^2. The exhibit was closed in April 2014. We archived the museum as 7,096 spherical images with a 360-degree spherical camera Ladybug5 (Point Grey Inc.), and developed a node-edge based walk-through system by using an appropriate arrangement of images (Fig. 1).

Spherical image viewer applications have several user interfaces for rotating the virtual camera such as a joystick, mouse, and on-screen buttons. In this research, the direction of the virtual camera is linked with the orientation of the tablet device. Therefore, when users move the device in a specific direction, the virtual camera moves in the same direction. Interactive interfaces that involve physical motion have been reported as encouraging users to develop a deeper understanding of geometric space and content

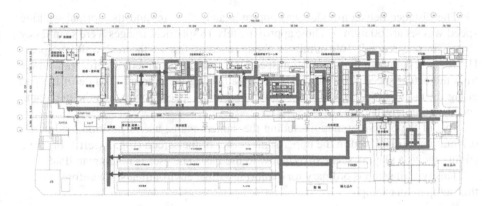

Fig. 1. Map of the reconstructed "Modern Transportation Museum (Osaka)" and camera paths (red lines). (Color figure online)

[1, 2]. The orientation of the tablet device in the real world is obtained from the built-in gyro and acceleration sensors in the device.

Moreover, to eliminate the effect of physical and spatial limitations, which would prevent users from rotating the virtual camera arbitrarily, only the angle around the vertical axis can be rotated by swiping the touch screen.

A virtual pad is used as an input interface for locomotion (Fig. 2 (left)). The virtual pad is a touch panel input interface designed to work as a joystick. Sliding the pad is equivalent to tilting a joystick [25]. Moreover, to inform users of the direction in which they can move from their node, arrows are shown around the virtual pad.

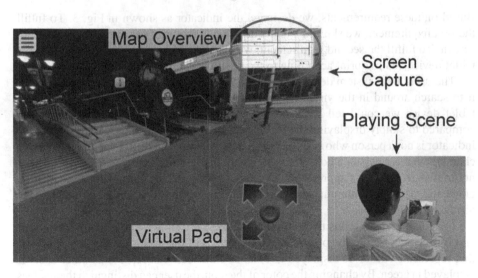

Fig. 2. Screen capture and playing scene of "Window to the Past."

The distance between nodes was approximately 0.15 m, and the normal walking speed was set at 160 m/min. Thus, approximately 18 spherical images were seamlessly shown in one second. 160 m/min is about twice as fast as the real walking speed. However, it is known that the motion speed in virtual environment is perceived slower than the actual speed [26]. Furthermore, by adjusting the amount of slide of the pad along the radial direction, users can move at arbitrary speed slower than the maximum speed setting (160 m/min).

Part of the overview map, including the camera paths, user's position, and user's orientation, is displayed in the upper-right corner of the screen (Fig. 2 (left)). Figure 2 (right) shows a playing scene of Window to the Past. The user is holding an iPad.

This type of setup is ordinary for exploring virtual environments. Therefore, we use this setup as an example.

2.2 Proposed Method for Sharing the Position and Gaze Direction of Other Users

The users perform two operations to explore the virtual environment: translation and rotation. Translation is an operation to move in the virtual environment. Rotation is an operation to look around in the virtual environment. Therefore, it is necessary to present information that shows the state of these two behaviors for sharing other user's experiences in the virtual environment. Then, in order to design an indicator for sharing other user's experiences, we considered the following two requirements:

- can be easily understood as it expresses other user who is interacting with the same system
- can be easily understood the position and gaze direction of other user

Based on these requirements, we designed the indicator as shown in Fig. 3. To fulfill the first requirement, we showed a tablet device and footprint per one user on the main screen. To fulfill the second requirement, we changed the position and direction of the tablet device and footprint according to the position and gaze direction of other user.

The user of the system described in previous chapter is holding an iPad and moves it to search around in the virtual environment. We considered that by displaying the tablet device we could tell the existence of others in at a minimum. By doing so, compared to simply displaying the model of a person, we can clearly express that the indicator is not a person who is simply placed in the virtual environment as a non-player character, but is a person who is interacting with the system as same as the user. In order not to disturb the user's appreciation as much as possible, we did not attach animation effect and made the minimum appearance to understand the position and direction in the virtual environment.

In addition, arrow icons that represent the users are shown in the map. They move and rotate according to the positions and directions of the users. On the map, the icon that represents oneself is displayed in blue, and the icon that represents other users is displayed in green. By changing the color of the icon, the user can distinguish themselves and others from the map.

This system can be used in two ways; real-time sharing and sharing with past experiences.

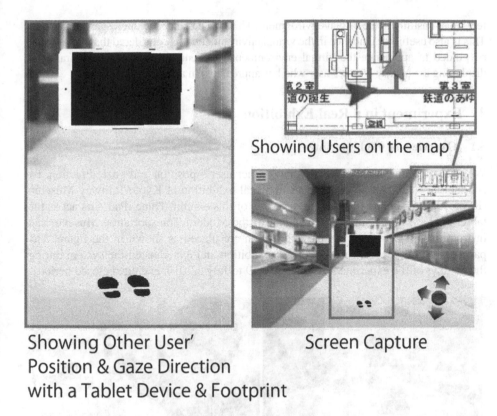

Showing Users on the map

Showing Other User'
Position & Gaze Direction
with a Tablet Device & Footprint

Screen Capture

Fig. 3. Showing other user's position and gaze direction with an transparent avatar with a tablet device and footprint on the main screen and arrows on the map view (Color figure online)

In real-time sharing, when this system is played at the same time on several tablet devices, the position and gaze direction of other users are immediately shared through the network. Based on the shared information, the indicators are drawn on the screen. Then the users can see each other's position and orientation in real time. The system can express the attention of people in the virtual environment by displaying position and orientation of others who are exploring the virtual environment together. By doing so, the system aimed to spark user's interest in the experiences in the virtual environment, extend the experience time of the system, and increase the number of interactions such as button operations.

Moreover, it is anticipated that synergistic effects due to communication in the real world between users will occur if the users who experience at the same time are nearby in the real exhibition space. For example, when one of the users has an impressive experience, s/he sometimes tells it to others around her/him. It will lead others to make the same interaction/experience. Then this kind of synergistic effect will make the interactive experience more effective.

In addition to sharing information on other users who are experiencing at the same time, by displaying the history of other users in the past, it is considered that the user can feel more bustling in the virtual environment. This will enhance the interest arousal effect. This is also useful for guidance in the virtual environment. It is considered that the user can be guided to appreciate the virtual environment as intended by a museum curator by displaying the history of other user who has appreciated in an appropriate way.

3 Experiment in a Real Exhibition

3.1 Overview of the Experiment

We evaluated our method, which shows other user's position and gaze direction, by conducting a large-scale experiment in a real exhibition at Kyoto Railway Museum (Kyoto, Japan). Figure 4 shows an overview of this exhibit. Three iPad Airs act as the tablet devices, and a simple explanation of the Modern Transportation Museum and instructions as to how to use the application are placed as shown in the figure. The participants are people who visited the exhibition and experienced the system during the 56 days of the experiment (From April 29 to July 3 2016, excluded closed period).

Fig. 4.   Overview of the exhibit and playing scene

The visitors varied from children to seniors. They did not know the purpose of this experiment and regarded it as a normal exhibit. To analyze the play log of the application, we set up the application to automatically terminate the experience when the user taps the finish button displayed at the upper left of the screen or returning the tablet to the display stand. During the user experience, the orientation and position in the virtual environment was logged. We only analyzed the data of first-time users because our focus was to capture user behavior when exploring the virtual environment without any previous knowledge. We identified first-time users by asking the subjects whether they had already experienced "Window to the Past" before starting their experience. Since the experiment was conducted in real museum in order to collect a large number of subjects, all conditions were not perfectly controlled. For example, although we show the explanations of the usage of the application and the input interfaces before subjects start their experience, it is not clear whether they really read and understand the explanations. The situation that users start to use applications without perfect understand often occurs in practical use, and it is meaningful to analyze a large number of data obtained from such practical situations.

We compared two conditions; with sharing and without sharing conditions. Under a with sharing condition, the position and gaze direction of other users are immediately shared through the network with the proposed method, as shown in Sect. 2.2 when the system was played at the same time on more than two tablet devices. Under a without sharing condition, the position and gaze direction of other users are not shared. Then all users played the system solely.

3.2 Results and Discussion

Under the with sharing condition, three users played at the same time in 49% of total experience time. Two users played at the same time in 34% of total experience time. Meanwhile, only one user played in 17% of total experience time. Maximum number of users who played at the same time was three in 64% of trials, two in 25% trials, and one in 11% of trials. Resulting in 11% of the participants under the with sharing condition were played as same as under the without sharing condition. However, assuming that the number of participants entering the exhibition room per unit time is constant, the probability of experiencing by only one person throughout the entire experience is considered to be higher for people with shorter experience time. If we analyze except these 11% of participants, it is considered that the experience time under the with sharing condition will be longer than actual. The sharing function was working in 83% of total experience time. It is considered that this rate is high enough to investigate the effect of the proposed system. We did not exclude these data from the sharing condition.

We excluded outliers for following analysis. Outliers are values that are 1.5 times greater than the third quartile of the interquartile range or 1.5 times smaller than the first quartile range of the quartile range. Moreover, we excluded data of users whose experience time is less than 10 s because the users do not appreciate the virtual environment properly in such cases. The total number of participants under the with sharing condition were 7,396, and 4,968 were the number of participants under the without sharing condition.

Figure 5 shows the box plot of the experience time per user by experimental conditions. The median of the experience time was 89.4 s for those under the with sharing condition and 70.6 s for those under the without sharing condition. Mann-Whitney's U test revealed that the experience time was significantly longer for those under the with sharing condition than for those under the without sharing condition ($p < 0.01$). Participants with experience time of less than 60 s were 33.3% of the total number under the with sharing condition and 44.0% under the without sharing condition. Because the number of users who finished with experiences of less than 60 s decreased, the proposed system has the effect of preventing loss of user's interest. These results suggested that the proposed method can increase the user's interest in the virtual environment, and lengthen the experience time.

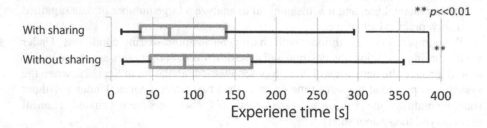

Fig. 5. Box plot of the experience time by the experimental conditions

Figure 6 (left) shows the average moving speed of the user for each elapsed time from the start of the trial. In the case of the system used in this experiment, it is rare that the user is constantly moving in the virtual environment. The users normally repeat moving and stopping. Therefore, it can be thought that the average moving speed is an indicator of activity level in the virtual environment (Higher moving speed indicates that the user moves more actively in the virtual environment). The result showed that average moving speed is higher for those under the with sharing condition than for those under the without sharing condition. In addition, the gap between average moving speeds under each condition increased with time. These suggest that the user moved more actively in the virtual environment under the with sharing condition, and the proposed method increased the moving distance in the virtual environment.

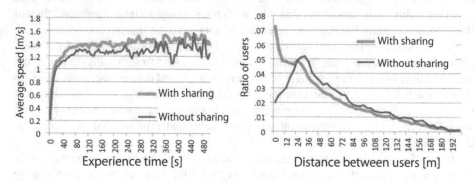

Fig. 6. Average moving speed (left) and Distance between users (right) in the virtual environment

Figure 6 (right) shows the distribution of distances between users who played at the same time. All subjects start moving from the same starting point. Therefore, in order to eliminate the effect of overlapping of positions immediately after the start, data of participants who are apart for more than 20 m from the start position were analyzed. These results suggest that the distance between the users tends to decrease for those under the with sharing condition. This effect might be utilized for guidance in the virtual environment because the users tend to move to other users shown in the environment.

4 Conclusion

In this paper, we proposed a new method of inherently encouraging users to continue their experience in a virtual environment while continuing to permit free exploration through social interactions. The proposed method generates a joint attention by displaying the movement of the position and gaze direction of other concurrent or previous user experiences. We introduced the proposed method into a virtual museum exploring system and demonstrated it in a real museum to evaluate the effectiveness of our method when used by a large number of people. The results showed that the proposed method prolonged the experience time of virtual museum exploring, and in particular, decreased the number of users who finished with experiences of less than 60 s. The results also suggested that the proposed method enhances users' interest and makes them move more actively in the virtual environment. In addition, the distance between the users in the virtual environment tends to be short when they use the proposed system in real-time sharing mode. These results showed the effectiveness of the proposed system.

In this study, we only investigated the proposed system in real-time sharing mode. Then, we need to investigate whether the proposed system in sharing with past mode also encourages users to continue their experience in a virtual environment. Moreover, the effect of shortening the distance between the users can be utilized for guidance in the virtual environment. We will seek a novel guidance method based on the attention sharing method and investigate its effectiveness in future work.

Acknowledgement. This work was partially supported by the MEXT, Grant-in-Aid for Scientific Research (A), 25240057.

References

1. Narumi, T., Hayashi, O., Kasada, K., Yamazaki, M., Tanikawa, T., Hirose, M.: Digital diorama: AR exhibition system to convey background information for museums. In: Shumaker, R. (ed.) VMR 2011. LNCS, vol. 6773, pp. 76–86. Springer, Heidelberg (2011). doi:10.1007/978-3-642-22021-0_10
2. Arakawa, T., Kasada, K., Narumi, T., Tanikawa, T., Hirose, M.: Augmented reality system for overlaying a scene in a video onto real world and reliving the camera operator's experience. Proc. IEEE Virtual Reality **2013**, 139–140 (2013)
3. Cairncross, S., Mannion, M.: Interactive multimedia and learning: realizing the benefits. Innovations Educ. Teach. Int. **38**(2), 156–164 (2001). Taylor & Francis
4. Kajinami, T., Hayashi, O., Narumi, T., Tanikawa, T., Hirose, M.: Digital display case: museum exhibition system to convey background information about exhibits. In: 2010 16th International Conference on Virtual Systems and Multimedia (VSMM), pp. 230–233 (2010)
5. Imura, J., Kasada, K., Narumi, T., Tanikawa, T., Hirose, M.: Reliving past scene experience system by inducing a video-camera operator's motion with overlaying a video-sequence onto real environment. ITE Trans. Media Technol. Appl. **2**(3), 225–235 (2014)
6. Hwang, J., Jung, J., Kim, G.J.: Hand-held virtual reality: a feasibility study. In: Proceedings of the ACM Symposium on Virtual Reality Software and Technology, pp. 356–363 (2006)

7. Chen, S.E.: Quicktime VR: an image-based approach to virtual environment navigation. In: Proceedings of the 22nd Annual Conference on Computer Graphics and Interactive Techniques, pp. 29–38 (1995)
8. Tanaka, R., Narumi, T., Tanikawa, T., Hirose, M.: Attracting user's attention in spherical image by angular shift of virtual camera direction. In: Proceedings of the 3rd ACM Symposium on Spatial User Interaction, pp. 61–64 (2015)
9. Okada, N., Imura, J., Narumi, T., Tanikawa, T., Hirose, M.: Manseibashi reminiscent window: on-site AR exhibition system using mobile devices. In: Streitz, N., Markopoulos, P. (eds.) DAPI 2015. LNCS, vol. 9189, pp. 349–361. Springer, Heidelberg (2015)
10. Shimojo, C., Simion, C., Shimojo, E., Scheier, C.: Gaze bias both reflects and influences preference. Nat. Neurosci. 6(12), 1317–1322 (2003). Nature Publishing Group
11. Zajonc, R.B.: Attitudinal effects of mere exposure. J. Pers. Soc. Psychol. 9(2p2), 1–27 (1968). American Psychological Association
12. Galyean, T.A.: Guided navigation of virtual environments. In: Proceedings of the 1995 Symposium on Interactive 3D Graphics, pp. 103–ff. ACM (1995)
13. Ropinski, T., Steinicke, F., Hinrichs, K.: A constrained road-based VR navigation technique for travelling in 3D city models. In: Proceedings of the 2005 International Conference on Augmented Tele-existence, pp. 228–235 (2005)
14. Abasolo, M.J., Della, J.M.: Magallanes: 3D navigation for everybody. In: Proceedings of the 5th International Conference on Computer Graphics and Interactive Techniques in Australia and Southeast Asia, pp. 135–142 (2007)
15. Chittaro, L., Burigat, S.: 3D location-pointing as a navigation aid in Virtual Environments. In: Proceedings of the Working Conference on Advanced Visual Interfaces, pp. 267–274 (2004)
16. Tanaka, R., Narumi, T., Tanikawa, T., Hirose, M.: Guidance field: potential field to guide users to target locations in virtual environments. In: Proceedings of 2016 IEEE Symposium on 3D User Interfaces (3DUI), pp. 39–48 (2016)
17. Milgram, S., Bickman, L., Berkowitz, L.: Note on the drawing power of crowds of different size. J. Pers. Soc. Psychol. 13(2), 79 (1969)
18. Narumi, T., Yabe, H., Yoshida, S., Tanikawa, T., Hirose, M.: Encouraging people to interact with interactive systems in public spaces by managing lines of participants. In: Yamamoto, S. (ed.) HIMI 2016. LNCS, vol. 9735, pp. 290–299. Springer, Cham (2016). doi: 10.1007/978-3-319-40397-7_28
19. Van Dijk, B., Zwiers, J., op den Akker, R., Nijholt, A.: Navigation assistance in virtual worlds. In: Boyd, E., Cohen, E., Zaliwski, A.J. (eds.) Proceedings 2001 Informing Science Conference, pp. 1–9 (2001)
20. Ibanez, J., Delgado-Mata, C.: Flocking techniques to naturally support navigation in large and open virtual worlds. Eng. Appl. Artif. Intell. 25(1), 119–129 (2012)
21. Narumi, T., Kasai, T., Honda, T., Aoki, K., Tanikawa, T., Hirose, M.: Digital railway museum: an approach to introduction of digital exhibition systems at the railway museum. In: Yamamoto, S. (ed.) HIMI 2013. LNCS, vol. 8018, pp. 238–247. Springer, Heidelberg (2013). doi:10.1007/978-3-642-39226-9_27
22. Endo, T., Katayama, A., Tamura, H., Hirose, M., Tanikawa, T., Saito, M.: Image-based walk-through system for large-scale scenes. In: Proceedings of 4th International Conference on Virtual Systems and Multimedia (VSMM 1998), vol. 1, pp. 269–274 (1998)
23. Anguelov, D., Dulong, C., Filip, D., Frueh, C., Lafon, S., Lyon, R., Ogale, A., Vincent, L., Weaver, J.: Google street view: capturing the world at street level. Computer 6, 32–38 (2010)

24. Uyttendaele, M., Criminisi, A., Kang, S.B., Winder, S., Szeliski, R., Hartley, R.: Image-based interactive exploration of real-world environments. IEEE Comput. Graph. Appl. **24**(3), 52–63 (2004)
25. Jankowski, J., Hulin, T., Hachet, M.: A study of street-level navigation techniques in 3d digital cities on mobile touch devices. In: Proceedings of 2014 IEEE Symposium on 3D User Interfaces (3DUI), pp. 35–38 (2014)
26. Banton, T., Stefanucci, J., Durgin, F., Fass, A., Proffitt, D.R.: The perception of walking speed in a virtual environment. Presence **14**(4), 394–406 (2005). MIT Press

Generating Rules of Action Transition in Errors in Daily Activities from a Virtual Reality-Based Training Data

Niken Prasasti Martono[1(✉)], Keisuke Abe[1], Takehiko Yamaguchi[2], Hayato Ohwada[1], and Tania Giovannetti[3]

[1] Department of Industrial Administration, Tokyo University of Science, Noda, Japan
niken.prasasti@sbm-itb.ac.id, 7416603@ed.tus.ac.jp,
ohwada@rs.tus.ac.jp
[2] Department of Applied Electronics, Tokyo University of Science, Tokyo, Japan
tk-ymgch@te.noda.tus.ac.jp
[3] Department of Psychology, Temple University, Philadelphia, USA
tgio@temple.edu

Abstract. Developments in virtual reality (VR) have advanced numerous applications in clinical settings in the areas of learning and treatment in neuropsychology. Emerging VR applications today focus on the challenge of diagnosis and cognitive training of mild cognitive impairment (MCI) and dementia patients and address navigation and orientation, face recognition, cognitive functionality, and other instrumental activities of daily living (IADL). The information recorded and captured by VR-based technology is real-time and can be advantageous for further analysis of patients' characteristics. The present study sought to utilize the data collected from VR-based software and a leap-motion device for learning in MCI cases to generate the rules for errors and action slips based on finger-action transitions when performing IADL. The finger motion was recorded as a time-series database, then an induction technique called Inductive Logic Programming (ILP), which uses logical and clausal language to represent the training data, was used to discover a concise classification rule using logical programming.

Keywords: Virtual reality · Inductive logic programming · Micro slips · Micro errors · Mild cognitive impairment

1 Introduction

Virtual reality (VR) as defined by [1] is "a scientific and technological domain, exploiting computer science and behavioral devices, allowing a person to interact multi-modally with a virtual world and its 3D entities that interact in real time by means of sensorimotor channels." As virtual reality has gained traction in the social sciences, scholars have begun to explore its viability for creating novel stimuli, treatments, and learning environments for use outside of the laboratory [2]. VRs have also been explored as a tool for cognitive behavioral therapy [2]. The use of VR-based technology in therapy is increasing in clinical settings because in some cases the technology is well-matched to the needs of clinical applications. In addition, the information recorded and captured

© Springer International Publishing AG 2017
S. Yamamoto (Ed.): HIMI 2017, Part II, LNCS 10274, pp. 166–175, 2017.
DOI: 10.1007/978-3-319-58524-6_15

by VR-based technology is real-time and can be advantageous for further analysis of patients' characteristics. Based on experiments and theoretical considerations, when VR-based technology is used in the learning process, useful data can be recorded automatically by software and can contribute to an analysis of each patient's state [3].

The purpose of the present study was to utilize data collected from VR-based software used for learning in Mild Cognitive Impairment (MCI) cases to examine whether such data can be successfully used in the task of generating rules of action transition in some types of errors made in the everyday actions of older adults. In this work, fourteen older adults completed a breakfast preparing task as an everyday action task in a designated virtual reality called the Virtual Kitchen (VK), equipped with a leap motion controller to record their finger motion. We took video recordings of the task and analyzed the motion-capture data, using these as inputs for inductive learning and using Inductive Logic Programming to produce rules for the errors.

The remainder of this paper is organized as follows. Section 2 reviews earlier work related to errors and slips in daily activities and summarizes the problem description of the study. Section 3 defines the experiments and data set used for analysis. Section 4 presents the process of ILP learning, including data preparation procedures. The resulting learned rules are provided in Sect. 5. Finally, the conclusion and further discussion are provided in the last section.

2   Problem Description

When doing daily activities such as making the bed, taking a shower, or preparing a meal, the process of action does not always go smoothly. For the most part, whether such goal-oriented tasks are completed with ease and according to a plan depends on the robustness and flexibility of human information processing. However, even in the most familiar of tasks, errors or slips of action do occur at a nontrivial rate [4].

Theories concerning the origins of action slips have been proposed by some preceding works [5–7] using the term "micro slips." Micro slips refer to the microscopic regulation of behavior. They are commonly observed in everyday sequential activities [8]. The first experimental research on micro slips was done by Reed and Schoenherr [9] and resulted in four classifications of micro slips: *hesitation*, *trajectory change*, *touch*, and *hand shape change*. These findings have been used in succeeding works on micro slips, especially on how a trajectory change in the hand has a significant relationship with the execution of micro slips. Some other works [10, 11] attempted to improve the classification of micro slips using three transition types. Nevertheless, the classification depended heavily on the direction of movement and did not give due weight to action transitions during sequential activities [8].

The study in [8] defined some new definitions for micro slips, using "motion" as a new coding scheme. Motion is a component of a sequential behavior and represents the manner in which a hand movement acts on an object. According to the scheme, micro slips are cases in which the motion does not proceed smoothly until the task is finished;

it often changes into another motion along the way. In the study results, five basic transition patterns were defined, depending on the specific action transition of the hand towards the object.

Such slips and errors have attracted the interest of psychologists and neuropsychologists [7, 12], and more recently they have become a focus as a predictor in analyzing the potential for Mild Cognitive Impairment (MCI) in older adults. For example, [13] presents a novel measure of slip and errors (called micro errors) in doing daily activities in order to improve the coding and monitoring of errors as an indicator of MCI. They defined five categories of micro errors: *Reach – Touch* errors, *Reach – No touch* errors, *Reach with Object* errors, *Extra Action* errors, and *Sequence* errors. They found that the micro errors could be reliable and sensitive, indicating their potential as a valid index of MCI. However, to date, there is no study examining how the new definition of micro errors relates to the direction of the hands nor to the hand action transition, which the present authors believe would be useful for better understanding in characterizing MCI patients.

This study has the goal of generating rules on the nature of micro errors by collecting finger movement and analyzing the basic transition patterns of study participants doing daily activity tasks in a virtual reality-based environment. Another purpose is to explore the use of analyzing finger speed when micro errors occur. In this study, the micro errors that will be used in the analysis are limited to two types: *Reach – Touch* (RT) errors and *Reach – No Touch* (RNT) errors.

3   Data Set

For this study, we asked fourteen ($n = 14$) older adults to complete the task of preparing a breakfast (breakfast task) in the VK environment as seen in Fig. 1. In performing the breakfast task, participants were expected to prepare a piece of toast and a cup of coffee. Toast preparation subtasks include putting the toast in the toaster, switching on the toaster, putting the toast on the plate, taking the butter and jelly with knife, and spreading the butter and jelly on the toast. Coffee-making subtasks include opening the coffee lid, scooping the coffee, putting the coffee in the mug, opening the sugar lid, scooping sugar with a spoon, stirring the coffee, putting in milk, and stirring the coffee.

From 14 older adults, based on a number of clinical tests and participants' historical data, four of them meet the criteria for Mild Cognitive Impairment, and three of them did not have MCI when the experiments were performed but did have MCI in the past.

Fourteen video clips were obtained for analysis from the breakfast preparing tasks. The basic motion units in the breakfast preparing task were determined based on preliminary observation of these video clips and adapting the work in [8]. There are five essential motions (*select, take, open, scoop, pour*) and no motion (*pause*). The finger movements all through the task were coded by watching the video in terms of these motion units. Uncompleted motions were coded using "-ing" in order to differentiate them from completed motions. Micro errors were coded over the whole task and classified into two types (*reach - touch (RT), reach - no touch (RNT)*), as defined in Table 1. A total of 116 micro errors

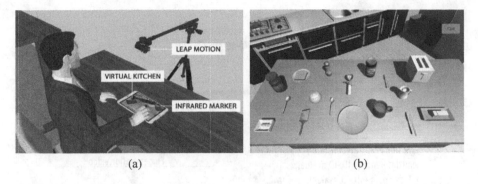

(a)   (b)

Fig. 1. (a) Configuration of the virtual kitchen environment [14] (b) Screen shot of the virtual kitchen breakfast task [14]

was observed throughout the video clips, including 93 RNT errors and 23 RT errors (Table 2).

Table 1. Definition of micro errors [13]

Micro-error type	Definition
Reach, touch	Unwanted object is reached for and touched (e.g., reaches for and touches cookies while making sandwich)
Reach, no touch	Unwanted object is reached for but not touched (e.g., reaches for cookies while making sandwich, but does not touch)

Table 2. Definition of motions coded from video

Motion type	Definition
Select	Finger reaching through an object
Take	Finger click an object and drag object to different position
Click	Finger click an object, usually to open (e.g. sugar jar, jelly jar)
Scoop	Finger hold an object (e.g. spoon, knife) and scoop something
Pour	Finger hold an object (e.g. cream) and pour it
Pause	Finger does not do any motion

4   Methodology

An overview of the methodology used in this study is presented in Fig. 2. We obtained several types of data as an input based on the interaction between the user and the Virtual Kitchen device, we then employed some preprocessing and learning to generate rules for the micro errors.

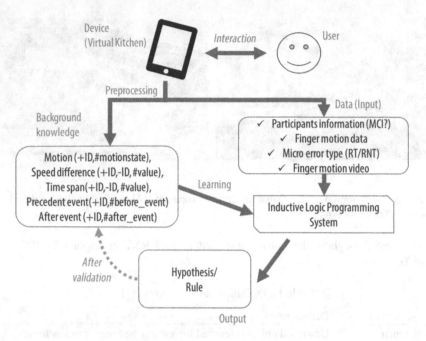

Fig. 2. Methodology overview

4.1 Motion Data Preprocessing

The VK system is equipped with a leap-motion sensor to collect finger movements and provide two-dimensional coordinate data. Data preprocessing of the motion data to obtain speed data is performed by data smoothing along each dimension using a moving-average filter to make data trends readable. After we calculated the speed from the motion data, we integrated the quantitative and qualitative motion data, executing the following steps.

Step 1. Collect a set of speed data and average each attribute value of the motion data
Step 2. Detect motion that reveals a micro error event and obtain a set of time codes
Step 3. Integrate the data from Steps 1 and 2 with the finger-motion state coding
Step 4. Add attributes indicating speed differences at the times when a finger motion is started and completed
Step 5. Integrate the data obtained in Step 4 into qualitative data (upLow, upMiddle, upHigh, downLow, downMiddle, downHigh)

The error detection in Step 2 and the finger-motion state coding in Step 3 were performed manually at the current stage. Detailed definitions of the subtasks are given in Table 4 in the Appendix. Table 3 gives an example of data integration after performing the five steps mentioned previously.

Table 3. Example on data integrating

Time	Time span	Subtask	Action	Speed diff	Error code
10:24:34	3 s	Toast 1	Select toast	upMiddle	
10:24:37	4 s	Toast 2	Take toast	upMiddle	
10:24:41	7 s	Toast 3	Pause	downLow	
10:24:48	4 s	Toast 3	Select knife	upLow	Reach - Touch
10:24:50	3 s	Coffee 1	Select coffee	upMiddle	
10:24:54	…	Coffee 2	Take coffee	upMiddle	

4.2 ILP Learning

Like other machine learning methods, ILP algorithms take examples of certain concepts, in our case related to two classes of micro errors, in order to construct a hypothesis that generalizes (the terms 'explains' or 'covers' are also used) the examples. Domain-specific knowledge, also called background knowledge, may be added in order to simplify the learning process; this kind of knowledge is given and does not have to be learned [15]. In this study, we used an ILP system called GKS [16, 17] to employ ILP and generate rules.

Coding micro-error as examples for ILP

Suppose, for example, that we want to learn the definitions of two types of micro-errors such as Reach – Touch and Reach – No Touch. As our aim is to recognize motion transitions in micro errors, the first task is to collect examples of these micro errors as well as motion examples associated with normal motion when no micro errors occur. Second, since ILP is a symbolic machine-learning method, we must generate a formal description of these micro errors.

To use symbolic data in ILP, the first task is to define a formal language in order to abstract the numerical data. The choice of language used in ILP is important because it can influence the learning results [15]. We chose to represent the temporal samples as a set of motion descriptions. A series of motions A is denoted with the following arguments:

- Subtask: a constant symbol set by looking at which subtask the motion belongs to.
- Motion: the state of hand motion; *select, take, open, scoop, pour, pause*.
- Speed difference: the qualifying value of finger speed while doing the motion; *low, middle, high* (both for positive and negative values of speed change).
- Time: the qualifying value of time length of a motion; *short, middle, long*
- Before: the name of the preceding subtask
- After: the name of the next subtask

The fourth and sixth arguments (before and after) specify even chaining in the finger motion. They are considered to provide important information as they reveal the symbolic temporal relationships between the elements of motion.

5   Learned Rules

We performed two experiments in using ILP for learning. First, we used only Reach –
Touch errors as positive examples, not considering any Reach – No Touch errors, and
therefore all examples other than RT errors are negative examples. In the second experiment, we used only Reach – No Touch errors as positive examples with all examples
other than RNT errors considered as negative examples. This process was used in order
to get a better result for the prediction rules. We present the rules that are the most
readable and are related to the real conditions of the experiments below. "[T, F]" denotes
the number of positive examples (T) and the number of negative examples (F) the rule
covers. "rt" represents the presented rules for the Reach – Touch errors, and "rnt" represents the presented rules for the Reach – No Touch errors.

5.1   Reach – Touch Error Rules

Several rules related to the Reach – Touch errors are listed below.

Rule 1

```
{7,1} +rt(A) :- motion(A,B,pause), before_event(A,
toast3), speed_diff(A,B,C,downlow,middle),
speed_diff(A,C,D,downlow,middle)
```

A Reach – Touch error happens if there is a pause motion (no motion of finger) after
performing subtask "Toast 3," which is turning the toaster on, and there is a decrease in
speed for a medium time range of the pausing motion.

Rule 2

```
{5,0} +rt(A) :- motion(A,B,take), after_event(A, sugar4),
speed_diff(A,B,C,upmiddle,long), speed_diff(A,C,D,upmid-
dle,middle)
```

A Reach – Touch error happens if there is a "take" motion before performing subtask
"Cream 1", which is selecting cream, and there is an increase in speed for a long time
range of the selecting motion. For example, after finishing whichever task was before
the cream task, the participants tend to take an unwanted object that is not related to the
previous or subsequent task.

5.2   Reach – no Touch Error Rules

Several rules related to Reach – No Touch errors are listed below.

Rule 3

```
{6,2} +rnt(A) :- motion(A,B,select), before_event(A, cof-
fee8), speed_diff(A,B,C,upMiddle,middle)
```

A Reach – No Touch error happens if there is a moderate speed increase over a
middle time interval when performing action "take" after performing "Coffee 8", which

is stirring the coffee. For example, after stirring the coffee in the mug, a participant may tend to select an unwanted object that is not related to the succeeding task.

Rule 4

```
{10,0} +rnt(A) :- motion(A,B,pause), after_event(A,
jelly1), speed_diff(A,C,D,downLow,long)
```

A Reach – No Touch error happens if there is a small speed decrease over a long time interval when performing no motion or pause before performing "Jelly 1," which is selecting jelly.

Rule 5

```
{11,1} +rnt(A) :- motion(A,B,select), before_event(A,
toast4), speed_diff(A,B,C,highlow,middle),
speed_diff(A,C,D,downlow,middle)
```

A Reach – Touch error happens if there is a selecting motion after performing subtask "Toast 4", which is taking toast to the plate, and there is a decrease in speed over a medium time range of the selecting motion. For example, after putting the toast on the plate, a participant may select an unwanted object that is not related to the succeeding task.

6   Conclusions and Discussion

We applied ILP to generate rules on how two types of micro errors happen in the task of learning in the virtual-reality environment called Virtual Kitchen. We described how to acquire motion data and transform the data into qualitative data that is useful for ILP learning. The focus of this study was to see how action transitions of the finger in the experiments were related to the pattern of micro errors.

For Reach – Touch errors, based on the learned results, the first rule suggests that there is a tendency for a micro error to happen after a medium-length pause. This rule naturally describes how participant motion is related to cognitive activity. When they pause, there seems to be a cognitive process going on while deciding what to do in the next step. Looking at the subtasks, the participants seem to make errors after the type of task in which they have to change the subtask (for example, from toast to coffee), which is supported by the fact that slips or errors tend to happen in between the decision points.

For Reach – No Touch errors, two rules represent how such errors tend to happen under the motion of selecting. This is also supported by the tendency of making errors at the decision point, because in subtask segmentation selecting is always put at the start of each subtask, meaning that the participants make errors just before they start to make a correct step at the beginning of small subtasks.

This study, however, has some limitations, including the fact that the task of action coding was still done manually. Also, the limited number of positive examples makes it seem that the rules cover only a few positive examples. Future work includes executing the action coding automatically, using available data from the virtual-kitchen device, and focusing on how to generate rules that can differentiate between patterns of micro errors involving healthy older adults and MCI patients

Appendix

Breakfast (toast and coffee) Subtasks.

1. Toast 1, select bread.
2. Toast 2, take and put bread into toaster.
3. Toast 3, click toaster on (move the lever down).
4. Coffee 1, select coffee (reach to and touch the coffee jar).
5. Coffee 2, take coffee (lift coffee jar and move it toward mug).
6. Coffee 3, open coffee (opening and placing lid on table).
7. Coffee 4, select spoon for coffee.
8. Coffee 5, scoop coffee (moving the spoon to the mug and adding coffee one or more times and placing the spoon down).
9. Sugar 1, select sugar.
10. Sugar 2, click to open sugar.
11. Sugar 3, select spoon for sugar.
12. Sugar 4, scoop sugar into mug.
13. Cream 1, select cream.
14. Cream 2, pour cream into coffee.
15. Coffee 7, select spoon for stir.
16. Coffee 8, stir mug.
17. Toast 4, take toast (remove bread from toaster and place it on plate).
18. Jelly 1, select jelly (touching the jelly before using it).
19. Jelly 2, move jelly.
20. Jelly 3, open jelly jar.
21. Jelly 4, select knife for jelly.
22. Jelly 5, scoop and spread jelly.
23. Butter 1, select knife for butter.
24. Butter 2, scoop and spread butter.
25. Quit, select quit.

References

1. Fuchs, P., Arnaldi, B., Tisseau, J.: La réalité virtuelle et ses applications. In: Fuchs, P., Moreau, G. (eds.) Le traité de la réalité virtuelle. Fondements et Interfaces Comportementales, vol. 1, pp. 3–52. Presse de l'Ecole des Mines de Paris, Paris (2003)
2. Fox, J., Arena, D., Bailenson, J.N.: Virtual reality' a survival guide for the social scientist. J. Media Psychol. **21**, 95–113 (2009)
3. Martono, N.P., Yamaguchi, T., Ohwada, H.: Utilizing finger movement data to cluster patients with everyday action impairment. In: 2016 IEEE 15th International Conference on Cognitive Informatics & Cognitive Computing, pp. 459–464 (2016)

4. Botvinick, M., Bylsma, L.: Distraction and action slips in an everyday task: evidence for a dynamic representation of task context. Psychon. Bull. Rev. **12**(6), 1011–1017 (2005). http://doi.org/10.3758/BF03206436
5. Norman, D.A.: Categorization of action slips. Psychol. Rev. **88**, 1–15 (1981)
6. Reason, J.T.: Human error. Cambridge University Press, Cambridge (1990)
7. Reason, J.T.: Cognitive underspecification: its varieties and consequences. In: Baars, B.J. (ed.) Experimental Slips and Human Error: Exploring the Architecture of Volition, pp. 71–91. Plenum, New York (1992)
8. Hirose, N.: Towards a new taxonomy of microslips. In: Cummins-Sebree, S., Riley, M., Shockley, K. (eds.) Studies in perception and action IX, pp. 91–96. Lawrence Erlbaum Associates, New York (2010)
9. Reed, E.S., Schoenherr, D.: The neuropathology of everyday life: on the nature and significance of microslips in everyday activities, unpublished manuscript (1992)
10. Hirose, N.: How to describe non-smooth action sequences: categorization of microslips. J. Ecol. Psychol. **1**, 19–24 (2004)
11. Hirose, N.: Effect of task and individual characteristics on microslips of action. In: Heft, H., Marsh, K.L. (eds.) Studies in perception and action VIII, pp. 199–202. Lawrence Erlbaum Associates, Mahwah (2005)
12. Baars, B.J.: Experimental Slips and Human Error: Exploring The Architecture of Volition. Plenum, New York (1992)
13. Seligman, S.C., Giovannetti, T., Sestito, J., Libon, D.J.: A new approach to the characterization of subtle errors in everyday action: implications for mild cognitive impairment. Clin. Neuropsychologist **28**(1), 97–115 (2014)
14. Martono, N.P., Yamaguchi, T., Maeta, T., Fujino, H., Kubota, Y., Ohwada, H., Giovanneti, T.: Clustering finger motion data from virtual reality-based training to analyze patients with mild cognitive impairment. Int. J. Softw. Sci. Comput. Intell. (IJSSCI) **8**(4), 29–42 (2016). doi:10.4018/IJSSCI.2016100102
15. Carrault, G., Cordier, M.O., Quiniou, R., Wang, F.: Temporal abstraction and inductive logic programming for arrhythmia recognition from electrocardiograms. Artif. Intell. Med. **28**(3), 231–263 (2003). http://doi.org/10.1016/S0933-3657(03)00066-6
16. Mizoguchi, F., Ohwada, H.: Constrained relative least general generalization for inducing constraint logic programs. New Gener. Comput. **13**, 335–368 (1995)
17. Nishiyama, H., Ohwada, H.: Yet another parallel hypothesis search for inverse entailment. In: ILP 2015 Short Paper (2015)

Navigation Patterns in Ederly During Multitasking in Virtual Environnment

Eulalie Verhulst[1](✉), Frédéric Banville[2], Paul Richard[1], Sabrina Tabet[2],
Claudia Lussier[2], Édith Massicotte[2], and Philippe Allain[1]

[1] Université d'Angers, Angers, France
`eulalie.verhulst@gmail.com`
[2] Université de Montréal, Montréal, Canada

Abstract. Cognitive assessment and screening can be realized with virtual environments (VE). These VE reproduce ecological situation and give an overview of participants difficulties through scoring systems. The most variables used to qualify participants performance are number of errors and time completion. These variables are link to cognition and navigation skill in VEs. We assessed navigation of adult and elderly in a multitasking VE. Navigation patterns were elaborate with diagram to visually detect differences between the two age groups. Elderly have poorer performance than adults.

1 Introduction

Cognitive assessment and screening is becoming a major challenge for the researchers to then adapt prevention and support of patients. For instance, to understand Mild Cognitive Impairment's (MCI) difficulties in their everyday life, they can be assessed during the realization of Instrumental Action of Daily Living (IADL) where errors are analyzed and characterized [1,2]. Belchior et al. [3] have listed 9 studies where MCI are assessed with IADL in real world situations. However, IADL can also be tested using virtual environment (VE) [4–8]. VEs are real time computer simulation in which users can navigate and interact with the use of specific 3D interaction technique [9,10]. 3D VEs and 2D computerized systems are mostly used in cognitive assessment and screening in dementia or MCI because they offer the possibility to automatically record behaviours in a database and to propose standardized measures [11]. Thus, numerous variables can be monitoring very precisely (e.g. completion time) and collected data can be easily analyzed. Most of the recorded data are linked to participants performance and are related to the usability of the proposed interaction technique. 3D interaction techniques are mainly characterized by 3 terms: navigation, selection and system control [12]. Navigation allows the users to travel in the VE from places to places adjusting his/her view point (i.e. steering) [13] which is fundamental to explore the VE and to navigate toward the chosen direction [14,15]. Navigation can be a goal itself or a way to managed a task, but in both cases, it has to be easy to use and to learn to reduce the cognitive resources associated

S. Yamamoto (Ed.): HIMI 2017, Part II, LNCS 10274, pp. 176–188, 2017.
DOI: 10.1007/978-3-319-58524-6_16

with the motor component (i.e. travel) [16]. So that users can easily be focused on the cognitive component of navigation (i.e. wayfinding) [17]. The imbrication of the travel and wayfinding component foster the creation of a cognitive map of the environment. The cognitive map is a mental representation of spatial information needed to navigate and to orient oneself in space [18]. Thus, navigation data are linked to the action plan and to the interaction technique used for travelling. Using VE permits to progress in the understanding of navigation patterns thanks to the recording of behavioral data. VEs are useful to collect data but the related behavioral analyses are sometime difficult to carry. Indeed, a lot of variables can be selected for analyses and results may be difficult to understand. Even if it is admitted that the users performance is linked to the task completion time [19] others variables can be extracted and analyzed such as log or time passed in each place of the VE. Having a better understanding of each variables recorded in a VE will allow us to apprehend participant's performance and adapt his support for instance by modified the interaction technique.

2 Related Work

2.1 Interaction Technique Used in Virtual Environment for Assessing Cognition

3D interaction techniques can be split in two categories according to the Jung et al.'s taxonomy [20]: egocentric and exocentric techniques. With exocentric techniques, the user's point of view is outside the VE citePoupyrev1998. For instance, the use of Ray Casting [16,21], mice or keyboard permits to easily interact with the VE. They are the most used because they are intuitive and easy to learn [20,22]. In a scoping review of VE for neuropsychological assessment, Valladeres et al. [23] showed that 47.7% of their studies, use mice and keyboard to interact with the VE and 20.75% use a touchscreen and a few the joystick. Moreover, some of them does not provide any indication about the way to interact in the VE. Indeed, 8 studies assessing MCI participants in VE have been listed (cf. Table 1) and participants with MCI could navigated using mice, keyboard, touch screen, joystick or motion capture tools (Kinect and Leap Motion) which makes it difficult to compare users performance in the several studies. Motion capture tools allow users to interact with the VE through Naturel User Interface such as walk simulation (e.g. walking-in-place, walking on a treadmill). These techniques are ecological with gestures very closed to the reality but can make user tired because of physical involvement to interact with the VE [24]. According Kulik et al. [15] interaction technique does not have to mimic reality but have to efficient and may also be fun. So, it may be preferable to have less ecological technique but more efficient.

To understand the impact of interaction technique on the participants performance it is necessary to give an exhaustive description of the system setup and the interaction technique used. The view point orientation can miss in the system description whereas this characteristic is primordial. Indeed, when a participant is navigating in a VE he must be able to move easily, looking around

Table 1. Interaction technique used in VE designed for assessing MCI

	Travel	Steering	Selection
Virtual supermarket [4]	Keyboard	*unknown*	Mouse clic
Virtual supermarket [5]	Keyboard	*unknown*	Mouse clic
Virtual supermarket [6]	Touchscreen (push on footprints)	Scrolling left and right on touchscreen	Push on touchscreen
Virtual museum [7]	Joystick	*unknown*	Mouse
Virtual day-out task [8]	Hand pointing gestures	Hand pointing gestures	Hand grasping gestures (leap motion)
Virtual day-out task [25]	Treadmill + kinect	*unknown*	Hand grasping gestures (leap motion)
Virtual park [26]	Joystcick	*unknown*	Push button
Serious game [27]	*not used*	*not used*	Push on touch screen

him [28]. Moreover navigation must be very easy allowing the participant to completely focus on the tasks to be achieved within the VE [29].

The challenge of human-machine interaction studies is to developpe and evaluate interaction techniques with a high usability and to understand how cognition is involved in the use of these interaction technique. Indeed, studies have shown that elderly and MCI can be uncomfortable with the use of mice [30] and can feel anxious about using it [31]. However, if some elderly has difficulties with technology acceptance, increasingly are using computer for instance to keep social link thanks to e-mail [32]. The use of computer and associated interaction technique such as mice and pads, is becoming very common in work as in private context. Moreover, mice could be used for screening MCI. Seelye et al. [33] found, with mouse data monitoring during web searching, that MCI make more resting time between mouse movements. Taken together these studies indicates that elderly can use various interaction technique and that navigational data could help to qualify users performance.

2.2   Cognitive Assessment in Virtual Environments

The use of VEs to assess cognitive functions specify to pick up variables used to score the performance of the participant. Indeed, these new tests recquire to readjust the scoring system from traditional tests especially in IADL tests. VEs permit to record a lot of variables but investigations are still needed to detect which variables are sensitive to correctly qualify the performance. Moreover, the recorded data are related both cognition and the use of interaction techniques. Indeed, the main variables used to qualify performance are completion time and number of error which are modulated by navigation efficiency in the VE.

Navigation efficiency is mainly assess by completion time and so, linked to the user's performance [19] where a long completion time is associated to a poor performance. These results are corroborated with some studies where MCI took significantly more time to complete the task than experimental participants [5–7]. For example, the navigation patterns can be shown with the Visualization of Users Flow (VU-Flow), a tool [34] which allow to analyze navigation patterns in 3D VE. VU-Flow records users position and orientation in logs so users path can be visualized as well as most visited routes. The path visualization leads to descriptive and quantitative data of navigational efficiency with fluid or saccadic paths and distance travelled [19]. Even if tools exist to visualize navigation data, it is still difficult to understand why patients took more time to realize the task. Is it because they are inefficient in the task realization (i.e. cognitive difficulties) or because the use of the interaction technique?

Variables used to assess participants performance in the 8 VE (cf. Table 1) were listed. Two methods can be used to qualify performance: created an efficiency ratio which is the compilation of several variables [8,25] or analyzed variables one by one where most variables are time completion and number of errors. Others collected data exist as number and rest periods [4,5] or distance travelled [4–6]. So, variables used in VE to qualify participants performance are related to quantitative navigation data. Mainly because monitoring data are linked to the tracking of participants position. Even if these data are difficult to appreciate because they are related to the use of the interaction technique, they can be reliable to qualify participants performance. For instance, Zygouris et al. [6] proposed an algorithm to detect MCI participant from elderly according time completion and age of the participants where a longer completion time is a sensitive variable to detect participants with MCI.

The present studys goal is to apprehend participants performance focusing on navigational data in a 3D EV. Results could help to have a better understanding of elderly performance and later compared them to MCI performance.

3   Method

The study was conducted with 13 young adults (4 men and 9 women) and 13 elderly (3 men and 10 women). Young participants (mean age: 25.16, SD: 6.14) were recruited in general population and elderly (mean age: 67.09, SD: 2.91) at the Alzheimer association. All participants are French speaker and have the same year of scolarity (mean 16.12 years for young adults and mean 15.25 years for elderly). Older with a MoCA less than 26 were excluded on this study. The participants realized IADL tasks during multitasking in the Virtual Multitasking Task-2 (VMT-2). The VMT-2 is a virtual apartment where prospective memory and executive functions are assessed during IADL. All trials begin with a familiarization stage where participants could visit the VMT-2, displayed on a full HD 27" monitor, without tasks to manage using mouse and keyboard and head-mounted display (HMD) (i.e. Oculus Rift). The goal of this preliminary step is to allow participants creating a cognitive map of the virtual apartment and to learn how to navigate select 3D objects (e.g. open/close a door). Then, all participants realized VMT-2 while navigation data and action were recorded in a csv database. Participants position was monitored in the x, z and y axis and transcribed on the apartment map. Collisions are marked using a red triangle on the map each time the user touch a 3D object such as a wall or a furniture. Total completion time and the time passed in each room of the virtual apartment were also recorded. Each participants had to perform the familiarization step in both a non-immersive and an immersive configuration. In the former case, the participants hat to navigate using mouse (travel) and keyboard (steering and selection), in the later case they had to navigate using the keyboard (travel), the HMD (steering) and the mouse (selection).

When the participant begins the VMT-2, he knows that he must answer to the phone if this one is ringing and to store the grocery. One minute after the beginning the phone rings and a voice asks the user to go to the main bedroom to feed the fishes and to dry on a shirt. Two minutes after the beginning, the voice on the phone asks to fax a document. Finally, after 15 min it asks to check if the tickets are properly placed on a shelf. The experiment ends when the participant think he has finished the tasks.

4 Results

All analyses were conducted using R software, at a significance level of 0.05. T modified was used to qualify errancies and U Mann-Whitney to compare elderly from young adult group.

4.1 Descriptive Analysis

Descriptive analysis was conduct on the map of the VE. We compared path with mouse and keyboard and path with HMD during familiarization stage where participants could visit the virtual apartment. Trajectory of adults and elderly present the same particularity when they navigate with the HMD (Fig. 1). Indeed, the path is more saccadic with right angle where it is smoother when participants use the mouse and keyboard to navigate.

4.2 Quantitative Analysis

Time Passed in Each Zone. Time passed in each zone was calculated to identified errancies. Errancy can be defined as a long time passed in one room including goings and comings without apparent goal. To qualify errancies, T modified test was conduct so that participant resting significantly more time than others in a room was doing errancy. There is no significantly difference of errancies between the 2 groups ($U = 83$; $p = 0.47$) or between immersion conditions (i.e. HMD and non-immersive) ($U = 41$; $p = 0.96$).

Completion Time. Elderly group took significantly more time to achieve the VMT-2 ($U = 126$; $p = 0.009$). We did not observe any effect of immersion ($U = 82$; $p = 0.40$).

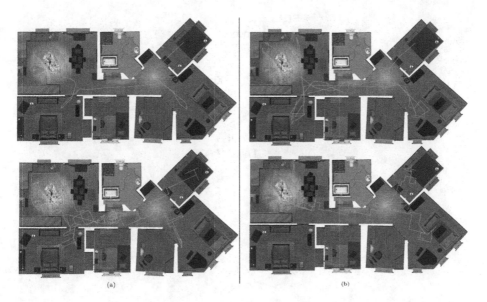

Fig. 1. Path of adults (a) and elderly (b) during familiarization step with mouse and keyboard and then with HMD.

Performance's Rate. To complete the VMT-2, elderly group took significantly more time to achieve the tasks in the VMT-2 (U = 126; p = 0.009). In addition, young adults realized more tasks than elderly (U = 32; p = 0.05). To know more about actions plan we analyzed logs recorded by the system and create activity diagram for adults(Fig. 2) and elderly (Fig. 3). In a first step, participants come in the apartment and go toward the kitchen to store the groceries. Only a few young adults begin to store the groceries when the phone is ringing to ask them to feed the fishes and dry the shirt which are in the main bedroom. Most young adults go in the main bedroom to do it and then go to the kitchen before answering on the second phone call whereas only half of elderly has the time to go in the bedroom or in the kitchen to begin some activities. The second phone call specify to go to the office to fax a document. During this time adults and elderly realize activities in a similar way. Indeed, they fax the document, feed the fishes, deposit the shirt if it is dry and continue or begin to store the grocery. It should be noted that half of the young adult group does not answer to the third phone call because these participants have already finish all activities in the apartment and so, stop the VMT-2. Others answer to the third phone call and go the entrance to check the tickets. At this point, if they finish all tasks they stop the VMT-2 or go back in the bedroom for finishing the shirt task and then go the kitchen for storing the last items before stopping the test. Focusing on the elderly group only 2 participants go to check the tickets. Others finish the tasks in the office or in the bedroom and then in the kitchen.

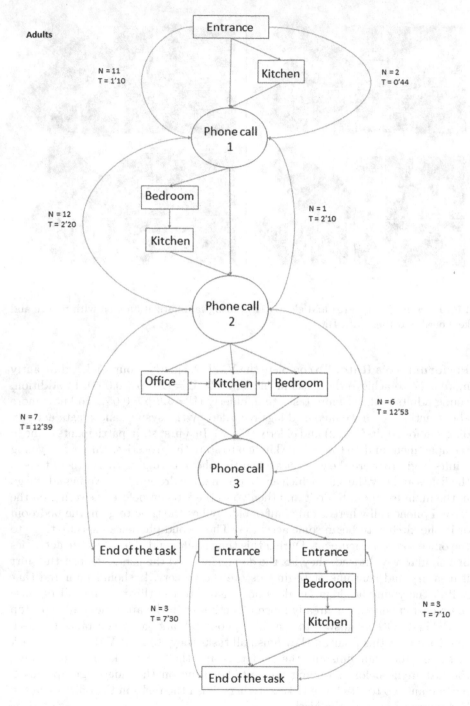

Fig. 2. Diagramm of the action realisation in the VMT-2 by adults. N = mean of participant. T = mean time.

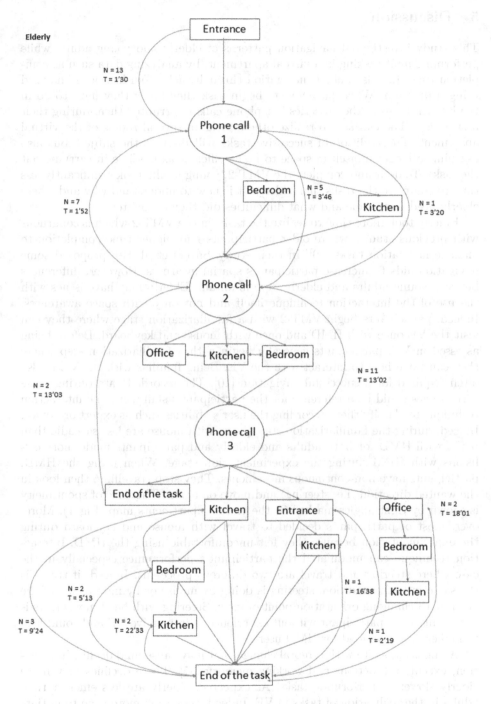

Fig. 3. Diagramm of the action realisation in the VMT-2 by elderly. N = mean of participant. T = mean time.

5   Discussion

This study investigated navigation patterns of elderly and young adults while performing multitasking in a virtual apartment, by analyzing data such as completion time. In this context, navigation through each room has been analyzed using a diagram. When participants begin task they know they have to go in the kitchen to store the groceries but phone calls interrupted them during their first action. The call ask to realize others tasks in several rooms of the virtual apartment. The addition of successive tasks will distract the subject but also ask him to locate himself in space to be as efficient as possible in carrying out the tasks. To do it and complete the VMT-2, young adults took significantly less time to complete the tasks than elderly. It is now to understand why and where elderly need more time and what difficulties did they encounter.

Elderly took more time to realize the tasks in the VMT-2 which is congruous with previous studies where older participants had higher time completion to manage navigation tasks [10]. In their study, Sayers et al. [10] proposed some navigation aids to increase participant's spatial awarness. However, differences between young adults and elderly were maintain. Elderly may have issues with the use of the interaction technique itself and not only with space awareness. Indeed, participants begin VMT-2 with a familiarization stage where they can visit the VE once with HMD and once with mouse and keyboard. Before being assessed in VE, participants generally begin with a familiarization step where they can learn how to interact with the VE. Being familiar with the VE is also often required for a successful navigation [10]. The recorded data during these early stages could be a reference for the participant's skill using the interaction technique to classify them according the user's abilities such as expert or novice. Indeed, during the familiarization step, paths with mouse are less saccadic than paths with HMD for both adults and elderly and participants made more collisions with HDM during the experimentation stage. When using the HMD, participants have non-continuous movements. They stop travelling, then look in the wanted direction (i.e. steering) and move on again. This lake of spontaneity is shown by right angles marked on the virtual apartments map (Fig. 1). Moreover, most of participants decided to travel with mouse and keyboard during the experimentation because they felt uncomfortable using the HMD. Interaction technique can modulated the participant's performance especially in the case where steering and travel are two different processus. Indeed, if travel is the same in both condition, steering is doing by mouse or by movements of the head, with changing orientation point of view. Steering with head movements is not intuitive for participant without experience in immersive VE and could lead to higher cognitive load for HMD users.

Aging is associate with cerebral change that may cause mild decline in attention, executive functions and working memory [35]. These declines may make elderly slower at performing tasks. As expected, elderly are less efficient than adults in the realization of tasks in VE. Indeed, they took more time to initiate tasks in the VMT-2 and half of elderly begin activities only after the second phone call. During the first and the second phone call, they stay in the same zone and seem to use the time to think. As they need more time to initiate activities in the end of the task the had several tasks to finish during the same time, so they are doing multitasking to manage all tasks. The multitasking context is present in IADL and is linked to independent living at home [36]. It requires several cognitive functions as executive functions, prospective and retrospective memory [37–39] and can lead to a higher cognitive load and difficulties to remember all the things to do. Indeed, most of elderly forget to realize the last task which is to check the tickets. Moreover, the multitasking context with unexpected events could lead to errancies for adults and elderly. During this time, they may think about the way to managed the next tasks. Indeed, when checking logs, we recorded any activities of the participant during errancy. However, we also observe another type of long time passed in a zone especially in the corridor or in the kitchen. According logs, in these room, participant had issue with item selection and orientation in space in these restricted places.

Taking together these results indicate that the elaboration of a EV for assessing cognitive functions is not an easy thing. Indeed, results showed that elerdly realized tasks in an inefficient way because phone calls were unexpected and disturbe participants but also because they need more time to be ready to act in the VE. In the VMT-2 the first phone call seems to occurs too early because the participants do not have the time to go in the kitchen to store the groceries. Moreover, adult participants finish the task quickly and the third phone call did not ring. Start actions in VE as function of time could lead to difficulties for participants to managed all the task. Actions could be launch not by time but by others actions. For instance, the first phone call ring after participant stored some grocery item instead of 1 min after the beginning of the VMT-2. A longer completion time is associated with cognition but also with the interaction technique. Analyze several variables instead of having a performances rate helps to make a distinction between cognition and abilities with the interaction technique. Understand how which part impacts more completion time could be make with analysis of collisions, time passed in each zone and logs. Collisions could be a quantitative indicator of usability of interaction technique and logs visualized with a diagramm could be a better indicator of participant's cognition. Analyze logs to construct diagram aims to be a useful method which allow to see where and what kind of difficulties the participant met.

As limitation, the study has not enough participant using the HMD. Complementary analyses should be conduct with more participants wearing the HMD. To avoid cybersickness with elderly the comparison could be done only with adults.

Acknowledgments. Thank to all students who work hard to make this research possible.

References

1. Seligman, S.C., Giovannetti, T., Sestito, J., Libon, D.J.: A new approach to the characterization of subtle errors in everyday action: implications for mild cognitive impairment. Clin. Neuropsychologist. **28**(1), 97–115 (2014)
2. Giovannetti, T., Bettcher, B., Briane, M., Brennan, L., Libon, D.J., Burke, M., Duey, K., Nieves, C., Wambach, D.: Characterisation of everyday functioning in mild cognitive impairment: a direct assessment approach. Dement. Geriatr. Cogn. Disord. **25**, 359–365 (2008)
3. Belchior, P., Holmes, M., Bier, N., Bottari, C., Mazer, B., Robert, A., Kaur, N.: Performance-based tools for assessing functional performance in individuals with mild cognitive impairment. Open J. Occup. Ther. **3**(3), 1–21 (2015)
4. Josman, N., Klinger, E., Kizony, R.: Performance within the virtual action planning supermarket (VAP-S): an executive function profile of three different populations suffering from deficits in the central nervous system. In: Proceedings of the 7th ICDVRAT (2008)
5. Werner, P., Rabinowitz, S., Klinger, E., Korczyn, A.D., Josman, N.: Use of the virtual action planning supermarket for the diagnosis of mild cognitive impairment. Dement. Geriatr. Cogn. Disord. **27**(4), 301–309 (2009)
6. Zygouris, S., Giakoumis, D., Votis, K., Doumpoulakis, S., Ntovas, K., Segkouli, S., Karagiannidis, C., Tzovaras, D., Isolaki, M.: Can a virtual reality cognitive training application fulfill a dual role? using the virtual supermarket cognitive training application as a screening tool for mild cognitive impairment. J. Alzheimers Dis. **44**(4), 1333–1347 (2015)
7. Tarnanas, I., Laskaris, N., Tsolaki, M., Muri, R., Nef, T., Mosimann, U.P.: On the comparison of a novel serious game and electroencephalography biomarkers for early dementia screening. In: GeNeDis (2015)
8. Tarnanas, I., Tsolaki, M., Nef, T., Muri, R., Mosimman, U.P.: Can a novel computerized cognitive screening test provide additional information for early detection of Alzheimer's disease? Alzheimer's Dement. **10**(6), 790–798 (2014)
9. Stanney, K.M., Kennedy, R.S., Kingdon, K.: Virtual environment usage protocols. Handbook of Virtual Environments: Design, Implementation, and Applications. Lawrence Erlbaum Associates Inc., New Jersey (2002)
10. Sayers, H.: Desktop virtual environments: a study of navigation and age. Interact. Comput. **16**(5), 939–956 (2004)
11. Morris, R., Kotitsa, M., Bramham, J., Brooks, B., Rose, F.: Virtual reality investigation of strategy formation, rule breaking and prospective memory in patients with focal prefrontal neurosurgical lesions. In: Proceedings of the 4th International Conference on Disability, Virtual Reality & Associated Technologies (2002)
12. Jankowski, J., Hachet, M.: A survey of interaction techniques for interactive 3D environments. In: Eurographics 2013-STAR (2013)
13. Bowman, D.A., Kruijff, E., LaViola, J.J., Poupyrev, I.: An introduction to 3-D user interface design. Presence: Teleoperators Virtual Environ. **10**(1), 96–108 (2001)
14. Liu, A., Fung, J., Lamontagne, A., Hoge, R., Doyon, J.: Brain regions involved in locomotor steering in a virtual environment. In: ICVR (2013)
15. Kulik, A.: Building on realism and magic for designing 3D interaction techniques. IEEE Comput. Graphics Appl. **29**(6), 22–33 (2009)
16. Bowman, D.A.: Interaction Techniques for Immersive Virtual Environments: Design, Evaluation, and Application. Invited Talk (1997)

17. Darken, R.P., Allard, T., Achille, L.B.: Spatial orientation and wayfinding in large-scale virtual spaces: an introduction. Presence: Teleoperators Virtual Environ. **7**(2), 101–107 (1998)
18. Tolman, E.C.: Cognitive Maps in Rats and Men. American Psychological Association (1948)
19. Patel, K.K., Vij, S.K.: Spatial navigation in virtual world. In: Advanced Knowledge Based Systems: Model, Applications and Research, TMRF e-Book, vol. 1, pp. 101–125 (2010)
20. Jung, J., Park, H., Hwang, D., Son, M., Beck, D., Park, J., Park, W.: A review on interaction techniques in virtual environments. In: 2014 International Conference on Industrial Engineering and Operations Management, pp. 1582–1590 (2014)
21. Poupyrev, I., Ichikawa, T., Weghorst, S., Billinghurst, M.: Egocentric object manipulation in virtual environments: empirical evaluation of interaction techniques. Comput. Graph. Forum (1998)
22. Roupé, M., Bosch-Sijtsema, P., Johansson, M.: Interactive navigation interface for virtual reality using the human body. Comput. Environ. Urban Syst. **43**, 42–50 (2014)
23. Valladares-Rodríguez, S., Pérez-Rodríguez, R., Anido-Rifón, L., Fernández-Iglesias, M.: Trends on the application of serious games to neuropsychological evaluation: a scoping review. J. Biomed. Inform. **64**, 296–319 (2016)
24. DSouza, L., Pathirana, I., McMeel, D., Amor, R.: Kinect to architecture. In: Twenty-Sixth International Conference Image and Vision Computing, pp. 155–160, New Zealand (2011)
25. Tarnanas, I., Schlee, W., Tsolaki, M., Muri, R., Mosimann, U., Nef, T.: Ecological validity of virtual reality daily living activities screening for early dementia: longitudinal study. JMIR Serious Games **1**(1), 1–14 (2013)
26. Weniger, G., Ruhleder, M., Lange, C., Wolf, S., Irle, E.: Egocentric and allocentric memory as assessed by virtual reality in individuals with amnestic mild cognitive impairment. Neuropsychologia **49**(3), 518–527 (2011)
27. Fukui, Y., Yamashita, T., Hishikawa, N., Kurata, T., Sato, K., Omote, Y., Kono, S., Yunoki, T., Kawahara, Y., Hatanaka, N.: Computerized touch-panel screening tests for detecting mild cognitive impairment and Alzheimer's disease. Intern. Med. **54**(8), 895–902 (2015)
28. Fischer, L., Oliveira, G., Osmari, D., Nedel, L.: Finding hidden objects in large 3D environments: the supermarket problem. In: Virtual Reality (SVR) XIII Symposium, pp. 79–88. IEEE (2011)
29. Santos Sousa, B., Dias, P., Pimentel, A., Baggerman, J.W., Ferreira, C., Silva, S., Madeira, J.: Head-mounted display versus desktop for 3D navigation in virtual reality: a user study. Multimedia Tools Appl. **41**(1), 161–181 (2009)
30. Smith, M.W., Sharit, J., Czaja, S.J.: Aging, motor control, and the performance of computer mouse tasks. Hum. Factors **41**, 389–396 (1999)
31. Wild, K., Mattek, N., Maxwell, S.A., Dodge, H.H., Jimison, H.B., Kaye, J.A.: Computer-related self-efficacy and anxiety in older adults with and without mild cognitive impairment. Alzheimer's Dement. **6**, 544–552 (2012)
32. Zickuhr, K., Madden, M.: Older adults and Internet use: For the first time, half of adults ages 65 and older are online. In: Pew Internet & American Life Project, Washington (2012)
33. Seelye, A., Hagler, S., Mattek, N., Howieson, D.B., Wild, K., Dodge, H.H., Kaye, J.A.: Computer mouse movement patterns: a potential marker of mild cognitive impairment. Alzheimer's Dement. Diagn. Assess. Dis. Monit. **1**, 472–480 (2015)

34. Chittaro, L., Ranon, R., Ieronutti, L.: VU-Flow: a visualization tool for analyzing navigation in virtual environments. IEEE Trans. Vis. Comput. Graphics **12**, 1475–1485 (2006)
35. Park, D.C.: The basic mechanisms accounting for age-related decline in cognitive function. Cognitive Aging: A Primer **11**, 3–19 (2000)
36. Esposito, F., Rochat, L., Van der Linda, A.-C.J., Lekeu, F., Quittre, A., Charnallet, A., Van der Linder, M.: Apathy and executive dysfunction in Alzheimer disease. Alzheimer Dis. Assoc. Disord. **24**, 131–137 (2010)
37. Burgess, P.W.: Real-world multitasking from a cognitive neuroscience perspective. In: Control of Cognitive Processes: Attention and Performance, pp. 465–472 (2000)
38. Vallejo, V., Wyss, P., Chesham, A., Mitache, A.V., Muri, R.M., Mosimann, U.P., Nef, T.: Evaluation of a new serious game based multitasking assessment tool for cognition and activities of daily living: Comparison with a real cooking task. Comput. Hum. Behav. **70**, 500–506 (2017)
39. Fortin, S., Godbout, L., Braun, C.M.J.: Cognitive structure of executive deficits in frontally lesioned head trauma patients performing activities of daily living. Cortex **39**, 273–291 (2003)

Recommender and Decision Support Systems

On Source Code Completion Assistants and the Need of a Context-Aware Approach

Fabio Villamarin Arrebola(✉) and Plinio Thomaz Aquino Junior

Centro Universitário da FEI – Fundação Educacional Inaciana Pe. Sabóia de Medeiros,
São Bernardo do Campo, Brazil
{fvarrebola,plinio.aquino}@fei.edu.br

Abstract. Source code completion assistance is a popular feature in modern IDEs. However, despite their popularity, there is little research about their key characteristics and limitations. There is also little research about the way software developers interact with code completion assistants, especially when considering the different techniques assistants use to populate the list of possible completions. This paper presents a study about the features of currently available code assistants and an experiment targeting professional Java developers familiar with the Eclipse platform that aims to collect and interpret usage data of two popular code completion assistants during the execution of three programming tasks. Results indicate that half the interactions with code assistants are either dismissed, interrupted or the completion proposals displayed have no direct contribution to the completion of the programming task. In that sense, we argue that code assistants still have a long road to pursue, since they seem to diminish the importance of the ultimate goals of the task at hand and also lack the ability of identifying and exploring the concepts of context-aware computing theory. The results of this paper can drive future HCI research to the design of adaptive code completion assistants that are able to respond to end user behaviors and preferences.

Keywords: Decision support systems · Evaluating information · Intelligent systems · Knowledge management

1 Introduction

Software practitioners consider that appropriate development tools play a major role in productivity [1, 2]. Such tools, which are often combined into Integrated Development Environments (IDEs), provide numerous features, and among them source code completion assistance is possibly the most prominent one. In fact, they gained so much popularity that it is safe to say that nowadays they are commonplace in modern IDEs. To support that claim, take the study [3] targeting the Eclipse platform – a popular IDE for the Java programming language. It observes that the source code completion assistant is the most executed command along with primary text editing commands like copy, paste and delete.

To this date all code completion assistants work essentially in the same way. Upon manual or automatic triggers they present to the software developer a list of possible

© Springer International Publishing AG 2017
S. Yamamoto (Ed.): HIMI 2017, Part II, LNCS 10274, pp. 191–201, 2017.
DOI: 10.1007/978-3-319-58524-6_17

suggestions given an input text. To do so they use a great variety of techniques that can be grouped into the lexical and semantic categories defined by [4], and while pure lexical assistants are now scarce possibly due to their simplicity, the literature regarding semantic alternatives is significant. It is easy to find alternatives like [5] and [6, 7], that provide a list of all the declarations that belong to a given type either in alphabetical order or according to some predefined statistical usage models. On the other hand, it is a little bit more challenging to find examples that offer features like method chaining [7, 8] and adaptive template completion [7], as well as sophisticated alternatives like [9, 10], that support a relaxed form of natural language input known as free-form queries[1]. Despite the alternative, code assistants provide an excellent tool to maximize source code composition speed [6]. But this is not their only contribution, and as [4, 11] observe, code assistants usage surpasses the faster typing goal and encompasses searching, exploring and correctness checking activities as well. Their importance is so evident that [11] points out that code assistants act as a real-time feedback system, and as such, software developers interpret failures in providing suggestions as an indication of erroneous source code.

However, despite their importance, there is little research about key characteristics and limitations of currently available code assistants. Additionally, there is little research about the way software developers interact with them. For that matter, determining how code completion assistants operate and how they influence the daily activities of software developers is crucial to drive future research on the topic, especially when considering the different techniques assistants use to populate the list of possible completions. With those statements in mind, the main goal of this paper is to highlight key characteristics and limitations of popular code assistants and to design and conduct an experiment with professional software developers. The experiment targets a very constrained environment that combines the Eclipse platform, the Java programming language and three fill-in-the-blanks programming tasks. It aims to collect and interpret usage data of popular semantic code completion assistants [5, 7] that differ in the approaches used to filter and sort the list of possible completions.

The results indicate that code assistants use a definition of context that is tightly coupled to source code structure. They also indicate that half of interactions with code assistants are either dismissed, interrupted or the completion proposals displayed have no direct contribution to the completion of the task at hand. These observations point out to the fact that semantic code assistants still have a long road to pursue, since they seem to diminish the importance of the ultimate goals of the task at hand and also lack the ability of identifying and exploring the concepts of context-aware computing theory [12, 13], especially considering qualities like the end user profile [14]. Additionally, results indicate that among participants code assistant [7] is the preferred choice over [5].

The contribution of this paper is twofold. First, there is a discussion about how code assistants operate and the design of an experiment that expands current literature regarding how code completion usage can be evaluated. Second, there are suggestions on how to improve code completion methods considering the key characteristics and

---

[1] Free-form queries can be defined as relaxed form of natural language input represented by a sentence of no more than ten words.

limitations of current alternatives and also exploring the concepts of context-aware computing theory. The results of this paper can drive future HCI (Human Computer Interaction) research to the design of adaptive code completion assistants that are able to respond to end user behaviors and preferences.

2   Related Work

For the purposes of this work related research can be divided in two categories. The first one comprises theoretical and empirical research aiming to highlight the overall importance and usage scenarios of code completion assistants. The second one considers the technical-driven research and the variety of distinct techniques used to populate the list of possible completions.

The empirical experiment [3] observes that code assistants are the most popular command used in the Eclipse IDE along with primary text editing commands like copy, paste and delete. This study measures the most frequent actions participants take while interacting with the IDE during ordinary programming sessions. However, as [4] observes, [3] presents no details about why and how code assistants are actually used. In that sense, [4] presents an experiment to evaluate four aspects of the interaction with code assistants, namely intentions, behaviors, breakdowns and recovery actions. It concludes through empirical evidence that software developers intentions mainly include faster typing and correctness checking. On the other hand, exploration activities are not that frequent as otherwise reported by [15], and this conflicting observation may be somehow related to the fact that the ultimate goal of [15] is to assess the usability implications of the presence of parameters in object constructor methods, and not to determine why code assistants are used. Indeed, [15] presents an interesting approach in tailoring their experiments using the systematic, pragmatic and opportunistic personas. Finally, [16] offers interest insights about the usability aspects of automatic completion, even though it is a study primarily designed to assess a search tool of an university library. This work suggests that automatic completion contributes to spell checking and general information search, as well as building confidence around unfamiliar topics and improving task execution speed.

The body of technical-driven research is quite vast, since it could safely embody pure code assistance literature and also a number of techniques primarily designed for the software synthesis domain [17, 18]. For the purposes of this work pure code assistance literature starts with [5] as the most basic form of semantic code completion. The code assistant [5] lists all the suggestions that match a given input while observing restrictions like code structure (e.g. suggestions differ if the assistant is invoked inside or outside a statement block), method and variable visibility and scope (e.g. suggestions exclude external, private and off-scope methods and variables) and so on. Once the list of suggestions is built it is sorted in alphabetical order. Eventually, the expected return type of an expression may precede the alphabetical sorting. Figure 1 illustrates both sorting scenarios regarding completion suggestions for type `java.nio.file.Files` of the Java standard API (Application Programming Interface).

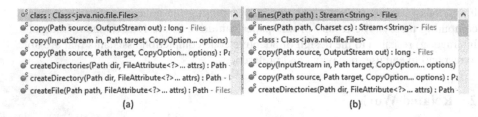

Fig. 1. Illustration of code completion assistant [5] and its (a) alphabetical and (b) expected type sorting features

Code Recommenders [7], which is often seen as a variant of [5], sorts suggestions according to predefined statistical usage models and also provides method chaining and adaptive template completion features. Figure 2 illustrates the statistical usage model filtering feature and the visual pointers it provides. It also illustrates the method chaining feature as an extension of the expected return type sorting of [5].

Fig. 2. Illustration of code completion assistant [7] and its (a) statistical usage model sorting and (b) method chaining features

Originally, [7] is the successor of [6], a work that is also worth mentioning due to two main reasons. First, it presents a comprehensive study of techniques that could improve code completion by mining information from large code bases. Second, it also presents a user study using questionnaires and interviews that observes that the subjective perception of the participants regarding speed improvements reaches 90%.

IntelliJ IDEA code assistant [8] is similar to the work of [7] with respect to the set of features it provides. A common feature between [5, 7] and also [8] is that they consider a definition of context that is tightly coupled to source code structure. The list of possible completions differ if the assistant is invoked inside or outside a statement block, and it also excludes external, private and off-scope methods and variables. Finally, the study [19] presents and evaluates a set of algorithms that suggest that source code change data history can improve the accuracy of code assistants.

Software synthesis research often cites [9] as an alternative in which a large database of sample source code is annotated with reference documentation information. The effectiveness of the approach is not only related to amount and quality of available data but also to the way the mapping between the user input and the annotated code base is performed. A more recent alternative is [10], which combines a handful of natural language processing techniques, like Part of Speech (POS) tagging, lemmatization, unigram declarations and Probabilistic Context-Free Grammar (PCFG) models. It considers that method signature information (e.g. method name and parameters names and types) and their eventual synonyms are the source of information upon which user input parsing occurs. Using static source code analysis techniques over a large dataset of training samples, the study [20] builds a N-gram language model and a Recurrent Neural Network (RNN) to support the intuition that the code completion problem can be reduced to predicting what would be the next statement given the nth previous ones.

In [21] the intuition is that some APIs (e.g. Java API) provide excellent documentation artifacts which are able to concisely describe their functionalities. After processing these artifacts, combining them into a map between keywords and their Abstract Syntax Tree (AST) primitives, and ultimately applying genetic programming algorithms, it is possible to mimic the same functionality that the original API provides. But the fact is that only a few APIs actually provide such useful documentation, and the technique heavily relies upon the manual definition of primitives, along with keywords-to-primitives mappings. SWIM [22] uses Q&A forums click-through data to build a probabilistic model between user queries and APIs, and this approach is in some sense a variation of [21]. Its ultimate goal is to map keywords and most frequent APIs to build what they call structured call sequences. And by doing so, it expands the capabilities of [10] in one of the first initiatives to produce code snippets with multiple statements. Domain Specific Languages (DSLs) and natural language descriptions [23] could also be cited since they are quite useful to enforce domain restrictions and thus reduce the search space.

3   Evaluating Code Assistants

The experiment this work presents targets the Eclipse platform and the Java programming language. It aims to collect and interpret usage information and the subjective impressions regarding two semantic code completion assistants that differ in the approaches used to filter and sort the list of possible completions. The first assistant is the longtime default option that ships with the Eclipse IDE [5] and it will thereon be simply called standard code assistant. It filters completions according to the restrictions of code structure and method and variable visibility and scope. In addition, it sorts completions alphabetically and eventually according to the expected return type of an expression. The second code assistant [7] will thereon be called intelligent code assistant. It is based on the work of [6] and it gained enough popularity to ship with the Eclipse IDE as well. It uses filtering approaches similar to [5] but instead of alphabetical sorting, it sorts completions according statistical usage models.

3.1   Participants

We studied 9 professional software developers. The average age was 29.2 years (range from 22 to 46), and among them 55.6% reported 4+ years of experience with the Java programming language. Additionally, 77.8% of them reported high (55.6%) to very high (22.2%) familiarity with Eclipse IDE, and 88.9% reported frequent (33.3%) to very frequent (55.6%) usage of code assistants features.

3.2   Environment

The experiment was designed to run in a custom distribution of Eclipse Java EE IDE for Web Developers version Neon 4.6.1 using the Java JDK 1.8.0_112. The distribution was customized in the sense it had two extended versions of the standard and the intelligent code assistants slightly modified to support event logging[2]. The events were recorded in log files and they included how many times the code assistant was invoked, how long it was active, the user input (if any) once the assistant was invoked and the eventual user choice.

3.3   Programming Tasks

Three programming tasks were designed to observe how software developers use code assistants. There was also a fourth task designed for practice purposes. All tasks considered the fill-in-the-blanks approach illustrated in Fig. 3, in which software developers should replace invalid or incomplete statements according to a set of given instructions. The open-question programming task format was refused since it could (in theory) maximize the overall task completion time for less experienced software developers.

```java
public static String encode(byte[] input) {

    if (input == null || Array.getLength(input) == 0) {
        throw new IllegalArgumentException();
    }
    // ********************************************************************************
    // * Find a method to get a Base64 encoder
    // ********************************************************************************
    // Once you find the right method, your statement will look like this:
    // (Please note that terms 'TYPE_OR_OBJECT' and 'METHOD' are to be replaced)
    //
    // Encoder encoder = TYPE_OR_OBJECT.METHOD;
    //
    // ********************************************************************************
    Encoder encoder = replaceMe_1;
```

Fig. 3. Illustration of a programming task fragment and the fill-in-the-blanks approach

Each programming task was represented as pair of Java classes: the main and the unit tests class. The main class had a general goal, which could be found in the comments section. The main class was incomplete as it presented at least two fill-in-blanks marks. The unit tests class was designed to assert whether the task was indeed complete without providing too detailed feedback as illustrated in Fig. 4.

---

[2] Supporting material can be found at https://github.com/fvarrebola/fei.

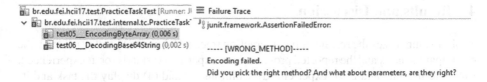

Fig. 4. Illustration of a programming task unit test and the feedback message

All programming tasks were designed to favor newly released APIs. The first task was designed to explore file handling features of the `java.nio` API introduced in Java 1.7. The second and third task were designed to explore `java.time` and `java.util` APIs and their date/time handling, streaming and functional programming features, all of them introduced in Java 1.8.

3.4 Procedure

Our experiment comprised three steps. The first one was a questionnaire designed to gather information on demographics and experience with the Java programming language and the Eclipse IDE. The second one comprised the actual programming tasks and it had an average duration of 90 min. The last one was a questionnaire designed to gather subjective impressions about the experiment, the programming tasks and also code assistants.

During the second step of the experiment participants were assigned at random to each programming task and each code completion assistant, and thus there was no proper balance. After disabling all remaining code assistants, a maximum adaptation period of 5 min was given so that the participant could read the instructions of the task at hand. Software developers were instructed to complete the main class of each programming task at their own pace using previous knowledge and also the features provided by the IDE. Since the main goal was to collect and observe how software developers use code assistants, participants were also instructed to avoid any form of external knowledge like search engines, Q&A forums and online source code samples. Finally, overall task completion time was recorded to facilitate data analysis.

3.5 Data Collection and Analysis

The second phase of the experiment resulted in 27 traces of interaction with code completion assistants. Each trace contained a set of events that indicated how many times the code assistant was invoked, how long it was active, the user input (if any) once the assistant was invoked and the eventual user choice. Traces were then parsed and grouped to provide insights about the average of displayed proposals per activation and the ratio between applied proposals and proposals that actually contribute to task completion.

4   Results and Discussion

Table 1 summarizes the results of the interaction traces. Columns (1) and (2) display the participant's index and the reported programming expertise (U stands for unexperienced, I for intermediate and E for experienced). Columns (3) and (4) display the task and its overall duration in seconds. Columns (5) and (6) display the code assistant (STD stands for standard and INT stands for intelligent) and how many times it was activated. Column (7) refers to the average display time of each code assistant. Column (8) displays the average number of proposals. Column (9) displays the ratio between applied proposals and the number of activations. Finally, column (10) displays the ratio of applied proposals that actually contribute to task completion.

Table 1.   Summary of interaction traces.

(1) Id	(2) Expertise	(3) Task	(4) Duration	(5) Assistant	(6) Activations	(7) Average display time	(8) Average proposals	(9) Applied proposals ratio	(10) Contributing proposals ratio
1	E	1	3511	STD	101	20.91	35.21	52.48%	18.87%
		2	2206	INT	40	30.73	37.38	45.00%	61.11%
		3	914	INT	22	19.91	49.00	54.55%	58.33%
2	I	1	503	INT	16	24.81	47.31	62.50%	70.00%
		2	691	INT	51	4.69	23.33	58.82%	63.33%
		3	225	STD	10	54.50	23.70	50.00%	80.00%
3	E	1	1539	STD	34	30.41	135.41	47.06%	43.75%
		2	2034	INT	57	14.98	59.05	45.61%	26.92%
		3	589	INT	13	35.08	46.08	46.15%	83.33%
4	E	1	1879	STD	116	12.21	72.95	34.48%	17.50%
		2	738	INT	51	9.71	70.96	43.14%	63.64%
		3	611	INT	34	14.97	29.74	29.41%	40.00%
5	E	1	664	INT	14	25.71	144.29	57.14%	87.50%
		2	2593	INT	86	20.30	52.01	51.16%	40.91%
		3	869	STD	25	28.04	108.88	60.00%	60.00%
6	I	1	6144	INT	194	17.29	52.07	43.30%	21.43%
		2	1930	STD	100	8.76	100.56	34.00%	38.24%
		3	471	INT	20	25.25	36.30	45.00%	55.56%
7	I	1	3749	INT	202	11.36	35.00	51.49%	21.15%
		2	1421	INT	66	7.85	40.41	56.06%	72.97%
		3	373	INT	19	7.63	38.63	52.63%	30.00%
8	U	1	2859	INT	88	13.90	51.06	68.18%	20.00%
		2	4066	INT	195	12.81	33.89	55.38%	44.44%
		3	1388	STD	56	11.50	116.39	71.43%	32.50%
9	E	1	3257	INT	103	16.40	67.86	56.31%	22.41%
		2	3232	STD	78	14.51	59.36	57.69%	48.89%
		3	890	INT	23	18.48	43.22	56.52%	30.77%
							AVERAGE	51.31%	46.43%
							STDEV	9.76%	21.50%

Discussion starts by stating that the experiment has a few shortcomings. First, it was designed to a single programming language and a single IDE. Second, it considered a very constrained scenario, in which participants were instructed to avoid any form of external knowledge like search engines, Q&A forums and online source code samples. Additionally, there is also the matter of the programming tasks, since they were not properly grouped according to complexity and they all targeted newly released APIs. In fact, during the third and final step of the experiment, 85.18% participants reported little (22.22%) to very little (62.96%) familiarity with the APIs involved. All these restrictions combined indicate that the scenario this experiment presents differs from ordinary activities performed by software developers. Finally, since programming tasks and code assistants were assigned at random, there was no proper balance between participants.

The high display time averages displayed on column (7) of Table 1 suggest that software developers intentions in constrained environments such as this experiment include exploration and documentation reading activities. The reason behind this observation may relate to a number of factors that include the quality of the information code assistants display, API usability characteristics as otherwise noted by [15], or simply lack of familiarity with APIs involved. For that matter, it is worth to note that participants reported subjective impressions that code assistants are not well suited for exploration activities, and once they are presented an unfamiliar task the tool of choice tends to be one of the many external forms of knowledge.

Discussion continues considering data displayed on columns (9) and (10). In this experiment, the average ratio of applied proposals is 51.31% (±9.76%). This ratio indicates the relation between the number of applied proposals and the number of code completion assistants activations. The average ratio of contributing proposals is a little lower at 46.43% (±21.5%). These numbers suggest that almost half of interactions with code assistants are either dismissed, interrupted or the proposals displayed have no direct contribution to the completion of the task at hand. However, additional criticism about this interpretation should also involve the actual user intentions behind each interaction, as otherwise reported by [4] and as noted during the interpretation of the average display time in column (7).

During the final questionnaire participants also reported overall satisfaction rates of 41.67% with respect to the standard assistant [5] and rates of 77.78% with respect to the intelligent assistant [7]. The reason behind this observation is possibly related to the subjective impressions of speed improvements as reported by [6], which are ultimately backed up by the sorting features based on predefined statistical usage models the intelligent assistant provide. Finally, participants observed that code assistants failed to provide adequate assistance for users that are unexperienced with the given programming language or that are unfamiliar with the task at hand or the APIs it involves.

5   Conclusion and Future Work

This paper presented the key characteristics and limitations of currently available code assistants and the design of an experiment aiming to collect and interpret code assistant completion usage data in three programming tasks. The experiment was conducted with 9 professional developers and the results indicate that half of interactions with code assistants are either dismissed, interrupted or the completion proposals displayed have no direct contribution to the completion of the task at hand. Results also indicate that among participates the intelligent code assistant [7] is the preferred choice over the standard alternative [5]. Additional observations also suggest that code assistants still have a long road to pursue. Since currently available alternatives use a definition of context that is tightly and exclusively coupled to code structure, they fail to explore high level qualities like the goals of the task hand, the end user role and his programming preferences.

Future work includes the design of a code assistant alternative that is able to infer the particular goals of the task at hand and to interact with end user to provide the most suitable completion suggestions. Future work also includes the design and conduction of longitudinal user studies that determine the actual influence code completion assistants play on task completion time. This type of study would likely require an alternative way to assert programming expertise as proposed by [24]. It would also require that tasks are grouped according to their complexity.

References

1. Trendowicz, A., Münch, J.: Factors influencing software development productivity – state-of-the-art and industrial experiences. In: Zelkowitz, M. (ed.) Advances in Computers, vol. 77, pp. 185–241. Springer, Heidelberg (2009). doi:10.1016/s0065-2458(09)01206-6
2. Paiva, E., Barbosa, D., Lima, R., Albuquerque, A.: Factors that influence the productivity of software developers in a developer view. In: Sobh, T., Elleithy, K. (eds.) Innovations in Computing Sciences and Software Engineering, pp. 99–104. Springer, Heidelberg (2010) doi: 10.1007/978-90-481-9112-3_17
3. Murphy, G., Kersten, M., Findlater, L.: How are Java software developers using the eclipse IDE? IEEE Softw. **23**(4), 76–83 (2006). IEEE, USA. doi:10.1109/ms.2006.105
4. Marasoiu, M., Church, L., Blackwell, A.: An empirical investigation of code completion usage by professional software developers. In: Coles, M., Ollis, G. (eds.) Proceedings of PPIG 2015, pp. 71–82 (2015)
5. Eclipse. http://www.eclipse.org. Accessed 16 Sept 2016
6. Bruch, M., Monperrus, M., Mezini, M.: Learning from examples to improve code completion systems. In: Vliet, H., Issarny, V. (eds.) Proceedings of the 7th Joint Meeting of the European Software Engineering Conference and the ACM SIGSOFT International Symposium on Foundations of Software Engineering, pp. 213–222. ACM, USA (2009). doi: 10.1145/1595696.1595728
7. Code Recommenders. http://www.eclipse.org/recommenders/. Accessed 16 Sept 2016
8. IntelliJ IDEA. https://www.jetbrains.com. Accessed 16 Sept 2016
9. Chatterjee, S., Juvekar, S., Sen, K.: SNIFF: a search engine for Java using free-form queries. In: Chechik, M., Wirsing, M. (eds.) FASE 2009. LNCS, vol. 5503, pp. 385–400. Springer, Heidelberg (2009). doi:10.1007/978-3-642-00593-0_26
10. Gvero, T.: Search Techniques for Code Generation. École Polytechnique Fédérale de Lausanne, Lausanne (2015)
11. Church, L., Nash, C., Blackwell, A.F.: Liveness in notation use: from music to programming. In: Lawrance, J., Bellamy, R. (eds.) Proceedings of PPIG 2010, pp. 2–11 (2010)
12. Schilit, B.N., Theimer, M.M.: Disseminating active map information to mobile hosts. IEEE Netw. Mag. Glob. Internetworking **8**(5), 22–32 (1994). IEEE Press, USA. doi: 10.1109/65.313011

13. Dey, A.K.: Understanding and using context. Pers. Ubiquit. Comput. **5**(1), 4–7 (2001). Springer. doi:10.1007/s007790170019
14. Aquino Junior, P.T.: PICaP: padrões e personas para expressão da diversidade de usuários no projeto de interação. Escola Politécnica da Universidade de São Paulo, São Paulo (2008). doi: 10.11606/T.3.2008.tde-15092008-144412
15. Stylos, J., Clarke, S.: Usability implications of requiring parameters in objects' constructors. In: 29th International Conference on Software Engineering, pp. 529–539. IEEE, USA (2007). doi:10.1109/icse.2007.92
16. Ward, D., Hahn, J., Feist, K.: Autocomplete as a research tool a study on providing search suggestions. Inf. Technol. Libr. **31**(4), 6–19 (2012). doi:10.6017/ital.v31i4.1930. Boston College University Libraries, USA
17. Gulwani, S.: Dimensions in program synthesis. In: Bloem, R., Sharygina, R. (eds.) Proceedings of 10th International Conference on Formal Methods in Computer-Aided Design, pp. 20–23. IEEE, Switzerland (2010). doi:10.1145/1836089.1836091
18. Bodik, R., Jobstmann, B.: Algorithmic program synthesis: introduction. Int. J. Softw. Tools Technol. Transf. **15**(5–6), 397–411 (2013). doi:10.1007/s10009-013-0287-9. Springer, Heidelberg
19. Robbes, R., Lanza, M.: How program history can improve code completion. In: 23rd IEEE/ACM International Conference on Automated Software Engineering, pp. 317–326. IEEE Computer Society (2008). doi:10.1109/ASE.2008.42
20. Raychev, V., Vechev, M., Yahav, E.: Code completion with statistical language models. In: O'Boyle, M., Pingali, K. (eds.) Proceedings of the 35th ACM SIGPLAN Conference on Programming Language Design and Implementation, pp. 419–428. ACM (2014). doi: 10.1145/2594291.2594321
21. Zhai, J., Huang, J., Ma, S., Zhang, X., Tan, L., Zhao, J., Qin, F.: Automatic model generation from documentation for Java API functions. In: Dillon, L., Visser, W., Williams, L. (eds.) Proceedings of the 38th International Conference on Software Engineering, pp. 380–391. ACM, USA (2016). doi:10.1145/2884781.2884881
22. Raghothaman, M., Wei, Y., Hamadi, Y.: SWIM: synthesizing what i mean: code search and idiomatic snippet synthesis. In: Dillon, L., Visser, W., Williams, L. (eds.) Proceedings of the 38th International Conference on Software Engineering, pp. 357–367. ACM, USA (2016). doi:10.1145/2884781.2884808
23. Aditya Desai, A., Gulwani, S., Hingorani, V., Jain, N., Karkare, A., Marron, M., Sailesh, R., Roy, S.: Program synthesis using natural language. In: Dillon, L., Visser, W., Williams, L. (eds.) Proceedings of the 38th International Conference on Software Engineering, pp. 345–356. ACM, USA (2016). doi:10.1145/2884781.2884808
24. Kuric, E., Bielikova, M.: Estimation of student's programming expertise. In: Proceedings of the 8th ACM/IEEE International Symposium on Empirical Software Engineering and Measurement. ACM, USA (2014). doi:10.1145/2652524.2652561

An Interactive Diagnostic Application
for Food Crop Irrigation

Nicolas Bain[(⊠)], Nithya Rajan[(⊠)], and Bruce Gooch[(⊠)]

Texas A&M University, College Station, TX, USA
{bain607,nrajan,goochq}@tamu.edu

Abstract. Agriculture is a major consumer of freshwater resources around the globe. This is especially true in Northern Texas and Oklahoma, where water withdrawl for agriculture purposes causes the continuous decline of aquifers. Information based irrigation management has the potential to conserve these vital resources. In this paper, we report on an interactive irrigation application that utilizes weather and LANDSAT data to calculate daily water needs for food crops. The work demonstrates that low-cost data can provide both basic, and advanced irrigation solutions via a web application.

Keywords: Irrigation · Food crops · Web-application · Water management

1 Introduction

As our population increases, so to does our production of food crops. This increase in demand for agriculture coincides with an increased demand for water resources. This has resulted in a continuous decline of aquifers, especially in Northern Texas and Oklahoma. Given the fact that our water resources are limited, it is in our best interest to allocate resources appropriately. Agriculture researchers have developed methods for more accurately determining irrigation needs, but these methods have previously been unavailable to the general public [4].

We report on an interactive web-application that is designed to put advanced irrigation tools into the hands of everyday farmers and crop scientists. We interviewed both types of users and found that they desired an application that was easy to use, quick in reporting results, and compatible with both computers and mobile devices. We also found that farmers generally don't want to input precise location data such as their address or map coordinates. On the other hand, crop scientists and plant breeders require the ability to input exact location data. We used this field study data to determine our design goals and process. The web-application was designed to be easily accessible to inexperienced web users and offers both basic, and advanced irrigation recommendations. The basic recommendations utilize location data limited to the user's zip code, whereas the advanced recommendation uses the exact latitude and longitude values for the user's field. To test and further develop our application, we implemented a user study that incorporated heuristic evaluation, application guidelines, cognitive walk-throughs, and usability testing. From this we were able to isolate and fix several issues, which ultimately lead to a streamlined, easy to use, widely accessible web-application.

© Springer International Publishing AG 2017
S. Yamamoto (Ed.): HIMI 2017, Part II, LNCS 10274, pp. 202–211, 2017.
DOI: 10.1007/978-3-319-58524-6_18

This paper is organized as follows: Sect. 2 introduces the system design, Sect. 3 describes the experimental setup, Sect. 4 is a discussion, and Sect. 5 examines the conclusions drawn from this work.

2   System Design

2.1   System Framework

To implement the system described above, we utilized Ruby on Rails™ (RoR). RoR is a web framework written in Ruby. It utilizes the model-view-controller (MVC) framework shown in Fig. 1. MVC offers Active Record database functionality, customizable web pages, and user interaction. RoR is exceptionally good for designing database-backed web applications due to its built in support the major database types. In our case, we chose to utilize PostgreSQL [1]. RoR is also open source software, which has resulted in community wide development of libraries. These libraries are collections of modules written in Ruby that can be easily incorporated into new or existing RoR applications. For example, our application utilizes geocoding and user authentication libraries to relieve some of the coding required while developing the application.

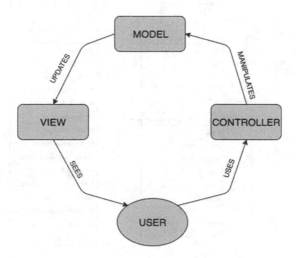

Fig. 1.   Model-view-controller framework.

2.2   Application Architecture

To describe the application architecture, we will begin with the database schema shown below in Fig. 2. There are four base models: crops, stations, Landsat, and users. Crops simply have a type (sorghum, cotton, or corn). However, each crop has a sub model associated with it called a KC coefficient. A KC coefficient is the ratio of evapotranspiration observed for a reference crop under similar conditions. There is a KC coefficient for each day of the crops growth. This is used in the irrigation recommendation calculations later down the line. There exists a station entry for each known station in Northern Texas. Every day these stations report on agriculture conditions for their area, which we have represented as the reading model. Daily readings can be found at the mesonet website for reference [2]. The Landsat model contains Landsat coverage metrics and their corresponding latitude and longitude values for Northern Texas. Last is the user model. This directly owns the farm and irrigation recommendation models, and indirectly owns the field model through the farm model. The user model contains standard user information such as username, email address, and an encrypted password. The farm model contains a farm name (to be easily recognizable), a zip code, the user ID of its owner, IDs of any associated fields, and the ID of the closest station. The closest station is found by performing a reverse geocode lookup using the provided zip code. Once a user has created a farm, they can begin creating fields. The field model contains a field name, the corresponding farm ID, a crop ID, the planting date, and an entry titled geometry, which is an instance of GeoJSON data. The final model is the irrigation recommendation. This model utilizes the reading, KC coefficient, and field (optional) models during its creation.

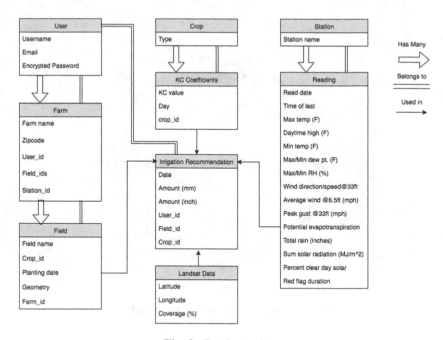

Fig. 2. Database schema

2.3   Application Flow

When utilizing the irrigation platform, users begin by creating an account. With an account, users can either generate a basic irrigation calculation, or create a farm and therein field for more accurate irrigation recommendations. Basic irrigation calculations take into account crop type, planting date, and the nearest station. The planting date and crop type can be selected through the use of a simple drop down menu, and the nearest station is found by performing a reverse geocode lookup using a user-entered zip code (this is the same way the farm model associates a station with itself). When the user has input the necessary parameters, they can generate an irrigation recommendation. This is done in the following manner: for every day since the planting date, grab the corresponding station reading and access its potential evapotranspiration value (in both mm and inches). Then grab the crop's KC value for the given day and multiply these two values. This gives irrigation recommendations in both mm and inches for every day since planting. These recommendations are presented to the user in an interactive

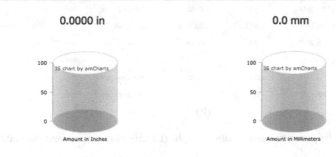

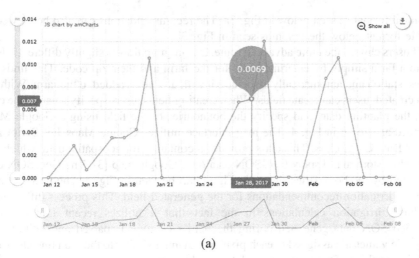

(a)

Fig. 3. (*continued*)

Past Irrigation Recommendations

Field	Date	Amount in	Amount mm	User			
Test	February 8th, 2017	0.0	0.0	test@email.com	Show	Edit	Destroy
Test	February 7th, 2017	0.0	0.0	test@email.com	Show	Edit	Destroy
Test	February 6th, 2017	0.0	0.0	test@email.com	Show	Edit	Destroy
Test	February 4th, 2017	0.0105	0.255	test@email.com	Show	Edit	Destroy
Test	February 3rd, 2017	0.0087	0.232	test@email.com	Show	Edit	Destroy
Test	February 1st, 2017	0.0	0.0	test@email.com	Show	Edit	Destroy
Test	January 31st, 2017	0.0	0.0	test@email.com	Show	Edit	Destroy
Test	January 30th, 2017	0.0	0.0	test@email.com	Show	Edit	Destroy
Test	January 29th, 2017	0.012	0.3	test@email.com	Show	Edit	Destroy
Test	January 28th, 2017	0.0069	0.1725	test@email.com	Show	Edit	Destroy
Test	January 27th, 2017	0.0066	0.176	test@email.com	Show	Edit	Destroy
Test	January 24th, 2017	0.0	0.0	test@email.com	Show	Edit	Destroy
Test	January 21st, 2017	0.0	0.0	test@email.com	Show	Edit	Destroy
Test	January 20th, 2017	0.0105	0.27	test@email.com	Show	Edit	Destroy
Test	January 19th, 2017	0.0042	0.105	test@email.com	Show	Edit	Destroy
Test	January 18th, 2017	0.0035	0.098	test@email.com	Show	Edit	Destroy
Test	January 17th, 2017	0.0035	0.091	test@email.com	Show	Edit	Destroy
Test	January 15th, 2017	0.0007	0.021	test@email.com	Show	Edit	Destroy
Test	January 14th, 2017	0.0028	0.07	test@email.com	Show	Edit	Destroy
Test	January 12th, 2017	0.0	0.0	test@email.com	Show	Edit	Destroy

(b)

Fig. 3. (a) Irrigation recommendation graph, (b) Irrigation recommendation table

graphical format as seen below in Fig. 3a. The recommendations can also be viewed in a table format below the graph as seen in Fig. 3b.

If users choose the more advanced route, the program flow is slightly different. Users create a farm simply by entering a title for the farm and their zip code. This finds the closest station and automatically associates it with any fields added to the farm. With the farm created, users can create fields. When creating fields, users specify a name, the crop type, the planting date, and specify the boundaries of the field using a Google Maps interface as shown in Fig. 4. The map interface utilizes Google Maps JavaScript API and its Data Layer class. This class provides a container for geospatial data, which can be used to store and display GeoJSON data on a Google map [3]. The GeoJSON data generated by the boundaries shown in Fig. 4 can be seen in Fig. 5. The user can now generate irrigation recommendations for the generated field. This process differs from the basic irrigation calculations in the fact that it utilizes recent Landsat data. The GeoJSON data generated during the field's creation is parsed and latitude and longitude values are assigned to each pixel in a manner similar to the scan line algorithm used in graphics. These latitude and longitude values are cross-referenced with the values stored in the Landsat model and the corresponding coverage values are pulled.

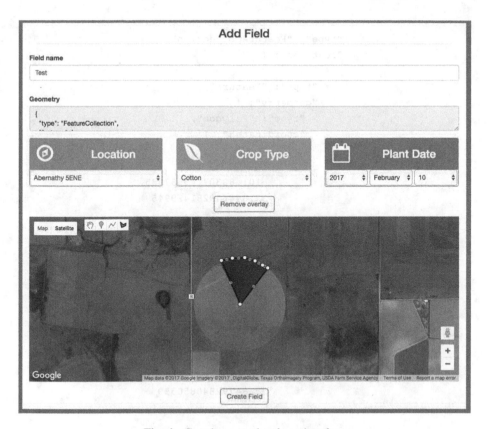

Fig. 4. Google maps data layer interface

These values, how they are determined, and how they are used to determine accurate KC values for the specified field, are outlined here [4]. Irrigation recommendations for every day since planting are generated and displayed for the user. These recommendations are displayed in the same manner as the basic irrigation calculations and can be seen in Fig. 3. Aside from the described pipeline, users can edit any farm or field, regenerate recommendations if necessary, view past recommendations, or delete old data.

3 User Study

Our irrigation tool was evaluated using heuristic evaluation, application guidelines, cognitive walkthroughs, and usability testing. In a heuristic evaluation, UI specialists study the interface in depth and look for properties that they know, from experience, will lead to usability problems. Our heuristic evaluators were skilled UI professionals, with advanced degrees and years of experience in evaluating digital interfaces. It was through their evaluation that we were able to simplify the UI design as much as possible before putting it into the hands of inexperienced testers. We went through

```
{
    "type": "FeatureCollection",
    "features": [
        {
            "type": "Feature",
            "geometry": {
                "type": "Polygon",
                "coordinates": [
                    [
                        [
                            -101.80307149887085,
                            33.844649281429945
                        ],
                        [
                            -101.8047022819519,
                            33.847750198310145
                        ],
                        [
                            -101.80311441421509,
                            33.84814226024592
                        ],
                        [
                            -101.8017840385437,
                            33.84792840850399
                        ],
                        [
                            -101.80049657821655,
                            33.8472868500664
                        ],
                        [
                            -101.80307149887085,
                            33.844649281429945
                        ]
                    ]
                ]
            },
            "properties": {}
        }
    ]
}
```

Fig. 5. GeoJSON data stored in geometry field of the field model

several UI design mock-ups before we were able to streamline the interface. We eventually settled upon a simple panel based UI and reduced necessary user input as much as possible. This went hand in hand with meeting our application's guidelines, which are listed below:

- The application must be compatible with both mobile and computer devices.
- The application must be easily accessible to inexperienced web users.
- The application must incorporate basic irrigation tools that limit the need for user input.
- The application must offer the option to use advanced irrigation calculation tools for users willing to input precise location data.

These guidelines were originally developed during our field study, where we met with crop scientists and farmers in order to determine what they would like to see in an online irrigation tool. We ensured that the application guidelines were met through the use of the cognitive walkthrough method and usability testing. The cognitive walkthrough method combines software walkthroughs with a cognitive model of learning through exploration [5, 6]. In this methodology, the developers of an interface walk through the application in the context of core tasks a typical user would need to accomplish. The respective actions and feedback from the interface are compared to the user goals and knowledge, and any discrepancies between the user's expectations and the steps required by the interface are documented.

For this evaluation we utilized professors of crop ecophysiology and precision agriculture from the agriculture departments at both Texas Tech University and Texas A&M University. Through this methodology we were able to identify a few issues early in development. The original map interface did not allow users to easily create a circular region. This is necessary as many crop fields are designed in a circular manner. We noted this and added in the functionality to lasso a section of the map by simply clicking a center point, and dragging to expand the radius of the circle. We also added the ability to pass in more parameters when creating a field. Crop scientists desired the ability to make notes pertaining to their field, which are unused in the irrigation calculations, but can help them with other analysis down the line.

Following the cognitive walkthrough testing, we moved on to usability testing. For this testing we used graduate agriculture students from Texas A&M. The usability testing was exceptional at finding recurring and general problems, and at avoiding low-priority problems. We found that occasionally, the map interface and other JavaScript elements would fail to load. This was actually two-pronged issue. The map interface was failing to load due to a new instantiation of the Turbolinks gem. This gem is a package for rails. "When you follow a link, Turbolinks automatically fetches the page, swaps in its <body>, and merges its <head>, all without incurring the cost of a full page load." [7] The gem's update included changes to function calls and had to be updated within our code. The other JavaScript elements that were failing were due to the use of an old build's navigation bar. To correct this, we removed the old Superfish navigation bar and replaced it with a custom designed bootstrap navigation bar. We also found that users desired an easy way to remove any drawing they had made on the map due to mistakes. To correct this, we simply added in a button that allowed for the removal of any overlay that had previously been drawn on.

4 Discussion

Dr. Rajan's previous work has shown that utilizing a KC value drawn from Landsat imagery is effective in estimating crop water usage [4]. She worked with the Texas Alliance for Water Conservation (TAWC) and its affiliates to test this. The team monitored three separate fields in three different conditions (fully irrigated, under irrigated, and dryland). Like our tool, they evaluated crop water usage from "standard weather observations from operational weather observing networks and readily available medium-resolution multispectral satellite imagery" (Landsat data). This is what allows the estimated crop water usage to be specific to an individual field, as opposed to the standard KC value approach which estimates crop evapotranspiration for a field in "standard conditions." These conditions are never met and certainly invariant from field to field. As Dr. Rajan noted in her paper, "The K_{sp} (KC value derived from using Landsat imagery and weather observations) is well-suited for operational applications such as irrigation scheduling, where its use could contribute to water conservation by minimizing over-irrigation" [4]. This is exactly what we aimed to do in creating this application. We think that one of the most important findings of our work is that software developers and agricultural specialists can easily work hand in hand to develop new-age tools for the agricultural work force. This is an ingenious way to incorporate emerging technologies with an older industry.

5 Conclusion

The irrigation scheduling application discussed throughout this paper has succeeded in placing new age irrigation science into the hands of everyday farmers. We were able to meet our design goals in both ease of access and efficiency. This resulted in a tool that is helpful to both inexperienced and power users. Farmers can utilize the basic irrigation tool while inputting minimal personal data whereas crop scientists and specialists can utilize the advanced tool for more accurate irrigation recommendations. As we continue to improve our tool and move it past the beta stage, it is our hope that this work will serve as a foundation for the development of interactive irrigation software in other agricultural heavy areas. This would result in decreased water usage and directly contribute to our ecological sustainability. We believe the development of this tool can also serve as a guideline for the implementation of additional agricultural research tools. There is a great deal of research that has been done, but has yet to make it into the hands of the public. Creating online tools to allow public access to such research would do wonders for the agricultural world.

References

1. www.rubyonrails.org. Last accessed 8 Feb 2017
2. http://www.mesonet.ttu.edu/Tech/1-output/climate.html. Last accessed 9 Feb 2017
3. https://developers.google.com/maps/documentation/javascript/datalayer. Last accessed 9 Feb 2017

4. Rajan, N., Maas, S.: Spectral crop coefficient for estimating crop water use. Adv. Remote Sens. **3**(3), 197–207 (2014)
5. Lewis, C., Polson, P.: Theory-based design for easily-learned interfaces. Hum. Comput. Interact. **5**(2–3), 191–220 (1990)
6. Lewis, C., Polson, P., Wharton, C., Rieman, J.: Testing a walkthrough methodology for theory-based design of walk-up-and-use interfaces. In: Proceedings of CHI 1990, Seattle, Washington, pp. 235–242. ACM, New York, 1–5 April 1990
7. https://github.com/turbolinks/turbolinks. Last accessed 9 Feb 2017

Wearable Computing Support for Objective Assessment of Function in Older Adults

Theodore Hauser[1], James Klein[1], Philip Coulomb[1], Sarah Lehman[1], Takehiko Yamaguchi[2], Tania Giovannetti[1], and Chiu C. Tan[1(✉)]

[1] Temple University, Philadelphia, USA
{tue69546,james.klein,tue49989,tug46038,tgio,cctan}@temple.edu
[2] Tokyo University of Science, Tokyo, Japan
tk-ymgch@te.noda.tus.ac.jp

Abstract. Naturalistic Action Test (NAT) is a diagnostic tool that involves a participant completing a common, everyday task under the observation of a trained clinician. The clinician can identify and quantify the severity of an individuals cognitive impairments based on the his or her actions while carrying out the task. Individuals with cognitive impairments have been shown to commit errors such as performing an incorrect sequence of steps when completing a task at greater rates than individuals without cognitive impairments. This paper describes our initial experiences in developing a wearable computing-based system to support NATs. The system's objective is to eventually help the clinician streamline the analysis of NATs by processing of the smartwatch collected sensor values to try and identify episodes that resemble errors.

Keywords: Wearable computing · Mild cognitive impairment · Naturalistic action test

1 Introduction

Managing the costs of dementia is a pressing problem facing many countries all around the world [29]. In the United States alone, there are an estimated 5.4 million Americans suffering from Alzheimer's Disease (AD), the most common cause of dementia today. The costs of managing AD is estimated to be as high as $236 billion dollars a year. This number is projected to continue to grow. By 2050, the number of AD sufferers is expected to reach to 13.8 million, and cost the country $1 trillion dollars [3]. Early detection of dementia can help patients, their families, and caregivers, better prepare for the disease to improve the overall quality of life [9,28]. The stage preceding dementia is termed *mild cognitive impairment* (MCI) [22]. Since age is the greatest risk factor for developing dementia, making screening of MCI more accessible to the larger older adult population is a priority.

The current approach for diagnosing dementia and MCI relies on accurate characterization of everyday functioning. Currently, self-reported and family-reported questionnaires are used to identify functional ability [15,19].

© Springer International Publishing AG 2017
S. Yamamoto (Ed.): HIMI 2017, Part II, LNCS 10274, pp. 212–222, 2017.
DOI: 10.1007/978-3-319-58524-6_19

Questionnaires have numerous advantages, including efficiency and low cost. However, they also have numerous drawbacks. Questionnaire data reflect ones appraisal of his/her ability to perform daily activities in the natural context. Limited insight, bias, and/or cognitive dysfunction may compromise the validity of self-reports [24,31]); consequently, caregiver-reports are generally preferred. However, some adults are not comfortable asking a relative to report on their functioning and many do not have a knowledgeable or healthy informant. As of 2014, over a quarter (28%) of non-institutionalized adults over age 65 live alone and the proportion of elders living alone increases with advanced age when functional difficulties may be more likely to emerge (e.g., 46% of women aged 75 and over lived alone). Even older adults who live with a close family member may not be observed when performing daily activities, particularly when functional difficulties are mild and do not disrupt independence. Additionally, older adults differ in their current and past daily routines, which may be problematic when assessing functioning with questionnaires. For example, a person who typically performs only a few simple tasks (e.g., making a sandwich for one person) throughout the day may be judged by an informant to be less impaired than a person who consistently is required to perform more complex tasks (e.g., preparing a full-course meal for a large family).

Performance-based tests address some of the drawbacks of questionnaires by recording participant behaviors while they perform standardized daily tasks in the laboratory [17]. The major limitation of performance-based tests is that they are time-consuming and require extensive training to score to identify subtle difficulties. This paper describes our initial experiences in developing a wearable computing-based system to address the limitation of the NAT and other performance-based tests. Our system consists of three components: (1) a smartwatch that collects and synchronizes the accelerometer and gyroscope data with the captured video; (2) a video annotation system that allows the clinicians to record notes while viewing the captured video; and (3) an analytical toolkit to sift through the sensor readings and identify features based on clinician-supplied input parameters. Our objective is to eventually help the clinician streamline the analysis of NATs by processing of the smartwatch collected sensor values to try and identify episodes that resemble errors.

2 Related Work

The popularity of smartphones and smartwatches has led to a new approach for monitoring human activity. These devices come with sensors that can detect, among other things, ambient light, acceleration, orientation, and so on. While these sensors cannot directly determine *what* the user is doing, there has been considerable research into algorithms that make use of these sensor data to *infer* human activity [2,14,18]. Most of existing work focused on recognizing common physical human activities like walking, jogging, biking, etc. [6,7,13,16,25]. More recent research has considered recognizing more complex human activities like eating [11,27] and smoking [23]. Our work differs from existing research in that

Fig. 1. Photograph of participant performing the NAT (breakfast preparation task). The left picture shows the start of the task. Note the presence of distractor objects (ice-cream scoop, paint brush, and salt shaker) found on the table. The right picture is the participant using his dominant arm to reach for the coffee. Participants are instructed to use their dominant arm as much as possible while carrying out the task.

we focus on identifying errors rather than activities. Compared to activities, e.g. walking, errors are more difficult to quantify, and are more personalized.

Another related area of research is the use of cameras to infer human activity [5,20,21]. Rather than infer human activities using sensors, this approach uses the captured camera images to classify human activities algorithmically. More recent work in this area has expanded beyond traditional cameras, towards using 3D cameras like the Microsoft Kinect, which can capture additional depth information [8,30]. We avoided using cameras for detection because of the lack of flexibility. The advantage of wearable devices is that they can be carried or worn unobtrusively on the person virtually all the time. This is unlike camera-based systems which can only record activities in a specific physical space.

Ubiquitous computing systems approach towards human activity recognition is a holistic approach that integrates different types of sensors and cameras together [1,10,12]. Work on "smart table" systems [4,26,32], for instance, which are used to track diet, can be also be repositioned to monitor the NATs. However, ubiquitous computing systems often require embedding sensors directly into the environment, which is expensive to deploy in practice. Our approach, on the other hand, uses consumer wearable devices like a smartwatch, which is readily available.

3   Background

The NAT is a standardized, performance-based measure of everyday functioning that requires participants to complete common tasks of increasing complexity with little guidance from the examiner. The clinician can identify and quantify the severity of a participants cognitive impairments based on the his or her

Table 1. Summary of errors used in NAT analysis

Overt errors	Omission errors: steps required to complete a task are not performed. E.g. does not add coffee grounds to coffee
	Commission errors: – Substitution: A similar, alternate object is used in place of target object to complete a task. E.g. spreads butter on toast with spoon instead of knife – Sequence: Anticipation of a step; steps or subtasks performed in reverse order. E.g. applies butter on bread without toasting – Perseveration: A step is performed more than once or for an excessive amount of time. E.g. adds butter/jelly repeatedly to toast
	Action-addition errors: The performance of an action not readily interpreted as a task step. E.g. puts toast in creamer
Micro errors	Initiating and terminating an incorrect action before the error is completed; picking up an incorrect item; initiating but not completing a behavior that is dissonant with the task goal. E.g. picks up garden shears instead of scissors, but never uses the garden shear to cut the wrapping paper

actions while carrying out the task. Participants with cognitive impairments have been shown to commit more errors while competing the NAT compared to participants without cognitive impairment. A wide range of error types have been reported and include overt errors, such as inaccurate task sequencing, use of distractor objects, and omissions of task steps. In people with more mild cognitive impairment micro-errors have been observed and shown to correlate with performance on cognitive tests. Micro-errors are more subtle than overt errors and include misreaching toward distractor objects and hesitations before reaching to target objects (see Table 1).

An example of a NAT task is to pack a lunch bag with the necessary objects (e.g., thermos lids) and distracting objects (e.g., spatula) distributed evenly on a large table. Figure 1 is a picture of a participant performing a breakfast preparation task involving making toast and coffee. A typical NAT session will involve the participant sitting at a table with the necessarily objects to complete the task, as well as additional objects to serve a distractors. For example, a coffee making task will include the coffee powder, milk, sugar, etc. within arms reach on the table, as well distractor objects like a salt shaker, a spatula, etc. that are not part of completing the task. The participant is told to complete the task by the clinician ahead of time. The complete instructions is shown in Fig. 2. The entire task is recorded on video for later analysis to evaluate the participants performance.

The NAT video is scored by trained coders blind to participant details (e.g., group membership, test scores, etc.). The video is scored for overt errors and micro-errors using standard scoring procedures. Scoring procedures focus on cognitive failures during the task and do not penalize participants for clumsiness or

Instructions for Conducting Lunch Task NAT

The following 10 points are read out verbatim to the participant.

1. I would like you to pack a lunch box. The lunch is for someone who wants a peanut butter and jelly sandwich, a snack, and a drink.

2. Can you repeat what you need to do? [*repeat the instructions for the participant until the participant shows that he/she understands the task instructions.*]

3. Now that you understand the task, you do not need to talk though the task. Remain silent and focus on what you are doing.

4. Do not touch or move any of the objects until you are ready to use them. Make your movements clear and precise.

5. Keep your hand at this resting position when you are not working with the objects. If **you need to think about what you're doing, place your hand back at the rest position** before you do the next step.

6. Do not use your non-dominant hand to do the steps of the task. We have put the bright bracelet on your non-dominant hand as a reminder for you not to use it. You may use the non-dominant hand to stabilize objects as you use them. For example, you may need to use it to stabilize a jar or the bread. But, do not use it to do meaningful task steps.

7. I will be timing you, so work as quickly as you can without making mistakes.

8. **Last, touch the "QUIT button" at the top right when you are finished working.**

9. Can you repeat the task rules? [*repeat the instructions for the participant until the participant shows that he/she understands the task instructions*]

10. Great. Go ahead and pack a peanut butter and jelly sandwich, a snack, and a drink.

Fig. 2. Verbal instructions to participant.

poor dexterity. Overt errors are grouped according to a widely published taxonomy that includes omissions, commissions, and action additions. Micro-errors include imprecise actions that do not reach the level of overt error. Table 1 summarizes these overt and micro-errors.

A key advantage of using NATs is that the tasks are sufficiently commonplace to be familiar to people across different socio-economic backgrounds, thus allowing a well-developed NAT to be used for a wide range of participants. However, the entire analysis process is both time consuming and labor intensive. Each video needs to be reviewed by multiple trained scorers, who then need to arrive at a consensus on the outcomes. Our system seeks to simplify this process through the use of smartwatch and analytical toolkit.

4   System Design

Our system consists of three components: a smartwatch component to collect the accelerometer and gyroscope orientation information; a video annotation program to facilitate the annotation and segmentation of the videos, and an analytical toolkit to process the resulting data.

4.1 NAT Workflow with Wearables

At the start of the experiment, the examiner will synchronize smartwatch and video recorder to the wall-clock time. The participant will be instructed to wear the smartwatch on his dominant wrist throughout the duration of the task. We also placed a brightly colored bracelet on the non-dominate hand with the words "DO NOT USE" printed on it to remind the participant not to use the non-dominant hand. The NAT was initially designed for stroke populations and was developed to be completed using only one hand in an attempt to accommodate people with hemiparesis following stroke. At the end of the experiment, the data from the smartwatch is extracted and archived.

The video annotation program is used to help divide a NAT task into small sub-tasks. Figure 3 illustrates the division of the breakfast preparation task into smaller sub-tasks. The coders will use the video annotation program to identify the start and end times for each sub-task. Since both the recorded video footage and smartwatch are synchronized to wall-clock time at the beginning of the experiment, we can associate each sub-task with the corresponding accelerometer and gyroscope data for the duration of that sub-task. This annotated date is fed into the analytical toolkit for later analysis.

The analytical toolkit uses the smartwatch data to identify videos, or segments of videos, that are suggestive of errors. The toolkit allows the coder to specify parameters to identify segments of interest. Figure 4 shows an example of the configuration file where the coder wants to determine the number of pauses, and the length of each pause, that occurred within each sub-task. The output

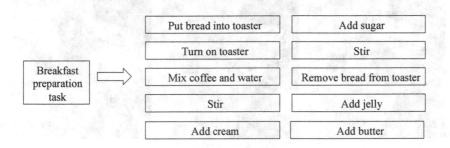

Fig. 3. Division of breakfast preparation task into sub-tasks.

| User Name | Data File Path | Subtasks | Type of analysis |

```
● ● ●                              config.txt ⌄
{Username = mc; File = /data/Breakfast1.csv ; Task = all; Analysis = Pause:2.5:2}
```

Fig. 4. Example of configuration file for the analytical toolkit.

also includes the timestamp of the video segments that correspond to each pause event so that the coder can return to the original video to review as needed.

4.2 Associating Smartwatch Data with Errors

Rather than attempting to match the accelerometer and gyroscope data with the errors listed in Table 1. Instead, our approach is to identify features that are suggestive of errors. To better understand errors and how they related to smartwatch data, we examined the collected videos to determine possible features which can be identified from the smartwatch data.

Figure 5 shows several frames of a video segment of a participant with MCI performing the NAT lunch sub-task of putting jelly onto toast. In Fig. 5(a) the participant is adding jelly to the toast, in (b) he places the knife down on the plate, and in (c) he starts to reach towards the jelly jar. This action was coded as a micro-error, because as shown in (d), even before touching the jelly jar, the

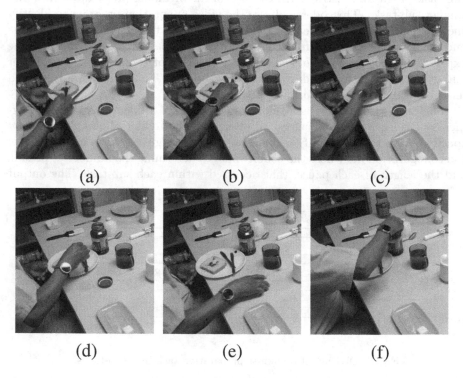

Fig. 5. Example of a micro-error from the "Add Jelly" subtask. Part (a) shows the participant adding jelly to the bread. In part (b), the participant is done with adding jelly and the next step is to replace the cap onto the jelly jar to complete the subtask. Part (c) shows the participant's hand reaching towards (but not touching) the jelly jar instead of the cap, and part (d) shows the participant quickly withdrawing his arm when he realizes this is a mistake. Parts (e) and (f) shows the participant performing the correct action of picking up the cap and placing it onto the jelly jar.

participant quickly redirects his reach towards the jelly jar lid. In (f), he places the lid onto the jelly jar. The micro-error depicted in (c) is characterized by a sudden and sharp arm movement from one object to another. From our preliminary observations of videos of participants with and without MCI performing NATs, we have identified two features that might be indicative of micro-errors. A micro-error is an imprecise action that do not reach the level of overt error, as described in Table 1.

The first are *pauses* where the participant's hand remains stationary in the air in the middle of completing a task. This could indicate a participant's hesitancy about the completing a sub-task, i.e. does salt or sugar go with coffee. The mobility of the arm can be measured by computing the magnitude of the x, y, and z-axis of the accelerometer, $\sqrt{x^2 + y^2 + z^2}$. A pause is a consecutive period of time where the arm remains static. This is determined by whether the magnitude of the accelerometer data is within a user-specified threshold value τ, i.e. $\sqrt{x^2 + y^2 + z^2} < \tau$.

The second feature is the presence of *sudden movements*, where the participant's hand moves accelerates in the same or opposite direction. This could indicate instances where the participant realizes a mistake before completing an action, e.g. initially reaching for the ice-cream scoop (instead of the spoon), but self-corrects before actually touching the ice-cream scoop. We determine a sudden movement when either consecutive x or y-axis accelerator values are larger than a user-supplied threshold value. We do not consider the z-axis values because a fast downward movement may be common when picking up objects.

4.3   Preliminary Results and Discussion

We tested our system on two older adults, OA2 and OA7, performing the lunch task NAT. One of the older adults (OA2) has mild cognitive impairment (MCI), whereas the other (OA7) does not. Figure 6 shows the demographics of the two older adults, as well as the differences in pauses and sudden movements based on the smartphone data. The Mini Mental Status Exam (MMSE) is a test of global cognitive status given to the older adults. Both OA2 and OA7 performed within the healthy range on this task. The Functional Assessment Questionnaire (FAQ) is a self-reported measure of functioning. A higher score indicates more functional problems. Both older adults performed within the normal range on the FAQ.

As shown in Fig. 6, the results of human error coding showed that the older adult with MCI committed 1 overt error and 9 micro-errors, whereas the healthy older adult made no overt or micro-errors. Data from the watch reveled that the older adult with MCI had approximately 50% more pauses than the healthy older adult, as well as 17% more sudden movements. The threshold for pauses and sudden movements is a magnitude of 1.0 and difference of acceleration of 0.5 m/s respectively.

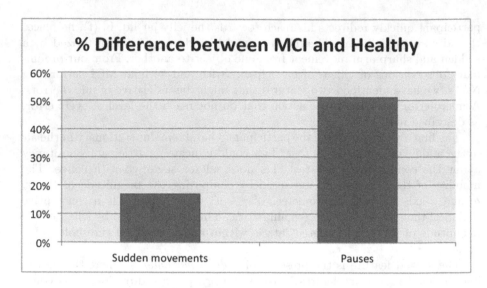

Fig. 6. Preliminary results from smartphone data.

Our preliminary findings indicate that the smartwatch can capture data from a NAT that can be indicative of MCI. However, we also identified two open issues. The first issue is the need to develop methods to individualized parameters and thresholds in the toolkit. Older adults differ in speed and dexterity of their physical movements, which may not be directly related to their cognitive abilities. However, the features of sudden movements and pauses are sensitive to these physical differences. One of our future aims is to explore ways of adjusting the parameters based on participant's physical capabilities. One approach is to include a profiling stage into the NAT to capture sufficient data to adjust the parameters. Another open issue is to identify a better method for accurately identifying episodes of overt and micro-errors. From Fig. 2, we see that the instructions to the participant's are fairly generic. This means that participants' arm movements may differ because they are completing a subtask differently than other older adults (e.g., adding two scoops of sugar rather than just one). Such individual differences may not be indicative of any difference in cognitive state. One approach we are considering is a finer-grain approach that examine a few specific sub-tasks, rather than the entire NAT trace, to identify errors.

5   Conclusion

Early detection of dementia is an important problem for many countries, especially countries with an aging population. Current methods of detection are not scalable to large population. This paper describes a system that uses consumer smartwatches to capture data from NATs to facilitate the identification of MCI among older adults. Preliminary experiments indicate that the approach is promising.

References

1. Alemdar, H., Ersoy, C.: Wireless sensor networks for healthcare: a survey. Comput. Netw. **54**(15), 2688–2710 (2010)
2. Anguita, D., Ghio, A., Oneto, L., Parra, X., Reyes-Ortiz, J.L.: Human activity recognition on smartphones using a multiclass hardware-friendly support vector machine. In: Bravo, J., Hervás, R., Rodríguez, M. (eds.) IWAAL 2012. LNCS, vol. 7657, pp. 216–223. Springer, Heidelberg (2012). doi:10.1007/978-3-642-35395-6_30
3. Alzheimer's Association, et al.: 2016 Alzheimer's disease facts and figures. Alzheimer's Dement. **12**(4), 459–509 (2016)
4. Chang, K., Liu, S., Chu, H., Hsu, J.Y., Chen, C., Lin, T., Chen, C., Huang, P.: The diet-aware dining table: observing dietary behaviors over a tabletop surface. In: Fishkin, K.P., Schiele, B., Nixon, P., Quigley, A. (eds.) Pervasive 2006. LNCS, vol. 3968, pp. 366–382. Springer, Heidelberg (2006). doi:10.1007/11748625_23
5. Chen, L., Wei, H., Ferryman, J.: A survey of human motion analysis using depth imagery. Pattern Recogn. Lett. **34**(15), 1995–2006 (2013)
6. Cho, Y., Nam, Y., Choi, Y.-J., Cho, W.-D.: Smartbuckle: human activity recognition using a 3-axis accelerometer and a wearable camera. In: Proceedings of the 2nd International Workshop on Systems and Networking Support for Health Care and Assisted Living Environments, p. 7. ACM (2008)
7. Choudhury, T., Consolvo, S., Harrison, B., Hightower, J., LaMarca, A., LeGrand, L., Rahimi, A., Rea, A., Bordello, G., Hemingway, B., et al.: The mobile sensing platform: an embedded activity recognition system. IEEE Pervasive Comput. **7**(2), 32–41 (2008)
8. Girshick, R., Shotton, J., Kohli, P., Criminisi, A., Fitzgibbon, A.: Efficient regression of general-activity human poses from depth images. In: IEEE International Conference on Computer Vision (ICCV), pp. 415–422. IEEE (2011)
9. Grossberg, G.T., Christensen, D.D., Griffith, P.A., Kerwin, D.R., Hunt, G., Hall, E.J.: The art of sharing the diagnosis, management of Alzheimer's disease with patients, caregivers: recommendations of an expert consensus panel. Prim. Care Companion J. Clin. Psychiatry, **12**(1) (2010)
10. Intille, S.S.: A new research challenge: persuasive technology to motivate healthy aging. IEEE Trans. Inf. Technol. Biomed. **8**(3), 235–237 (2004)
11. Kalantarian, H., Sarrafzadeh, M.: Audio-based detection and evaluation of eating behavior using the smartwatch platform. Comput. Biol. Med. **65**, 1–9 (2015)
12. Korhonen, I., Parkka, J., Van Gils, M.: Health monitoring in the home of the future. IEEE Eng. Med. Biol. Mag. **22**(3), 66–73 (2003)
13. Kwapisz, J.R., Weiss, G.M., Moore, S.A.: Activity recognition using cell phone accelerometers. ACM SigKDD Explor. Newsl. **12**(2), 74–82 (2011)
14. Lara, O.D., Labrador, M.A.: A survey on human activity recognition using wearable sensors. IEEE Commun. Surv. Tutorials **15**(3), 1192–1209 (2013)
15. Lawton, M.P., Brody, E.M.: Assessment of older people: self-maintaining and instrumental activities of daily living. Nurs. Res. **19**(3), 278 (1970)
16. Long, X., Yin, B., Aarts, R.M.: Single-accelerometer-based daily physical activity classification. In: Annual International Conference of the IEEE Engineering in Medicine and Biology Society, EMBC, pp. 6107–6110. IEEE (2009)
17. Moore, D.J., Palmer, B.W., Patterson, T.L., Jeste, D.V.: A review of performance-based measures of functional living skills. J. Psychiatric Res. **41**(1), 97–118 (2007)
18. Mukhopadhyay, S.C.: Wearable sensors for human activity monitoring: a review. IEEE Sens. J. **15**(3), 1321–1330 (2015)

19. Pfeffer, R.I., Kurosaki, T.T., Harrah, C.H., Chance, J.M., Filos, S.: Measurement of functional activities in older adults in the community. J. Gerontol. **37**(3), 323–329 (1982)
20. Popoola, O.P., Wang, K.: Video-based abnormal human behavior recognition - a review. IEEE Trans. Syst. Man Cybern. Part C (Appl. Rev.) **42**(6), 865–878 (2012)
21. Poppe, R.: A survey on vision-based human action recognition. Image Vis. Comput. **28**(6), 976–990 (2010)
22. Roberts, R., Knopman, D.S.: Classification and epidemiology of MCI. Clin. Geriatr. Med. **29**(4), 753–772 (2013)
23. Saleheen, N., Ali, A.A., Hossain, S.M., Sarker, H., Chatterjee, S., Marlin, B., Ertin, E., al'Absi, M., Kumar, S.: Puffmarker: a multi-sensor approach for pinpointing the timing of first lapse in smoking cessation. In: Proceedings of the ACM International Joint Conference on Pervasive and Ubiquitous Computing, pp. 999–1010. ACM (2015)
24. Sands, L.P., Ferreira, P., Stewart, A.L., Brod, M., Yaffe, K.: What explains differences between dementia patients' and their caregivers' ratings of patients' quality of life? Am. J. Geriatr. Psychiatry **12**(3), 272–280 (2004)
25. Shoaib, M., Bosch, S., Incel, O.D., Scholten, H., Havinga, P.J.: Fusion of smartphone motion sensors for physical activity recognition. Sensors **14**(6), 10146–10176 (2014)
26. Steurer, P., Srivastava, M.B.: System design of smart table. In: Proceedings of the First IEEE International Conference on Pervasive Computing and Communications, (PerCom), pp. 473–480. IEEE (2003)
27. Thomaz, E., Essa, I., Abowd, G.D.: A practical approach for recognizing eating moments with wrist-mounted inertial sensing. In: Proceedings of the ACM International Joint Conference on Pervasive and Ubiquitous Computing, pp. 1029–1040. ACM (2015)
28. Vickrey, B.G., Mittman, B.S., Connor, K.I., Pearson, M.L., Della, R.D., Penna, T.G., Ganiats, R.W., DeMonte, J.C., Cui, X., Vassar, S., et al.: The effect of a disease management intervention on quality and outcomes of dementia carea randomized, controlled trial. Ann. Intern. Med. **145**(10), 713–726 (2006)
29. Wimo, A., Jönsson, L., Bond, J., Prince, M., Winblad, B., Alzheimer Disease International: The worldwide economic impact of dementia 2010. Alzheimer's Dement. **9**(1), 1–11 (2013)
30. Xia, L., Aggarwal, J.K.: Spatio-temporal depth cuboid similarity feature for activity recognition using depth camera. In: Proceedings of the IEEE Conference on Computer Vision and Pattern Recognition, pp. 2834–2841 (2013)
31. Zanetti, O., Geroldi, C., Frisoni, G.B., Bianchetti, A., Trabucchi, M.: Contrasting results between caregiver's report and direct assessment of activities of daily living in patients affected by mild and very mild dementia: the contribution of the caregiver's personal characteristics. J. Am. Geriatr. Soc. **47**(2), 196–202 (1999)
32. Zhou, B., Cheng, J., Sundholm, M., Reiss, A., Huang, W., Amft, O., Lukowicz, P.: Smart table surface: a novel approach to pervasive dining monitoring. In: IEEE International Conference on Pervasive Computing and Communications (PerCom), pp. 155–162. IEEE (2015)

Introducing a Decision Making Framework to Help Users Detect, Evaluate, Assess, and Recommend (DEAR) Action Within Complex Sociotechnical Environments

Ryan A. Kirk[1(✉)] and Dave A. Kirk[2]

[1] Kirk Enterprises, LLC, Seattle, USA
info@ryankirk.info
[2] Consul Pack, Inc., Minneapolis, USA
dave.kirk1@comcast.net

Abstract. As causality becomes non-linear, data-driven decision making becomes challenging because traditional Decision Support Systems (DSSs) do not support these environments. Existing analytical methods struggle in complex environments where variables that interact with each other as well as themselves. DEAR is a new framework that supports complex decision making. This framework performs change detection, evaluates causal relationships and interactions, assesses the risk of known interventions, and recommends action using a guided exploration strategy that blends historically successful solutions with possible alternatives.

Fear of viral outbreaks drove the need for public policy to mitigate mosquito populations in Columbus, OH. Through monitoring environmental variables, this approach detected changes in precipitation and temperature. Using CCM to assess causality, this approach determined that temperature was the primary driver of the complex mosquito population ecosystem. It determined the probability that mosquito populations would also rise. Through forming a risk assessment based upon the historic success of mosquito control systems, this approach is able to offer real-time guidance as to which vector-based mitigation strategy to pursue.

Keywords: Causality · Decision-making · Decision support systems · DSS · Complex systems · Causal inference · Vector-based transmission · Disease · Viruses · Zika · West nile virus · Mosquitoes

1 Introduction

This paper will discuss the ongoing development of the DEAR decision making framework intended to facilitate decision making amidst complex and uncertain environments. Systems are becoming increasingly interactive. The feedback from one set of decisions becomes input for another. These problems span different industries such as: web-based advertising, automated investing techniques, real-time user recommendations, industrial processes, etc. When it comes to facilitating decision making using Decision Support Systems (DSSs) most techniques assume that the input data is neither complex or non-linear [1, 2]. As data becomes increasingly novel, voluminous, and complex and as

© Springer International Publishing AG 2017
S. Yamamoto (Ed.): HIMI 2017, Part II, LNCS 10274, pp. 223–239, 2017.
DOI: 10.1007/978-3-319-58524-6_20

feedback becomes increasingly common within online systems, researchers and practitioners need techniques to help users to confidently take action. Through incorporating a technique for complex causal inference, and through incorporating risk mitigation recommendations into a DSS, this research aims to help extend the usefulness of DSSs to these modern data domains.

Beneath the concerns about facilitating decision-making in complex systems is the challenge that comes with supporting causal inference and risk assessment. A technique called Convergent Cross-Mapping (CCM) allows for causal analysis amidst non-linear systems [3, 4]. The authors have already applied this technique to novel domains and have extended the scalability of this technique so that it can apply to larger data sets [5, 6]. The authors have also used Kelly's equations to govern the optimal level of action to take in a given environment given the desired level of risk. Through using a combination of these two techniques, the authors propose a DEAR framework that allows the creation of DSSs to support inference in non-linear systems.

This paper will first discuss some background information related to DSSs, non-linear systems, decision-making loops, and to CCM. Then it will define the problem and recommend the DEAR approach as a solution. It will discuss how this framework helps solve problems and it will present an example use case. Finally, it will discuss the results of the application of this framework to that use case and will summarize the next steps related to further refining this set of ideas.

1.1 Decision Support Systems

There are several primary ways that DSSs can facilitate decision making. First they can help to reduce cognitive load. Well known information visualization techniques allow users to quickly compare the differences in behavior of data defined concepts. For example, showing multiple line charts on the same chart can help the user spot changes both in individual and in groups of time series. Second, DSSs can support cognitive scaffolding through using language and page layouts to augment a users' ability to understand the relationship between data points. For example, an interface may include a language tree of terms related to the decision space. Third, DSSs can support attribution formation through helping users to form and evaluate hypotheses. This can be done through including information from multiple sources within a single chart. Finally, DSSs can support the decision making process when it guides a user from exploration to hypothesis formation, to evaluation, and ultimately towards action. While these four types of cognitive support are powerful, they have pronounced and limitations when applied to complex, non-linear domains.

The need for action recommendations. While DSSs often do a good job of providing context and at helping users compare alternative hypotheses, they typically end up leaving it to the user to figure out which decision to make [1, 7, 8]. Without clear support for considering the likely impacts and marginal contribution of specific sets of actions, DSSs force the user to guess which action type to take and how much of that action to engage. This can result in a lack of confidence in the decision, a decline in trust in the

DSS, and lack of adoption of the proposed solution. For this reason this paper proposes an approach to supporting decision making that helps guide actions.

The need for detection-oriented approaches. Another challenge facing DSSs is the number of variables present in many modern systems. This makes it challenging to visualize information and to support hypothesis generation and evaluation. For this reason, many DSS systems have recently begun incorporating machine-assisted qualities that will recommend areas of consideration. While this is a good first step, it does not scale well since the number of possible interactions is combinatorial. For this reason, this paper proposes an approach that helps minimize the computational effort required to form comparisons through limiting the number of possible combinations considered.

The need for concept learning. One of the reasons it could be hard to recommend an action is that there is limited or no historic data for actions and their success. However, in complex or non-linear environments, the user may encounter concepts or types of interactions that they have not seen before. Such concepts are novel and typically have no names. A limit of most modern DSS tools that utilize ontological scaffolding is that it requires both the knowledge of a comprehensive domain and the mappings of this domain to the data set [1]. Recent examples of cognitive tools suggest that such tools are beginning to infer groups of examples based upon relations between their properties [8]. This form of unsupervised learning is helpful since it allows for structured inference to take place in the absence of clearly defined or clearly mapped topologies.

1.2   Linear and Non-Linear Decision Making Contexts

A complex system is one that contains many processes or components whose behavior is a function both of each other's states, but also of their own previous states [3]. The feedback of information from previous states to future states creates non-linear dynamics s.t. traditional causal analysis becomes much more difficult [2]. In such systems stable states, called attractors, tend to emerge around the boundaries within this system where the feedback force is much stronger than the noise within the system. The converse point where noise is similar to or greater than the feedback force represents the periods of phase transition within such systems. In such systems, if one variable causes another then there will be a tendency for embedded states of these variables to concomitantly be either a part of an attractor or of a phase shift. Through examining historically offset time series values of process or component, a non-linear causal technique can examine the relationship between variables in complex systems. Taken's theorem describes and proves the efficacy of this type of complex inference.

As data becomes increasingly novel, voluminous, and complex, the presence of non-linear effects tends to increase. Non-linear systems are those whose previous states substantially effect their current state. Reducing cognitive load is challenging since it becomes unclear which data to concomitantly display. It is challenging to facilitate attribution formation since it is difficult to infer how to sample data to prevent certain paradoxes, such as Simpson's paradox, from affecting the validity of analysis [10]. Scaffolding is challenging in complex systems since many of the interactions between various data types results in novel interactions that do not map well onto existing topologies. Finally, the decision-making process itself is more circuitous and it is difficult to figure out where to recommend intervention.

1.3 Decision Making Feedback Loops

In complex environments feedback from users related to the usefulness of DSSs is often either that they result in output that is not actionable or that the system does a poor job of communicating the relationships between variables. Either way, users are unsure which action to take. DSSs for non-linear environments that can offer clear action recommendations need to scaffold two things. First, the decision making process should have a full scaffold from problem identification through to action orientation. To orient an action requires both focusing upon where to act and then upon recommending the degree of action to take. Second, there is an emphasis upon creating models whose results becomes a part of the future model. Both of these concepts relate to the uncertainty about which action to take. A common approach to solving both of these problems is the use of decision making loops. In addition to creating a feedback-based approach, this approach will also need to account for action constraints such as the need to explore and the limited ability to take action.

The OODA loop. This is one example of action-oriented loop [7]. This framework asks the user to observe, to orient, to decide, and to act. This process is intended for individuals making real-time decisions within their working environments. The loop is critical to this framework since it suggests historic outcomes factor into future decisions.

Analyst loops. Intelligent systems that actively involve the analyst in a decision-making loop have recently received increased attention [8]. This type of approach is naturally congruent with complex environments since in such environments the future state depends upon a function of other variables as well as upon the previous state of itself.

Action budgets. In order to truly capture the constraints that users often face in applied settings, this approach must recognize that the user can typically only take one or a few actions [8, 9]. This limited ability to act results in constraints characterized by the action budget for a given environment. Such constraints occur because of any number of limitations: time, computational power, human attention, process constraints, etc. Whatever the source, the take away is the presence of an upper limit on the number of simultaneous actions a user can take. This means this approach must account for the conditional and the marginal effects of an action or of inaction.

Reinforcement learning. If the outcome of an action informs the future prediction as to which action a system should take, then this system engages in reinforcement learning [11]. The typical problem with such exploratory approaches is that they need to somehow balance pursuing the historically optimal solution with the need to ensure that the system has explored all possible solutions for a given problem. While outside the specific context of the problem that this approach strives to solve, the contrast between exploration and exploitation is one that algorithms such as online bandit approaches strive to solve. Nonetheless, this approach does learn from this work and recommends that DSSs balance the potential reward for an action with the underlying risk associated with both taking the action and with taking no action.

1.4 Problem Statement

Driving actions in complex systems is challenging because the future state of these systems is highly dependent upon the former states. Thus, control variables are often a function not only of the other variables but also of their own former states. In such environments traditional causal methods break down. This leads to a lack of interpretability and an inability to take action based upon the results from traditional DSSs. To combat this, this approach needs to consider practical factors such as the computational complexity of the model and the organizational risk associated with certain actions. Finally, this approach needs to account for the ability of the user or of the system to take action as a part of its recommendations.

2   Description of DEAR Framework

The DEAR framework proposes a four-step approach to guiding non-linear decision making that extends the OODA loop framework. In the OODA loop framework the user observes, orients, decides and then acts. DEAR stands for Detect, Evaluate, Assess, and Recommend. This framework strives to detect opportunities for action, evaluates root cause, assesses risk, and then recommends a degree of action to take. It starts by initially assessing the causal relationship between multitudes of variables in real time. Second, the system evaluates each concept for changes over time. Third, if the system detects an unexpected change it then examines which factors could plausibly explain the change. Fourth it recommends an action that balances the need to balance exploration with exploitation. This final step acknowledges the iterative nature of decision making necessary to achieve success in non-linear systems. Through providing mathematical definitions alongside practical examples, the authors hope to present an approach upon which researchers and practitioners can build.

2.1 Detecting Changes

The first technique used to facilitate DSSs in non-linear environments is the incorporation of automated change detection techniques. The goal is to detect meaningful changes in real time so that users or machines can take action using the subsequent stages of this approach. Thus, change detection is critical for increasing awareness of unexpected events and for reducing the number of subsequent comparisons.

Detecting changes can take place using any of a variety of techniques. Regardless of change detection method, this approach starts by initially building a model of each of the variables [12]. Next, this approach detects and notifies the system when incoming examples are unexpected based upon historic context. In this case a variable can be substantially different for a couple of reasons: combination of features is rare, magnitude of event is statistically unlikely, rate of occurrence is unlikely, change is larger than normal, etc. In such a case we can think of this either as anomaly detection or as outlier detection. Two common techniques are outlier detection and surprise-based techniques.

Outlier detection. There are many forms of outlier detection [12]. Each form typically examines the related distribution and then examines the percentile at which incoming values fall on that distribution. If the position of the incoming value is above a certain, pre-defined threshold, then that example is an outlier [10]. Here are several forms of outlier detection: value-based using the normal distribution, variance-based using the F-distribution, rate-based using the Poisson distribution, etc. If an example exceeds the threshold on the relevant distribution, then it is considered rare. Optionally, this technique comes in one-tailed or two-tailed variants.

Surprise-based detection. In addition, certain unsupervised clustering techniques group variables into various sets based upon the properties of their attributes [12]. By examining the frequency of occurrence for sets of values, these techniques can determine whether a certain set of attributes is unlikely. Unlike the outlier detection technique, similarity-based techniques typically have some final objective used to determine the rarity of a set of variables. The simplest example would be the chain product rule. Similar to outlier detection there is a threshold past which example are rare.

Since this approach is primarily concerned with combing several different processes together, the rest of this paper will consider one of the simpler possible forms of detection: value-based outlier detection using the normal distribution. Rarity will be set at a $p = 0.99$ level meaning that, on average, this approach will only consider about 1% of incoming examples. Future work may focus upon automatically learning this threshold so that it results in less subsequent computational effort.

2.2 Evaluating Causality

Once this approach detects an unexpected change, the next step is to examine which variables could have caused this to take place. This evaluation process uses causal inference to determine which factors could have contributed to the observed outcome. Two common types of causal inference are probabilistic or frequentist methods. Both methods have experimental design constraints. Frequentist methods such as ANOVA analysis require the use of either a within group or between groups experimental design [10]. Probabilistic methods such as Bayesian inference require a proper understanding of a priori independence. While both techniques are useful, they are not helpful for complex environments where traditional design of experiments approaches are not possible and where a priori knowledge of independence is challenging to surmise. For this reason, this approach uses the CCM technique for causal inference.

Convergent Cross-Mapping (CCM). Traditional experimental design focuses upon understanding the direct relationship between a dependent and independent variable. In such a case any change in the dependent variable must precede a related change in the independent variable. Over time this precedence will lead to a parametric relationship upon which researchers can establish significance. This approach will run into problems if used to analyze complex environments. For example, it could lead to the identification of spurious relationships. Paradoxically and perniciously it can also result in the inability to define causal relations for systems with longer embeddings. For this reason, a DSS designed for us in complex environments must use a different technique for assessing causality.

Fortunately, there are already approaches researchers can use. CCM is one such approach that primarily considers the level of embedding between variables [2–5]. This technique starts by creating a set of time-delayed embeddings, or manifolds, of the variables in question. It then uses the manifold for the test variables to predict the manifold for the control variables. Through performing this process many times this technique then has a set of predicted variables alongside a set of actual variables. It then examines the correlation between the prediction and the actual values. The reason for this is that correlation represents the unit-normalized covariance between variables.

An astute reader may question why this technique uses correlation to test for causation. Because this technique considers the correlation of the embedded manifold, it is effectively examining the postulates presented within Taken's theorem [2]. Broadly stated, if one variable causes another then that variable being influenced will contain information about its cause. This is an information-based approach to establishing causal relationships. Through discovering the rate at which the test variables are able to predict the control variables it is examining the amount of information present in the test variables related to the location of the control variables as they vacillate between being bound to an attractor or undergoing phase shifts. CCM provides the correlation between the predicted and actual value of the control variable (Table 1).

Table 1. CCM output for variables A and B alongside the related causal inference.

A xmap B	B xmap A	Causal inference
Low	Low	No causality
Low	High	Unidirectional (A → B)
High	Low	Unidirectional (B → A)
High	High	Bidirectional

The CCM technique outputs a correlation value for a set of increasingly large library lengths. While each length yields a value, the output is value from the final, largest library length. By examining the manifold relationship between variables with various numbers of examples, this technique can examine the rate at which the CCM relationship converges to a stable value. Consider two variables A and B. By using CCM to test for causality in both direction (ie. A xmap B and B xmap A), CCM can determine:

Whereas correlation is symmetrical, the output of CCM is not. Recall that CCM tests for causality by examining the flow of information between variables. Because of this, and seemingly paradoxically, if the value for A xmap B is high then this implies that B is driving A since A contains information about B. The definition of high is left to the user to interpret. As with other measure of correlation, one could examine the significance of this value at a p = 0.05 level to determine that this causal relationship is stronger than a random interaction.

2.3 Assessing Relative Risk

At this point the DSS has detected an unexpected event and has established the causal relations between this event and other known variables. Before the DSS can move towards figuring out which action to take, it needs to first figure out whether taking an action is likely to be successful. Doing this will require forming probabilistic inference.

The output of the CCM technique represents the probability of explaining the variance in one set of variables given knowledge of a different set. However, CCM also offers a stronger assertion: this value is the probability that the information in one set will carry through to another. This is related to the probability that the movement in one set will cause another to move in the same direction. Thus, the square of the CCM output represents the expected amount of variance that the source variables can control.

Kelly's criterion. This formula is a probabilistic technique that will determine the ideal action to take given a set of constraints [9]. There are two input for this formula: the probability the action will result in success and the payout if the action is successful. Used in conjunction it will determine the degree to which an agent should commit to an action related to a specific outcome based upon the likelihood of that outcome to effect change and the expected payout for that outcome. The more accurate one can get in terms of determining the odds of success and the likely payout, the more useful this formula becomes. Where w is the total funds available to invest, p is the probability of success, b is the odds or payout, and k is the funds to invest this criteria states:

$$k = w\frac{p(b+1) - 1}{b} \tag{1}$$

As mentioned above the CCM correlation value is synonymous with causation. Furthermore, recall that each edge is the normalized correlation value s.t. it represents the probability that one variable can control another variable of interest.

The expected payout is an external factor determined by the user. This factor should be a function of the expected gain if the action taken is as successful as possible. The units for this gain are not important so long as it is continuous and there is a return on investment using the same units. If the investment is time the return is time savings. If this factor is negative it will effectively force the agent to take action to avoid this outcome. If the payout is the probability that an intervention will succeed then convert it to the odds value using this equation:

$$\text{Odds} = \text{Probability} / (1 - \text{Probability}) \tag{2}$$

Once this approach incorporates these factors within the formula, the results tell the user how much of an action to take given a limited pool of resources to commit. Called a wallet, express this pool of resources using the same units as the units for the payout factor. The size of the wallet should represent the total risk the user is willing to lose over a long period of time. For example, if the unit for risk is dollars, then this wallet may represent a budget used for maintaining infrastructure. The result of this equation determines which variable the user should action and the degree to which the user should commit resources to take action given a fixed budget. This approach works well for cases where the agent only takes one type of action.

Multiple actions types. There are multiple ways to consider the application of Kelly's criteria to multiple action types. First, select the single action that has the highest expected payout. Note that payout is the result of the equation. An alternative approach is to combine the expected return from a number of different options. So far this approach has assumed that all causal variables act independently. Testing interaction effects is a good way to examine independence [10, 13]. With this knowledge, the DSS can normalize the expected payout for each variable by its marginal contribution. The marginal contribution would be that contribution above and beyond the interaction contribution. The resultant normalization the percentage of action to direct towards each option.

Unintended consequences. Finally, this approach can also estimate the potential conse-quences of taking action(s) upon other variables. Since users may wish to take the action that maximally changes one variable while leaving others unaffected. DSSs can use this approach combined with the knowledge of interaction effects from above to help users prevent unintended consequences. Doing this would require setting negative expected odds for the variables the user wants to leave alone. Then the total expected payout becomes the sum of the expected payout from the action or set of actions along with the expected loss from the optional, negative payout variables.

2.4 Recommending Action

At this point the DSS has detected unexpected changes in one or more variables and it has expressed the causal relations between them. This allowed the DSS to determine which set of actions had the highest expected payout. However, the system cannot simply recommend the highest payout. The reason for this is that the approach would not account for the remaining uncertainty related to whether or not there are better options that the model has never considered [11]. To account for these factors the approach must balance pursuing the optimal action with the need to occasionally explore alternatives. This requires choosing an initial minimum threshold with which to pursue an entirely random course of action. Next, through keeping track of the actual payout for each action, this approach can determine whether the model is likely accounting for external factors. If the difference between actual and expected payout does not decrease as the model continues to learn, then this can inform the model that it should increase the rate at which it takes random actions. This approach is similar to how multi-armed bandit algorithms hone in on the correct balance between exploratory and exploitational actions.

Sampling saves time. Machine simulation using sampling techniques such as the Monte Carlo method or via implementing Gibbs sampling will allow this approach to explore the possible outcomes associated with a series of actions [10]. While this approach can directly model the result of a given action, it requires many computations to consider the possible payouts for a series actions. Use sampling techniques to simplify computational complexity.

2.5 Integrating the Framework

This approach recommends the possible use of a variety of techniques. Not all of these techniques are necessary for a majority of use cases. Nonetheless they are tools that, when used in conjunction with the DEAR framework, will result in a method that can consistently deliver insights that are simultaneously actionable and parsimonious. In order to integrate this approach within an existing DSS, consider focusing upon each stage of this approach as a discrete set of functional processes. While each stage is conceptually separate, they are also computationally separable. Treating each stage as separate will allow this approach to build models that are more scalable. This is because each stage will then contain only the information necessary for performing its operations. This will reduce the storage, computational, and transportation costs.

3 Method

3.1 Context

Many scenarios benefit from risk mitigation. One area that influences both public policy and corporate decision making is the reduction of mortal risk. One of the leading causes of unexpected deaths comes from vector-borne diseases carried by insects [14]. The incident rate of these diseases is in the hundreds of millions per year with about a million annually attributable fatalities. By far the largest contributor to these diseases is mosquitoes. Mosquitoes are ubiquitous throughout the world and carry many diseases including: the Zika virus, West Nile virus, Chikungunya virus, dengue, yellow fever, malaria, lymphatic filariasis, and Japanese encephalitis [14–16].

Preventing mosquito-borne diseases could focus upon preventing mosquitoes, preventing mosquitoes from contracting viruses, or upon preventing humans from coming in contact with mosquitoes. This paper does not focus upon preventing mosquitoes from contracting viruses since that is intractable enough that it requires specialized knowledge. While there are methods to prevent humans from contacting mosquitoes, the likelihood that humans will come into contact with mosquitoes is also a function of mosquito populations [14]. Therefore, this paper focuses upon mosquito populations.

There are many hypotheses about what factors cause mosquito populations to effect humans. Example hypotheses include precipitation, weather, geography, human population density, and time of year [15]. Since it is challenging to obtain precise geographical data, this paper will focus upon weather and upon precipitation [17, 18]. However, the population of mosquitoes has been shown to thrive in and near urban areas due to the prevalence of favorable environmental conditions [16]. Researchers find it challenging to prove that weather or that precipitation cause influxes in mosquitoes since it has proved hard to control for these variable. Additionally, natural systems are complex enough that natural experiments are hard to come by and the few good examples become difficult to reconcile with the general population. Finally, this is of particular concern due to the close proximity of mosquitoes and potential transmission of disease to humans.

3.2 Application

The previous section discussed the importance of this scenario. This scenario is also important from an application perspective. Public policy struggles to balance competing approaches to increase public safety. In complex and uncertain environments the unambiguous solutions, even if less efficacious, are easier to justify to critics. Furthermore, because there are many competing hypotheses regarding the cause of large changes in mosquito populations, this will represent a good opportunity to test this framework on a socially impactful problem. The method of this paper will be applied to the mosquito population in the United States. Weather data consists of Fahrenheit temperature and inches of precipitation.

In order to exercise the full DEAR framework, four different algorithms will examine this scenario. First it will detect large changes in mosquito populations using a statistical outlier detection technique. This simple technique will test for values that are beyond the 95th percentile. Second, it will apply the CCM technique to evaluate causal relations between these variables and the mosquito population. Third, it will model the risk associated with taking actions based upon these causal relationships. Fourth, it will examine several possible actions in order to recommend a policy action.

4 Results

4.1 Detecting Percentile-Based Outliers

Detection techniques are both statistical and user-driven. In July of 2015 in Columbus, OH the population was aware of a large increase in mosquitoes [19]. There was fear about West Nile Virus and an observed case of Zika virus. The precipitation had also markedly increased by nearly 50% year over year. This discovery led to the use of causal inference techniques.

4.2 Evaluating Causality Using CCM

To interpret CCM plots, examine the strength of correlation across increasing library lengths. If this correlation value increase as the library length increases, it suggests that information about one variable is increasingly found in the other. If the line for A xmap B increases but B xmap A does not, it suggests uni-directional causality (B causes A). Recall from above that there are four possible interpretations. Recall also that significance is still assessed at the 0.05 level. With a library length of 25, the correlation value has to be greater than 0.46 to achieve significance.

Initial investigation did not show any relationship between precipitation and mosquito populations or between temperature and population. However, subsequent analysis considered the degree days and cumulative mosquito population. Degree days is the cumulative sum of average daily temperatures. Turning these variables into cumulative variables immediately revealed causal relationships.

Figure 1 shows the discovery of evidence for non-linearity and the presence of a complex attractor in the phase portraits for Daily Precipitation, Mean Daily Temperature, Daily Mosquito Count, and a plot showing the relationship between Mean Daily Temperature and Daily Mosquito Count. This qualifies the datasets as suitable candidates for CCM analysis. The authors have discovered attractors with similar characteristics in other industrial and physical systems [5, 6].

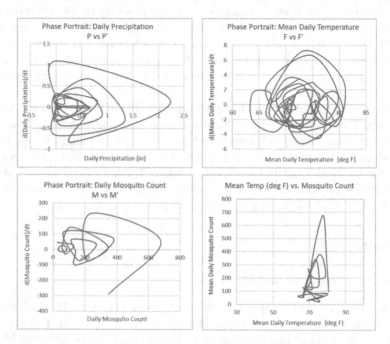

Fig. 1. Phase portraits for Daily Precipitation, Mean Daily Temperature, Daily Mosquito Count, and a plot showing the relationship between Mean Daily Temperature and Daily Mosquito Count.

Figure 2 illustrates that while mosquito population data contain information about seasonal precipitation, that seasonal precipitation does not contain very much information about mosquito populations. This implies seasonal precipitation has a causal effect on mosquito population. Cumulative mosquito population xmap cumulative precipitation is significant (0.73) while the inverse is not significant. This asymmetrical pattern of information re-occurs throughout other variables.

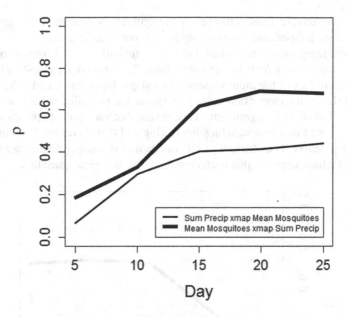

Fig. 2. Causality of cumulative seasonal rainfall on mosquito population based on convergent cross mapping.

Figure 3 illustrates that the cumulative mosquito population xmap degree days is significant (0.80). This means that mosquitos contains information about temperature;

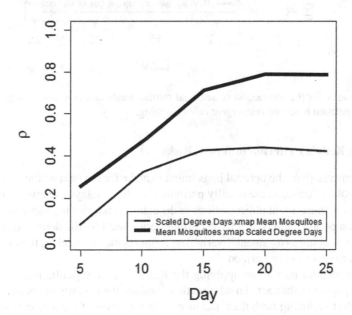

Fig. 3. Causality for cumulative degree days on mosquito population based on convergent cross mapping.

changes in temperature cause changes in mosquitoes. Notice there is informational asymmetry since temperature xmap mosquitoes is not significant.

Since both temperature and precipitation significantly affect mosquito population, the next step was to check for two-way interactions. This approach can test for interaction by taking the product of the input variables as a single input into CCM [13].

Figure 4 shows that interaction xmap population is not significant but that population xmap interaction (0.7) is significant. This means that mosquito populations contain information about these two variables interacting and that therefore these interactions affect this population. The strength of this interaction is smaller than either of the two direct effects which suggests that each contains some marginal causality.

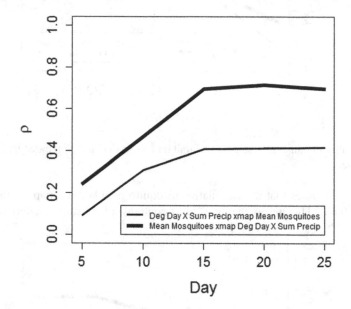

Fig. 4. Causality for the interaction of seasonal rainfall totals and cumulative degree days on mosquito population based on convergent cross mapping.

4.3   Using Kelly's Criterion to Assess Risks

The Kelly criteria gives the optimal investment to make for the next action. It is a kinetic approach. Policy decisions are usually periodic with long delays in between decisions. For that reason, think about policy actions as the action to take for the subsequent period. This decision period should match the polling period used by the detection framework to notice changes in environmental variables. If data comes in weekly, then recommendations can have a weekly horizon.

Another peculiar part about applying the Kelly criteria to public policy is that the notion of a payout is abstract. To address this consider the investment as that of organizational effort including both time and money. If the result of the action is successful, then the need to take that action in the future should be reduced relative to the amount of action taken and the expected payout determined by the Kelly criteria.

Effective planning suggests implementing control systems in anticipation of peak mosquito population should have the most beneficial result in terms of minimizing the disease vector prevalence. Fortunately, the DSS knows the probability that an increase in temperature will lead to an increase in mosquito population from the causal analysis phase. Recall that cumulative mosquito population xmap degree days was 0.80. The square of this offers a 0.64 probability information in temperature will be found in mosquitoes. Now the DSS can now use Kelly's criteria to examine preventative actions.

Mosquito Control authorities have numerous options at their disposal for mosquito population control including biological, environmental, and chemical remediation systems. The historical success rate of these control systems has been 90% [20]. Although effective, these control systems represent significant expenditures of resources. Nonetheless, the odds associated with these interventions are 9:1. Given these favorable odds, Kelly's equation suggests investing up to 60% of resources during this cycle.

4.4 Recommending Mosquito Control Action

Given the results of the risk analysis this approach recommends that the responsible agency spend 60% of its funds for preventing vector-based diseases on mosquito control systems. Since this data updates weekly this decision can also update weekly. The shorter the decision period, the faster this approach will find the correct set of actions to take. If successful, this will prevent the need to take future action relative to the payout. It also saves the remaining funds for use with alternative initiatives that might be more successful. Finally, record the result of actions in order to further refine future risk models.

5 Conclusions

5.1 Conclusions Related to Applying the DEAR Framework to This Context

Monitored changes in environmental variables led to subsequent causal analysis regarding mosquito populations in Columbus, OH. This revealed that while both temperature and precipitation exhibit a causal effect on mosquito populations, temperature is slightly more explanatory. These variables also interact. By translating the degree of control discovered using CCM into Kelly's criteria, this approach was able to recommend data-driven policy for mosquito mitigation efforts.

5.2 Conclusions Related to the DEAR Framework

Treating each stage as separate within this model made it easy to integrate different stages of the analytical process. Separating each component made this approach more scalable and will allow the creation of models for larger data sets since each stage only contains the information necessary for performing its operations. This will reduce the storage, computational, and transportation costs of data while empowering researchers.

6   Next Steps

A substantial area for future work relates to applying this technique to systems containing many simultaneous variables. This will require an understanding of marginal causality. Preliminary plans involve building graphical models containing the causal information from the evaluation phase of this approach. Once a graph exists, this approach should be able to leverage graph-based processing techniques to perform the necessary likelihood estimations.

Finally, while there are good methods for doing the detection in real-time, CCM remains a computationally complex process and future work will also focus upon building a more scalable version of CCM with similar guarantees.

References

1. Kirk, R.A.: Evaluating a cognitive tool built to aid decision making using decision making approach as a theoretical framework and using unobtrusive, behavior-based measures for analysis. Doctoral Dissertation. Retrieved from ProQuest (3684297) (2015)
2. Takens, F.: Dynamical Systems and Turbulence. Lecture Notes in Mathematics, vol. 898, p. 366. Springer, Heidelberg (1981)
3. Sugihara, G., May, R., Ye, H., Hsieh, C., Deyle, E., Fogarty, M., Munch, S.: Detecting causality in complex ecosystems. Science **338**, 496–500 (2012)
4. Ye, H., et al.: Distinguishing time-delayed causal interactions using convergent cross mapping. Sci. Rep. **5**, 14750 (2015)
5. Pesheck, P.S., Kirk, R.A., Kirk, D.A.: Multiphysics modeling to improve MW heating uniformity in foods. In: Transformative Food Technologies to Enhance Sustainability at the Food, Energy, and Water Nexus, Lincoln, Nebraska, USA, 22–24 February 2016
6. Kirk, Ryan A., Kirk, Dave A., Pesheck, P.: Decision making for complex ecosystems: a technique for establishing causality in dynamic systems. In: Stephanidis, C. (ed.) HCI 2016. CCIS, vol. 617, pp. 110–115. Springer, Cham (2016). doi:10.1007/978-3-319-40548-3_18
7. Boyd, J.: A discourse on winning and losing. (Working Air University Library No. M-U 43947). Maxwell Air Force Base, Montgomery (1987)
8. Veeramachaneni, K., et al.: AI^2: Training a big data machine to defend. In: 2016 IEEE 2nd International Conference on Big Data Security on Cloud (BigDataSecurity), IEEE International Conference on High Performance and Smart Computing (HPSC), and IEEE International Conference on Intelligent Data and Security (IDS), New York, pp. 49–54, (2016). doi:10.1109/BigDataSecurity-HPSC-IDS.2016.79
9. Zeckhauser, R.: Investing in the unknown and unknowable. Capitalism and Society **1**(2), 5 (2006)
10. Pearl, J.: Causality. Cambridge University Press, New York (2000)
11. Jaderberg, M., et al.: Reinforcement learning with unsupervised auxiliary tasks. Computing Research Repository, 1611 (2016)
12. Thompson, D.R., Mandrake, L., Green, O.R., Chen, S.A.: A case study of spectral signature detection in multimodal and outlier-contaminated scenes. IEEE Geosci. Remote Sens. Lett. **10**(5), 1021–1025 (2013)
13. Hargens, L.: Product-variable models of interaction effects and causal mechanisms. (CSSS Working Paper No. 67R). Center for Statistics and the Social Sciences, Seattle (2008)

14. A global brief on vector-borne diseases. [Editorial]. World Health Organization (2014). http://apps.who.int/iris. Accessed
15. Lindsey, N.P., Staples, E., Lehman, J., Fischer, M.: Surveillance for Human West Nile Virus Disease — United States, 1999—2008. CDC Surveillance Summaries 59(SS02), 1–17 (2010). Accessed
16. Mosquito-Borne Diseases. National Institute for Occupational Saftey and Health, 8 November 2016. https://www.cdc.gov/niosh/topics/outdoor/mosquito-borne/. Accessed
17. Weather history for Columbus, OH. The old Farmer's Almanac (2015). http://www.almanac.com/weather/history/OH/Columbus. Accessed
18. Esri:. ArcGIS weekly mosquito density maps – Columbus 2015 [computer software]. California, Redlands (2017). http://www.arcgis.com. Accessed
19. Ohio department of health: Wet summer = more mosquitoes = risk of West Nile Virus. Fox 8 News Cleveland (2015). http://fox8.com/2015/07/10/ohio-department-of-health-wet-summer-more-mosquitoes-risk-of-west-nile-virus/. Accessed
20. Frieden, T.R., Schuchat, A., Ptersen, L.R.: Zika virus 6 months later. The JAMA Network (2016). http://jamanetwork.com/journals/jama/fullarticle/2543301. Accessed

Data Sources Handling for Emergency Management: Supporting Information Availability and Accessibility for Emergency Responders

Vimala Nunavath$^{(\boxtimes)}$ and Andreas Prinz

CIEM Research Group, Department of ICT,
University of Agder, Grimstad, Norway
{vimala.nunavath, andreas.prinz}@uia.no

Abstract. Information is an essential component for better emergency response. Although a lot of information being available at various places during any kind of emergency, many emergency responders (ERs) use only a limited amount of the available information. The reason for this is that the available information heterogeneously distributed, in different formats, and ERs are unable to get access to the relevant information. Moreover, without having access to the needed information, many emergency responders are not able to obtain a sufficient understanding of the emergency situation. Consequently, a lot of time is being used to search for the needed information and poor decisions may be made. Therefore, in this paper, our research focuses on bringing the available heterogeneously dispersed information together to improve the information accessibility for ERs. In this study, we present an approach for integration of heterogeneous databases in the Semantic Web context using a Model-driven data integration approach based on an information model. We propose an architecture using the Enterprise Services Bus (ESB) and web service technologies for facilitating knowledge sharing and data exchange between different ERs. Based on the proposed architecture, we developed a system prototype and presented it with an indoor fire emergency response scenario.

Keywords: Indoor fire emergency · Model-driven data integration · Information accessibility · Situational awareness · Information exchange · Mule ESB · Enterprise-Service-Bus (ESB) · Data mapping · Service-Oriented Architecture (SOA) · Human-Centered Design (HCD) · Model-Driven Architecture (MDA)

1 Introduction

Recently, many countries have been impacted by various natural and man-made disasters which caused immense damage [1]. If we consider fire emergency, it has become one of the major challenges in today's world that causes loss of lives and devastating impacts on infrastructures and economies. In 2014, all over the world, almost 28 million fire emergencies occurred with a total of 21000 fatalities and losses of 110 billion US\$ worldwide [2]. According to the Center of Fire Statistics of CTIF report [2],

© Springer International Publishing AG 2017
S. Yamamoto (Ed.): HIMI 2017, Part II, LNCS 10274, pp. 240–259, 2017.
DOI: 10.1007/978-3-319-58524-6_21

the second largest fire emergency occurrence type is in structures i.e., in buildings. If we consider Norway as a case, the fire statistics for the year 2015 shows that, in total, 2717 building fire emergencies were occurred and caused 35 fatalities [3]. Almost four billion NOK economic damage were paid for the year 2014 [4].

Generally, to mitigate the emergency impacts and damages, a complex network of emergency responders (ERs) from different emergency response organizations (EROs) such as fire and rescue service, police service, health care service, and municipality personnel work together in teams for managing emergency efficiently. During emergency response, these involved ERs collaborate and coordinate by share right information to the right person at the right time to obtain a common operational picture, to make decisions, and to perform tasks such as protecting the life of the people, reducing the property damage, extinguishing the fire, rerouting the traffic, aiding victims, transporting the victims to nearest hospitals, supporting emotionally affected victims at the operational level [5, 6]. The example information that is exchanged among different ERs could be victim information, information about location and condition of the victim, resource information, building information, information about hazardous goods inside the building and information about victims' medical condition and so on. However, one of the key challenges faced by involved ERs is often lacking adequate information [7].

According to the Utøya incident report [8] and Statens havarikommisjon for transport (SHT) report [9], one of the key challenges for the involved ERs during the Utøya disaster and fire in the Gudvangatunnel was not having access to the adequate information. Consequently, 77 fatalities occurred in Utøya disaster and 23 were seriously injured, while 5 were severely injured due to smoke in the Gudvangatunnel emergency. So, from both these reports it is evident that ERs did not access appropriate information in a timely manner. As a result, the information flows were broken down and it was difficult to make timely decisions during emergency response [1, 9].

Another challenge that ERs encounter is that even though the needed emergency related data is available, it is difficult for ERs to access it as the data is heterogeneous and distributed at various places [10]. However, to solve this problem, a data integration framework was proposed by authors of this paper and can be sound in [11]. In addition, another challenge is that misunderstanding between ERs is caused due to semantic differences of distributed data [12, 13]. Moreover, the involved ERs do not use common terminology for representing same thing. This semantic inconsistency data make ERs' decision making process slow, thereby, results in inefficient emergency management. However, to solve the semantic inconsistency problem, an information model was developed by authors of this paper and can be found in [14]. Apart from them, in this paper, we focus on the process of connecting existing data sources with the developed information model. So, the research question is formulated as: "*How to connect the existing data sources with the developed information model?*"

The purpose of addressing this research question is to provide a holistic way for improving access to the needed/relevant information for enabling the data exchange and knowledge sharing among different emergency responders who are at both onsite and off-site i.e., at Control and Command Center. The rest of the paper is organized as follows. Section 2 presents background for the emergency management operations and information access challenges, current ICT tools that are in use in Norway. Section 3 presents the proposed framework for understanding the data source handling process, and Sect. 4 presents the results of data source handling development and implementation. Literature review and the results are discussed in Sect. 5. Finally, conclusion part summarizes the lessons learned from this research and discusses directions for future research in Sect. 6.

2 Data Integration for Emergency Management

In this section background to emergency response operations and existing ICT tools used by ERs in Norway are presented. After that, we discuss the challenges that ERs face during emergency response. In this paper, information needs of involved ERs who are at emergency site are handled.

2.1 Emergency Management Operations in Norway

As mentioned in earlier paragraphs, when emergency occurs, lot of information is generated at diverse sources. Despite the rapid development of Information and Communication Technology (ICT), the data is manually collected by the ERs at the emergency site [6, 15].

To deal with emergency, at first, one Crew Manager (CM) and two Smoke Divers (SDs) from the fire and rescue service go to the emergency site immediately after receiving the emergency fire alarm or call from either the Command and Control Center (110) or from the emergency location. After reaching the site, they evaluate the situation by collecting the information manually from those who are at the emergency scene (either from victims or from witnesses or from the owner of the place). The collected information could be about number of people, fire location, fire cause, access routes, building map, hazardous goods and so on. This manually collected information is then passed to the fire chief with a hand-held device such as either mobile or walkie-talkie to make him obtain the overview of the situation and to make decisions. The CM acts as an On-Scene Commander (OSC) until the Fire Chief (FC) arrives at the emergency site. The FC arrives at the emergency location only if he thinks that the emergency is not minimal and will create major impact.

When the FC arrives at the emergency site he/she takes over the OSC responsibilities from the CM and acts as an OSC until ERs from police services and ambulance services arrive to the scene. However, in the Agder region of Norway, all EROs are so far using their own customized information systems [16]. So, collected information is manually documented first on a paper and then in a Microsoft word document by fire personnel. This electronic report is called a situational report which is stored in their information systems. This report is accessible only internally and not available for other emergency organizations. When police staff arrives at the emergency site, leader of the police takes over the OSC responsibilities from the FC and acts as an OSC. The OSC makes all the decisions at the emergency site and guides other EROs such as fire and protection services, ambulance services, and municipality staff. A conceptual model of data exchange and knowledge sharing among different ERs is shown clearly in Fig. 1.

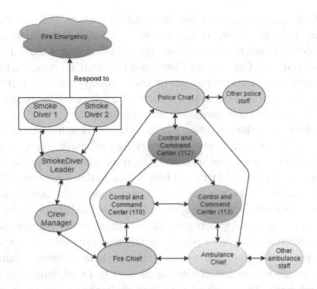

Fig. 1. A conceptual model of emergency organizational partners' information communications.

The tasks of each organization are documented in Table 1. In addition, based on the fire and rescue protection report [17] and police services book [18] the conceptual model (Fig. 1) for various ERs information communication is formulated. In this conceptual model, the data exchange and knowledge sharing among ERs of each individual organization is being sketched. Information communication between ERs of each emergency organization may have similar characteristics and requirements and the shown information flows, however, are bidirectional.

Table 1. Involved emergency organizations and their tasks during fire emergency response.

Emergency organization	Tasks at emergency site
Fire protection service	– Extinguishing the fires – Saving lives, averting danger and limiting damage – Evacuating victims from the buildings
Police service	– Saving lives, averting danger and limiting damage – Maintain peace, order and security on site – Assist with salvage of cargo so far, the service and circumstances warrant – Issue death notification of accidents, Disasters and criminal acts – Register fatalities, injured and missing – Investigation – Distributing information with media and others
Health care service	– Provide first-aid – Transportation of victims to health centers
Municipality personnel	– Noting down the details of incoming victims – Informing details about saved victims to police

When the OSC commander receives information such as fire and victims' information from the FC and victim transportation information from ambulance service chief, he or she notes downs this information manually and shares that information with other operational staff and Control and Command Center (CC) personnel (112). When the CC staff receive this information, he or she manually stores the received information in their information systems in the form of a Microsoft word document. This document will be available and accessible only internally.

A similar information storage process is done by the health care (113) and municipality staff as well. Despite each emergency organization being equipped with advanced information technologies to support their emergency response activities, the stored information is not accessed by other EROs. Due to this limitation, ERs often have out-of-date information. In such case, they cannot make right decisions and cannot manage the emergency efficiently. In addition, lack of sufficient on-site information for the ERs might be due to not upgrading the off-site information systems as well.

In Norway, different ERs from police, health and fire services use different terminology for representing the same words (semantic heterogeneity), thereby creating uncertainties in collaboration and communication [19]. In addition, due to syntactic, schematic heterogeneity, the involved ERs face challenges at emergency site. Moreover, large amounts of information from various ERs make it difficult to orient themselves during emergency response. Therefore, information must be provided quickly, actively and periodically, to ensure that everyone takes accurate and relevant information, thereby enhancing the emergency management operations effectively. This can be achieved only by enabling the semantic, syntactic and schematic interoperability between different systems.

2.2   ICT Solutions Used by Emergency Responders in Norway

In Norway, the following ICT systems are mainly have been used for emergency management. Those ICT systems are: (1) A crisis incident management (CIM) tool used by the police and municipality staff, (2) LOCUS used by the fire and rescue service, and the health service, (3) BRIS used by the fire and rescue service, and (4) VISION BOSS used by the fire and rescue service.

- **CIM:** It is a software program for crisis management support, produced by One Voice AS, a company delivering crisis management solutions for a variety of organizations. It supports aspects of crisis management such as quality assurance, risk and vulnerability analyses, emergency planning, training, and evaluation. The purpose of this tool is to notify police personnel when major incidents occur. It supports notification and alerting of personnel through distribution lists for sending messages by email, SMS, and phone. The system provides the receiver with several response alternatives which are logged, so that the sender of a message can keep track on the status of each alerted individual [20, 21]. It is currently used by many organizations that the police collaborate closely with, among others, the Directorate for Civil Protection and Emergency Planning (DSB), The Norwegian Civil Defense, and all Norwegian municipalities and county governors.

- **LOCUS:** It is a company delivering mission-critical solutions and products to the fire and rescue service as well as to the health service, among others (e.g. transport and logistics, security service companies). The solutions are designed to reduce time constraints through being a tool for the emergency agencies to make the right decisions in relation to resource allocation. The LOCUS' solutions are directed towards use by the 110 and 113 emergency call centrals (TransFire for the fire and rescue service and TransMed for the health service) and mobile devices installed in vehicles for the tactical personnel (TransMobile 7). The detailed information about the solutions can be found in [21].

- **BRIS:** It is a reporting system with an overview of the missions that the fire and rescue handle. All assignments that got recorded in 110 control project management tool are automatically transferred to the BRIS. This facilitates the reporting of employees of fire and rescue services. The data collected via the BRIS, should provide a better basis for carrying out preventative work, and to develop fire and rescue service at local, regional and national levels. This tool is mainly used during emergency recovery [22].

- **VISION BOSS:** It is a project management tool which is used by the 110 operators for creating incident reports. These reports are made available both during and after an emergency event. This tool also includes crew-lists with contact details and their competence information. It also contains information about resources such as vehicles and equipment content [23].

The drawbacks of these above-mentioned ICT tools are that they do not give automatic real-time information from the emergency site to provide awareness of the situation. They do not support the ERs who are facing operational problems in accessing information from various sources. So, the vision of a common emergency response system with common terminology available for all emergency stakeholders in Norway is still not available [16]. Therefore, in this work we proposed a data integration framework and implemented a prototype to realize efficient timely information access.

3   A Proposed Data Integration Framework

Before proposing and developing any kind of information system, as per the Human-Centered Design (HCD) approach [24], it is necessary to understand the domain in which the system is being used. So, we considered the emergency management domain and particularly, the response phase.

3.1   Emergency Scenario

We used an indoor fire emergency (i.e., in educational building) as a use-case for domain analysis which was as follows.

"Imagine there is a big fire in the university building. This fire emergency happens in building A at the University of Agder Grimstad campus. There are 100 persons stuck inside the university. From these people, 10 persons are vulnerable (vulnerable are old people, children, pregnant, allergic to smoke and heat, physically-challenged person).

These vulnerable people cannot reach the exit quickly and are spread over the whole building. Visitors are also there and stuck inside the building. They are not aware of the evacuation procedures and exit routes to escape. After lot of people self-evacuated, 50 victims are still trapped in each floor in the university building. As the university building has several floors, at least 10 victims got stuck inside each room. However, first responders are unaware of total number of victims, the number of persons inside each floor of the building and their exact location to get an overview of the situation and to evacuate them".

The detailed emergency scenario description can be found in our previous research [25]. To deal with this kind of emergency situation, ERs should have access to different university's information systems in order to know how many people are still inside the building and also their location. However, in reality, the data resides in several systems and ERs do not have access to these systems. In addition, the ERs cannot get a unified view of the several systems' data. Therefore, there is a need of a way of integrating and handling data from different sources with different formats via a unified system is essential.

Furthermore, with the help of this scenario, information needs of various ERs were identified. After identifying the information needs, a data integration framework was proposed. To develop an information system, the authors of this paper could not get access to different EROs' databases and applications due to security and privacy barriers. Therefore, for data integration, different applications and databases of University of Agder (UiA) have been used as a proof-of-concept to provide a holistic way to access the relevant information in a timely-manner.

3.2 Information Requirements and Model

Information is the content of the communication that takes place within the framework of emergency response. The following information is essential to obtain situational awareness and for decision making. The information requirements are about *who, where, when, what, and how*. Here, *who* means the information related to the involved people and organizations. *Where* means, the information related to the location of the emergency. *When* is, the information related to the date and time of the emergency. *What* means, the information related to the type of the event, needed resources (material) and what kind of activities should be involved. *How* means the information related to the cause of the event and performing tasks. The detailed description of the acquired information needs and the developed information model can be found in our previous research [14, 25].

3.3 Data Integration Framework

Based on the proposed reference architecture for emergency management operations a data integration framework was proposed which can be seen in [17]. The proposed framework consists of three components i.e., the first part is data sources handling component, the second part is semantic model component, and the last one is information presentation component.

- The data source handling component handles different applications or data sources of different EROs such as fire and protection services, police services, ambulance services and municipality.
- The semantic model component represents the key concepts in the emergency response domain and their semantic relationship. By using this semantic model, a centralized database (CDB) will be developed. This CDB is an instance of the developed semantic data model. The input data for the CDB is provided by the data source handling layer which fetches data from the different EROs' databases and stores in CDB.
- In information provisioning component, the data which is stored in CDB is provided to ERs on a web-application for supporting different purposes such as getting overview of the situation, for decision making, setting up the shelters, and arranging ambulances for transporting victims. The acquisition and availability of the needed data supports ERs in managing the emergency efficiently and effectively.

4 System Implementation

In this section, we present the results of data source handling development and implementation part of the proposed framework.

4.1 Data Sources

As mentioned in the previous section, we consider fire in a university building use case as a proof of concept for handling existing data sources.

The reason for selecting the university building as a use case is that, university consists of several floors, blocks (buildings) and several people. If any emergency occurs inside the building, it is difficult for the emergency responders to locate the victim's location as they are wide spread in the entire area. To fulfil the above-mentioned information needs of the ERs, we considered a semantically-enhanced mediator-based data integration approach for handling data sources in Enterprise Service Bus (ESB). The detailed description of the mediator based data integration approach can be found in [27]. The six different applications that used are: *FS system, SAP portal, Syllabus system, UiA system, Sensor database and Cisco Prime Infrastructure Application.* The description of each system is given in Table 2.

4.2 System Description

During implementation, we used connectors to provide access to the above-mentioned data sources such as FS, SAP, Syllabus, UiA and Cisco Prime Infrastructure application (Cisco PIA). This can be seen in Fig. 2. For the schematic mapping from the local databases, we have used mule ESB. Mule ESB is an open source lightweight integration framework that combines messaging, web services, data transformation, and intelligent routing to reliably connect and coordinate the interaction of significant numbers of diverse applications across extended enterprises with transactional integrity [53].

Table 2. Used data sources for data integration [26]

Used applications	Description
FS system	It contains information related to students who have registered to the courses and program at the university
SAP portal	It contains information related to the full time and part time employees
Syllabus system	It contains information related to the time plan of the scheduled courses
UiA system	It contains information related to university building information, resources information and hazardous material information
Sensor database	It contains information related to the smoke, fire, and temperature inside the room
Cisco Prime Infrastructure application	It contains information related to the connected users over Wi-Fi

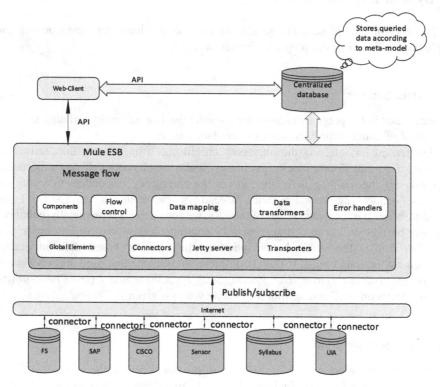

Fig. 2. A data integration prototype for fire emergency management.

In our system development, a message flow was implemented to specify how a service request is to be parsed in the system. Mule uses message flows to plug together a series of message processors. The typical message flow has a message source (usually connectors), which accepts messages from an external source (e.g., databases or applications or third party APIs) either via standard protocol i.e., HTTP and triggers the execution of the flow. It also typically includes a series of message processors which transforms (i.e., convert message payload data to a format that another application can understand), filters, and enriches messages. The message flow for the implementation included an HTTP endpoint component as message source, which made the flow available as an HTTP service. In addition, there are two types of endpoint-based connectors i.e., inbound endpoints and outbound endpoints in mule ESB. Here, inbound endpoints serve as a message source for a flow and outbound endpoints send information to the external systems (i.e., web services or files or databases). The final prototype implementation in mule ESB can be seen in Fig. 3.

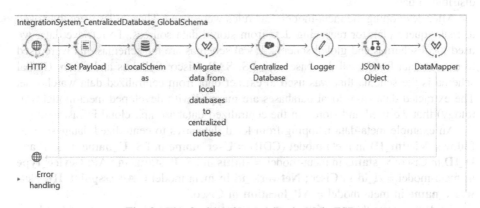

Fig. 3. The final implementation in Mule ESB

In Mule ESB, *HTTP endpoint* connector was used in collaboration with the Simple Object Access Protocol (SOAP) component, where the service was configured with an appropriate jetty transport representing the different operations that could be invoked on the service bus. The SOAP component would make the service available for cross-computer communication. *Transformers and jetty transport* were being used to perform data conversion (i.e., from JSON to Object) and to expose Mule Services over HTTP using a Jetty HTTP server. *Data mapper* takes data in a specific format and outputs the same data in the format of our choice. Therefore, we have used this component to resolve semantic heterogeneity. *Data Sense* uses message metadata to facilitate application design. With this functionality, Anypoint Studio proactively acquires information such as data type and structure, to prescribe how to accurately map or use this data in your application.

4.3 Data Mapping

To integrate the data from different databases, we first developed a meta-model which can be found in our previous research [25]. The reason for developing the meta-model was, when the data are stored in individual databases, then these databases are simple and good enough to handle queries against them. But, when it comes to integrate these individual databases into different systems or vice versa, there will be problems with mapping different database structures due to mismatch in naming domain concepts. For an example, user name in one data can be named as *"user_name"*, but in another database, it can be named as *"u_name" or "u_id"*. It is obvious that these concepts have the same semantic i.e., information about the user_name. But syntactically, they are different. This difference is not easy for a human-being to recognize the similarity when they are from different organizations. Moreover, it is also not an easy task for a machine to integrate. Therefore, resolving semantic heterogeneity not only helps machines understand the domain concepts, but also give users a unified way to access distributed data.

After developing the meta-model, few rules were made. These rules were then used to make query plan for retrieving data from stored data sources. To retrieve data, we used local schemas and global schema. Local schemas are the schemas that were used to extract data from local databases i.e., FS, SAP, Cisco, Syllabus and so on. Global schema is the schema that was used to extract data from centralized data warehouse. The extracted data from local databases are mapped with developed meta-model (ontology) that we used and stored in the centralized database i.e., cloud infrastructure.

An example meta-data mapping from local databases to centralized database is as follows. **Victim_ID** in meta-model (CDB) = **User_name** in FS, **U_name** in SAP and **U_ID** in Cisco; **v_status** in meta-model = **status** in FS, **P_status** in SAP; **Device_type** in meta-model = **d_id** in Cisco; **Network_id** in meta-model = **Accesspoint_ID**; **Network_name** in meta-model = **AP_location** in Cisco.

To demonstrate the use of the prototype system, an example case is considered i.e., if ERs request the following information on the GUI: *"the persons and their location inside the building during fire emergency which occurred between 9 to 10 am"*. To present this information, first a global schema was created and then local schemas. Here, queries against the database were made by using Structured Query Language (SQL). The rules (query plan) that used to extract data from local databases and store them in CDB and present on GUI are as follows.

- A Student is identified with username in the FS and in the Cisco database (**user_name** in FS = **u_id** in Cisco).
- An Employee is identified with username in the SAP and in the Cisco database (**u_id** in Cisco = **u_name** in SAP).
- The Student location should be matched with the location of any registered course (if he/she is registered to any course) (if **u_id** in Cisco = **user_name** in FS; then **course_id** of connected user in FS = **c_id** in Syllabus; **r_location** in cisco = **room_location** in syllabus).

- The Employee location should be matched with the location of any teaching course (if he/she teaches any course) (**u_id** in Cisco = **u_name** in SAP; **course_name** in SAP = **coursename** in Syllabus; **r_location** in cisco = **room_location** in syllabus).
- If an employee is not teaching any course, then the location of the employee should be matched with the employee's office (**r_location** in Cisco = **room-location** in SAP).

If a victim is connected to the Cisco network with several devices, and these devices are shown at two different locations at the same time, then we choose the victim's location based on the following criteria. However, in this criterion, first we check what kind of devices and how many are connected to Cisco network with one username. (we assume that the user is always connected to wi-fi with two devices i.e., mobile and laptop and carries mobile phone with him/her). If user is connected to wi-fi with two devices to Cisco network, then we check the location of the connected mobile and laptop as follows.

For employee:

- First, we check the location of the connected devices (*in Cisco db*). If both the connected devices' location (*in Cisco db*) is matching with location of employee's office room (in *SAP db*) then we assume that the user is at office room and show that information on the GUI.
- If the connected laptop's and mobile phone's location is not matched with employee's office room location, then check whether this employee has any class to teach at that time (in *Syllabus db*). If employee has class to teach and both devices' location is matched with teaching room location, then we consider teaching room's location information and show it on the GUI.
- If the connected laptop's location matched with office room's location and mobile phone location matched with teaching room location, then check whether this employee has any class to teach at that time (in *Syllabus db*). If employee has class and mobile phone location is matched with teaching room location, then we consider location of the mobile phone and show it on GUI.
- If both connected laptop's and mobile phone's location is not matched with employee location, then we check whether laptop's and mobile phone's location is moving from one place to other. If yes, then we consider the location of both devices' information and show it on the GUI.
- If the connected laptop's location is matched with employees' office room and mobile phone's location is in other location, then we check whether mobile phone's location is moving from one place to other. If yes, then we consider the mobile phone's location information and show it on the GUI.

For student:

- If student is connected the cisco network with laptop and mobile, then check the location of the laptop and mobile. Now, check whether this student has any classes to attend. If yes, then check whether the student's mobile phone and laptop's location is matching with course class room's location. If yes, then show the course class room's location on GUI.

- If student is connected to the cisco network with laptop and mobile, then check the location of the laptop and mobile. Now check whether this student has any classes to attend. If not, then show the current location of student on GUI.
- If student is connected to the cisco network with laptop and mobile, then check the location of the laptop and mobile. Now check whether this student has any classes to attend. If yes, then check whether the student's laptop's location is matching with course class room's location. If no, then check whether the mobile is matching with course class room's location. If yes, then show location of mobile on GUI.
- If student is connected to the cisco network with laptop and mobile, then check the location of the laptop and mobile. Now check whether this student has any classes to attend. If yes, then check whether the student's laptop's location is matching with course class room's location. If no, then check whether the mobile is moving from one place to other. If yes, then show location of mobile on GUI.

In Fig. 3, the used components in the message flow perform the following actions.

- *HTTP:* It is a connector which can send and receive HTTP and HTTPS requests given a selected host, port, address. With this connector, we can choose the methods such as GET, POST, DELETE. In addition, this connector can be configured to listen for incoming HTTP requests that can be expected to reach a given HTTP address.
- *Set Payload:* This is a transformer which is used to set the payload. The payload can be a string or a mule expression. Here, mule expression is a language which can be used to access and evaluate the data in the payload to filter, route, or otherwise act upon the different parts of the Mule message object.
- *Local Schemas-* It is a database connector which connects to all databases separately and queries data as local schemas into a flow.
- *Migrate data from local databases to centralized database* – It transforms message i.e., transforms data structure and format to produce the output Salesforce connector expects.
- *Centralized database* – It is a Salesforce connector used as outbound connector which connects with Salesforce cloud, and performs an operation to push data into Salesforce according to the developed meta-model.
- *Logger:* It is a component reference which is used to log messages such as error messages, status notifications, or exceptions.
- *JSON to Object:* It is a transformer which converts a JSON encoded object graph to a java object.
- *Data mapper:* It is a tool to query and transform data inside Mule. Data transformation can be done graphically mapping the fields by dragging and dropping them inside the mule.
- *Error Handling:* In mule, if faults occur, they are referred to as exceptions. When an activity in the Mule instance fails, Mule throws an exception. To manage these exceptions, Mule allows to configure exception strategies [28].

5 Discussion and Related Work

Emergency response operations depend on the availability of relevant information in order to support search and rescue tasks and decision-making at the emergency site and at the Command and Control Center [29]. Data from diverse sources are an essential input for the ERs' decision making and situational awareness. However, to make relevant information available and accessible for ERs during emergency response is challenging as the data reside in different sources and these sources belong to different organizations. Consequently, getting access to those organizational data sources is difficult due to technological, political and organizational barriers. In addition, these organizations mostly use different terminology (semantics) for managing/storing their data. Utilization of such data during emergency response turns into a manual and intensive work for ERs in order to make it understandable to one another.

During the last years, researchers have proposed and developed various information systems by using different integration approaches to solve syntactic, schematic and semantic heterogeneity problems. Casado et al. [30], proposed and developed a data interoperability software solution for cross-border collaboration. The main goal of their work was to translate emergency related terms and symbols from one language to other language with the help of a common and modular ontology called EMERGency in case of a border fire. In addition, also to translate emergency related symbols from one country to other country. For data interoperability, service-oriented architecture has been used for solving mediation issues. In addition, in this project, semantic mapping for different predefined information artefacts, information representations and languages between countries in Europe was focused. However, if their work is compared with our work, semantic mapping of the incident information was left out.

Balogh et al. [31], proposed to use an agent-based infrastructure for supporting interoperability as part of the SECRICOM project. The data sources that were used for integration were not EROs' data sources. Moreover, the authors have used agent-based integration approach and did not look into the semantic differences of the data sources.

Fahland et al. [32], developed a prototype system called HUODINI for the flexible integration and visualization of heterogeneous data sources for disaster management. HUODINI collects information from several freely available data sources on the web, such as news feeds, personal blogs, tagged images, and seismo-graphic information. However, in their work, textual and multimedia data was integrated. Moreover, the developed and used ontology provides only event and object related information. The other information such as where, when, how and who are left out.

Romanowski et al. [33], implemented a web-based decision support tool for emergency managers by using data fusion, data mining and data integration techniques. The purpose of this developed system was to build scenarios based on the integrated data (historical data). However, in their work, the authors did not look into the semantic differences of the data sources.

Ashish et al. [34], developed an information system that provides integrated access to a wide variety of information sources. With this developed system, both previous data and real-time information are integrated. However, the purpose of the developed system was to provide information related to the location such as maps of the location and facility, floor plans of buildings in the area, hazardous material location information, and other potentially useful information such as work schedules and shift timing information. Moreover, real-time sensor data such as surveillance cameras in a building at the incident site also made available to the fire brigades. However, in their work, the authors look into the geospatial aspects, but neglects the deep semantics of the emergency.

Li et al. [10], proposed and implemented a decision support system by integrating diverse EROs data sources to enable the collaborative information sharing among community-based NGOs, public, and private organizations within a community. However, we consider the used point-to point integration approach as not scalable, that means, when the number of applications increases, the complexity of the whole system increase. In addition, any change in one application will make the whole system change. Moreover, new connection between the that application and others need to be reestablished. This can result in high maintenance costs and a lack of flexibility when it becomes necessary to make changes [35].

Mecella et al. [36], proposed and developed a 2 layer peer to peer service-oriented software infrastructure to support decision making during emergency situations. It provides a decentralized, event-driven information integration environment. In this project, task analysis technique called Hierarchical Task Analysis was used to identify the task requirements for various emergency scenarios. However, the developed solution partially solves semantic mapping of the geo-data, but neglects deep semantics of the emergency.

Alamdar et al. [37] integrated geospatial data of different sensor databases and used for a flood use-case and Lezcano et al. [38], proposed an archetype approach for integrating different sensor data sources for solving semantic heterogeneity. However, both these solutions, tried to solve semantic heterogeneity of different type of sensor data.

In [39–43], the authors integrated different spatial data sources for providing spatial data to the emergency responders, Kou et al. [44], proposed a heterogeneous data integration framework for providing video and audio data. However, to our knowledge, this framework has not yet been developed and tested with a use-case.

Raman et al. [45], proposed and developed a web-based disaster management system called CEMAS for providing resource related information to the emergency responders. The information provision was done by integrating different data sources. The main objective of their system is to provide emergency alert about surrounding area via SMS or email to the emergency responders in case of natural disasters.

Christman et al. [46], proposed a methodology to integrate tactical level information integration from two systems i.e., Civil Information Management (CIM), and Data Processing System (DPS). For data interoperability, a data exchange format called National Information Exchange Model (NIEM) was used. However, the used NIEM data model solves semantic heterogeneity partially when compared to our solution.

Subik et al. [47], provides multi-disciplinary rescue teams with an integrated and intelligent communication and information system for efficient data sharing and emergency process management before, during and after major incidents. Their developed system allows mapping internal onto an external data structures and vice versa for achieving technical and syntactical interoperability. However, their work completely neglects the semantic one.

SINTEF [48], proposed and built a middleware which allows data, system and network interoperability for multi-agency emergency collaboration and decision-making. In their project, multimedia information has been integrated by using SOA paradigm and web services technology. For requirement analysis, participatory design methodology and ethnographic studies were being used. In addition, they use EDXL standard for information exchange. This project provides data from the social media to the involved ERs for situational awareness social-media data integration. However, in their work, semantic mapping was done on unstructured data i.e., social media data. Whereas in our solution, semantic heterogeneity of structured data of existing systems is solved.

Apisakmontri [49], proposed and developed an ontology to integrate different humanitarian aid information and disaster management systems However, in their work, semantic mapping was done on unstructured data i.e., social media data. Whereas in our solution, semantic heterogeneity of structured data of existing systems is solved.

Erskine et al. [50], used a hybrid approach for aggregating data from social networks for natural disasters. Here, hybrid approach means utilizing automated data mining tools and crowdsourcing to optimize the information. However, in this study, solving semantic heterogeneity aspect was not considered.

Careem et al. [51] developed a software application called SAHANA for managing resources and information in disaster response, but does not address the semantic integration of content.

Although various information systems have been developed by introducing novel ideas to provide information to the emergency responders in order to improve emergency management, there are still gaps: (1) deep analysis of the semantics of the technological/man-made emergency domain and (2) disseminating the needed/relevant information to the involved ERs at the right time to the right person at the right time. So, we presented a methodology and developed a prototype. The novelty of our methodology lies in providing functionality for more data usage in terms of on-the-fly integration of different data sources and analysis.

Here, on-the fly data integration means, for example, after the emergency occurrence, the involved ERs realize that extra information is available at the emergency site for example, information related to victim and resources inside the building. The involved ERs could think that they can use this extra available information in their search and rescue operations. Although this information is available at the emergency site, involved ERs do not have access to that kind of information. In such a scenario, ERs could consider our implementation part, particularly the domain analysis aspect. Here, the domain analysis aspect is nothing but knowing the involved stakeholders, their information needs and so on in advance in case of an emergency.

If 90% of the emergency domain analysis is done before the emergency occurrence for all types of emergencies, then it is easy for the involved stakeholders to manage the emergency. Here 90% of the analysis is nothing but *partially who (analysis on who should involve from organizations), partially how (performing tasks depending on the emergency type), where (location of the emergency), partially what (needed resources and activities depending on the emergency type).* However, some information is generated just before the emergency i.e., when (date and time of the emergency). In addition, some information is generated during the emergency i.e., partial information of who (involved victims) and is not known by the ERs before the emergency. So, after the emergency, including this extra information in the developed system is not that difficult as the ERs get to know about the emergency situation and the needed information. This is because the implementation is something that can be automatized or modularized.

If we compare our solution with the commercial tools e.g. CIM [20], Esri's ArcMap [54], Map info [55], WebEOC [56], Crisis Commander [57] and so on, they typically have all-in-one approach i.e., in these developed tools, the information is taken in from other sources and claim that the data belongs to them at the end. Consequently, again poor access to the needed information. Furthermore, since these systems are commercial, it is not clear to us whether the semantic consistency issue has been taken in to consideration in the development of these systems. If we consider our work as whole, we find out that Xchangecore [52] is related to our work. It is an open source system developed by XchangeCore Community. Xchangecore is widely used in USA for supporting data orchestration for emergency management. This system is based on international data exchange standards such as Common Alerting Protocol (CAP), Emergency Data Exchange Language – Distribution Element (EDXL-DE), and Emergency Data Exchange Language – Resource Management (EDXL-RM). One of the components of this solution is similar to our solution i.e., information interoperability for providing real-time information. In this system, data sharing agreements are made in advance for accessing the information and for sharing. To use Xchangecore, a complex installation process is involved. Moreover, to integrate any other application to the Xchangecore, a connector has to be implemented, which can not be done by non-programmer. Furthermore, guidance is required to understand the whole systems and components. However, in our solution, different data get linked easily with the information model to present an holistic overview. In addition, all our interviews with ERs revealed that the domain analysis part can be done in advance i.e., for all kind of emergencies where ERs can be prepared.

6 Conclusions

In this paper, the authors studied a process for bringing inter-agency data together as a potential source for providing real-time information for emergency management. Based on an indoor fire emergency case study, the issues, information and functional requirements regarding access, dissemination and usage of data from existing data sources for managing emergency were identified. To address the investigated challenges and requirements, a data integration framework was proposed by using Model-driven data integration and a prototype was developed. This data integration framework consists of three components. (1) the data source handling component, (2) the semantic model component, and (3) the information presentation component. The implementation was done based on an approach called semantically-enhanced mediator-based data integration. Based on the presented approach, a prototype is developed by integrating existing data sources with the developed information model in real-time to support ERs for situational awareness and for decision-making.

In conclusion, having information from various places through mediator-based data integration approach would give more efficient access to the information during emergency management. The presented approach would also provide improvement in inter-agencies' knowledge sharing and data exchange through providing more automation in the interaction among organizations involved in emergency management. As future work, we plan to evaluate the prototype and the methodology with a questionnaire based survey and prototype demonstration workshop session with various ERs to get their feedback and recommendations for further improvements.

Acknowledgment. We would like to owe our gratitude to the Grimstad fire and rescue service personnel, and Kristiansand police staff who allocated their time and supported us during our research work. We would also like to appreciate Tina Comes and Jaziar Radianti for providing their support and help throughout our research.

References

1. Tsai, M.-K., Yau, N.-J.: Improving information access for emergency response in disasters. Nat. Hazards **66**(2), 343–354 (2013)
2. CTIF, World fire statistics. International Association of Fire and Rescue Services, p. 62 (2016). ctif.org
3. DSB. Brann_Statistikk (2016). https://www.dsb.no/menyartikler/statistikk/branner/. [cited 06.09.2016]
4. Norskbrannvernforening.   Skadeutbetalinger_etter_branner   (2015).   http://www.brannvernforeningen.no/index.asp?mal=3&fane=1&id=38636&nl=&menyfane=1
5. Nunavath, V., Radianti, J., Comes, M., Prinz, A.: Visualization of information flows and exchanged information: evidence from an indoor fire game. In: Proceedings of the 12th International Conference on Information Systems for Crisis Response and Management, Kristiansand, Norway, May 2015
6. Comes, T., et al.: Decision maps: a framework for multi-criteria decision support under severe uncertainty. Decis. Support Syst. **52**(1), 108–118 (2011)
7. Comes, T., Vybornova, O., Van de Walle, B.: Bringing structure to the disaster data typhoon: an analysis of decision-makers' information needs in the response to Haiyan. In: Proceedings of the AAAI Spring Symposium Series (SSS 2015) on Structured Data for Humanitarian Technologies: Perfect Fit or Overkill (2015)
8. Gjørv, A.B.: Evaluation report on the events of 22 July 2011, Oslo (2012)
9. SHT, Rapport om brann i vogntog på E16 i Gudvangatunnelen i Aurland (2015)
10. Li, J., et al.: Community-based collaborative information system for emergency management. Comput. Oper. Res. **42**, 116–124 (2014)
11. Nunavath, V., Prinz, A.: Reference architecture For emergency management operations. In: Nunes, M.B., Isaías, P., Powell, P. (eds.) 8th IADIS International Conference on Information Systems. IADIS, Madeira, Portugal (2015)
12. Ram, G.M., et al.: A road crisis management metamodel for an information decision support system. In: 2012 6th IEEE International Conference on Digital Ecosystems and Technologies (DEST) (2012)
13. Weick, K.E.: The collapse of sensemaking in organizations: the Mann Gulch disaster. Adm. Sci. Q. **38**, 628–652 (1993)

14. Nunavath, V., et al.: Representing fire emergency response knowledge through a domain modelling approach. In: Norsk konferanse for organisasjoners bruk av IT (2016)
15. Van de Walle, B., Turoff, M.: Decision support for emergency situations. ISeB 6(3), 295–316 (2008)
16. Meum, T., Munkvold, B.E.: Information infrastructure for crisis response coordination: a study of local emergency management in Norwegian municipalities. In: Fiedrich, F., Comes, T., Fortier, S., Geldermann, J., Müller, T. (eds.) ISCRAM, Baden-Baden, Germany (2013)
17. Beredskap, D.f.s.o., Veiledning til forskrift om organisering og dimensjonering av brann-vesen (2003)
18. NPD, Police emergency preparedness system, Part I. Guidelines for police contingency planning and incident management, ed. A.c.o.p.J. W.kluver and A.c.o.p.J. Starheimsæter. NPD, pp. 1–225. Police Directorate Publication, Norway (2011)
19. Borén, M.: Intertwining paths towards a common goal: Three emergency units side by side. University of Oslo, Oslo (2012)
20. OneVoice. Crisis Incident Management Tool (2016). https://onevoice.no/en/focus/crisis. [cited 06.09.2016]
21. Boden, A., Buscher, M., Zimmermann, M.L.A.: Domain analysis II: User Interfaces and Interaction Design (2013). http://www.sec-bridge.eu, http://www.sec-bridge.eu/content/d02.3_domain_analysis_ii.pdf
22. DSB. BRIS (2016). https://www.dsb.no/lover/brannvern-brannvesen-nodnett/artikler/bris/
23. DSB, Viktig med gode rutiner for Vision Boss og tidsplaner (2015)
24. ISO/IEC, ISO 9241-210 ergonomics of human-system interaction – part 210: Human-centered design for interactive systems (2010)
25. Nunavath, V., Prinz, A., Comes, T.: Identifying first responders information needs: supporting search and rescue operations for fire emergency response. Int. J. Inf. Syst. Crisis Response Manag. (IJISCRAM) 8(1), 25–46 (2016)
26. Nunavath, V., Prinz, A.: LifeRescue: a web based application for supporting emergency responders during indoor fire emergency management. In: 3rd International Conference on Information and Communication Technologies for Disaster Management (ICT-DM). IEEE, Vienna (2016)
27. Bertossi, L.: Virtual Data Integration, p. 144 (2003)
28. Mule. Error Handling (2017)
29. Seppänen, H., Virrantaus, K.: Shared situational awareness and information quality in disaster management. Saf. Sci. 77, 112–122 (2015)
30. Casado, R., et al.: Data interoperability software solution for emergency reaction in the Europe Union. Nat. Hazards Earth Syst. Sci. 15(7), 1563–1576 (2015)
31. Balogh, Z., et al.: Agent-based integration of rescue systems for first responders. In: Proceedings of the IEEE 10th Jubilee International Symposium on Applied Machine Intelligence and Informatics, SAMI 2012 (2012)
32. Fahland, D., et al.: HUODINI–Flexible information integration for disaster management. In: 4th International Conference on Information Systems for Crisis Response and Management (ISCRAM), Delft, NL (2007)
33. Romanowski, C.J., et al.: Information management and decision support in critical infrastructure emergencies at the local level. In: 2013 IEEE International Conference on Technologies for Homeland Security (HST). IEEE (2013)
34. Ashish, N., et al.: The software EBox: integrated information for situational awareness. In: 2009 IEEE International Conference on Intelligence and Security Informatics, ISI 2009 (2009)
35. Kress, J., et al.: Enterprise Service Bus (2013)

36. Mecella, M., et al.: Workpad: an adaptive peer-to-peer software infrastructure for supporting collaborative work of human operators in emergency/disaster scenarios. In: International Symposium on Collaborative Technologies and Systems, CTS 2006. IEEE (2006)
37. Alamdar, F., Kalantari, M., Rajabifard, A.: Towards multi-agency sensor information integration for disaster management. Comput. Environ. Urban Syst. **56**, 68–85 (2016)
38. Lezcano, L., Santos, L., García-Barriocanal, E.: Semantic integration of sensor data and disaster management systems: the emergency archetype approach. Int. J. Distrib. Sens. Netw. **9**, 1–11 (2013)
39. Bakillah, M., et al.: Mapping between dynamic ontologies in support of geospatial data integration for disaster management. In: Li, J., et al. (eds.) Geomatics Solutions for Disaster Management. Lecture Notes in Geoinformation and Cartography, pp. 201–224. Springer, Heidelberg (2007)
40. Vatseva, R., et al.: Applying GIS in seismic hazard assessment and data integration for disaster management. In: Zlatanova, S., et al. (eds.) Intelligent Systems for Crisis Management. Lecture Notes in Geoinformation and Cartography, pp. 171–183. Springer, Heidelberg (2013)
41. Stancalie, G., Craciunescu, V., Irimescu, A.: Spatial Data Integration for Emergency Services of Flood Management. In: Jones, J.A.A., Vardanian, T.G., Hakopian C. (eds.) Threats to Global Water Security. NATO Science for Peace and Security Series C: Environmental Security, pp. 155–165. Springer, Dordrecht (2009)
42. Jiping, L., et al.: Research and prospect on multi-source geospatial data integration for emergency services. In: Cartography Beyond the Ordinary World, p. 163 (2015)
43. Zhinong, Z., et al.: Integration of GIS/RS/GPS for urban fire response. In: 2012 International Conference on Computer Vision in Remote Sensing (CVRS) (2012)
44. Kou, G., et al.: A heterogeneous information integration framework for emergency management. In: Proceedings of the 3rd International Conference on Information Sciences and Interaction Sciences, ICIS 2010 (2010)
45. Raman, M., et al.: Web-based community disaster management and awareness system (CEMAS) in Malaysia. In: Proceedings of the 11th International ISCRAM Conference. University Park, Pennsylvania (2014)
46. Christman, G.J., Fila, B.D.: Civil information integration and interoperability. In: Proceedings of the 4th IEEE Global Humanitarian Technology Conference, GHTC 2014 (2014)
47. Šubik, S., et al.: SPIDER: Enabling interoperable information sharing between public institutions for efficient disaster recovery and response. In: 2010 IEEE International Conference on Technologies for Homeland Security (HST). IEEE (2010)
48. BRIDGE Project. http://www.bridgeproject.eu/en/about-bridge/objectives
49. Apisakmontri, P.: Ontology-based integration of humanitarian aid information for disaster management systems. School of Knowledge Science, p. 135. Japan Advanced Institute of Science and Technology, Japan (2016)
50. Erskine, M.A., Sibona, C., Kalantar, H.: Aggregating, Analyzing, and Diffusing Natural Disaster Information: A Research Framework (2013)
51. Careem, M., et al.: Sahana: overview of a disaster management system. In: 2006 International Conference on Information and Automation (2006)
52. Xchangecore. Data Archestration tool. http://www.xchangecore.org/
53. MuleESB. https://www.mulesoft.com/integration-solutions/dataweave-integration
54. Esri's ArcMap. http://www.esri.com/arcgis/about-arcgis
55. Map info. http://www.mapinfo.com/
56. WebEOC. https://www.intermedix.com/solutions/webeoc
57. Crisis Commander. http://usa.autodesk.com/adsk/servlet/item%3FsiteID%3D123112%26id%3D12236790

User Context in a Decision Support System
for Stock Market

Percy Soares Machado[✉], Nayat Sanchez-Pi[✉], and Vera Maria B. Werneck[✉]

Instituto de Matemática e Estatística –IME, Mestrado em Ciências Computacionais,
Universidade do Estado do Rio de Janeiro – UERJ, Rua São Francisco Xavier 524 – 6°
Andar – Bl. B, Rio de Janeiro, RJ 20550-013, Brazil
percy.trainee@gmail.com, {nayat,vera}@ime.uerj.br

Abstract. This paper presents a proposal for a Decision Support System sensitive to the user's context in the area of investment. This area is especially complicated due to the complex nature of the stock market. Therefore, a context-sensitive
decision support can be a great support for investors. In the literature survey on
DSS for investments in the stock market could be found that very little has been
explored regarding the investor profile in financial decisions-making systems.
Any practical experiment was not found where the investor profile has been
applied on the recommendations for investment in the stock market. The work
emphasized the main points to be considered in the User Context implementation
for decision support systems development. The main motivation for this work
was to demonstrate how the performance of Decision Support Systems for investment in stock market could be improved through the application of user context
to their recommendation models. A recommendation system for buying and
selling of stocks, based on genetic algorithms, was implemented and measured
the performance in various test scenarios, with user profiles and without user
profile features. The system configured without user profile, often performed
below results than the different profiles modeled and implemented. To confirm
the preliminary results, the ANOVA test was conducted and the null hypothesis
was refuted at 0.0001 level.

Keywords: User context · Genetic algorithm · Stock market investment

1 Introduction

Context-aware computing is an important area for Decision Support Systems (DSS).
These systems often help people make decisions by analyzing the several options with
greater speed, in order to obtain better results for their problems. By using the user
context, the solution employed is closest to the user reality and expectations.

This paper presents a proposal for a Decision Support System sensitive to the user's
context in the area of investment. This area is especially complicated due to the complex
nature of the stock market, being very difficult to elaborate a model able to predict the
stock price. Therefore, a context-sensitive decision support can be a great support for
investors.

© Springer International Publishing AG 2017
S. Yamamoto (Ed.): HIMI 2017, Part II, LNCS 10274, pp. 260–271, 2017.
DOI: 10.1007/978-3-319-58524-6_22

The work emphasized the main points to be considered in the context of User implementation for decision support systems in a context user. Therefore, the main motivation for this work was to demonstrate how the performance of Decision Support Systems for investment in stock market could be improved through the application of user context to their recommendation models.

During the research, some tests was applied to measure and compare the results of the application of user context in Decision Support Systems. In this simulation, a recommendation system of buying and selling of stocks, based on genetic algorithms, were implemented and measured the performance in various test scenarios, with investor profile configuration and without user profile features. The work identified and modeled different investor profiles and their features by creating classes in JAVA programming language to encapsulate all aspects related to the user profile for investment in stocks.

In the literature survey on DSS for investments in the stock market could be found that very little has been explored on the profile of the investor in financial decision-making systems (Lipinski 2008; Louwerse and Rothkrantz 2014; Baba et al. 2002). However, the research of Samaras and Matsatsinis (2004) addressed the subject in a theoretical form, modeling a portfolio allocation system based on the investor profile. Any practical experiment was not found where the investor profile has been applied on the investment recommendations in the stock market.

In order to evaluate the results of user context adoption in decision support systems for investment, the system based on Genetic Algorithms of Lipinski (2008) was implemented and extended with characteristics of Conservative, Moderate and Aggressive. Several simulations were done in different time scenarios, comparing the profitability of the system with user profile and without user profile features. In the end, the results were analyzed and submitted to the ANOVA test.

2 Related Works

A literature survey was done in order to evaluate the Decision Support systems for investment in the stock market. This paper sought an overview of the strategies and techniques used by these systems and identify possible improvement opportunities.

The search process of this survey was done through consulting the data sources from August to October 2015, being revised in November 2015. After applying the inclusion and exclusion criteria, there were 80 articles found. From there, all selected papers were read to perform the collection of information.

The analyzed papers developed Decision Support Systems for stock trading. In general, the systems succeeded in their recommendations, so that simulations made with real data were able to get attractive earnings. After processing the results, it was possible to verify that Artificial Intelligence (AI) is present in most of the works found. This is in line with the tendency of Decision Support Systems to embody AI techniques to aggregate knowledge into decision-making, verified by Perraju (2013). Some authors even (Huang 2012; Lipinski 2008; Baba et al. 2002) use more than one IA technique to compose the solution model for the problem.

The most used techniques are Neural Networks, Genetic Algorithms and Fuzzy Logic. Together they are present in 70% of the total. The Fig. 1 shows the graph with the main techniques of Artificial Intelligence used on the development of Decision Support Systems for investment. This metric counts only traditional Artificial Intelligence techniques, it does not consider new techniques developed by the authors.

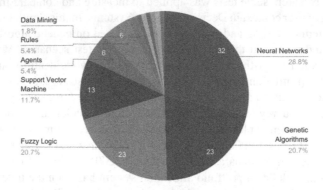

Fig. 1. Artificial intelligence techniques used in decision support systems

It is possible to verify a tendency of the more recent works to be more complex and to use hybrid models (two or more AI technique). While older papers employed simple models (only one AI technique). Most of the works found (65%) still have simple AI models, while the remaining ones (35%) innovated adopting hybrid models.

These systems are recommended for all investors who wish to invest in stocks. However, considering the articles found in the literature survey, there is no distinction among the types of users that may be using the system. That is, the investor is treated in a generic way, and his personal characteristics are not considered.

3   User Context

Context-sensitive computing is a paradigm defined by Schilit (1995) that studies methods for modeling and using context information. The context consists of the following components: where the user is, with whom the user is and what resources are nearby (Schilit 1995). According to Sánchez-Pi et al. (2012), context information can be user location, time, space, device type, meteorological conditions, user activity, what people or devices are nearby, etc. However, Dey (2001) defines context as any information that can be used to describe the state of an entity. Chen et al. (2000) still classifies the context in Physical (environmental factors, usually captured by sensors), Computational (hardware resources available) or User (user profile, focused on his needs, preferences, and mood).

Considering the user as part of the context, Kang (2008) differentiated context into two types: internal and external. Internal context describes the user's state, for example, his emotional state. The external context refers to the state of the environment, such as location, time, etc.

Within the computational area, it is possible to say that a system is sensitive to context if it offers relevant information and services to the user. This relevance depends exclusively of the user preferences (Dey 2001). Sánchez-Pi et al. (2012) state that context-sensitive systems must be able to adapt to context changes in order to maintain quality of service for users.

In the Stock Market environment, the user context concept is clearly perceived in the investor personal characteristics. Although there are several types of financial investments available to the investor. Not all investment are recommended for all people, because each type of investment has its peculiarities. In order to know if an opportunity is right for a particular person, it is important that the investor knows his profile. After performing this analysis, it is possible to select the best investment options, avoiding possible future frustrations with an inappropriate recommendation to the investor profile (Rambo 2014).

According to Haubert et al. (2014), it is fundamental to choose the investment according to the investor characteristics and needs. Thus, it is possible to recommend riskier or more conservative assets, according to the individual preferences of each person.

The Como Investir (2014) website did a survey of the main factors that affect the profile of the investor. According to this research, the characteristics found that most exert influence are age, value available for investment, horizon, risk tolerance and prior knowledge.

One of the currently used techniques by financial institutions to assist the profile identification is the Investor Profile Analysis (IPA) questionnaire (Como Investir 2014). The work of Souza (2005) compared three risk tolerance questionnaires from different US financial institutions. According to the research, after analyzing the questionnaires answered, these institutions classify investors into three groups: Conservative, Moderate and Aggressive.

In the Conservative profile, investors are mainly looking for security and liquidity in their investments, not being willing to take risks in their applications in a way that prioritizes the preservation of equity to the detriment of portfolio profitability (Frankberg 1999). According to Frankberg (1999), in general, they are adults over 40 years of age, married with children and financially stabilized.

The Moderate profile look for a balance between security and profitability. People in this profile are willing to take some risk in order to get better returns. They have some knowledge about the market and evaluate in each investment whether the risk outweighs the profitability (Frankberg 1999). According to Frankberg (1999), individuals between 30 and 40 years old, with children and married form this group. They are susceptible to small losses due to the search for greater profitability.

The Aggressive profile is made up of investors that aim at maximum profitability and have high-risk tolerance. Most of your portfolio is for riskier applications, and especially for stocks. Therefore, this profile is subject to greater losses than the others (Frankberg 1999). According to Frankberg (1999) the Aggressive is the profile that most dedicates time to their investments and, generally, they are the youngest investors, singles and without children.

4 Evolutionary Decision Support System for Stock Trading Using User Context

4.1 Methodology

A paper from the literature review was selected to be implemented and become possible the comparison of the results of the system with user profile and without user profile features. The following selection criteria was used: the works should provide their algorithms in order to allow the system to be implemented and tested, use some of the most used Artificial Intelligence techniques in DSS for investment, and more recent publications were selected instead of old ones.

From the described criteria, the following work was selected for the implementation and execution of the simulation: Evolutionary Decision Support System for Stock Market Trading (Lipinski 2008). This system used Genetic Algorithms in its development. This technique is one of the most used by the authors in the development of Decision Support Systems for investment, according to literature survey (Sect. 2).

4.2 Evolutionary Decision Support System for Stock Market Trading (Lipinski 2008)

Lipinski (2008) proposed a Decision Support System, based on Genetic Algorithms, to recommend buy and sell stocks on the Paris Stock Exchange. This system works by analyzing the signals given by the technical analysis indicators, and consolidates this information to compose recommendations for buying and selling stocks.

The system treat the individuals as a set of weights associated with the indicators of technical analysis:

$$y = (w_1, w_2, \ldots, w_n)$$

where w represents the weight associated with each indicator of the technical analysis. Initially, random weights are assigned to each individual chromosome. From there, output signals are calculated through the weighted average of the indicators multiplied by their respective weights:

$$s = (w_1.f_1(K) + w_2.f_1(K) + \ldots + w_n.f_n(K))$$

where K represents historical stock price data and f are the indicators of technical analysis. The algorithm recommends buy stocks if the output signal s is greater than the upper limit (0.5), and recommends sell stocks if the signal is less than the lower limit ($-$0.5). The author tested the *Sharpe, Sortino* and *Sterling* metrics for the fitness function, achieving the best results with the latter.

The algorithm (Fig. 2) adopted a very simple stock trading strategy. Whenever a buy recommendation is made, the algorithm simulates the purchase of half of the available equity capital. Similarly, when there is a sell recommendation, the algorithm simulates the sale of half of the stocks it owns.

```
1  P ← RANDOM-POPULATION(N);
2  POPULATION-EVALUATION(P, ϱ);
3  while not TERMINATION-CONDITION(P)
4  do
5      P(P) ← PARENT-SELECTION(P, M);
6      P(C) ← CROSSOVER(P(P));
7      MUTATION(P(C), τ, τ₀);
8      REPLACEMENT(P, P(C));
9      POPULATION-EVALUATION(P, ϱ);
```

Fig. 2. Investment strategy based on genetic algorithms. font: LIPINSKI, Lipinski 2008

The first step of the algorithm is to create the initial population P. This population of solutions is generated with N individuals of random weights between 0 and 1, giving rise to M "child" individuals. After creation, the performance of P is evaluated by the fitness function chosen. Then, several genetic operations are performed with the population so that it evolves. Firstly, the selection of M individuals of P is done to compose the population Pp, so that the fittest individuals are more likely to be selected. Then, crossover of Pp is done to create a new population Pc, this also goes through the process of mutation. Finally, the sets of solutions P and Pc are compared, remaining only the fittest individuals. This process is repeated until the solution population stops evolving.

In order to test the system effectiveness, the author performed an experiment with *Renault* (RNO.PA) stock from September 03 to November 23, 2007. The best results occurred when the algorithm was configured with 200 individuals, 300 children individuals, and using *Sterling* as fitness function. The system achieved a return of 0.1734%, above the –6.0% loss on the stock price in the same period.

This low return may even be enough for conservative investors, but it would certainly displease the more bold investors. Despite this, the algorithm was able to make a profit for the investor, while in the same period, only buying and holding the stock would mean a loss of 6.0%.

4.3   Implementation of Evolutionary Decision Support System for Stock Trading

The JAVA programming language was chosen for the implementation. A free technology allows the development of Genetic Algorithms, essential for the accomplishment of this work. As data source, the paper used historical stock price data, provided by Yahoo Finance (2016). These data were useful both for the training of the algorithm and to perform all the test scenarios of this work.

In order to verify if the system implementation is in accordance with the algorithm proposed by Lipinski (2008), the same test performed by the author was repeated with the implemented system. Thirty simulations were performed with the RNO.PA stock, in order to confirm if the same results would be obtained in both cases. Unfortunately, as the author did not inform the period that he used to train the algorithm, the training period was established from January to November 2005. The results of the simulations are available in Fig. 3 and it can be considered close to the results obtained by Lipinski

(2008). The difference found in some values can be justified by some possible difference in the period used for training the algorithm that is not specified and cannot be found.

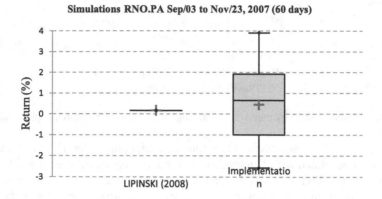

Simulations RNO.PA Sep/03 to Nov/23, 2007 (60 days)

Fig. 3. Boxplot chart of simulations RNO.PA Sep/03 to Nov/23, 2007

Once the system was completed, the focus turned to the development of the User Profile. The inheritance and polymorphism features of object-oriented programming were used to allow the system to support different user profiles. Thus, the abstract class *Strategy* has been created, and all other user profile classes inherit from that same "model" class, but each has its own peculiarities. The *AutorStrategy* class implements the original model without a User Profile, and the other classes *ConservativeStrategy*, *ModerateStrategy*, and *AggressiveStrategy* represent respectively the investor profiles. The user profile classes differ from the system developed by Lipinski (2008) on the following questions: fitness function, limits for output signals, and stock trading strategy.

In the Conservative profile, the fitness function was not changed, that is, used the Sterling index that measures the risk and return ratio of the investment. However, the buy signal limit was increased from 0.5 to 0.8 and the sell signal limit decreased from –0.5 to –0.4. These changes intend to provide more confidence to the Conservative investor, increasing the degree of certainty required to buy stocks and reducing the level of certainty required for sale. The stock trading strategy has not changed.

For the Moderate profile, it was observed that *Sterling* metric is not related to the increase of the returns and, therefore, does not agree with the objectives of the profile. Thus, return was chosen as a fitness function for the Moderate profile. The output signal limits were set at 0.6 for buy and –0.5 for sell. The stock trading strategy was also modified in order to achieve higher returns. At each buy signal, all available equity is invested in stocks, rather than just half as the author suggests, likewise, at every sell signal, all stocks in portfolio are sold.

In the Aggressive profile the return was also used as fitness function, and the output signal limits are 0.6 for buy and –0.6 for sell. The main change in this profile was the stock trading strategy. If a sell signal is identified, but the user does not have any action, the algorithm perform a short selling of stocks corresponding to 80% of the available capital. This strategy, while profitable in times of falling stock prices, is also more risky and has an additional cost of 0.5% of the value of the transaction. After the user profile implementation in the system, it was possible to perform the simulations.

5 Evaluation of Evolutionary Decision Support System for Stock Trading

The Ibovespa index (BVSP) was chosen to simulate stock buy and sell orders to test the system. Unlike the simulation done by Lipinski (2008), which tested the *Renault* (RNO.PA) stock, the choice of a stock index was adopted to any particular event of a specific stock do not influencing the results. In the literature review it was possible to find other works (Kara et al. 2011, Boyacioglu and AVCI 2010, Chen et al. 2007), who also chose to use stock index rather than simply stock.

The first step of the system execution was to generate and train the population of possible solutions. The system requests the user profile that will be evaluated. Each population is trained to achieve the objectives of a specific profile and, therefore, the entire process is performed for each of the four profiles identified in this work (Conservative, Moderate, Aggressive and without user profile). The training was performed considering the historical Ibovespa index data from January 2012 to August 2016. This training process continues until the population's fitness stabilizes.

After training, the best individual in the population is selected and submitted to the test scenarios. Different periods were evaluated, as discussed in the investor characteristics, different profiles have different investment terms.

In order to ensure consistency of results, 30 simulations (training and test) were done for each scenario, and for each investor profile. Each simulation takes around 9 min to train the algorithm, and a few seconds to test. Considering the 30 simulations done, the process lasted about 4 h and 30 min for each user profile in each test scenario below.

5.1 One Month Scenario

The Fig. 4 shows that the short period of 1 month was inconclusive, because the configurations without user profile, Conservative and Moderate, did not make any recommendation of buy or sell stocks in most of the simulations (0.0%). On the other hand, the Aggressive profile achieved an average return of 148%. This result is extremely positive, and much higher than the other profiles and Ibovespa.

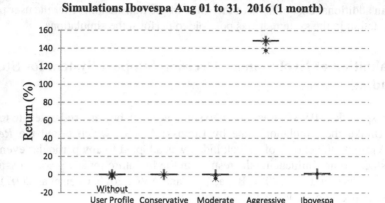

Fig. 4. Boxplot chart of simulations Ibovespa August 01 to 31, 2016

5.2   One Year Scenario

The Fig. 5 shows that Aggressive profile increased its gains so far and achieved an average return of 166% in the period. The Moderate profile obtained 3.5%, however, below the Ibovespa (13.8%). Conservative profile remained stable. The average return of the system without user profile was a little below zero.

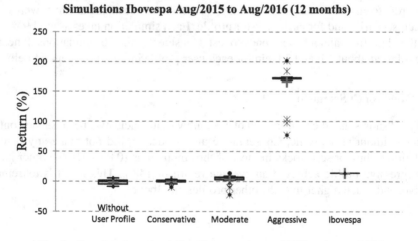

Fig. 5. Boxplot chart simulation Ibovespa August 2015 to August 2016

5.3   Five Years Scenario

In 5 years, it is possible to see in Fig. 6 that all the profiles had a profit, Aggressive 256%, Moderate 38% and Conservative 13.5%. This performance was above the 9.7% achieved by the system without a user profile. However, the Ibovespa had a loss of –16% in the period.

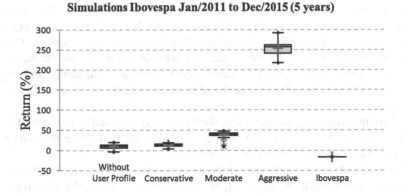

Fig. 6. Boxplot chart of simulations Ibovespa January 2011 to December 2015

5.4 Result Analysis

The results of the simulations indicate that it is possible to improve the recommendations of Decision Support Systems for investment in stocks market through the implementation of user context. In the most of test scenarios performed, the user profiles were able to have an average return higher than the return of the system without user profile features. In some cases, the result of the system without user profile was equivalent to the result of the user profiles and in isolated cases; the Moderate profile had the worst performance.

In order to confirm the preliminary results obtained in the simulations, the test results with the Ibovespa index from January 2011 to December 2015, using four different user profile configurations, were submitted to ANOVA test (analysis of variance). From the test result (Table 1), it is possible to refute the null hypothesis at the significance level of 0.0001. That is, there is evidence of significant differences among the means of returns of the four groups of users, with the probability less than 0.01% that these results are the same. Therefore, it is possible to conclude that the results are different. If the results are different and the median of return was higher using the user profile, then the hypothesis that it is possible to improve the recommendations of Decision Support Systems for stock market using User Context is true.

Table 1. ANOVA test (analysis of variance) returns of different user profile configurations from January 2011 to December 2015 (5 years)

Source	DF	Sum of squares	Mean squares	F	Pr > F
Model	3	362108,005	120702,668	896,169	**<0,0001**
Error	116	15623,746	134,687		
Total corrected	119	377731,751			

6   Conclusion

The work proposed to improve the recommendations made by Decision Support Systems for investments through the implementation of user profile. To verify this hypothesis, the investment system of (Lipinski 2008), based on Genetic Algorithms, was chosen to be implemented and tested with User Context and without User Context.

In order to create a model for the system, the investor's behavior and characteristics were studied. The investor profiles identified were Conservative, Moderate and Aggressive. Each profile was properly analyzed and modeled with its own characteristics and objectives.

The Java programming language was used for the system and User Context implementation. Classes with each of the profiles were developed in order to promote the configuration and reuse of the investor profiles.

In the most test scenarios, the user profile settings worked as expected and they were able to achieve their goals. As expected, no investor profile was the best in all circumstances. The Aggressive profile achieved excellent returns in short periods, accounting for 148% in 1 month and maximum yield of 256% in 5 years, but it did not perform as well in longer periods. The Moderate profile had returns close to zero in the short term, however, it had significant returns in the medium and long term, with the user profile having the best performance in 5 years (38%), surpassing the Ibovespa index (-16%). The Conservative profile also had near zero yields in the short term; however, in the long term it achieved 13.5% of return investing only in low risk applications.

The system configured without user profile had results lower than the Aggressive, Moderate, and Conservative profiles. Only in isolated and short-term cases, the system without user profile was able to overcome the Moderate profile. This demonstrates the relevance the User Context implementation was for the simulations results. To confirm the preliminary results, the ANOVA test was performed and the null hypothesis was refuted to the 0.0001 level. As differences were found between the results and the median of the return was higher using user profile, so the hypothesis that it is possible to improve the recommendations of Decision Support Systems for stock market using User Context is accepted.

Instead of selecting some stock to perform the simulations, the paper chose to use the Ibovespa index to perform the test scenarios. In practice, the results found in this work are close to the results that would be obtained if were invested in the stock of any big company, which follow the Ibovespa index. However, for predictions of smaller companies that do not follow the index variation, new simulations with these stocks would be necessary. Considering that Genetic Algorithms search for to provide optimized solutions for any problem, it is very likely that the system also have good results with stocks of smaller companies.

As future works, it is possible to improve the training time of the algorithm. Each test scenario needs about 4 h and 30 min to train each user profile. If multiplied by the four profile settings, each simulation took a total of 18 h to execute. This delay in an investment application on the stock market can be harmful to the user. Perhaps the combination of Genetic Algorithms and Neural Networks could create a system that does accurate recommendations and requires less training time.

References

Baba, N., Inoue, N., Yanjun, Y.: Utilization of soft computing techniques for constructing reliable decision support systems for dealing stocks. In: Proceedings of the 2002 International Joint Conference on Neural Networks, pp. 2150–2155. IEEE (2002)

Chen, Y., Yang, B., Abraham, A.: Flexible neural trees ensemble for stock index modeling. Neurocomputing 70(4), 697–703 (2007)

Como Investir. Análise de perfil do investidor (2016), disponível em. http://www.comoinvestir.com.br/investidores/analise-de-perfil/paginas/default.aspx. Accessed 23 May 2016

Dey, A.K.: Understanding and using context. Pers. Ubiquit. Comput. 5(1), 4–7 (2001)

Frankenberg, L.: Seu futuro financeiro: você é o maior responsável. Gulf Professional Publishing (1999)

Lipinski, P.: Evolutionary decision support system for stock market trading. In: Dochev, D., Pistore, M., Traverso, P. (eds.) AIMSA 2008. LNCS (LNAI), vol. 5253, pp. 405–409. Springer, Heidelberg (2008). doi:10.1007/978-3-540-85776-1_39

Louwerse, V.; Rothkrantz, L.: Intraday stock forecasting. In: Proceedings of the 15th International Conference on Computer Systems and Technologies, pp. 202–209. ACM (2014)

Haubert, F.L.C., de Lima, M.V.A., Herling, L.H.D.: Finanças comportamentais: um estudo com base na teoria do prospecto e no perfil do investidor de estudantes de cursos stricto sensu da grande Florianópolis. Revista Eletrônica Estratégia e Negócios. Florianópolis 5(2), 171–199, mai/ago (2012)

Huang, C.: A hybrid stock selection model using genetic algorithms and support vector regression. Appl. Soft Comput. 12(2), 807–818 (2012)

Kang, H., Suh, E., Yoo, K.: Packet-based context aware system to determine information system user's context. Expert Syst. Appl. 35(1), 286–300 (2008)

Perraju, T.: Artificial intelligence and decision support systems. Int. J. Adv. Res. IT Eng. 2(4), abr 2013

Rambo, A.C.: O perfil do investidor e melhores investimentos: da teoria à prática do mercado brasileiro. Monografia do curso de Ciências Econômicas. Universidade Federal de Santa Catarina, Florianópolis (2014)

Samaras, G.D., Matsatsinis, N.F.: Intelligent investor: an intelligent decision support system for portfolio management. Oper. Res. Int. J. 4(3), 357–371 (2004)

Sánchez-Pi, N., Carbó, J., Molina, J.M.: A knowledge-based system approach for a context-aware system. Knowl.-Based Syst. 27, 1–17 (2012)

Schilit, W.N.: A System Architecture for Context-Aware Mobile Computing. Universidade de Columbia, Departamento de Ciência da Computação, Tese de Doutorado (1995)

de Souza, C.R.V.: Avaliando Questionários de Risco e o Comportamento do Investidor sobre a Ótica de Behavioral Finance. FGV, Rio de Janeiro (2005)

Yahoo Finance. Historical Stock Data. http://finance.yahoo.com, Accessed 11 Aug (2016)

Designing a Predictive Coding System for Electronic Discovery

Dhivya Soundarajan and Sara Anne Hook(✉)

Department of Human-Centered Computing,
Indiana University School of Informatics and Computing,
535 W. Michigan Street, Indianapolis, IN 46202, USA
dsoundar@umail.iu.edu, sahook@iupui.edu

Abstract. This paper presents the preliminary results of a pilot project to design a predictive coding system for electronic discovery (e-discovery) that will be able to handle potentially relevant evidence in a myriad of formats and that will have the features and functionality that lawyers and members of the legal team will find most useful. We developed our predictive coding system to combine available software tools with particular emphasis on usability and in making the user interface as intuitive, attractive and user-friendly as possible. Future work will include a survey and interviews with potential users, testing the system with larger sets of files and documents, and continued refinement of the user interface and backend processing.

Keywords: Electronic discovery · Predictive coding · Technology-assisted review · Legal technology · Law firms

1 Introduction

Over the past year, we have been designing a predictive coding system based on readily available software and natural language processing. Our paper provides a brief overview of existing predictive coding/TAR systems, comparing these systems to what lawyers who are responsible for an electronic (e-discovery) process actually need and highlighting the shortcomings in existing systems that our system will attempt to address in its special features and functionality. We demonstrate the current iteration of our predictive coding system using a typical set of documents and file formats, with screenshots to show our system's information architecture and user interface, how the results of a query are presented to users and the balance between recall and precision. Particular issues that guided our decision-making as we designed our system were security, especially given the lawyer's duties with respect to confidentiality, ease of use, ability to limit access to certain materials and how to train the system itself as well as to provide guidance to potential users. As part of the paper, we outline plans for future work, including more extensive development and testing of our system with larger sets of documents and a broader range of types of files and formats beyond traditional text-based materials and incorporating continuous active learning and built-in alerts, reminders and tips for using our system more effectively.

© Springer International Publishing AG 2017
S. Yamamoto (Ed.): HIMI 2017, Part II, LNCS 10274, pp. 272–287, 2017.
DOI: 10.1007/978-3-319-58524-6_23

2 Background

Although questions about evidence in digital format were raised in cases as early as the 1980s and 1990s, the emerging area of law known as electronic discovery (e-discovery) did not begin to find its way into the typical lawyer's lexicon until the mid-2000s. Two major events occurred during this time that marked the true beginning of the field of e-discovery and that continue to form the foundation of how the process is handled today. In Zubulake v. UBS Warburg, Judge Shira A. Scheindlin articulated major principles and themes regarding e-discovery, including the responsibilities of lawyers and clients, sanctions for spoliation of evidence and what constitutes accessible versus inaccessible data [1]. In 2006, the Federal Rules of Civil Procedure were amended to incorporate Judge Scheindlin's rulings and to establish the discoverability of Electronically Stored Information (ESI) as an umbrella term intended to encompass both current and future technology and the data that it generates. E-discovery is something that impacts everyone, whether they know if or not, because it deals with the proper collection, preservation, analysis and production of evidence in digital form. To put it bluntly, if you are sued, the opposing party's lawyer will request nearly every piece of digital evidence in any format that might be relevant to the case, including email and text messages and social media. Anyone can find himself/herself needing to comply with requests for potentially relevant evidence – in electronic or paper/hard copy form.

One of the special concerns with e-discovery is that a faulty and incomplete process, particularly during the review stage, can result in sanctions and waive the attorney-client privilege or other confidentiality doctrine if ESI that could and should have been protected is inadvertently produced to the opposing party. Such failures, especially for breaches in confidentiality, can result in disciplinary action being taken against the lawyer in the states where he/she is licensed [2]. The Federal Rules of Civil Procedure were amended again in December 2015 to shorten the timeframes for various stages in an e-discovery process, to place a greater emphasis on proportionality and to provide clarity on when and what kinds of sanctions the court can impose for spoliation of evidence [3]. Courts are already applying the amended version of the Federal Rules of Civil Procedure, which means that an e-discovery process must now be completed in a significantly reduced period of time and with greater specificity required for requests and objections [4]. The e-discovery process becomes increasingly complex as lawyers and clients deal with wearable devices and the Internet of Things, which create and store even more potentially relevant electronic evidence in a wider variety of files and formats.

There have been many attempts to use technology to address the complexity, time commitment, risk and expense of an e-discovery process. In the past ten years, vendors have improved and enhanced the services and software they offer for e-discovery, digital forensics, litigation support and information governance [5]. One of the services that some vendors provide is predictive coding, which is often referred to or included as part of Technology-Assisted Review (TAR). Predictive coding combines computer speed with human reasoning in the form of artificial intelligence and allows the computer to learn and make decisions [6]. Initially, such tools were looked at with considerable suspicion, even though information retrieval, indexing, machine learning and data analytics have been used in other disciplines for many years [7]. Fortunately, the reticence to use these types of systems in litigation has faded somewhat, illustrated by a long line of cases that start with strong support of computer-assisted review articulated in Da Silva Moore v. Publicis Groupe, which is described as the first published opinion recognizing TAR as "an acceptable way to search for relevant ESI in appropriate cases." [8–10]

Summaries of recent cases about predictive coding/TAR can be found in The Sedona Conference's new publication, TAR Case Law Primer [11]. However, concerns remain about whether predictive coding systems are as effective as they could be, although the court in the Dynamo Holdings case noted that the gold standard of human review is a myth as is the expectation that e-discovery requires a perfect response [12, 13]. Other courts have held that while the use of predictive coding is permissible, a responding party cannot be forced to use it [14].

Predictive coding can be used throughout an e-discovery process, including early case assessment, reviewing ESI before production, prioritizing pre-production review, sorting ESI for privilege, for overall quality control, such as comparing human review with predictive coding results, and in reviewing production from the opposing party as well as during other stages of litigation, such as preparing for depositions, responding to summary judgment motions and working with expert witnesses. Some common features of predictive coding/TAR systems are concept searching, contextual searching, metadata searching (ESI must usually be produced in native format with the metadata intact), relevance probability and ranking, clustering, and sorting ESI by the issues and arguments in a case.

3 Methods

In order to design the interface, the first step was to conceptualize our ideas based on factual user data rather than grounding it only on technical assumptions. Although several vendors provide predictive coding/Technology Assisted Review (TAR) software as part of their overall electronic discovery services, we were especially concerned about developing a predictive coding system that is user-friendly and in keeping with proper usability principles for interface design. In setting our strategy, it was essential that our preliminary design be based on clear, unbiased feedback obtained from a passionate specialist within the field of e-discovery. Given that there are similar kinds of software already in the legal technology marketplace, we started our project by conducting research on several existing exemplary models for predictive coding, comparing their features and functionality and noting gaps in what users might require. From here, we identified our problem space.

4 The Problem Space

A typical predictive coding system uses analytics to assist lawyers in collecting, preserving, reviewing and analyzing the relevancy of the Electronically Stored Information (ESI) in a particular legal case. It is important to note that ESI can encompass a wide range of documents and file types. In a manual system, the lawyer reviews all potentially relevant ESI by hand, classifies the ESI as relevant or not relevant, and indicates whether the ESI can be protected under one of the confidentiality doctrines. In predictive coding system, the lawyer reviews and develops a model with a preliminary set of documents that train the system. The machine routines this analysis model as its algorithm and categorizes the documents appropriately, thus drastically reducing the overall cost and time required to perform these phases of an e-discovery process, hopefully ensuring its accuracy and avoiding either failing to include potentially relevant ESI or inadvertently producing ESI that could and should be protected. One issue with existing predictive coding services is the user interface. These predictive coding services tend to focus more on yielding high throughput, but seem less concerned about the ease with which users interact with the system.

5 The Overall Framework

We can first look at the overall system architecture that we conceived of to acquire a deep understanding of the purpose of the user interface (Fig. 1).

The model accepts multimodal input, henceforth referred to as Electronically Stored Information (ESI) of any data format that can be stored in the repository by using the Hadoop Distributed File System (HDFS). The natural language processing component incorporates the supervised machine learning algorithms that support conceptual search. Conceptual search is an automated information retrieval method to search electronically stored, unstructured text that is conceptually similar to the

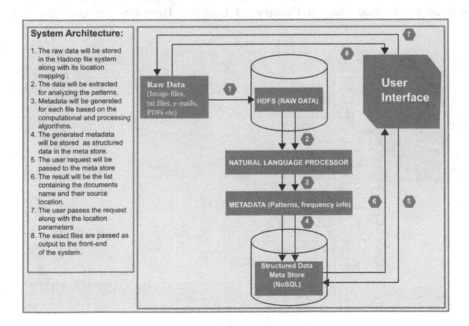

Fig. 1. Architecture of the system

information provided in a search query. A supervised learning algorithm promotes not only passive analysis of data, but also accepts a lawyer's periodic input to enhance the accuracy and efficiency of the process. The robust algorithms for the predictive analysis are applied to this huge "raw data store." The resulting metadata informs the frequency of a particular keyword for a file and is stored as structured metadata in a "meta store." Communications between the "metadata store – interface" and the "interface – raw data store" are parameterized to support more reliable storage and retrieval of data from different servers since data is in a law firm may be distributed and stored in multiple servers or even in the cloud.

A "Weka tool" generates a sample report that shows the recall and precision rate of passing an absolute training set to a model that uses classifiers to group files based on most frequently occurring common words in the files (Fig. 2).

An initial interface was developed only to verify that the basic functional needs for testing the model were met, rather than incorporating usability considerations (Figs. 3 and 4).

As outlined in the Background section above, even though there are many benefits to using predictive coding/Technology Assisted Review(TAR), lawyers still hesitate to use it because of their unfamiliarity with the technology. Thus, an optimal solution to this problem must focus on hiding technical complexities from users by designing an intuitive, attractive, easy-to-navigate interface that will give users comfort in having control over the system. To understand the key requirements of the system, one of the authors, who has considerable experience with e-discovery, provided extensive insights and feedback on the design and development process of the system over several months. In addition to the findings from our review of the literature and existing predictive coding services, we relied on books by Levy and Nunnally and Farkas as well as the Nielson Norman Group's 10 Usability Heuristics for User Interface

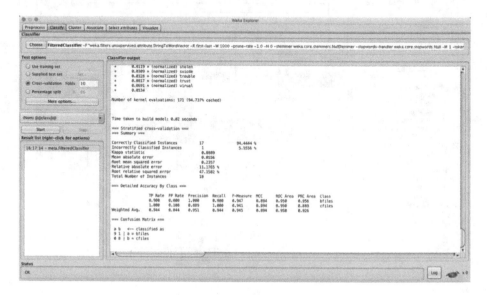

Fig. 2. Weka tool report

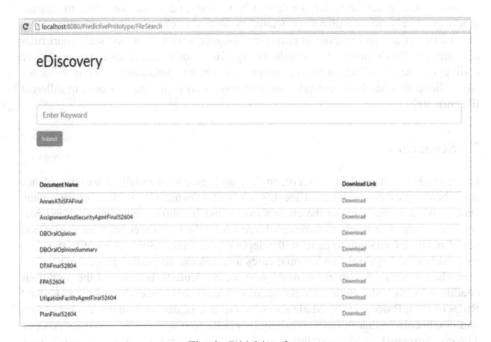

Fig. 3. Initial interface

Fig. 4. Initial interface

Design [15–17] During the first phases of the development of our system, we were fortunate to be able to present our work at two local conferences to audiences with expertise in data mining, interaction design and usability testing.

The interface encompasses the following modules:

- Search
- Upload
- List
- Tag
- Inline tooltip

6 Persona

To understand the behavior of our prospective users and their mental models in interacting with each of these modules, we developed a persona of a law firm employee who would be working in e-discovery and followed this persona through a typical e-discovery scenario.

Marie is paralegal working for a law firm that concentrates its practice on general business law, bankruptcy and creditors' rights. She has a certificate in Paralegal Studies and several years of experience. She facilitates and manages e-discovery processes, under the guidance and supervision of the lawyers who are responsible for the cases she works on. Her roles may encompass educating clients on e-discovery policies, drafting litigation hold procedures for the lawyer's review and communication to clients, working closely with e-discovery teams to assess a client's electronically stored information (ESI), and helping to ensure compliance with federal and state court rules and the law firm's protocols for e-discovery. Her motivation is to use a predictive coding system to collect, preserve, analyze and review potentially relevant evidence from clients that has been generated by a variety of software and is stored in different file formats.

7 Scenario

Marie needs to help collect, preserve, analyze and review potentially relevant evidence for a bankruptcy case. She must identify a set of relevant files such as client's bank statements and details about the client's assets and liabilities, including real and personal property. She needs to retrieve a large set of the client's email transactions and social media information to increase the depth of the search. She will identify the most frequently used keywords from similar cases to accelerate the search process. There is a very short timeline for an e-discovery process, particularly because of the ambitious deadlines for each step in the process articulated in the 2015 amendments to the Federal Rules of Civil Procedure [3]. Marie also needs to consolidate and maintain a list of files and documents so that in future recalling this collection will not be a tedious process. The law firm must avoid transmitting certain documents and files to the opposing party because they may be protectable under attorney-client privilege, as attorney work-product or because of another confidentiality doctrine. Thus, downloading those documents should be restricted in order to avoid inadvertently including them in the set of ESI to share with the opposing party's lawyer.

Based on the presented scenario, we have identified design goals for each module that may be useful as part of Marie's efforts.

8 Discussion

We discuss the design goals for each module as follows. At this point in the design of the system, we relied extensively on Nielson Norman Group's 10 Usability Heuristics for User Interface Design [17].

8.1 Search Module

This module addresses the main purpose of the system, to search a file or files of the listed category. An "autocomplete suggestion widget" is a good choice for promoting usability because it guides the user in building the search query. To make it manageable, special attention is required in designing the autocomplete widget. Avoiding the scroll bars for the autocomplete search box promotes an optimized search. Including scroll bars in our system would make the search process more cumbersome, since it would require continuous manual scrolling on a user's computer that most users dislike.

We plan to offer two types of categories in the search bar. These two options are machine-generated and user-generated categories. Differentiating the categories with different colors or styles aids the user in identifying the more prominent category (machine-generated category). Not only do the different types of categories require a color or style variation, but also the search key and the category need to be distinguished. The suggested categories need more focus than the user-typed search key, because users are already aware of the words they typed in the bar and thus it needs no highlighting. This reduces the cognitive overload for users. These variations provide a clear perception of the search suggestion by converging the user's focus on the categories rather than the search key. Finally, the more important component is the widget label. It communicates the type of suggestion that the interface is providing to the user, averting unnecessary confusion for users in understanding autocomplete suggestions. The widget's label should clearly mention the purpose of the user's search.

8.2 Upload Module

This module has three options for users. They can upload a document or file, a selected list of documents and files or an entire folder of documents and files. To achieve optimal usability, users are provided with options based on their goals. In our scenario, one of the tasks for our user is uploading huge volumes of files and documents, selectively uploading a list of files and documents or bulk uploading of all of this material through folders. All three methods for uploading potentially relevant ESI are supported by allowing users to either select the files and documents from directories by meticulous clickable options or to "drag and drop" to upload the materials. In this way, we promote mapping real-world actions to the system and reduce the number of operations involved in uploading content to the repository.

Another feature of our system is the progress bar. The progress bar indicates the status of the loading process. It will not only indicate the status of the uploading process itself, but also the status of different procedures that are happening within the backend of the system while a file or document is being uploaded. The different stages that a file passes as it is entered into the repository are visible to users as icons with a green checkmarks over it to indicate that the file is moving from one stage to another. These icons help a user clearly understand the process that is happening behind the interface, thus encouraging users to trust the system and giving the user a greater sense of control. The four stages represented by the icons correspond to the backend processes that we developed for the system. These designations are for ESI transferred across the security layers, ESI stored in the database, ESI categorized based on the computed model, and ESI encrypted and stored in the repository.

8.3   Tag Module

This module addresses the problems with organizing files and documents based on a user's preferences. By default, the system is programmed to be able to organize files and documents based on a training or seed set of files that have been input into the system through the initial model improvement progression. However, the system needs frequent interventions by the manual reviewers (lawyers or their paralegals) to calibrate the precision and recall rate of the model. The tag module takes care of this calibration process over time. It takes the input for calibration from all the users of the system who are collaborating on the same case, but at different times during the case. Users are adding files and documents to existing established categorization, increasing the precision rate, or generating a new category for the files, increasing the recall rate.

The "list" module has the tag module embedded within it. Users may select and tag an unlimited number of files and documents for future reference. To facilitate usability, users can either add a new tag or attach an existing tag to the file or document selected. The tag option is available for a file when it is selected using a checkmark. This supports "multi-file" tagging and "select file" tagging. Thus, the system spares users from redundant iterative monotonous tagging activity. A label's success depends on using it properly, so designing the tag module needs considerable care. Users will note the significance of the tag because tags will be displayed by the frequency of use or its latest use information. Both kinds of data inform the user how that tag is being interpreted and applied by other users, which influences the user's decision in choosing a tag for his/her selected files and documents. The more often a tag is used, the more chances for the system to learn that category and prepare the search hierarchy accordingly. If a user believes that he/she has selected or added a tag in error, an option to delete a tag allows the user to correct his/her error.

8.4   List Module

The list module has all the files and documents listed in order of choice preferred by the user. To achieve additional usability, users are given the freedom to order files and documents according to their needs in a case. Users should be able to sort based on relevancy, frequency of use, most recent and alphabetical order. Users might also require more sophisticated filtering options. They should able to filter the files and documents based on their file structure, file type or protected or unprotected as confidential, as attorney-client privilege or as attorney work-product. The view of the list bar must be scalable. Users can be provided with the option to vary the number of files and documents that could be listed for a page. The system will provide a download option. Users can select files or documents to either download or tag. Thus, the system needs to provide users with the functionality to easily select files and documents. To facilitate this function, we included an option to select and de-select files and documents using checkboxes.

8.5   Inline Tooltip Module

This module ensures that the users are aware of every possible interaction that they could execute to attain their search and retrieval goals as seamlessly and effortlessly as possible with minimal need to consult system documentation. To achieve usability, note that although one aspect of good practice when designing an interface is that it must be self–explanatory, it is also good practice to provide users with proper documentation and training materials on how to use the system. Instead of confronting users with non-intuitive, immense documentation on how to use the features and functionality of a system, introducing inline tool tips motivates a new user to get started with the system without any struggles. The inline tooltip feature can be turned off, so that experienced users will not perceive it as an inconvenient element.

9   Results

After identifying the design requirements and features of the system, we began the initial design phase of the project by outlining a basic layout.

9.1   The Conceptualization

A user can begin with "suggestion widget" as a search bar to type in the keywords (terms, party names, dates) of the files or documents that he/she requires. The "suggestion bar" is activated when it senses that there is text in the text field of the "search bar." The user chooses the particular category from the widget and clicks on the search button. The "list" module lists the files that are relevant or related conceptually to the keywords searched. Users can modify the list based on two sorting criteria – the relevancy of the keyword (more frequently used) and ascending/descending order of the file. Users can filter files and documents based on such attributes as whether an item is protected/privileged or not and file and format types. They have the option to mark a file as protected. They can click on the lock icon to protect it. The lock icon indicates the status of the file or document as either protected or not protected. The download option is available for all files except protected materials.

Tagging a file is permissible for all types of files and documents. The inline tool tips are activated when a user interacts with the system for the first time at the following functional points (Figs. 5 and 6).

1. When a user logs into the system, the tooltip greets the user and requests that the user type a keyword into the text field of the search bar.
2. It shows the user how to upload a file or document when the user clicks on the upload option.
3. Similarly, an inline tooltip is activated when the user hovers over the protected, sort, tag or download user interface (UI) controls.

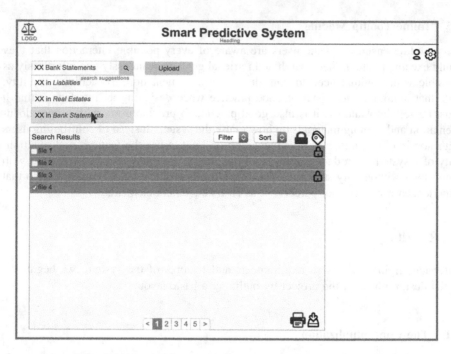

Fig. 5. Conceptual design of the "Smart Predictive System"

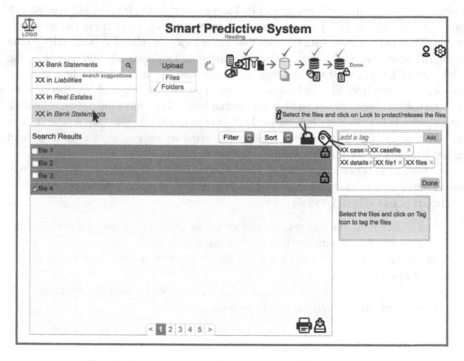

Fig. 6. Conceptual design of the "Smart Predictive System"

10 Future Work

Up to this point in the project, we have been working with a limited set of files and documents that we created, primarily files and documents that relate to bankruptcy law. In addition to testing and refining the system, particularly the backend processes, we need to gather a broader range of ESI, including files and documents from other areas of the law and materials that can be clearly identified as being those that need special protection due to confidentiality concerns. We also need to test a range of non-text-based items, because dealing with increasingly complex formats is another challenge to the e-discovery process and to predictive coding/Technology Assisted Review (TAR) services. Another step is to better integrate all of the modules and parts of our system, such as the database, the logic and algorithms, natural language processing and conceptual searching. Once the system is fully developed, we will test it again with a group of lawyers who practice bankruptcy law.

Some specific activities that will be part of our future work include the following.

10.1 Initial Evaluative User Testing

Even though the basic requirements of the system have been identified and conceptualized, in order to make the system more effective and efficient, additional insights into user preferences and the rationale for final design choices need to be validated before developing the low-fidelity prototype and testing the flow of a user's interactions with the system. To obtain feedback about a user's preferences for the modules, two variations of key modules will be shared with a group of users. This feedback will also reveal any features and functionality that we may have overlooked in our initial planning and design approaches. A survey will be created and follow-up one-on-one interview sessions with potential users will be conducted. The questions in the survey and interviews will attempt to understand a user's choice of one type of module over the other and the rationale behind it, except for the "list module." The design of the list module will be demonstrated to users to verify the accuracy of the reflections obtained as the result of the interview data synthesis phase (Fig. 7).

10.2 The Two Variations of the Autosuggestion Widget

The first variation has categories presented based on the most frequently used order. The second variation has the categories listed bas on alphabetical order.

10.3 The Two Variations of the Tab Module

The first variation lists the previously used tags with a number appended to it. The number indicates how often people have used that tag. The second variation lists the previously used tags with color intensity variation. The more frequently used tags have more intensity when compared with other less used tags. The color intensity is directly proportional to frequency of usage of that respective tag (Fig. 8).

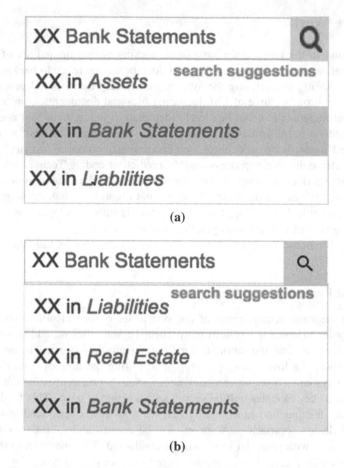

Fig. 7. (a) and (b) are two Variations of the Autosuggestion Widget

10.4   The Two Variations of the Upload Module

The first variation of the upload module has a normal progress bar indicting the status of the upload process whereas the second variation has different icons each indicating the progress, acknowledging to users the completion of each stage of the upload process that the files and documents pass through that is happening behind the interface of the system (Fig. 9).

After the final version of each module is determined, we will develop a low-fidelity prototype and test the flow of the interaction. After that, a high-fidelity prototype will be designed and a "think-aloud session" will be conducted to obtain direct input on how users actually perceive the system.

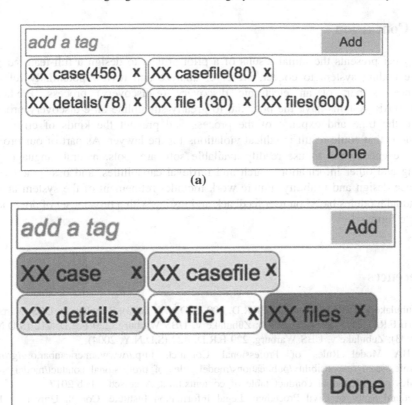

Fig. 8. (a) and (b) are two variations of the tab module

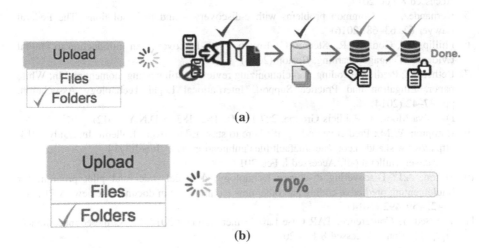

Fig. 9. (a) and (b) are two variations of the upload module

11 Conclusion

This paper presents the initial results of a pilot project to design a full-featured predictive coding system to collect, preserve, analyze and review potentially relevant evidence as part of an electronic discovery (e-discovery) process. Predictive coding/TAR systems have the potential to greatly streamline an e-discovery process, reduce the time and expense of the process and prevent the kinds of errors and omissions that could result in ethical violations for the lawyer. As part of our project, we have endeavored to use readily available software tools, natural language processing and other information search and retrieval capabilities, and best practices in interface design and usability. Future work includes refinement of the system and its individual modules based on user feedback and testing with a broader set of documents and file formats.

References

1. Zubulake v. UBS Warburg, 217 F.R.D. 309 (S.D.N.Y. 2003); Zubulake v. UBS Warburg, 216 F.R.D. 280 (S.D.N.Y. 2003); Zubulake v. UBS Warburg, 220 F.R.D. 212 (S.D.N.Y. 2003); Zubulake v. UBS Warburg, 229 F.R.D. 422 (S.D.N.Y. 2004)
2. ABA Model Rules of Professional Conduct. http://www.americanbar.org/groups/professional_responsibility/publications/model_rules_of_professional_conduct/model_rules_of_professional_conduct_table_of_contents.html, Accessed 8 Feb 2017
3. Federal Rules of Civil Procedure, Legal Information Institute, Cornell University Law School, 1 December 2015. https://www.law.cornell.edu/rules/frcp, Accessed 8 Feb 2017
4. Fuchs, J.L., McLean, C.G., Fiorentinos, I.S., FitzGerald, J.W., Heintz, A.F., Marino, E.J.: Noteworthy trends from cases decided under the recently amended federal rules of civil procedure, Jones Day, September 2016. http://www.jonesday.com/noteworthy-trends-from-cases-decided-under-the-recently-amended-federal-rules-of-civil-procedure-09-06-2016/, Accessed 8 Feb 2017
5. Hernandez, A.: Common problems with e-discovery – and their solutions. The Federal Lawyer **63**, 63–68 (2016)
6. Phillips, A., Godfrey, R., Steuart, C., Brown, C.: E-Discovery: An Introduction to Digital Evidence. Cengage Learning, Boston (2014)
7. Bethea, D.: Predictive coding: Revolutionizing review or still gaining momentum? In: White paper, Litigation and Practice Support, International Legal Technology Association, pp. 37–42 (2014)
8. Da Silva Moore v. Publicis Groupe, 287 F.R.D. 182, 183 (S.D.N.Y. 2012)
9. Hampton, W.M.: Predictive coding: it's here to stay. E-Discovery Bulletin, June/July 2014. https://www.skadden.com/sites/default/files/publications/LIT_JuneJuly14_EDiscoveryBulletin.pdf, Accessed 8 Feb 2017
10. Sutton, A.J.: Discovering discovery technology: a model order and pilot program for implementing predictive coding and other new technologies in document review. AIPLA Q. J. **42**, 459–492 (2014)
11. The Sedona Conference. TAR Case Law Primer, January 2017, https://thesedonaconfence.org/publcations. Accessed 8 Feb 2017

12. Dynamo Holdings Limited Partnership v. Commissioner of Internal Revenue, 2016 WL 4204067 (T.C. 13 July 2016)

13. Grant, D.: Seeing is believing: using visual analytics to take predictive coding out of the black box. LegalTech News, pp. SS1–SS4, December 2015

14. Hyles v. New York City, 10 Civ. 3119 (S.D.N.Y. 1 August 2016)

15. Levy, J.: UX Strategy: How to Devise Innovative Digital Products That People Want. O'Reilly Media, Sebastopol (2015)

16. Nunnally, B., Farkas, D.: UX Research: Practical Techniques for Designing Better Products. O'Reilly Media, Sebastopol (2016)

17. Nielsen, J.: 10 Usability Heuristics for User Interface Design. Nielson Norman Group, 1 January 1995. https://www.nngroup.com/articles/ten-usability-heuristics/, Accessed 8 Feb 2017

Hazards Taxonomy and Identification Methods in Civil Aviation Risk Management

Yuan Zhang[✉], Yijie Sun, Yanqiu Chen, and Mei Rong

China Academy of Civil Aviation Science and Technology, Beijing, China
zhangyuan@mail.castc.org.cn

Abstract. The SMS requirements and implementation of ICAO, FAA, Transport Canada, EASA, CAAC, etc. are summarized, and the problems existing in the definition, classification and identification method of hazards put forward by ICAO, SMICG, ECAST, CAAC and FAA are analyzed. Based on the analysis to the definitions of system safety and safety attributes, the definition of system elements is put forward. Then, the hazard taxonomy is set up, which are procedure, responsibility, personnel, and equipment, supervision and inspection, operation environment and effect. Meanwhile, the secondary taxonomy is given. According to the established hazard taxonomy, three hazard identification methods are set up, which are system and job analysis, unsafe events analysis and safety information statistical analysis. For each method, applicable objects, working process and application example are given respectively. The hazard taxonomy and identification methods have been put into practice in a number of service providers in China, the results show that the taxonomy and identification methods have highly practicability.

Keywords: Hazard · Hazard taxonomy · Hazard identification method · Risk management · SMS

1 Introduction

1.1 The Current SMS Implementation

In recent years, with the rapid development of world's air transport industry and aviation industry, the current focus is on improving the level of safety management and preventing serious unsafe events.

Now, service providers from every state are implementing the Safety Management System (SMS). The main elements include safety management policy, safety management organization, safety management responsibility, safety management procedures and standards, etc., and in which the key works are safety risk management, safety information management and safety education. Finally, a positive safety culture is built in the organization, and then reduces the risk of operation.

ICAO. In order to maintain and improve safety in civil aviation, International Civil Aviation Organization (ICAO) developed a new annex to safety management (Annex 19) [1]. Annex 19 requires the implementation of a SMS in civil aviation serves providers and a State Safety Programme (SSP) in Contracting States.

© Springer International Publishing AG 2017
S. Yamamoto (Ed.): HIMI 2017, Part II, LNCS 10274, pp. 288–301, 2017.
DOI: 10.1007/978-3-319-58524-6_24

Annex 19 specifies the framework of a SMS. The framework contains four components and twelve elements as the minimum requirements for SMS implementation, in which the safety risk management is the core component of SMS.

Risk management comprises three elements, which are hazard identification, safety risk assessment and mitigation. Risk management differs from previous methods of safety management and is a proactive safety management method based on the safety data. It is not taking measures after the accident or incident, but identifying hazards and controlling associate risk in advance, so as to prevent the serious unsafe event.

Currently, most contracting states of ICAO have established the SMS requirements to service provider respectively, such as the United States, Canada, European Union, China, Australia, England, etc.

FAA. Federal Aviation Administration (FAA) issued the "Safety Management Systems for Aviation Service Providers" (AC 120-92B) [2]. This advisory circular (AC) provides information that air carriers are required to implement SMS. At same time, FAA issued the "Introduction to Safety Management Systems (SMS) for Airport Operators" (AC 150/5200-37) [3]. This AC introduces the concept of SMS for airport operators.

In order to promote SMS implementation smoothly in airports, from 2006 to 2011 FAA carried out two stage pilot [4] of airport SMS construction. In 2006, FAA selected 26 airports to participate the first stage pilot, and in 2008 the number is 9 in the second stage pilot. Parts of airports participating in the pilot developed their own SMS Manual and implementation plan. Through the pilot FAA gathered information on practice and experience of how to implement SMS in airports.

In 2009, FAA conducted a SMS implementation study for airports. The aim of the study is to gain the procedures and methods of how airports implement the SMS throughout their own operational environment. 14 airports those had participated in the first or second stage pilot were involved in the study. Based on the study, FAA developed the draft of "Safety Management Systems for Airports" (AC 150/5200-37A) [5]. The AC provided detailed guidance to develop and implement SMS on an airport and explained how to develop a proactive way to identify and control potential hazards in a systematically way.

Transport Canada. Canada belongs to the states those implement SMS earlier. Canada has released a large number of rules and guidance aiming at promoting SMS construction. The rules and guidance [6] comprise "Introduction to Safety Management Systems" (TP 13739), "Guidance on safety management systems development" (AC 107-002), "Safety Management Systems for Small Aviation Operations - A Practical Guide to Implementation" (TP 14135), "Implementation procedures for airport operators" (AC 300-002), "Implementation procedures guide for air operators and approved maintenance organizations" (TP 14343) and "Implementation procedures for air traffic services operations" (AC 800-001). At the same time, Canada has taken a lot of measures to SMS construction of service provides.

EASA. European Aviation Safety Agency(EASA)has issued the SMS requirements [7] to flight, cabin crew and air operations in the form of Regulation. The European Commercial Aviation Safety Team (ECAST), the European Helicopter Safety Team

(EHEST) and the International Helicopter Safety Team (IHST) who are the components of the European Strategic Safety Initiative (ESSI), have published some materials and toolkits aiming at promoting the best practices of SMS.

- **Air operators**-Commission Regulation (EU) defined the SMS organization and technical requirements for air operators. The requirements will apply to all operators who are required to hold an AOC/organization certificate under the new EU rules.
- **Airports**-EU has published the "Authority, Organization and Operations Requirements for Aerodromes" with Regulation (EC) No 139/2014. The rules required that airport operators shall implement and maintain a SMS.
- **ATM**-The "Common requirements for the provision of air navigation services" Regulation (EC) No 1035/2011 published by EU mandated Air Traffic Management providers to have a SMS and Quality Management System (QMS). At same time, the management systems of safety, security and quality are required to be integrated.

CAAC. Civil Aviation Administration of China (CAAC) [8] began the SMS construction in 2005. The SMS pilots in Hainan airlines, Hunan airport and Nanjing airport were carried out successively. On the basis of the SMS pilots, the SMS requirements for each type of service provider were issued, which include:

- **Aviation Operators**-"SMS Requirements on Aviation Operators" (AC-121/135-FS-2008-26)
- **Airports**-"Civil Airport Operation Safety Management" (CCAR-140) and "Guidelines for Airport SMS Development" (AC-139/140-CA-2008-1)
- **ATC Providers**-"Guiding Manual for Civil Aviation ATM SMS Development V3" (MD-TM-2011-001) and "Guidance for Civil Aviation ATM SMS Audit" (AP-83-TM-2011-02)
- **Maintenance Organizations**-"SMS of Maintenance Organizations" (AC-145-15)
- **Aviation Security Units**-"Guidelines for Aviation Security Management System (SEMS) Implementation" (AC-SB-2009-1)

CAAC is developing the SMS requirements to Aircraft Manufacturers and General Aviation.

Up to the end of 2016, the SMS of all the Aviation Operators, Airports, ATC Providers, Maintenance Organizations and Aviation Security Units in China have been certificated by CAAC. In order to promote the quality and performance of SMS, CAAC is carrying out the SMS performance oversight to the above service providers through the toolkit of SMS audit. The toolkit is based on a computer server and associate pad clients. The check list contained in this toolkit includes more than 300 check items which covers all the SMS elements from document, responsibility, staff, implement to effect. In the past six years, CAAC has used the toolkit to carry out the SMS audits to more than 30 service providers. At the same time, from 2014 to 2016 CAAC has been carrying out safety performance management pilots in 13 service providers which include aviation operators and airports, which aimed at that SMS can be really in place and play a role.

Others. Meanwhile, Civil Aviation Authority (CAA) [9] and Australian Civil Aviation Safety Authority(CASA) [10] have also done a lot of work to promote service providers to develop SMS. Some Organizations have carried out more research work on SMS, such as EUROCONTROL [11], Flight Safety Foundation (FSF) [12] and Safety Management International Collaboration Group (SMICG) [13], etc.

1.2   The Current Hazards Definition, Classification and Identification

Risk management is the core component of the SMS, which is the key role of transforming safety management from passive to active. As Fig. 1, through the process of hazard identification, risk evaluation and risk control, risk management takes the initiative to find the hazards in operational, and then the risk mitigation measures are taken beforehand. The ultimate goal is to reduce the risk of system operation and prevent the occurrence of accidents or incidents.

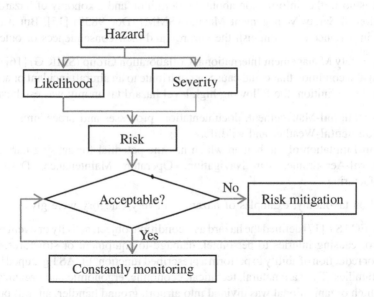

Fig. 1. Risk management process

Hazards identification is first process of risk management. At present, some organizations have carried out some research on the definition and classification of hazards, such as ICAO, SMICG, ESSI, etc.

ICAO. In the second edition of Safety Management Manual (SMM) (Doc 9859) [14], ICAO defined the hazard as a condition or an object with the potential to cause injuries to personnel, damage to equipment or structures, loss of material, or reduction of ability to perform a prescribed function. ICAO also pointed that it is not reasonable to confuse hazards with their consequences. In this situation, the hazard reflects its consequences rather than the hazard itself.

In the Doc 9859 V2, Hazards are divided into three groups, which are natural hazards, technical hazards and economic hazards.

- **Natural hazards** are the consequences of the environment within which operations take place. Examples are adverse weather conditions, geographical conditions, environmental events, public health events, etc.
- **Technical hazards** are the results of energy sources or safety-critical functions. Examples are deficiencies of aircraft, facilities and related equipment, etc.
- **Economic hazards** are the consequences of the socio-political environment within which operations take place. Examples are the growth and recession of economic and the cost of material or equipment.

It also discussed that the scope of hazards in aviation is wide. The factors should be looked into in hazard identification include design, procedures and operating practices, communications, personnel, organizational, work environment, regulatory oversight, defenses, human performance, etc.

There is no further information about the definition and taxonomy of hazard in the third edition of Safety Management Manual (SMM) (Doc 9859) [15]. But it emphasized the importance of distinguish the hazards and their consequences or outcomes.

SMICG. Safety Management International Collaboration Group (SMICG) [16] defined the hazard as a condition that could cause or contribute to an aircraft incident or accident. Based on this definition, the following high level hazard taxonomy was established:

- **Organizational-**Management, documentation, processes and procedures.
- **Environmental-**Weather and wildlife.
- **Human-**Limitation of the human which has the potential for causing harm.
- **Technical-**Aerodrome, Air Navigation, Operator, Maintenance, Design and Manufacturing.

Based on taxonomy, examples of hazards to every category were given.

ECAST. ECAST [17] defined the hazard as a condition, object, activity or event with the potential of causing injuries to personnel, damage to equipment or structures, loss of material, or reduction of ability to perform a prescribed function. ECAST grouped hazards into five families. They are natural, technical, economic, ergonomic and organizational, among which organizational was divided into airport, ground handler, aircraft operator, ANSP, maintenance organization. Examples of hazards were given to every category.

After that, ECAST provided some information about the tools and techniques of hazards identification, such as brainstorm, hazard and operability study (HAZOPS), checklist, failure modes and effects analysis (FMEA), structured what-if (SWIFT), dynamic models, future hazards identification through FAST method, etc. But the introduction is simple and not enough to guide the actual work of hazard identification.

CAAC. In the "SMS Requirements on Aviation Operators" (AC-121/135-FS-2008-26) CAAC given the definition of hazards, that is any existing or potential condition may cause personnel injury, illness or death, or system, equipment or property damage, or environmental damage. But there was no specific and clear category and identification method of hazard.

In terms of hazard classification, service providers in China basically group hazards through the following three ways at present.

- There is no specific hazards category. Hazards are listed one by one, other than in form of category. Only the number statistics can be conducted to hazards, there is no way to carry out the statistics on category, and the common, multiple hazards cannot be identified.
- Hazards are classified in accordance to the business process. First, operation system is divided into subsystems, primary processes and the secondary processes, etc. Then, hazards belong to every processes are identified. The advantage of this method is that it can identify the hazards existing in each business process, but cannot carry out the statistics and management to common hazards in the scope of whole organization.
- Hazards are classified in according to the SHEL model or the man-machine-environmental-management model. Through these models hazards can be classified, but these taxonomies are oversimplified and lack of a more detailed secondary classification standards. For example, the staff is not divided into more detailed classification standard, such as number, qualification, ability and fatigue, etc. It results in more difficult in hazards identification and statistical analysis later.

On the other hand, service providers identify hazards mainly in some subjective ways, such as brainstorm and experience discussion, etc. There is not some clear and scientific methods to insure the comprehensiveness and accuracy of hazard identification.

FAA. In the Safety Assurance System (SAS) [18] FAA defined the hazard as a condition that could foreseeably cause or contribute to an aircraft accident. Meanwhile, FAA Air Traffic Organization [19] defined the hazard as any real or potential condition that can cause injury, illness or death to people; damage or loss to system, equipment, property or environment. FAA ATO given some methods to identify hazard, which are comparative safety assessment, failure model and effect analysis, job task analysis, scenario analysis and what-if analysis, etc. But there is only sample description to these methods, and no detailed implementation procedures.

1.3 The Problems in Hazards Identification

Although there are some hazard definitions and taxonomies, the definitions are not clear enough, the taxonomies are lack of operability and do not cover all types of hazards. And they are lack of adequate guiding significance to the risk management of service providers. In terms of hazards identification, there are some introductions of methods, but they are not detailed and clear enough to guide services providers to identify hazards.

There are also some problems in service provider's daily hazard identification.

- Due to the lack of clear definition and taxonomy of hazard, there is no unified standard for hazards currently. Some service providers take a seriously unsafe event as a hazard, such as runway excursion, etc. Some service providers take a process unsafely event as a hazard, such as human error, equipment failure, etc. Inaccurate hazards identification affects the subsequent hazards assessment and risk control seriously.

- Because of the lack of scientific and feasible methods for hazards identification, many service providers cannot identify all the hazards in civil aviation operation comprehensively, which influence the effect of risk management.

Based on the above problems, in order to improve effectiveness and actual effect of hazards identification, it is necessary to establish a set of comprehensive hazards taxonomy. At the same time, it is needed to establish some scientific and practical methods of hazard identification to ensure the comprehensiveness and effective of hazards identification. This paper focuses on the establishment of the hazards taxonomy and identification methods.

2　Set Up Hazard Taxonomy

2.1　Put Forward the Definition of System Element

In the Safety Assurance System (SAS) [18] FAA defines the system safety as the application of special technical and managerial skills to identify, analyze, assess, and control hazards and risks associated with a complete system.

At same time, FAA put forward the concept of safety attributes, which are the qualities of a system that should be present in a well-designed certificate holder system and process. The safety attributes are:

1. Responsibility—a clearly documented person who is accountable for a process.
2. Authority—a clearly documented person who has the authority to manage a process.
3. Procedures—the methods which are used to accomplish a particular process.
4. Controls—checks and restraints aiming to ensure a desired result.
5. Process Measures—validate a process and identify problems or potential problems, and then correct them.
6. Interfaces—interactions between different processes and units.

Based on the concepts of system safety and safety attributes, the definition of system elements is put forward. System elements are the necessary factors to assure organization function will be achieved. The organization function will be not achieved or achieved partially if all or some system elements are absent. Based on this concept, in the area of civil aviation safety if we want to assure the operation safety, firstly there should be a set of detailed regulations and procedures to tell employees what and how to do. Then, the responsibilities should be allocated to tell employees who to do. At same time, the organization should make sure that there are enough and qualified persons to do the job though recruitment and training. In order to accomplish the organization function, necessary hardware and software should be equipped. After that, what is most important is that employees do the job according to the rules; in order to achieve this supervision is essential. Environment factor should be taken into account in the whole operation process. At last, what we do not want to face is that all the above elements are there but the effect is not accomplished. So, achieve the desired effect is the most impartment.

According to the above ideas, the system elements may contain procedure, responsibility, personnel, implementation, facility, supervision, environment and effect. Only these elements all be there every organization function can be come true.

2.2 Set Up the Hazard Taxonomy

Based on the concept of system safety, safety attributes and system elements above, the hazard taxonomy is put forward, which includes procedure, responsibility, personnel,

Table 1. Hazard taxonomy

First-level taxonomy	Explanation	Secondary taxonomy
1. Procedure	The detailed content, process and standard of operation should be documented.	• Safety policy • Procedure • Standard
2. Responsibility	The safety responsibility should be documented, and the safety personnel should be authorized.	• Responsibility assignment • Rationality of responsibility
3. Personnel.	The abundant, qualified and health personnel should be equipped with, in order to implement system operation.	• Number • Ability • Qualification • Psychological factor • Physical factor • Physical limit • Fatigue • Pressure
4. Implementation	Personnel should implement system operation according to the established procedures and standards.	• Violation • Error • Human-computer interaction • Team cooperation
5. Facility	There should be abundant tools that satisfy the requirement of working and are regular maintained and calibrated.	• Software • Hardware
6. Supervision	The first line operation should be supervised to ensure that all the operations are in accordance with established procedures, responsibilities and standards.	• Mechanism • Inspector • Implement • Effect
7. Environment	The environment factors that influence the safety operation should be considered.	• Working environment • Natural environment • Social environment • Airspace environment
8. Effect	The actual effect of system operation should be considered.	• Lack of effect standard • Not achieves the desired effect

implementation, facility, supervision, environment and effect. At the same time, the secondary taxonomy is put forward (As Table 1).

3 Set Up Methods of Hazard Identification

According to the actual situation of safety and operation of civil aviation, three methods of hazard identification are set up. For each method, the applicable objects and working process are given. Meanwhile, the specific application examples are described in detail respectively.

3.1 System and Job Analysis

Applicable Objects. This method is suitable for the hazard identification of service provider in the following situations:

1. The initial setting up of systems, such as the new company or department. The comprehensive hazard identification is required to search all the hazards existing.
2. The significant changes, such as the adjustment of organization framework, new business, new operation procedure, new equipment, which need hazards identification and management to ensure that there is no safety issues after the change is put into practice.
3. Hazard identification on a regular basis, such as every year or every two years.

Table 2. Decomposition of flight operation system

System	First-level process	Second-level process
Flight operation	Implementation of flight	Preflight preparation
		Flight
		Evaluation after flight
	Pilot scheduling	Airlines analysis
		Pilots qualification analysis
		Develop pilots flight plan
		Adjust pilots flight plan in abnormal situation
	Pilot training	Flight training
		Flight theory training
		Simulator training
	Safety management	Safety information management
		Risk management
		Safety education

Working Process and Application Example.

Decomposition of work process. For a particular operation system, such as flight operation system or maintenance system, etc., the work process is decomposed into some specific work units. It is appropriate that the system is broken down into three levels or four levels process according to the complexity of the system. Take the flight operation system as an example (As Table 2).

Hazard identification. Base on the decomposition of work process, hazards are identified for each minimum level work process in accordance with the above hazard taxonomy.

Take the pilot scheduling as an example to identify hazards for its four second-level processes from the aspects of procedure, responsibility, personnel, implementation, facility, supervision, environment and effect (As Table 3).

Table 3. Hazards identification to pilot scheduling

Work process		Procedure	Responsibility	Personnel	Implementation	Facility	Supervision	Environment	Effect
Pilot scheduling	Airlines analysis	Lack of procedures and standards of airline analysis							
	Pilots qualification analysis		Lack of responsibility of pilot qualification analysis						
	Develop pilots flight plan				There is violation in developing pilots flight plan	The software of developing pilots flight plan is not appropriate			
	Adjust pilots flight plan in abnormal situation			Staff capacity can't meet the requirement of adjusting pilots flight plan in abnormal situation			Lack of supervision to adjusting pilots flight plan in abnormal situation		

So, there are six hazards in the work process of pilot scheduling (As Table 4). The blanks show that there is no hazard.

Table 4. Hazards in pilot scheduling

Hazard taxonomy	Hazards
1. Procedure	• Lack of procedures and standards of airline analysis
2. Responsibility	• Lack of responsibility of pilot qualification analysis
3. Personnel	• Staff capacity can't meet the requirement of adjusting pilots flight plan in abnormal situation
4. Implementation	• There is violation in developing pilots flight plan
5. Facility	• The software of developing pilots flight plan is not appropriate
6. Supervision	• Lack of supervision to adjusting pilots flight plan in abnormal situation

3.2   Unsafe Event Analysis

Applicable Objects. This method is suitable for the hazards identification of service provider in the following situations:

1. For the unsafe event that has happened, the root causes analysis according to the Fault Tree Analysis (FTA) is needed to identify the hazards. The aim is to prevent such event do not happen again.
2. For the unsafe event that has not happened but is unwished and serious, the hazards identification should be carried out to prevent such event do not happen.

Working Process and Application Example.

Construct FTA. For an unsafe event, construct FTA and analysis every causes of the event. Take the vehicle scrape aircraft as an example.

The Fig. 2 shows that the event covers multi-level causes. Vehicle speeding, brake failure, driving not along the route are the direct causes of the event, and the personnel violation, lack of vehicle speed limit, wet ground, vehicle lack of maintenance and the unreasonable route are indirect causes. The cause analysis will find the reasons in the organizational level finally, which includes safety policy, education, resources, etc.

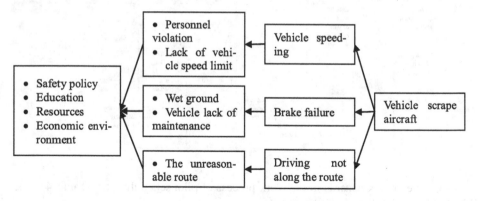

Fig. 2. FTA analysis to vehicle scrape aircraft

Hazard identification. Base on the FTA, the hazards are identified from the aspects of procedure, responsibility, personnel, implementation, facility, supervision, environment and effect, and four hazards are identified (As Fig. 3).

Hazard taxonomy	Hazards
1. Procedure	• Lack of vehicle speed limit
2. Implementation	• Personnel violation
3. Facility	• Vehicle lack of maintenance • The unreasonable route
4. Environment	• Wet ground

Fig. 3. Hazards in vehicle scrape aircraft

3.3   Safety Information Statistical Analysis

Applicable Objects. Service providers collect some kinds of safety information in the daily operation, including:

- Unsafe event;
- Safety check;
- Flight quality monitoring;
- Service difficulty reports (SDR);
- Equipment operation;
- Safety audit;
- Government oversight;
- External safety information; etc.

Statistical analysis is carried out to above information to find common safety issues and tendencies, then the hazards in the daily operation are identified, evaluated and managed.

Working Process and Application Example

Safety information collection and statistics. Collect all kinds of safety information in the daily operation, and carry out statistical analysis regularly. Statistical analysis methods including:

- Quantity statistics;
- Comparison analysis;
- Correlation analysis;
- Trend analysis;
- Principal component analysis; etc.

Through the analysis, some common safety issues existing in the daily operation can be found. Such as:

- The hard landing, in which the vertical overload is form 1.6G to 1.8G, in the fourth quarter is more than that in the third quarter;
- Safety information report delay is more in the second half of the year;
- There are more violations in daily operation; etc.

FTA analysis. For the safety issues got from safety information statistics, the FTA model is used to analysis and identify hazards. Take the safety information submitted not in time as the example to identify hazards.

As shown in Fig. 4, the immediate cause of the event include: lack of information submit standards, inconvenient information submit tools, lack of supervision to information submit and lack of responsibility of information submit. Meanwhile, there are some deeper reasons from the organizational level.

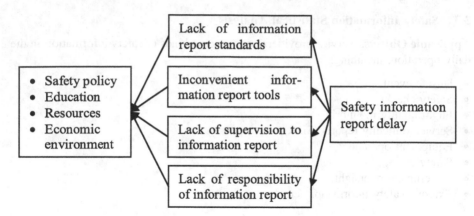

Fig. 4. FTA analysis to safety information report delay

Hazard identification. Base on the above causes analysis, the hazards are identified from the aspects of procedure, responsibility, personnel, implementation, facility, supervision, environment and effect, and four hazards are identified (As Table 5).

Table 5. Hazards in safety information report delay

Hazard taxonomy	Hazards
1. Procedure	• Lack of information report standards
2. Responsibility	• Lack of responsibility of information report
3. Facility	• Inconvenient information report tools
4. Supervision	• Lack of supervision to information report

4 Conclusion

1. The SMS regulations and requirements issued by ICAO, FAA, Canada, EASA, CAAC, etc. and implementation of SMS are summarized. The definition, classification and identification method of hazard put forwarded by ICAO, SMICG, ECAST, CAAC and FAA are summarized, the defects in hazard definition and classification and the problems in the service provider's hazard identification are analyzed.
2. Based on the analysis to the definition of system safety and the safety attributes, the definition of system elements are put forward. Then, the hazard taxonomy is set up, which are the procedures, responsibilities, personnel, and equipment, supervision and inspection, operation environment and effect. Meanwhile, the secondary taxonomy is given.
3. According to the established hazard taxonomy, three hazard identification methods are set up, which are the system and job analysis, unsafe events analysis and safety information statistical analysis. Applicable objects, working process and application example for each method are given respectively.

4. The established hazard taxonomy and identification methods can assist service providers to carry out hazard identification more systematically and comprehensively, which could improve the effectiveness of risk management.
5. The hazard taxonomy and identification methods have been put into practice in a number of service providers in China, the results show that the taxonomy and methods have highly practicability.

References

1. ICAO. ANNEX 19: Safety Management, February 2013
2. FAA. AC 120-92B: Safety Management Systems for Aviation Service Providers (2015)
3. FAA. AC 150/5200-37: Introduction to Safety Management Systems (SMS) for Airport Operators, February 2007
4. External SMS Efforts - Part 139 Rulemaking Airport SMS Pilot Studies. https://www.faa.gov/airports/airport_safety/safety_management_systems/external/pilot_studies/
5. FAA. AC 150/5200-37A: Safety Management Systems for Airports. Draft
6. Easy Reference Guide of Safety Management System-related Documents. https://www.tc.gc.ca/eng/civilaviation/standards/sms-guide3665.htm
7. Safety Management System (SMS). http://www.easa.europa.eu/easa-and-you/safety-management/safety-management-system-sms
8. CAAC. http://www.caac.gov.cn
9. CAA. http://www.caa.co.uk
10. CASA. https://www.casa.gov.au
11. Eurocontrol. http://www.eurocontrol.int
12. FSF. https://flightsafety.org
13. Safety Management International Collaboration Group (SMICG). http://www.skybrary.aero/index.php/Safety_Management_International_Collaboration_Group_%28SM_ICG%29
14. ICAO. Doc 9859 2nd edn. Safety Management Manual (2009)
15. ICAO. Doc 9859 3rd edn. Safety Management Manual (2013)
16. SMICG: Hazard Taxonomy Examples, April 2013
17. ECAST: Guidance on Hazards Identification, March 2009
18. FAA: Safety Assurance System Policy and Procedures, vol. 10. Order 8900.1, September 2016. http://fsims.faa.gov/PICResults.aspx?mode=EBookContents&restricttocategory=general ~ menu
19. FAA Air Traffic Organization: Safety Management System Manual Version 4.0 (2014)

Can Travel Information Websites Do Better?
Facilitating the Decision-Making Experience for Tourists

Lanyun Zhang and Xu Sun[✉]

University of Nottingham, Ningbo, China
{Lanyun.Zhang,Xu.Sun}@nottingham.edu.cn

Abstract. Tourists tend to spend a significant amount of time engaging in information searches during their trip planning process. This research adds to the knowledge of tourism information presentation through studying different types of available online textual tourism information, examining their characteristics, and exploring their influence on tourists' desires to visit a destination. Two studies were conducted in total, in which Study 1 employed a mixed-method approach to extract the values of online data. Study 2 employed a scenario-based experiment with a follow-up questionnaire and interview to obtain the perceived values of the different types of textual information. This research categorises the online textual tourism information into four types: *blogs*, *reviews*, *messages*, and *articles*. *Blogs* tend to present tourism information using first person narratives, displaying a strong sense of affection and positive emotions with a touch of sincerity and excitement. *Reviews*, as the easiest to understand and most useful type of textual tourism information, have a significant influence on tourists' desires to visit a particular destination.

Keywords: Textual information presentation · Tourism · Empirical study · Design

1 Introduction

Tourism is a highly hedonic activity that people like to think about and prepare for in advance, and will later talk about their trip experiences [6]. During the trip planning process, tourists tend to make trip-related decisions beforehand, taking into account the opinions and reviews of the tourists who have already visited the potential destinations. To systematically understand the trip planning processes of individual tourists, Mathieson & Wall [11] and Mansfeld [8] investigate the tourism-related product purchasing, information searching and decision-making. The view of the tourism information search process has been expanded into a broader communication scale [19], in which tourism information search behaviour satisfies the following needs: functional, hedonic, innovative, aesthetic, and sign, and they are realised through the following information sources: social, personal, marketing, and editorial. Due to the fact that information searches play an important role during the trip decision-making processes [6] and following the development of the Web 2.0 and social media, existing studies have explored trip decision-making and tourists' information needs in the context of

© Springer International Publishing AG 2017
S. Yamamoto (Ed.): HIMI 2017, Part II, LNCS 10274, pp. 302–313, 2017.
DOI: 10.1007/978-3-319-58524-6_25

using online systems [2, 14]. Different types of online tourism information (online texts, videos, photo slides, and panoramas) have been investigated in terms of their influences on tourists' desires to visit a particular destination [9], and it has been found that textual descriptions lead to more positive attitudes towards making a visit. Therefore, we aim to focus on the different types of textual tourism information that are available on existing online websites, and then to classify them, examine their characteristics, and explore their effects on tourists' desires to visit a potential destination.

With regard to the different types of textual tourism information, current online services and platforms provide enormous opportunities to allow publication from various information sources, including social, personal, marketing and editorial [19]. From the perspective of social sources, Xiang & Gretzel [20] investigate the extent to which social media appear in search engine results in the context of tourism searches. However, the literature has not explored comprehensively the textual tourism information across current online services. Further, it lacks an analysis of the characteristics of each type of textual tourism information, although it has drawn attention to studies which examine how travel blogs affect tourists' desires to visit a particular destination. Chen et al. [5] examine the characteristics (such as reliability, interestingness, novelty, etc.) of travel blog content which have an influence on tourists' decision-making. However, since travel blogs are not the only form of textual tourism information which is available online, this study aims to explore all relevant such information, with a specific focus on how they influence tourists' perceptions while reading the same, and their desires to visit destinations thereafter.

We have conducted two studies to contribute to the knowledge of: (1) identifying the different types of textual tourism information and understanding their characteristics; and (2) exploring the perceived characteristics of the identified textual tourism information and their different influences on tourists' desires to visit a destination.

2 Background and Literature Review

2.1 Tourism Information Websites

Tourism is an 'Information-Intense Industry' [16] and online resources provide many platforms where tourism information can easily be both distributed and consumed. Websites stimulate the creating and sharing of tourism information (Pen et al. 2007) and serve as an important information source in tourists' decision-making processes.

Web 1.0 allows users (tourists, marketers, official managers, etc.) to publish tourism-related information online, but it is only a 'readable' system and information is only updated once in a while. Web 2.0 allows users to interact with the websites, such that it is a dynamic 'writable' system which encourages free participation, collaboration, and information sharing. 'Social media', created by Web 2.0, consists of Internet-based applications that carry consumer-generated content. Xiang & Gretzel [20] propose a typology of online 'social media' websites, based on search engine results: 40% virtual community sites (e.g., LonelyPlanet), 27% consumer review sites (e.g., TripAdvisor), 15% blogs (e.g., TravelPod), 9% social networking sites (e.g., Twitter, Facebook) and only 7% media sharing sites (e.g., Youtube, Flickr, Arounder). In this research, the aim is to explore online tourism information from websites that are in the category of either Web 1.0 or Web 2.0, or social media.

2.2 Online Tourism Information

Since tourists generally have limited knowledge of any detailed information about potential destinations, they tend to seek out and be significantly influenced by online tourism information [22]. Online information, whether it is generated by peer tourists or by official marketers, is important for tourists' information searches and decision-making processes [13].

Existing researches have explored the different types of online tourism information that are widely used by tourists, both in terms of how their characteristics are perceived by the users, and their overall effects on tourists' desires to visit a particular destination. Marlow & Dabbish [9] compare four types of tourism information: texts, photo slides, videos, and panoramas. They find that across the four types of information, vividness and interactivity are the two characteristics that most influence users' attitudes towards visiting an unfamiliar destination, and they also report that readers of text and panorama descriptions of destinations tend to have significant positive attitudes about visiting such places. Further, they explain that text descriptions are more likely to help readers to form vivid mental images in their minds, while panorama descriptions are more likely to allow interaction between the users and any relevant information.

With regard to the written descriptions of a destination, there are different types of textual information, such as blog content, review content, official introduction content, etc. Chen et al. [5] focus on blog text content, and investigate which characteristics of the travel blogs attract tourists' attention and influence their decisions. They find that the novelty, understandability, and interestingness are the perceived characteristics that have a positive influence on tourists' desires to visit a destination.

In this research, we aim to explore all types of textual tourism information that are available online, and then to classify them, examine their characteristics and understand how they influence tourists' decisions.

3   Study 1

3.1   Objectives

With the various types of tourism information that are available on websites to help tourists' decision-making, Study 1 aims to identify the different types of online textual tourism information on a number of representative websites, and to examine their characteristics in terms of their linguistic features, the emotions presented, and the brand personalities of the destinations described in the information.

3.2 Method

We adopted a mixed-method approach that has been applied previously in collecting and analyzing social media data [3], which consists of online data crawling, text mining, and content analysis. Firstly, a manual content analysis was carried out through Affinity Diagram, to classify the available online textual tourism information. Secondly, text mining was employed to examine the characteristics of the identified types of online textual tourism information in a large scale using two processes: automatic online data crawling and WordStat data analysis.

3.3 Procedure

We selected one non-social website: *Wikitravel (WT)*, and six social media websites: *TripAdvisor (TA), Virtualtourist (VT), LonelyPlanet (LP), TravelPod (TP), Facebook (FB)*, and *Arounder (AD)*, based on Xiang & Gretzel's [20] work. In this study, we first collected small samples of tourism-related information to conduct a manual content analysis for the purposes of identifying the different types of textual tourism information. We collected different types of textual information about the same destination (London), and the same tourist attraction (the Tower of London). For the manual content analysis, we searched for tourism information across the aforementioned websites, browsed the webpages, observed their information formats and summarised the textual content forms of the websites.

For text mining, we chose to expand the scale and crawl 313,117 words' text from the same websites. We developed and utilised a framework to collect data from WWW sites with unique domains. Web crawler is an automatic process of parsing HTML webpages and then extracting relevant information [18]. HTML skeleton patterns in each of the target websites were identified for the purposes of writing the parsing code fragment. The crawling framework was installed on a dual core CPU with 4 GB RAM included. The HTML parser was written in Eclipse Java and we deployed a multi-threaded version of the web crawler to make it scalable. We applied an existing core algorithm for fast reading the HTML skeleton on an Eclipse platform and embedded our own regular expressions in the system. For example, any white spaces between paragraphs on the *TripAdvisor* website should be ignored and skipped. For textual pre-processing, we removed any hash tags, eliminated any non-relevant pictures, user profile information and advertisements. This pre-processing was also machine coded.

3.4 Analysis

For the manual content analysis, we applied Affinity Diagram [15] to classify the online textual tourism information. For the text mining, WordStat 2010 was used to analyse the crawled 313,177 words text data separately into the groups of the classifications. To investigate the characteristics of the different types of textual information from the perspective of their linguistic features, WordStat is able to count the frequency of each word and calculate the percentage of its appearance. In this study, we only focused on the frequencies of the pronouns, namely the first person (e.g., *I, our, my*), the second person (e.g., *you*), and the third person (e.g., *he, it*). To investigate the emotions and personalities presented by the textual information, external dictionaries were installed in WordStat. We used the Regressive Imagery Dictionary [10, 17] to examine the emotions identified in the information, and the Brand Personality Dictionary [1, 12] to examine the brand personalities that were evident in the different types of textual information. Brand personality contains five traits with which to describe a brand or a product: sincerity (displaying feelings of kindness and thoughtfulness), sophistication (signifying something which is elegant and prestigious), excitement (indicating a carefree, spirited and youthful attitude), competence (suggesting success, accomplishment and leadership), and ruggedness (something which is rough, tough, outdoorsy and athletic).

3.5   Results and Discussions

Through the manual content analysis, four types of online textual tourism information were identified: *blogs* (i.e., personal blogs), *reviews* (i.e., review comments), *messages* (i.e., commercials and notifications), and *articles* (i.e., official introductions and comprehensive descriptions). This classification is consistent with the conclusion by Vogt & Fesenmaier [19], that tourism information is derived fundamentally from four sources: social (reflecting the *reviews*), personal (reflecting the *blogs*), marketing (reflecting the *messages*), and editorial (reflecting the *articles*).

This study shows that the four types of textual tourism information have different characteristics with regard to one particular destination in terms of: (1) the linguistic features - the narrators' viewpoints, namely the first person, second person and third person; (2) the emotions expressed via the information - the intangible environments that the information creates; and (3) the brand personality - a set of human characteristics that are attributed to a brand name, in this case - London. The following presents and discusses the characteristics detected by WordStat across the four types of textual tourism information (see results in Table 1):

- *Blogs* tend to describe tourism information using first person narratives, displaying a strong sense of affection and positive emotional effect, and presenting a destination with sincerity and excitement. Due to the nature of blog content, which normally consists of tourists' personal travel stories, experiences, and journals, they often present a trip in a first person narrative. Blogs, written in the first person, place the readers read as the narrators so they will associate closely with the travel stories. Readers will immerse themselves spontaneously in the blog contents, will feel what the narrators have experienced and will be affected easily. Meanwhile, blogs usually contain a mixture of objective facts (destination facilities, environments and services) and subjective opinions (tourists' personal experiences and feelings) regarding a particular destination. Therefore, readers will find *blogs* to be very affective, and in this particular case, the destination of London was presented with a sense of sincerity and excitement.
- *Reviews* tend to describe tourism information using first and third person narratives, often displaying aggression and anxiety, and presenting a destination with sophistication and excitement. Review comments contain the travel experiences and opinions

of a substantial number of tourists who have been to a particular destination. Meanwhile, the nature of writing review comments means they are not limited to making compliments, but rather expressing genuine opinions based on real experiences, whether good or bad. Therefore, the content of any review comments may vary dramatically due to the various perspectives of different users, and may even show polarisation regarding one destination. It is reflected in this result that review comments reveal emotions of aggression and anxiety to readers, and in this case the destination of London was presented with a sense of sophistication and excitement.

- *Messages* tend to describe tourism information using first and second person narratives, displaying a sense of affection and positive emotional effect, and presenting destinations with sophistication and excitement. Due to the nature of commercials and notifications on social media, the goals of managers sending this type of information are to promote the tourism industry of a particular destination and to attract more tourists. It is logical that *messages* use first and second person points-of-view (POV) to shorten the distances between readers (potential customers) and destinations.

- *Articles* tend to describe tourism information using third person narratives, presenting a destination with sincerity, but the emotions cannot be detected. It reflects the nature *articles* that they will normally introduce a tourism destination from a distance, from a third person POV with very few personal opinions, with the majority of the information content being factual, accurate and reliable. Therefore, the results from this study show that *articles* display no emotions, and the destination of London was presented with a sense of sincerity.

Table 1. Study 1 results

	Websites (in short forms)	Characteristics		
		Word frequency pronouns	RID - Emotion	Brand personality
Blogs	TP	'I': 3.6%	Affection, Positive effect	Sincerity, Excitement
Reviews	TA, VT, TP, FB, AD	'It': 3.4%, 'I': 1.8%	Aggression, Anxiety	Sophistication, Excitement
Messages	FB	'You': 2.9%, 'our': 1.3%	Affection, Positive effect	Sophistication, Excitement
Articles	WT, LP	'It': 1.2%	N/A	Sincerity

4 Study 2

4.1 Objectives

Based on the results of Study 1, four types of online textual tourism information were identified, each of which exhibit different characteristics to readers. To examine how these four types of textual information have an influence on tourists' decision-making,

Study 2 aims to empirically explore how the users perceive both their characteristics and their impacts on tourists' desires to visit a destination.

4.2 Hypotheses

Existing studies have identified many information quality variables from tourists' perspectives, in which the variables have an influence on their reading experiences and further impact on their behavioural intentions to visit a destination [5, 7, 9]. Chen et al. [5] find that the perceived reliability and understandability of tourism blog content will influence the blog usage enjoyment, and will further influence tourists' intentions to visit the destination described. Since the information search behaviour of a tourist usually has a specific purpose of finding sufficient information to allow decisions to be made, the functional need (i.e., the usefulness of the information in terms of tourism decision-making) is a fundamental factor in the examination of tourism information [19]. Meanwhile, Marlow & Dabbish [9] find that the perceived vividness of a piece of information has a positive influence on tourists' desires to visit a destination through the concept of psychological distance. Therefore, in Study 2, we aim to investigate how different types of information content (based on the results of Study 1: *blogs*, *reviews*, *messages*, and *articles*) influence tourists' reading experience and their desires to visit a destination. The following hypotheses are offered:

H1a. The form of information content influences the perceived reliability of the tourism information.

H1b. The form of information content influences the perceived understandability of the tourism information.

H1c. The form of information content influences the perceived vividness of the tourism information.

H1d. The form of information content influences the perceived usefulness of the tourism information.

H2. The form of information content influences tourists' desire to visit a destination.

4.3 Method

An empirical scenario-based experiment was carried out, in which each participant was asked to read all four types of textual tourism information. After they finished reading each type of information, they were required to complete a questionnaire regarding the characteristics of the given information and their desires to visit the destination described therein. Therefore, this is a within subject study with non-parametric data, and it has one testing variable with four levels (four types of textual tourism information). This experiment contained three parts. The first part presented the scenario to the participants (see Table 2). The second part displayed four pieces of tourism information to the participants, based on the textual information identified in Study 1. The four pieces of information were randomly shown to the participants, and after each piece of information had been read, closed-end questions (see Table 2) were posed to investigate participants' opinions and desires towards visiting the destination featured in the information. Finally, the third part entailed a follow-up interview (see Table 2), to obtain the in-depth knowledge of why the participants formed certain impressions and made particular decisions after reading the different types of information.

Table 2. Study 2 material

Part 1: Scenario	You have a 3-week holiday that you are **free to arrange**, and you have decided to travel to a destination that is **far away** and **totally new** to you. During the information search period, you have found several very attractive destinations in Mexico, Peru, and Brazil (the **cost is within your budget**). You start searching more detailed information about these destinations, so that you are able to **make decisions**. Now you have found four pieces of information, please read them carefully and answer one page of the questionnaire after you finish reading each piece of information.
Part 2: Questionnaire	*Characteristics*: Reliability; Understandability; Vividness; Usefulness.
	Decision: Desire to visit the destination.
Part 3: Interview	*Characteristics: Which type of information is the most* Reliable; Easy to understand; Vivid; Useful *to you? Why?*
	Decisions: Please explain why you had more desire to visit XXX rather than XXX?

4.4 Participants

Sixteen participants (8 males, 8 females, aged 18 to 39) were recruited through emails and posters for this within-subject experiment. All participants were Chinese, who had neither been to Mexico, Peru, or Brazil, nor had any prior knowledge about the detailed tourism information in these countries.

4.5 Material

The four pieces of tourism information used in Study 2 were designed based on the four types of textual tourism information identified from Study 1: *blogs*, *reviews*, *messages*, and *articles*. In this study, we selected four destinations in Mexico, Peru, and Brazil, for which similar tourism content was chosen: natural landscapes and heritages. The actual information content for the chosen destinations was downloaded from TravelPod (*blogs*), TripAdvisor (*reviews*), WikiTravel (*articles*), and a travel agent website (*messages*). The questionnaires were designed in English and later translated to Chinese for the participants, who were more comfortable with their first language.

4.6 Data Collection and Analysis

The questionnaire data was collected by 7-point Likert questions, each time a participant finished reading a piece of information. A Freidman's test was employed to analyse the one variable, within-subject, and non-parametric ordinal data. The follow-up interview was carried out after each participant finished reading all four pieces of information and had completed the questionnaires. Due to the nature of the qualitative data, interviews were audio-recorded, fully transcribed by the first author, and analysed based on an Emergent Themes Analysis [21].

4.7 Results and Discussions

The results from Study 2 (see Table 3) indicate that there are significant differences in how users perceived the four types of textual tourism information identified in Study 1, and how the four types of information had different influences on tourists' desires to visit a destination.

Table 3. Study 2 results

		Median values (scale: 1 to 7)			
	Sig. (P values)	Messages	Reviews	Articles	Blogs
Reliability	0.004**	5	6	6	6
Understandability	***	5	6	5	6
Vividness	***	3.5	5	4	6
Usefulness	0.005**	5.5	6	5	5
Desire to visit	0.004**	5	5	4	5.5

* P value < 0.05; ** P value < 0.01; *** P value < 0.001

Reliability. AFreidman's test shows that the perceived reliability is significantly different across the four types of textual tourism information ($X^2_{(3)} = 13.336, p = .004$), where pairwise tests reveal that the textual tourism information in the forms of *articles* is perceived the most accurate, reliable, and closest to the facts. It reflects the finding from Study 1 that tourism information in the form of *articles* presents a destination with sincerity. Due to the nature of *articles*, they tend to narrate the facts of a destination, in terms of history, location, culture, population, etc., so it is quite reasonable that *articles* are the most reliable type of information source. Interestingly, the form of *review* comments and personal *blogs* are also perceived to be very reliable, and are significantly more reliable than *messages* (i.e., commercials and travel agent notifications). It can be explained by Cheong et al.'s [4] findings that users have more trust in product information created by other consumers than in information generated by manufacturers, and this trustworthiness attributed to user-generated content (including blogs and peer comments) remains, regardless of whether the particular views are positive or negative.

Understandability. A Freidman's test shows that the perceived understandability is significantly different across the four types of textual tourism information ($X^2_{(3)} = 19.465, p = .000$), where pairwise tests reveal that the textual tourism information in the forms of *reviews* and *blogs* is perceived to be the easiest to understand and to follow with little effort. It can be explained by the comments of one participant, who described how *"Blogs and review comments are written by other travellers, as tourists with the same perspectives of myself. The language is easy and straightforward, and it* *feels like I am experiencing their trips through the words*". This comment reflects the finding from Study 1 in which *blogs* and *reviews* tend to use first person narratives, so that readers feel closer to the information, as if they are the narrators throughout the whole reading. Therefore, it is easier to understand the content in *blogs* and *reviews*.

Vividness. A Freidman's test shows that the perceived vividness is significantly different across the four types of textual tourism information ($X^2_{(3)} = 21.613, p < .000$), where pairwise tests reveal that the textual tourism information in the forms of *blogs* is perceived to be the most likely to create images, sounds, or smells in users' minds, and make the users feel like they are immersed in the environment/activity/location while reading the information. It can be explained by one participant, who stated that "*Blogs tend to describe the process of a trip, how the authors get to the destination, how the trip begins, what they experience... in an order. So it is very easy and natural to create a sequence of images of their trips*".

Usefulness. A Freidman's test shows that the perceived usefulness is significantly different across the four types of textual tourism information ($X^2_{(3)} = 12.780, p = .005$), where pairwise tests reveal that the textual tourism information in the forms of *reviews* is perceived to be the most useful while undertaking the tasks for making tourism decisions. Most of the participants expressed the view that all four types of information were useful, to some extent, at different stages of their trip planning processes. However, *review* comments played the most influential and useful role in the decision-making process, and as one participant explained, "*No matter how good a destination is as a travel agent claims, or as an official article introduces, or even as a personal blog describes, all these types of information come from one or a very limited number of sources. I cannot make decisions based on this small amount of information. What I like about reviews is that I can get many up-to-date pieces of information from the viewpoints of different tourists, which are very straightforward, quick to access, and also comprehensive. I would still eliminate a destination after reading an article emphasising how good it is, if the review comments from most of the peer travellers were negative*".

Desire to visit. A Freidman's test shows that the tourists' desire to visit a destination is significantly different across the four types of textual tourism information ($X^2_{(3)} = 13.489, p = .004$), where pairwise tests reveal that the textual tourism information in the forms of *reviews* and *blogs* has the most significant influence on tourists' desires to visit a destination. The desire to visit a destination has been shown to be positively associated with vivid mental imagery [9], and the perceived understandability of the information [5]. This study shows that *blogs*, which are the easiest to understand and have the most vivid type of textual tourism information, have a significant influence on tourists' desires to visit a particular destination. Meanwhile, *review* comments, which are the easiest to understand and have the most useful type of textual tourism information, also have a significant influence on tourists' desires to visit a destination. Reliability, as one of the most important characteristics of online tourism information, does not have any effect on blog usage enjoyment, nor on tourists' desires to visit a destination [5]. It is consistent in Study 2 that *articles*, as the most reliable type of information, do not exert much influence on tourists' desires to visit a destination. One participant explained that, *"The reliability of information is very important, but it is more like an initial condition. I won't even read it carefully if I believe the information is fake, dodgy, or exaggerating the truth. But it does not mean that I would like to go there if I believe the information is true"*.

5 Conclusion

This research first investigated the online textual tourism information through a mixed-method approach that has previously been applied in collecting and analysing social media data [3]. Study 1 identified and classified four types of textual tourism information: *blogs*, *reviews*, *messages*, and *articles*, in which we found that their characteristics varied between in terms of the linguistic features, the emotions contained, and the brand personality presented in the case of one common destination. Study 2 empirically explored how tourists perceived the four types of textual tourism information, and we found that: (1) *articles* are perceived as the most reliable type of information; (2) *reviews* and *blogs* are perceived as the easiest to understand; (3) *blogs* are perceived as the best for creating image in users' minds; and (4) *reviews* are perceived as the most useful resource when making tourism decisions. Finally, Study 2 empirically explored how the four types of textual tourism information influence on the tourists' levels of desire to visit a destination. The results show that *blogs* and *review* comments have a significant influence on tourists' desires to visit a destination.

The investigation of online textual tourism information in this paper provides knowledge of how the different types of textual tourism information differ in terms of the presentations of the information, how tourists perceive them, and how they are affected by them. Technology designers may consider combining different types of textual tourism information to users at different stages in the trip planning process, so that tourists feel more comfortable that their needs are being met while reading any such customised information.

Acknowledgement. The authors would like to thank Xinyu Fu for his help with data collection, the participants for the empirical study, the paper reviewers, and the support of International Doctoral Innovation Centre at the University of Nottingham, Ningbo, China. We also acknowledge the financial support from National Natural Science Foundation of China for a Grant awarded to the authors (Grant No. 71401085).

References

1. Aaker, J.L.: Dimensions of brand personality. J. Mark. Res. **34**(3), 347–456 (1997)
2. Borràs, J., Moreno, A., Valls, A.: Intelligent tourism recommender system: a survey. Expert Syst. Appl. **41**(16), 7370–7389 (2014)
3. Chan, H.K., Wang, X., Lacka, E., Zhang, M.: A mixed-method approach to extracting the value of social media data. Prod. Oper. Manag. **25**(3), 568–583 (2015)
4. Cheong, H.J., Morrison, M.A.: Consumers' reliance on product information and recommendations found in UGC. J. Interact. Advertising **8**(2), 38–49 (2008)

5. Chen, Y., Shang, R., Li, M.: The effects of perceived relevance of travel blogs' content on the behavioral Intention to visit a tourist destination. Comput. Hum. Behav. **30**, 789–799 (2014)
6. Decrop, A., Snelders, D.: Planning the summer vacation an adaptable process. Ann. Tourism Res. **31**(4), 1008–1030 (2004)
7. Grant, R., Clarke, R.J., Kyriazis, E.: A review of factors affecting online consumer search behaviour from an information value perspective. J. Mark. Manag. **23**(5–6), 519–533 (2008)
8. Mansfeld, Y.: From motivation to actual travel. Ann. Tourism Res. **19**, 399–419 (1992)
9. Marlow, J., Dabbish, L.: When is a picture not worth a thousand words? The psychological effects of mediated exposure to a remote location. Comput. Hum. Behav. **30**, 824–831 (2014)
10. Martindale, C.: Romantic Progression: The Psychology of Literary History. Hemisphere, New York (1975)
11. Mathieson, A., Wall, G.: Tourism, Economic, Physical and Social Impacts. Longman, Harlow (1982)
12. Moya, M.D., Jain, R.: When tourists are your "Friends": exploring the brand personality of Mexico and Brazil on Facebook. Public Relat. Rev. **39**(1), 23–29 (2013)
13. Yoo, K.H., Gretzel, U., Zanker, M.: Persuasive Recommender Systems: Conceptual Background and Implications. Springer, Heidelberg (2012)
14. Pudliner, B.A.: Alternative literature and tourist experience: travel and tourist weblogs. J. Tourism Cult. Change **5**(1), 46–59 (2007)
15. Shafer, S.M., Smith, H.J., Linder, J.C.: The power of business models. Bus. Horiz. **48**(3), 199–207 (2005)
16. Sheldon, P.J.: Tourism Information Technology. CAB International, Oxon (1997)
17. Stigler, M., Pokorny, D.: Emotions and primary process in guided Imagery psychotherapy: computerized text-analytic measures. Psychother. Res. **11**(4), 415–431 (2001)
18. Thelwall, M.: A web crawler design for data mining. J. Inf. Sci. **27**(5), 319–325 (2001)
19. Vogt, C.A., Fesenmaier, D.R.: Expanding the functional information search model. Ann. Tourism Res. **25**(3), 551–578 (1998)
20. Xiang, Z., Gretzel, U.: Role of social media in online travel information search. Tourism Manag. **31**(2), 179–188 (2010)
21. Wong, B.L.W., Blandford, A.E.: Analysing ambulance dispatcher decision making: trialing emergent themes analysis. In: Presented at HF 2002: Joint Conference of the Computer Human Interaction Special Interest Group and The Ergonomics Society of Australia, Melbourne (2002)
22. Um, S., Crompton, J.L.: Attitude determinants in tourism destination choice. Ann. Tourism Res. **17**(3), 432–448 (1990)

A New Information Theory-Based
Serendipitous Algorithm Design

Xiaosong Zhou[1], Zhan Xu[1], Xu Sun[1(✉)], and Qingfeng Wang[2]

[1] Faculty of Science and Engineering,
University of Nottingham Ningbo China, Ningbo, China
Xu.sun@nottingham.edu.cn
[2] Business School, University of Nottingham Ningbo China, Ningbo, China

Abstract. The development of information technology has stimulated an increasing number of researchers to investigate how to provide serendipitous experience to users in the digital environment, especially in the fields of information research and recommendation systems. Although a number of achievements have been made in understanding the nature of serendipity in the context of information research, few of these achievements have been employed in the design of information systems. This paper proposes a new serendipitous recommendation algorithm based on previous empirical studies by taking into considerations of the three important elements of serendipity, namely "unexpectedness", "insight" and "value". We consider our design of the algorithm as an important attempt to bridge the research fruits between the two areas of information research and recommendation systems. By applying the designed algorithm to a game-based application in a real life experiment with target users, we have found that comparing to the conventional designed method; the proposed algorithm has successfully provided more possibilities to the participants to experience serendipitous encountering.

Keywords: Serendipity · Recommendation system · Information theory

1 Introduction

Serendipity is widely experienced in human history, it is defined as "an unexpected experience prompted by an individual's valuable interaction with ideas, information, objects, or phenomena" [1]. So far studies relating to serendipity mainly focus on the following two directions: theoretical studies in the area of information research which aim to investigate the nature of serendipity [2–4], and the empirical studies with the purpose to develop applications or algorithms that provide users with serendipitous encountering especially in the digital environment [5–7].

One of the areas which try to employ serendipity applications is the design of recommender system. The overloaded information in the cyber space has made current users no longer satisfied by recommending them those "accurate" information, instead, users aims to be recommended with the information that are more serendipitous and interesting to them [8–10]. However, a rising concern identified in our reviewing of relevant studies is that those discoveries from information research regarding the nature

© Springer International Publishing AG 2017
S. Yamamoto (Ed.): HIMI 2017, Part II, LNCS 10274, pp. 314–327, 2017.
DOI: 10.1007/978-3-319-58524-6_26

of serendipity do not receive sufficient attentions in the recommender system designs. This paper proposes a new algorithm to support serendipitous recommendation by applying recent research fruits on serendipity in the area of information research.

2 Problem and Research Question

Recommender system researchers often consider serendipity as "unexpected" and "useful" [11], and have designed recommendation algorithms through either content-based filtering [12] or collaborative filtering [13]. However, most of the recommendation algorithms mainly focus on providing "unexpectedness" to the users, and treated the "usefulness" as only a metric value to measure the effectiveness of their algorithms rather than considering it as a design clue [14].

As a comparison, serendipity in information research is often considered with three main characteristics: unexpectedness, insight and value [4]. "Unexpectedness" is considered as the encountered information should be unexpected or a surprise to the information actor, while "value" specifies that the encountered information should be considered as useful and beneficial to the information actor. These two understandings of "unexpectedness" and "value" consist with the current view of serendipity in designing recommender systems [11, 14]; however, the "insight" aspect tends to be neglected.

"Insight" is considered as an ability to find some clue in current environment, then "making connections" between the clue and one's previous knowledge or experience, and finally shift the attention to the new discovered clue [15]. Some researchers have found such ability of "making connections" is actually a key facet in experiencing serendipity [4] and can be quite different among individuals and result in a range of serendipity encounterers from the super-encounterers to occasional-encounterers [16]. The connections can be made between different pieces of information, people and ideas [3]; therefore, to support or "trigger" connection-making in order to bring more possibilities of experiencing serendipity have always been considered as an important design clue for those information researchers [17, 18].

Based on the discussed issues, we then raise our research question: is it possible to combine the theoretical studies of serendipity in information research, especially the ignored aspect of "insight" or "making connection", into the recommender system design?

Followed by our research question, we proposed a collaborative-filtering based algorithm by considering the theoretical discoveries of serendipity from the area of information research. Based on the discovery from information research that serendipity is often encountered in a relaxed and leisure personal state [1, 3], we then applied the algorithm into a game based application and conducted an empirical experiment.

3 Proposed Algorithm

There are two major concerns in providing serendipitous encountering in the recommendation system design: the first concern is how to balance "unexpectedness" and "useful". As pointed out by [14], there should be "a most preferred distance" between the two values, as the high level of unexpectedness may cause user's dissatisfaction of the recommended information, while users may also lose interest to that information with a low unexpectedness. The second concern is how to combine "insight" into system design to stimulate the process of "making connections".

The two concerns are addressed from the following perspective of "relevance" with two hypotheses:

- Hypothesis 1: Given the information that is highly relevant to a user's personal profile, the information would also of a high potential value to the user;
- Hypothesis 2: A user will be unexpected to the information that is relevant to his profile while is not previous acknowledged or known by the user.

Consider a target user A, who is the user that will be provided with the recommended information, a user B who is highly relevant to user A and a user C who is highly relevant to user B while is not known by user A. The user A may experience serendipity by providing the information of user C, which is unexpected to him/her, and by providing the relationship between user B and user C, which may further cause interestingness or usefulness to user A. The following part of this section illustrates a detailed implementation of the algorithm.

1.   Target user

Consider a table of a target user profile U_1 with a category set $C = \{C_1, C_2, C_3...C_i... C_n\}$, where C_i represents the i-th category of the user profile. All the categories are arranged through the value of their weights in the user profile. The weight can either be a given weight by the dataset or calculated through clustering analysis [19]. In order to simplify the introduction of our proposed algorithm here, it is more convenient to set the weight for each C_i which is given by the dataset in the very beginning. The weight of C_i is larger than C_j ($i > j$) in C set:

$$w_c = \left\{ w_{C_1}, w_{C_2}, \ldots, w_{C_i}, \ldots, w_{C_i}, \ldots, w_{C_n} \middle| w_{C_i} \geq w_{C_j}, i > j \right\} \tag{1}$$

For each category set C_i, consider $C_i = \{a_1, a_2, a_3... a_i ... a_n\}$, where a_i is the corresponded attribute to each vector C_i. In particular, for each a_i represents the dimension according to which a new user profile may be produced (i.e. author of literatures; musicians). The values for each a_i are also arranged by their weight in each vector C_i and can be calculated through semantic analysis such as the tf^*idf weight (term-frequency times inverse document frequency) calculation [20]:

$$w(t, d) = \frac{tf_{t,d} \log\left(\frac{N}{df_t}\right)}{\sqrt{\sum_i \left(tf_{t_i,d}\right)^2 \log\left(\frac{N}{df_{t_i}}\right)^2}} \tag{2}$$

Where $w(t,d)$ represents for the weight of a term t in a document d, and it is a function of the frequency of t in the document (tf_t,d), the number of documents that contain the term *(dft)* and the number of documents in the collection *(N)*. As a result, the weight for a category set C_i is determined by the weight of each attribute in the set:

$$w_{c_i} = \left\{ w_{a_1}, w_{a_2}, \ldots, w_{a_i}, \ldots, w_{a_j}, \ldots, w_{a_n} \middle| w_{a_i} \geq w_{a_j}, i > j \right\} \tag{3}$$

2. *Screen the weight*

As been pre-defined that C_1 with the largest weight in the C set and a_1 with the largest weight in the C_i set. Set a threshold τ to eliminate the low weight value from the user profile U_1:

$$w_{c_i} = \left\{ w_{a_1}, w_{a_2}, \ldots, w_{a_i}, \ldots, w_{a_j}, \ldots, w_{a_n} \middle| w_{a_i} \geq w_{a_j}, i > j \right\} \tag{4}$$

Similarly, set a threshold θ to eliminate the low weight value from the C_i set:

$$w_{c_i} = \left\{ w_{C_i a_1}, w_{C_i a_2}, w_{C_i a_3}, \ldots, w_{C_i a_i} \middle| w_{C_i a_i} \geq \theta \right\} \tag{5}$$

3. *Generate a new user profile*

A new user profile U_{i+1} is produced according to each a_i in the C_i set. Here, the generation of the user profile arranges from the largest weight of w_{C_i,a_1} to the smallest weight of w_{C_i,a_i}.

4. *Iteration and End condition*

Based on the weight arrangement in a user profile, it is intuitional that for an attribute a_i with a large weight, it is also with more possibility for the current user to have acknowledged about the information of a_i. In other words, the probability for a current user U_i to make connection with the next user profile U_{i+1} is proportional to the weight of the attribute in current user profile:

$$P(U_{i+1} | U_i) = \lambda w_{c_i} * w_{c_i,a_i} \tag{6}$$

where λ is the proportionality coefficient of the probability to the relevant weight.

The probability of making connections by target user U_1 to i-th user can be further extended if only the generated user is always new to the prior generated ones:

$$P(U_i | U_1) = P(U_2 | U_1) * P(U_3 | U_2) * \ldots * P(U_i | U_{i-1}) \tag{7}$$

The iteration to find the next user would not continue until it meets the following two end conditions:

- the generated user is no longer new to all the previous generated users;
- $P(U_i | U_1)$ comes to a threshold δ, where δ represents an appropriate threshold of the probability.

The reason to set the threshold δ is to ensure the effectiveness of the iteration process. This is because if $P(U_i|U_1)$ comes too large, the recommended information may fail to bring the target user with the sense of unexpectedness, as the recommendation may probably have been acknowledged by the user; however, if the value of $P(U_i|U_1)$ is too small, the recommended information may be too irrelevant to the target user and he/she may lose interest on it. Hence the setting of the threshold δ is a very important step for the iteration process and it needs to be further identified based on empirical studies in the future. Once the recommendation list is generated within the threshold δ, they can be recommended to the target user by selecting the item with the highest values of $P(U_i|U_1)$.

5. Recommendation

When the iteration is finished, the content with the largest weighted category in current candidate will be provided to the target user, in addition with the relevant information of the previous searched users that result in the current user.

6. An example of the proposed algorithm

An example of the proposed algorithm is provided in Fig. 1. Consider *Ann* as the target user (U_1) with different literature categories of $\{A, B, C\}$ in her personal library, whose weight is $\{0.5, 0.3, 0.2\}$ (Fig. 1a). The author names of the literatures are set as the attributes for each category and according to the *tf*idf* weight calculation, there are three values $\{a_1, a_2, a_3\}$ in category A with the weight $W'A = \{0.6, 0.3, 0.1\}$. Set $\lambda = 1$ for each probability of the current user to find the next user profile, the probability for *Ann* to find *a1*'s profile (U_2) can be calculated according to Eq. (6):

$$P(U_2|U_1) = w_A * w_{A,a_1} = 0.5 * 0.6 = 0.3 \tag{8}$$

The profile of *a1* is then produced as Fig. 1b. Likewise, among the four authors in the D category, author *d1* (U_3) weights largest and then produce *d1*'s profile (Fig. 1c):

$$P(U_3|U_2) = w_D * w_{D,d_1} = 0.4 * 0.5 = 0.2 \tag{9}$$

According to Eq. (7), the probability for *Ann* (U_1) to find *d1*'s profile (U_3) is:

$$P(U_3|U_1) = P(U_2|U_1) * P(U_3|U_2) = 0.3 * 0.2 = 0.06 \tag{10}$$

Set the threshold δ as 0.06, then the iteration of the algorithm stops and recommend literatures of category F in *d1*'s profile to *Ann*, in addition with the relevant information of *d1* and *a1*. For example, the recommended information can be "these papers (category F) are most stored by *d1*, who had published papers *(d1, d2, d3, d4)* with *a1* before".

7.   Description of the Proposed Algorithm

The proposed algorithm is collaborative filtering based, hence it is more appropriate to those dataset whose content is generated by different users, according to which the next user's profile will be easier to produce for a current user.

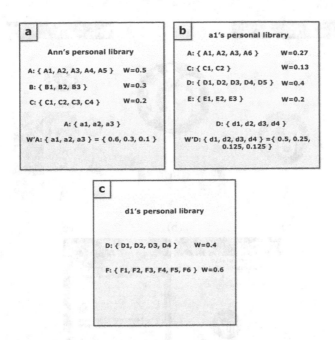

Fig. 1. An example of the proposed algorithm: (a) target user *Ann*'s personal library; (b) user *a1*'s personal library generated by *Ann*; (c) user *d1*'s personal library generated by *a1*

The proposed algorithm relates with serendipity from the following three aspects:

- *Unexpectedness*: by setting the value of probability. In an identified threshold δ, the unexpectedness of the information to a target user is inversely related to the magnitude of probability. The smaller probability for a target user to find another user, the more unexpectedness he/she receives from the provided information of the current candidate.
- *Insight*: by providing the information of the searched clues which demonstrates the relationship between the provided user (recommendation source) and the target user. As aforementioned that the ability to connect the new clue with previous knowledge/experience is a key element in the occurrence of serendipity, and thus there is a necessity for the designers to provide the design clues can contribute to a customer's noticeability or attention to connect the provided information with his/her personal profile. In the provided example of Fig. 1, such insight is provided by showing the relationship between *d1* and the target user, who had published paper together before.
- *Value*: by generating the next user's file according to the weight arrangement of the attributes; those with larger weights are considered as priorities. This is because the larger weight the attribute is, the more possibility it may have to satisfy the target user's need/concern, and finally brings more potential value to the user.

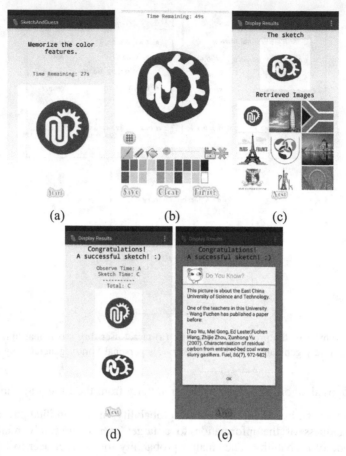

Fig. 2. Different stages of the designed sketch application: (a) Memorised picture; (b) Participant's sketching; (c) Retrieving; (d) Sketching result and game score; (e) provided picture information

4   Empirical Study

A problem that the developed algorithm confronted is how to evaluate it successfully in a real life environment. According to the information research, studying serendipity in a controlled experiment always has negatively influences on the participants [21, 22]; in addition, serendipity is such a subjective phenomenon that it is tightly closed to the participant's own experience or knowledge [4, 15]. A hint to address the problem may rise from Shute's [23] stealth assessment theory where the assessments or inferences of conceptions or models that is elusive to humans is embedded into new computer-based technologies such as games. In the centre of Shute's theory is the Evident-Centred Design (ECD), where a player's abilities and understandings, especially those that cannot be directly observed by researchers (e.g. critical thinking, problem solving) is reflected through the embedded tasks or situations in the design, such as the interaction processes of the game. Serendipity is exactly such a phenomenon that cannot be observed directly by the researchers; however, during the process of game-playing, participants would naturally produce sequences of actions while performing the designed tasks and hence provides us with possible evidences to access the encounter of serendipity. In addition, there is also evidence from the information research that serendipity is often experienced by those participants who are in a relaxed and leisure state [1, 3], and playing games can bring participant to such a relaxed state comparing with other activities. Based on the above discussion, we have then employed the algorithm into a game-based application and have conducted an empirical experiment to investigate whether our proposed algorithm could provide serendipitous encountering to researchers. The study is described in details below:

4.1 Participant

28 PhD students (14 males and 14 females) from different disciplines are invited to the study. They were asked to conduct a drawing game on a mobile application which was developed by the research group.

4.2 Game-Based Application

The developed game is an android-based drawing game, which involves the following stages:

- Memorising and sketching

Each participant was given a picture in the very beginning for observation. Participant was then asked to layout the colour features of the picture based on the memory. A time clock is set during this stage where the maximum observation time is 30 s and the maximum sketch time for each participant is 120 s.

- Retrieving

When a participant finishes sketching, a group of 30 images is displayed to the participant for retrieving whether or not his/her drawing picture was contained in the provided pictures. If the picture is contained in the group, he/she may click on the picture to pick it out. Or the participant only needs to click "Next" button.

- Sketching result

Participant's finial sketching result is provided after retrieving. A winning game means the participants has successfully retrieved the drawing picture, and then he/she will be given a game score based on the observation time and sketching time. Otherwise, the participant will be noticed he/she has failed in the sketching.

- Providing picture information

The last stage of the application provides participants the related information of the picture, in regardless of whether or not the participant has made a successful sketching.

4.3   Embedded Algorithm and Comparison

– *Embed proposed algorithm into the developed application*

The next step is to embed the proposed algorithm into the application. As all the participants are PhD researchers, the algorithm is designed based on three assumptions:

- Assumption 1: For each PhD student, their supervisor's information is a large weight attribute in their personal profile.
- Assumption 2: For each PhD's supervisor, the co-author from their publications is a large weight attribute in the supervisor's profile.
- Assumption 3: For each co-author's personal profile, their working institution is a large weight attribute.

Therefore, each PhD student supposed to be provided with the information of their supervisor's co-author's institution. Figure 3 shows the design of the study including how the proposed algorithm is embedded into the game-based application and the sketch game process. Based on each participant's information, we start our study by providing them with the pictures which show the institution badge (Fig. 2a). Each participant was then asked to draw the picture out within 120 s (Fig. 2b). After retrieving (Fig. 2c) and showing the result of the sketch (Fig. 2d), the serendipitous information to the pictures was provided to the participant (Fig. 2e). The given information related to the picture includes two levels: (1) the introduction of the institution; (2) the publications of both the participant's supervisor and the co-author, as is shown in Fig. 5a.

– *A comparison of the proposed algorithm*

As a comparison, each participant was also given the pictures that without the serendipitous information from our proposed algorithm (Fig. 4). Two cover pictures from the "Nature" website (www.nature.com) were selected to the participant, together with the description of the picture on the website (Fig. 5b). We consider such provision as the conventional way to introduce the relationship between the picture and the information (pic-and-info). As a result, each participant should draw two pictures with our proposed algorithm and two with the conventional way of "pic-and-info".

4.4   Evaluation

The traditional measurement of serendipity in the area of recommender systems is often based upon the conventional perception on serendipity, where it is considered with the two main characters of "unexpected" and "useful" [11, 14, 24]. However, information research on serendipity has found that an important characteristic of serendipity is the element of time. The considered serendipity at a certain time may be changed with time [3, 4]. Therefore, [17] argued that apart from "unexpectedness" and "useful", "interesting" and "relevant" should also be taken into considerations as new measurements of serendipity, this is because their studies have shown that users may keep or follow up the information that is "relevant" or "interest" to them and lead to serendipity at a

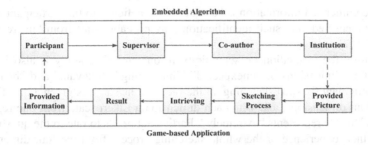

Fig. 3. Process of the study and the embedded proposed algorithm

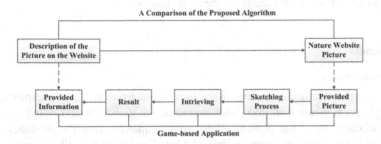

Fig. 4. A comparison of the proposed algorithm

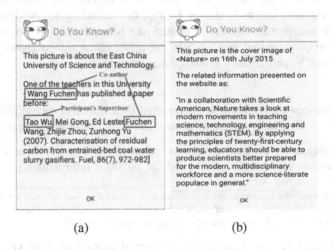

(a)   (b)

Fig. 5. Provided information: (a) designed algorithm; (b) information from the nature website

different time. They consider such serendipity as "pseudo-serendipity" which refers to "*encounters experienced by users that have the potential of being serendipity in that users intended to do something in the future with those encounters*" [17, 25].

In this paper, we tend to argue that both "pseudo-serendipity" and "serendipity" would happen in recommendation systems. This is because in some cases, whether or not the recommended information is "useful" or "beneficial" to the participant needs to be further identified, and such identification may probably start from "interesting" or "relevant" [17].

Therefore, the evaluation on serendipity in our empirical study is also identified from the four dimensions of "unexpected", "interesting", "relevant" and "beneficial". After a participant finished sketching all the pictures, he/she was given a questionnaire with the four dimensions, and with each dimension a Likert scale from one represents "not at all" to five represents "extremely". Participant needs to rate in the questionnaire based on their experience of the whole sketching process from the four dimensions.

In addition, a 15 min post-interview is carried out right after each participant finished their sketching. The interview explored participant's subjective experience and the further reason for their ratings of the four dimensions.

4.5   Results

1.   Questionnaire

In total, 20 effective questionnaires were picked out from the 28 participants, as the other eight participants were too concentrated in the gameplay and failed to read the related information of the picture. These questionnaires were the feedbacks of 40 pictures of the conventional way of "pic-and-info" and the other 40 pictures based on our designed algorithm.

Only the marks of four or five are considered to be effective values on the corresponding dimension, which is shown in Fig. 6. According to the four identified dimensions of unexpected, interested, related and beneficial, it is obvious that comparing with the conventional way of "pic-and-info", our designed algorithm is more possible to result in participant's serendipitous encountering.

2.   Interview

During the interviews, most participants reported their senses of serendipity relating to the serendipitous algorithm designed pictures from the following two perspectives:

- All the participants reported that they had experienced "unexpectedness" because of the relationship between the picture and the provided information:

  I've never thought the picture is related to my supervisor! I've just taken it as a drawing game…… The information in the end really surprised me and I really think this is a very good design to provide me with the information in such a context! (Participant 3)

In addition, 12 out of 20 participants reported another level of unexpectedness existing in the content of the information, as the provided information was previously unacknowledged to them:

  I never know that my supervisor had published such a paper with him (the co-author) before…… I'm interested about it and will check the details of the paper later. (Participant 10)

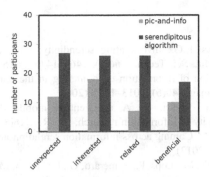

Fig. 6. Questionnaire result

- The result of the sketching game:

Over eight participants expressed their requirements to add an external link of the presented information (e.g. published paper of ...). One participant even asked us to send him the detailed information after the study.

By contrast, most participants have reported a less interest in the conventional "pic-and-info", this also reflects the important role of "relatedness" played in the design of the algorithms. As a result, the feedbacks from the participants have demonstrated that our proposed algorithm can effectively support the design strategies for serendipity.

5 Conclusion and Future Work

In this paper, we have presented a new serendipitous recommendation algorithm by combining the theory of serendipity in information research. In particular, our proposal extended the design of such serendipitous recommendation by including two other vital aspects in serendipity, namely, "insight" and "value".

We also performed an empirical experiment with target users by employing the proposed algorithm to a game-based application. The result demonstrates that comparing with the conventional design of "pic-and-info", our algorithm has effectively encouraged our participants to experience serendipitous encountering However, the study is limited by the small sample number of participants, so our future work will aim to explore the algorithm through more datasets, and to investigate the appropriate thresholds (e.g. τ, θ, δ) which have been set in current algorithms. We will also compare our proposed algorithm with other existing algorithms so as to better evaluate and optimize the algorithm in different situations.

Acknowledgments. We acknowledge the financial support from a NSFC grant with code 71401085.

References

1. McCay-Peet, L., Toms, E.G.: Investigating serendipity: how it unfolds and what may influence it. J. Assoc. Inf. Sci. Technol. **66**(7), 1463–1476 (2015)
2. Erdelez, S.: Investigation of information encountering in the controlled research environment. Inf. Process. Manage. **40**(6), 1013–1025 (2004)
3. Sun, X., Sharples, S., Makri, S.: A user-centred mobile diary study approach to understanding serendipity in information research. Inf. Res. **16**(3) (2011)
4. Makri, S., Blandford, A.: Coming across information serendipitously – Part 1. J. Documentation **68**(5), 684–705 (2012)
5. Iaquinta, L., De Gemmis, M., Lops, P., Semeraro, G., Filannino, M., Molino, P.: Introducing serendipity in a content-based recommender system. In: Proceedings of the 8th International Conference on Hybrid Intelligent Systems, HIS 2008 (2008)
6. Yamaba, H., Tanoue, M., Takatsuka, K., Okazaki, N., Tomita, S.: On a Serendipity-oriented recommender system based on folksonomy and its evaluation. Procedia Comput. Sci. **22**, 276–284 (2013)
7. Makri, S., Blandford, A., Woods, M., Sharples, S., Maxwell, D.: Making my own luck: serendipity strategies and how to support them in digital information environments. J. Assoc. Inf. Sci. Technol. **65**(11), 2179–2194 (2014)
8. Lu, Q., Chen, T., Zhang, W., Yang, D., Yu, Y.: Serendipitous personalized ranking for Top-N recommendation. In: IEEE/WIC/ACM International Conferences on Web Intelligence and Intelligent Agent Technology, pp. 258–265, IEEE Computer Society (2012)
9. Sun, T., Zhang, M., Mei, Q.: Unexpected relevance: an empirical study of serendipity in retweets. In: *ICWSM*, pp. 592–601 (2013)
10. de Gemmis, M., Lops, P., Semeraro, G., Musto, C.: An investigation on the serendipity problem in recommender systems. Inf. Process. Manage. **51**(5), 695–717 (2015)
11. Ge, M., Delgado-Battenfeld, C., Jannach, D.: Beyond accuracy: evaluating recommender systems by coverage and serendipity. In: Proceedings of the fourth ACM Conference on Recommender systems (2010)
12. Jenders, M., Lindhauer, T., Kasneci, G., Krestel, R., Naumann, F.: A serendipity model for news recommendation. In: Hölldobler, S., Krötzsch, M., Peñaloza, R., Rudolph, S. (eds.) KI 2015. LNCS (LNAI), vol. 9324, pp. 111–123. Springer, Cham (2015). doi:10.1007/978-3-319-24489-1_9
13. Oku, K., Hattori, F.: Fusion-based recommender system for improving serendipity. In: Proceedings of the Workshop on Novelty and Diversity in Recommender Systems (DiveRS 2011), 5th ACM International Conference on Recommender Systems (2011)
14. Adamopoulos, P., Tuzhilin, A.: On unexpectedness in recommender systems: or how to better expect the unexpected. ACM Trans. Intell. Syst. Technol. **5**(4), 1–32 (2014)
15. Rubin, V.L., Burkell, J., Quan-Haase, A.: Facets of serendipity in everyday chance encounters: a grounded theory approach to blog analysis. Inf. Res. **16**(3) (2011)
16. Erdelez, S.: Information encountering: a conceptual framework for accidental information discovery. In: Proceedings of an International Conference on Information Seeking in Context. Taylor Graham Publishing (1997)
17. Pontis, S., Kefalidou, G., Blandford, A., Forth, J., Makri, S., Sharples, S., Woods, M.: Academics' responses to encountered information: context matters. J. Assoc. Inf. Sci. Technol. **67**(8), 1883–1903 (2016)
18. Kefalidou, G., Sharples, S.: Encouraging serendipity in research: designing technologies to support connection-making. Int. J. Hum. Comput Stud. **89**, 1–23 (2016)

19. Rohlf, F.J.: NTSYS-pc numerical taxonomy and multivariate analysis system, version 2.0. Appl. Biostatistics, 23 (1998)
20. Pazzani, Michael J., Billsus, D.: Content-Based Recommendation Systems. In: Brusilovsky, P., Kobsa, A., Nejdl, W. (eds.) The Adaptive Web. LNCS, vol. 4321, pp. 325–341. Springer, Heidelberg (2007). doi:10.1007/978-3-540-72079-9_10
21. McCay-Peet, L., Toms, E.G.: Uses and gratifications: measuring the dimensions of serendipity in digital environments. Inf. Res. **16**(3) (2011)
22. Bogers, T., Rasmussen, R.R., Jensen, L.S.B.: Measuring serendipity in the lab: the effects of priming and monitoring. In: Proceedings of the iConference 2013 (2013)
23. Shute, V.J.: Stealth assessment in computer-based games to support learning. Comput. Games Instr. **55**(2), 503–524 (2011)
24. Murakami, T., Mori, K., Orihara, R.: Metrics for evaluating the serendipity of recommendation lists. In: Satoh, K., Inokuchi, A., Nagao, K., Kawamura, T. (eds.) JSAI 2007. LNCS (LNAI), vol. 4914, pp. 40–46. Springer, Heidelberg (2008). doi:10.1007/978-3-540-78197-4_5
25. André, P., Schraefel, M.C.: Designing for (un)serendipity - computing and chance. Biochem. Soc. **31**(6), 19–22 (2009)

Intelligent Systems

Discovering Rules of Subtle Deficits Indicating Mild Cognitive Impairment Using Inductive Logic Programming

Keisuke Abe[1(✉)], Niken Prasasti Martono[1], Takehiko Yamaguchi[2],
Hayato Ohwada[1], and Tania Giovannetti[3]

[1] Departement of Industrial Administration, Tokyo University of Science,
Katsushika, Japan
7416603@ed.tus.ac.jp, niken.prasasti@sbm-itb.ac.id,
ohwada@rs.tus.ac.jp
[2] Department of Applied Electronic, Tokyo University of Science,
Katsushika, Japan
tk-ymgch@te.noda.tus.ac.jp
[3] Department of Psychology, Temple University, Philadelphia, USA
tgio@temple.edu

Abstract. Recently, Japan has been experiencing a declining birthrate and an increasingly aging population; as a result, the number of dementia patients is increasing. Current medical science has no way to treat dementia completely after onset. Therefore, it is necessary to detect mild cognitive impairment (MCI) in the early stage just before dementia develops. It is clear that MCI patients who exhibit subtle deficits in daily living behavior (in this study, micro-errors (MEs)) have declining cognitive function associated with cognitive impairment. Virtual reality (VR) technology has been actively utilized in rehabilitation and therapy, and here we use an application known as Virtual Kitchen (VK). In this work, we analyze how ME happens. We use finger movement data and subtask information from VK. Our methodology proposes a combination of inductive logic programming (ILP) and the sliding window algorithm. Because ILP can extract expressive rules but is susceptible to noise and memory hog, it is difficult to use sensor data directly for learning. Sliding window is used as its ability to reduce the amount of data while holding the shape of original time series data. From preliminary experiments, we obtained some rules of ME occurrence that are related to differences in speed, time interval, and subtask. We obtained results that explain how ME occurrence is generally related to subtask and finger speed. In the future, we will use more positive samples and conduct more experiments to obtain better and more accurate results.

Keywords: Cognitive impairment · Virtual reality · Time series · Data mining

1 Introduction

Recently, Japan has been experiencing a declining birthrate and an increasingly aging population; as a result, the number of dementia patients is increasing. Current medical science has no way to treat dementia completely after onset. Therefore, it is necessary

© Springer International Publishing AG 2017
S. Yamamoto (Ed.): HIMI 2017, Part II, LNCS 10274, pp. 331–340, 2017.
DOI: 10.1007/978-3-319-58524-6_27

to detect mild cognitive impairment (MCI) in the early stage just before dementia develops. If treatment or prevention can be done early in the MCI stage, there is a possibility that dementia will not develop. However, MCI is diagnosed subjectively by a doctor. Recent quantitative research indicates that MCI patients who exhibit subtle deficits in daily living behavior (in this study, micro-errors (MEs)) have declining cognitive function associated with cognitive impairment. Sara et al. demonstrated that there was a high possibility that participants experiencing a large number of MEs had lower cognitive function [1].

In recent years, virtual reality (VR) technology has been actively utilized in rehabilitation and therapy, and VR applications corresponding to human physical and cognitive functions have been developed [2]. In this study, we use an application known as Virtual Kitchen (VK) [3] to analyze how ME occurs. VK is used as an application for participants to perform daily living tasks, such as making breakfast, in virtual space [4]. VK is equipped with a leap motion sensor, and we are able to record finger movements to obtain useful information.

This study utilizes finger movement data and subtask information from VK to analyze how ME occurs. First, we performed data smoothing to reduce sensor noise. Second, we segmented speed data according to subtask completion time. Third, we employed the sliding window algorithm to use Inductive Logic Programing (ILP). Finally, we used ILP to visualize rules and to use qualitative and quantitative data.

2   Finger Movement and VK Data

2.1   Raw Data

The VK system is equipped with a leap motion sensor to collect finger movements and provide two-dimensional coordinate data. This sensor records data at 0.01 per second and contains much noise; thus, data preprocessing is necessary. We performed data smoothing for each dimension using a moving average filter to make data trends easier to understand. Figure 1 plots the results of moving average filter using a span of 50 points. We then calculated speed data from the preprocessed data.

We obtained finger movement data and VK information data that included the state of the finger when touching the screen of the VK application. Thirteen healthy young adults, the pilot participants, prepared breakfast as everyday action tasks in the VK.

2.2   VK Data

Breakfast tasks analyzed in this work consist of preparing toast and making coffee (Table 1). Toast preparation subtasks include putting the toast in the toaster, switching on the toaster, putting the toast on the plate, taking the butter and jelly with knife, and spreading the butter and jelly on the toast. Coffee making subtasks include opening the coffee lid, scooping the coffee, putting the coffee in the mug, opening the sugar lid, scooping sugar with a spoon, stirring the coffee, putting in milk, and stirring the coffee. Figure 2 depicts the configuration of the VK system and the leap motion devices.

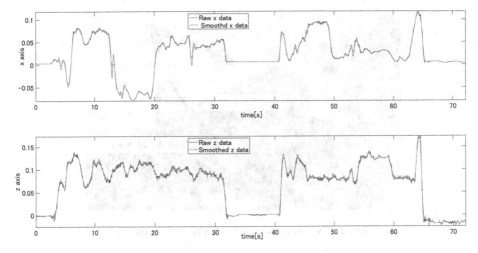

Fig. 1. Result of moving average filter

Table 1. Subtasks of toast and coffee preparation

Variable	Description	Variable	Description
Toast 1	Putting the toast in the toaster	Coffee 1	Opening the coffee lid
Toast 2	Switching on the toaster	Coffee 2	Scooping coffee
Toast 3	Putting the toast on the plate	Coffee 3	Putting coffee into mug
Toast 4	Taking the butter with knife	Coffee 4	Opening the sugar lid
Toast 5	Spread the butter on toast	Coffee 5	Scooping sugar with a spoon
Toast 6	Taking the jelly with knife	Coffee 6	Stirring the coffee
Toast 7	Spread the jelly on toast	Coffee 7	Putting in milk
		Coffee 8	Stirring the coffee

2.3 Segmentation by Subtask

In this study, we segmented completion time by subtask and used segmented data as sample data for the data-mining method. The time frame in Fig. 3 represents finger speed until completion of the breakfast task. For example, the leftmost frame separates the speed of the fingers until finishing subtask toast 1. The yellow segments indicate that ME was observed during the subtask.

We found 45 positive examples that represent ME events in the subtasks and 168 negative examples of events other than ME.

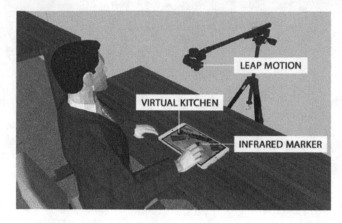

Fig. 2. System configuration of VK application [3]

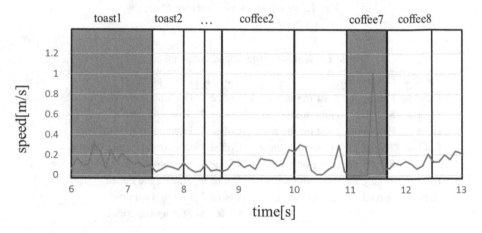

Fig. 3. Segmentation

3 Method

Our methodology proposes a combination of inductive logic programming (ILP) and the sliding window algorithm. Because ILP can extract expressive rules using background knowledge but ILP is susceptible to noise and memory hog, it is difficult to use sensor data directly for ILP. Sliding window is used to reduce the amount of data retaining shape of original time series data. The details are discussed in the next section. To use ILP, we must define some background knowledge that is obtained from finger speed and subtask information: speed, difference in speed, time intervals, the current subtask, the previous subtask, and the next subtask. In the final process, we use ILP to extract rules covering positive data. We used the parallel ILP system known as GKS [5, 6].

3.1   Sliding Window Algorithm

The sliding window algorithm is a piecewise linear approximation algorithm that is often used for machine learning and data mining for preprocessing sensor data [7]. In this study, it is used as it has the ability to reduce the amount of data while holding the shape of original time series data. We used the sliding window algorithm with interpolation against each segmented data [7]. Figure 4 plots the result of the sliding window algorithm with interpolation to reduce noise.

In this study, sliding windows are used on the original finger speed data in an effort to produce the smallest number of time points that will be used in ILP background knowledge.

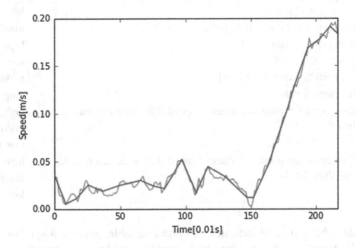

Fig. 4. Example of sliding window result with interpolation

3.2   ILP

ILP is a machine learning method that uses logic as the input. This method can extract rules explaining positive samples but not negative samples, and is a method to express time series data using flexible background knowledge. We defined two categories of predicate: movement and subtask. Table 2 lists predicates of ILP background knowledge. The movement category represents the quantitative data related to finger speed. The speed predicate represents the speed at a certain point in time. The diff_span predicate has two constants that exhibit difference between speed at a certain time point and speed at the adjacent time point, and time intervals between them. The subtask category includes predicates that explain qualitative data. We defined current subtask, previous subtask, and next subtask. By combining finger movement and subtask information, we can determine trends in type of subtask and type of movement when ME occurs.

ILP cannot deal with a continuous value; thus, we must transform data into discrete values. Table 3 lists descriptions of data transformation. The + symbol denotes an

Table 2. Predicates and mode declarations in background knowledge

Type	Predicate
Movement value	speed (+time, #value)
	diff_span (+time, -time, #value, #value)
Subtask	current_subtask (#value)
	previous_subtask (#value)
	next_subtask (#value)

Table 3. Descriptions of transformed values

#value	Range	Definition
speed	value < 0.02 [m/s]	low
	0.02 [m/s] ≦ value < 0.06 [m/s]	middle
	0.06 [m/s] ≦ value	high
span	value < 0.2 [sec]	short
	0.2 [sec] ≦ value < 0.5 [sec]	middle
	0.5 [sec] ≦ value	long
diff	Categorize the positive values of speed difference (increasing) into three levels	high_up
		middle_up
		low_up
	Categorize the positive values of speed difference (decreasing) into three levels	high_down
		middle_down
		low_down

input variable, the − symbol indicates an output variable, and the # symbol denotes a constant. We transformed speed into high, middle, and low. We transformed the difference value into three stages so as to be equal frequency, depending on whether it was positive or negative. We transformed time intervals into long, middle and short.

For example, in diff_span, we express change of speed as

```
speed(1,low)
diff_span(1,2,high_up,short)
diff_span(2,3,low_down,middle).
```

The upper expression indicates that time series point 1 is low speed. The middle expression indicates that from time series point 1 to time series point 2 there is a high speed increase at short time intervals. The second expression indicates that from time series point 2 to time series point 3 there is a speed decrease at medium time intervals. We can express the time series change as described above.

4   Results

As a result, we obtained rules using the ILP learning result. "{T, F}" means the number of positive examples and the number of negative examples explained by the rule. The obtained results from ILP are as follows.

Rule 1:

```
{5,0}+pos(A) :- speed(A,B,low), diff_span(A,B,C,high_up,
short), diff_span(A,D,B,middle_down,short),
diff_span(A,E,D,high_up,middle)
```

ME occurs when there is a high speed increase in a short time interval from the middle point, a moderate decrease occurs at a short time interval, and speed rises greatly in short time intervals.

Rule 2:

```
{7,2} +pos(A) :- speed(A,B,middle), diff_span(A,B,C, mid-
dle_up,short), diff_span(A,D,B,middle_down, middle),
diff_span(A,E,D,high_up,middle)
```

ME occurs when there is a moderate speed decrease at a middle time interval from the middle point, speed increases moderately in a short time interval, and then it increases greatly in a middle time interval.

Rule 3:

```
{6,2} +pos(A) :- diff_span(A,B,C,middle_down,short),
previous_subtask(A,toast2), diff_span(A,C,D,middle_up,
short)
```

ME occurs when there is a moderate speed decrease at a short time interval from the previous time series point; then it increase moderately at short time interval after performing subtask toast 2.

Rule 4:

```
{5,2} +pos(A) :- speed(A,B,middle), next_subtask(A,
toast3), diff_span(A,B,C,high_up,middle),
diff_span(A,C,D,middle_down, middle)
```

ME occurs when there is a high speed increase at a short time interval from the middle point; then speed decreases moderately at a middle time interval before performing subtask toast 3.

Rule 5:

```
{5,1} +pos(A):- speed(A,B,high), current_subtask(A, cof-
fee2),diff_span(A,B,C,middle_down,middle),
diff_span(A,D,B,high_up,short)
```

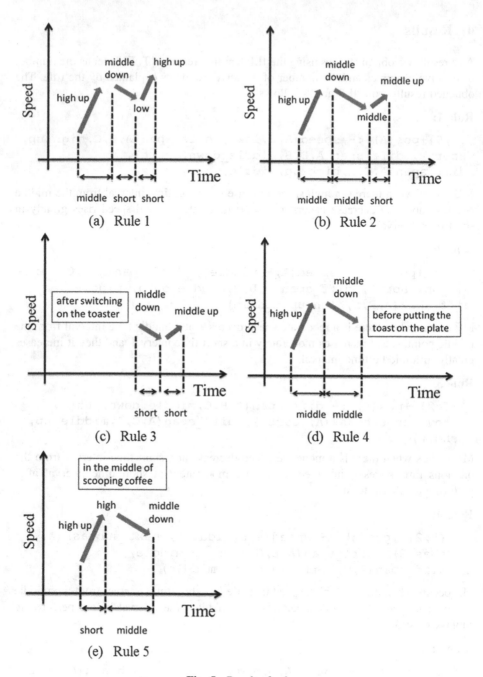

Fig. 5. Result of rules

ME occurs when there is a high speed increase at a short time interval, and then speed decreases moderately from the low point in a short time interval in the middle of subtask coffee 2.

Figure 5 presents these results in a time frame.

5   Discussion

From the preliminary experiments, we obtained some rules related to speed change and time interval. Rule 1 and Rule 2 indicate that ME tends to occur when speed rapidly increases and decreases in a short time interval. Also, regarding subtasks, Rule 3 and Rule 4 indicate that ME occurred after toast 2 (when the participant changed from toast task to coffee task) and before toast 3 (when the participant changed from coffee task to toast task). These results indicate that ME occurs during changing of subtasks, when there is much cognitive load. Rule 5 indicates that ME occurred in the middle of performing coffee 3.

Some MEs occur when there is no change in finger speed. Therefore, MEs can be roughly divided into two groups: those that involve speed change and those that involve no speed change. In the group that involves speed change, speed tends to increase and decrease in a short time interval, and ME occurs at the time of task switching.

However, in this study, the number of positive examples and the number negative example are unbalanced, because the amount of positive data was small and only a few samples were covered by the rule. In the future, we will work with more samples to obtain better results.

6   Conclusion and Future Work

This study used ILP to extract rules for subtle deficits occurring during performance of cognitive tasks in a VR environment. We arranged raw data and transformed data into discrete values for use in ILP. We defined background knowledge such as speed, difference, time interval, and subtask; then we used ILP to learn rules that define the occurence of ME. We obtained rules regarding finger movement and subtask in relation to ME occurence. ME tends to occur when movement changes in a short time interval (less than 0.5 s) and when the participant switches from one task to another. We obtained some preliminary results that explain how ME is generally related to subtask and finger speed. However, we had only a small amount of positive data in this pilot experiment. In the future, we will use more positive samples and conduct more experiments to obtain better and more accurate results.

References

1. Seligman, S.C., Giovannetti, T., Sestito, J., Libon, D.J.: A new approach to the characterization of subtle errors in everyday action: implications for mild cognitive impairment. Clin. Neuropsychologist **28**(1), 97–115 (2014). https://doi.org/10.1080/13854046.2013.852624

2. Faria, A.L., Andrade, A., Soares, L., i Badia, S.B., Langhorne, P., Bernhardt, J., Hsieh, C.: Benefits of virtual reality based cognitive rehabilitation through simulated activities of daily living: a randomized controlled trial with stroke patients. J. NeuroEng. Rehabil. **13**(1), 96 (2016). https://doi.org/10.1186/s12984-016-0204-z
3. Foloppe, D.A., Richard, P., Yamaguchi, T., Etcharry-Bouyx, F., Allain, P.: The potential of virtual reality-based training to enhance the functional autonomy of Alzheimer's disease patients in cooking activities: a single case study. Neuropsychol. Rehabil. 1–25 (2015). https://doi.org/10.1080/09602011.2015.1094394. November 2011
4. Martono, N.P., Yamaguchi, T., Ohwada, H.: Utilizing finger movement data to cluster patients with everyday action impairment. In: 2016 IEEE 14th International Conference on Cognitive Inlormatics & Cognitive Computing, pp. 459–464 (2016). https://doi.org/10.13140/RG.2.1.2084.5684. (August)
5. Mizoguchi, F., Ohwada, H.: Constrained relative least general generalization for inducing constraint logic programs. New Gener. Comput. **13**(3–4), 335–368 (1995). https://doi.org/10.1007/BF03037230
6. Nishiyama, H., Ohwada, H.: Module … Module Worker. In: CEUR Workshop Proceedings of the Late Breaking Papers of the 25th International Conference on Inductive Logic Programming, pp. 86–94 (2015)
7. Keogh, E., Chu, S., Hart, D., Pazzani, M.: An online algorithm for segmenting time series. In: Proceedings of the 2001 IEEE International Conference on Data Mining, pp. 289–296 (2001). https://doi.org/10.1109/ICDM.2001.989531

Vector Representation of Words for Plagiarism Detection Based on String Matching

Kensuke Baba[1(✉)], Tetsuya Nakatoh[2], and Toshiro Minami[3]

[1] Fujitsu Laboratories, Kawasaki, Japan
baba.kensuke@jp.fujitsu.com
[2] Kyushu University, Fukuoka, Japan
[3] Kyushu Institute of Information Sciences, Dazaifu, Fukuoka, Japan

Abstract. Plagiarism detection in documents requires appropriate definition of document similarity and efficient computation of the similarity. This paper evaluates the validity of using vector representation of words for defining a document similarity in terms of the processing time and the accuracy in plagiarism detection. This paper proposes a plagiarism detection algorithm based on the score vector weighted by vector representation of words. The score vector between two documents represents the number of matches between corresponding words for every possible gap of the starting positions of the documents. The vector and its weighted version can be computed efficiently using convolutions. In this paper, two types of vector representation of words, that is, randomly generated vectors and a distributed representation generated by a neural network-based method from training data, are evaluated with the proposed algorithm. The experimental results show that using the weighted score vector instead of the normal one for the algorithm can reduce the processing time with a slight decrease of the accuracy, and that randomly generated vector representation is more suitable for the algorithm than the distributed representation in the sense of a tradeoff between the processing time and the accuracy.

Keywords: Text processing · Plagiarism detection · Document similarity · Score vector · Vector representation of words

1 Introduction

Plagiarism detection for a huge amount of document data requires efficient methods. An approach to a fast plagiarism detection is finding "similar" documents using statistics of word occurrences, such as the bag-of-words model [11]. Similar documents in the statistical sense can be found from a large dataset in a practical time using suitable data structures, such as indices based on locality sensitive hashing [9]. This kind of detection is expected to be effective against plagiarisms of ideas or rough structures of documents. The target of our study is plagiarisms of superficial descriptions such as "copy and paste", which can be detected more accurately using techniques based on pattern matching on strings [7].

© Springer International Publishing AG 2017
S. Yamamoto (Ed.): HIMI 2017, Part II, LNCS 10274, pp. 341–350, 2017.
DOI: 10.1007/978-3-319-58524-6_28

A difficulty in applying string matching-based techniques to plagiarism detection for general documents lies on setting the similarity between words; we need to define a similarity between words so that the document similarity based on the word similarity is computed as fast as possible while keeping acceptable accuracy. The edit distance [17] and its weighted and local version [15] are the bases of sequence alignment in bioinformatics [13], and the weight, that is, a kind of similarity between words is often given as substitution matrices [8] on the basis of expert knowledge. There exist some plagiarism detection methods based on the edit distance with a weight [10,16]. However, the processing time of computing the document similarity for these methods is $O(mn)$ for the lengths m and n of the target documents.

We proposed a plagiarism detection algorithm that runs in $O(n \log m)$ time with acceptable accuracy. The algorithm uses a document similarity based on the score vector [8] with a weight defined by vector representation of words. For two documents, the ith element of the score vector is the number of matches between corresponding words in the documents aligned with the gap i between the start positions. The vector is computed in $O(n \log m)$ time using the convolution theorem [6] and a fast Fourier transform (FFT) [8]. We represented a weight for the score (that is, a similarity between two words) by the inner product of the vectors mapped from the words, and the document similarity based on the word similarity is also computed in $O(n \log m)$ time using the FFT-based computation.

The aim of our study is to clarify what kind of vector representation of words is suitable for plagiarism detection. In the experiments, we evaluated two types of vector representation based on the score vector with a weight for the proposed algorithm. One uses the vectors generated randomly in order that those would represent the match and mismatch of words approximately with a small dimensionality. The idea of this vector representation corresponds to the randomization of the FFT-based algorithm for the score vector [4]. The other was a distributed representation generated by a neural network-based method word2vec [12]. We applied the plagiarism detection algorithm with the two types of vector representation and a naive vector representation that corresponds to the score vector without weight, to the dataset for a plagiarism detection competition in PAN [14] to investigate the processing time and the accuracy of plagiarism detection.

This study tried to find an application of distributed representation of words which is attracting attentions as a key technology for statistical processing on document data. A distributed representation is regarded as a function that maps a word to a numerical vector with a small dimensionality, and the distance between vectors represents a similarity between the words correspond to the vectors. A simple distributed representation is available by reducing the dimensionality of a straightforward vector representation based on word frequency [11]. The recent work [12] in neural networks made easy to achieve a distributed representation that represents a word similarity well from actual document data, and the tool for generating the distributed representation is available from the Internet [3].

As the result of the evaluation, we achieved a tradeoff between the processing time and the accuracy of plagiarism detection, which is affected by the dimensionality of vector representation of words. We found that the proposed algorithm based on the weighted score vector could reduce the processing time extremely with a slight decrease of the accuracy from that based on the normal score vector, and that the randomized vector representation could generate a better tradeoff than the distributed representation. For example, the proposed algorithm with the randomized vector representation could reduce about 90% of the processing time required for the algorithm with the normal score vector with a decrease of only 1% in the accuracy.

The rest of this paper is organized as follows. Section 2 introduces the plagiarism detection algorithm based on the weighted score vector. This section also describes the methods of experiments to evaluate the algorithm. Section 3 reports the experimental results. Section 4 gives considerations on the results and future directions of our study.

2 Methods

We proposed a plagiarism detection algorithm based on a document similarity, that is, a weighted version of the score vector between documents. This section introduces the document similarity and the plagiarism detection algorithm, and describes the methods to evaluate the proposed algorithm.

2.1 Preliminaries

W is a finite set of words. $x \notin W$ is the *never-match word*. δ is a function from $(W \cup \{x\}) \times (W \cup \{x\})$ to $\{0, 1\}$ such that $\delta(v, w)$ is 1 if $v, w \in W$ and $v = w$, and 0 otherwise.

A *document* is a list of words. The length of a document is the size of the list. W^n for an integer $n > 0$ is the set of the documents of length n over W. For a document p of length n, p_i for $1 \leq i \leq n$ is the ith word of p. pq is the concatenation of documents p and q. w^n for a word w and an integer $n > 0$ is the document of n w's.

2.2 Score Vector

The *score vector* between $p \in W^m$ and $q \in W^n$ is defined to be the $(m + n - 1)$-dimensional vector whose ith element is

$$\sum_{j=1}^{m} \delta(p_j, q'_{i+j-1}), \tag{1}$$

where $q' = x^{m-1} q x^{m-1}$.

Example 1. Let p and q be the documents "I have a pen I have an apple" and "I have a pineapple", respectively. Then, q' is "$x\ x\ x\ x\ x\ x\ x$ I have a pineapple x $x\ x\ x\ x\ x\ x$" and the score vector between p and q is $(0, 0, 0, 2, 0, 0, 0, 3, 0, 0, 0)$.

Let ϕ be a function from $W \cup \{x\}$ to $\mathbf{R}^d$ for the set $\mathbf{R}$ of the real numbers. Then, the *weighted score vector* between $p \in W^m$ and $q \in W^n$ with ϕ is defined to be the $(m+n-1)$-dimensional vector whose ith element is

$$\sum_{j=1}^{m} \langle \phi(p_j), \phi(q'_{i+j-1}) \rangle. \tag{2}$$

We call ϕ a *vector representation of words*.

Example 2. Let ϕ be a vector representation of words such that $\langle \phi(v), \phi(w) \rangle$ is 1 if $v, w \in W$ and $v = w$, 0.9 if v and w are "an" and "a", 0.5 if v and w are "apple" and "pineapple", and 0 otherwise. Then, for the documents p, q in Example 1, the weighted score vector between p and q with ϕ is $(0, 0, 0, 3.4, 0, 0, 0, 3, 0, 0, 0)$.

The processing time for computing the normal score vector between $p \in W^m$ and $q \in W^n$ is $O(|W|n \log m)$ by using the algorithm for the match-count problem based on the convolution theorem and an FFT [8]. Practically, $|W|$ can be reduced to the number of the different words that occurred in both of the documents. The processing time for the weighted score vector with a vector representation of words of dimensionality d is computed in $O(dn \log m)$ time in the same way as the FFT-based algorithm. The size of the alphabet or the dimensionality of vector representation equals to the number of $O(n \log m)$ computations for convolutions repeated in the algorithm.

2.3   Vector Representation of Words

To implement a plagiarism detection algorithm, we defined the vector representation ϕ of words in the following three methods:

– *Naive* vector representation of words,
– *Randomized* vector representation of words, and
– *Distributed* representation of words.

The naive vector representation ϕ_n is defined as follows. Let φ be a bijective function from $W \cup \{x\}$ to $\{0, 1, \ldots, |W|\}$ and $\varphi(x) = 0$. Then, ϕ_n is the function from $W \cup \{x\}$ to $\{0, 1\}^{|W|}$ such that, the ith element of $\phi_n(w)$ for $w \in W \cup \{x\}$ is 1 if $i = \varphi(w)$, and 0 otherwise. Then, $\langle \phi_n(v), \phi_n(w) \rangle = \delta(v, w)$ for any $v, w \in W \cup \{x\}$.

Example 3. W in Example 1 is regarded as $\{I, \text{have}, a, \text{pen}, \text{an}, \text{apple}, \text{pineapple}\}$. Then, an example of the naive vector representation is the function from $W \cup \{x\}$ to $\{0, 1\}^7$ such that $\phi_n(x) = (0, 0, 0, 0, 0, 0, 0)$, $\phi_n(I) = (1, 0, 0, 0, 0, 0, 0)$, $\phi_n(\text{have}) = (0, 1, 0, 0, 0, 0, 0)$, and so on. For computing the normal score vector, we can reduce W to $\{I, \text{have}, a\}$, and then ϕ_n can be the function from $W \cup \{x\}$ to $\{0, 1\}^3$ such that $\phi_n(x) = (0, 0, 0)$, $\phi_n(I) = (1, 0, 0)$, $\phi_n(\text{have}) = (0, 1, 0)$, and $\phi_n(a) = (0, 0, 1)$.

The randomized vector representation ϕ_r is defined to be the function from $W \cup \{x\}$ to $\{-1, 0, 1\}^d$ for an integer d such that, $\phi_r(x)$ is the d-dimensional zero-vector, and $\phi_r(w)$ for $w \in W$ is a vector chosen randomly from $\{-1, 1\}^d$. Then, for any d, $\langle \phi_r(v), \phi_r(w) \rangle$ for $v, w \in W$ is d if $v = w$, and the expectation of the inner product is 0 otherwise. The idea of this vector representation corresponds to the randomization of the FFT-based algorithm for the score vector proposed by Atallah et al. [4], and we used the function with integers proposed by Baba et al. [5].

Example 4. In the case of Example 3, an example of ϕ_r with $d = 4$ is the function such that $\phi_r(x) = (0, 0, 0, 0)$, $\phi_r(\mathrm{I}) = (1, 1, 1, 1)$, $\phi_r(\text{have}) = (1, 1, -1, -1)$, $\phi_r(\mathrm{a}) = (1, -1, 1, -1)$, and so on.

The distributed representation ϕ_d was implemented by using word2vec [12]. We configured the dimensionality d in the available tool, and normalized the output vectors. Therefore, the ϕ_d is defined to be a function from $W \cup \{x\}$ to $[-1, 1]^d$ such that, $\langle \phi_d(v), \phi_d(w) \rangle$ for $v, w \in W \cup \{x\}$ is 1 if $v, w \in W$ and $v = w$, 0 if $v = x$ or $w = x$, and a value in $[-1, 1)$ otherwise.

2.4 Plagiarism Detection Algorithm

A *plagiarism detection* is, for a pair of documents, to predict "positive" (that is, there exists a plagiarism in a document from the other document) or "negative".

The plagiarism detection algorithm in this paper is, for two input documents,

1. Calculate the weighted score vector between the documents with a vector representation of words, and
2. Predict positive or negative using the obtained vector and a threshold.

In Process 1, we used the three vector representations defined in Subsect. 2.3. In Process 2, we determined the threshold from training data by applying a support vector machine with a linear kernel to pairs of the peak value of the obtained vector and the length of the shorter document, where the *peak value* of a vector v is the minimal element in v'' and $v'_i = v_{i+1} - v_i$ for $1 \le i < |v|$.

Example 5. The peak value of the weighted score vector in Example 2 is -6.8. In the proposed algorithm, the support vector machine is applied to the pair of the peak value -6.8 and the length 4 of the shorter document.

The processing time of the proposed algorithm is mainly due to the $O(n \log m)$ computation for the (weighted) score vector. Additionally, we need an $O(m + n)$ computation for the detection of the peak value in the computed score vector.

2.5 Experiments

We applied the plagiarism detection algorithm defined in Subsect. 2.4 to a dataset to measure the accuracy for the three vector representations of words defined in Subsect. 2.3.

We used a dataset of a plagiarism detection competition in PAN 2013 [14] which is available from the Internet [1]. The dataset contains pairs of documents with a plagiarism of "copy and paste" (*positive pairs*) and pairs with no plagiarism (*negative pairs*). We picked 2,000 positive pairs and 2,000 negative pairs, and then divided the data equally into training and test data for validation of the algorithms. The average length of the documents was 1,432. We used the training data for learning in word2vec to generate ϕ_d in addition to fitting the support vector machine for the prediction.

The *accuracy* of a plagiarism detection algorithm is defined to be the ratio of the number of the correct predictions to the number of the total predictions. The processing time of the algorithms is proportional to the dimensionality d of the vector representation of words, while the accuracy of the proposed algorithm is expected to be better for a larger d. Therefore, this experiment clarifies the relation between the processing time and the accuracy of the proposed algorithm.

We also applied the algorithm to other data in the competition that include plagiarisms with some kinds of obfuscations. We had expected that the accuracy would be improved by

- Using the weighted score vector generated by the distributed representation instead of the normal score vector,
- Increasing the dimensionality of the distributed representation, and
- Using a larger training data for generating the distributed representation instead of the given data.

The new dataset for plagiarism detection contains 8,370 positive pairs and 2,000 negative pairs. We generated three types of distributed representation of words: one for the dimensionality 100 and 200 trained with the given data of PAN, and one of dimensionality 200 trained with an archived data in Wikipedia [2]. The size of the extra data of Wikipedia was 13.1 GB while that of the training data of PAN was 30 MB.

3 Results

Figure 1 shows the accuracy of the proposed algorithm for the three vector representations of words, that is, the naive, the randomized, and the distributed one: The dimensionality for the naive vector representation was fixed to the "restricted" alphabet (vocabulary) size. The alphabet size of the document data and the average number of the different words that occurred in both of the input documents were 143,600 and 96, respectively. Then, the result for this vector representation is the point of the accuracy 1 at the dimensionality 96. For the other vector representations, the graph shows the accuracy against the dimensionality

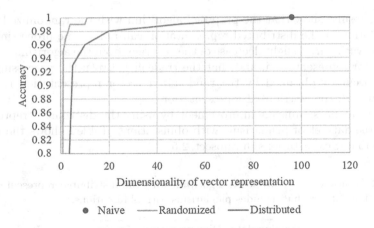

Fig. 1. Accuracy of the proposed algorithm against the dimensionality of vectors for the three types of vector representation of words.

of the vector representations, where the accuracy is assumed to be 0.5 for the dimensionality 0 and 1 for any dimensionality larger than 100.

Figure 2 shows the relation between the processing time of the algorithm and the dimensionality of vector representation of words. The results were generated by the algorithm with the randomized vector representation. The computation with the other types of vector representation can be simulated by this case because the difference is only the values of vectors by the definition in Subsect. 2.3. We can estimate that the processing time is proportional to the dimensionality with an overhead of about 10 ms, corresponding to the theoretical analysis in Subsect. 2.4. Therefore, the dimensionality of vector representation can be used as the measure for the processing time of the algorithm.

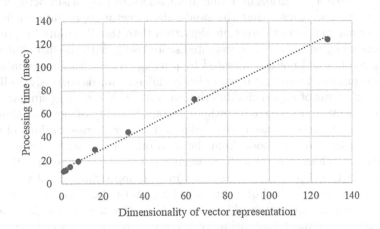

Fig. 2. Processing time of the proposed algorithm with the randomized vector representation of words against the dimensionality of vectors.

These results show that the proposed algorithm with the randomized vector representation or the distributed representation can reduce the processing time extremely with only a slight decrease of the accuracy from the algorithm with the naive vector representation, and that the tradeoff between the processing time and the accuracy obtained by the randomized vector representation is better than that with the distributed representation.

There was no significant improvement by using the distributed representation for the dataset of plagiarisms with obfuscations. Table 1 shows the results opposite to our expectations in Subsect. 2.5.

Table 1. Accuracy of the proposed algorithm with the distributed representation of words for the dataset that includes plagiarisms with obfuscations.

Training data	Dimensionality	Accuracy
(Naive)	96	0.89
PAN	100	0.87
	200	0.87
Wikipedia	200	0.87

4   Discussion

From the experimental results in Sect. 3, we can conclude that the processing time for detecting plagiarisms in documents can be reduced extremely by using the weighted score vector for the document similarity, although the accuracy decreases slightly. For example, the processing time and the accuracy of the proposed algorithm with the randomized vector representation of dimensionality 4 can be respectively about 10% and 99% of those with the normal score vector, which is a probable situation in actual applications of plagiarism detection.

Additionally, we found that the randomized vector representation is more suitable for our plagiarism detection algorithm than the distributed representation generated by word2vec. The weighted score vector with the distributed representation contained noises generated by putting scores also on mismatches of words. It is supposed that finding completely-different words correctly is effective against plagiarisms of superficial descriptions rather than finding similar words.

One of our future work is to investigate the applicability of our idea, that is, to combine string matching-based techniques and vector representations obtained by statistical learning methods from data, to other tasks with documents. In this study, we achieved a tradeoff between the processing time and the accuracy of plagiarism detection, which yields just an approximation of the process based on the simple method of string matching. Actually, using the distributed representation generated by word2vec was not effective against plagiarisms with obfuscations. We expect that using vector representation of words may obviously improve an accuracy in some other tasks that treat a kind of semantics in addition to the syntax of documents.

5 Conclusion

In this paper, we evaluated the validity of using vector representation of words for setting a document similarity. We proposed a plagiarism detection algorithm that uses a document similarity based on the score vector with the weight defined by vector representation of words. We experimented the processing time and the plagiarism detection accuracy of the proposed algorithm with the three types of vector representation of words. The results show that the proposed algorithm based on the weighted score vector can detect plagiarisms in an extremely shorter time with a slightly worse accuracy than the algorithm based on the normal score vector. Additionally, we found that the randomized vector representation is more suitable for the plagiarism detection algorithm than the distributed representation. To take a concrete example, the proposed algorithm with the randomized vector representation can reduce about 90% of the processing time required for the algorithm with the normal score vector with a decrease of only 1% in the accuracy.

Acknowledgement. This work was supported by JSPS KAKENHI Grant Number JP15K00310.

References

1. Evaluation data, originality: PAN. http://pan.webis.de/data.html. Accessed Feb 2017
2. Wikimedia downloads: Wikipedia. https://dumps.wikimedia.org/backup-index.html. Accessed Feb 2017
3. word2vec: Google Code Archive. https://code.google.com/archive/p/word2vec/. Accessed Feb 2017
4. Atallah, M.J., Chyzak, F., Dumas, P.: A randomized algorithm for approximate string matching. Algorithmica **29**(3), 468–486 (2001)
5. Baba, K., Shinohara, A., Takeda, M., Inenaga, S., Arikawa, S.: A note on randomized algorithm for string matching with mismatches. Nord. J. Comput. **10**(1), 2–12 (2003)
6. Cormen, T.H., Stein, C., Rivest, R.L., Leiserson, C.E.: Introduction to Algorithms, 2nd edn. McGraw-Hill Higher Education, New York (2001)
7. Crochemore, M., Rytter, W.: Jewels of Stringology. World Scientific, Singapore (2003)
8. Gusfield, D.: Algorithms on Strings, Trees, and Sequences: Computer Science and Computational Biology. Cambridge University Press, New York (1997)
9. Indyk, P., Motwani, R.: Approximate nearest neighbors: towards removing the curse of dimensionality. In: Proceedings of the Thirtieth Annual ACM Symposium on Theory of Computing, STOC 1998, pp. 604–613. ACM, New York (1998)
10. Irving, R.W.: Plagiarism and collusion detection using the Smith-Waterman algorithm. Technical report, Department of Computing Science, University of Glasgow (2004)
11. Manning, C.D., Raghavan, P., Schütze, H.: Introduction to Information Retrieval. Cambridge University Press, New York (2008)

12. Mikolov, T., Sutskever, I., Chen, K., Corrado, G.S., Dean, J.: Distributed representations of words and phrases and their compositionality. In: Burges, C.J.C., Bottou, L., Welling, M., Ghahramani, Z., Weinberger, K.Q. (eds.) Advances in Neural Information Processing Systems, vol. 26, pp. 3111–3119. Curran Associates Inc. (2013)

13. Pearson, W.R., Lipman, D.J.: Improved tools for biological sequence comparison. Proc. Natl. Acad. Sci. USA **85**(8), 2444–2448 (1988)

14. Potthast, M., Gollub, T., Hagen, M., Tippmann, M., Kiesel, J., Rosso, P., Stamatatos, E., Stein, B.: Overview of the 5th International Competition on Plagiarism Detection. In: Forner, P., Navigli, R., Tufis, D. (eds.) Working Notes Papers of the CLEF 2013 Evaluation Labs, September 2013

15. Smith, T., Waterman, M.: Identification of common molecular subsequences. J. Mol. Biol. **147**(1), 195–197 (1981)

16. Su, Z., Ahn, B.-R., Eom, K.-Y., Kang, M.-K., Kim, J.-P., Kim, M.-K.: Plagiarism detection using the Levenshtein distance and Smith-Waterman algorithm. In: Innovative Computing Information and Control, p. 569 (2008)

17. Wagner, R.A., Fischer, M.J.: The string-to-string correction problem. J. ACM **21**(1), 168–173 (1974)

Map Uncertainty Reduction for a Team of Autonomous Drones Using Simulated Annealing and Bayesian Optimization

Jordan Henrio[✉] and Tomoharu Nakashima

Osaka Prefecture University, Sakai, Japan
jordan.henrio@cs.osakafu-u.ac.jp, tomoharu.nakashima@kis.osakafu-u.ac.jp

Abstract. This research focuses on the problem of reducing the uncertainty rate of an environment in the context of surveillance. A human operator designates a set of locations to be checked by a team of autonomous quadcopters. The goal of this work is to minimize the uncertainty rate of the environment while penalizing solutions whose the total travelled distance is large. To cope with this issue, the A* algorithm is employed to plan the shortest path between each pair of points. Then, a simulated annealing algorithm is used to allocate tasks among the team of drones. This paper discusses three different objective functions to solve the problem whose cost-efficient and feasible solutions can be obtained after a few minutes. The presented work also deals with optimization of the simulated algorithms parameters by using Bayesian optimization. It is currently the state-of-the-art approach for the problem of hyperparameters search, for expensive to evaluate functions, since it allows to save computation time by modeling the cost function. The Bayesian optimizer returns the best parameters within one day, while the use of grid search methods required weeks of computations.

Keywords: Surveillance · Path planning · Task allocation · A* algorithm · Simulated annealing algorithm · Bayesian optimization

1 Introduction

Conventional surveillance systems use fixed-position cameras. Although they have a pan-and-tilt feature in order to record large-plan videos or even 360-degree-view videos, they still suffer from their "fixed geographical position" characteristic. Thus, it is difficult to track a particular object or to record information about blind spots.

Recently, drones have become more and more popular and this trend is still continuing. It exists a large range of different drones, including ones with embedded tools for video recording. Such a system could be used as a moving surveillance camera. In this context, using a drone instead of, or coupled with, usual systems could improve the security level. Drones can perform better object tracking since they can follow the object of interest and they can also fly around this

© Springer International Publishing AG 2017
S. Yamamoto (Ed.): HIMI 2017, Part II, LNCS 10274, pp. 351–370, 2017.
DOI: 10.1007/978-3-319-58524-6_29

object in order to record various views of it. In addition, because of their flying capacity, they can record information on the ground as well as at heights and as they are small they can also record information in narrow locations as well as indoor areas.

Most of the drones have a feature allowing the user to design a flight path. In the case of this research, a human supervisor selects a set of locations that should be visually checked by a team of autonomous drones. These points are called check points. Each of them is associated with a real value that increases as the time elapses after the last visit increases. This value is used as the uncertainty rate of the corresponding point which represents how confident we are that the information about the point is up to date.

The problem of finding a permutation that minimizes the energy consumption of drones as well as the travelled distance have been largely tackled in the literature, often by suggesting to use complex solvers like memetic algorithms [1–3]. This work proposes a path planning method using a simple simulated annealing algorithm to minimize the average of the check points.

A large grid, presented in Sect. 3, is used as a discrete representation of the environment and the path between every possible pair of points is computed by the application of the A* algorithm. A centralized task allocation system using a simulated annealing algorithm searches for the optimal permutation of the check points according to their uncertainty rate. Section 4 discusses three solvers with different objective functions. One is for the case of minimization of the travelled distance, another for the case of minimization of the uncertainty rate and the last solver mixes the two functions. In Sect. 5, we describe the solver's hyper-parameter optimization process by using Bayesian optimization. Such a method is becoming more and more popular to deal with hyper-parameter optimization issues and saved us a large amount of time compared to the use of a grid search method. Section 6 presents the different experiments conducted during this research.

2   Related Work

The problem of optimal path planning for a team of autonomous drones has been largely tackled in the literature by various approaches. A common approach is employing generally mixed linear integer programming as in Richards et al. [4,5]. While this kind of methods provides an optimal solution, the computation time is often unfeasibly long. Other work have proposed to solve the problem of path planning with a reasonable computation time by computing an approximation of the optimal solution as in [6].

Recent works have suggested to focus on the allocation of points to visit, considering the path to join each point is already known. Then, the problem of interest is similar to the well-known Travelling Salesman Problem (TSP). Since this class of problem is NP-complete, there is no known method that can provide the optimal solution in a polynomial time. Therefore, most of the suggested works solve the problem by using meta-heuristic algorithms as the ant colony algorithm in Jevtic et al. [7], and the more recent firefly algorithm as in Osaba et al. [8,9]. A large number of works rather propose to use memetic algorithms as in [1–3].

The method proposed in this paper is similar to the work of Liu et al. [2] and Jose et al. [3] except that the desired solution is not the one that minimizes the traveled distance by the teams of robots, but minimizes the uncertainty rate of the check points. However, the method also focuses on the reduction of the travelled distance. Furthermore, memetic algorithms are relatively complex because they require to develop several methods such as solutions' reproduction, mutation, crossover and local optimization. This work rather suggests to use a modest simulated annealing algorithm which allows to find nearly optimal solutions.

3   Representation of the Environment

This research aims to plan paths for a team of autonomous drones that monitor the Osaka Prefecture University campus for surveillance. The campus location can be found at (34.545412, 135.506348) in the latitude/longitude system. It is about a 858×624 m^2 area and contains different buildings of different sizes and heights, trees, a pond, a farming area, stables, a large sports ground, etc. Since some of these elements, as buildings and trees, could represent a danger for the drones, they are considered as *non-admissible areas*, in contrast with clear zones which are considered as *admissible areas*.

The environment of interest is shown in Fig. 1. In this figure, the environment is delimited by a large rectangle containing smaller rectangles and triangles representing the non-admissible areas. The black circle represents the starting point of the drones and the grey circles are the check points. It is important to

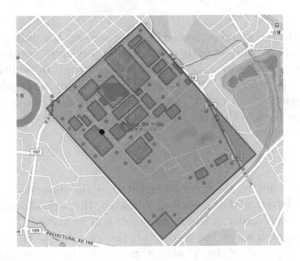

Fig. 1. Map of the environment of interest

note that the map used in this research is not up-to-date and some buildings are missing. We are considering to use a more recent map for future works.

The environment is represented by using a grid of 1716×1248 cells. Thus, one cell represents a 50×50 cm^2 area of the environment. The admissible and non-admissible areas are shown in Fig. 2. The black cells represent non-admissible areas and the white areas admissible ones. For simplification only the buildings and the pond are considered as non-admissible areas. Also the black triangles in the top-right and bottom-left corners as well as the rectangle in the bottom-right corner are not buildings, but only delimitation of the map which considers the boundary of the campus.

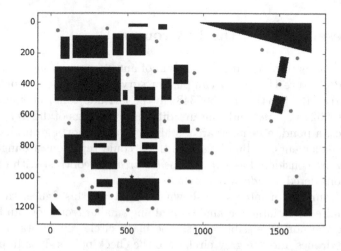

Fig. 2. Discretized representation of the environment with the 32 check points

Once the map has been represented in the above way the path planning module is used to find the shortest path, or at least a short path, between all possible pairs of the check points by applying the A* algorithm. In addition, the path between each check point and the starting point of the drones is also computed. For the implementation of the A* algorithm, the Python library developed by Careaga [10] was used in the computational experiments of this research.

4   Solvers

Once all the paths linking the points designated by the supervisor, as well as the start point, are determined as described in Sect. 3, the task allocation module is called to compute the order in which the points will be visited. The search space can be seen as a graph where the vertices are the locations to visit and the edges are the paths computed by the A* algorithm. Then, the goal is to find the path passing through every vertex, which minimizes the average uncertainty rate as well as travelled distance.

Each check point is associated to a real number u. This value is used to represent the uncertainty about the situation at this particular location in the environment. This uncertainty rate increases according to the elapsed time after the last visit by any drone to this particular point as defined in Acevedo et al. [11]. At the very first time, the uncertainty rate of every check point is initialized to 1, which is equivalent to consider that the situation at these points is unknown. The value of a point i falls directly to 0 when a drone arrives at the point's location and checks the situation. Then, the uncertainty rate will gradually grow up to 1 as the elapsed time increases. This process is mathematically expressed as in (1):

$$u_i(t) = 1 - e^{-\eta t}, \tag{1}$$

where t is the elapsed time after the last visit and η is a decay constant. As depicted in Fig. 3, this function defines an inverted exponential growth of the uncertainty rate. In other words, an event is unlikely to occur right after the situation has been checked, but the environment state can rapidly change after a few minutes. In this work, the uncertainty rate is considered to return to its original state (i.e., 1.0) after one hour since the last visit. In this case, $\eta = 0.001279214$.

The task allocation module's role is to find the permutation which minimizes the estimated average uncertainty rate of the check points at the end of the mission. To do so, we describe three objective functions in the following subsections. The optimization problem with the three objective functions is solved by using a simulated annealing algorithm where the neighbor solutions are obtained by swapping two check points in the permutation. For the implementation of the algorithm, the Python Simanneal library [12] was used.

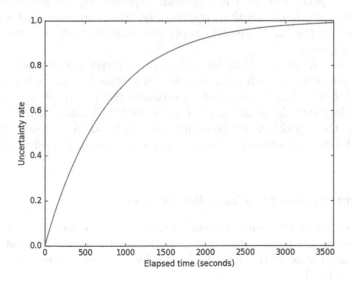

Fig. 3. Uncertainty rate's evolution over one hour

In the following, we search for an approximation of the optimal solution using the check points located as depicted in Fig. 2. In this paper, two drones are involved that monitor the situation of the environment at the 32 check points, starting from the star symbol located in (528,999).

In this paper, the drones are assumed to fly at a constant speed of 1 m/s and their battery is assumed to have 25 min of autonomy. Since the size of one cell in the map is a 50×50 cm^2 area, the drones can travel 3000 cells with one single battery load. In addition, they are assumed to fly at different altitudes to avoid collision issues.

4.1 Tasks Allocation

The problem treated in this section is similar to a TSP. However, in our case the traveling salesman has a limited budget (the drone's energy) and need to return to its start point before running out of money. After he has withdrawn some money (battery replaced), he can resume his travel. Furthermore, in our case, the cities to visit are shared by two salesmen.

The task allocation is done as presented in Algorithm 1. This algorithm cuts the permutation (a single list of several points) in a set of routes (several lists of several points). Here, *permutation* is considered as a queue. The algorithm dequeue the elements while the battery has enough energy to go to the permutation's next point and return to the start point from there. By doing so, every solution returned by this algorithm is feasible. In order to compute the distance between two given points the algorithm takes as input, *distance*, the matrix distance obtained after application of the A* algorithm as explained in Sect. 3. *start* is the start point, *pos* the current position, *battery* the current energy consumption and *limit* is a constant representing the drone autonomy. *list*(), *push*(*a*) are functions that, respectively, create an empty list and insert an element *a* at the tail of the list. *pop*() is a function that removes the head element of a queue.

It is important to note that for a fixed drone's speed it is possible to estimate the time at which each point is visited since the distance is known. Thus, Algorithm 1 can be easily extended to estimate the points of interest's average uncertainty rate. In addition, the total travelled distance with the solution returned by the algorithm can be easily computed too. As a result, this algorithm can be used as a base for the evaluation function of the solvers described below.

4.2 Minimization of the Travelled Distance

In order to minimize the environment's uncertainty rate, one could intuitively think to search the permutation which minimizes the total travelled distance and thus the duration of the mission. The problem of distance minimization can be defined as in (2):

$$p^* = \arg \min_p distance(p), \tag{2}$$

Algorithm 1. Task Allocation

1: Input: *permutation, distance, start, limit*
2: *solution, route* ← list()
3: *pos* ← *start*
4: *route*.push(*pos*)
5: *battery* ← 0
6: **while** *permutation*.length > 0 **do**
7:     *target* ← *permutation*.head
8:     **if** *battery* + *distance$_{pos,target}$* + *distance$_{target,start}$* < *limit* **then**
9:         *battery* ← *battery* + *distance$_{pos,target}$*
10:         *pos* ← *target*
11:         *route*.push(*pos*)
12:         *permutation*.pop()
13:     **else**
14:         *pos* ← *start*
15:         *route*.push(*pos*)
16:         *solution*.push(*route*)
17:         *route* ← list()
18:         *route*.push(*pos*)
19:         *battery* ← 0
20:     **end if**
21: **end while**
22: **return** *solution*

$$distance(p) = \sum_{i=2}^{n} d(p_{i-1}, p_i), \qquad (3)$$

where p^* is the optimal permutation, n the number of points in the permutation and $d(p_{i-1}, p_i)$ a function returning the number of cells in the path linking points p_{i-1} and p_i, computed by the A* algorithm in Sect. 3.

The simulated annealing algorithm is a meta-heuristic method. Thus, the returned solution is not guaranteed to be optimal. In addition, since the process employs probabilities, solutions returned from one application of the algorithm to another can vary. A typical solution obtained is represented in Fig. 4. The solution is formed by two routes for each drone. Drone 1's routes are represented by a succession of triangles and those of Drone 2 by a succession of crosses. The differences in colors indicate the different routes of each drone. Then, the Drone 1 and Drone 2's black routes are executed in a first time and grey routes are executed after. This solution tries to visit points located on the extremities of the map while visiting points which are on the way.

4.3   Direct Minimization of the Average Uncertainty Rate

The estimated average uncertainty rate at the end of the mission for the solution obtained by the previous solver is about 89.56%. Since this result is relatively high, one can legitimately consider the use of another objective function as described in (4):

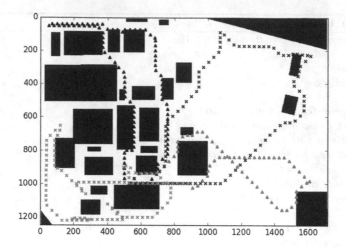

Fig. 4. Solution of the solver minimizing the travelled distance (i.e., (2))

$$p^* = \arg \min_{p} uncertainty(p), \tag{4}$$

$$uncertainty(p) = \frac{1}{n} \sum_{i=1}^{n} 1 - e^{-\eta(T - t_{p_i})}, \tag{5}$$

where T is the estimated number of elapsed seconds between the beginning and the end of the mission, t_{p_i} is the estimated number of elapsed seconds between the beginning of the mission and the moment when point i will be visited. Thus, this new objective function tries to directly minimize the estimated average uncertainty rate. A typical solution is represented in Fig. 5. The solution tries at first to visit points which are at the extremities of the map without visiting points which are on the way. Since the number of points far away from the start point is lower than the number of points near the start point, this solver "sacrifices" their uncertainty rate in order to maximize the number of points which can be visited quickly just before the end of the mission. This solution has an average uncertainty rate of about 61.61% for a traveled distance of more than 17,000 cells while the first solver finds a solution about two times lower (8392 cells).

4.4   Mixing the Two Objective Functions

By sacrificing the uncertainty rate of points far away from the start point, the previous solver returns solutions which have routes visiting only a single point before returning to the start point like the Drone 1's first route (black triangles path in Fig. 5). This implies that the battery of the drones should be frequently replaced or charged. To cope with this issue, one possible idea is to use an objective function which minimizes the average uncertainty rate while penalizing solutions whose travelled distance is large, by using a positive constant λ

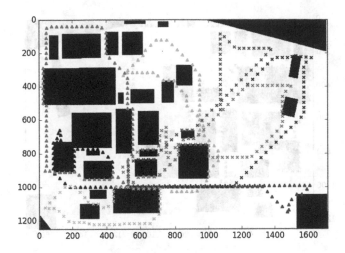

Fig. 5. Solution of the solver minimizing the average uncertainty rate (i.e., (4))

controlling the penalization strength as described in (6):

$$p^* = \arg\min_{p} \left\{ uncertainty(p) + \lambda distance(p) \right\} \tag{6}$$

In our implementation, the average uncertainty rate in (4) and (6) is multiplied by 10000, for two reasons. Firstly, the employed library for the simulated annealing algorithm seemed to have difficulty in optimizing a cost function whose range is between 0 and 1. Secondly, it allows the uncertainty rate to play a more important role in the cost function than the distance. However, this issue could be treated by using a smaller penalization coefficient λ.

A typical solution by using $\lambda = 0.1$ is depicted in Fig. 6. As it can be observed, it looks like the solution found by the first solver (i.e., Fig. 4), but it requires two additional routes (then two additional battery changes). The average uncertainty rate is about 61.76% and the total traveled distance is 13426 cells. Thus, this solution is better than the second solver's solution in terms of travelled distance, but slightly lower in terms of uncertainty rate. Table 1 summarizes the results of the optimization with the objective functions that were presented in this section.

Table 1. Summary of typical solutions with by the different objective functions

Objective function	Distance (#cells)	Uncertainty rate (%)	#routes
Distance	8392	89.56	4
Uncertainty rate	17565	61.61	8
Mix	13426	61.76	6

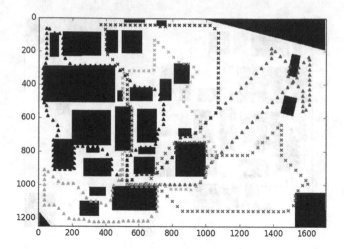

Fig. 6. Solution of the two mixed objective functions (i.e., (6))

5   Hyper-parameter Optimization

The method proposed in Sect. 4 requires the definition of four hyper-parameters. The first one is the penalization coefficient used in the third objective function defined in (6). The three other hyper-parameters come from the simulated annealing algorithm. One is the number of iterations spent by the algorithm to find the best solution. In our implementation, during one iteration, the algorithm swaps two points in the permutation and evaluates the cost of the resulting solution from the new permutation. The simulated annealing as originally defined in Kirkpatrick, Gelatt, Vecchi et al. [13] accepts solutions whose cost is higher than the best solution found with a probability in order to avoid local optima. A new solution so-far with the higher cost is accepted with a probability depending on the current system's temperature, as defined in (7):

$$P(e_{\text{best}}, e_{\text{current}}, T) = \exp\left(-\frac{(e_{\text{current}} - e_{\text{best}})}{T}\right), \tag{7}$$

where e_{best} is the best encountered state's cost, e_{current} is the current state's cost and T is the current system's temperature. This temperature decreases linearly (exponentially) along the iterations, leading to lower and lower exploration. Then, the two other hyper-parameters are the start temperature ($T_{\max}$) and the final temperature ($T_{\min}$) of the system.

In this section, the choice of the penalization coefficient value is presented. Then, we discuss the influence of the number of iterations. Finally, Bayesian optimization is used to optimize the temperature interval.

5.1   Trade-Off Between Uncertainty Rate and Distance

In order to investigate the effect of the penalization coefficient on the cost function, the simulated annealing algorithm was applied several times to the problem defined in Fig. 2 with different values of λ. As explained above, the simulated annealing algorithm induces probabilities in the process and thus solutions resulting from multiple applications of the algorithm are generally slightly different. Therefore, for each tested λ, the algorithm is applied ten times on random starting solutions in order to calculate an average cost.

As depicted in Fig. 7, the traveled distance decreases as the penalization coefficient strength increases. On the other hand, the average uncertainty rate increases. Therefore, there is a trade-off between average uncertainty rate and the traveled distance of solutions.

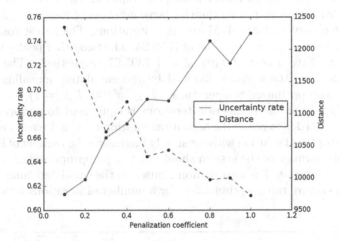

Fig. 7. Influence of the penalization coefficient on the average uncertainty rate and the total traveled distance

Our main goal is to minimize the average uncertainty rate while the distance minimization is a second goal for convenient reasons. Furthermore, the average solution for $\lambda = 0.1$ has a total traveled distance of 12347.5 cells while without penalization the traveled distance was above 17500. Thus, with the drones' characteristics established in Sect. 4, even the lower coefficient in the interval [0.1, 1] saves two routes (i.e. two battery loads) in the plan. Actually, the choice of this hyper-parameter depends on how much the uncertainty rate can be sacrificed in favor of shorter traveled distances, and this choice is arbitrary.

5.2   Effect of Iterations on the Search Performance

The next step consists in analyzing the gain in cost by increasing the number of iterations. While the simulated annealing algorithm could find the optimal solution for an infinite computation time and a temperature range large enough such that the acceptance rate is not null, we can accept an approximation of the best solution to reduce computation time. Thus, one can legitimately wonder how many iterations it is necessary until the satisfactory solutions are obtained. To do so, the simulated annealing algorithm is applied to the problem defined in Fig. 2 by testing different numbers of iterations in the interval [100000, 20000000]. For each test the algorithm is applied ten times in order to calculate an average solution.

The results of this experiment are depicted in Fig. 8. This figure represents the evolution of the cost function according to the number of iterations. In addition, the gain over the additional computation time implied by the increasing number of iterations is also depicted. The gain changes quickly during the stage of the search process, but tends towards 0 after around 10M iterations (represented by the horizontal dotted line). In other words, the improvement in the cost is smaller than the additional computation time for large numbers of iterations. Also, some peaks can be observed at 8M, 12M and 16M iterations. The lowest cost is found at 16M iterations for an average cost of 7359.24. The two other peaks at 8M and 12M iterations have a cost of 7408.33 and 7395.97 respectively. These abrupt changes come from the variance induced by the simulated annealing which is applied with non optimized temperatures ($T_{\max} = 100$, $T_{\min} = 1$).

To simply rely on the number of iterations is equivalent to perform a brute-force search. In order to refine the algorithm solution cost and reach an approximation of the optimal solution without simply increasing the number of iterations, the temperature range of the system should be setup appropriately according to the problem of interest. The next section focuses on the simulated annealing algorithm's temperature range optimization for a number of iterations fixed to 3M.

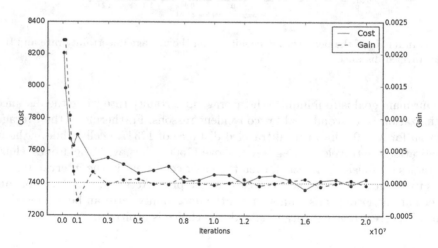

Fig. 8. Cost evolution according to the number of iterations

5.3   Temperature Optimization by Using Bayesian Optimization

As explained above, the system's temperature range is an important setup since it controls the algorithm exploration behavior. If the temperature is too high, most of the new states are accepted and the simulated annealing algorithm acts in a similar way to random search method. On the other hand, if the temperature is too low the algorithm behavior becomes similar to a greedy search method.

Our first attempts for the system's temperatures optimization were done by using a grid search technique. However, since the algorithm takes about 4 min to perform 3M iterations on a core-i7 computer, it is relatively time expensive to test it several times with different hyper-parameters. Thus, the grid search application took several weeks of computations. In addition, the grid search algorithm should be avoided since the optimal values of the hyper-parameters could be outside the grid definition.

Recent researches, especially in the field of machine learning, suggested the use of Bayesian optimization to cope with the issue of function optimization in an intelligent way. This method is efficient for time-consuming task as the simulated annealing algorithm since it takes benefit from inferential probabilities to reduce the number of evaluations at the cost of a relatively expensive sample preparation. The core idea of Bayesian optimization is to first model the cost function, generally with a Gaussian process as defined in (8):

$$f(x) \sim GP(\mu(x), k(x, x')), \ \ \forall x, x' \in X^2, \tag{8}$$

given some prior sample data $x \in X$ where X is the search space, $\mu(x)$ the mean function and $k(x, x')$ a covariance function. Then, the optimization process involves sampling data as defined in (9):

$$x_{\text{next}} = \arg \max_{x \in X} a(x) \tag{9}$$

where x_{next} is the next iteration to try and $a(x)$ is an acquisition function whose role is to evaluate the search space according to some criteria given the model of $f(x)$. After sampling data where the acquisition function is maximized, the model defined in (8) is updated with the observed results and the search space is reevaluated by the acquisition function. This process is repeated until convergence or any other termination criteria.

For our implementation we used the Python library GpyOpt [14]. In our case $f(x)$ is the function returning the average cost obtained after five applications of the simulated annealing algorithm with 3M iterations to the problem defined in Fig. 2. x is a vector containing the temperature boundaries, T_{max} and T_{min}. The search space ranges in [0.01, 400] for both temperatures and is constrained by (10):

$$T_{\text{min}} < T_{\text{max}}, \ \ \forall \, T_{\text{min}}, T_{\text{max}} \in [0.01, 400] \tag{10}$$

The function $f(x)$ is modeled by using a Gaussian process whose covariance function is the square exponential kernel. The acquisition function used is the *expected improvement* acquisition function, as defined in Snoek et al. [15] (11):

$$a(x; \{x_n, y_n\}, \theta) = \sigma(x; \{x_n, y_n\}, \theta)(\gamma(x)\phi(\gamma(x)) + \mathcal{N}(\gamma(x); 0, 1)), \tag{11}$$

$$\gamma(x) = \frac{f(x_{\text{best}}) - \mu(x; \{x_n, y_n\}, \theta)}{\sigma(x; \{x_n, y_n\}, \theta)}, \tag{12}$$

where $x \in X$, $\{x_n, y_n\}$ is the pair of prior sample point x_n and its outcome y_n, θ represents the Gaussian process parameters, $\phi(\cdot)$ is the cumulative distribution function of the standard normal distribution, $\mathcal{N}(\cdot)$ is the standard normal distribution and x_{best} designates the best iteration observed during the optimization process. $\mu(\cdot)$ and $\sigma(\cdot)$ are the predictive mean and the predictive variance functions of the Gaussian process respectively.

Since the evaluation function is expensive to compute, one could want to take advantage from processor architectures and performs several evaluations in parallel. Some works suggested different methods for batch Bayesian optimization as in Snoek et al. [15] as well as González et al. [16]. As stated in [16], Batch Bayesian optimization is very helpful since the acquisition can be multi-modal especially during the first steps of the optimization process when the model is quite rough. In our case we used the local penalization method defined in [16]. This method consists in building, at each iteration, a batch of sample points by penalizing the acquisition function for each element in the batch as in (13):

$$x_k = \arg\min_{x \in X} (a(x) \prod_{i=1}^{k-1} \varphi(x; x_i)), \tag{13}$$

where x_k is the k-th element in the batch and $\varphi(x; x_i)$ ranges in $[0, 1]$. This function tends towards 0 when x_i is far from x. Thus, it reduces the acquisition function in a neighborhood where $f(x)$ will be tested by a batch's element already prepared. As a result, the several acquisition function's modes are explored since after being penalized the best mode could become lower than the second best. In our case, we used batches of six elements distributed over six cores on a single machine.

The resulting Gaussian process is depicted in the two first subplots of Fig. 9. The first contour plot represents the Gaussian process mean function and the second its standard deviation function. The x-axis corresponds to T_{max} and the

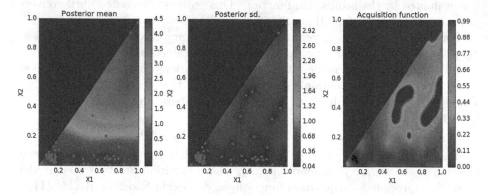

Fig. 9. Gaussian process, sample locations and acquisition function

y-axis to T_{min}. During our first applications of the Bayesian optimization method we encountered difficulties by using directly the domain $X = [0.01, 400]$. However, scaling the search space between 0 and 1 produced smoother models. Also, the simulated annealing algorithm's outcomes are automatically scaled by the Bayesian optimization algorithm, according to the outcomes encountered during the optimization process. Since the aim is to find solutions that minimize the objective function, we are interested in low values of the mean function's contour plot. The dots in the contour plots represent the different observed iterations during the optimization process. It started by sampling 12 points in X and building a prior Gaussian process according to the observed simulated annealing outcomes. Then, by applying the local penalization algorithm the optimization converges around $T_{max} = 45.58$ and $T_{min} = 21.56$, as it can be seen in Fig. 9 where a large number of iterations are gathered in the corresponding region in the scaled search space ($T_{max} = 0.1139$, $T_{min} = 0.0539$). Thus, it is interesting to note that even by penalizing five times the acquisition function around $T_{max} = 0.1139$ and $T_{min} = 0.0539$, the optimizer still samples in this region of the search space.

The Gaussian process representation indicates that large values of T_{min} produce poor outcomes. In addition, the optimization process spent a considerable number of iterations in sampling values for T_{max} around 300. Such values give an acceptance rate of nearly 50% during the first iterations of the simulated annealing. Actually, such values of T_{max} seem to be a waste of iterations in the case of our problem since the optimizer concluded that an acceptance rate of 5% ($T_{max} \sim 50$) is much more efficient. On the other hand, too low values of T_{max} yield relatively poor outcomes. Thus, it is important to have a non null acceptance rate during the first steps of the simulated annealing algorithm. The third subplot represents the acquisition function. While probabilities of sampling large T_{max} for low T_{min} are high, the next iterations (represented by dots in the left bottom corner) still gather around $T_{max} = 0.1139$ and $T_{min} = 0.0539$.

The first subplot in Fig. 10 depicts the distance, in the search space, between the different iterations over the optimization process. From 0 to 12, the optimizer did a random sampling in order to build a prior model. The 60 next iterations alternate between short and long distances. Since the optimizer evaluated iterations six by six, the differences in distances are due to the exploration of the different modes of the acquisition function. Actually, from the 70th iteration the distance between iterations remains low (excepted one peak around 80). Thus, it can be interpreted that the optimizer converged to the optimal solution. The second subplot indicates the best outcome encountered over the optimization process. During the last iterations, $f(x_{best}) = 7344.57$ which is lower than the average cost for 16M iterations in Fig. 8. Therefore, by using Bayesian optimization, we obtained a temperature configuration helping the simulated annealing algorithm to find cost-efficient solutions within a reasonable number of iterations. In addition, the optimization process took 15 h to find the best setup, saving us a considerable amount of time compared to the application of grid search methods.

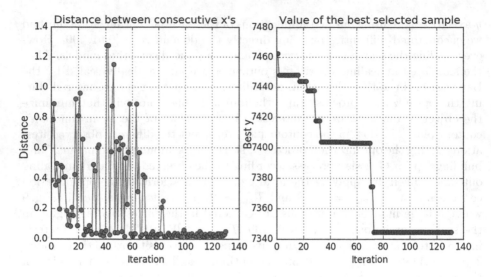

Fig. 10. Optimization convergence

6 Experiments

This section first investigates the effect of drones team's size on the average uncertainty rate by using the method presented in Sect. 4 as well as the hyper-parameters optimization in Sect. 5. The second experiment focuses on the system's abilities to generalize for other random problems' configuration. The third and the last experiment verifies the Bayesian optimizer convergence speed remains unchanged even for problems requiring more check points.

6.1 Team Size Effect

Table 2 summarizes the effect of team size on the cost, uncertainty rate and distance. The results are the average outcomes of ten applications of the simulated annealing algorithm by using the hyper-parameters determined in Sect. 5. Increasing the number of drones largely decreases the uncertainty rate since more locations can be checked in parallel, however, the uncertainty rate stagnates around 46.5% from a team of five drones. On the other hand, the distance explodes as the team's size increases. Since the uncertainty rate plays a larger part in the objective function than the distance, $\lambda = 0.1$, the simulated annealing returns obvious solutions having a low cost but a large distance. Increasing the value of the penalization coefficient λ fixed this problem. For example, by using three drones and $\lambda = 0.2$ the simulated annealing returned an average solution of cost 15788.49 with an uncertainty rate of 51.26% and a distance of 12552 cells. Thus, the value of λ plays an important role and should be chosen according to the problem.

Table 2. Cost evolution according to the team size

#drones	Cost	Uncertainty rate (%)	Distance (#cells)
1	8416.4	73.93	10229.8
2	7374.95	61.42	12323.2
3	6674.15	53.46	13280
4	6460.39	48.6	15998.5
5	6578.21	46.55	19222.4
6	6573.17	46.5	19224

6.2   Setup Limits

Similarly to the experiment in Sect. 5, this second experiment focuses on the influence of the number of iterations in the simulated annealing on the search performance. In the experiment of this subsection, we do not use the problem depicted in Fig. 2 anymore. The problem of interest here is for a team of two drones to visit 50 check points that are randomly selected.

Figure 11 represents the cost evolution over the number of iterations and the gain in improvement according the number of iterations. Since the number of locations to check is larger than the problem represented in Fig. 2, solutions are more expensive. A peak at 15M iterations indicates it exists solutions with a cost at least equal to a cost of 8057. The gain drops to 0 quickly since the improvement in cost has become smaller and smaller compared to the incremental computation time. On the other hand, there is a considerable gap between outcomes from simulated annealing algorithm applied with few iterations (1M~3M) and applications with further iterations. While outcomes could be improved by optimizing the temperature range, more complex problems require more iterations.

6.3   Efficiency of Bayesian Optimization

One could wonder if the Bayesian optimizer in Sect. 5 requires more iterations to optimize the temperature range according to more complex problems. To check this ability, this experiment runs a new Bayesian optimization on a simulated annealing algorithm spending 3M iterations to find the best permutation on the 50 random check points problem used in the last section.

The first subplot of Fig. 12 represents the distance between two consecutive iterations during the optimization process. The first 12 iterations were selected randomly to explore the search space and build a prior Gaussian process. Until the 53th iteration the distance between them is large due to the exploration of four different modes in the acquisition function. However, from the 54th iteration and until the end of the optimization process the distance is nearly equal to zero. The optimizer focused every iteration in $T_{min} \in [6, 29]$ and $T_{max} \in [29, 52]$ during 13 epochs (78 iterations). The second plot represents the minimum cost encountered at each iteration. At the moment of the prior Gaussian process

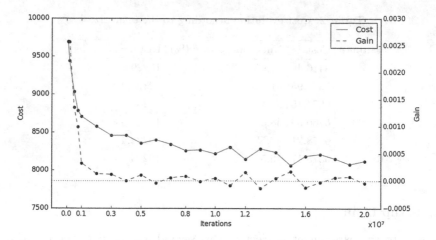

Fig. 11. Cost evolution according to the number of iterations for 50 random check points

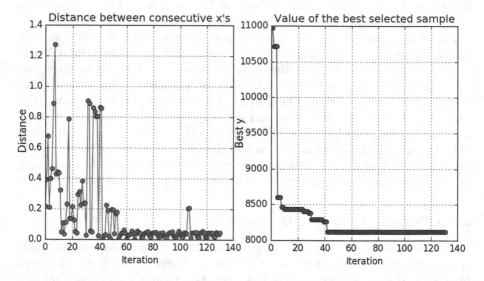

Fig. 12. Optimization convergence for a more complex problem

construction the minimum encountered cost is slightly lower than the one for the same number of iterations in Fig. 11. Actually, the best outcomes obtained at the end of the optimization process is equal to 8119.65 and then equivalent to the cost obtained for 12M iteration in Fig. 11. However, this best cost is larger than 8057 (best outcomes obtained in the previous experiment). Therefore, even by optimizing the temperature range 3M iterations is not enough to get the global optimum. On the other hand, the convergence speed is equivalent than the one in Sect. 5. Thus, the Bayesian optimization convergence speed seems independent from the permutation size treated by the simulated annealing algorithm.

7   Conclusion

This paper proposed a method representing the environment as a graph whose vertices are locations for which the situation has to be checked by a team of autonomous drones and edges are built by the A* algorithm. Thus, the problem of finding a path in the graph passing through every node is similar to a TSP. A simulated annealing algorithm is used to find the path which minimizes the environment's average uncertainty rate while considering the total travelled distance.

Whereas the simulated annealing algorithm's number of iterations plays an important role on the solution's quality, the temperature adjustment is also very important since it avoids getting blocked in a local optimum. In addition, the temperature range optimization allows to speed up convergence and then to reduce the number of iterations.

The temperature optimization problem was addressed by using Bayesian optimization. This method has shown capacities to find the optimum in a relatively low number of iterations. Furthermore, it saved us weeks of computations compared to the use of grid search methods. On the other hand, in its current definition the optimization process requires to fix the simulated algorithm's number of iterations, but this number depends on the problem. Further work would consist in making the optimization process more general. To do so, the Bayesian optimizer should consider both the number of iteration and the temperature range. However, to simply search the optimal number of iterations would always results on the search space upper bound. To cope with this issue, a possible idea is the optimization of the *expected improvement per second* as proposed in Snoek et al. [15]. By doing so, the optimizer looks for a setup which provides good outcomes of the function to optimize (in our case the simulated annealing algorithm) while requiring its computation time to be as low as possible.

Finally, the algorithm used for the task allocation is too simple and reconsidering this step would certainly improve the solution quality. However, the proposed method is adjustable. Thus, it is independent from the used task allocation algorithm as well as the A* algorithm or the simulated annealing algorithm. Further work would consist in proposing a task allocation algorithm which considers different drones' start points, different drone's characteristics (autonomy, speed, ...) and which allocates tasks in a less greedy way.

References

1. Castro, M., SöRensen, K., Vansteenwegen, P., Goos, P.: A memetic algorithm for the travelling salesperson problem with hotel selection. Comput. Oper. Res. **40**(7), 1716–1728 (2013)
2. Liu, C., Kroll, A.: Memetic algorithms for optimal task allocation in multi-robot systems for inspection problems with cooperative tasks. Soft Comput. **19**(3), 567–584 (2015)
3. Jose, K., Pratihar, D.K.: Task allocation and collision-free path planning of centralized multi-robots system for industrial plant inspection using heuristic methods. Robot. Auton. Syst. **80**, 34–42 (2016)

4. Richards, A., How, J.P.: Aircraft trajectory planning with collision avoidance using mixed integer linear programming. In: Proceedings of the 2002 American Control Conference (IEEE Cat. No. CH37301), vol. 3, pp. 1936–1941. IEEE (2002)
5. Richards, A., How, J., Schouwenaars, T., Feron, E.: Plume avoidance maneuver planning using mixed integer linear programming. In: Proceedings of the AIAA Guidance, Navigation, and Control Conference, pp. 6–9 (2001)
6. Richards, A., Bellingham, J., Tillerson, M., How, J.: Coordination and control of multiple UAVs. In: AIAA guidance, navigation, and control conference, Monterey, CA (2002)
7. Jevtić, A., Andina, D., Jaimes, A., Gomez, J., Jamshidi, M.: Unmanned aerial vehicle route optimization using ant system algorithm. In: 2010 5th International Conference on System of Systems Engineering (SoSE), pp. 1–6. IEEE (2010)
8. Osaba, E., Carballedo, R., Yang, X.-S., Diaz, F.: An evolutionary discrete firefly algorithm with novel operators for solving the vehicle routing problem with time windows. In: Yang, X.-S. (ed.) Nature-Inspired Computation in Engineering. SCI, vol. 637, pp. 21–41. Springer, Cham (2016). doi:10.1007/978-3-319-30235-5_2
9. Osaba, E., Yang, X.S., Diaz, F., Onieva, E., Masegosa, A.D., Perallos, A.: A discrete firefly algorithm to solve a rich vehicle routing problem modelling a newspaper distribution system with recycling policy. Soft Comput. 1–14 (2016)
10. Careaga, C.: Python A* pathfinding (with binary heap). ActiveState Code. http://code.activestate.com/recipes/578919-python-a-pathfinding-with-binary-heap/
11. Acevedo, J.J., Arrue, B.C., Maza, I., Ollero, A.: Distributed approach for coverage and patrolling missions with a team of heterogeneous aerial robots under communication constraints. Int. J. Adv. Robot. Syst. **10**, 1–13 (2013)
12. Perry, M.T.: simanneal. https://github.com/perrygeo/simanneal
13. Kirkpatrick, S., Gelatt, C.D., Vecchi, M.P., et al.: Optimization by simulated annealing. Science **220**(4598), 671–680 (1983)
14. The GPyOpt authors: GPyOpt: a Bayesian optimization framework in python (2016). http://github.com/SheffieldML/GPyOpt
15. Snoek, J., Larochelle, H., Adams, R.P.: Practical Bayesian optimization of machine learning algorithms. In: Advances in Neural Information Processing Systems, pp. 2951–2959 (2012)
16. Gonzalez, J., Dai, Z., Hennig, P., Lawrence, N.: Batch Bayesian optimization via local penalization. In: Proceedings of the 19th International Conference on Artificial Intelligence and Statistics, pp. 648–657 (2016)

A New Approach to Telecommunications Network Design Automated and Data Driven

Fabion Kauker[1]([✉]), Chris Forbes[1], Matthew Blair[1], and Danny Huffman[2]

[1] Biarri Networks Pty Ltd, Melbourne, Australia
{fabion.kauker,chris.forbes,matt.blair}@biarri.com
[2] ONUG Solutions, Raleigh, USA
dhuffman@onugsolutions.com

Abstract. Globally there has been a significant increase in the number of Fiber to the Home (FTTH) projects. These projects are very expensive, take a long time to complete and require vast amounts of communication and documentation. Standards and processes vary greatly per project. The impact of this variability on the above factors is exacerbated by the use of manual tools with varying levels of data creation and interaction. Existing tools utilize either a Geographic Information System (GIS) or a Computer-Aided Design (CAD) approach. Both rely on user expertise, bespoke data models and process. We present a data driven automated optimization software based approach which generates designs. This is compared to a manual alternative on the basis of time, quality, workflow and usability. Both are then broken down into their primitives. Whilst using existing interaction paradigms the software is able to shift the user's role from intensive input to minimal input and review. The new approach is able to reduce the time taken by 34% and the material construction costs by 28% for the FTTH design.

Keywords: HCI · AI · Operations research · MIP · Human–computer interaction · Human computation · FTTx · GPON

1 Introduction

Humans have been building complex structures for a long time; this could not have been possible without the utilization of tools. These can range from paper and pencil to more advanced tools like software and simulation. The creation of new technologies has led to new engineering and construction methods but also the motivation for more ambitious endeavors. As demand for new technologies grows including transportation, power and communications networks so does the number of projects. Overall this process can be seen as somewhat cyclical.

When a new technology is discovered applications are consequently developed. These must then be engineered into use and in the course of this new discoveries are made. In today's context engineering has been broken into various specializations, all having their roots in hard sciences like chemistry, physics and biology. Some examples include, civil, chemical, mechanical, electrical, robotic and aeronautic engineering. In most large scale projects it will take specialized team of engineers to develop and

S. Yamamoto (Ed.): HIMI 2017, Part II, LNCS 10274, pp. 371–389, 2017.
DOI: 10.1007/978-3-319-58524-6_30

implement a solution. One of the essential parts of a successful project is the communication and documentation throughout. There are now multiple professional bodies which create and/or maintain standards and provide membership for individuals and entities. Each industry and/or specialization may have multiple standards which can be driven by region. A good example of this is power and energy [23], where standards bodies set rules and regulation with regard to the applications, ratings, connections, testing, current and voltage. This has been made possible by engineering tools which can be used to design and measure products and systems.

It is currently a unique time in history with the availability of inexpensive computation resources, however access to these resources is not always guaranteed. Since the invention of computer networks the use of these has evolved from projects like ARPANET to the modern internet where consumers access content and communication [8]. Whilst the applications grow, so does the demand for bandwidth (Fig. 1).

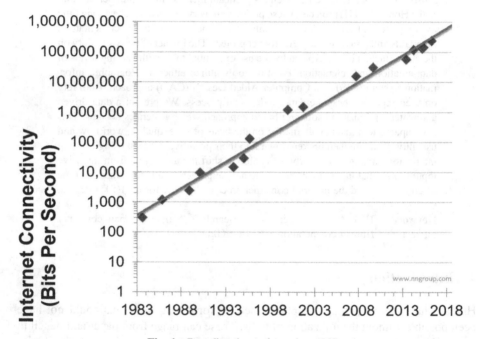

Fig. 1. Broadband speed vs. time [13]

The tools used to design and build these networks have not changed significantly since the deployment of power networks. In the United States the roll out of the power grid based off the Electricity Supply Act of 1926 relied largely on human labor both in design and deployment. Further to this the interaction of previous undertakings with new deployments is always a challenge. Put simply each time a new network is rolled out, the superseded network and surrounding infrastructure must be remediated to accommodate the new infrastructure. This poses a challenge as the effort is highly visible and can create a severe inconvenience for the community in the short term. The development of manual systems and the eventual computerization of these has been advantageous but inadvertently created its own set of challenges. The process has been expedited however the scale and scope of the projects requires vast amounts of human labor both in planning and execution. The ongoing training and education of users across systems and processes can at times cause parties involved to succumb to the status quo. Put simply the investment into software and structure prevents the application of new technologies. Often the use of systems which are familiar and replicate pencil and paper are adopted rather than having users encouraged to replace them and move to new paradigms. By using manually generated outcomes stakeholders favor investing additional manual effort rather than starting a new design, this can be viewed from the point of view of sunk costs [4, 9]. This is contrasted against the manufacturing industry which in some instances has seen entities/manufacturers move to a fully digital process [12]. In civil engineering there is still a reliance on paper based communication, which causes significant challenges to implementing fully digital processes in the field. Some factors include user resistance, the need for retraining, as well as the lack of consistent user friendly applications [15]. However, simple tools have proven to be effective and facilitated the deployment of multiple networks. The challenge comes when comparing the civil engineering capabilities to that of physical network design functionality. It is still difficult and time consuming to model scenarios and compare alternatives without repeating manual effort. The application of engineering standards, business rules and quality control can differ across teams. Further to this the work must be effectively partitioned, assigned, managed and reconciled. This is often done by multiple parties with their own sets of governing rules and motivating factors. For example many cities still require the submission of paper or flat files for construction permits. Organizing and ensuring access to these presents challenges. These documents whether paper or electronic, do not have a common industry standard for the layout and components; therefore it can be timely and challenging to ensure compliance on a project-by-project basis.

Generally, industry challenges include the shortage of qualified engineers, the variance of standards, process and quality, and extensive investment in human labor to accurately estimate cost incrementally for a potential network deployment. This research seeks to clarify the toolkit available for potential projects and also share learnings with the broader research community. This paper will specifically focus on the creation of a FTTH design by using algorithms to enhance and augment human capability.

The current manual process and solution for creating a FTTH design are comprised of multiple pieces of software or processes, each of which has its own set of caveats. By utilizing the current engineering tools used that have an established user base the manual process is replicated as per current industry practice. Tools like AutoCAD provide a foundation on which a set of domain requirements are customized for. On top of this a data model is created so that other stakeholders can utilize the information communicated [1]. Through our experience it is observed that this varies on a project by project basis.

Creating a FTTH design consists of drawing objects which represent cables and their connectivity. By using graphs and geometry as the representation for the objects, the software applies algorithms to create potential designs. The data is geo-referenced and stored in a GIS format allowing the visualization plus measurement of the inputs and outputs. The algorithmic approach utilizes Mixed-Integer Programming.

This enables the expressive construction of a mathematical formulation to express parts of the design requirements. This is combined with functionality that is created to give the user the ability to influence a solution.

Each of the above mentioned concepts are discussed and pieced together for both the manual and augmented approach. The potential for improvement and demand for connectivity is real. By sharing this work the goal is to create further discussion about the ability of computing to transform an industry and the specific tools that could be enhanced or developed. The interface between domain experts, computers and algorithms provides a vast opportunity for enhanced productivity.

2 Graphs and Geometry

From a mathematician's viewpoint, in order to take a data driven approach to design FTTH networks the method must expresses the fundamentals of network design as graphs and geometry. This is the contrasted against the viewpoint of the engineer. Graphs are utilized to represent the connectivity between multiple points of service and their interconnectivity. Geometry is used when relating to the physical shape and routes of the components, a fiber cable can be visualized with a linestring. By using these key concepts the information can be expressed as data and therefore can be used in computation. Both are domains of academia in their own right, each has an extensive amount of knowledge and research to support the field. Some of which can be applied to designing networks, or creating the tools to do so. Including graph traversal algorithms, which enable the navigation of a network [9]. Furthermore many algorithms have implementations developed and supported by the open source community.

The base components of graphs used are nodes and edges. These refer to a specific item, for example a location in space, component, cable or a customer. The nodes are connected by edges which represent the linkage from one node to another. These edges can be used to express direction such that nodes can only be accessed in a specified direction. For example take the nodes A, B, C and the set of edges ((A, B), (C, B)) which is equivalent to A → B ← C. It is not possible to go from B to the other nodes. It is also useful to think of these concepts in terms of the information they are trying to express. Specifically if the objective is to model a telecommunications network there can be multiple ways of expressing the same information. It is important therefore to create a standard. Questions that should be addressed and that have implications include, how are node names generated? How are connections between objects modeled? How will additional data be stored? Does the data need to be human and/or machine readable? There are many software libraries that can be used to assist, which have support for the base implementation of these concepts and algorithms which can be used on the graph once generated (Fig. 2).

Geometry is used to express the shape of items and their location relative to one another. The geometric two dimensional types used include points, line strings and polygons. By using shapes with coordinates relative to each other many geometric operations can be performed. Some of which include, intersection, union, derivation and modification. Further to this there are techniques that can be used to increase the speed of computation for these [6] (Fig. 3).

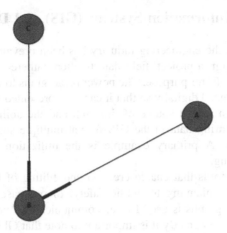

Fig. 2. An example of a directed graph

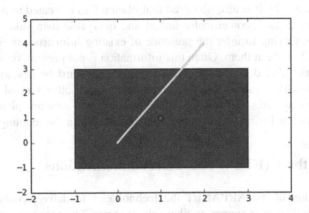

Fig. 3. An example of a polygon, line string and point visualization

Graphs and geometry can be combined, in this instance the graph is derived by intersecting the geometry, points and line strings. By defining when objects intersect they can be transformed into a graph object. The linkage of edges is also commonly done via lookup tables, generally when creating designs these linked values are created from the design. Thus when completing a new design this information must be created and derived from existing data. In order to utilize computation both on the graph and geometry, the access methods between them should be defined. By using these concepts and combining them with GIS the objects can be visualized at their location with maps. Once the data is used throughout the process it is possible to build functionality and conduct analysis.

3 Geographical Information Systems (GIS) and Data

The use of data within the engineering industry has been prevalent for some time; in order to accurately design a project, field data is often gathered. This is then used to ensure that the design is fit for purpose. The newer paradigm is to have that data located in space and geo-referenced digitally so that it can be represented visually onto satellite imagery. This enables a shared source of the truth and the ability to compose maps from the data. By capturing data in the GIS format multiple sources can be brought together and analyzed. A primary example is the utilization of satellite imagery combined with designing.

There are multiple tools that enable creation and editing of GIS data. The applications range from city planning to public safety. In our case the combination of location, geometry and graphs is used for telecommunications network design. However, when working with geometry it is important to note that GIS relies on a spheroid and projections of it. This is important when computing distances and even when ensuring the source data is correct. Multiple systems and tools exist for the manipulation of GIS data [17]. It is also observed that often a GIS is treated as a drawing tool rather than a relational, geometrically linked and queryable data store. This is very challenging when trying to infer the presence of existing infrastructure like poles and the links (strand) between them. Often this information is not present, or it is structured incorrectly for the fiber design use case. Therefore tools must be developed to assist. Having accurate GIS data is a highly valued asset which allows rapid and accurate assessment of many tasks including business cases, costs, network planning, market analysis, targeted marketing and detailed construction costing/scheduling.

4 Fiber to the x (FTTx) and Telecommunications

Since the creation of the ARPANET the technologies to deliver connectivity have evolved, from dial up over copper, to fiber (glass) optics. The core concepts remain the same, a location is connected to another which enables the transmission of data packets between them. With the rapid increase in demand for bandwidth many communities and telecommunications companies are deploying fiber optic networks. This deployment translates into extensive civil works, installing cables underground in conduit or suspended aerially between poles. In both urbanized and rural areas this can be time and cost intensive. The networks being created now connect subscriber locations back to a central office; these areas are referred to as 'serving areas' and can contain connections for tens of thousands of residents. This is highly dependent on location and the technologies utilized. The configuration of the network varies however the general concept is that there is an optical path from one end to the other. As the network is built up from the subscriber side, paths are combined either onto a fiber via optical splitting of the wavelengths of light or onto a cable via a terminal or splice [4]. The route the connections take can be determined from the street network data; there are also multiple commercial vendors who provide base routes for where cable can be installed. However the core data is not often routable. This means that potential routes must be derived from street, city, customer, open and commercial data. There are many unique possible combinations of configurations to connect subscribers. These are driven by the selection of components from manufacturers, this combination is termed 'architecture'. One of the challenges in effectively deploying a network is selecting the correct architecture. This can be done by comparing multiple alternative designs and is also part of the data driven design process but is not explored in this paper.

5   Operations Research (OR) and Mixed-Integer Programs (MIPs)

OR is defined as the application of advanced mathematics to solving complex decision making problems to/or near optimal values. The term is also analogous to analytics. To model the FTTH design problem a combination of heuristics and MIPs are used to model the network and find design solutions. By using leading edge commercial solvers, models can be created, evolved and solved rapidly. The combination of multiple techniques and models yields near optimal results which are better than current alternatives, including manual experts [5].

5.1   Problem Definition

It is challenging to define and model the complete network design problem. Further to this even if it is possible to do so the reliance on the completeness and accuracy of data can be a fundamental flaw. Therefore we have decomposed the problem into parts. The complete problem can be modeled as a MIP however the problem is significantly large enough that the time taken to find a solution is too large. Where "too large" is expressed as the time taken to give the user an output such that this can be quantified and the input data modified to generate suitable design iterations. Lowest optimal values are not always able to be directly translatable into real world solutions. Therefore tools and functionality have been created to assist in expressing real world constraints and designer preferences. The problem can be defined as:

Definition: *Minimize cost by finding the minimum number of edges to be used such that the problem constraints are met.*

Edges represent the physical location of segments of cable to be constructed. The nodes which edges link are potential locations for components and/or demand points. Though the problem constraints may vary on a per project basis the core concepts are reusable. The core mathematical concepts applied are minimum spanning tree, flow modeling and assignment algorithms. The input, combination and parameters of these vary on a case by case basis.

6   Python and Software Development

By utilizing Python, a high level language with open source principles and library support we are able to rapidly construct software functionality to both automate and reconfigure processes. This is further enabled by inbuilt Python environments in programs like QGIS (an open source GIS software program), source control, versioning, deployment systems and cheaply available hosted computing. The software solution can be decomposed into the following subcategories: input, solver, output, and infrastructure.

6.1   Input and Output (IO)

The objectives of IO are to input and transform data. Data is received from multiple sources and in multiple formats/structures. In order to be able to perform computation on the data it must be read and transformed into a consistent form. The requirements for data derivation vary from application to application but the core ideas are the same. The first process is defined as the preprocessor. This is where the input data is transformed into a candidate network which consists of a graph representation which models the demand locations, possible routes for cables and locations for components. This information can then be fed to the solver. Upon finding a solution the result must be matched with its matching data to then create the derived outputs. Specifically, cables are composed of the edges in the graph selected by the solver. However, geometrically the cables must be one continuous geometric object which terminates at either end at a component which is also represented as a geometric point. The specifics regarding the geometry, how it is represented, what attributes are assigned/derived are determined by the application. The format is also determined by the end use of the output. Generally there are three objectives of the output. Communicate the information such that the network can be costed, built and store the information so the network can be operated and maintained.

6.2   Solver

The creation of a solver is defined as the use of advanced mathematical algorithms to model the FTTx network design problem domain. Given the inputs have been created these must be transformed into a structure that can be used to create the MIP. There may be multiple heuristics applied to create a set of inputs so that the model can be solved faster. Examples include graph simplification and candidate component or cable generation. The data is used to generate a formulation which is then solved by a commercial solver. This can be done in multiple stages based on the business rules and specifics being modeled.

6.3   Infrastructure

Relates to the physical and virtual machines, software functionality and how it is used, deployed, supported and maintained. In order to develop and utilize the software systems that are developed the methods of doing so must be created and supported.

This can be local or remote programming in an editor or IDE through to deploying the packaged versioned pieces of functionality and accessing them in the deployed environment. Further to this each user must have access and the system must be versioned to ensure consistent results. Much of the incremental design work requires the interaction with drawing tools and as such a mouse is a much need addition to increase productivity. Workflows can also be improved by using large desktop monitors. As much of the design effort is spent verifying data on satellite images or viewing streets on Google Street View, fast internet connections also assist with the transfer of data between subscribers and devices.

7 Human Computer Interaction (HCI)

When developing the system and software the focus initially started on building a system that would automate and capture the knowledge of the domain expert, their knowledge and expertise. Much like the initial Artificial Intelligence (AI) or knowledge systems where rules were captured and then implemented using logic, (if p then q) [10] this was then combined with MIPs which created a solution and provided automation with regard to the design creation. Thus taking a rationalistic [20] approach where key actions and aspects of thoughts were encoded. It quickly became apparent that on two dimensions the system would need to evolve to be effective for users. Firstly the decomposition of the functionality into steps rather than a one click solution. This gave the ability to influence what were mathematically near optimal solutions which respected the rules. However domain expertise was applied and the output did not look right to the human engineer. The experience and knowledge of the engineering requirements could not be expressed in the mathematical modeling due to the lack of data or the complexity that it would create. These additions are referred to as functionality additions. When creating a design it was also observed that it is important to give users rapid feedback on the design. This was made possible by having solvers that found good solutions in less than five minutes. This gave users an output that could be reviewed and then iterated on. The completion of design in a required format and with various attributes presents a challenge for manual design. As the values are complex and inter-related it is common place to defer the effort and therefore make mistakes in design. By using software and creating solutions programmatically the attributes can be created based on the design solution. This provides enormous value when storing and accessing the designs in a database. However, each end user often has their own standard and the requirements may lack documentation.

8 Process Decomposition

The network design process is separated into stages that can be followed in a linear flow to derive solutions. It is however sometimes necessary to backtrack due to new information provided by the outputs. This then makes the process iterative. The first step is to turn the data into a suitable input which can be turned into a graph with the required amounts of fiber at each termination point. As previously described this is referred to as preprocessing and there are multiple steps each of which derives additional information. Each of these processes can be run individually or in series and range from simple scripts to more complex pieces of software. It is important to note that the data structures throughout enable the user to customize the functionality so that the results can be altered to meet requirements. The design is also decomposed into tiers such that the user can design different parts of the network and then combine them to get to the end result. The data may also be partitioned to enable a user to be more thorough and also create a design more quickly by parallelizing the effort [11].

9   Functionality Additions

Throughout the design process the data must be manipulated. Often it is a matter of adjusting the inputs to get a new result. For example changing from aerial to underground routing would mean removing the aerial option and creating an underground one. There are also other techniques used to enable the desired result. This functionality includes forcing a link between a subscriber and terminal, providing fixed component locations, increasing the cost of an edge deterring its use, removing an edge and fixing a network footprint for a tier. This functionality is created based on the graph and geometry models discussed earlier. The interaction with the data is primarily done in QGIS.

10   Human Computation

Another way of viewing the software is through the lens of human computation, whilst falling short in terms of a large scale automated system, the method and use of the tools can be seen to be analogous to human computation, whereby incremental decisions are made which contribute to the large objective of creating a network design [2, 3, 7].

11   Tools and Examples

Area partitioning is an example of the use of graph partitioning algorithms [11] to fragment work from a larger set. This is often utilized when planning areas larger than 5,000 premises as time constraints and the complexity of detail can be overwhelming for the individual designing the area. However, the challenge is to bring the pieces together again. The engineer faces the same issue when completing a manual design. It is also possible to segment the problem based on the tier of design, lead-in or service design, letting the user focus purely on where the endpoint will connect to and how they can be combined optimally. This takes into account the maximum length of service from a terminal and also the maximum number of connections of a terminal. The terminals must then be connected and often geographic areas are utilized to create boundaries based on property development and other natural or man-made boundaries, for example railways. However, this can lead to additional costs when designing the cable routes and connecting the components to one another.

12 Experiment Design

Given areas of 500 and 2,000 premises compare manual design with an algorithmically-generated/auto design. Both methods utilize the same data, same base tool set, design rules, and output requirements. It is assumed that attributes can be programmatically generated. The designs are comprised of the cable and component but layouts for support assets are part of a later detailed design process. The design requirements are fixed as depicted below in Fig. 4. This is termed a centralized splitter network. The base premises are combined to at most 12 connections made by cables with one fiber. These terminals are then combined into groups of 48 which are served by a 576 cabinet. These cabinets are then served by a central active location.

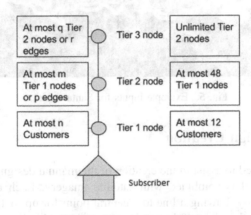

Fig. 4. A network topology

13 Method

In order to complete a design data must be accessed from available sources. Data was sourced from the City of Santa Cruz [22], Open Street Map (OSM) [21] and Open Address [24]. This was then exported using QGIS. The area of Santa Cruz has been selected as it contains a suitable area of approximately 2,000 premises. The design manual and auto process are compared in two scenarios. 500 subscribers, this reflects a design for a single serving area. A typical working unit for a FTTH project where a physical cabinet with 576 ports is utilized. Then 2,000 subscribers are designed to highlight the subtlety of deciding how to select multiple areas of 500 subscribers and interconnecting them (Fig. 5).

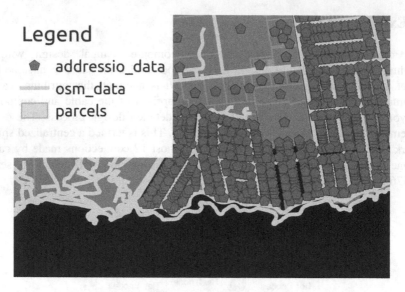

Legend

● addressio_data

━━ osm_data

▢ parcels

Fig. 5. Example inputs for Santa Cruz

14 Manual Design Creation

The base data was used to assist in the creation of the manual design. This was used to guide the process and is combined with satellite imagery. Each address point and rooftop is connected by drawing a line to a central point for up to 12 units. These are selected by starting at the edges of the service area and working inwards. Once all units have been served the service points need to be combined into the next tier. This is a more complex macro task as it requires the routing of the cable and the tracking of fiber usage. In the larger area this process is repeated for the next tier. This process can be broken into the following primitives and workflow per Figs. 6 and 7.

Each step is fully manual, creating a high chance for error. This can be minimized by utilizing tools such as snapping. This allows the drawing of connected geometries by hand. Components are also separated into layers so that they can be worked with independently. Once the design is complete it is challenging to rework as choices made previously must be interpreted and then either adjusted or deleted. Therefore each design increment requires significant design knowledge and effort. It is also assumed that a designer has knowledge regarding the best practices for component placement and cable routing.

Attribute creation and tracking can be one of the most time consuming tasks. But it is often very useful for validation and measuring compliance. In this manual design however it is assumed that the attributes can be created programmatically.

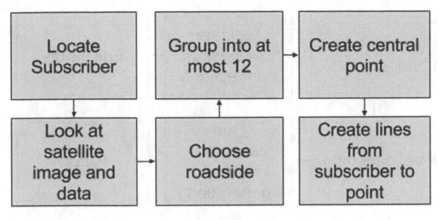

Fig. 6. Tier one primitives

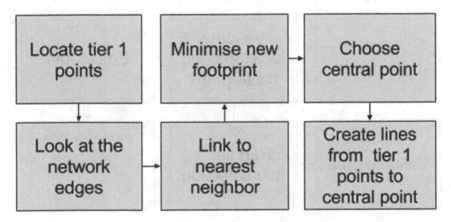

Fig. 7. Tier two and above primitives

15 Auto Design Creation

The data is used as direct input into the software functionality. The first step is to turn the street centerlines into geometry that represents the possible routes for the cable. Along this route the components can also be placed. Upon some iterations and the addition/removal of streets that were missing or incorrect, the next step is to connect the address points to the potential routes. These are then connected into Tier 1 nodes, with capacity n, in this case $n = 12$. Upon some iteration these can then be connected back to a Tier 2 node followed by a Tier 3 node. See Figs. 8 and 9 below.

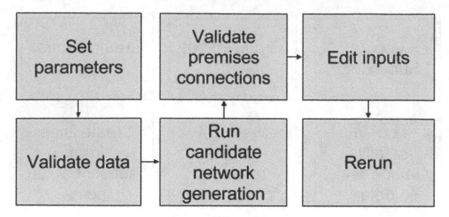

Fig. 8. Auto design data input iteration & drop creation

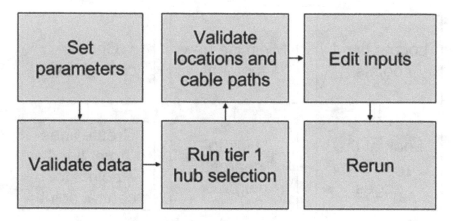

Fig. 9. Auto design tier one primitives

16 Findings

Both manual and auto designs are referred to as planning or high level design that can be used to create a business case or guide the downstream engineering design creation. The designs are compared on a quantitative level, by comparing the number of components, length and the time taken for each design. The processes also differ in approach. The manual design creation is linear as the design is created incrementally whereas the auto design outputs are generated and iterated. It is also easy to create design variations using the auto design methodology. The total design time for the area of 2,000 premises in Santa Cruz took 5 h and 30 min to complete manually. Whereas using the auto design software the design was completed in 3 h and 10 min (see Appendix A). This is approximately a 42% reduction in the time taken. Further to this the majority of time taken was making minor changes to data rather than intently drawing the design. This can lessen the cognitive complexity for the individual/group by removing menial work

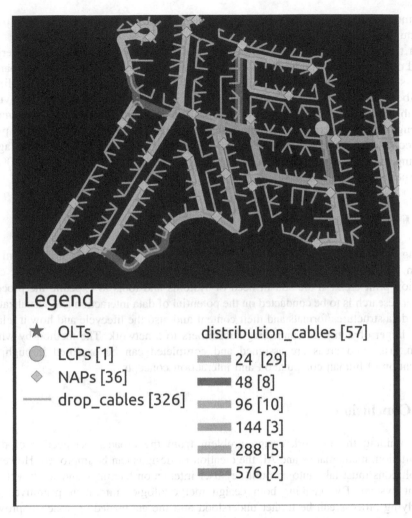

Fig. 10. Sample design output for Santa Cruz

and utilizing macro specialization skills [14, 18, 19]. The overall cost of the design has been compared also and the cost was able to be reduced by approximately $170,000 which translates to a 7% reduction (see Appendix B) (Fig. 10).

17 Industry Application

There are existing unique solutions to quickly finding high level designs [16] however very few look at the larger business problem and the usability of software and delivering it to a user base. Currently the software and process has been used to design more than 5 million households across six continents, including internal use and multiple customer deployments. This requires multiple users at various stages of the process communicating and collaborating.

In the United States Biarri has been actively working with ONUG Engineering. Based on the analysis conducted by ONUG when compared with the previous manual process the auto design is up to 28% more cost efficient and can be constructed utilizing less fiber. When combined with the time reduction for planning and design the savings are substantial. Infact the automated optimization solution, with real world planning and engineering experience programmatically applied, assisted in reducing the planning completion time by over 50% and the engineering time by 34%. Once again restating the substantial benefits put forward by Ferris et al. [5] saving at least 10% in construction and material cost.

18 Future Work

Having delivered a large volume of designs the process bottleneck is shifted from the design creation to the design ingestion. Such tasks as quality assurance and construction print creation are still in need of systems and tools to expedite the process. Further research is to be conducted on the potential of data interaction and visualization tools, data structures/formats and their content and also the lifecycle and how it relates to the larger objective of connecting subscribers to a network. The method by which design tasks and areas are assigned and completed can be explored through the application of human computation and interaction concepts.

19 Conclusion

By examining the network design problem from the broader perspective of data, computation, mathematics and AI, the creation of designs can be improved. However, the solutions must take into account key user interaction learnings and work within a current system. By breaking both design methodologies into their primitives, the underlying process can be further understood and the automated approach improved. Existing software and tools used by the industry, as well as the availability of data has created an effective starting point for the application of the methodology.

Appendix A

See Table 1.

Table 1. Times measure to complete designs manual and auto

	500 manual	500 auto	2,000 manual	2,000 auto
Drop creation	1:30:00	0:30:00	3:00:00	0:30:00
LCP location and cabling	1:30:00	0:30:00	1:30:00	0:30:00
Create candidate network	N/A	0:30:00	N/A	1:00:00
Data preparation	0:30:00	0:30:00	1:00:00	1:00:00
OLT location and cabling	N/A	N/A	1:00:00	0:10:00
Total	**3:30:00**	**2:00:00**	**6:30:00**	**3:10:00**

Appendix B

See Table 2.

Table 2. The Analysis and comparison of designs

	500 manual	500 auto		Costs	Manual 500 cost	Auto 500 cost	% Difference
NAPs	33.00	36.00	−3.00	500.00	16,500.00	18,000.00	9.09%
LCPs	1.00	1.00	0.00	2,000.00	2,000.00	2,000.00	0.00%
Drops	322.00	326.00	−4.00	100.00	32,200.00	32,600.00	1.24%
Drop length	19,057.17	19,412.12	−354.94	5.00	95,285.87	97,060.60	1.86%
Distribution length	3,905.66	3,560.27	345.38	50.00	195,282.80	178,013.59	−8.84%
Distribution splices	26.00	21.00	5.00	500.00	13,000.00	10,500.00	−19.23%
Feeder length	0.00	0.00	0.00	50.00	0.00	0.00	
Feeder splices				500.00	0.00	0.00	
					354,268.67	338,174.19	−4.54%
	2,000 Manual	**2,000 Auto**			**Manual 2,000 Cost**	**Auto 2,000 Cost**	**% Difference**
NAPs	216.00	212.00	4.00	500.00	108,000.00	106,000.00	−1.85%
LCPs	7.00	6.00	1.00	2,000.00	14,000.00	12,000.00	−14.29%
Drops	2,069.00	2,068.00	1.00	100.00	206,900.00	206,800.00	−0.05%
Drop length	122,973.17	132,368.51	−9,395.35	5.00	614,865.83	661,842.56	7.64%
Distribution length	25,056.60	21,771.38	3,285.22	50.00	1,252,830.18	1,088,569.08	−13.11%
Distribution splices	180.00	120.00	60.00	500.00	90,000.00	60,000.00	−33.33%
Feeder length	3,285.07	2,866.76	418.31	50.00	164,253.63	143,337.98	−12.73%
Feeder splices	2.00	1.00	1.00	500.00	1,000.00	500.00	−50.00%
					2,451,849.64	2,279,049.62	−7.05%
						172,800.02	

Appendix C

Complete input and output data.
https://drive.google.com/file/d/0Bz-HHuLfMk2PdE00SHF2NDVvUU0/view.

References

1. Bahr, G.S., Wood, S.L., Escandon, A.: Design engineering and human computer interaction: function oriented problem solving in CAD applications. In: Antona, M., Stephanidis, C. (eds.) UAHCI 2015. LNCS, vol. 9175, pp. 13–24. Springer, Cham (2015). doi:10.1007/978-3-319-20678-3_2
2. Blumberg, M.: Patterns of connection. In: Michelucci, P. (ed.) Handbook of Human Computation, pp. 5–12. Springer, New York (2013)
3. Blumberg, M.: Foundations in human computation. In: Michelucci, P. (ed.) Handbook of Human Computation, pp. 3–4. Springer, New York (2013)
4. Bulletin, T.: The Fiber Optic Association, Inc., pp. 1–7 (2011)
5. Ferris, P., Forbes, C., Forbes, J., Forbes, M., Kennedy, P.: Optimizing network designs for the world's largest broadband project. Interfaces (Providence) **45**(1), 83–97 (2015)
6. Finkel, R., Bentley, J.: Quad trees a data structure for retrieval on composite keys. Acta Inform. **4**, 1–9 (1974)
7. Grier, D.: Human computation and divided labor. In: Michelucci, P. (ed.) Handbook of Human Computation, pp. 13–23. Springer, New York (2013)
8. Hafner, K., Lyon, M.: Where wizards stay up late: The origins of the Internet (1998)
9. Hart, P., Nilsson, N., Raphael, B.: A formal basis for the heuristic determination of minimum cost paths. IEEE Trans. Syst. Sci. Cybern. **4**, 100–107 (1968)
10. John, M.: Machines of Loving Grace: The Quest for Common Ground Between Humans and Robots (2015)
11. Karypis, G., Kumar, V.: A fast and high quality multilevel scheme for partitioning irregular graphs. SIAM J. Sci. Comput. **20**, 359–392 (1998)
12. Lohr, S.: G.E., the 124-Year-Old Software Start-Up, The New York Times (2016). http://www.nytimes.com/2016/08/28/technology/ge-the-124-year-old-software-start-up.html. Accessed 10 Sep 2016
13. Nielsen, J.: Nielsen's Law of Internet Bandwidth (1998). https://www.nngroup.com/articles/law-of-bandwidth/. Accessed 10 Sep 2016
14. Nyerges, T., Mark, D., Laurini, R.: Cognitive aspects of HCI for GIS: an introduction. In: Nyerges, T.L., et al. (eds.) Cognitive Aspects of Human-Computer Interaction for Geographic Information Systems. NATO ASI Series, vol. 83, pp. 1–8. Springer, Netherlands (1995)
15. Pascoe, J., Ryan, N., Morse, D.: Using while moving: HCI issues in fieldwork environments. ACM Trans. Comput. Hum. Interact. **7**, 417–437 (2000)
16. Poon, K.F.(Danny), Ouali, A., Chu, A., Ahmad, R.: Application of AI methods to practical GPON FTTH network design and planning. In: Owusu, G., O'Brien, P., McCall, J., Doherty, N.F. (eds.) Transforming Field and Service Operations, pp. 133–151. Springer, Heidelberg (2013). doi:10.1007/978-3-642-44970-3_9
17. Sadoun, B.: GIS applications to city planning engineering. In: Encyclopedia of Human-Computer Interaction (2005)

18. Sanderson, P.: Cognitive work analysis and the analysis, design, and evaluation of human-computer interactive systems. In: Conference on Human-Computer Interaction (1998
19. Turk, A.: An overview of HCI for GIS. In: Nyerges, T.L., et al. (eds.) Cognitive Aspects of Human-Computer Interaction for Geographic Information Systems. NATO ASI Series, vol. 83, pp. 9–17. Springer, Netherlands (1995)
20. Winograd, T.: Shifting viewpoints: artificial intelligence and human-computer interaction. Artif. Intell. **170**, 1256–1258 (2006)
21. OpenStreetMap. http://www.openstreetmap.org/#map=13/36.9866/-122.0690. Accessed 10 Sep 2106
22. Open Data - County of Santa Cruz, California - Assessor Parcels. http://data.sccgis.opendata.arcgis.com/datasets/b8127236e33544e3a24bdd0f0cfa6ac2_28. Accessed 10 Sep 2016
23. IEEE SA - Power and Energy Standards. https://standards.ieee.org/findstds/standard/power_and_energy.html. Accessed 10 Sep 2016
24. OpenAddresses — Download Data. https://github.com/openaddresses/openaddresses/blob/6ed079787f8bcf7dcdd14d296a4364765d1cc144/sources/us/ca/santa_cruz.json. Accessed 10 Sep 2016

A System Description Model with Fuzzy Boundaries

Tetsuya Maeshiro[1,2(✉)], Yuri Ozawa[3], and Midori Maeshiro[4]

[1] Faculty of Library, Information and Media Studies, University of Tsukuba,
Tsukuba 305-8550, Japan
maeshiro@slis.tsukuba.ac.jp
[2] Research Center for Knowledge Communities, University of Tsukuba,
Tsukuba 305-8550, Japan
[3] Ozawa Clinic, Tokyo, Japan
[4] School of Music, Federal University of Rio de Janeiro, Rio de Janeiro, Brazil

Abstract. Describing phenomena of interest as a system is valuable to analyze using system science methodologies. The boundary is considered as the necessary component of a system, through which the system interacts with its environment. Although system based analysis is applicable, not all phenomena seem to present boundaries. We discuss boundary description of two phenomena, namely the lifestyle disease and the music composition process. The hypernetwork model homogenizes boundaries and relationships, and boundaries can be treated as an instance of relationships.

1 Introduction

System science assumes that a given system has boundary that separates the system from its environment. This assumption further enables the inference that the boundary can be identified and extracted. This paper discusses phenomena that the concept of a well-defined boundary cannot be applied. We treat these phenomena because we are representing them as systems to analyze and understand their characteristics.

1.1 Boundary Definition

There are cases that the boundary of a system is a physical object or entity, and the boundary is clearly identified. For instance, a cell of a living organism has the cell membrane as the boundary between the cell and the environment. There are, however, cases that the boundary cannot be explicitly identified. For instance, when a person is treated in a social context, we understand that a boundary exists among individuals, between an individual and the society, among others. However, we cannot identify and point exactly these boundaries. The boundaries in these cases are describable, but ungraspable. Then these boundaries are not directly describable since they are subjective entities (not consisting of objects), but can only be described using the elements belonging to the both sides of the boundary. Therefore, we define two classes of boundaries:

© Springer International Publishing AG 2017
S. Yamamoto (Ed.): HIMI 2017, Part II, LNCS 10274, pp. 390–402, 2017.
DOI: 10.1007/978-3-319-58524-6_31

(i) Class-I: physical boundary
(ii) Class-II: conceptual boundary

Both types of boundaries actually exist. This paper discusses the boundary representation of both classes. Description of lifestyle diseases belongs to the class-I, and music composition process belongs to the class-II.

1.2   Boundary Description

Suppose we are modeling person-person interactions, and treating a person as a system (Fig. 1). In this case, the boundary between the system (person) and the environment is clear, as the body shape and the skin serve as the boundary of the system. Not only the physical substances but also abstract entities such as information is input to and output from the system, and the body contour is interpreted as the membrane that input and output *"matters"* pass through. When these "matters" pass from outer side of the membrane to the inner side, it is interpreted that these "matters" were input to the system. Similarly, when the direction is from the inside to the outer side of the membrane, it is the output of the system.

Now consider the modeling of interactions among individuals, for instance among two persons (Fig. 2). When modeling direct interactions between two people, the boundary is set in somewhere between the persons, such as the dotted line in Fig. 2(A). Another possible modeling is to include the environment (Fig. 2(B)), and to model the boundary as in the single person case (Fig. 1). The advantage of including the environment is that the boundary is modeled intuitively as in the single person case, but the direct interaction between persons is not modeled, as any exchange of "matters" between persons is intermediated

Fig. 1. A person surrounded by environment.

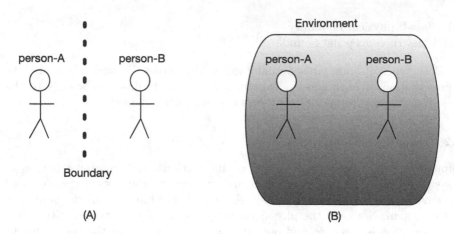

Fig. 2. Boundary between two persons. (A) The boundary exists between person-A and person-B. (B) Extension of the illustration of one person case, where both persons are surrounded by an environment.

by the environment, introducing inaccuracy into the model. The boundary in Fig. 2(A) is conceptual and imaginative, differing from the boundary between a person and environment (Fig. 1). In Fig. 2(B)), it is also possible to interpret the entire environment as the boundary between persons. The difference from Fig. 1 emerges, as the body shape would no longer function as the boundary in Fig. 2(B).

Now consider the modeling of interactions among groups of people, for instance among families (Fig. 3). Clearly, there are interactions among groups of people, which is different from interactions among individuals. In interactions among groups, the unit of interaction is the group of people, therefore there is a boundary that distinguishes a group of people from other groups. However, differing from the case of individual person's interactions where the body shape of each person could be interpreted as the boundary, it is difficult to find similar physical entity that represents the boundary of the group of people. Suppose the interaction between two families. A family is a set of people with consanguineous or legal relationship. We recognize the members of a family, and looking at the family members makes us recognize them as a single family. However, the concept of the family is virtual, and there is no physical entity that encompasses the family members, or something analogous to body shape that helps us identify as a single family.

But when treating interactions among families, where the representation unit is family, we interpret two families as distinct entities although the boundary between them cannot be described. Analogous to person-person interaction case, the interactions are executed through the boundary between two families, although it is a conceptual boundary.

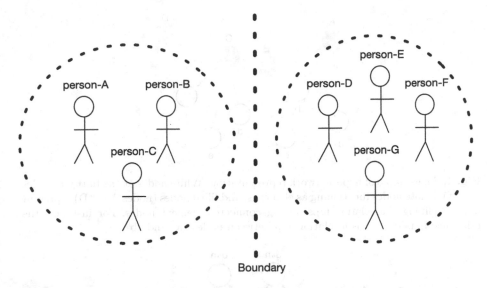

Fig. 3. Boundary between two group of people, one consisting of three persons, and the other of four persons. Dotted circles denote the groups. The location of the dotted line denoting the boundary is arbitrary.

2 Methods

The representation model to describe the boundaries is the hypernetwork model, an extended model derived from graph theory [6,7], but with more representation capabilities. The hypernetwork model allows multiple viewpoints to comprehend the target phenomena. Representation is viewpoint dependent, and representations are generated from the same set of elements. Its advantage is the freedom of the representation viewpoint to analyze the system.

The system description of a given viewpoint is realized by a set of elements of the system and relationships among them. Relationships are N-ary, and are also represented as an element of the system. Elements can be generated, modified and deleted.

Mathematically, the elements that constitute a system is a set

$$V = \{v_1, v_2, \ldots, v_N\} \tag{1}$$

where N is the number of elements.

Then a viewpoint is a subset of the elements whose relationships are defined by the relationship nodes (colored nodes in Fig. 4). The collection of the elements with relationship nodes constitute an interpretation of a system under certain viewpoint. The relationship nodes in Fig. 4 is colored for illustration purpose, but these nodes are also elements. The function of an element is viewpoint dependent.

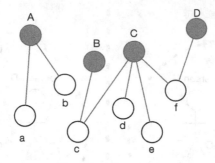

Fig. 4. An example of hypernetwork representation. White nodes at the bottom (nodes a ⋯ f) denote nodes functioning as elements, and filled nodes (nodes A ⋯ D) represent nodes defining the relationships among connected element nodes. For instance, the relationship node "A" is a relationship between nodes "a" and "b".

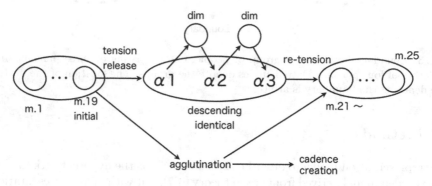

Fig. 5. An example of hypernetwork representation of a decision during music composition.

A viewpoint P is defined as

$$P = E \times R, \text{ where } E \subseteq V, R \subseteq V, E \cap R = \emptyset \qquad (2)$$

Thus the set of elements E and the set of relationships R are non-overlapping subsets of V.

Multiple viewpoints $P_1, P_2, \ldots P_M$ exist for V. The details of an element and a relationship can be specified by connecting other elements as attribute nodes. Let $A \subseteq V$ denote the set of attribute nodes. An attribute may specify multiple nodes, and element and relationship nodes function as attribute nodes of other nodes. Figure 5 is a representation of a decision in music composition process.

2.1   Describing Boundaries

The description of the boundary depends on the boundary type whether it is conceptual or not. In the case of person-person interaction, the boundary is

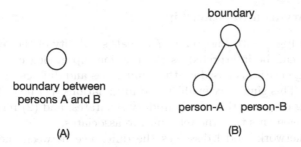

Fig. 6. Two representations of the boundary between persons A and B of Fig. 2.

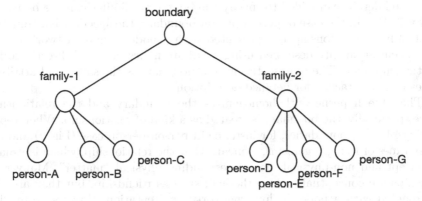

Fig. 7. Representation of the boundary between two groups of people illustrated in Fig. 3.

physical, so the boundary can directly be described using entities that constitute the boundary. Another possible description of the boundary is the external space that surrounds the persons (Fig. 6). On the other hand, the same description is unapplicable for family interactions, because the shape of the boundary cannot be defined.

Since the boundary between families is conceptual, one representation of the boundary is to describe using the descriptions of families that the boundary separates. More specifically, we describe each family using corresponding family members, and then use the family descriptions to represent the boundary between them. The description of the boundary is indirect in this representation scheme, and requires two steps. The step is defined as the number of intermediated links from the node representing the entity to the elements used in description. The step in hypernetwork model corresponds to the node level. Figure 7 illustrates the representation of the boundary between families. This is because the family is a concept and no physical entity exists.

2.2   Boundary as a Relationship

Comparison of Fig. 5 with Figs. 6 and 7 reveals similarity of the representation. The boundary can be interpreted as the relationship among elements. A relationship among entities is based on the similarities and differences of properties of the entities. This similarity enables two formulations: (1) boundary is a relationship among elements that the boundary separates; and (2) relationship is a border among elements that the relationship associates.

The hypernetwork model dissolves the difference between the relationship and the boundary. It enables the understanding that the gap is a kind of relationship. If the boundary is conceptual, it is analogous to conventional relationships, and details can added to specify the boundary. Similarly, if the boundary is physical, as in the case of person-person boundary, the specifications function identically. A relationship is represented with a node in hypernetwork model, and specifications are described using attribute nodes attached directly to the relationship node. The representation of a boundary is the same, and attribute nodes can be attached for detailed description.

Then the hypernetwork homogenizes the boundary and the relationship. More specifically, the boundary is treated as a kind of relationship. When representing physical boundaries, for instance in person-person case (Fig. 2) and cell membranes of living organisms, it means that the relationship, which is usually a concept and non-physical, has corresponding physical "matter". Many relationships are conceptual or hypothetical, such as friendship, but they are also represented with a node. In hypernetwork representation, there is no explicit distinction between representations of conceptual and physical boundaries. As previously explained in this paper, the hypernetwork model is able to represent duals. In dual representation, the boundary becomes the entity, and the elements represented as entities are treated as relationships.

Representing the boundary between two entities is simple compared to more entities. A node represents the boundary, and it connects the nodes representing the two entities (Fig. 8). Multiple possibilities or representation arise for boundaries among more than two entities. The boundary among N entities can be treated as a single boundary (Fig. 9(A)), or the boundary can be split and treated as a set of boundaries between pair of entities (Fig. 9(B)). For boundaries among $N > 2$ entities, both interpretations are possible, and both representations can

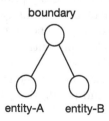

Fig. 8. Boundary representation between two entities.

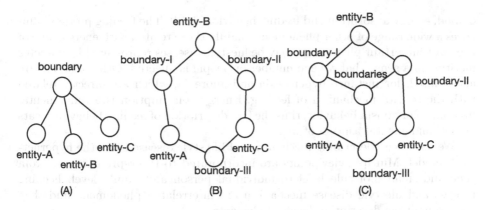

Fig. 9. Boundary representation between three entities. Three examples are shown.

coexist in hypernetwork model. A node representing all pairwise boundaries can be added (Fig. 9(C)).

Treating the boundary as an entity or a relationship depends on the viewpoint to treat the system. When visualizing the boundary as an entity, each boundary will be treated as distinct ones, and each will be identified with the specific label. For instance, the representation of Fig. 9(B) has three boundaries (I, II and III) and three "matters" (A, B and C). Suppose the three "matters" represents persons, and the boundaries denote the boundaries among persons. When treating the boundaries I, II and III as entities to analyze the nature of these boundaries, the persons A, B and C function as relationships or boundaries.

The advantage of the hypernetwork model is that it allows the representation of boundary as the relationship or the entity, and the "matter" as the relationship of the boundary, even if the interpretation of a viewpoint lacks immediate meaning.

3   Boundaries in Actual Phenomena

This section describes the application of the model to actual phenomena. The objective of describing as a system is to understand the phenomena by analyzing how the changes in properties of elements that constitute the system influence the phenomena. It is to observe the phenomena as a whole, the *"global behavior"*, by modifying the behavior of individual elements that constitute the phenomena and relationships among elements.

The boundary of the system is one of global behaviors to analyze. Then the goal is defined as the analysis of how the boundary behaves due to changes in elements' behaviors.

3.1   Lifestyle Disease

We are currently describing the feeding process of human beings. The feeding process refers to all functions, processes and control mechanisms regarding intake of food, energy absorption and feeding behavior [8–14]. The feeding process influences a wide range of other phenomena, mainly those related with energy. One of the most important phenomena may be lifestyle diseases represented by diabetes meritus, in a sense that a huge number of people is affected. Other diseases are also related, for instance hyperorexia and anorexia, which are directly related with the control mechanism of feeding. Energy consumption is a fundamental function of organism behavior, thus the fact description of feeding behavior treats one of fundamental aspects of life.

We have been describing mechanisms of life style disease using the hypernetwork model. Multiple viewpoints are incorporated to the representation, from gene and small molecule level to individual person and family level. Feeding process and lifestyle disease mechanism are interrelated phenomena and they involve multiple description levels of elements.

Genes, proteins and molecules constitute the lowest description level, and a group of people the highest description level. Cells, organs and persons, which belong to intermediate levels, are also used for descriptions. Besides the processes based on molecular biology, we are also integrating process related to oriental medicine, the meridian treatment.

Boundaries are clearly defined in descriptions based on molecular biology of levels below single person. However, descriptions based on meridian present no corresponding physical "matters". Figure 10 is an illustration of meridian, where the black dots represent the meridian points. The body shape may function as the boundary, and its description can be incorporated to the representation.

On the other hand, when a part of meridian points is of interest, the body shape can no longer be used as the boundary, and the use of conceptual boundary is required. The shape of the boundary is undefined, and can be freely defined.

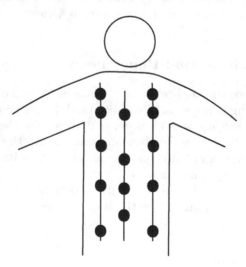

Fig. 10. A part of meridian in human body. A line denotes the grouping of meridian points represented by dots.

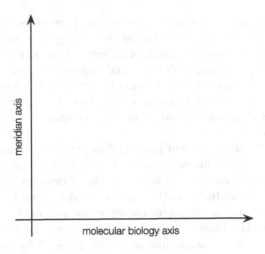

Fig. 11. Two perpendicular axes in lifestyle disease description.

The question is whether the boundary is necessary in this description, and our study suggests that the boundary is not a requirement for the analysis.

We are also conducting the integration of descriptions based on molecular biology and meridian. The problem of defining the boundary also arises in integrated representation. A possible visualization is the two dimensional space, each in perpendicular axes (Fig. 11). The boundaries used in descriptions based on molecular biology is unsuitable for integrated description because of the incorporation of meridian. Visualization of integrated model is necessary to analyze the influence of change in meridian to molecular biological phenomena and vice-versa.

3.2   Music Composition Process

We are analysing the music composition process of professional composers, treating the composition process as a sequence of decision makings. We focus on the creation process or composition process, from a blank music sheet to the final work. This is a "creation history" of musical piece, where the simultaneous employment of knowledge and imagination are essential [1].

Musical score is the de facto representation of musical pieces. Musical score encompasses every aspect of the musical piece, and it describes what to be performed, how to be performed, and composer's intentions. Many works on music analysis have been published, including the description model of music structure. For instance, Generative Theory of Tonal Music (GTTM) [2] is a model to describe the structure of musical pieces based on linguistic theory. Conventional works try to represent this type of knowledge as the static entity, usually treating as a structure of notes, chords and groups of these elements [2]. Typical structure is hierarchical, where the whole musical piece is positioned at the top of the hierarchy.

Music composition process presents following properties: (i) it is a creative process, and because of its artistic nature, sensitivity and emotion is strongly involved; (ii) there is a solid foundation of music theory, differing from other Arts fields such as paintings, sculptures and dances. Harmony of tonal music, for instance, involves mathematics of sound frequencies. The liberty and amount of sensitivity that is involved in music composition is higher than engineering process, industrial design and product design, for example, which have strong theoretical bases.

In the present work, a musical piece is represented by relationships among decisions. Such a creation history is more valuable than static structures generated by conventional methods. The disclosure of description of intermediate composition process is useful for both composers and players. For composers, it is valuable to overview and clarify his own composition process to improve the composed opus, besides the benefit to reorganize his ideas. For musical instrument players, the acquisition of background and underlying philosophy is invaluable, because deeper understanding of musical piece is fundamental and crucial for good execution.

In the description of the music composition process based on decision makings, the granularity of described decisions correspond to the description level in feeding process. There are decisions that involve a small number musical elements, for instance a single note, and others that affect the entire music. The former is fine granularity, and latter the coarse granularity. Then the boundary would be defined as the boundary of decision makings. The decision making is already conceptual, so its boundary is also necessarily conceptual.

Similar to the description of lifestyle disease, two aspects are represented in the description of the music composition process (Fig. 12): (1) decision elements

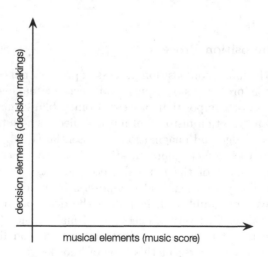

Fig. 12. Two perpendicular axes in music composition process description.

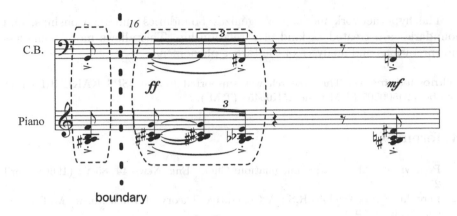

Fig. 13. An example of boundary between two adjacent music elements.

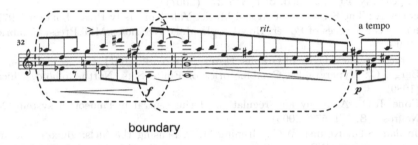

Fig. 14. An example of boundary between two overlapping music elements.

that describe decisions during composition; and (2) musical elements, such as music notes, that describe the composed music.

The boundary in representation of musical elements are intuitive because we can draw described regions on musical score. For adjacent and partially overlapped representations, the boundary is the intersection between the relevant elements. For instance, the boundary between adjacent elements can be traced as in Fig. 13. If an overlap exists, the overlap would be the boundary (Fig. 14). In both cases, the shape of elements and boundaries are conceptual.

4   Conclusions

This paper discussed the validity of boundaries in system representation of two phenomena, the lifestyle disease with feeding process and the music composition process. While the former belongs to the phenomena analyzed in classical system theory, the latter one is of different class. The conventional concept of the boundary, which functions to intermediate input and output from the system, does not apply to all system descriptions.

The hypernetwork model homogenizes boundaries and relationships, and boundaries are treated as kind of a relationship. This allows more boundless interpretations and analyses of the target phenomena.

Acknowledgments. This research was supported by the JSPS KAKENHI Grant Numbers 24500307 (T.M.) and 15K00458 (T.M.).

References

1. Polanyi, M.: The creative imagination. Chem. Eng. News **44**, 85–93 (1966). April 25
2. Lerdahl, F., Jackendoff, R.S.: A Generative Theory of Tonal Music. MIT Press, Cambridge (1996)
3. Christakis, N.A., Fowler, J.H.: The spread of obesity in a large social network over 32 years. N. Engl. J. Med. **357**, 370–379 (2007)
4. Forte, A.: The Structure of Atonal Music. Yale University Press, London (1977)
5. Klein, G.: Sources of Power: How People Make Decisions. MIT Press, Cambridge (1999)
6. Berge, C.: The Theory of Graphs. Dover, New York (2001)
7. Berge, C.: Hypergraphs: Combinatorics of Finite Sets. North-Holland, Chicago (1989)
8. Cone, R.D.: Anatomy and regulation of the central melanocortin system. Nat. Neurosci. **8**, 571–578 (2005)
9. Jordan, S.D., Konner, A.C., Bruning, J.C.: Sensing the fuels: glucose and lipid signaling in the CNS controlling energy homeostasis. Cell. Mol. Life Sci. **67**, 3255–3273 (2010)
10. Porte, D., Baskin, D.G., Schwartz, M.W.: Insulin signaling in the central nervous system: a critical role in metabolic homeostasis and disease from c. elegans to humans. Diabetes **54**, 1264–1276 (2005)
11. Sainsbury, A., Cooney, G.J., Herzog, H.: Hypothalamic regulation of energy homeostasis. Best Pract. Res. Clin. Endocrinol. Metab. **16**, 623–637 (2002)
12. Badmin, M.K., Flier, J.S.: The gut and energy balance: visceral allies in the obesity wars. Science **307**, 1909–1914 (2005)
13. Demuro, G., Obici, S.: Central nervous system and control of endogenous glucose production. Curr. Diab. Rep. **6**, 188–193 (2006)
14. Lam, T.K., Schwartz, G.J., Rossetti, L.: Hypothalamic sensing of fatty acids. Nat. Neurosci. **8**, 579–584 (2005)
15. Karr, J.R., et al.: A whole-cell computational model predicts phenotype from genotype. Cell **150**, 389–401 (2012)
16. Schierenberg, E.: Embryological variation during nematode development. In: WormBook (2006)

Towards User Interfaces for Semantic Storytelling

Julián Moreno-Schneider[✉], Peter Bourgonje, and Georg Rehm

German Research Center for Artificial Intelligence (DFKI),
Alt-Moabit 91c, 10559 Berlin, Germany
{julian.moreno_schneider,peter.bourgonje,georg.rehm}@dfki.de
http://digitale-kuratierung.de

Abstract. Digital content and online media have reached an unprecedented level of relevance and importance. In the context of a research and technology transfer project on Digital Curation Technologies for online content we develop a Semantic Storytelling prototype. The approach is based on the semantic analysis of document collections, in which, among others, individual analysis results are, if possible, mapped to external knowledge bases. We interlink key information contained in the documents of the collection, which can be essentially conceptualised as automatic hypertext generation. With this semantic layer on top of the set of documents in place, we attempt to identify interesting, surprising, eye-opening relationships between different concepts or entities mentioned in the document collection. In this article we concentrate on the current state of the user interfaces of our Semantic Storytelling prototype.

Keywords: Digital Curation Technologies · Linked data · Natural language processing · Semantic storytelling

1 Introduction

Digital content and online media have reached an unprecedented level of relevance and importance, especially with regard to commercial, political and societal aspects, debates and collective decisions. In that regard, one of the many technological challenges refers to better support and smarter technologies for knowledge workers, i.e., persons, who work primarily at and with a computer, who are facing an ever increasing stream of heterogeneous incoming information and who create, based on the specific requirements and expectations of the sector they work in and their job profile, in a rather general sense, new information. For example, experts in a digital agency build mobile apps or websites for clients who provide the digital agency with documents, data, pictures, videos and other assets. Knowledge workers in a library digitise a specific archive, augment it with additional information and publish the archive online. Journalists need to stay on top of the news stream including blogs, microblogs, newswires, websites etc. in order to produce a shorter or longer article on a breaking topic. All these different professional environments and contexts can benefit immensely from semantic

© Springer International Publishing AG 2017
S. Yamamoto (Ed.): HIMI 2017, Part II, LNCS 10274, pp. 403–421, 2017.
DOI: 10.1007/978-3-319-58524-6_32

technologies that support the knowledge workers in their respective activities: finding relevant information, highlighting important concepts, sorting incoming documents in multiple different ways, translating articles in foreign languages, suggesting interesting topics. We call these different semantic services, that can be applied in multiple different professional environments that all have to do with the processing, analysis, synthesis and production of digital information, *Curation Technologies.*

In the context of our research and technology transfer project Digital Curation Technologies we develop a Curation Platform that offers language- and knowledge-aware services such as semantic analysis, search, analytics, recombination and generation (e.g., thematic, chronological and spatial) for the curation of various types of digital content. Our goal is to shorten the time it takes knowledge workers to familiarise themselves with a potentially large collection of documents by extracting relevant data and presenting it in a way that allows them to be more efficient, especially in the situation when the respective knowledge worker is not a domain expert with regard to the topics discussed in the document collection. In the project we work with data sets provided by the project partners, four SME companies active in different sectors.[1] The data sets cover multiple domains, some are publicly available, others are not.

In addition to semantic text analytics there has been, in recent years, a renewed interest in Natural Language Generation applications, especially with regard to content generation based on structured data sets. At the same time there is a growing need for semantic technologies that help content curators and knowledge workers to make the most of their time, to support them by automating or semi-automating some of the more time-consuming tasks and to accomplish them in a more efficient way, ideally also by providing content products that are of higher quality. There are multiple potential use cases for these technologies in many different sectors [3,4,18,20]. In this paper we focus upon the semantic analysis of document collections in order to suggest interesting story paths between different entities mentioned in the collection. We call this approach *Semantic Storytelling.*

The immediate availability of large amounts of semantic data and knowledge bases makes this approach possible by applying semantic analysis methods, most of them based on Natural Language Processing (NLP). The annotation of semantic information in the source documents provides the necessary additional knowledge needed to tackle the ambitious task of computing and recommending potential story paths. Let us consider the example of the Panama Papers.[2] It is virtually impossible for one or even a team of investigative journalists to go through 11.5 million documents (2,6 TB of data) to find all the relevant information needed to prepare a report, news article or book on the investigation of the collection. Especially in this but also in many other use cases it would save a lot of time and resources to make use of a system that can, ideally automatically,

---

[1] The four SME partners are ART+COM AG, Condat AG, 3pc Neue Kommunikation GmbH and Kreuzwerker GmbH.
[2] https://panamapapers.icij.org.

process the whole collection and offer the investigators potential story paths in order to use them as starting points for their own articles.

The remainder of this paper is structured as follows. Section 2 covers related work. Section 3 provides a description of the current state of our curation platform. In Sect. 4 we discuss our results. Section 5 concludes the article and presents suggestions for future work.

2   Related Work

There are several approaches that are closely related to our Semantic Storytelling concept, all of them concentrating on their own specific objectives and providing solutions for their respective challenges. Our key challenge is to generate, ideally with limited or no human intervention at all, a story based on semantically annotated natural language text collections.

Some systems focus on providing content or applications for entertainment purposes. For example, Wood [32] uses a collection of pictures, videos and other media to generate albums, Gervás et al. [9] focus on storytelling in the gaming domain. Other groups use story structuring methods as part of therapy programs such as Kybartas et al. [13]. Other approaches focus on storytelling in a particular domain, typically recipes [7,8] or weather reports [1,11,22,30], requiring knowledge about characters, actions, locations, events, or objects that exist in this particular domain [10,23,31].

A notable exception to relying on domain knowledge is Li et al.'s approach [15], who attempt to construct plot graphs from a set of stories annotated using a crowd sourcing approach. The resulting plot graphs are used to generate alternative versions of the annotated stories, which are then evaluated again using a crowd sourcing approach. The evaluation task consists of either accepting a story as a logical piece of content, or making changes to the ordered list of events to make it a logical sequence (e.g., deleting events or re-ordering them). The authors report no statistically significant difference in the number of changes made to an automatically generated story compared to the number of changes made to a human-generated story. Important notions in the construction of a story plot are the logical ordering of events (a criminal has to be arrested before a conviction can occur) and the mutual exclusiveness of events (one cannot simultaneously be dead and alive). While some authors include the order of events [6], we currently do not take it into account.

In this paper, we focus on the user interface for story generation systems. Most similar interfaces focus on the final visualisation of the story as a game or a visual element but not on a graphical user interface for the, in a general sense, content management. Ma et al. [16] present several alternative visualisation scenarios for stories. Similarly, Segel and Heer [26] demonstrate different visualisation options for data in a narrative way. What they do not present, however, is an interface for the management of the content for these stories. Tanahashi and Ma [29] provide a detailed description of an approach for arranging events onto time lines, not taking into account the management of the content (events) itself.

Kybartas and Bidarra [14] present two different interfaces for semantic storytelling, both different to our approach. They concentrate on novel visual interactivity methods for end users. Their first interface, Smart Storybook, is a storytelling prototype designed specifically to enable children to experience storytelling in a creative and exploratory way, while the second, Improv Game is the prototype of a casual improvisational multi-player storytelling game, in which players take turns in building segments of a story.

In addition to these research activities, the area of Content Management Systems is of relevance to our project. With regard to our goals, a web-based solution for curating smaller content pieces or atomic content modules would be ideal. There are, of course, many Content Management Systems available on the market (e.g., Joomla, Drupal, Wordpress, Typo3 and many others), that all have different sets of features. What they lack, however, is the possibility of handling and managing semantic information. The core of our project, curation technologies and curation services, are not yet a typical feature or set of features of Content Management Systems.

The results presented by Mulholland et al. [17] are similar to the idea of story content management that we have developed. They describe an ontology for the definition and curation of stories in museum exhibits. Besides the ontology, it also presents a graphical interface, based on the CMS Drupal, in which the events that make up a story can be managed. Events can be added, deleted or modified. In our approach, we manage events in a similar way, but we cannot import them from external sources yet (this functionality is under development). However, we offer users the option of ranking events (positive, negative) and make the underlying engine aware of these positive or negative scores.

The most closely related approach is the one developed by Poulakos et al. [19], which presents "an accessible graphical platform for content creators and even end users to create their own story worlds, populate it with smart characters and objects, and define narrative events that can be used by existing tools for automated narrative synthesis". Its functionality is divided in three parts: Story World Creation, Smart Object Creation and Event Creation. The first part defines the states and relationships in the story world, the second defines the objects and characters of the story, and the third defines the events that create the story. The generation of new events is similar to our approximation, because it is also done in a new window where values are assigned to the properties of the event. Conversely, their consideration of event is wider than ours, because they regard an event as an action happening in the story, while we currently still consider events as semantic triples.

3   Architecture and System Description

In this section we briefly describe the current prototype of our interactive, semi-automatic semantic storytelling system. It can be used to analyse document collections of almost arbitrary sizes, ranging from a few files to collections comprising millions of documents, in order to generate story paths that can be further explored interactively. The system is still under development. We re-arrange and present the information extracted through the semantic analysis in a structured way. This is why we refer to our approach as semantic storytelling. Its foundation is the digital curation platform also developed in the project [2,5,25]. The platform offers multiple curation services [18,20], linked data extraction [5], machine translation [28] and natural language processing [3,4].

In addition to the storytelling system based on several NLP components (Named Entity Recognition, temporal expression analysis, linked data integration etc.), a second key contribution of this article is a user interface (UI) that allows the interaction with potential story paths to modify their content and structure and the user interaction mechanisms. The system architecture is shown in Fig. 1. It consists of three main parts, the NLP engine for analysing the documents, the storytelling module, that is responsible for creating story paths out of collections and the user interface (UI), which is handling the interaction between users and the system.

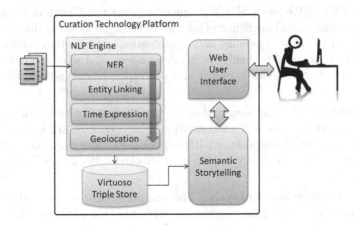

Fig. 1. Architecture of the interactive semantic storytelling engine

3.1 Natural Language Processing Engine

Our platform consists of a set of NLP modules to analyse documents and extract information to be used in several digital curation scenarios, among others, for generating stories. Interoperability between the modules is realised through the NLP Interchange Format (NIF) [24], i.e., all modules accept NIF as input and return NIF as output. The shared usage of NIF allows for the combination of web services in a decentralised way without hard-wiring specific workflows or pipelines. In the following we describe the modules to put together a semantic analysis workflow.[3]

Named Entity Recognition. First we convert every document to NIF and then perform Named Entity Recognition (NER). The NER module currently consists of two different approaches (additional ones to be added as part of future work). If annotated data is available, we train models to use in the NER task to deal with disambiguation and spotting of previously unseen entities. If we have a lexicon, dictionary or list of words (as is the case in one of our SME partner's use cases and data sets), we can use the dictionary for lexicon-based proper noun identification (with limited mechanisms for disambiguation). Both approaches are based on OpenNLP modules.[4] For entities that were spotted using the trained model approach, we proceed to look up the entity on its (language-specific) DBPedia page using DBPedia spotlight [27]. This allows us to retrieve relevant information using a SPAQRL query. For our current use cases and domains we use domain-specific dictionaries with names and URIs, i.e., we upload this dictionary in a key-value format, enabling the annotation of a spotted entity with the URI as additional information. In the case of locations the system points to Geonames URIs.[5] We use a SPARQL query against the Geonames ontology to retrieve the latitude and longitude of entities of the type location that we identify in the text. In the case of persons and organisations, our system points to URIs at Deutsche Nationalbibliothek[6]. As document-level statistics, we calculate the average latitude and longitude points and corresponding standard deviations.

Entity Linking. The next step within the workflow is Entity Linking. As input it receives the text annotated with entities. These entities are looked up in an ontology to retrieve, if available, a URI, depending on the presence of the entity in the ontology. This module was also implemented using DBPedia Spotlight.

Temporal Expression Analysis. The temporal expression analyser uses a regular expression based grammar that is currently able to process German and English natural language text. After the identification of temporal expressions, these are normalised to a shared machine readable format and added to the NIF representation. In this step we also add document-level statistics based on the normalised temporal values. The specific value is the mean date range; it is a range consisting of the average date in the document minus the standard deviation as the starting point, and the average date in the document plus the standard deviation as the end point of the range.

---

[3] Interested readers are invited to experiment with the API: http://dev. digitale-kuratierung.de/api/e-nlp/namedEntityRecognition. The documentation is available on Github: https://github.com/dkt-projekt/e-OpenNLP/tree/master-architecture-update.

[4] https://opennlp.apache.org.

[5] http://www.geonames.org.

[6] http://www.dnb.de.

Geographical Localisation Module. The geographical location module uses a SPARQL query to retrieve the latitude and longitude of the location as specified in the DBpedia entry (see above). This information is then added to the entity annotation in NIF. After the identification of geolocation entities, the module calculates the mean and standard deviation value for latitude and longitude of all location entities of a document for which a DBpedia entry could be found. This information is also added to the NIF representation.

Annotated Final Document. An example of an annotated document after processing with the NLP engine is shown below. The red text denotes the annotated entities, the green text denotes the annotated temporal expressions, the blue text denotes the information added by the entity linking module and the orange text shows the information added by the geolocation module

```
@prefix rdf:    <http://www.w3.org/1999/02/22-rdf-syntax-ns#>.
@prefix xsd:    <http://www.w3.org/2001/XMLSchema#>.
@prefix itsrdf: <http://www.w3.org/2005/11/its/rdf#>.
@prefix nif:    <http://persistence.uni-leipzig.org/nlp2rdf/
                ontologies/nif-core#>.
@prefix rdfs:   <http://www.w3.org/2000/01/rdf-schema#>.
@prefix geo:    <http://www.w3.org/2003/01/geo/wgs84_pos/>.
<http://link.omitted/documents/document1#char=0,26>
    a          nif:RFC5147String , nif:String , nif:Context;
    nif:beginIndex       "0"^^xsd:nonNegativeInteger;
    nif:endIndex    "26"^^xsd:nonNegativeInteger;
    nif:isString    "Welcome to Berlin in 2016."^^xsd:string;
    dfkinif:averageLatitude    "52.516666666666666"^^xsd:double;
    dfkinif:averageLongitude   "13.383333333333333"^^xsd:double;
    dfkinif:standardDeviationLatitude  "0.0"^^xsd:double;
    dfkinif:standardDeviationLongitude  "0.0"^^xsd:double;
    nif:meanDateRange      "20160101010000_20170101010000"
                        ^^xsd:string.
<http://link.omitted/documents/document1#char=21,25>
    a      nif:RFC5147String , nif:String;
    nif:anchorOf       "2016"^^xsd:string;
    nif:beginIndex     "21"^^xsd:nonNegativeInteger;
    nif:endIndex       "25"^^xsd:nonNegativeInteger;
    nif:entity     <http://link.omitted/ontologies/nif#date>;
    itsrdf:taIdentRef   <http://link.omitted/ontologies/nif#date=
                        20160101000000_20170101000000>.
<http://link.omitted/documents/#char=11,17>
    a          nif:RFC5147String , nif:String;
    nif:anchorOf    "Berlin"^^xsd:string;
    nif:beginIndex  "11"^^xsd:nonNegativeInteger;
    nif:endIndex    "17"^^xsd:nonNegativeInteger;
    itsrdf:taClassRef    <http://dbpedia.org/ontology/Location>;
    nif:referenceContext <http://link.omitted/documents
                        /#char=0,26>;
```

```
geo:lat          "52.516666666666666"^^xsd:double;
geo:long         "13.383333333333333"^^xsd:double;
itsrdf:taIdentRef     <http://dbpedia.org/resource/Berlin>.
```

3.2   Towards Semantic Storytelling

The storytelling module makes use of the analysis information to generate potential story paths. This generation is based on templates. Templates are JSON files defining the fields that compose every event involved in the story. These fields also define the type of the entities involved in the events. These can be constructed in two different ways, i.e., through manual definition or through the semi-automatic generation based on events from previously annotated documents. The manually defined templates are used as an initial point for the semantic storytelling and they include the most frequent events (entities and relations) mentioned in the collections of documents that we had available from our SME partners. The semi-automatic approach, which is currently under development, takes a collection of documents annotated with entities, relations (verbs) and events and infers a template structure. This inference is made using clustering algorithms to group the events and filtering based on frequency of appearance. Using clusters we can classify those events belonging to different parts of a story type.

In the following we present, as an example, the Biography template in a triple-based format, omitting some information for readability.

```
biographyTemplate_V1
    mainEntity: PERSON
    Events:
        PERSON(met)PERSON
        PERSON(born)LOCATION
        PERSON(study)LOCATION
        PERSON(joined)UNKNOWN
        PERSON(moved)LOCATION
        [...]
        PERSON(employed)LOCATION
        PERSON(marry)PERSON
        PERSON(lived)LOCATION
        PERSON(died)LOCATION
```

A story is defined as a structured set of events which contain entities and relations. In the current version of the system, relations are constituted by specific groups of verbs that relate entities with one another.[7] This generic template is filled using information semantically extracted from the document collection. The first step of the template filling process is searching the most common entity that matches the mainEntity type of the template. For example, in the case of

---

[7] This approach will be augmented with a more rhetorical or discourse-oriented approach as part of future work.

Biography the mainEntity is PERSON, so the system retrieves all the entities of type PERSON appearing in the collection and selects the most frequent one. After selecting the main entity, the system iterates over the events in the template and looks for other events matching the main entity and the relation (verb). If there is more than one suitable event, it selects the most frequent. Once the system has tried to fill all the events of the template, it returns the story path containing the information. This approach cannot be considered full Natural Language Generation because the typical last step of surface realisation is not included. Our main goal is to increase the efficiency in knowledge acquisition for human users, not the fully automatic generation of natural language text.

3.3   User Interfaces for Semantic Storytelling

During the runtime of the project we have implemented several different semantic storytelling interfaces. The initial prototype is shown in Fig. 2.

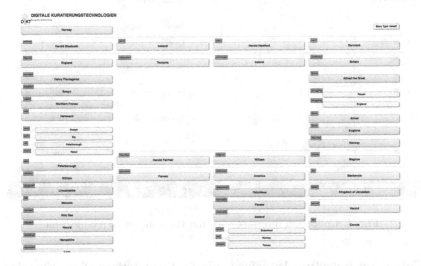

Fig. 2. The initial semantic storytelling prototype

The prototype presents a semantic story using a tree structure. The blue, green and yellow boxes are entities, which are interlinked by relations (specific classes of verbs), shown in the purple boxes. A detailed example can be seen in Fig. 3, which shows three events: Odin → *traced* → Loki, Loki → *chagrined* → Balder, Balder → *found* → Nanna.

This initial prototype interface lacked interactivity, i.e., users could not modify the content or the structure of stories. In order to solve the lack of interactivity, we developed a second version. The new UI was designed to be simple and intuitive. It is composed of three main parts.

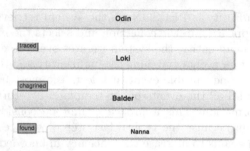

Fig. 3. Detail of the previous figure showing the relations Odin → *traced* → Loki, Loki → *chagrined* → Balder and Balder → *found* → Nanna

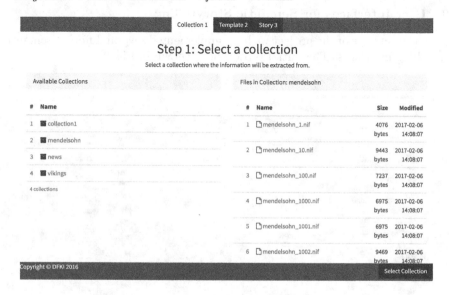

Fig. 4. Collection interface showing the content of a collection

1. **Collection Selection Interface** (Fig. 4): this interface allows the selection of an information source (i.e., a collection of documents) to use for generating stories. Users can navigate through the available collections, visualise documents and inspect their content and annotations. Users can also modify the annotated information.
2. **Template Selection Interface** (Fig. 5): this interface allows users to select a story template to be filled with the information of the collection previously selected. Templates are associated with story types. Templates cannot be modified directly in the interface; this feature will be added in a future iteration of the interface.
3. **Story Management Interface** (Fig. 6): this interface allows users to visualise the automatically generated story in a list or tree version.

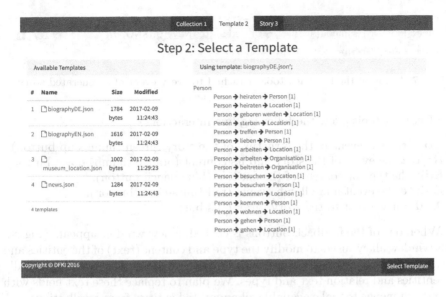

Fig. 5. Template interface showing the content of a template

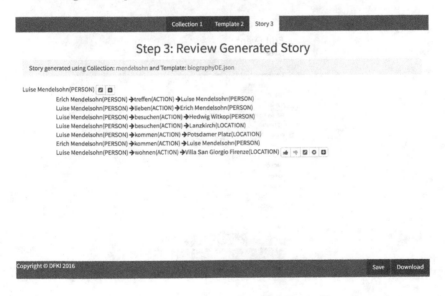

Fig. 6. Story interface showing the content of an automatically generated story using a specific collection and template

Enabling Interactivity. When the knowledge worker is presented with the generated story, we also provide interactive mechanisms to allow the user to modify the story efficiently. The interactivity was implemented as a set of feedback tools that are attached to every event in the storyline (shown in Fig. 7).

Cassady(PERSON) →born(ACTION) →Salt Lake City(LOCATION)
Kerouac(PERSON) →joined(ACTION) →<u>United States Navy(UNKNOWN)</u> 👍 👎 ✏ ✖ ➕
Kerouac(PERSON) →moved(ACTION) →College Park(LOCATION)

Fig. 7. Detail of the feedback tools attached to every event of a generated story

The feedback tools allow the following five interactions.

1. **Confirm** the event in the structure of the story (green thumbs-up button).
2. **Reject** the event of the story and its content (orange thumbs-down button).
3. **Edit** the type or content of the entities (blue pencil button).
4. **Delete** the event and all sub-events (red times-circle button).
5. **Add** a new event to the story (gray plus button)

When one of the feedback buttons is clicked, a new window appears (Fig. 8). This window allows users to modify the type and content (text) of the entities and the relation (verb) involved in the event. Currently, the user has to write manually the entities and relation text and types. We plan to replace these text fields with drop down menus to make available all annotated entities from a collection.

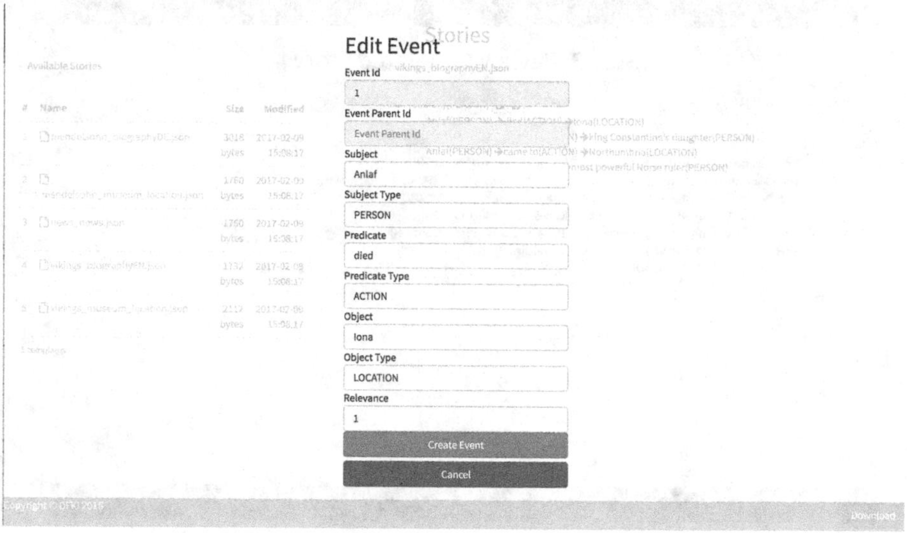

Fig. 8. Detail of the "Edit event" window

4   Experiments

We evaluated the current version of the dashboard using users. We have not yet applied a user-centric evaluation because we are still in the process of defining and shaping the technology behind this new type of interaction interface and visual metaphor [21]. The goal was to measure the usability of the new visual metaphor. We applied the methods described by Kelly [12], who measures usability in three dimensions: *effectiveness, efficiency* and *satisfaction*. In this preliminary study we focus upon satisfaction.

Users were asked to apply the system to create stories based on a variety of document collections and story types. Users were also asked to use the interactive controls: accepting or rejecting information, deleting or adding fields. Finally, users were asked to fill in a questionnaire. We recruited 15 subjects, aged between 23 and 47, with different educational backgrounds (engineering: 7, linguistics: 5, other: 3; 8 female, 7 male). All participants had been using computers for five to ten years. None of them had ever used a system like or similar to our semantic storytelling prototype. The users were asked to apply the system to create stories based on various combinations of a template and one of the following document collections:

- *Mendelsohn Letters:* a collection of 5144 personal letters written by the well known architect Erich Mendelsohn and his wife, Luise. Most of the letters are short. Topics range between architecture, travels and personal events. Language: German.
- *Vikings:* a collection containing seven longer documents (ca. 40,000 words on average). The collection is about Vikings, their history and culture. Language: English.
- *News:* a set of 2352 online news articles in German. Language: English.

Users were asked to apply the following templates:

- *Biography:* this template is characterised by having a main entity of type PERSON and a set of events that are related to the main entity. Because of that, this template is composed by a set of events related to the main entity, such as, *born → LOCATION, marry → PERSON* or *work → ORGANISA-TION* among others.
- *Museum Exhibit:* this template is also characterised by a central information, but contrary to the biography, it is not an entity but a whole topic. An example of museum exhibit covers the topic of Vikings. This exhibit does not only present a single Viking, but the entire Viking civilization, including all the famous Vikings, the locations where they lived, etc. In this sense, a template covering this kind of story is much more generic, and needs much structure than a single list. Because of that, this template contains a tree structure where there are nested events. A nested event is an event where the subject of the nested event is the object of a previous event.
- *News:* like the stories it generates, this template is the most generic and in which it is difficult to define a structure. Therefore, we have tried to keep this template open to facilitate news from different domains and topics. Therefore, this template also organises the events in the form of a tree, but with a peculiarity: events do not have to belong to the same topic, in contrast to the museum exhibit.

The detailed characteristics of the templates are shown in Table 1.

Table 1. The templates used in the evaluation

Name	# Events	Lang	Domain	Description
Biography	16	EN/DE	Biography	Specifies the entities and events that make up a biography
Museum exhibit	9	EN/DE	Single topic	Typical entities and events relevant for a museum exhibit
News	11	EN/DE	General	Typical entities and events in news articles

The workflow of the interface starts by selecting a collection and a template. Once these are selected, an automatically generated storyline is presented to the user in the interface shown in Fig. 6. Users are asked to verify the extracted storyline in two different ways: first, to check if the structural elements (entities and events) and their organisation is correct and, second, check if the content (text and URL) of the elements (events) is correct. Users are asked to explore all possibilities offered by the platform. After completing the task, users were asked to fill in a questionnaire with ten questions, allowing to score the respective system feature with a numeric value (between 0 and 10), and also to provide comments (see Table 2).

Table 2. The post-task questionnaire

	Question	Evaluated feature
Q1	How easy was it to generate a story using the interface?	Story generation
Q2	How intuitive was it to select a collection?	Collection selection
Q3	How intuitive was it to select a template?	Template selection
Q4	How easy was it to positively/negatively rank an event?	Event ranking
Q5	How easy was it to add new events to the story?	Add event
Q6	How easy was it to edit an event?	Edit event
Q7	How easy was it to delete an event?	Delete event
Q8	Inside the new event window, how easy was it to select information for filling the event properties (predicate, object, etc.)?	New event window
Q9	Inside the edit event window, how easy was it to change the information contained in the event (predicate, object, etc.)?	Edit event window
Q10	Was it intuitive to use the download story button?	Download button

The numerical scores were used to assess users' perception of a certain interface feature (Fig. 9). The free text comments were analysed manually and qualitatively to draw conclusions about users' perceptions.

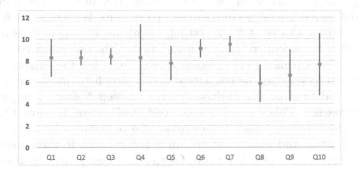

Fig. 9. Average and standard deviation of the scores assigned to the ten questions

It can be seen that users value the interface in a positive way (average value of 8.2), although there is also some disparity with a high standard deviation (1.75). The selection of collections and templates (Q2, Q3) have been positively scored (8.25 and 8.375) by all users (standard deviation: 0.7 and 0.74). As regards the event management buttons (Q4–Q7) the average values are high (8.25, 7.75, 9.13, 9.5) and the standard deviations are small (1.6, 0.83, 0.75) with only one exception in the ranking button (3.1). This indicates a high degree of general satisfaction among users. In contrast, the event management window (Q8 and Q9) and the download button (Q10) get lower scores on average (5.9, 6.6, 7.6). The qualitative analysis of the comments of the questions provides interesting insights:

- There was a general feeling that the interface was not finished yet. This makes sense since the full integration of the semantic storytelling prototype into the curation dashboard [21] is still pending.
- The current graphics and visual design of the interface was commented upon ("it is a little 90 s style").
- Negative remarks arose from the difficulty of including the text of the entities and relations or of the types, by not having access to the content of the documents of the collection.
- The high standard deviation in Q4 is due to a very low value given by a user who specified that "using the button was easy, but the internal functionality of the button was not clear".
- Another general comment was the lack of information about what the functionality of each button was.

These results will be taken into account in the next iteration of the user interface [21].

5   Conclusions

In this paper we present the first prototype of a novel type of application: semantic storytelling. This curation service is developed in the context of a research and technology transfer project on Digital Curation Technologies. The approach is based on the semantic analysis of document collections. With this semantic layer in place, we attempt to identify interesting, surprising, eye-opening relationships between different concepts or entities mentioned in the document collection.

Especially with regard to the discourse level analytics, the current approach at relation extraction must be considered rather simplistic in nature, especially when compared to more knowledge-intensive or deep Natural Language Generation approaches. This was a conscious technical design decision. One of the key ideas behind our approach is to explore the boundary of what is possible, technically feasible and implementable, in a generic way, in the curation technology platform and what will remain, for the time being, more in the realm of experimental software [21].

With regard to the evaluation, we have gained several conclusions. The three main findings are that users find the semantic storytelling prototype interesting and, generally, useful, but many improvements need to be applied before we can consider the approach a final product, rather than an evaluation interface or experimental prototype. Second, the "edit event" window is difficult to use. It is not intuitive and the information that can be included in entities and relations is not clear, which suggests a redesign of the approach. The visual and graphics design (including colours, typefaces etc.) of the prototype needs to be updated.

The approach to a semantic storytelling interface presented in this paper has created very useful results for defining the next steps and several novel future approaches that we had not considered previously. The most important one is that the storytelling interface can not function as a stand-alone UI, i.e., it has to be integrated into a larger curation framework or dashboard, so that users can develop a much better and deeper understanding of the information that has been or can be included in the storytelling interface and how it was processed.

Acknowledgments. The project "Digitale Kuratierungstechnologien" (DKT) is supported by the German Federal Ministry of Education and Research (BMBF), "Unternehmen Region", instrument Wachstumskern-Potenzial (no. 03WKP45). More information: http://www.digitale-kuratierung.de.

References

1. Belz, A.: Automatic generation of weather forecast texts using comprehensive probabilistic generation-space models. Nat. Lang. Eng. **14**(4), 431–455 (2008). http://dx.doi.org/10.1017/S1351324907004664
2. Bourgonje, P., Moreno-Schneider, J., Nehring, J., Rehm, G., Sasaki, F., Srivastava, A.: Towards a platform for curation technologies: enriching text collections with a semantic-web layer. In: Sack, H., Rizzo, G., Steinmetz, N., Mladenić, D., Auer, S., Lange, C. (eds.) ESWC 2016. LNCS, vol. 9989, pp. 65–68. Springer, Cham (2016). doi:10.1007/978-3-319-47602-5_14

3. Bourgonje, P., Schneider, J.M., Rehm, G.: Digital curation technologies for forensic linguistics. In: 13th Biennial Conference of the International Association of Forensic Linguists, Porto, Portugal, July 2017 (in Print)

4. Bourgonje, P., Schneider, J.M., Rehm, G.: Semantically Annotating heterogeneous Document Collections - Curation technologies for digital humanities and text analytics. In: CUTE Workshop, 2017 - CRETA Unshared Task zu Entitätenreferenzen. Workshop bei DHd2017, Berne, Switzerland., February 2017 (in Print)

5. Bourgonje, P., Schneider, J.M., Rehm, G., Sasaki, F.: Processing document collections to automatically extract linked data: semantic storytelling technologies for smart curation workflows. In: Gangemi, A., Gardent, C. (eds.) Proceedings of the 2nd International Workshop on Natural Language Generation and the Semantic Web (WebNLG 2016), pp. 13–16. The Association for Computational Linguistics, Edinburgh (2016)

6. Chambers, N., Jurafsky, D., Manning, C., Ng, A.: Inducing Event Schemas and Their Participants from Unlabeled Text. Computer Science Department, Stanford University (2011). https://books.google.de/books?id=3cc3yEErDX8C

7. Cimiano, P., Lüker, J., Nagel, D., Unger, C.: Exploiting ontology lexica for generating natural language texts from RDF data. In: Proceedings of the 14th European Workshop on Natural Language Generation, pp. 10–19. Association for Computational Linguistics, Sofia, Bulgaria, August 2013. http://www.aclweb.org/anthology/W13-2102

8. Dale, R.: Cooking Up Referring Expressions. In: Proceedings of the 27th Annual Meeting on Association for Computational Linguistics, ACL 1989, pp. 68–75. Association for Computational Linguistics, Stroudsburg (1989). http://dx.doi.org/10.3115/981623.981632

9. Gervás, P.: Stories from games: content and focalization selection in narrative composition. In: I Spanish Symposium on Entertainment Computing. Universidad Complutense de Madrid, Madrid, September 2013

10. Gervás, P., Díaz-Agudo, B., Peinado, F., Hervás, R.: Story plot generation based on CBR. In: Macintosh, A., Ellis, R., Allen, T. (eds.) Applications and Innovations in Intelligent Systems XII, pp. 33–46. Springer, London (2005). http://dx.doi.org/10.1007/1-84628-103-2_3

11. Goldberg, E., Driedger, N., Kittredge, R.I.: Using natural-language processing to produce weather forecasts. IEEE Expert Intell. Syst. Appl. **9**(2), 45–53 (1994)

12. Kelly, D.: Methods for evaluating interactive information retrieval systems with users. Found. Trends Inf. Retr. **3**(1–2), 1–224 (2009)

13. Kybartas, B., Bidarra, R., Eisemann, E.: Integrating semantics and narrative world generation. In: Proceedings of FDG 2014 - Ninth International Conference on the Foundations of Digital Games, Fort Lauderdale, FL, April 2014. http://graphics.tudelft.nl/Publications-new/2014/KBE14

14. Kybartas, B., Bidarra, R.: A semantic foundation for mixed-initiative computational storytelling. In: Schoenau-Fog, H., Bruni, L.E., Louchart, S., Baceviciute, S. (eds.) ICIDS 2015. LNCS, vol. 9445, pp. 162–169. Springer, Cham (2015). doi:10.1007/978-3-319-27036-4_15

15. Li, B., Lee-Urban, S., Johnston, G., Riedl, M.O.: Story generation with crowdsourced plot graphs. In: Proceedings of the Twenty-Seventh AAAI Conference on Artificial Intelligence, AAAI 2013, pp. 598–604. AAAI Press (2013). http://dl.acm.org/citation.cfm?id=2891460.2891543

16. Ma, K.L., Liao, I., Frazier, J., Hauser, H., Kostis, H.N.: Scientific storytelling using visualization. IEEE Comput. Graph. Appl. **32**(1), 12–19 (2012)

17. Mulholland, P., Wolff, A., Collins, T.: Curate and storyspace: an ontology and web-based environment for describing curatorial narratives. In: Simperl, E., Cimiano, P., Polleres, A., Corcho, O., Presutti, V. (eds.) ESWC 2012. LNCS, vol. 7295, pp. 748–762. Springer, Heidelberg (2012). doi:10.1007/978-3-642-30284-8_57

18. Neudecker, C., Rehm, G.: Digitale Kuratierungstechnologien für Bibliotheken. Zeitschrift für Bibliothekskultur 4(2), 48–59 (2016). http://0277.ch/ojs/index. php/cdrs_0277/article/view/158

19. Poulakos, S., Kapadia, M., Schüpfer, A., Zünd, F., Sumner, R., Gross, M.: Towards an accessible interface for story world building. In: AAAI Conference on Artificial Intelligence and Interactive Digital Entertainment, pp. 42–48 (2015). http://www. aaai.org/ocs/index.php/AIIDE/AIIDE15/paper/view/11583

20. Rehm, G.: Flexible Digitale Kuratierungstechnologien für verschiedene Branchen und Anwendungsszenarien. In: Bienert, A., Flesser, B. (eds.) EVA Berlin 2016 - Elektronische Medien & Medien, Kultur, Historie, Berlin, Germany, pp. 19–22, 23. Berliner Veranstaltung der internationalen EVA-Serie. 09–11 November (2016)

21. Rehm, G., He, J., Schneider, J.M., Nehring, J., Quantz, J.: Designing user interfaces for curation technologies. In: 19th International Conference on Human-Computer Interaction - HCI International 2017, Vancouver, Canada, July 2017 (in Print)

22. Reiter, E., Sripada, S., Hunter, J., Davy, I.: Choosing words in computer-generated weather forecasts. Artif. Intell. **167**, 137–169 (2005)

23. Riedl, M.O., Young, R.M.: Narrative planning: balancing plot and character. J. Artif. Int. Res. **39**(1), 217–268 (2010). http://dl.acm.org/citation.cfm?id= 1946417.1946422

24. Sasaki, F., Gornostay, T., Dojchinovski, M., Osella, M., Mannens, E., Stoitsis, G., Richie, P., Declerck, T., Koidl, K.: Introducing FREME: deploying linguistic linked data. In: Proceedings of the 4th Workshop of the Multilingual Semantic Web, MSW 2015 (2015)

25. Schneider, J.M., Bourgonje, P., Nehring, J., Rehm, G., Sasaki, F., Srivastava, A.: Towards semantic story telling with digital curation technologies. In: Birnbaum, L., Popescuk, O., Strapparava, C. (eds.) Proceedings of Natural Language Processing meets Journalism - IJCAI-16 Workshop (NLPMJ 2016), New York, July 2016

26. Segel, E., Heer, J.: Narrative Visualization: Telling Stories with Data, vol. 16, pp. 1139–1148. IEEE Educational Activities Department, Piscataway, NJ, USA, November (2010). http://dx.doi.org/10.1109/TVCG.2010.179

27. Spotlight, D.: DBPedia Spotlight Website (2016). https://github.com/ dbpedia-spotlight/

28. Srivastava, A., Sasaki, F., Bourgonje, P., Moreno-Schneider, J., Nehring, J., Rehm, G.: How to configure statistical machine translation with linked open data resources. In: Proceedings of Translating and the Computer 38 (TC38), pp. 138–148, London, UK, November 2016

29. Tanahashi, Y., Ma, K.-L.: Design considerations for optimizing storyline visualizations. IEEE Trans. Visual. Comput. Graphics **18**(12), 2679–2688 (2012). http:// dx.doi.org/10.1109/TVCG.2012.212

30. Turner, R., Sripada, S., Reiter, E., Davy, I.P.: Generating spatio-temporal descriptions in pollen forecasts. In: Proceedings of the Eleventh Conference of the European Chapter of the Association for Computational Linguistics: Posters & #38; Demonstrations, EACL 2006, pp. 163–166. Association for Computational Linguistics, Stroudsburg (2006). http://dl.acm.org/citation.cfm?id=1608974.1608998

31. Turner, S.: The Creative Process: A Computer Model of Storytelling and Creativity. Taylor & Francis (2014). https://books.google.gr/books?id=1AjsAgAAQBAJ

32. Wood, M.D.: Exploiting semantics for personalized story creation. In: Proceedings of the 2008 IEEE International Conference on Semantic Computing, ICSC 2008, pp. 402–409 (2008). http://dx.doi.org/10.1109/ICSC.2008.10

Towards Adaptive Aircraft Landing Order with Aircraft Routes Partially Fixed by Air Traffic Controllers as Human Intervention

Akinori Murata[✉], Hiroyuki Sato, and Keiki Takadama

The University of Electro-Communications,
Building W-6, 1-5-1 Chofugaoka, Chofu, Tokyo 181-8585, Japan
kouho.aki@cas.hc.uec.ac.jp

Abstract. This paper focuses on how cognitive loads of air traffic controllers can be reduced when optimizing both aircraft route and landing order in the airport landing problem (ALP), and proposes its method which can adaptively change the optimized aircraft landing order according to the aircraft routes partially fixed by air traffic controllers as human intervention. Though the intensive simulation on Haneda Airport in ALP, the following implications have been revealed: (1) our proposed optimization method succeeded to mostly maintain the same level of the results without fixing some of aircraft routes (i.e., the mostly same total distance of all aircrafts from the start position to the destination airport) even if air traffic controllers fixed some of aircraft routes; and (2) this result indicates that our proposed method has a great potential of reducing the cognitive loads of air traffic controllers by reducing the number of aircrafts that should be watched with fixing some of aircraft routes.

1   Introduction

For safe aircraft control, air traffic controllers give appropriate directions to aircrafts because they cruise at high velocity and it is difficult for pilots to independently operate aircrafts without aircraft collision. Since environment has occasionally changed by (e.g., sudden turbulence or a congestion of aircrafts), air traffic controllers consider safety for aircraft as a primary option. When the number of aircrafts in the airspace increase, cognitive loads of air traffic controllers extremely increase, which may prevent from keeping their concentration. Furthermore, air traffic increases every year, which demands more liability of air traffic controllers. For this issue, it is needed to reduce their cognitive load while optimizing both aircraft routes and their landing order [1]. Regarding the landing order optimization problem for aircrafts, Xiao proposed the binary-representation-based genetic algorithm method that can evolve the landing orders of the aircraft by evolutionary computation as the aircraft arrival order and scheduling problem [4].

© Springer International Publishing AG 2017
S. Yamamoto (Ed.): HIMI 2017, Part II, LNCS 10274, pp. 422–433, 2017.
DOI: 10.1007/978-3-319-58524-6_33

2   Current Air Traffic Management

A method of air traffic control is different from Regarding to a method of air traffic control, it differs according to countries. Airspace is divided into some segments called sector and aircrafts are managed every sector. The air traffic controllers instruct appearance of aircrafts in this sector to change directions and velocity adjustment. In an airport, air traffic controllers consider a relation between aircrafts and should determine landing routes and an order for aircrafts. For this reason, air traffic controllers have a great work load of air traffic control in the airport. They determine the order for aircrafts based on FCFS(First Come First Serve). FCFS is a rule to determine order of arrival aircrafts based on estimated arrival time. If the aircraft's landing interval to the airport is short, air traffic controller gets the aircraft to take a detour route in order to change the arrival time. This is the rule to reduce the cognitive loads of air traffic controllers but this rule has a problem in a point of efficiency of a runway capacity. In rush hour of arrival and departure aircrafts on an airport, ATFM (Air Traffic Flow Management center) command to delay aircrafts in Japan to avoid being crowded aircrafts in the particular area. However this system does not deal with increasing the demand for aircrafts for these reason, Air traffic controllers hope the system which is less cognitive loads of air traffic controllers and the landing order optimization method to reduce the occupancy time of an arrival airport. From an interview with air traffic controller, the main three factor effect on their workload are the number of tasks at the same time, constraint on time and duration of time. There is a high relation between the number of aircrafts and the mental workload [3].

3   Conventional Method

L. Bianco proposed a scheduling model for aircraft which simulates a real environment to generate landing order [2]. H. Xiao proposed an optimization method which is based on Genetic Algorithm (GA) using Bianco's model. His optimization method successfully produced a landing order to minimize the occupancy time of a destination airport because this method takes into consideration a size of aircraft [4]. The Size is a significant impact on landing time interval (LTI), also different interval by the leading and follower of the aircraft. For example, LTI of 228s is needed for a category 1 to follow a category 4. This asymmetric relation is a key factor in this optimization. To solve ALP, the total airborne delay has to be minimized. The following formula represents the total airborne delay.

$$A_{Q(n)} = \begin{pmatrix} P_{Q(n)} & n = 1 \\ max(P_{Q(n)}, A_{Q(n-1)} + S(C_{Q(n-1)}, C_{Q(n)})) & n > 1 \end{pmatrix} \quad (1)$$

$$D_i = A_i - P_i, \qquad i = 1, 2, ..., N_{AC} \quad (2)$$

$$\min_{Q(1),...,Q(N_{AC})} J_1 = \min_{Q(1),...,Q(N_{AC})} \sum_{i=1}^{N_{AC}} D_i \quad (3)$$

Table 1. Minimum LTI

(seconds)   Category of following aircraft

		1	2	3	4
	1	96	200	181	228
Category of leading aircraft	2	72	80	70	110
	3	72	100	70	130
	4	72	80	70	90

1;B747 2;B727 3;B707 4;DC9

N_{AC} aircrafts are planning to land an destination airport during operation day, and Ci, Pi and Ai are the category of aircraft size, the predicted landing time and the ALT of the ith aircraft in the first predicted arrival order. $Q(n)$ is the nth aircraft in the optimized landing order. $S(i, j)$ is the LTI for an aircraft of category j to follow an aircraft of carefory i to land. D_i is a difference of ith aircraft optimization time and the original prediction arrival time. The initial landing time is setting on by the principle of FCFS. Note that this method does not consider the landing route of aircraft. This means, it can produce an adequate landing order so that reducing the occupancy time, and so it is still unclear how a landing route should be designed to follow the decided the landing order (Table 1).

4   Proposed Method

4.1   Aircraft Routes as Path Planning

As shown in Fig. 1, This figure shows the overview of the previous method, which consists of landing route and the landing order unit as a hierarchical structure. First, Landing route unit generates candidates of each aircraft landing route, for example, X candidates represented by blue, red and green line routes are generated as shown in this figure. After such a generation, the unit selects the top some amount of candidates, for example, the top Y amount of X candidates are selected as shown in this figure. Finally, the selected main route as appropriate landing order is added sub-routes. Then the candidates are evaluated in terms of two aspects; (1) the total distance of main route from the current position to the destination airport and (2) the diversity of the routes can be quantified based on novelty search [5]. Thus, this unit eventually produces the landing routes which indicates small distance to the destination airport and can be customized for adapting as many situations as possible. Note that the routes that pass on the prohibit area is identified as infeasible solution. Each candidate of main landing route (i.e., the gene) is generated by NSGA-II [6]. Then, if the generated route is feasible solution, sub-routes are added to the generated main landing route (see Fig. 3) by the following steps; Sub-route algorithm (Fig. 2).

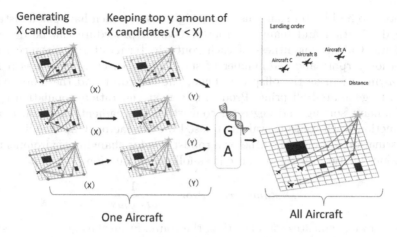

Fig. 1. Overview (Color figure online)

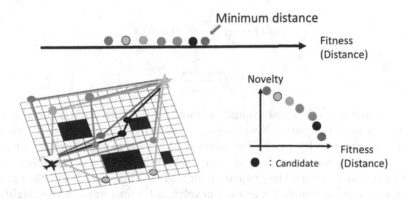

Fig. 2. Evaluating candidates of route

Step 1: For one of main route, calculating each the distance between the way points.

Step 2: Creating a square of distance r that center is a midpoint between the way points and a point on the vertical bisector randomly is determined. This point becomes new way point.

Step 3: New route that the new way point created in Step 2 is added is calculated the evaluation value.

Step 4: This route is saved as one of sub-route if the limitations of this route are met.

Step 5: Repeating from Step 2 to Step 4 until the termination condition is satisfied.

After adding the sub-routes to each landing route, they are evaluated with the fitness function and applied to genetic operators (i.e., the crossover and mutation) to find better solutions with a high fitness which have small distances to the destination and many sub-routes. Overall procedure can be described as follows; Calculating fitness of each route in terms of the distance to the destination airport and the number of sub-routes. Selecting routes as parents and copying them as the offspring. Then, the crossover and the mutation are applied to generated offspring. Producing a next generation population by the non-dominant sorting and degree of congestion tournament selection. Evaluation function Each route is evaluated based on two factor. One is a distance to the destination airport. The other is a robustness for changing environment. An evaluation function for the distance is as following equation.

$$Distance\ evaluation = \frac{1}{distance} \tag{4}$$

Where distance indicates total length of the route. From the equation, the shortest distance to the destination airport is the maximum evaluation value of the candidates. Next, an evaluation function of the diversity is calculating as follow.

$$\rho(x) = \frac{1}{K} \sum_{n=1}^{k} dist(x, \mu)\alpha \tag{5}$$

$$\alpha = a^{(\frac{distance}{d\_min} - 1)} \tag{6}$$

Novelty-search is the radical evaluation method for individual solutions corresponding to landing routes. Novelty-search measures how solution is unique in all of them and novelty metric for solution Where ρ is calculated as shown in this equation, μ_i indicates the individual which is ith-nearest neighbor in the population and x means the evaluated individual. The "dist" function is used $Euclid(\|x - \mu_i\|)$ as usual. For scoring novelty, a target group as the neighbor is used an archive or the population which is current generation. The number of K is vary from the population and problems, and algorithms. K value is most used 15 [7].

4.2   Arrival Sequence Optimization

Figure 4 shows the overview of the arrival sequence optimization unit. This unit execute GA to search appropriate combination of routes for aircrafts. The arrival sequence optimization unit picks out the top N candidates by the non-dominant sorting and degree of congestion tournament selection and searches the best combination of landing routes for some aircrafts by GA [8]. Each solution is represented in the integer type of gene and each locus indicates the selected route with each aircraft. This unit takes the following steps;

Step 1: Selecting one route for each aircraft.
Step 2: Checking on interval of aircraft whether meet constraint condition or not.

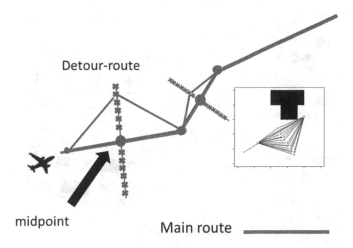

Fig. 3. Detour routes

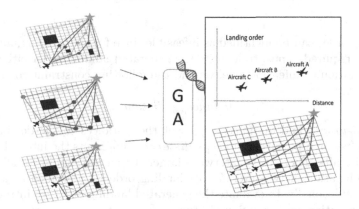

Fig. 4. Select arrival order

Step 3: Calculating evaluation value that meets limitation.
Step 4: Selecting parents from among solutions that meet limitation by using tournament selection.
Step 5: Crossing between parents and mutation.
Step 6: Repeating from Step 2 to Step 5 until the termination condition is satisfied.

The following is described the limitation condition that a solution meet, how to calculate evaluation value of the solution (Step 2 and Step 3) and how to mutate and crossover (Step 5) in detail. Constraints and evaluation value after generating of the combination of routes for some aircrafts, the arrival sequence optimization unit determines the landing order of aircrafts. Here, when the landing order indicates that the interval between each aircraft's landing is small,

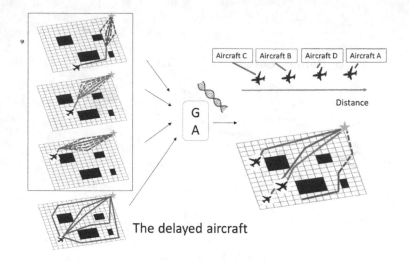

The delayed aircraft

Fig. 5. Select detour route (Color figure online)

its landing order can be identified as infeasible since for safe landing, an enough interval is required. Thus, to identify the generated landing order either one of feasible solution or infeasible one, we add the following constraint condition for landing order;

$$r > distance_p - distance_n \qquad (7)$$

Symbol $distance_n$ and $distance_p$ represent the distances to the destination of two aircrafts n and p; thus $distance_p - distance_n$ represents the interval between the two aircrafts. Then, if the interval is larger than a threshold r for all possible route combination of two aircrafts, its landing order is identified as a feasible solution. Additionally, to evaluate the generated landing order we introduce the following equation as calculation of fitness;

$$Fitness = \sum_{n=1}^{m} distance_n \qquad (8)$$

The fitness of landing order is simply calculated as the summation of distance of each aircraft. It is the distance of main route. Thus, the small value of fitness means that its landing order can reduce the occupancy time of the destination airport. Crossover and mutation This employ the uniform crossover and the mutation changes each gene locus to a random value with a certain probability. After this step, main route of each aircraft is determined and these aircrafts are cruising on landing route. If it occurs unexpected situations such as appearance of new aircrafts, the aircraft which determined main route takes an opportunity to select sub-route. In case of this, arrival order generating unit replace sub-routes for main routes and research the best combination of landing routes by GA (See Fig. 5). The landing order optimization unit recalculates the landing order applying detour routes. In this figure, three, blue, green and red aircrafts select their own detour routes and the other delayed purple aircraft selects a landing route. Such an appropriate combination of all routes is searched by GA. Then the landing order is determined.

5   Experiment

5.1   Experiment Setting

We conduct experiments on the grid map as introduced in [9]. As shown in Fig. 6 is a grid-map where the aircraft was flying. Noted that the black squares represent obstacles which indicate a prohibit area. Around Haneda airport, are set up outbound aircraft from this airport and for military purpose. Two dimensions map and this map we use here is a 250 km × 250 km. In this experiment, we use Haneda airport as a reference. This airport is highest air traffic in Japan. Aircrafts which arrives at Haneda airport come from east or west. There are four runways so from east and west side aircraft can own runway separately. Given this situation, we take scheduling only west side.

Table 2. Parameter

Path Planning		Arrival Schedule Sequence	
parameter	value	parameter	value
populationsize	100	population size	100
generation	500	generation	1000
crossoverrate	1	crossover rate	1
mutationrate	0.7	mutation rate	0.3
k	15	constraint	9.26
a	10		

We define forty aircrafts are staying at the starting area denoted by the blue-rectangle in the figure. To investigate whether our method successfully optimizes its order that reduces the occupancy time of the destination airport, we conduct the following one experimental case; This system optimizes each aircraft route and arrival order at five minutes intervals The maximum number of appearance aircrafts is three at one time. About thirty aircrafts land on Haneda airport per an hour, therefore average appearance aircraft is considered three. Each aircraft chooses an appropriate route which is considered interval of length of another aircrafts routes. Once aircraft routes had been determined, the aircraft must cruse along the course of chosen route. We conduct three steps per one seed and 10 trials. In comparison to proposed method, we conducted four methods. (1) the first method is the all fixed landing route method. Once the arrival optimization unit determine each landing route, Aircrafts does not select a detour route in this method. (2) this method is called the partially fixed landing route.

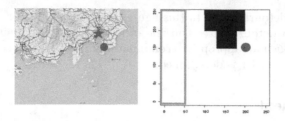

Fig. 6. Map (Color figure online)

This method is almost identical to the all fixed landing route method. This method is different in that some aircraft have a opportunity to select a detour route in comparison to that. In this experiment, the one aircraft selected randomly does not select at one step. (3) Third method is called No fixed landing route. This method selects a detour route of all aircrafts. (4) In this method, we change the evaluation which use only *Distance evaluation*.

We used the following parameter setting for NSGA-II and simple GA (Table 2).

6   Result

Table 3 indicates the value of the total distance every step for each method. Figure shows the experiment result. Figure 7 indicates the total distance for each

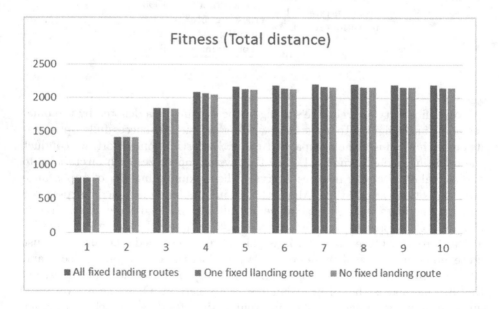

Fig. 7. Total distance (Color figure online)

Table 3. Total distance value

Step	All fixed landing route	One fixed landing route	No fixed landing route
1	799.886	799.886	799.886
2	1410.877	1410.877	1410.877
3	1843.04	1838.889	1832.655
4	2083.344	2066.65	2053.593
5	2166.057	2134.609	2127.239
6	2182.452	2144.567	2136.06
7	2200.697	2168.342	2156.187
8	2200.414	2162.278	2158.935
9	2196.006	2162.478	2159.398
10	2191.331	2152.006	2149.272

Table 4. The number of feasible solution (GA)

Step	The number of feasible solution (GA)
1	2
2	1
3	0
4	0
5	0
6	0
7	0
8	0
9	0
10	0

step. The vertical axis means averages of total distance over 10 experiments and horizontal axis means each step. The blue bar shows the total distances by all fixed landing route (without employed detour routes), The orange bar shows the total distance by a part of fixed landing route and the black shows the total distance by applied detour routes. Table 4 indicates the number of feasible solution of the arrival order.

As you can see this Fig. 7, the result of No fixed landing route is the best performance in all step of all and it found that detour routes contributed to reduce the occupancy time of the arrival airport. The result of all fixed landing routes was worst performance of the three, but this method could generate feasible solution of the arrival order in all steps. Because, Each aircraft generated a variety of landing routes of distance. The less aircrafts employed the detour route, the less air traffic controllers have cognitive loads. That is, to employ much detour routes cause increasing the directions. On the other hand, The GA hardly generated a feasible solution because this method could find the shortest route from to the destination airport and this had not mechanism to search a variety of candidates of distance. For this reason the evaluation based on novelty search had a good effect on generating diversity of distance and it is useful to reduce the cognitive loads of air traffic controllers.

7   Conclusion

This paper focused on how cognitive loads of air traffic controllers can be reduced when optimizing both aircraft route and landing order in the airport landing problem (ALP), and proposes its method which can adaptively change the optimized aircraft landing order according to the aircraft routes partially fixed by air traffic controllers as human intervention. Concretely, our proposed method consists of the aircraft route and the landing optimization units as a hierarchical structure. In this method, some aircrafts select detour routes, while the other aircrafts do not select detour routes. To investigate effectiveness of the proposed method, we tested it on the grid map of Haneda Airport in ALP. The experimental results revealed the following implications: (1) our proposed method could optimize the aircraft routes and their landing order even if the aircraft routes are fixed by the air traffic controllers. In detail, our proposed optimization method succeeded to mostly maintain the same level of the results without fixing some of aircraft routes, i.e., the total distance of all aircrafts (from the start position to the destination airport) with fixing some of aircraft routes is a little bit worse than without fixing some of aircraft routes. which some aircrafts are fixed landing route is as short as that one which all aircraft can select the detour route. (i.e., the mostly same total distance of all aircrafts even if air traffic controllers fixed some of aircraft routes; and (2) this result indicates that our proposed method has a great potential of reducing the cognitive loads of air traffic controllers by reducing the number of aircrafts that should be watched with fixing some of aircraft routes. What should be noticed here is that the result has only been obtained from the specific case, i.e., the Haneda Airport. Therefore, further careful qualifications and justifications, such as an investigation to the other airports, are needed to generalize our results. For an actual application, the advices or comments from air traffic controllers are needed.

References

1. Bennell, J.A., Mesgarpour, M., Potts, C.N.: Airport runway scheduling. Ann. Oper. Res. **204**(1), 249–270 (2013)
2. Bianco, L., Dell'Olmo, P., Giordani, S.: Scheduling models and algorithms for TMA traffic management. In: Bianco, L., Dell'Olmo, P., Odoni, A.R. (eds.) Modelling and Simulation in Air Traffic Management. Transportation Analysis, pp. 139–167. Springer, Heidelberg (1997)

3. Aoyama, H., Shiomi, K., Iida, H.: Study on Cognitive Process of Air Traffic Controller in En-route Control, Technical report of IEICE. SANE, vol. 107(67), pp. 7–12 (2007)
4. Hu, X.-B., Chen, W.-H.: Genetic algorithm based on receding horizon control for arrival sequencing and scheduling. Eng. Appl. Artif. Intell. 18(5), 633–642 (2005)
5. Lehman, J.: Evolution Through the Search for Novelty. University of Central Florida Orlando, Florida, Diss (2012)
6. Deb, K., Pratap, A., Agarwal, S., Meyarivan, T.: A fast and elitist multiobjective genetic algorithm: NSGA-II. IEEE Trans. Evol. Comput. 6(2), 182–197 (2002)
7. Cuccu, G., Faustino, G.: When Novelty Is Not Enough. Springer, Heidelberg (2011)
8. Golberg, D.E.: Genetic Algorithms in Search, Optimization, and Machine Learning, p. 102. Addison-Wesley, Reading (1989)
9. Tajima, T., Nakano, K., Ichikawa, M.: A real-time path planning using genetic algorithms. J. Jpn. Soc. Artif. Intell. 10(14) (1995)

Analysis of the Quality of Academic Papers by the Words in Abstracts

Tetsuya Nakatoh[1]([✉]), Kenta Nagatani[2], Toshiro Minami[3], Sachio Hirokawa[1], Takeshi Nanri[1], and Miho Funamori[4]

[1] Research Institute for Information Technology, Kyushu University, 744 Motooka, Nishi-ku, Fukuoka 819-0395, Japan
nakatoh@cc.kyushu-u.ac.jp
[2] Graduate School and Faculty of Information Science and Electrical Engineering, Kyushu University, Fukuoka, Japan
[3] Kyushu Institute of Information Sciences, Fukuoka, Japan
[4] National Institute of Informatics, Tokyo, Japan

Abstract. The investigation of related research is very important for research activities. However, it is not easy to choose an appropriate and important academic paper from among the huge number of possible papers. The researcher searches by combining keywords and then selects an paper to be checked because it uses an index that can be evaluated. The citation count is commonly used as this index, but information about recently published papers cannot be obtained. This research attempted to identify good papers using only the words included in the abstract. We constructed a classifier by machine learning and evaluated it using cross validation. As a result, it was found that a certain degree of discrimination is possible.

Keywords: Bibliometrics · Research investigation · SVM · Citation

1 Introduction

The investigation of related research is a very important task for researchers. Therefore, databases of academic papers are now indispensable for researchers. Appropriate keywords generate lists of papers related to keywords from these databases. They may be very long, but in general, several scales are provided.

The citation count [1] is the most widely used evaluation scale for an paper. Many databases have a function for sorting the search results of papers by the number of citations. Although the citation count is a useful and objective measure, newly published papers cannot be evaluated. One solution to this problem may be an assessment of the journal in which it was published as a substitute for evaluating the paper directly. The impact factor (IF) is a typical measure used to evaluate academic journals, which reflects the annual average number of citations of papers published in that journal. It is the most frequently used standard. The IF has the ability to imply the relative importance of journals within

S. Yamamoto (Ed.): HIMI 2017, Part II, LNCS 10274, pp. 434–443, 2017.
DOI: 10.1007/978-3-319-58524-6_34

a specific field but is not appropriate for comparison across fields. Therefore, the IF is not suitable for ranking a paper search. Another alternative evaluation method would be to use the researcher's evaluation. A symbolic example of this approach is the h-index [4] proposed by Hirsch. Alternatively, the usefulness of orthometrics [15] has been demonstrated in recent years.

These measures are also very useful for researchers. However, the collection and analysis of such information incurs a large cost. In fact, it is said that the number of citations that are still emphasized is already a mechanism for information gathering because it has already been created [7]. Here, we thought that it would be impossible to determine the quality of a paper more directly from the information contained within the paper. The information in the paper is the following information described in the published paper: the title of the paper, the name of the author, the affiliation of the author, the keywords specified by the author, the abstract, and the text. We have evaluated the quality of papers by using data excluding the text of this bibliographic information [8]. In this research, it became clear that the influence of the journal and year of publication is strong.

In this paper, we attempt to classify papers more purely using only the words included in the abstract of the paper. We define good papers as papers with many citations and construct classifiers based on a support vector machine (SVM), featuring words contained in the abstract. The performance of the classifier is evaluated by 10-fold cross validation. In addition, we conduct a qualitative analysis on the words effectively acting on the classification of the paper.

2   Classification Method

An SVM is a pattern recognition model using supervised learning. In this study, we attempt to classify collected papers into two groups: excellent papers and not excellent papers using an SVM.

It is difficult to define an excellent paper. We decided to use a large number of citations for the definition of an excellent paper only in the evaluation of the method. The purpose of this study is to find excellent papers from only the information included in the paper without external information such as the citation count, so it may seem like a contradiction. However, since Citation Count is not used when actually classifying an paper according to this method, there is no inconsistency.

Paper having a citation count equal to or larger than a given threshold is defined as excellent paper. Based on the threshold, classifiers that organize the papers into two groups are constructed by machine learning. The attribute set used for learning is the frequency vector of words contained in the abstract. We use a 10-fold cross-validation for various thresholds and find the optimal parameters for the threshold.

3   Experiment

3.1   Experimental Data

The papers used for the experiments were collected for two different perspectives. One is the papers extracted from the paper database Scopus including the keyword bibliometrics, and the other is the papers published in 15 international conferences and 5 journals, which we believe are important in the computer science field, also extracted from Scopus. We select only the papers with the abstract. The former paper database is called DB_Bibliometrics, and the latter is called DB_CS. DB_Bibliometrics and DB_CS contain 8,072 and 38,766 papers, respectively. A list of journals selected for DB_CS is presented in Table 1.

All papers are classified by a threshold T for the number of citations and constructed as data input into the SVM, where an paper having a number of citations of T or more is positive; otherwise, it is negative. In this study, the classification performance at multiple thresholds T is analyzed, and the following list is used as the threshold: (1, 2, 3, 4, 5, 6, 7, 8, 9, 10, 20, 30, 40, 50, 60, 70, 80, 90, 100).

3.2   Classification

The SVM has multiple kernels available. In the pilot survey, we used the following four general kernel functions using LIBSVM[1]. The parameter used the default value of LIBSVM.

- linear
- polynomial
- radial basis function
- sigmoid

Four classes of kernels were applied to positive/negative split paper sets, and the classification performance was measured by 10-fold cross validation. As a result, it was almost impossible to classify papers, except with the linear kernel. Therefore, we analyzed the linear kernel in more detail. In the subsequent analysis, SVM^{perf2}, which can classify the linear kernel at a high speed, was used.

In the linear kernel, there is a normalization parameter C to be set. For the default setting, $C = 0.01$, the following list of C values was used as a candidate determined to be useful in the preliminary analysis: (0.01, 0.02, 0.03, 0.04, 0.05, 0.06, 0.07, 0.08, 0.09, 0.1, 0.2, 0.3, 0.4, 0.5, 0.6, 0.7, 0.8, 0.9, 1, 2, 3, 4, 5, 6, 7, 8, 9, 10, 20, 30, 40, 50, 60, 70, 80, 90, 100).

In the following, we show the normalization parameter C and performance graphs for the classification performance obtained for the chosen citations.

---

[1] http://www.csie.ntu.edu.tw/~cjlin/libsvm/.
[2] https://www.cs.cornell.edu/people/tj/svm_light/svm_perf.html.

Table 1. Experimental data1 about computer science

Name of journal	# of papers
Journal of the ACM	1,217
VLDB Journal	617
ACM Transactions on Database Systems	776
IEEE Transactions on Knowledge and Data Engineering	2,436
Name of proceedings	# of papers
International Conference on Information and Knowledge Management	1,563
International Conference on Very Large Data Bases	854
Data Mining and Knowledge Discovery	466
European Conference on Research and Advanced Technology for Digital Libraries	424
International Conference on Asian Digital Libraries	438
International Conference on Data Engineering	2,225
IEEE International Conference on Data Mining	2,184
International Conference on Machine Learning	1,376
International Joint Conference on Artificial Intelligence	3,220
ACM IEEE International Conference on Digital Libraries	652
Pacific-Asia Conference on Knowledge Discovery and Data Mining	1,323
European Conference on Principles and Practice of Knowledge Discovery in Databases	1,027
SIAM International Conference on Data Mining	781
Annual International ACM SIGIR Conference on Research and Development in Information Retrieval	6,647
ACM International Conference on Knowledge Discovery and Data Mining	2,178
ACM International Conference on Management of Data	4,916
International Conference on Theory and Practice of Digital Libraries	201
International Conference on World Wide Web	3,245

Classification for DB_Bibliometrics. Figure 1 shows the classification performance with the regularization parameter C when classifying papers with given CC (Citation Count) in DB_Bibliometrics as positive. Of the many types of CC used for the calculation, 1, 10 and 100 are picked up and shown in the Fig. 1. A larger value of C enables stable classification. However, if the value of CC is large, classification is impossible regardless of the value of C.

On the basis of the above results, it can be seen that while the classification performance increases as the regularization parameter C increases, the

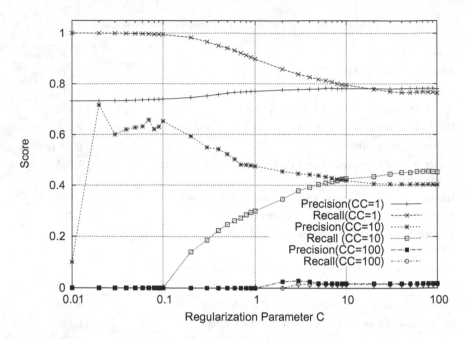

Fig. 1. Search of the regularization parameter for DB_Bibliometrics

classification performance rapidly decreases above a certain level. The relationship between the number of citations and the classification performance when $C = 10$, which seems to result in easier classification performance, is shown in Fig. 2. Although the classification performance is significant compared to the baseline (rate of positive: this is consistent with this line), it may be difficult to extract excellent papers with this classification performance.

Classification for DB_CS. Figure 3 shows the classification performance with the regularization parameter C when classifying papers with given CC (Citation Count) in DB_CS as positive. Of the many types of CC used for the calculation, 1, 10 and 100 are picked up and shown in the Fig. 3. A larger value of C enables stable classification. Regarding $CC = 10$ and $CC = 100$, there is a part where Precision goes down as C increases. However, since Recall is close to zero there, it is not a very good classification. Relatively around $C = 100$ is stable.

On the basis of the above results, we select $C = 100$, which seems to result in easier classification performance, and Fig. 4 shows the relation between the number of citations and the classification performance. Although this is also classified significantly compared with the baseline (rate of positive), it may be difficult to actually extract excellent papers with this classification performance.

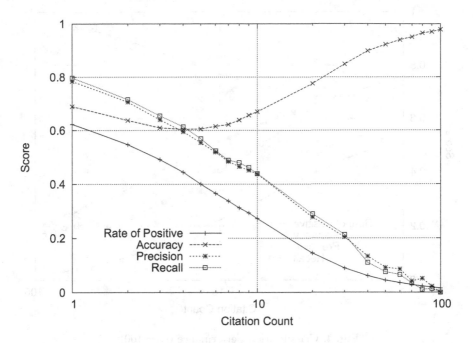

Fig. 2. Classification performance $(C = 10)$

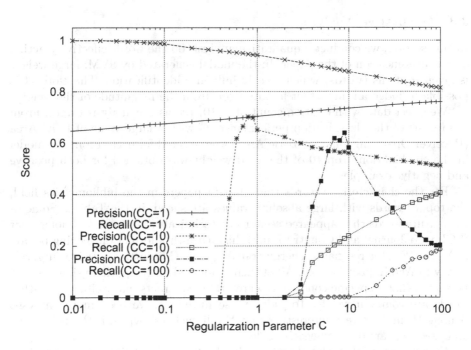

Fig. 3. Search of the regularization parameter for DB_CS

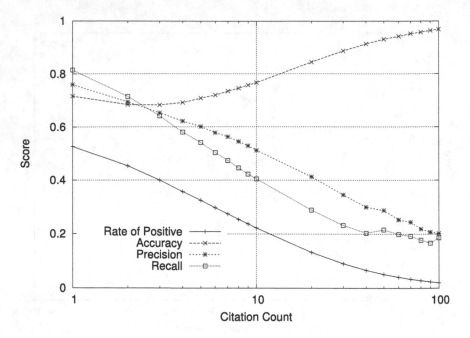

Fig. 4. Classification performance ($C = 100$)

3.3   Qualitative Analysis

In this section, we conduct a qualitative analysis on the words effectively acting on the classification of the paper. In the model generated by SVM, large weight is given to items (words) which greatly influence identification. Therefore, it is possible to judge an important feature word from the magnitude of the weight.

We select data with citation count of 1, 10, 100 as the analysis target. From the results of the classification performance, C with a large value of ROC Area (Receiver Operating Characteristic Area) was selected for each. From the model in the combination, Top 10 of the word weight was obtained for both positive and negative example.

For the characteristic words that classify papers in the bibliometrics field, the top 10 words with large absolute values are shown in the Table 2. Some of the feature words that appeared seem to be technical terms: nanotechnology, sjr (SCImago Journal and Country Rank), hisb (health information-seeking behavior), fret (Forster resonance energy transfer), mis (Minimally-invasive surgery), and wif (Web Impact Factor). All of them appeared on the positive side. It must be shown that a specific concrete research theme attracts many citations. Other words are common words. To judge these meanings, we need more analysis. Among them, it is very interesting that "bibliometrics" which is the field to be analyzed appears on the negative side.

Feature words that classify papers in the Computer Science field are similarly shown in the Table 3. More terms related to specialty appear here: imecho

Table 2. Feature Words for DB_Bibriometrics

CC	C	Polarity	Feature words
1	0.3	+	discuss, spain, terrorism, background, bias, basic, change, attempt, multiple, nature
1	0.3	−	bibliometrics, chinese, right, cooperation, cloud, hypertension, edit, literatures, reserve, imaging
10	0.2	+	nanotechnology, peer, site, percent, bias, illness, background, cocitation, firm, locate
10	0.2	−	bibliometrics, good, aim, education, secondary, mendeley, especially, hospital, big, explore
100	2	+	gs, sjr, hisb, innovative, fret, reconstruction, mis, actor, clear, wif
100	2	−	possible, accord, visibility, category, item, find, bibliometrics, importance, state, important

(a kind of search system), reproduction, yeast, clouddb, congruence, congruence, occf (One-Class Collaborative Filtering), kddcs (K-D tree based Data-Centric Storage), softrank, TAGME (a kind of system), TwitterRank, UMICs (upper-middle-income countries), MWEs (Mulberry water extracts), hilbert, vfdt (variance fractal dimension trajectory), edutella (a P2P network), diffsets, closegraph, sdms (Species distribution models), webml (Web Modeling Language), ordpath (a hierarchical labeling scheme). Many of these appear on the positive side, which seems to indicate that a specific concrete research theme attracts many citations. On the other hand, the negative side seems to contain a lot of sensuous words: noteworthy, metastories, reasonably, reformulate.

Table 3. Feature words for DB_CS

CC	C	Polarity	Feature words
1	60	+	imecho, reproduction, sbook, profitable, typology, yeast, clouddb, cap, holder, redescription
1	60	−	proceeding, copyright, eac, mwes, whilst, sampler, inewsbox, noteworthy, metastories, matrixnet
10	30	+	congruence, epic, illustration, occf, insecure, kddcs, softrank, selector, tagme, twitterrank
10	30	−	copyright, proceeding, γ, ga, reasonably, sampler, reformulate, compactly, bis, umics
100	20	+	acquisitional, hilbert, vfdt, edutella, diffsets, closegraph, splay, sdm, webml, ordpath
100	20	−	copyright, ssl, baseline, denote, historical, recursive, centers, immediate, piece, dnf

4   Related Work

There are many works aiming at research investigation. The citation count is useful for evaluating scientific research. Martin [7] reported that the citation count has gained support as a criterion. Kostoff [5] showed that the citation count as a measure of evaluation has some problems.

It is more appropriate to find related papers if we restrict the papers in a specific research area. Nakatoh et al. [10] proposed the focused citation count (FCC), which restricts the research area of the cited papers by keywords, and showed that more appropriate papers could be extracted.

Even with such examples of the use of the citation count as a measure of an paper's importance, it is not almighty. For example, it is not appropriate to use it as a measure to evaluate a new paper. Therefore, it is common to use an evaluation of the scientific journal in which the paper was published or the researcher who wrote the paper.

A journal's IF [1,3,6] is one of the most popular evaluation measures of scientific journals. Thomson Reuters updates and provides the scores of journals in the Journal Citation Reports every year. Hirsch [4] defined the h-index of a researcher as the largest number h such that the researcher wrote h papers and each of the papers is cited from h papers or more. Scopus provides the h-index score of researchers.

For the detection of appropriate journals, there are also studies that have conducted analyses focused on a research area. Nakatoh et al. [9] proposed a method for selecting appropriate journals by using the citation, which focuses on a specific field to evaluate a journal.

In this study, we attempted to determine the quality of a paper from only the information in the paper. Regarding the judgment of the quality of a paper, there are several studies using checklists [16–18]. However, creating a checklist for each field is a laborious task. Otani et al. [14] considered the important expressions that represent important sentences in scientific papers. Ashok et al. [13] pointed out that it is possible to identify successful novels by their style. These studies support the position of this research.

5   Conclusion

The investigation of related research is very important for research activities. The number of citations is commonly used as an index, but information about recently published papers cannot be obtained. In this study, we attempted to identify good papers using only the words included in the summary. After constructing a classifier utilizing machine learning and evaluating using the cross validation, it became clear that some degree of discrimination is possible.

On the other hand, the discrimination performance is low, and it is difficult to use it to extract papers that are good as it is. It is possible to improve the method using the words used for extraction. In addition, we are planning to evaluate a paper in combination with its other attributes.

Acknowledgement. This work was partially supported by JSPS KAKENHI Grant Number 24500176.

References

1. Garfield, E.: Citation indexes for science: a new dimension in documentation through association of ideas. Science **122**(3159), 108–111 (1955)
2. Garfield, E., Sher, I.H., Torpie, R.J.: The Use of Citation Data in Writing the History of Science. Institute for Scientific Information, Philadelphia (1964)
3. Garfield, E.: The history and meaning of the journal impact factor. J. Am. Med. Assoc. **295**(1), 90–93 (2006)
4. Hirsch, J.E.: An index to quantify an individual's scientific research output. Proc. Natl. Acad. Sci. USA **102**(46), 16569–16572 (2005)
5. Kostoff, R.N.: Performance measures for government-sponsored research: overview and background. Scientometrics **36**(3), 281–292 (1996)
6. Marshakova-Shaikevich, I.: The standard impact factor as an evaluation tool of science fields and scientific journals. Scientometrics **35**(2), 283–290 (1996)
7. Martin, B.R.: The use of multiple indicators in the assessment of basic research. Scientometrics **36**(3), 343–362 (1996)
8. Nakatoh, T., Hirokawa, S., Minami, T., Nanri, T., Funamori, M.: Assessing the significance of scholarly articles using their attributes. In: 22nd International Symposium on Artificial Life and Robotics (AROB 2017), pp. 742–746 (2017)
9. Nakatoh, T., Nakanishi, H., Hirokawa, S.: Journal impact factor revised with focused view. In: 7th KES International Conference on Intelligent Decision Technologies (KES-IDT 2015), pp. 471–481 (2015)
10. Nakatoh, T., Nakanishi, H., Baba, K., Hirokawa, S.: Focused citation count: a combined measure of relevancy and quality. In: IIAI 4th International Congress on Advanced Applied Informatics (IIAI AAI 2015), pp. 166–170 (2015)
11. Newman, M.E.J.: The structure of scientific collaboration networks. Proc. Natl. Acad. Sci. USA **98**(2), 404–409 (2001)
12. Wuchty, S., Jones, B.F., Uzzi, B.: The increasing dominance of teams in production of knowledge. Science **316**(5827), 1036–1039 (2007)
13. Ashok, V.G., Feng, S., Choi, Y.: Success with style: using writing style to predict the success of novels. In: 2013 Conference on Empirical Methods in Natural Language Processing, pp. 1753–1764 (2013)
14. Otani, S., Tomiura, Y.: Extraction of key expressions indicating the important sentence from article abstracts. In: IIAI 3rd International Conference on Advanced Applied Informatics, pp. 216–219 (2014)
15. Zahedi, Z., Costas, R., Wouters, P.: How well developed are altmetrics? A cross-disciplinary analysis of the presence of 'alternative metrics' in scientific publications. Scientometrics **101**(2), 1491–1513 (2014)
16. Schulte, J.: Publications on experimental physical methods to investigate ultra high dilutions – an assessment on quality. Homeopathy **104**(4), 311–315 (2015)
17. Zorin, N.A., Nemtsov, A.V., Kalinin, V.V.: Formalised assessment of publication quality in Russian psychiatry. Scientometrics **52**(2), 315–322 (2001)
18. Dasi, F., Navarro-García, M.M., Jiménez-Heredia, M., Magraner, J., Viña, J.R., Pallardó, F.V., Cervantes, A., Morcillo, E.: Evaluation of the quality of publications on randomized clinical trials using the Consolidated Standards of Reporting Trials (CONSORT) statement guidelines in a Spanish tertiary hospital. J. Clin. Pharmacol. **52**(7), 1106–1114 (2012)

A Web-Based User Interface for Machine Learning Analysis

Fatma Nasoz[1(✉)] and Chandani Shrestha[2]

[1] University of Nevada-Las Vegas, Las Vegas, NV, USA
fatma.nasoz@unlv.edu
[2] Microsoft, Seattle, WA, USA
chshrest@microsoft.com

Abstract. The purpose of this study is to develop a user-friendly web application that follows human computer interaction design guidelines and principles and is used to recognize patterns in datasets and to predict outputs of instances that it hasn't previously encountered. The application design follows human computer interaction design guidelines and principles and it employs supervised machine learning algorithms linear regression, logistic regression, and backpropagation for prediction. Java is used in the backend to create a model that maps the input and output data based on any of the machine learning algorithms while Play Framework and Bootstrap are used to display content in frontend. The application allows users to upload datasets that will be used to train and test the system. Each column of an uploaded dataset represents an attribute and each row represents an instance. The system is also developer friendly and allows changes be made to the source code for a more customized interaction.

Keywords: Machine learning · Classification · Regression · Web-based graphical user interface

1 Introduction

Machine learning systems are used to solve a variety of learning tasks [11]. For any given application, the main goal of machine learning is to build a model that represents and generalizes the training examples [7] and the performance of the model is measured by how well it generalizes when tested on new data.

In this study, we develop a web-based graphical user interface that allows its users to utilize machine learning algorithms to solve regression and classification problems. The supervised machine learning algorithms used to build the predictive models are linear regression [13], logistic regression [1], backpropagation [14].

This application can be used for classification problems like predicting whether a tumor with certain attributes is benign or malignant. In supervised machine learning techniques, each data instance used for training must have both input and output values, meaning all instances which are being used to train the machine learning model for breast tumor data have a set of features describing the tumor and an attribute stating if the tumor is cancerous or not.

© Springer International Publishing AG 2017
S. Yamamoto (Ed.): HIMI 2017, Part II, LNCS 10274, pp. 444–453, 2017.
DOI: 10.1007/978-3-319-58524-6_35

As for the interface, in the backend, Java is used to create a model that maps the input and output data based on any of the machine learning algorithms. In the frontend, Play Framework and Bootstrap are used to display content. Play Framework is chosen because it is based on web-friendly architecture. As a result, it uses predictable and minimal resources (CPU, memory, threads) for highly scalable applications. It is also developer friendly where changes can be made in the code and hitting the refresh button in browser will update the interface. Bootstrap is used to style the web application and it adds responsiveness to the interface with added feature of cross-browser compatible designs. Thus, the website has a responsive design and suitable for any device.

The interface design is guided by the "Eight Golden Rules of Interface Design" for improved universal usability [16]. The interface is more focused towards novice and intermediate users. Following are the list of implemented design rules:

- **Consistency:** Font size, color of text, button, input box size, alignment of content, background color, margin and organization of content is consistent. Similar sequence of actions is used to predict outcome in all machine learning algorithms. The flow of entering inputs and moving from one screen to the next page is also consistent throughout the application. Headers and footers are also consistent throughout.
- **Simple layout:** Contents in the application are short and descriptive so that users don't skip or get annoyed with lengthy information. A design is simple more appealing and loads faster as web application should give access to the information not abundance of information. Simple well organized display is used where left section of the interface shows stage of the application and right side shows information related to current stage of the application. Cluttered display of interface elements is also avoided.
- **Reduce short term memory load:** Users don't have to memorize steps to reach "Result" screen, which displays the predicted value. The progress towards prediction is displayed on the left side of each interface inside "Steps" section. Steps are listed in ascending order in which they will be executed. It informs users the step they are currently in, the previous step they completed, as well as the upcoming step.
- **Error prevention and error checking:** Each input box has a placeholder which gives user an idea of what kind of information needs to be entered there. Additionally, error checking is done to prevent users from submitting invalid information or missing required information.
- **Compatibility of data entry and data display:** The format of data entered as input to the application is compatible with the format of data displayed as output. On the "Result" screen the format of predicted value is similar to the format of value in the column representing dependent variable (output column) of data file.

Figure 1 shows the home screen of the application, which provides information on the functionality of the system. To see the available machine learning analysis options the users need to click the "Get Started" button and Fig. 2 displays the steps and available options.

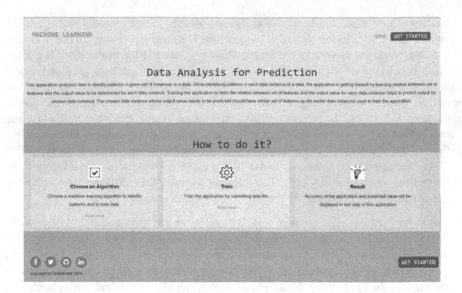

Fig. 1. Home screen

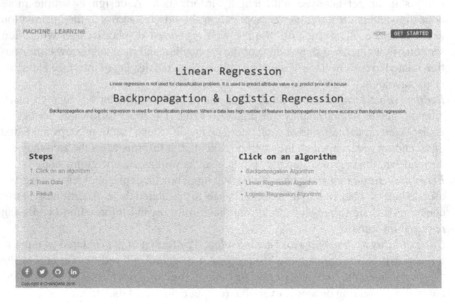

Fig. 2. Content displayed after clicking the "Get Started" button

Figure 3 displays the interface screen during data analysis with one of the algorithms. This screen allows the user to input the parameters for the chosen machine learning algorithm.

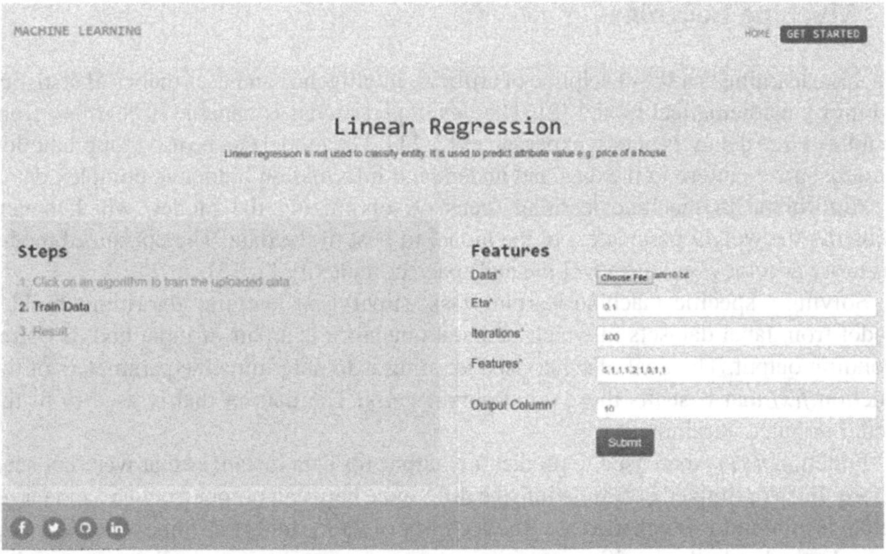

Fig. 3. Analyzing the data

2 Motivation

There are massive collections of data related to health [2, 10], business [3], education [2], etc. Each of these datasets has some patterns that can reveal cause of certain disease [15], cause of business failure [3], relation between customers and products [2, 3, 17], relationship between education and career opportunities [2], etc.

Machine learning helps to detect patterns and regularities and make good approximations or predictions. It is used in data analysis of retail, finance, credit application, fraud detection, stock market, medical data [2]. It is also used to process large datasets where it is not obvious how information is interrelated [6]. Similarly, neural networks are used to analyze imprecise, fuzzy, imperfect knowledge where there is a lack of mathematical algorithm to perform the analysis [8].

In order to serve the individual needs of individuals and organizations, there is a need to extract information from this huge volume of data sets in digital world [9]. There are many research studies conducted in machine learning and advanced desktop applications like MATLAB and SASS have been developed to detect patterns and predict outcome; however not all users have are trained in using the advanced methods and applications. The main of this study is to design and develop a web-based application that follows human computer interaction design guidelines and principles [16] and can learn patterns in the data and utilize these patterns to make prediction.

3   Machine Learning

Machine learning is a sub-discipline of artificial intelligence and uses theory of statistics to build a mathematical model [2]. The developed model is capable of learning from complex large data sets or past experiences [2, 11]. The model can be used for prediction or to visualize pattern in the data and understand information hidden in complex data.

Algorithms in machine learning focus on optimizing the model, which means adjusting the weight parameters of the model to best fit the data. The optimized model has more accuracy and has low time and space complexity [2, 15].

Solving a specific machine learning task, supervised learning algorithms build a model from label datasets in which each data instance is a pair of input and its corresponding output. The goal of supervised learning is to determine the parameters of the function $f(x)$ that best fits those input-output pairs. The dataset that is used to fit the model is called a training set.

Function $f(x)$ is then used to predict the output for data instances that were not seen before. In an optimized cost function, the difference between output from $f(x)$ and target output is minimum, which increases the accuracy of the system [12]. Supervised learning is used to solve both classification (i.e., output values are categorical) and regression (i.e., output values are continuous) problems. Three supervised learning algorithms (linear regression, logistic regression, and backpropagation) were implemented to be used with the interface. The models were optimized with gradient descent [11].

4   Results

The system application is tested using two different publicly available breast cancer data sets found at University of California, Irvine Machine Learning Repository.

4.1   Dataset with Nine Attributes

The properties of the first data set [4] are:

- Number of Instances: 699
- Number of Attributes: 9 (input features with values ranging 1–10: Clump Thickness, Uniformity of Cell Size, Uniformity of Cell Shape, Marginal Adhesion, Single Epithelial Cell Size, Bare Nuclei, Bland Chromatin, Normal Nucleoli Mitosis)
- Missing values: 16
- Class distribution: 458 Benign and 241 Malignant

  The data set is divided into three groups using k-fold method

- Training data is 80% of total data
- Cross validation is 10% of total data
- Test data is 10% of total data

  The models are tested on the test data with 70 instances (10% of the dataset) that have not been used to train the model. Table 1 shows the number of correctly predicted instances in both benign and malignant classes with logistic regression, which corresponds to an overall accuracy of 98.6%. Figures 4 and 5 show the interface screens during logistic regression training and prediction, respectively.

Table 1. Prediction accuracy with logistic regression on breast cancer data with 9 attributes

Class	Correctly predicted instances	Total instances
Benign	55	56
Malignant	14	14

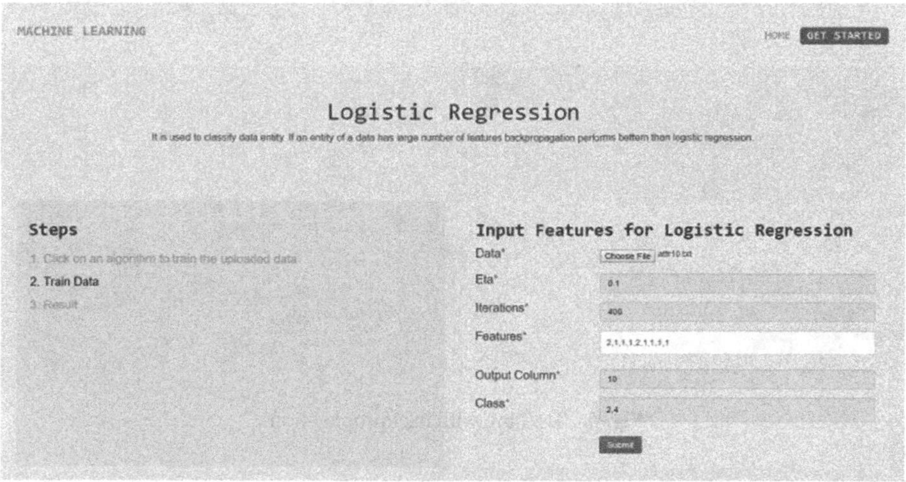

Fig. 4. Training with logistic regression

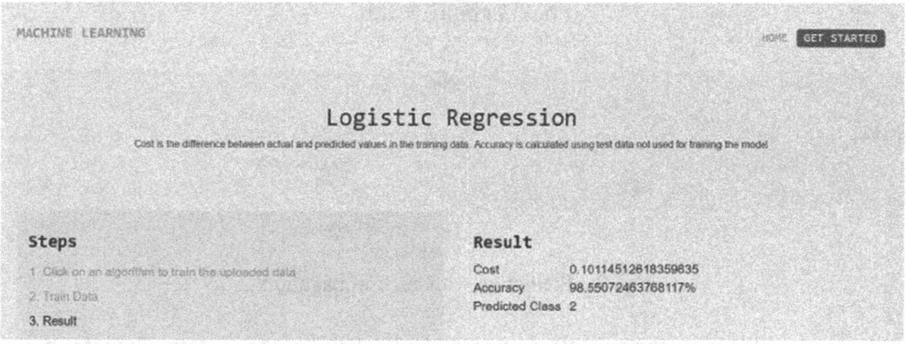

Fig. 5. Prediction with logistic regression

Table 2 shows the number of correctly predicted instances in both benign and malignant classes with backpropagation, which corresponds to an overall accuracy of 98.6%. Figures 6 and 7 show the interface screens during backpropagation training and prediction, respectively.

Table 2. Prediction accuracy with backpropagation on breast cancer data with 9 attributes

Class	Correctly predicted instances	Total instances
Benign	55	56
Malignant	14	14

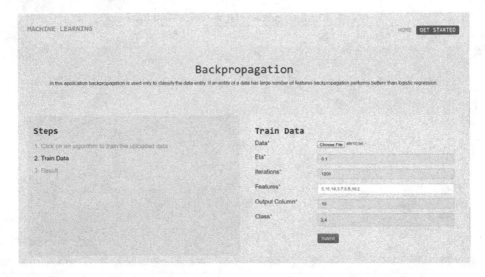

Fig. 6. Training with backpropagation

Fig. 7. Prediction with backpropagation

Users can also view the console section of the backend of the system when it is being trained. The console displays the decreasing value of cost in each iteration of gradient descent, as well as the number of correctly predicted benign and malignant data instances, and overall accuracy. Figure 8 shows the console during back analysis of breast cancer data with 9 attributes.

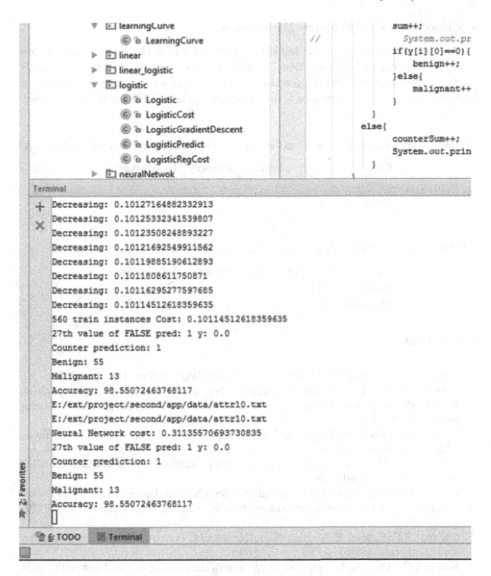

Fig. 8. Console view during training with backpropagation on breast cancer data with 9 attributes

4.2 Dataset with Thirty-One Attributes

The properties of the second data set [5] are:

- Number of instances: 569
- Number of attributes: 31
- 30 real value-valued input features: radius, texture, perimeter, area, smoothness, compactness, concavity, concave points, symmetry, fractal dimension, etc.
- Missing values: none

- Class distribution: 357 benign, 212 malignant

The models are tested on the test data with 57 instances (10% of the dataset) that have not been used to train the model. Tables 3 and 4 show the number of correctly predicted instances in both benign and malignant classes with logistic regression and backpropagation, which corresponds to overall accuracies of 91.2% and 75.4%, respectively.

Table 3. Prediction accuracy with logistic regression on breast cancer data with 31 attributes

Class	Correctly predicted instances	Total instances
Benign	39	44
Malignant	13	13

Table 4. Prediction accuracy with backpropagation on breast cancer data with 31 attributes

Class	Correctly predicted instances	Total instances
Benign	30	44
Malignant	13	13

References

1. Agresti, A.: Categorical Data Analysis, 3rd edn. John Wiley & Sons, Hoboken (2012)
2. Alpaydin, A.: Introduction to Machine Learning, 3rd edn. The MIT Press, Cambridge (2014)
3. Bose, I., Mahapatra, R.K.: Business data mining: a machine learning perspective. Inf. Manag. **39**(3), 211–225 (2001)
4. Breast Cancer Wisconsin (Diagnostic) Data Set. https://archive.ics.uci.edu/ml/datasets/Breast+Cancer+Wisconsin+(Original)
5. Breast Cancer Wisconsin (Original) Data Set. https://archive.ics.uci.edu/ml/datasets/Breast+Cancer+Wisconsin+(Diagnostic)
6. Chester, M.: Neural Networks: A Tutorial. Prentice-Hall, Inc., Upper Saddle River (1993)
7. Domingos, P.: A few useful things to know about machine learning. Commun. ACM **55**(10), 78–87 (2012)
8. Eberhart, R.C., Robbins, R.W. (eds.): Neural Network PC Tools: A Practical Guide. Academic Press, Cambridge (1990)
9. Kausnal, C., Arya, A., Pathania, S.: Integration of data mining in cloud computing. Adv. Comput. Sci. Inf. Technol. (ACSIT) **2**(7), 48–52 (2015)
10. Magoulas, G.D., Prentza, A.: Machine learning in medical applications. In: Paliouras, G., Karkaletsis, V., Spyropoulos, C.D. (eds.) ACAI 1999. LNCS (LNAI), vol. 2049, pp. 300–307. Springer, Heidelberg (2001). doi:10.1007/3-540-44673-7_19
11. Mitchell, T.M.: Machine Learning. McGraw-Hill, New York (1997)
12. Reed, R.D., Marks, R.J.: Neural Smithing: Supervised Learning in Feedforward Artificial Neural Networks. The MIT Press, Cambridge (1998)
13. Rencher, A.C., Christensen, W.F.: Methods of Multivariate Analysis, 3rd edn. John Wiley & Sons, Hoboken (2012)
14. Rumelhart, D.E., Hinton, G.E., Williams, R.J.: Learning representations by back-propagating errors. Nature **323**(6088), 533–536 (1986)

15. Sajda, P.: Machine learning for detection and diagnosis of disease. Annu. Rev. Biomed. Eng. **8**, 537–565 (2006)
16. Shneiderman, B., Plaisant, C., Cohen, M., Jacobs, S., Elmqvist, N., Diakopoulos, N.: Designing the User Interface: Strategies for Effective Human-Computer Interaction, 6th edn. Pearson, Hoboken (2016)
17. Witten, I.H., Frank, E.: Data Mining: Practical Machine Learning Tools and Techniques, 3rd edn. Morgan Kaufmann, Cambridge (2016)

On Modeling the Evolving Emotion on Literature

Tiffany Y. Tang[1(✉)] and Lotus Xinhe Zhou[2]

[1] Media Lab, Department of Computer Science, Wenzhou Kean University, Wenzhou, China
yatang@kean.edu
[2] Department of English, Wenzhou Kean University, Wenzhou, China
zhouxin@kean.edu

Abstract. A number of prior research have revealed that emotion and literature intertwine with each other during humans' reading experience. However, there have been yet still in dearth of research efforts in an attempt to understanding and modeling temporal emotional changes in literary texts which motivates this study. Through computerized mood emotion visualization, we are able to probe into he general emotional changes of a single character in literary texts. The research results adds to the richness of understanding of emotion changes in literature and provides directions for future development of computer algorithm in testing emotional dimensions in literature reading.

Keywords: Emotion · Literature · Analysis · Emotion lexicon · Experiment

1 Introduction and Background

In recent decades, research efforts on studying the relationships between literature and emotion, music and emotion are plentiful, at the same time numerous researches of emotional analysis of music and literature are theorized and applied in various fields, especially on in-class pedagogy and sentiment analysis of online social networks; music-generated computational algorithm like TransProse try to reproduce the same or least similar emotions contained in the selected literary text [4]; some edgy and innovative English literature or poetry courses in university try to bring music into classes as prelude of their literary readings, practicing the idea that the music contains the similar emotions as the literary text may involve students better in the comprehension of the text [5].

In this paper, we start by previewing the current research efforts on sentiment analysis and discuss the relationship between emotion and literature and how emotions function in literature. Then we bring up the conjecture that there might be possibilities for computer algorithms to visualize emotional changes in literature based on computer programming on an emotion lexicon. We describe the mechanism (the process of testing emotions changes in literary texts) and justify our selections. After that we present our testing results and draw conclusions on whether computer algorithm can perceive emotion changes in literary texts like human brains. Finally, we provide the limitation and scope of our research which are supposed to offer suggestions for future work.

© Springer International Publishing AG 2017
S. Yamamoto (Ed.): HIMI 2017, Part II, LNCS 10274, pp. 454–463, 2017.
DOI: 10.1007/978-3-319-58524-6_36

2   Related Work

2.1   Sentimental Analysis on the Social Networking Sites

Sentiment analysis of texts aiming at certifying attitudes of the speaker or the writer is prevalent for its ambidextrous applications, such as legal matters, business advertisements and government intelligence [2–4]. The texts deemed to have value for sentiment analysis varied from Twitter feeds [12], online news [12], diary-like blog posts [3] and fairy tales [1]. Reliable sentiment analysis requires not just the simple algorithms that categorize the scanned keywords as positive or negative, but more sophisticated filtering mechanisms that reaches parsing linguistic precision and allow the differentiation of irony, slang and idiomatic expressions [12]. Currently there have been many researchers and computer scientists designing different projects with the purpose of identifying emotions within texts using various sophisticated algorithms. For example, TSA (Twitter Sentiment Analysis) project functions as analyzing sentiments of any keyword across twitter and news reports from Google news, helping its users to determine the positive and negative reactions towards a particular keyword appearing in the tweets and news [12]. Another example would be Affect Analysis Model (an emotion recognition algorithm) designed based on the compositionality principle to recognize personal emotional state or sentiment conveyed through "informal messages written in an abbreviated or expressive manner" like "diary-like blog posts and fairy tales" [1]. However, these prior works all have their temporarily inextricable limitations that wait for future modification, including too much dependence on the emotion lexicon and data-mining bases and lack of contextual knowledge of the texts [1]. Identifying emotions changes occurring in literary texts are rare, which motivates our research.

2.2   Temporal Emotion Changes in the Process of Literature Reading

Reading literature is a splendid procedure during which emotion responses generated by readers towards the reading text become an indispensable consequence [8]. Even for pure music with mere melody and no lyrics such as piano pieces, happy or sad emotions may be evoked in a listener, strange as it seems and curious are researchers in finding out how human brains work to attach certain emotions to music pieces that are not substantial or concrete in seemingly any sense. Not to mention readers' emotional reactions towards literary texts which contain substantial words and sentences that convey more concrete emotions than melodies. Johnson et al. say that readers understand the text on the premise of understanding the writer's propositional contents and the appeal planted within the text, which implies that understanding the emotional environment built by the writer is essential to a reader's understanding of a literary text [7]. His team argues that any successful literary piece creates an emotional impact on its readers, and affirms that literature is an ideal case study for researchers to approach links between human brains mechanisms and emotional analysis in various ways [7].

Many papers have discussed the relationships between emotion and literature, mostly with a focus on the application of emotions that facilitate humans' understanding of literature. McGregor argues that teachers in junior high school reading classes may evolve the techniques of playing appropriate music to enhance students' understanding of the assigned poetry [9]. McGregor regards students' comprehension of the reading as inspirational task. One criterion to determine whether the inspirational task is achieved is whether the students sense the feelings and emotions revealed within the text. She holds that using music as a prelude to poetry reading will result in students' deeper understanding of that poetry, for that the carefully selected music will set the right mood and lead students into the circumstance of the poetry quickly [9].

Similarly, Bellver holds that the prevalent use of music in introductory literature class provides students with emotion within readings and unknowingly engages them in understanding the central idea of the readings, transcending the obstacles of the past and the unknown. She argues that music used as a pedagogical tool serves to underscore the emotion conveyed in literary treads and to spur students' interest in literature. There have been courses opened by professors on exploring emotions aroused in readers by English literature [2].

There have also university courses provided to teach students how emotions work in their appreciation of literature. A syllabus of an experimental course ENGL 680 in Kansas State University aims to show students functions of emotions in reading literature and how emotion conveyed in literature influence its readers [5]. Reading materials in the course extend from Aristotle to Darwin to the contemporary theories involving emotion theories in psychological and neurobiological area. More courses like this arise to form the trend of informing their students of ways to think of their reading behaviors with a focus on emotional feedbacks, yet researches in the field is in dearth.

2.3 How Emotion Functions During the Reading Experience

Robinson develops a theory of the composition/structure of emotion, and examine emotion's function in an interdisciplinary circumstance [11]. She holds that emotion is composed of an "affective appraisal" and a corresponding physiological arousal, followed by a cognitive appraisal, with all appraisals being non-cognitive (the appraisals occurred without awareness and extra efforts to further information processing) [11]. These appraisals potentially trigger physiological and behavioral responses, which continue to induce cognitive monitoring of the situation, pushing human brains to reassess the initial response made under non-cognitive state due to the circumstances and individual beliefs. This sets the foundation for her later argument that certain literature works need to be read emotionally in order to be understood. It also underscores the importance of cognitive monitoring to assess whether the brain performs its duty on feeling the "suitable" emotions for the text. Robinson backs up her philosophical opinions using psychological research results, saying that emotions are more of emotion processes than emotion states, and that through the process of reading literature, complex cognitions enable humans to react emotionally to the texts [11]. Robinson also holds that emotions are individuated by cognitions, saying that unlike other sentient creatures, humans are capable of applying complex cognitions to generate emotions based on personal interests and later feedbacks on the suitability of that emotion, and it's the humans' capability to use complex cognitions to constitute the initial stage of an emotion that allow them to be able to respond emotionally to literature [11]. Similarly, Hogan thinks that literature offers a unique insight on how emotions are produced and experienced by human beings [6]. By examining a list of highly esteemed literary works under the context of mainly neurobiological, psychological and sociological field, Hogan systemically interprets a series of emotions appearing in the texts—romantic love, grief, mirth, jealousy, compassion and so on, and how they function in human experiences in different ways due to individuality and personality of different people [6]. Hogan relates scientific research with complementary literary works on the function and structure of emotions, and brings new light on the field's research directions, indicting the possibility of exploring emotions in the interdisciplinary context [6].

Currently there are have been many theories developed of how emotions act during the process of reading and appreciating literary works, but few study emotion changes in literary texts, which have extensive applications in many multiply fields, such as pedagogy and creative writing. Doing research with a focus on emotional changes will help the exploration of the subject and facilitate its application process.

3 Our Approach at a Glance

3.1 Emotion Lexicon-Based Approach and Text Corpus

Following the protocols suggested in [10], we conduct the sentimental analysis based on the NRC's word-emotion association lexicon to test emotions indicated by words in the literary texts.

In this research, the chosen literary texts are two classic world literature pieces: *Oedipus the King* and *King Lear*. The former is an Athenian tragedy written by Sophocles around 5 BC, and the latter is a tragedy written by William Shakespeare. These two specific literary texts are chosen mainly because of two reasons: (1) These texts contain emotions that are currently considered operable by the algorithm during the first phase of testing, meaning that words in these texts be detected as emotional by the emotion lexicon, though there are more sophisticated emotions such as nostalgia, jealousy, and disappointment that cannot be captured or interpreted by the algorithm; (2) We have a relatively controlled understanding and interpretation of the themes and emotions conveyed within the texts. What's worth attention is that we read these texts based on a contextualized and well-informed literature background of that certain piece of literature, and widely accepted interpretations and criticisms were involved during the learning process. As a result, our feedbacks on these literary texts can be consolidated. This added both convenience and disadvantages to our research, thus validating the professionalism and universality of literary texts we choose, meanwhile the research results may appear to be coincidental due to the influence of the standardized teaching of these texts. This is one of the limitations of our research and it needs to be considered in future work [5].

3.2 Detecting Emotion in Texts: The Algorithm

We used the NRC Emotional Lexicon to test general emotions and potential emotion changes in the selected literary texts [10]. We divide each text into different parts in two ways: in the first approach, we divide the text by words said by each character, part 1 contains all the paragraphs said by the first character appear in the text, part 2 contains all the paragraphs said by the second character, the rest of the text is disposed in the same manner; in the second approach, we pick out a particular character with obvious emotional change throughout the text using human emotional judgements, respectively *Oedipus the King* and *King Lear*, and then divide all the paragraphs he says once at a time during his conversation with other characters. By the second approach, we hope to find anastomosis between the results produced by the computer algorithm and produced by human brains.

After collecting the results of algorithm, we manually attempted to analyze the results through a human expert, and then compared it to the results produced by the algorithm.

4   The Temporal Emotion Trend in Texts: Data Visualization

4.1   General Findings

Figures 1, 2, 3 and 4 show the general findings on one of the literature text, the King Lear, including its main character (Fig. 3) and the evolving emotional trend in the text (Fig. 4).

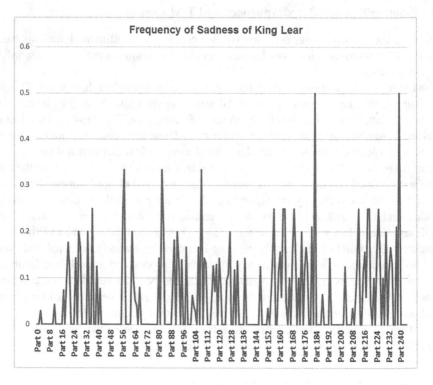

Fig. 1. Frequency changes of sadness in the character King Lear

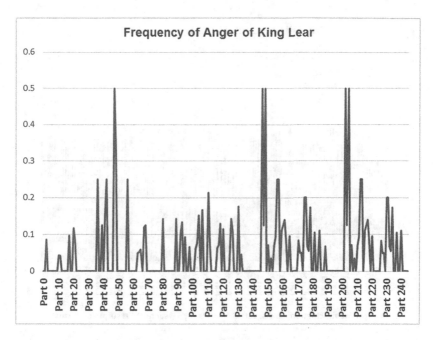

Fig. 2. Frequency changes of anger in the character King Lear

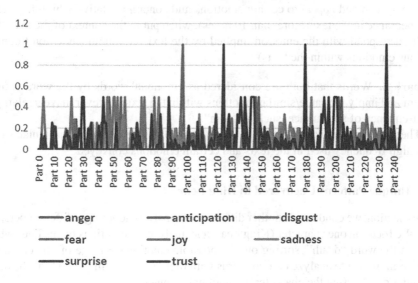

Fig. 3. Overall emotion changes of the character King Lear

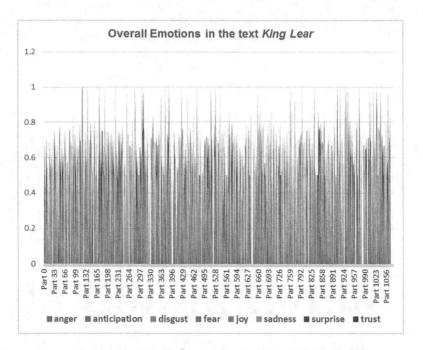

Fig. 4. Overall emotion changes of the character King Lear

Remark 1. Words like "evil" that both are considered as emotional words by the word lexicon system and appeal to certain emotions and contain a relatively high frequency of appearance in the text (more than 10 times), when put in the context of the text, they don't correspond with the emotion implied by the lexicon system (they don't convey obvious emotions within the texts).

Remark 2. Words that both are considered as emotional words by the word lexicon system and imply the same/similar emotions within the text, however, have a relatively low frequency of appearance, such as "pain".

Therefore, it's unlikely that there is necessary links between the particular words with high frequency used in the texts and certain emotions conveyed.

4.2 Unique Patterns Uncovered in King Lear

In this section, we conducted another different test analysis adopting a different perspective. We focus on one character (King Lear) and analyze his emotions by his lines which contain the word "death", sorting out the possible emotional change of this character. In general, we try to analyze certain words with high frequency in the text that have the potential of reflecting the character's emotional changes.

Throughout the whole tragedy, King Lear goes through a drastic change of fate and living, his power and kingship being deprived by his two daughters, his mental state goes from high-spiritedness to madness, in the end he is too sad for his stupidity and loss of his youngest daughter that he dies. Throughout the play, Lear's emotions in general changes from excessively high-spiritedness (happiness) to sadness and depressiveness. This emotion change can be reflected by his wording that containing the word "death", which goes from anticipation to excessive anger to eventual sadness. Therefore, there contains certain connections between emotion changes of the character with certain words used in the text that perceived as emotional by the emotion lexicon.

Despite a few differences, our judgement largely coincides with the result produced by the emotion lexicon. The emotions changes of the character King Lear can be reflected in both our manual reading tests and our approach. Both the human reader and the lexicon are able to test the emotional changes of the character. However, the way the human reader and the lexicon work on producing feedback on the literary text are different. The former reads the text and interprets the emotions of the character based on the work of human brains mechanisms, and he makes connections among changes of plot and the phrase used by the character. In comparison, the emotion lexicon produces the test result based on the designed running algorithm, and the process involves no sentient emotional analysis. It's the researchers who compare the results produced by the two and claims the similarities and differences.

5 Discussions

5.1 General Findings

In both texts, the following observations were made:

1. Words like "evil" that both are considered as emotional words by the word lexicon system and appeal to certain emotions and contain a relatively high frequency of appearance in the text (more than 10 times), when put in the context of the text, they don't correspond with the emotion implied by the lexicon system (they don't convey obvious emotions within the texts).
2. Words that both are considered as emotional words by the word lexicon system and imply the same/similar emotions within the text, however, have a relatively low frequency of appearance, such as "pain".
3. Therefore, it's unlikely that there is necessary links between the particular words with high frequency used in the texts and certain emotions conveyed.

5.2 Limitation of the Use of the Emotion Lexicon in Detecting Emotion

Firstly, the emotion lexicon cannot test the frequency of each word appear in the separated sections of the text. Because of this, designing the method using which to test emotion changes throughout the text can be difficult.

Secondly, common words like "home", "king", "wife" that don't have emotional implications yet with high frequency of appearing in the text are collected by the lexicon, while words that appeal to certain emotions like "pity", "wreck", "bloody", "deadly", "evil", "cruel", "grief", "guilt" and "terror" "murderous", "slaughter", "slayer", "distress", "violent", "defy" and "disease" have relatively low frequency of appearance in the text (less than ten times) aren't emphasized on by the lexicon, which makes it hard to find necessary link between the particular words used in the texts and certain emotions conveyed.

6   Limitations of Our Study

Human beings are subjective, and individual perceptions towards which emotion is conveyed with most frequency and emotion changes within the text inevitably differ from one another. Therefore, what students personally think of the texts more or less differ from the standard/mainstream thoughts, the thoughts produced by their professors or the textbooks.

During the research, we ask the students to choose one out of five kinds of emotions based on what they learned from their literature classes. In a word, students who attach the emotions to the texts may be influenced by their professors or the prevalent public thoughts. It is one limitation of our research, that there are not enough students who have the autonomy or authority to judge whether the emotions contained within the piano pieces is corresponding to that conveyed within the texts based on their personal opinions. Future work may be conducted in consideration of how to resolve this concern.

English is an ever-changing language with new words and phrases constantly added into its lexicon. It's obvious that Old English, contextualized in this research Elizabethan language used to write King Lear by William Shakespeare differed greatly from English we use today, English translation of Oedipus the King tend to adopt a traditional English style of using English. Therefore, emotion(s) evoked by a word in old English also differed from that of the same word in today's English. The emotion lexicon used are programmed by today's computer science researchers, as a result, putting old English texts through a modern-programmed emotion lexicon seems to produce inaccurate outcomes, which future researchers may take into consideration. Future research may consider creating an Old English lexicon to more accurately test the research result.

7   Concluding Remarks

Prior research focus on theorizing the relationships between literature and emotion, in both algorithmic and literary approaches, and on putting theories into practice, applying emotions conveyed in the literary texts into numerous fields especially pedagogy and sentiment analysis for online social media. However, few researchers aim to test the efficiency of current inventions that aim to humanize computer algorithms and endow them with humans' sensibility and perceptions. This paper examines the potential of emotion lexical-based approach in testing the overall emotions and emotion changes of certain characters in literary texts through a series of testing. Future works will expand the genres of literary texts being tested using the emotion lexicons.

Acknowledgments. We thank all the volunteers who participated in the research process. Thanks also go to Relic Yongfu Wang for his generous help in designing the computer algorithm to run the emotion lexicon and his valuable insights in the design of the testing.

References

1. Alm, C.O., Sproat, R.: Emotional sequencing and development in fairy tales. In: Tao, J., Tan, T., Picard, R.W. (eds.) ACII 2005. LNCS, vol. 3784, pp. 668–674. Springer, Heidelberg (2005). doi:10.1007/11573548_86
2. Bellver, C.G.: Music as hook in the literature classroom. Hispania **91**(4), 887–896 (2008)
3. Pang, B., Lee, L.: Opinion mining and sentiment analysis. Found. Trends Inf. Retrieval **2**(1–2), 1–135 (2008)
4. Hannah, D., Mohammad, M.S.: Generating music from literature (2014). arXiv preprint: arXiv:1403.2124
5. Gregory, E.: Topics in American Literature: Emotion and American Literature (2014). http://www.k-state.edu/english/eiselei/engl680/. Accessed 17 May 2015
6. Colm, H.P.: What Literature Teaches Us about Emotion (2011). http://www.cambridge.org/us/academic/subjects/psychology/cognition/what-literature-teaches-us-about-emotion?format=HB. Accessed 17 May 2015
7. Johnson-Laird, P.N., Oatley, K.: Emotions, music and literature. In: Michael, L., Haviland-Jones, J.M., Feldman Barrett, L. (eds.) Handbook of Emotions, 3rd edn., pp. 102–113. The Guilford Press (2010)
8. Lewis, M., Haviland-Jones, M.J., Feldman Barrett, F.L.: Handbook of Emotions. The Guilford Press (2008)
9. Laura, M.A.: A lesson series: the correlation of music and literature. Engl. J. **13**(7), 489–493 (1924)
10. Mohammad, S.M., Turney, P.D.: NRC Emotion Lexicon. NRC Technical report (2015). http://www.saifmohammad.com/WebPages/ResearchInterests.html. Accessed 17 May 2015
11. James, H.: Review of Jenefer Robinson's book Deeper Than Reason: Emotion and Its Role in Literature, Music, and Art (2007). https://ndpr.nd.edu/news/25307-deeper-than-reason-emotion-and-its-role-in-literature-music-and-art/. Accessed 17 May 2015
12. Sureka, R., Kaushik, G., Patira, S.: Twitter Sentiment Analysis (2014). https://wiki.cc.gatech.edu/designcomp/images/2/2c/Twitter_Sentiment_Report.pdf. Accessed 17 May 2015

Supporting Collaboration and User Communities

User Experience (UX) of a Big Data Infrastructure

Hashim Iqbal Chunpir[1,2,3(✉)], Dean Williams[4], and Thomas Ludwig[2,3]

[1] Department of Computer Science, Federal University of São Carlos, São Paulo, SP, Brazil
[2] Faculty of Informatics, University of Hamburg, Vogt-Kölln-Straße 30, Hamburg, Germany
[3] German Climate Computing Centre (DKRZ), Bundesstr. 45a, Hamburg, Germany
{chunpir,ludwig}@dkrz.de
[4] Lawrence Livermore National Laboratory, Livermore, CA, USA
williams13@llnl.gov

Abstract. Earth System Grid Federation (ESGF), a well-known e-infrastructure provides open data to study the future anthropogenic climate change. Data are accessed by the research communities to produce sophisticated simulations of the Earth system. This study is based on the survey questionnaire taken by 357 researchers (end-users) who interact with the interfaces provided by ESGF e-infrastructure. Despite the evolution as well as development in the components, applications and user interfaces provided by the e-Science infrastructure, the barriers exist and they limit and delay the research process of scientists while they interact with the e-infrastructure. Hence, the full benefit of the terabytes of data projects hosted by the e-infrastructure is not realized. This study suggests a dire need to do improvements in the e-infrastructure particularly in the human computer interaction (HCI) components such as user interfaces of applications, webpages, ingestion of/access to large volumes of scientific data, collaborative tools, web documentation and others. If these improvements are made the user's research process using an e-infrastructure will be quadrupled and due to better researchers' experience using e-infrastructures e-research can thrive. Thus, bringing in timely research results and scientific discoveries.

Keywords: User experience (UX) · Big data · Open data · e-Science infrastructure · Cyber-infrastructure · Virtual research environment (VRE) · Collaboratory · Open science

1 Introduction

Users need an interface to access e-Science resources usually data and computation power. It is essential to know how the e-infrastructures are really used and who the users are. While there can be thousands of users of an e-infrastructure, the users who use e-infrastructure extensively can be very few [1]. The interface to access e-Science resources includes command line tools, web portals and User Interfaces (UIs) to access data assets; hosted by an e-infrastructure. These interfaces provided by an e-infrastructure are the key gateways to perform e-Science operations such as: Creating data, collecting, storing data, sharing data, publishing data, searching data sets, visualizing data and processing data. The UIs of e-infrastructure are designed, developed by the developers and designers.

© Springer International Publishing AG 2017
S. Yamamoto (Ed.): HIMI 2017, Part II, LNCS 10274, pp. 467–474, 2017.
DOI: 10.1007/978-3-319-58524-6_37

This study explores the interaction and the User eXperience (UX) of users of an e-Science infrastructure: Earth System Grid Federation (ESGF) [2, 3]. ESGF is a global climate e-Science infrastructure that offers climate data projects, computing and visualization facilities to climate scientists. ESGF is currently also being extended to serve other domains such as biology, chemistry and astronomy. The UI of e-Science infrastructures in general have not been adequately researched [4] and there is hardly any study that points at the UX of e-Science and especially in the domain of climate science. These UIs of e-Science infrastructures, however, play a central role for the success of e-Science as e-Science is considered a new paradigm in doing research and helps to fulfill the Science 2.0 vision. Science 2.0 is a term under which more collaboration amongst scientists using technology, especially Web 2.0 technologies is expected; as opposed to traditional laboratory science which is termed as Science 1.0.

This study shows that the end-users of ESGF experience problems with the UIs and HCI components to get the needed data and information via web documentation. Therefore, they send requests to the user support centre or help desk in a hope to get their problems solved. Consequently, offering a better UX and establishing an efficient support in a wider scope are one of the major challenges to be dealt with to make e-Science an established significant scientific method in the highly digitalized and open data society of the 21st Century. This paper evaluates the UX and usability of UI of the applications offered by ESGF e-Science infrastructure and highlights the parts of infrastructure and applications that need further enhancement.

This paper is structured as follows: In the Sect. 2 the background of the context and terminologies of e-Science, UI and UX is provided. Also in this section an overview of related work to the research question is given. Subsequently the research steps taken to generate recommendation are explained in Sect. 3. The results of this research study are then shown and explained in Sect. 4. Future work and conclusion are elaborated in Sect. 5 and Sect. 6, respectively.

2 Background and Related Work

Access to big data of scientific nature to enable e-research is conducted via e-Science infrastructures that are deployed to access and share the data, high performance computing (HPC) facilities and human resources to facilitate interdisciplinary and interdisciplinary research to harvest knowledge [2, 3, 5–7]. Users need an interface to access its resources usually data. The interface includes command line tools, web portals and Graphical User Interface (GUI) to access data assets which are the main resources hosted [8]. However, during an interaction of a user with an e-Science infrastructure, a user may require help due to outages of some resources e.g. servers or any other anomaly and even difficult user interfaces. In other case: a user requires particular scientific or technical information [1]. In order to meet these user challenges, e-Science infrastructures also known as cyber-infrastructures (CI) or virtual research environments (VREs) offer UIs and user support in the form of a help-desk, which have not received adequate attention to include users' point of view since the inception of cyber-infrastructures [9].

Nevertheless, the aspect of interaction with UI of an e-Science infrastructure is not limited to the end-users. Indeed, it has been observed that also other stakeholders, e.g. data publishers, data curators, need better UI of tools and applications to properly publish data and make it accessible the users of an e-Science infrastructure [3, 10–12]. Moreover, e-Science infrastructure is mostly a decentralized structure of multiple organizations as well as data centers worldwide and there are diverse users with diverse needs interested in doing e-research at multiple sites world-wide [5, 13]. The users and employees of research laboratories and data centers such as Lawrence Livermore National Laboratory (LLNL), the German Climate Computing Centre (DKRZ), British Atmospheric Data Centre (BADC), Jet Propulsion Laboratory (NASA-JPL) and other are generally scientists and they contribute towards publishing big data on one hand and on the other they use it [5, 10]. All these facts lead to the motivation to study the current UX, UI and other related areas in the domains of cyber-infrastructures.

In this study we take Earth System Grid Federation (ESGF) as a use case in the form of a single case study. ESGF is an important open data infrastructure in the field of climate science. ESGF facilitates to study climate change and impact of climate change on human society and Earth's eco-system [14]. In the case study of ESGF, it was previously felt that the UIs and tools to support users including the user support process and information on the web documentation to guide users of a distributed, multi-organizational research-oriented, non-commercial, collaborative environment needs an overhaul [3]. Consequently, new UI called CoG was suggested and implemented. Moreover, suggestions were also made to improve the user support process and Federated e-Science User Support Enhancement (FeUSE) framework was suggested [3, 15]. Better the user experience (UX) of the tools offered by ESGF, better the GUI and more productive can be the e-research environment that can lead to the boom.

There are many books as well as articles that provide guidelines to design an effective Graphical User Interface (GUI) in order to enhance the user experience and the usability e.g. [16–18]. A study about the guidelines to provide reliable information for users, displayed on the UI is found in [19] and significance of line length for tablet PC users is found in [20]. However, it is not known that whether these guidelines have been applied to the UIs of e-Science infrastructures that serve big data to a wide variety of users. Systematic evaluation of e-infrastructure UIs are needed to be done. There is hardly any study that discussed the UX of e-Science UIs previously. Nonetheless, former studies relevant to UX in e-Science and other issues pertaining particularly to ESGF are: The study about the governance scheme of ESGF [6, 21], the user support process of ESGF was thoroughly examined [2, 3, 10, 11, 15], the evaluation of the user support unit i.e. helpdesk process [8], the user interface of the tools used by the help desk unit [22], the model tasks can be coordinated, prioritized and accomplished [20], the visualization challenges of ecosystems [7] and others. The state of the art on the current challenges in the field of open data and e-infrastructures are indicated by [14]. The problems with the web documentation for seeking relevant information on the web are also common. Moreover, apart from better usability, User experience (UX), the possibilities of UI customization, UI as well as software extension, and collaboration features amongst users of e-Science infrastructures are very important in choosing the suitable UI.

In the last decade, the UIs as well as user-support in ESGF has been evolving mainly due to the changes in the governance scheme and technology employed by ESGF cyber-infrastructure. For instance, looking at the history of ESGF development, due to the technological cum organizational changes and especially the introduction of new data projects served by the ESGF data archive system, the number of users and their new types of needs as well as requirements have been on the constant upsurge. The technology and its use can affect the business model, service orientation and the policies of organizations [23] and this is true for e-Science infrastructures as well. Consequently, up until now the employees of ESGF are designing and developing the UIs, on a free will basis. This survey questionnaire conducted revealed number of issues especially related to UX and UIs.

3   Research Methods

An online survey of data providers and consumers supported by ESGF was conducted in December 2016. The intent of the survey was to provide the ESGF community of developers with anonymous feedback about how ESGF can improve its core services and to ascertain what scientists believe is the greatest strengths and weaknesses of the ESGF enterprise. The Executive Committee (EC) distributed the survey via mailing lists associated with ESGF projects, resulting in a representative sampling of geographically and topically diverse responders. Descriptive results from the global survey attempt to shed light on the data needs of national and international projects. Action items generated from the survey results are intended to bridge the gap between short and long term development and operations.

For this survey, the request for feedback went out to: (1) several World Climate Research Programme (WCRP)-endorsed Model Intercomparison Projects (MIPs) including Coupled Model Intercomparison Project (CMIP), the Atmospheric Model Intercomparison Project (AMIP), and Input for Model Intercomparison Project (Input4MIPs); (2) Coordinated Regional Climate Downscaling Experiment (CORDEX); (3) the NASA-led Observations for Model Intercomparisons (Obs4MIPs); (4) the Accelerated Climate Modeling for Energy (ACME) project; and (5) the Collaborative RE-Analysis Technical Environment Intercomparison Project (CREATE-IP). Most questions asked researchers to rate their need for a specific support or service on a six point Likert scale i.e. scale from 1 to 6; 1 indicated little or no interest, while 6 indicated high interest or need. Other questions required yes or no responses. The survey also presented open-ended questions. Weighted average values were calculated for each question across all responses (e.g., a value of 4.54 for a particular topic would indicate that most participants for that question would rate the topic as being of high or very high interest). Also calculated was the percentage of participants that gave a topic a particular rank (e.g., 37% ranks as a very high response). Merging the weighted average with the percentage of responses gave yet another perspective on the value of the survey response (e.g., 1.49 constitutes a very high community interest, taking into consideration the combined weighted average and the percentage of participants).

4 Results and Discussion

Respondents were asked to identify themselves as a data provider, data consumer, or both. The survey also asked the respondents to best describe their profession (e.g., undergraduate or graduate student, postdoctoral scholar, academic scientist, governmental scientist, or other) and type of affiliation (e.g., governmental agency, university and the private sector). Results show that Linux was the most commonly used platform among the respondents, followed by Windows and Mac OSX.

The bulk of the survey consisted of 42 questions listed under several subcategories that asked respondents to rate the importance of the service or tool. These subcategories included:

- User interface (UI) (websites, CoG)
- Ingestion of and access to large volumes of scientific data (i.e., from data archive to supercomputer and server-side analysis)
- Web documentation
- Improved UI designs and principles to enable easier access to computer and software capabilities (e.g., recommendation systems, more flexible and interactive interfaces)
- Distributed global search
- Unified data discovery for all ESGF data sources to support research.
- Quality control (QC) algorithms for data
- Reliability and resilience of resource
- Data access and usage
- Remote computing capability
- Data transport
- QC issues

The first step in evaluating the responses was to list the subcategories in terms of need on a scale of 1 to 6:

- 10 of the subcategories earned an average response rating of 4.1 or higher.
- 17 earned between 4.1 and 3.7.
- Remaining responses earned less than 3.6.

This spread indicates that ESGF users have diverse needs and priorities. Roughly 40% of responses with a combined weighted score of 1.49 indicated that *the ESGF UI also known as CoG (*www.earthsystemcog.org*) was the most difficult feature to use and needs improvement*. About 35% of responses, with a combined weighted score of 1.46, pointed to *the need for sufficient access to large volumes of data with computational resources for server-side (i.e., remote) analysis and visualization*. Also notable at a combined weighted score of 1.46 was *the emphasis on better, more reliable online documentation*. Related to these changes, *respondents requested an environment that supports more effective collaboration and sharing within and between science teams (e.g., collaborative tools)*, at a combined weighted score of 1.11. Of relevance to efforts to design a more integrated data and computing infrastructure was the finding that *most respondents access data and compute resources via web interfaces or remote login along with application programming interfaces (APIs)*.

The question identified as the area of greatest need overall was "How important is knowledge gathering, managing, and sharing?" All questions in this category were rated less than 4.06 but higher than 3.8; no other category had such a high average. The topics included:

- Direct data delivery into ESGF computing systems from distributed data resources —3.99/27.7%.
- Data sharing—3.96/27.99%.
- Web documentation—3.89/37.61%.
- Data publishing (long-tail publishing for individual scientists)—3.89/27.41%.
- QC algorithms for data—3.86/32.07%.
- Ancillary data products (e.g., data plots, statistical summaries)—3.84/30.32%.

A question raising significant interest among the survey participants was "How good are human-computer interactions?" Respondents identified collaborative environments, in particular, as a key requirement (3.63). The new ESGF mandate regarding data management and sharing clearly has penetrated the community and raises questions for many, as evident by high scores for several related survey topics:

- Easy way to publish and archive data using one of the ESGF data centers— 3.89/27.41%.
- User support for data access and download—4.21/29.45%.
- Access to enough computational and storage resources—3.89/28.96%.

5   Future Work

From the results of this study further research directions in future for the enterprises and big data infrastructures based on fog, cloud and grid computing can be guided by a significant research objective that is how users' view can be incorporated in the design and development of the components, application, processes and interfaces of e-infrastructures. The survey conducted in this study was instrumental in providing users' feedback to guide software developers to let them know that what they need. The detailed analysis report of the results of this survey is marked as a future work, which will be published in future. It is recommended by other e-Science initiatives to conduct users' survey at regular intervals to gauge the usability and UX of e-infrastructures to provide better services to users.

Additionally, it is proposed to focus on encouraging and persuading users of big data infrastructures to participate in the design, development and evolution of the applications related to data infrastructures and the underlying processes in the future research. Furthermore, it is an interesting aspect to study that how the software designers and developers especially people who design UIs of design interfaces and other components of software are currently meeting users' requirements in order to allow users to interact with applications without any trouble. And how it can be done better. The process of development of software and interfaces, whether related to e-Science or not, needs to incorporate user's point of view in the form that the developers can address users' UI requirements. Since there are different types of users in e-Science it is important to consider all groups of users

[3]. Most of the stakeholders e.g. in e-Science and ICT infrastructures include data scientists, data curators, computer scientists, domain experts, managers and most importantly interface designers as well as software engineers, who can provide input to enable better usability to the users.

6   Conclusion

In this study users' survey was applied to observe the user experience (UX) in a federated e-Science environment of the climate science domain. It was observed that the features regarding HCI, UI of ESGF applications and web documentation need further improvement in order to enhance user experience. In this direction, the documentation is needed to be updated regularly, made reliable and accessible to all types of users. Furthermore, ingestion of large volumes of scientific data and access to large volumes of scientific data (i.e., from data archive to supercomputer and server-side analysis) need to be improved. The respondents also indicated the need of an environment that supports more effective collaboration and sharing within and between science teams (e.g., collaborative tools). In essence, the concepts of service orientation and meeting user's needs should be incorporated in the business models of big data enterprises particularly governmental e-Science facilities.

Acknowledgement. We appreciate the sincere participation and support of the ESGF colleagues and the users of ESGF in the survey. We also acknowledge the contribution of members of the executive committee of ESGF such as Luca Cinquini, Dan Duffy, Sandro Fiorre, Alexandra Nuzzo, Sebastian Denvil, Michael Lautenschlager and other colleagues in distributing the survey and analyzing the results.

References

1. Freeman, P.A.: Is it possible to define cyberinfrastructure? First Monday **6**(12) (2007)
2. Chunpir, H.I., Ludwig, T., Curri, E.: Improving processes for user support in e-Science. In: IEEE 10th International Conference on e-Science (e-Science), vol. 2, pp. 87–90 (2014)
3. Chunpir, H.I.: Enhancing User Support Process in Federated e-Science. University of Hamburg (2015)
4. Xie, M., Bodenheimer, B.T.M.: Interface design for a modern software ticketing system. In: Proceedings of the 42nd Annual Southeast Regional Conference, pp. 122–127 (2004)
5. Chunpir, H.I., Ludwig, T., Williams, Dean N.: Evolution of e-Research: from infrastructure development to service orientation. In: Marcus, A. (ed.) DUXU 2015, Part III. LNCS, vol. 9188, pp. 25–35. Springer, Cham (2015). doi:10.1007/978-3-319-20889-3_3
6. Chunpir, H.I., Ludwig, T.: Reviewing the governance structure of end-user support in e-Science infrastructures. In: Informatik 2014 Proceedings of Mastering Big Data Complexity. Lecture Notes in Informatics (LNI), vol. 232 (2014)
7. Chunpir, H., Moll, A.: Analysis of marine ecosystems: usability, visualization and community collaboration challenges. Procedia Manuf. **3**, 3262–3265 (2015)
8. Chunpir, H.I., Rathmann, T., Ludwig, T.: The need for a tool to support users of e-Science infrastructures in a virtual laboratory environment. Procedia Manuf. **3**, 3375–3382 (2015)

9. Soehner, C., Steeves, C., Ward, J.: e-Science and Data Support Services, Washington, DC, USA (2010)
10. Chunpir, H.I., Ludwig, T., Badewi, A.: A snap-shot of user support services in Earth System Grid Federation (ESGF): a use case of climate cyber-infrastructures. In: Proceedings of the 5th Applied Human Factors and Ergonomics (AHFE) Conference, July 2014
11. Chunpir, H.I., Ludwig, T., Badewi, A.A.: Using soft systems methodology (SSM) in understanding current user-support scenario in the climate science domain of cyber-infrastructures. In: Marcus, A. (ed.) DUXU 2014, Part III. LNCS, vol. 8519, pp. 495–506. Springer, Cham (2014). doi:10.1007/978-3-319-07635-5_48
12. Chunpir, H.I.: Prioritizing tasks using user-support-worker's activity model (USWAM). In: Yamamoto, S. (ed.) HIMI 2016. LNCS, vol. 9735, pp. 379–390. Springer, Cham (2016). doi: 10.1007/978-3-319-40397-7_36
13. Chunpir, H.I., Badewi, A.A., Ludwig, T.: User support system in the complex environment. In: Marcus, A. (ed.) DUXU 2014. LNCS, vol. 8520, pp. 392–402. Springer, Cham (2014). doi:10.1007/978-3-319-07638-6_38
14. Schulte, F., Chunpir, H.I., Voß, S.: Open data evolution in information systems research: considering cases of data-intensive transportation and grid systems. In: Marcus, A. (ed.) DUXU 2016. LNCS, vol. 9748, pp. 193–201. Springer, Cham (2016). doi: 10.1007/978-3-319-40406-6_18
15. Chunpir, H.I., Zaina, L.: Assisting users in open data infrastructures: a management perspective. In: 15th International Conference WWW/Internet 2016, pp. 27–34 (2016)
16. Shneiderman, B.: Designing the User Interface, vol. 2, no. 2 (1998)
17. Nielsen, J.: Iterative user-interface design. Computer (Long Beach, California), **26**(11), 32–41 (1993)
18. Finstad, K.: Interacting with computers the usability metric for user experience. Interact. Comput. **22**, 323–327 (2010)
19. Karbay, E.B., Chunpir, H.I.: Gauging the reliability of online health information in the turkish context. In: Yamamoto, S. (ed.) HIMI 2016, Part II. LNCS, vol. 9735, pp. 423–433, Springer, Cham (2016). doi:10.1007/978-3-319-40397-7_40
20. Sahito, W.A., Chunpir, H.I., Hussain, Z., Hassan, S.R., Schulte, F.: Significance of line length for tablet PC users. In: Marcus, A. (ed.) DUXU 2015, Part II. LNCS, vol. 9187, pp. 587–596. Springer, Cham (2016). doi:10.1007/978-3-319-20898-5_56
21. Williams, D.N.: ESGF: ESGF governance model, Livermore, CA, USA (2013)
22. Chunpir, H.I., Curri, E., Zaina, L., Ludwig, T.: Improving user interfaces for a request tracking system: best practical RT. In: Yamamoto, S. (ed.) HIMI 2016. LNCS, vol. 9735, pp. 391–401. Springer, Cham (2016). doi:10.1007/978-3-319-40397-7_37
23. Bartens, Y., Chunpir, H.I., Schulte, F., Voß, S.: Business/IT alignment in two-sided markets: a cobit 5 analysis for media streaming business models. In: Strategies Information Technology (IT) Governance and Alignment in Business Settings, IGI Global, pp. 82–111 (2017)

Expanding Scientific Community Reach Based on Web Access Data

Vagner Figueredo de Santana$^{(\boxtimes)}$ and Leandro Marega Ferreira Otani

IBM Research, IBM, Tutóia St., 1157 São Paulo, SP, Brazil
{vagsant,lmarega}@br.ibm.com

Abstract. Knowing the main characteristics of a scientific community, how it reaches all stakeholders, and understanding how individuals engage around a subject is needed in order to support decision makers to plan strategies to maintain and nurture the community. This work presents a new way of interpreting the reach of a scientific community by incorporating Web access data to the co-author network commonly considered. The case presented involves the Brazilian Human-Computer Interaction (HCI) community and the access to the website of the XV Brazilian Symposium on Human Factors in Computer Systems, the main HCI conference in Brazil. The proposed method is grounded on Organizational Semiotics and differs from the existing works because it considers a wider population than the conference authors. Inspired by the Organizational Onion, it considers three different levels of connection: Informal, Formal, and Technical. In the presented case, the reach commonly used (i.e., author-author network) counts on 257 authors while the total of people orbiting the event involved 5,432 unique visitors, in other words, the co-author network represents approximately 5% of the population orbiting the event. The presented method shows that data originated from Web accesses support a different way of representing a scientific community reach, including multiple segments that are commonly not considered as the target-audience, resulting in a more inclusive approach in the sense of considering the plurality of people orbiting an event, mediated or not by a computer. Our contribution shows a data informed approach of expanding the scientific community reach in order to characterize people orbiting the conference.

Keywords: Organizational semiotics · Log analysis · Social network · Author network

1 Introduction

Bibliometrics is a discipline that involves multiple methods to describe characteristics and identify patterns from published documents. Norton [11] defines Bibliometrics as the set of the various methods of measurement applied to artifacts of human communication forms. In Computer Science, much of the work performed in Bibliometrics involves the use of DBLP Computer Science Bibliography[1], which is an online reference for bibliographic information on major Computer Science publications. In addition, works

---

[1] http://dblp.uni-trier.de/.

© Springer International Publishing AG 2017
S. Yamamoto (Ed.): HIMI 2017, Part II, LNCS 10274, pp. 475–492, 2017.
DOI: 10.1007/978-3-319-58524-6_38

involving the analysis of DBLP, including analyzes of community and relationship among people, uses co-author (or author-author) network. In these works, authors are connected when authored a paper, book, chapter, among other types of documents. Examples of works based on DBLP performing such analysis are [3, 10, 16].

In the literature, when the term 'scientific community' takes place, either it is used broadly as anyone doing research or, in more data-oriented approaches, it is restricted to the ones publishing in certain conferences or journals. According to Barbosa and Souza [2], Human-Computer Interaction (HCI) researchers themselves should have a deep understanding of the context in which the object of their investigation is placed. Thus, we are proposing an extension to the co-author network to represent the people orbiting a given scientific subject (e.g., conference, discipline), highlighting characteristics often not covered in co-author network analysis.

In this work, we present a new way of interpreting the reach of a scientific community by incorporating Web access data. The Web access considered was captured using Google Analytics, which is one of the many analytics existing tools, and people that liked the conference page in the Facebook[2]. The case presented involves the characterization of the Brazilian Human-Computer Interaction community based on the access to the website of the XV Brazilian Symposium on Human Factors in Computer Systems (aka IHC), the main HCI conference in Brazil.

In the last years, the conference counted on more than 200 attendees. Since it very beginning it is promoted by Brazilian Computer Society. Since 2006 it has been organized in cooperation with SIGCHI (Special Interest Group in Computer Human Interaction) and ACM (Association of Computer Machinery)[3]. The most frequent keywords of papers published in the Symposium are the following: (1) Semiotic Engineering, (2) Human-Computer Interaction, (3) Accessibility, (4) Usability Evaluation, and (5) Interface [5]. They represent the focus of the Brazilian HCI Community and how researchers are engaged to HCI topics and methods.

The main contribution of this work is a data informed approach of expanding the scientific community reach in order to represent from co-author network to people orbiting the conference. The next section presents the related works, Sect. 3 describes the theoretical background, Sect. 4 details the proposed method, Sect. 5 presents the results and, finally, Sect. 6 concludes.

2   Related Work

Next we present works related to the characterization of the Brazilian HCI community, focusing on Bibliometrics involving the IHC conference.

Henry et al. [8] present an analysis of the main HCI conferences (i.e., ACM SIGCHI Conference on Human Factors in Computing Systems, User Interface Software and Technology, Advanced Visual Interfaces and IEEE Symposium on Information Visualization). The work also has a focus on visualization of information related to

---

[2] www.facebook.com/2016IHC/.

[3] www.sbc.org.br/ihc.

published works. This section will focus on presenting details of Brazilian HCI community. For a broader review of works involving the ACM SIGCHI conference and the international HCI community, refer to [1].

Barbosa et al. [1] explored the metadata of **340 full papers** published in the first **14 editions** of IHC. The work details the authorship profile of the Brazilian HCI community and how it changed over time, including the evolution of co-author network and characterization of the community.

Gasparini et al. [4] present a descriptive analysis of the first **11 editions** of IHC, focusing on the visualization of all editions of the event by the time the work was published. The data set analyzed involved **236 full papers** published and **398 authors**. The characterization had shown authors that play a central role in the community, main research themes, and geographical distribution of authors, among other information.

Considering co-author network studies, Gasparini et al. [5] analyzed the co-author network regarding **12 editions** of IHC. The data set considered as composed of conference **full papers**. In the study authors present the researchers that are central do the co-author network, connection trends, institutions, and acting fields of IHC authors (e.g. computer science, design, engineering, psychology, etc.).

Beyond the co-author network, Gasparini et al. [6] listed the **authors with more than one full paper** in the IHC, inspected the Lattes Curriculum Vitae[4] of each one of **105 authors**, gathering data about institution, advisor, and title. In addition, authors applied an online questionnaire to the ones that have changed institution, state, or region (**36 authors**). The questionnaire counted on **21 participants**. The work shows that migration occurred changed the collaborations among authors, fostering emerging HCI research groups and diffusing HCI in Brazil.

Considering citations of works published in IHC editions, Gasparini et al. [7] studied whether and how the IHC publications cite publications from IHC itself. The data set considered in the work involves **340 full papers** published in the first **14 editions** of the IHC, summing up to **7,350 authors**. The work describes a citation profile of the event and point to the growth of the community. However, it also presents that research produced by Brazilian HCI community should widen its visibility by its peers.

The existing works consider a restrict scope of the HCI Brazilian community when relying only on full papers or full paper authors information. Hence, people that act in the subject but are not present in the conference proceedings, participating, presenting, in multiple levels of engagement (e.g., demos, posters, and workshops), were not considered in previous analysis. It is also worth mentioning that these "soft connections" regarding people orbiting the conference were hard or even impossible to obtain in early editions of IHC. However, in this paper we present an approach that combines additional data to the co-author network to better characterize the reach of the conference.

According to Souza et al. [13], due to the large size of Brazil, IHC has been the main venue for HCI researchers to meet and discuss their works. However, for the same reason, people that orbit the IHC and are impacted by decisions taken considering only full paper authors. The proposed method differs from the existing ones because it

---

[4] http://lattes.cnpq.br/.

considers a wider population than the full paper authors, which is a group of people commonly considered in reports and studies to characterize scientific community or to build co-author networks.

3 Theoretical Background

Following the tradition of HCI in Brazil of being inspired and expanding the boundaries of Semiotics [13], this work is grounded on Organizational Semiotics (OS). OS is a discipline that deals with information and information systems in such a way it takes into account from technical to human and social aspects. OS supports the understanding on how individuals behave, norms governing behaviors, characteristics and functions of signs used [8, 14, 15]. According to Liu [9], *"an organization is a social system in with people behave in an organized manner by conforming to a certain system of norms."* Moreover, an organization can be seen as an information system where people use signs with some purpose [9]. In this sense, organizations count on regular norms and processes that can be automated and supported by computer-based systems. However, the introduction of computer-based systems is just part of the solution, since informal and formal layers encompass this technical aspect. In OS, this view of organization is referred as the Organization Onion (Fig. 1).

The informal layer takes into account cultural aspects, values, habits and behavior of each individual member of the organization. In the informal layer the intentions are understood and emerging protocols and patterns are taken into account. The formal layer is within the context of informal layer. In the formal layer the literate culture plays the central role; rules are created to replace intentions. People involved in the formal layer function as sign-token transmitters in this organization. The technical layer is

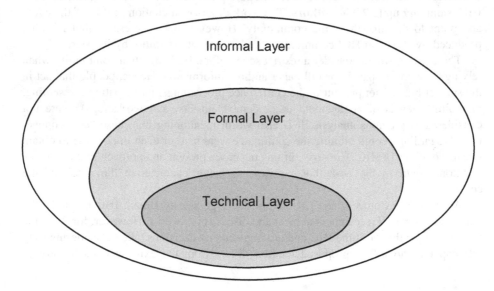

Fig. 1. Organizational Onion.

within the context of formal layer. The technical layer encompasses the system programmed according to rules and processes of the said organization. In the technical layer routine and repetitive tasks of well-defined work processes are coded. In sum, a technical system presupposes a formal system, which, in turn, relies on an informal system [9].

The Organizational Onion provides a rich framework to understand organizations and, specially, to consider the multiple aspects related to information systems and **how human perform tasks in these systems**, from well-defined tasks, reaching rules, behavior and intentions emerging from interactions among humans.

The rationale of applying the Organizational Onion to study the reach of a scientific community resides in the fact that, by studying the connections between authors (co-author network), only the technical information is considered; rules and processes are well-defined to be there. The role of sign-token transmitters is not considered, i.e., communications emerging when people interact among each. In this regard, the formal layer is considered. Finally, traces of interactions that are not mapped are taken into account by Web access data analysis.

4 Proposed Method

The method places accesses of people orbiting the subject in the informal layer, people formally engaged in the subject are placed in the formal layer, and, finally, people that publish at the conference are placed in the technical layer. Accordingly, based on the Organizational Onion, we propose the placement of connections and people around a scientific subject according to the three layers, thus, representing the reach of a community: informal, formal, and technical (Fig. 2).

- **Informal:** the set of people with some interest in the subject orbiting the subject in an informal way, mainly by the use of Web access data and Online Social Networks (OSN) data.
- **Formal:** the set of people with interest in the event, mainly represented by people attending to the event, having a formal connection with the subject.
- **Technical:** the set of people that strongly engaged in the subject, represented by people that published a work at the conference (i.e., co-author network).

Considering the works in the literature regarding the co-author network, the people and relationships are mapped to a graph. This mapping represents people as nodes (or vertices) and edges (or links) connect these people. In a co-author network, each author is represented as node and two nodes are connected if they published a work together. Hence, the technical layer is mapped according to the co-author network.

The formal layer considers people that participated in the event without publishing papers, representing a different engagement and sign-token transmission. The informal layer is represented by people orbiting the event, with no formal connection with the event, mapped by considering Web access and OSN connections.

The data set considered combines access data to the conference website in conjunction with the data coming from conference proceedings and participation reports prepared by session chairs during the conference. When author name conflict (such as

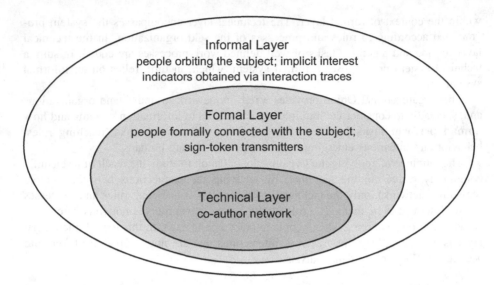

Fig. 2. Organizational Onion applied in the context of scientific community reach.

name similarity and/or abbreviation), last names were compared and, on of further conflicts, authors' CVs were checked. When conflicts persisted, the most recently mapped name was discarded.

For the analysis regarding co-author network, IHC and OSN participants, the data set consists of 276 Facebook users, 105 conference works, and a total amount of 120 authors that presented, 32 authors that did not present but participated in the event, 105 authors that were not present and 61 people that participated in the event without any publication in the conference. The works were distributed as follows: 34 full papers, 24 short papers, 2 workshops, 3 short courses, 6 works presented during the workshop of thesis and dissertation, 8 works presented during the workshop on HCI education works, 6 reports part of the evaluation competition, 4 works of the HCI in practice track, and 18 posters/demos.

The tool used was Google Analytics and the data set considered involves 10 months of Web access, from the publication/announcement of the website to December 21st. Google Analytics was chosen because it is the most popular analytics tool and it is being used by 54.5% of the websites in the whole Web [17].

In order to use the Google Analytics, it is required the insertion of a line of code in all Web pages of the website to analyze. This line of code refers to the JavaScript library responsible for logging Web data access. Google Analytics offers multiple features as history analysis, real time access view, demographic analysis, visitors interests, navigation flow, among others. However, in specific occasions it is not possible to capture data related to user profile due to privacy or technologic characteristics of users' device. Demographic data and topics of interest, for instance, are not identified by Google Analytics service, instead, Google partners as DoubleClick use mobile apps and cookies to obtain this data. In addition, the use of Google Analytics was considered over other solutions based on Web server logs considering the short-comings presented in [12].

The data capture started from the moment the website was published aiming at constant evaluation of the website usage and characterization of the access. The analysis was postponed until the access started to decay, representing the decrease of interest a couple of weeks after the conference. Moreover, in the process of data cleaning, sessions with duration of 10 s or less where removed from the data set, as these accesses usually come from Web crawlers or developers debugging the website.

The data considered from OSN refers to the likes given by people to the event page on Facebook. Event participants were not included in the likes counting. The goal is to map also people interacting with the event only via OSN, given that people are using more and more such pages instead of navigating through the website (see the trend of searches regarding last editions of the event, even when the number of participants remains stable over the last IHCs[5]).

5   Results

Next we present the results from the characterization of people involved in the three layers, from informal, to formal, and then technical. Moreover, we discuss character-istics of different layers. The focus is on characterizing the informal layer and con-trasting with basic characteristics of formal and technical layers.

5.1   Informal Layer

The Web data access considered in the analysis was captured during 10 months. It involves 25,519 sessions, 141,079 page views (mean number of pages per session 5.53), 10,904 unique visitors, 57.8% of returning visitors, and bounce rate of 12.02%. Figure 3 shows the number of daily sessions in the period versus mean session time. Before disclosing the website to the public, the website counts on low number of sessions and high duration time compared to the rest of the sessions, showing the activity of developers and the organizing committee reviewing the website content. Thus, to remove this effect from the data set, the period considered in the analysis is from February 22nd to October 18th. Hence, to select the proper data, the Google Analytics segment feature was used. An additional exclusion condition for sessions with duration of 10 s or less. The referred period is related to 11,461 sessions, 106,711 page views (mean of 9.31 pages per session), 5,432 users, mean visit time of 6 min 28 s and bounce rate of 0.01%. It is worth noting the reduction of the bounce rate from 12.02% (the whole data set) to 0.01% (after filtering), which highlights the role played by this segment feature. Thus, for the next analysis informing user details, the data set considered is related to this segment of the data set.

---

[5] https://www.google.com/trends/explore?date=all&q=ihc%202016,ihc%202015,ihc%202014,ihc%202013.

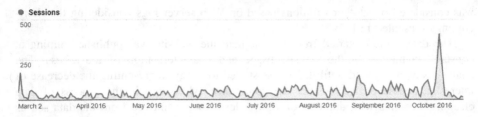

Fig. 3. Daily sessions; the peak is related to the period in which the conference occurred.

In Fig. 3 it is possible to verify that the number of accesses is reduced in the weekends and that the accesses increase in the first days of the week (Monday, Tuesday). On the other hand, the mean session time is greater in the weekends. In Fig. 4 it is possible to see that the mean session time decreases as time passes. This behavior is expected given that the website counts on 57.8% of returning visitors. Next, we present the characterization of accesses according to the following: demographics, topics of interest, geography, engagement and flow of users, technology, and device.

Regarding demographics and interests, the group of people from 25 to 34 years has the greater participation in this layer (Fig. 5). Also, it was computed that 59.4% of the accesses are related to male and 40.6% are related to female. The distribution considering age and number of sessions throughout time (Figs. 6 and 7) shows peaks related to important dates of the event and the predominance of people from 25 to 34 years old in terms of activity. In addition, the 35 to 44 years old group accessed the website mainly during week days. No differences in the access behavior considering gender. Visitors interests involve technology (4.8%), movies (4%), and TV (3.7%)

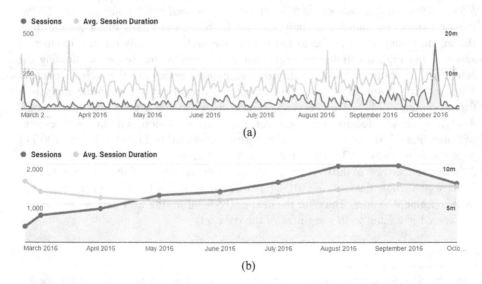

Fig. 4. Daily sessions versus mean time (a) and monthly sessions versus mean session time (b).

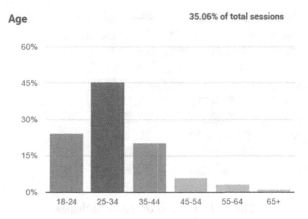

Fig. 5. Distribution of users by age.

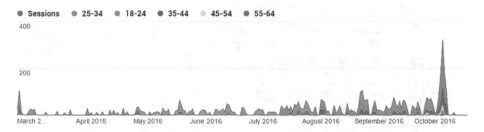

Fig. 6. Distribution of sessions by age.

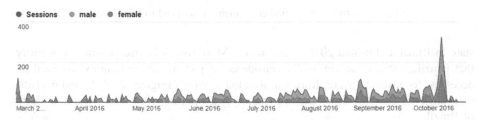

Fig. 7. Distribution of sessions by gender.

(Fig. 8). Considering market segments, education (5.15%), travel (3.47%), and consumer electronics (3.42%) are the top segments related to the website visitors (Fig. 9).

Considering geography, as expected, most of the access came from Brazil; 10,683 sessions (93.21%). In this group, 71.27% use Portuguese as default browser language and 20.68% use English as default browser language. Figure 10 shows the distribution of visits considering the Brazilian state that originated the accesses. From the 10,683 accesses containing information regarding the state of origin, 4,039 are attributed to the state of Sao Paulo (37.81%); this is expected since that Sao Paulo is the most populated

484   V.F. de Santana and L.M.F. Otani

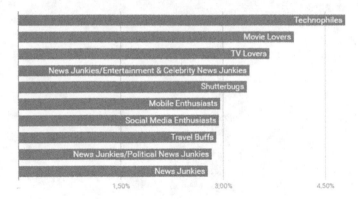

Fig. 8. Distribution of visitors' affinities.

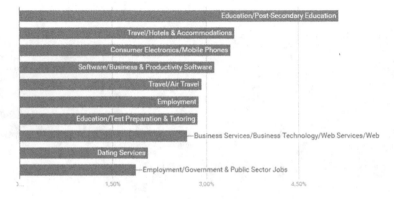

Fig. 9. Distribution of market segments associated to the visitors.

state in Brazil and hosted 2016's conference. Moreover, it is also possible to identify that Brazilian states that are hardly considered as part of the community, counted on accesses, for instance, Acre, Roraima, Rondonia, which originated (3, 5, and 6 visits, respectively). This highlights the importance of supporting HCI research in the North of Brazil.

Considering engagement, Fig. 11 shows the filtered sessions (0-10 s) and that the majority of visits are in the interval between 11 and 1800 s (30 min). In addition, the most common duration is in the interval of 1 to 3 min. Figure 12 shows the flow of users from the homepage of the conference's website. More than 6,200 accesses were originated at Google (56.36%). In addition, the pages that users reached most commonly from google were the homepage and the call for papers page. The next pages accessed involve important dates, venue, and program information. Figure 13 shows the origin of accesses and the following flow of users. Beyond accesses originated in Brazil, the website also counted on accesses coming from United States (410 visits), Canada (61 visits), Russia (46 visits), and United Kingdom (28 visits).

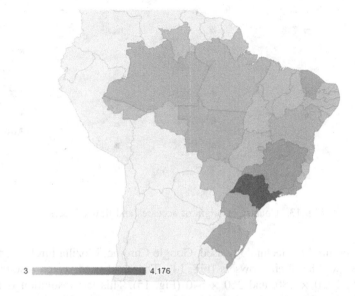

Fig. 10. Accesses by Brazilian states.

Session Duration	Sessions	Pageviews
0-10 seconds	0	0
11-30 seconds	2,430	11,837
31-60 seconds	1,793	10,698
61-180 seconds	2,618	20,356
181-600 seconds	2,359	23,416
601-1800 seconds	1,836	23,481
1801+ seconds	425	16,923

Fig. 11. Duration of visits and visualizations of pages.

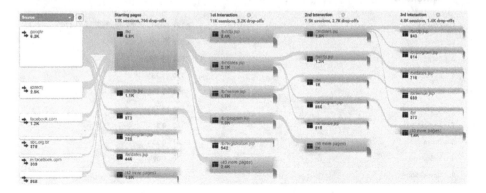

Fig. 12. Flow of users across website pages.

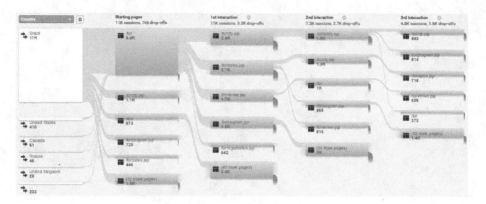

Fig. 13. Country of origin of accesses and flow of users.

Bearing in mind the technology used, Google Chrome, Mozilla Firefox, and Safari are the most popular Web browsers (Fig. 14). The most used screen resolutions are 1366×768, 1920×180, and 360×640 (Fig. 15). This last resolution is an interesting result, probably related to the use of mobile devices (Fig. 16), which occurred in 17.55% of the visits; tablet accesses represent 1.88% and desktop accesses represent 80.57% of the visits.

Figure 17 shows the view of the informal layer, omitting nodes related to unique visitors. In the image, it is possible to see how authors are positioned in the center, and how conference participants and people that followed information of the conference via Facebook distance from them. The graph has 6,026 nodes (i.e., the sum of authors, participants, unique visitors, and Facebook users), 382 edges, density of 2.10×10^{-05}, and 5831 connected components.

Browser	Sessions ▼	↓	Sessions ▼
filtered results	**11,461** % of Total: 47.79% (23,984)		**11,461** % of Total: 47.79% (23,984)
1. Chrome	8,191		71.47%
2. Firefox	1,923		16.78%
3. Safari	923		8.05%
4. Internet Explorer	130		1.13%
5. Safari (in-app)	114		0.99%
6. Edge	83		0.72%
7. Android Browser	42		0.37%
8. Opera	41		0.36%
9. YaBrowser	10		0.09%
10. Opera Mini	3		0.03%

Fig. 14. Web browsers used to access the conference website.

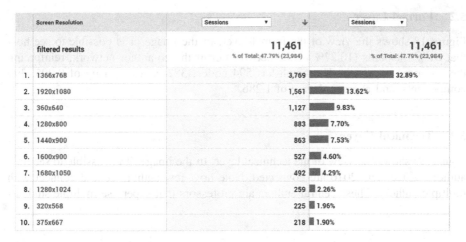

Fig. 15. Screen resolutions used by visitors.

Fig. 16. Devices used by users to access the conference website.

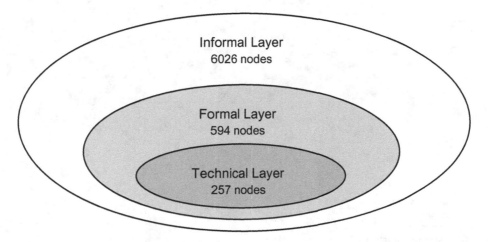

Fig. 17. Representation of the universe related to the IHC conference. Nodes represent authors, participants, authors that presented during the conference, and people that liked the conference page in the Facebook

5.2 Formal Layer

Figure 18 shows the view of the formal layer. In the image, it is possible to see how that 61 participants (10.27% of the network) orbit the co-author network, reinforcing the proposed approach. The graph has 594 nodes, 382 edges, density of 0.005, 399 components, and average degree of 1.286.

5.3 Technical Layer

Figure 19 shows the view of the technical layer. In the image, it is possible to see how authors of the IHC 2016 are connected. Note how few authors central connect with multiple authors. These central authors are professors that supervise multiple students

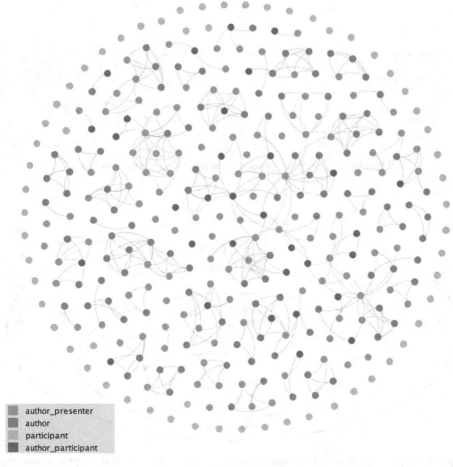

author_presenter
author
participant
author_participant

Fig. 18. Connections among authors, authors that participated in the conference, and the authors that presented during the conference.

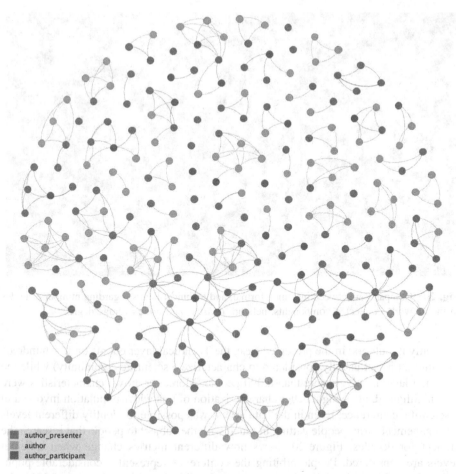

Fig. 19. Connections between authors, authors that participated in the conference, and the authors that presented during the conference.

in HCI. The graph has 257 nodes, 382 edges, density of 0.012, 62 connected components, and average degree of 2.973.

6 Discussion

The presented method shows that data originated from Web accesses support a different way of characterizing a community, considering people that are interested in the subject and that are touched somehow by the conference and actions taken having in mind only the authors. In sum, the method places accesses of people orbiting the subject in the Informal Layer, people formally engaged in the subject are placed in the Formal Layer, and, finally, people that are present in the conference proceedings are placed in the Technical Layer. The results show that a scientific community touches more people

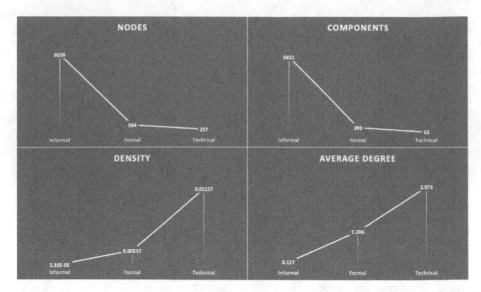

Fig. 20. Comparison between informal, formal, and technical layers regarding number of nodes in the network, connected components, network density, and node average degree.

than only its authors. In the presented case, the Technical layer counts on few hundreds of authors (the set usually considered to characterize a scientific community) while the Informal layer involves more than 6,000 people. Moreover, novel characteristics were also highlighted, allowing a better characterization of this wider population involved in a scientific conference. Even in the data access was possible to identify different levels of engagement, from people getting in touch with the subject to people that research the subject for decades. Figure 20 shows how different metrics change when different levels are considered. People orbiting the conference represent a considerable population. In addition, given that the edges are only related to the conference of 2016, the number of edges do no alter, thus, the number of connected components represents the same situation as the graph nodes chart. When considering density, it is interesting to see how sparse such network is; the technical layer, which is the most connected one counts on 1% of all possible connections. Moreover, regarding average degree, the technical layer points that in the technical layer that each author of IHC 2016 co-authored a paper with 2.973 other authors.

The proposed approach has some limitations. The presented analysis was performed considering only one year of the conference. An interesting approach involves analyzing the history of a conference, especially if the conference website stays at the same domain, which enables a long-term analysis. It's also valid to notice that, since Google Analytics define new website visitors based on cookies, the differentiation of a new visitor from a returning visitor connecting from a different browser or device is not possible. However, due to technology (i.e., Javascript is enabled in almost all modern browsers) and adoption characteristics (i.e., requiring authentication), this is the best method for identifying visitors at scale.

This work has an especial value in the context of accessibility, given that it includes people that are away of the venue. Knowing characteristics of the whole audience and expanding the reach of the scientific community might leverage policies that promote the participation of people that are interested in the subject, but struggle to enter the community. Future work involves the analysis of more than one year in order to evaluate trends and how people orbiting the subject became authors or participants over time.

Finally, our contribution shows a data informed approach of expanding the scientific community reach in order to foment strategies of bringing more and more people to the core of the community.

References

1. Barbosa, S.D.J., Silveira, M.S., Gasparini, I.: What Publications Metadata Tell Us about the Evolution of a Scientific Community: The Case of the Brazilian Human-Computer Interaction Conference Series. Scientometrics **110**(1), 275–300 (2016). doi:10.1007/s11192-016-2162-4
2. Barbosa, S.D.J., Souza, C.S.: Interacting with public policy: are HCI researchers an endangered species in Brazil? Interactions **18**(3), 69–71 (2011). http://dx.doi.org/10.1145/1962438.1962454
3. Elmacioglu, E., Lee, D.: On six degrees of separation in DBLP-DB and more. ACM SIGMOD Rec. **34**(2), 33–40 (2005)
4. Gasparini, I., Kimura, M.K., Pimenta, M.S.: Visualizando 15 anos de IHC. XII Simpósio Brasileiro sobre Fatores Humanos em Sistemas Computacionais (IHC) (2013)
5. Gasparini, I., da Cunha, L.F., Kimura, M.H., Pimenta, M.S.: Análise das redes de coautoria do simpósio brasileiro sobre fatores humanos em sistemas computacionais. In: Proceedings of the 13th Brazilian Symposium on Human Factors in Computing Systems, pp. 323–332. Sociedade Brasileira de Computação (2014)
6. Gasparini, I., Silveira, M.S., Barbosa, S.D.J.: Caminhos Migratórios da Comunidade Brasileira de IHC. In: Proceedings of the 14th Brazilian Symposium on Human Factors in Computing Systems (IHC 2015), pp. 242–251 (2015)
7. Gasparini, I., Barbosa, S.D. J., Silveira, M.S., Mendonça, F.C.: Auto(re)conhecimento: refletindo sobre a influência das publicações do IHC no próprio IHC. In: Proceedings of the 15th Brazilian Symposium on Human Factors in Computing Systems (IHC 2016) (2016)
8. Henry, N., Goodell, H., Elmqvist, N., Fekete, J.D.: 20 Years of four HCI conferences: a visual exploration. Int. J. Hum.-Comput. Interact. **23**(3), 239–285 (2007)
9. Liu, K.: Semiotics in Information Systems Engineering. Cambridge University Press, Cambridge (2000)
10. Liu, X., Bollen, J., Nelson, M.L., Van de Sompel, H.: Co-authorship networks in the digital library research community. Inf. Process. Manage. **41**(6), 1462–1480 (2005)
11. Norton, M.: Introductory Concepts in Information Science. Information Today Inc., Medford (2000)
12. Santana, V.F., Baranauskas, M.C.C.: WELFIT: A remote evaluation tool for identifying web usage patterns through client-side logging. Int. J. Hum. Comput. Stud. **76**, 40–49 (2015)
13. Souza, C.S., Baranauskas, M.C.C., Prates, R.O., Pimenta, M.S.: HCI in Brazil: lessons learned and new perspectives. In: Proceedings of the VIII Brazilian Symposium on Human Factors in Computing Systems (IHC 2008), pp. 358–359. Sociedade Brasileira de Computação, Porto Alegre, Brazil (2008)

14. Stamper, R.K.: A semiotic theory of information and information systems/applied semiotics. In: Invited Papers for the ICL/University of Newcastle Seminar on 'Information', 6–10 September (1993)
15. Stamper, R.K.: Extending semiotics for the study of organisations. In: Proceedings of Conference on Semiotics and the Information Sciences (1998)
16. Sun, Y., Barber, R., Gupta, M., Aggarwal, C.C., Han, J.: Co-author relationship prediction in heterogeneous bibliographic networks. In: 2011 International Conference on Advances in Social Networks Analysis and Mining (ASONAM), pp. 121–128. IEEE (2011)
17. W3TECHS—Web Technology Surveys. Usage of traffic analysis tools for websites (2016). https://w3techs.com/technologies/overview/traffic_analysis/all

Infrastructure for Research Data Management as a Cross-University Project

Thomas Eifert[1(✉)], Ulrich Schilling[2], Hans-Jörg Bauer[3],
Florian Krämer[1], and Ania Lopez[4]

[1] IT Center, RWTH Aachen University, Aachen, Germany
{eifert,kraemer}@itc.rwth-aachen.de
[2] Centre for Information and Media Services,
University of Duisburg-Essen, Essen, Germany
ulrich.schilling@uni-due.de
[3] Regional Computing Centre, University of Cologne, Cologne, Germany
bauer@uni-koeln.de
[4] University Library, University of Duisburg-Essen, Essen, Germany
ania.lopez@uni-due.de

Abstract. Research Data Management (RDM) receives more and more attention as a core component of scientific work. This importance equally stems from the scientific work with ever-increasing amounts of data, the value of this data for subsequent use, and the formal requirements of funding agencies. While these requirements are widely accepted among the research communities in general, the individual acceptance depends on many factors. In particular, we found that the ratio between the benefits achieved by RDM and the burdens imposed is not equal among the different roles that participate in the scientific process. In consequence, we analyse how we can optimize this ratio by different factors. Despite these different factors, common to all solutions is the demand for accessible and persistent storage that suits the particular needs imposed by RDM. At the Universities of Aachen, Bochum, Dortmund, Duisburg-Essen, and Cologne, we started a joint project to build up a distributed storage infrastructure dedicated to the needs of RDM and to address some of the acceptance factors.

Keywords: Research data management · Collaboration · Extended domain model

1 Introduction

Research data (RD) is the outcome as well as the foundation of scientific work. Researchers need an environment that enables them to work efficiently and securely with their research data (cf. [KE13, EU10]. National and international research funding institutions, such as the European Union program Horizon 2020, the German Research Foundation, the HRK, the German university rectors' conference [Ho14, Ho15] and the Federal Ministry of Education and Research as well as various publishers (e.g. NATURE[1]), are increasingly requiring scientists and scholars to plan and execute good

---

[1] http://www.nature.com/srep/journal-policies/editorial-policies.

© Springer International Publishing AG 2017
S. Yamamoto (Ed.): HIMI 2017, Part II, LNCS 10274, pp. 493–502, 2017.
DOI: 10.1007/978-3-319-58524-6_39

data management practices. An obligation to archive produced data already exists by carrying out "good scientific practice" [RW11], some even ask for the publication of primary data, e.g. the Open Data Pilot of the EU[2].

To fulfill these growing requirements and thus make research data accessible and usable for subsequent research projects has become an inevitable objective for all scientific institutions. Thus, structures and processes have to be established to relieve the scientists from these tasks and let them focus their primary work. For this reason, there are many (inter-)nationally coordinated activities as well as activities at German federal state and local levels to tackle these questions. The coordinating activity in the state of Northrhine-Westphalia takes place in the context of "DH-NRW" ("Digitale Hochschule NRW" ⇔ "Digital University – Northrhine-Westphalia"). Here, activities at various levels, from communication and awareness-building activities, the compilation of a central, structured information repository about the requirements as well as of possible methods and tools scientists can use, up to detailed process charts to help scientists as well as central units within the universities to understand their mutual demands.

This contribution presents the approach of our universities to build a local infrastructure that integrates with these activities.

2 Requirements by Users

In many surveys and interviews [ES16], we tried to learn the users' needs and requirements. All responses summed up, users primarily like to keep their current workflow (which is "best" supported by their local solution), and so any RDM infrastructure is expected to fit into whatever.

In essence, that means a user interface individually tailored at least to the requirements of a scientific community, ideally to a department's habits. Such a level of customization currently does not seem a realistic requirement, so we need to establish ways to support the researchers by more standardized solutions.

In order to draft such a solution – or a set of solutions – we first tried to translate the scientists' requirements into processes and activities. At this level, RDM software should be easy to use and capable of supporting the scientists in managing their data. For the process level, we tried to model the various roles that participate within the scientific process (s. Fig. 1) in order to better structure and understand the scientists' needs.

The most important roles are the Scientist and the Science-/project manager. Further roles are the society, i.e. anyone interested in results and data, and the external scientist.

The scientist generates data, makes annotations (i.e., generates metadata) and, at a later stage in a project, evaluates the data, tries models and parameters and so on. The science manager is involved in that evaluation process, too. Furthermore, he might manage several projects in parallel or in sequence, so he needs to be able to find and analyze data across several projects, a task often hindered by simple directory structures with implicit knowledge (sometimes buried in paper notebooks).

These various activities are not equally distributed over the lifecycle of research data.

---

[2] http://europa.eu/rapid/press-release_IP-13-1257_en.htm.

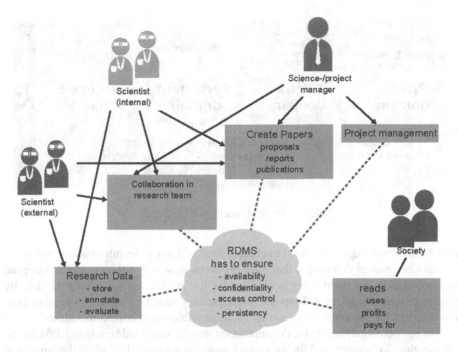

Fig. 1. Roles and activities

The well-known domain model [KE13] visualized in Fig. 2 has proven to be a valuable means to a common understanding and basic structuring of research data management and the lifecycle of research data. In our context, it helps to structure demands and solutions according to their occurrence during the information life cycle. It distinguishes four domains where researchers act: the private domain, the group domain, the persistent domain, and the public domain enabling access and reuse. In our understanding, this domain model tries to capture the phases data and metadata undergo. The research process itself has much more loops and iterations like getting a set of data, evaluating, getting more data, perhaps with different experimental settings, and so on.

Research typically starts in the private domain where a researcher mainly works alone or in very small teams on his data. In most cases, the data is then with more collaborators, most often of other institutions or organizations. This phase is typically residing within the group domain. This wider sharing usually causes to add metadata well known to the individual researcher but essential to get an understanding by collaborators and thus has to be available with the shared data. Due to the duality of external collaborators being colleagues as well as competitors, identity based authentication and role based access control is important to participate in identity lifecycle management, role management etc. in order to have traceable access to data.

Once publications have been written or, at least, at the end of a project, good scientific practice and formal requirements asks for long-term storage of primary research data. At least the data that has led to the results of the project or the publication

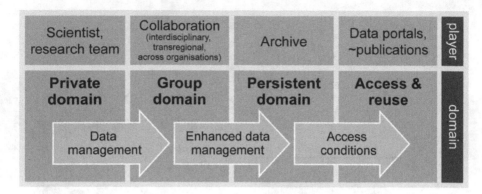

Fig. 2. Domain model [KE13, ES16]

must be archived. Again, the need to capture further descriptive information rises since it cannot be ensured that people that have produced data will still be available once the data needs to be accessed. This is obvious for the public domain. Using the data by other researchers requires a thorough understanding based on an encompassing documentation with comprehensive and as far as possible standardized metadata.

The previous analyses lead to the impression that the value and benefit of RDM for the organization, for society, and for the project manager are very clear while the individual benefit for a scientist is not as obvious. We further followed this idea and tried to name the benefits and burdens, sorted by the domains of the domain model and by role (s. Table 1). Here, we split up the Project Manager role – often being a university professor – into the role of the principal investigator within a scientific context, the role of the head/manager of his department, and, eventually, the role of the organization's head. With this structure, Table 1 shows a sketch of benefits (denoted by "+") and burdens ("−").

Table 1. Benefits (+) and burdens (−)

	Scientist	Science/Project manager		
		PI	Head of dept.	Head of organisation
Private domain	− Generate − Annotate + Use + Proof of priority	+ Use annotated data + Better data exploitation	− Workload + Compliance	+ Compliance + Intellectual property + Good science
Group domain	− Annotate + Use − Share + Use colleague's shared data	+ Use + Access control	+ Handover	+ Reputation
Persistent dom.		+ Store + Reuse	+ Store + Reuse	
Access & reuse	+ Reputation	+ Good science + Reputation		

Despite the uncertainty of entries in this table, we see the workload to feed the RDM process lying mainly on the scientist where the individual benefit, in particular for scientists that leave the university after their graduation, appears to be marginal. On the other hand, a broad acceptance by the scientific community at our universities seems to be crucial for a successful implementation of RDM. Archives with just the mandatory fields filled to comply with the regulations appears to be too little to be useful.

With this background, we started our project with the aim to increase the benefit and to lower the burden for scientists.

3   Joint Project

When we look at the domain model (Fig. 2), an implicit assumption is that the "research" – i.e., the project – has already started somehow and that the infrastructure is aware of this project as well as of all other projects (Fig. 3).

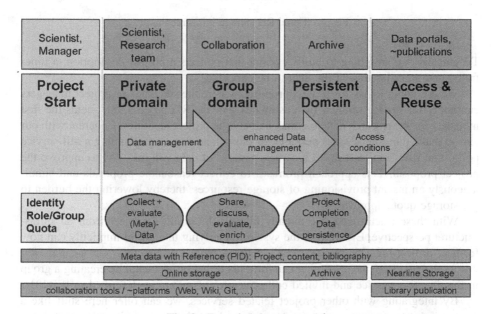

Fig. 3. Extended domain model

However, besides the eventual project proposal and approval process, the incarnation of a project in an infrastructure at least has the potential of being a quite tedious task. After all interviews with researchers that is a strong reason why projects are not reflected in the technical and process infrastructure. On the other hand, as an institution we are highly to be able to differentiate each project since this gives a chance for any further treatment in a structured manner.

We therefor suggest to introduce a sort of a "0th domain" like depicted in Fig. 4. In particular, this domain should cover the technical instantiation of a project.

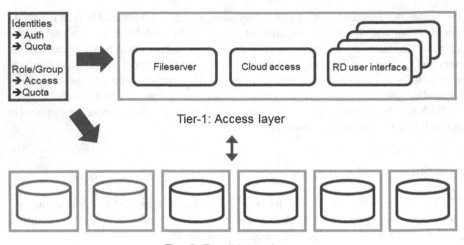

Tier-1: Access layer

Tier-2: Persistency layer

Fig. 4. Tiered RD storage infrastructure

Technically, we are going to build a portal that collects a project description, a time-frame and an estimation of the data to be expected.

We are going to ask for project proposals where the scientists or project managers can apply for storage on their own estimates. For the RD process, this yields the first metadata for the research data to come, namely the project identifier. Coherent with our aim to make things as easy as possible for our scientists we are planning a self-service portal that uses – at least up to a certain amount of data volume – AI to approve the project proposal. This approach promises to collect reasonable proposals and simultaneously an instant provisioning of storage resources, thereby lowering the burden to get storage quota approval.

With these (meta) data, we already know a lot about a project from an infrastructural perspective. Even more, the system underlying that portal implicitly can now form a "project lifecycle management", delivers reports and so on.

As the next step, the researcher can form his or her project team by creating a group in the directory service and invited colleagues to this group as described in [EB13].

By integrating with other project related services, we can offer here stuff like a project web site, a groupware group for mails and appointments, a git project and so on.

Figure 4 also depicts the different infrastructure levels that support the data handling in the domains. The bar that runs along all the domains is labelled "Meta data": Starting from the information collected during the project initialization in the "0th domain" we have to keep as much meta data as possible, either for the researcher himself, in order to support the evaluation of his experimental data, for team members or successors to make a use of the data and, when eventually published, to find and understand the data. The storage level in comparison in more segmented. Here we plan an online storage for the active project phase. After completion of a project or a thesis, the relevant data is put into an archive system. Currently, this is a dedicated tape based system, but the most important aspect here is that here long-term lifecycle management is handled like "keep at least for 10 years".

Six Universities of the German state of North Rhine -Westphalia, Aachen (RWTH + Uni of applied Science), Bochum, Dortmund, Duisburg-Essen, and Cologne embarked to build modules and in particular the one named "online storage" as an infrastructure for RD-storage and RDM.

The RD-storage will be a 2-tier solution with an access layer as tier 1 and a persistency layer as tier 2. In that model, tier 1will offer access by NAS protocols and web/cloud protocols. In addition, community specific tools and portals are located in this tier to offer means to handle data and metadata and thus enable aspects of RDM. Common to all functions on tier 1 is a single authentication and authorization service that provides identities and identity based role information.

Tier 2 will be realized by a distributed object storage system. Due to the amount of "hot" research data at out universities, the total amount of storage will be in the 10 PB range. This tier addresses the above-mentioned "capacity, persistency, and security" aspect.

At each of our universities, we will realize this tiered configuration. The main advantages of the joint project is the co-operation at gaining expertise in running such a complex system in a way that it fits to the specific demand of RDM as well as in creating new solutions. Furthermore, we will use cross-site replication for protection of selected data.

As said, most important for our project is the goal to make RDM an integral part of every scientist's workflow [RW11, RW16]. To reach this, an inevitable requirement to convince scientists is an availability very near 100%. This also requires an adequate availability of technical experts, which is much easier to accomplish by a larger – virtual – team.

A common question for all teams running storage infrastructure is how to manage the amount of data. There are techniques like billing for used space, setting quotas (by which rules ever) etc. Since we see the depicted RD storage infrastructure different from general-purpose storage but as a scientific resource, the "0th domain" will implement a process similar to the one which is established in the high performance computing regime since long and which matches perfectly with current funding regulations.

As said above, a project will start in the "0th domain". Therefore, we expect to have a project id before data arrived. A side effect of this is that we can implement only project based storage quota and thereby avoid the difficulties that arise when mixing user quota with group (i.e., group) quota.

While technical parameters are necessary to be met, the scientists also ask for processes that support them doing science. Here, specific tools for every special field come in where the specialties how research data is handled, annotated, and used in this field are supported in a way that its use generates a value for the scientist. Due to the multitude of these tools, we are working closely together with researchers from different communities to implement a sufficient set of these.

The blocks named "RD user interface" will be systems that connect the scientists' with their data beyond file access. We are planning a range from quite customizable web tools that allow managing meta data and connect it to data. We also see the opportunity for server based data analysis tools, either as PaaS or as SaaS. In any case, by being tied to one authentication service, all access methods on this layer will enforce consistent access rules.

To benefit from this, the logical interfaces must be the same across all sites, so besides technical co-operation we are also in the process of implementing matched change processes.

Common to all domains are the aspects of user-orientation or community orientation. The first means handling as well as the functional perspective, and integration into existing personal workflows. The second means the ability to integrate in the workflows that are established within a scientific community. This ability appears to be much more important than an institutional view.

This said, a strong focus of our RDM activities is about workflows, processes, metadata, and user interfaces.

However, every data has to be stored in a persistent and convenient manner and in a way, which fits the specifics of RDM. In particular, we see here the necessity to offer a broad range of protocols to access the storage by either legacy as well as modern, REST aware software. In our opinion, this is a prerequisite to offer services to the multitude of community specific software layers.

On the other hand, key aspects of RDM are the knowledge about the persons involved in the scientific workflow, and the ability to create cross references between stored data and metadata stored anywhere.

The cross references have to be inert against the specific location of the data in the storage hierarchy. This is achieved by storing the data in object storage and linking persistent, resolvable identifiers to the object id.

The knowledge about the persons start with the identity management systems established at our universities, relying on well-established methods of integrating another organization's members in an identity management system [EB13]. However, since scientific collaboration depend on cross-university access, we have set up a concept for mapping the partner university's users to each other's user directory. In a next step, we are evaluating whether we can better support the scientific collaboration to have these resources linked to common scientific identity providers like Orchid or ResearcherID. This could pave the way to link directly a scientist's results to his publication list and thus contributing to the individual benefit.

In general, we discuss data and their descriptions and annotations, i.e. their metadata. In this context, "data" is often understood as "original" data as obtained from experiments or simulations. However, a lot of research is made by using existing data, e.g. by applying a new analysis, a new way of combining information and so on. Regardless of the fact that this type of scientific work generates new data and metadata and results, these results rely on the previous generation of that data. Even with proper citation, it's not trivial to keep track of such a dependency, in particular in cases when there are multiple layers of data dependency. Here, the blockchain technology could be a method to create a link chain for data citations, so that derived data can be tracked down to the original raw data even across multiple "hops". Even more, starting from any point in that chain it allows finding dependent data. Due to the blockchain concept, such a link chain would even be institution agnostic.

As said, scientists and project managers have to rule with the regulations on RDM imposed by funding agencies etc. Here we see a way to support and thus lower the burden by taking (partial) responsibility in such a way that using the centrally supplied tools and infrastructure for research data will help the scientists to do things in a compliant way. Of course, that means an appropriate "Service level agreement" that goes significantly beyond the traditional "uptime and backup" promise.

4 Conclusion

In many cases, the "RDM process" is entered when the "real science" is done, namely when a project or a partial project has been completed and is due for archival and, eventually, for publication. In the common domain model, it is domains 3 and 4.

In our project, we are trying to "push" the entry point into RDM closer to the scientists' workplace. From an institutional perspective, this improves the chance to get more data with better annotations as early as possible and thus allows protecting that data from being lost. From the individual scientists' perspective, this approach has the downside that the daily work must be adopted to such a framework. However, is offers the great chance that the scientists have an individual benefit from using RDM. These benefits might stem from data analysis tools that use the aggregated metadata for better analyzing the data, from the safekeeping of data by the storage infrastructure, and by helping the scientist adhering to compliance rules.

Our next steps in that project are to implement the storage components and to combine software and APIs to use our growing RDM infrastructure as seamless as possible, where this will be a long-running project where the tool part will grow and develop incrementally as more and more scientists adopt to the RD process and articulate specific demands.

Acknowledgements. A joint project group of our universities has carried out the depicted work. Our thanks go to J. Kather, B. Magrean, M. Politze, R. Reinecke, and M.S. Müller for the many fruitful discussions.

References

[EU10] European Union: Riding the Wave. How Europe can gain from the rising tide of scientific data (2010). http://ec.europa.eu/information_society/newsroom/cf/document.cfm?action =display&doc_id=707. Last Access 11 Jan 2016

[Ho14] Hochschulrektorenkonferenz: Management of research data – a key strategic challenge for university management (2014). http://www.hrk.de/positionen/gesamtliste-beschluesse/ position/convention/management-von-forschungsdaten-eine-zentrale-strategische-herausforderung-fuer-hochschulleitungen/. Last Access 12 Jan 2016

[Ho15] Hochschulrektorenkonferenz: How university management can guide the development of research data management. Orientation paths, options for action and scenarios (2015). http://www.hrk.de/positionen/gesamtliste-beschluesse/position/convention/ wiehochschulleitungen-die-entwicklung-des-forschungsdatenmanagements-steuern-koennen-orientierung/. Last Access 12 Jan 2016

502   T. Eifert et al.

[ES16]   Eifert, T., Muckel, S., Schmitz, D.: Introducing Research Data Management as a Service Suite at RWTH Aachen University. GI Lecture Notes in Informatics – Proceedings, vol. P-257, pp. 55–64, ISSN (Print) 1617-5468, ISBN (Print) 978-3-88579-651-0

[RW11]   RWTH Aachen University: Grundsätze zur Sicherung guter wissenschaftlicher Praxis der Rheinisch-Westfälischen Technischen Hochschule Aachen. Amtliche Bekanntmachung vom, 11 January 2011. http://www.rwth-aachen.de/global/show_document.asp?id=aaaaaaaaaaaaoyxb. Last Access 12 Jan 2016

[RW16]   RWTH Aachen University: Leitlinien zum Forschungsdatenmanagement für die RWTH Aachen. Rektoratsbeschluss vom, 08 March 2016. http://www.rwth-aachen.de/global/show_document.asp?id=aaaaaaaaaaqwpfe&download=1. Last Access 10 March 2016

[EB13]   Eifert, T., Bunsen, G.: Grundlagen und Entwicklung von Identity Management an der RWTH Aachen. PIK - Praxis der Informationsverarbeitung und Kommunikation. Band 36, Heft 2, Seiten 109–116 (2013). doi:10.1515/pik-2012-0053

[KE13]   Klar, J., Enke, H.: Rahmenbedingungen einer disziplinübergreifenden Forschungsdateninfrastruktur. Report Organisation und Struktur (2013). doi:10.2312/RADIESCHEN_005. Last Access 12 Jan 2016

Semiotic Engineering to Define a Declarative Citizen Language

Lilian Mendes Cunha[1]([⊠]), Claudia Cappelli[1,2]([⊠]),
and Flávia Maria Santoro[2]([⊠])

[1] Systems Information Post Degree Program, Federal University of the State
of Rio de Janeiro (UNIRIO), Rio de Janeiro, Brazil
lilian.cunha@uniriotec.br
[2] Departament of Applied Informatics, Federal University of the State
of Rio de Janeiro (UNIRIO), Rio de Janeiro, Brazil
{claudia.cappelli,lavia.santoro}@uniriotec.br

Abstract. The Brazilian Public Administration (PA) intends to turn
its business process transparent, but the language choice was BPMN.
Current research observes that the declarative language can partially
fit the PA's constraints. However declarative language is not easy for
the citizen to understand. In our case study, we found evidence of it by
using the Communicability Evaluation Method. Thus, in this paper, we
propose a preliminary version of a new declarative language.

Keywords: User-friendly · Declarative process · HCI · Semiotics ·
Govern

1 Introduction

In recent years, research has become increasingly focused on the legal aspect of
Public Administration (PA) worldwide, which is the management of public services. The citizens have been the major stakeholders using the public services [1, 2].
On the grounds of transparency, the Brazilian public organisations have to
publish their services' information as established at the Transparency Law [3]
and the Access Law [4]. In this sense, the organisations have to guarantee, among
other things, that the citizens understand what is happening inside the organisation and how information is generated and used [5], i.e. processes performed as well
as services offered. Furthermore, Brazilian government established a norm which
demands that public business process has to be represented with Business Process
Management Notation (BPMN) [6]. Equally important, since 2005, the European
countries PA's (Spain, Germany, Switzerland, and Austria) is organising its activities modelling process also with BPMN [7]. On the other hand, Mendling et al.
[8] suggest that business process models are difficult to understand caused by a
formal description weakness.

Business process models represent activities (actions performed by roles) and
the relations among them called execution flows [9]. Currently, literature distinguishes two types of process modelling. The imperative process defines the

© Springer International Publishing AG 2017
S. Yamamoto (Ed.): HIMI 2017, Part II, LNCS 10274, pp. 503–515, 2017.
DOI: 10.1007/978-3-319-58524-6_40

sequence of activities that should be executed in a structured form. In contrast, the declarative process only determines the mandatory actions, leaving the users free to chose how to execute them [9,10]. A business process is modelled with specific languages, and each language has a notation with a formal grammar [9]. The imperative business process languages are, for example, BPMN [10] and, Petri Net [11], among others. In addition, for instance, the declarative business process language can be ConDec [12] and DCR Graphs [13] among others.

In the PA's context, the BPMN has been extensively studied, represented as imperative processes [14]. Ahrend [15] argued that BPMN did not cover all situations proposed due to the inconsistency of data. Nevertheless, recent research appears with insights on the declarative process to address the limitation of BPMN, as shown in Cognini [16]. One of those limitations is related to the fact that the regulation has several genres of writing.

In fact, when the focus is on the citizens, both declarative and imperative business process languages have proved to fail. They do not seem appropriate to show information to society. The demand of imperative processes approach for the citizens have been developed, e.g. [17,18]. Nonetheless, the declarative processes still claiming to it. As government uses imperative and declarative written languages, we understand that a citizen language to represent imperative and declarative business processes is needed.

Following this line of argumentation, this paper proposes to extend a declarative language based on characteristics of human communication to improve citizen understanding. We use the Communicability Evaluation Method (CEM) [19] from Semiotic Engineering methods for testing the signs of a declarative language. Our goals were to discover the characteristics of understandability and to comprehend how we can improve the language by the inclusion of new elements to promote more understandability and to provide better communication between the government and the society.

The remaining of this paper has been structured as follows. Section 2 provides an overview of Declarative Process. Section 3 presents the characteristics of understandability in process models, introducing patterns for modelling better. Section 4 explains the concepts of semiotics used. Section 5 describes an example to explain the preliminary proposal. Finally, Sect. 6 presents conclusions.

2   Declarative Languages

The Declarative Process Modelling Language has a large body of knowledge in the Business Process Management (BPM) field. Although in literature, we observe different designations for raw language, for example, Declarative Process Modelling Language [20], Declarative Process Modelling [21] and the shorter Declarative Language [22], we will use the short name.

We decided to study from Pesic [23] until nowadays, around 2006 2016, due to the ConDec language, designed with the aim to be comprehensible for users [24, p. 25]. Pesic [12] describes Declare as a Workflow Management System (WMS), used as a template for any business process modelling language based on Linear Temporal Logic (LTL) [25], shown Fig. 1.

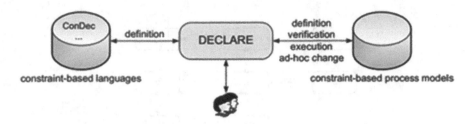

Fig. 1. DECLARE as a WMS [24]

The LTL is an extension of classical logical with atomic propositions and the standard Boolean operators ($\neg$, $\wedge$, $\vee$, $\rightarrow$, $\leftrightarrow$) well-defined in the literature. The operators used for the extension were always ($\square$), next time ($\bigcirc$), eventually ($\diamond$) and next ($\sqcap$) [28].

In addition, she defined three types of behaviours: undesired, called as "forbidden"; alternative, called as "optional"; and accepted, called as "allowed". Table 1 shows the distinction between them.

Table 1. Explanation about the behaviours

Behaviour	Explanations
Undesired	The situation might never happen in all instances of the process
Alternative	Something can happen but does not occur frequently and in some cases, could be not appropriate
Accepted	The situation will occur naturally in all instances

The process of modelling business with declarative languages might be represent the business rules throught sign usage to introduce specified behavior. It must define what the process should not do. In other respects, not all the relations are connected and there is no order of execution illustrated in Fig. 2(a) [23,26]. An important point of view is the execution order of the activities that must be tacit defined by constraints [12]. Figure 2 depicts a timeless representation of differences between imperative and declarative process modelling language. Conversely, the declarative process modelled automatically in the ConDec language is shown in Fig. 3 [30].

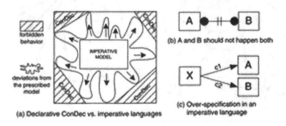

Fig. 2. Differences between Imperative and Declarative perspective

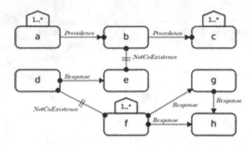

Fig. 3. ConDec automatically generated

The ConDec language, as we already mentioned, was the pioneer of the languages with the focus on the user and has been updated along with languages based on LTL as well, such as PICTURE [27], DCR Graphs [13] and so on. In our case study, we choose the ConDec, because it has a larger number of elements to represent the process than the others languages, and we argue that they can be useful in our context.

3   Characteristics of Understandability

"Transparency through computerised systems is supposed to improve governments all over the world by reducing corruption and enhancing accountability to citizens" [28]. Cappelli et al. [29] argued that for the organisations give transparency they need to make many steps in their business process. Accessibility, usability, informativeness, understandability and audibility are characteristics that contribute to transparency [30]. Figure 4 presents Transparency SIG where these relationships are depicted.

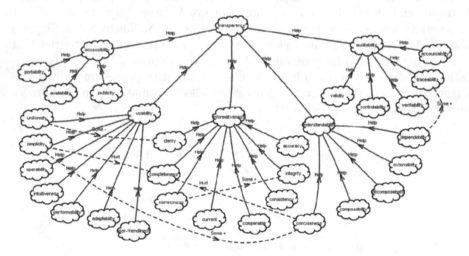

Fig. 4. Adapted from Organisational Transparency SIG [5], where the hierarchy means the sub-element helps the element

Fig. 5. The Catalogue of Understandability [18]

Based on Cappelli et al. [5] definitions, Engiel et al. [18] developed a Understandability Catalogue [Fig. 5] applied to public services process models.

They defined not only the characteristics but also operationalizations and implementation mechanisms. Table 2 explains how to insert or change elements in business process models to give citizens more understanding about that processes. Their proposal uses the complete catalogue during modelling step to increase an Imperative process model into a new model easier to citizen readable.

Table 2. Some examples of operationalizations and implementation mechanisms [18]

Characteristic	Operationalization	Implementation mechanisms
Adaptability	Define different views of the process model according to the target audience	(i) Identify the target audience – who, in the external environment, interested in information about the process; describing the profile of each audience group; (ii) Associate which process elements/information (activity, flow, rules, actors, etc.) are relevant to each profile; (iii) Define ways by which each element will be identified (colour, size, etc.) in the model, considering each profile
	Explain the process model	(i) Provide a textual description of the overall model
Clarity	Associate each activity to its actor/responsible party	(i) Use the same colour to identify activities and the party responsible for their execution; or (ii) Associate activities and their actor with arrows
Clarity	Associate each activity to its rules	(i) Associate activities to their rules using an arrow; or (ii) Create a table associating each activity with the rules which apply to them
Conciseness	Reduce process complexity	(i) Present the process model with the minimum number of activities/flow required for its execution; or (ii) Do not include subprocesses.
Intuitiveness	Build models independent of notations	(i) Use known metaphors/icons to represent elements of the process
Uniformity	Standardise elements of the process model	(i) Determine the shape, size and colour of each the element of the process

Carvalho et al. [17], based on Engiel et al. [18], added some new operationalizations and implementations mechanisms creating an Imperative Citizen
Language. This language transforms BPMN flows, which are based on an imperative logic in a very simple flow giving more clarity, conciseness and intuitiveness
for the process. Figure 6(a) and (b) represent this transformation.

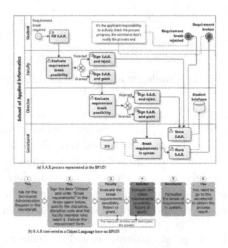

Fig. 6. Citizen Language based on BPMN

In this paper, we argue that the same could be done for declarative languages,
aiming to transform a Declarative flow into a Declarative Citizen Language. In
this sense, we present the background of Semiotic Engineering used for proposing
this transformation.

4   Semiotic Engineering

The Semiotics deals with the whole creation process of a sign, which is: processing,
their usage and the emphasis on the reaction suffered in dealing with them. A sign
is something that serves or gives a definition of something to someone [31].

The signs are the primary source of communication between the members of
an organisation, as shown in the Organizational Semiotics which is the related
subject in Semiotic [32]. According to Sjöström [33], the interpretation and creation of a picture are a consequence of pragmatic and social aspects that come
from the Semiotic Framework. The Semiotic Framework is not used in our work
yet because we focus on finding the problems with communication between a
process model and the citizen. It seems appropriate to use the communicative
perspective, in Fig. 7, to simulate some questions about the declarative business
models based on Communicability Evaluation Method (CEM) [34].

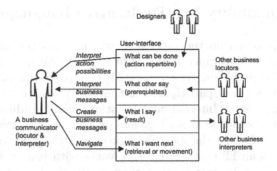

Fig. 7. A communicative perspective on user interfaces [33]

The effects of CEM have been the communication appraisal between the designer and user using an Information System interface, for interaction. It occurs by the expressions that the users make while doing a task. For each expression, CEM proposes a tag as a result for indicating the feeling of the message received from the designer [34]. Figure 8 show the CEM tags categorised. The method indicates the problems of communication called as a breakdown.

Category type	Sub-Category		Distinctive Feature	Tag
(I) Complete / Persistent Failures		(a)	User is conscious of failure.	"I give up."
		(b)	User is unconscious of failure.	"Looks fine to me."
(II) Temporary Failures	1. User's semiosis is temporarily halted	(a)	because he cannot find the appropriate expression for his illocution.	"Where is it?"
		(b)	because he does not perceive or understand the designer's deputy's illocution.	"What happened?"
		(c)	because he cannot find an appropriate intent for illocution.	"What now?"
	2. User realizes his illocution is wrong	(a)	because it is uttered in the wrong context.	"Where am I?"
		(b)	because the expression in illocution is wrong.	"Oops!"
		(c)	because a many-step conversation has not caused the desired effects.	"I can't do it this way."
	3. User seeks to clarify the designer's deputy's illocution	(a)	through implicit metacommunication.	"What's this?"
		(b)	through explicit metacommunication.	"Help!"
		(c)	through autonomous sense-making.	"Why doesn't it?"
(III) Partial Failures		(a)	User understands the design solution.	"Thanks, but no, thanks."
		(b)	User does not understand the design solution.	"I can do otherwise."

Fig. 8. The tags categorised [35]

Ferreira et al. [36] used this method to appraise the Unified Modeling Language (UML). In our case, we are doing a similar research with the declarative process model, aiming to find the breakdown to reach business process understandability. Thus, the first step was to use a case study described in the next section.

5   Understandability in a Declarative Language

The case study is based on the process in which a tourism agency needs to address a demand for insurance health care (Fig. 9). We used this exercise to find communication problems. We represented these problems using tags as used in CEM. Four participants participated in this study. All of them are 26 ~ 35 years old. Person 1 is an International Relations undergraduate student and she does not have knowledge about business process models. Person 2 is an IT professional who works with databases and knows a little about business process models. Person 3 is an IT professional who works with tests case and has also some knowledge about business process models. Person 4 is an IT professional who works at Secondary School and does not have any knowledge about business process models. The tags were created based on CEM tags.

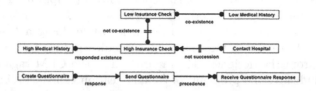

Fig. 9. ConDec applied to people [22]

They all received the same instructions in order to describe their understanding of the process based on the model of (Fig. 9). The first person said that she could not understand the model at all. So she did not create any tag. The other three participants asked some questions like: **"Where is the beginning?"**, **"Why the process has two lines"**, **"Where is the end"**, **"Why are the tasks not all connect"**, **"What are the questionnaires?"**, **"Who did the questionnaire?"**, **"Who received?"**, **"How to know the next activity"** and **"Who should to fill up the questionnaire?"**. We used these questions as CEM tags with the purpose to identify breakdown structures in the process model.

After analysing the results, we could end up with some remarks. The questions about responsibility for an activity can be answered using the notation of DCR Graphs [13]. Thus, we based on DCR graphs for adding new elements, which we think, could help to improve the understandability. With this in mind, the languages SBPMN [37], eCRG [38], PICTURE [27] also gave us insights into new elements to propose.

For each question, we suggested inserting new elements in the process model. Each one has a correspondence with one characteristic of understandability defined by Engiel et al. [18]. Table 3 shows these correspondences.

Table 3. Elements created to give understandability to a Declarative Language

Elements	Operat. Component	Tag correspondent
[37]	Intuitiveness	"Where is the beginning?"
[37]	Intuitiveness	"Where is the end?"
[38]	Clarity	"Who should to fill up the questionnaire?"
[38]	Clarity	"Who did the questionnaire?"
not co-existence	Conciseness	"Why the process has two lines?"
precedence	Conciseness	"Why the process has two lines?"
Next Responded existence	Conciseness	"Why the process has two lines?"
co-existence	Conciseness	"Why the process has two lines?"
Int. Employee CheckHigh Insurance Status	Clarity	It represents an activity of start and did not represent a tag. Also, the activi-ty always has the status, a role and a label
Int. Employee Create Questionnaire Status	Clarity	It represents an alternative activity of start and did not represent a tag. Also, the activity always has the status, a role and a label
File Inputs: XPTO Output: WPTO	Conciseness	"What are the questionnaires?"

At the end, we applied these new elements to build a new diagram. Figure 10 depicts the preliminary example of the new language.

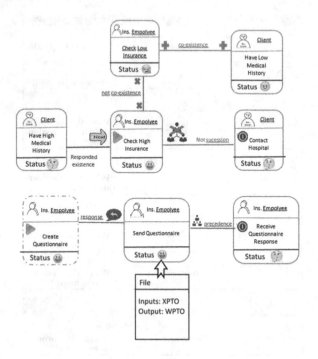

Fig. 10. New model proposed (transformed from Fig. 9)

6   Conclusions

The results of case study show us that the ConDec, despite being designed to be understood by the user, in fact when the people saw they did not recognise the tasks that should be done. We start to build a new declarative language, and our future work will bring concepts of Semiotic Framework to help formal explanations about it.

Future work also includes to formally write this new language and evaluate it with users.

Acknowledgement. We would like to thank the participants of the case study, and also, to CNPq for the research scholarship.

References

1. Shafritz, J., Russell, E., Borick, C.: Introducing Public Administration. Taylor & Francis, Hoboken (2015)
2. Petruşel, R.: A framework for researching public administration decision making processes. Transylvanian Rev. Adm. Sci. **39**, 128–146 (2013)
3. Rousseff, D., Cardoso, J.E., Amorim, C.L.N., de Aguiar Patriota, A., Belchior, M., Silva, P.B., Hoffmann, G., Siqueira, J.E.C., Chagas, H., Adams, L.I.L., Sobrinho, J.H., Nunes, M.d.R.: Law 131 Transparency Law (2011)
4. Rousseff, D., Cardoso, J.E., Amorim, C.L.N., de Aguiar Patriota, A., Belchior, M., Silva, P.B., Hoffmann, G.: Access Law - LEI N° 12.527, DE 18 DE NOVEMBRO DE 2011 (2011)
5. do Prado Leite, J.C.S., Cappelli, C.: Software transparency. Bus. Inf. Syst. Eng. **2**(3), 127–139 (2010)
6. Simão, V.M., Filho, L.A.F.N.D., Britto: Instrução Normativa - CGU MPOG 01–2016 (2016)
7. Villa, M.: Process modelling in the public administrations & e-government gateways: ICTE-PAN. In: Proceedings of the eGovInterop, vol. 5 (2005)
8. Mendling, J., Reijers, H.A., Cardoso, J.: What makes process models understandable? In: Alonso, G., Dadam, P., Rosemann, M. (eds.) BPM 2007. LNCS, vol. 4714, pp. 48–63. Springer, Heidelberg (2007). doi:10.1007/978-3-540-75183-0_4
9. Weske, M.: Business Process Management: Concepts, Languages, Architectures. Springer Publishing Company Incorporated, Heidelberg (2010)
10. Fahland, D., Lübke, D., Mendling, J., Reijers, H., Weber, B., Weidlich, M., Zugal, S.: Declarative versus imperative process modeling languages: the issue of understandability. In: Halpin, T., Krogstie, J., Nurcan, S., Proper, E., Schmidt, R., Soffer, P., Ukor, R. (eds.) BPMDS/EMMSAD 2009. LNBIP, vol. 29, pp. 353–366. Springer, Heidelberg (2009). doi:10.1007/978-3-642-01862-6_29
11. Desel, J., Reisig, W.: Place/transition petri nets. In: Reisig, W., Rozenberg, G. (eds.) ACPN 1996. LNCS, vol. 1491, pp. 122–173. Springer, Heidelberg (1998). doi:10.1007/3-540-65306-6_15
12. Pesic, M.M.: Constraint-based workflow management systems: shifting control to users. Ph.D. thesis, Technische Universiteit Eindhoven (2008)
13. Slaats, T., Mukkamala, R.R., Hildebrandt, T., Marquard, M.: Exformatics declarative case management workflows as DCR graphs. In: Daniel, F., Wang, J., Weber, B. (eds.) BPM 2013. LNCS, vol. 8094, pp. 339–354. Springer, Heidelberg (2013). doi:10.1007/978-3-642-40176-3_28
14. Torres, V., Giner, P., Bonet, B., Pelechano, V.: Adapting BPMN to public administration. In: Mendling, J., Weidlich, M., Weske, M. (eds.) BPMN 2010. LNBIP, vol. 67, pp. 114–120. Springer, Heidelberg (2010). doi:10.1007/978-3-642-16298-5_11
15. Ahrend, N.: Opportunities and limitations of BPM initiatives in public administrations across levels and institutions. Ph.D. thesis, Humboldt-Universität zu Berlin, Wirtschaftswissenschaftliche Fakultät (2014)
16. Cognini, R., Hinkelmann, K., Martin, A.: A case modelling language for process variant management in case-based reasoning. In: Reichert, M., Reijers, H.A. (eds.) BPM 2015. LNBIP, vol. 256, pp. 30–42. Springer, Cham (2016). doi:10.1007/978-3-319-42887-1_3
17. Carvalho, L.P., Santoro, F., Cappelli, C.: Using a citizen language in public process models: the case study of a Brazilian University. In: Kő, A., Francesconi, E. (eds.) EGOVIS 2016. LNCS, vol. 9831, pp. 123–134. Springer, Cham (2016). doi:10.1007/978-3-319-44159-7_9

18. Araujo, R., Cappelli, C., Engiel, P.: Raising citizen-government communication with business process models. In: Handbook of Research on Democratic Strategies and Citizen-Centered E-Government Services, pp. 92–106 (2015)
19. Souza, C.S.D., Leitão, C.F., Prates, R.O., Silva, E.J.D.: The semiotic inspection method. In: Proceedings of VII Brazilian Symposium on Human Factors in Computing Systems, IHC 2006, p. 148 (2006)
20. Schunselaar, D.M.M., Maggi, F.M., Sidorova, N., Van Der Aalst, W.M.P.: Configurable declare: designing customisable flexible process models. In: Meersman, R., Panetto, H., Dillon, T., Rinderle-Ma, S., Dadam, P., Zhou, X., Pearson, S., Ferscha, A., Bergamaschi, S., Cruz, I.F. (eds.) OTM 2012. LNCS, vol. 7565, pp. 20–37. Springer, Heidelberg (2012). doi:10.1007/978-3-642-33606-5_3
21. Schönig, S., Jablonski, S.: Comparing declarative process modelling languages from the organisational perspective. In: Reichert, M., Reijers, H.A. (eds.) BPM 2015. LNBIP, vol. 256, pp. 17–29. Springer, Cham (2016). doi:10.1007/978-3-319-42887-1_2
22. De Leoni, M., Maggi, F.M., Van Der Aalst, W.M.P.: An alignment-based framework to check the conformance of declarative process models and to preprocess event-log data. Inf. Syst. **47**, 258–277 (2015)
23. Pesic, M., Schonenberg, H., Van Der Aalst, W.M.P.: DECLARE: full support for loosely-structured processes. In: Proceedings of the IEEE International Enterprise Distributed Object Computing Workshop, EDOC, pp. 287–298 (2007)
24. Pesic, M., Van Der Aalst, W.M.P.: A declarative approach for flexible business processes management. In: Eder, J., Dustdar, S. (eds.) BPM 2006. LNCS, vol. 4103, pp. 169–180. Springer, Heidelberg (2006). doi:10.1007/11837862_18
25. Maggi, F.M., Mooij, A.J., Van Der Aalst, W.M.P.: User-guided discovery of declarative process models. In: IEEE SSCI 2011: Symposium Series on Computational Intelligence - CIDM 2011: 2011 IEEE Symposium on Computational Intelligence and Data Mining, pp. 192–199 (2011)
26. Goedertier, S., Vanthienen, J.: Declarative process modeling with business vocabulary and business rules. In: Meersman, R., Tari, Z., Herrero, P. (eds.) OTM 2007. LNCS, vol. 4805, pp. 603–612. Springer, Heidelberg (2007). doi:10.1007/978-3-540-76888-3_83
27. Becker, J., Pfeiffer, D., Räckers, M.: PICTURE - A new approach for domain-specific process modelling. In: CEUR Workshop Proceedings, vol. 247, pp. 45–48 (2007)
28. Meijer, A.: Understanding modern transparency. Int. Rev. Adm. Sci. **75**, 255–269 (2009)
29. Aló, C.C.: Uma Abordagem para Transparência em Processos Organizacionais Utilizando Aspectos. Ph.D. thesis, PUC-Rio (2009)
30. Cappelli, C., Leite, J.: Transparência de processos organizacionais. In: II Simpósio Internacional de Transparência nos Negócios, Universidade Federal Fluminense, LATEC, Niterói, RJ, Brasil (2008)
31. Liu, K.: Semiotics in Information Systems Engineering. Cambridge University Press, Cambridge (2000)
32. Stamper, R., Liu, K., Hafkamp, M., Ades, Y.: Understanding the roles of signs and norms in organisations - A semiotic approach to information systems design. J. Behav. Inf. Technol. **19**(1), 15–27 (2000)
33. Sjöström, J., Goldkuhl, G.: The semiotics of user interfaces - a socio-pragmatic perspective. In: Liu, K. (ed.) Virtual, Distributed and Flexible Organisations, pp. 217–236. Springer, Netherlands (2004)

34. Prates, R.O., de Souza, C.S., Barbosa, S.D.J.: Methods and tools: a method for evaluating the communicability of user interfaces. Interactions **7**(1), 31–38 (2000)
35. Souza, C.S., Laffon, R.F., Leitão, C.F.: Communicability in multicultural contexts: a study with the International Children's Digital Library. In: Forbrig, P., Paternò, F., Pejtersen, A.M. (eds.) HCIS 2008. IFIP AICT, vol. 272, pp. 129–142. Springer, Boston, MA (2008). doi:10.1007/978-0-387-09678-0_12
36. Ferreira, J.S.J., de Araujo, R.M., Baião, F.A.: Comunicaçã através de modelos no contexto do desenvolvimento software. Master's thesis, Federal University of the State of Rio de Janeiro (UNIRIO) (2015)
37. Fernández, H.F., Palacios-González, E., García-Díaz, V., G-Bustelo, B.C.P., Martínez, O.S., Lovelle, J.M.C.: SBPMN - an easier business process modeling notation for business users. Comput. Stand. Interfaces **32**, 18–28 (2010)
38. Knuplesch, D., Reichert, M.: A visual language for modeling multiple perspectives of business process compliance rules. Softw. Syst. Model., 1–22 (2016)

The Participatory Sensing Platform Driven by UGC for the Evaluation of Living Quality in the City

Yang Ting Shen[1(✉)], Yi Shiang Shiu[2], Wei Kuang Liu[1], and Pei Wen Lu[3]

[1] School of Architecture, Feng Chia University, Taichung, Taiwan
{yatishen,wkliu}@fcu.edu.tw
[2] Department of Urban Planning and Spatial Information,
Feng Chia University, Taichung, Taiwan
ysshiu@fcu.edu.tw
[3] Department of Geography, National Changhua University of Education, Changhua, Taiwan
peiwenlu@cc.ncue.edu.tw

Abstract. In this paper, we present a mobile-based participatory sensing method to engage citizens' participation in the living quality evaluation. The system called City Probe consists of the APP and the platform to provide the location-based services. City Probe allows citizens to identify and assess the spatial issues. By using the rating function of City Probe APP, citizens can turn the qualitative spatial issues into measurable UGC data. In addition, the UGC data are visualized as (1) rating value map, (2) rating amount map, and (3) rating heat map to present the different quantitative patterns of city. The experiment of arcade survey verifies the value of City Probe by locating and assessing the OCCUPANCY issue.

Keywords: Participatory sensing · Crowdsourcing · VGI · Decision support system · UGC

1 Introduction

By contributing recent convergence of greater access to web-enabled and GPS-enable mobile devices connections, vast numbers of individuals became able to create and share Volunteered Geographic Information (VGI) [22]. The use of mobile devices to upload VGI data gives citizens the ability to act as sensors. Thus, the term citizen-sensor network refers to an interconnected network of people who actively observe, report, collect, analyze, and disseminate information via text, audio, picture, video, or even score messages [24]. Comparing with the expert-driven data, the user-generated contents (UGC) [5, 27] show less authoritative but more commonsense in the description of daily information. As we know, the identification referring to city events or activities may need general agreements as much as we can, not specific perspectives. Therefore, if we look forward the general investigation of city phenomenon, the ubiquitous citizens who deeply engage their daily life in the city will be the most powerful sensors. All we need is to provide the proper tool which can turn citizens' perception into quantifiable statistics.

In this paper, we propose a novel system called City Probe for the participatory sensing of citizens. We try to engage citizens to identify and quantify the complex issues

© Springer International Publishing AG 2017
S. Yamamoto (Ed.): HIMI 2017, Part II, LNCS 10274, pp. 516–527, 2017.
DOI: 10.1007/978-3-319-58524-6_41

based on their perception. The system including APP and platform is developed for citizens' participation and data collection. A field study operated by City Probe is conducted to collect the citizens' feedback for the special issue.

2   Literature Review

Researchers, policymakers and the public use data to understand and persuade. Higher quality data tend to generate more significant action and better understanding [4]. A new architecture for data collection in regard to UGC can enhance and systematize existing methodology by increasing the quantity, quality and credibility. In addition, inspired by the development of mobile technology and its popularity, the UGC data carrying the geographical information make the applications of location-based service (LBS) possible. In this section, we will discuss the trend of UGC and how participatory sensing and VGI turn it into LBS applications.

2.1   User-Generate Contents

User-generated content (UGC) refers to media content created or produced by the general public rather than by paid professionals and primarily distributed on the Internet [7]. With the emergence of Web 2.0, UGC has been, and will likely be, increasingly changing the way that people search, find, read, gather, share, develop, and consume information.

Some websites or platforms take the advantages of UGC to build up their contents or services. YouTube is a content community that allows users to post, view, and comment to videos on the platform. Facebook is a social networking platform that users can create profiles featuring personal information, interests, photos, and the like. Twitter is a micro-blogging site that allows people to publish (tweet), reply to, and forward posts. Wikipedia is an online encyclopedia that allows users to co-work with the produce of knowledge. All the websites or platforms mentioned above use the UGC to support their contents or service and profit from them. Some commercial websites use UGC technologies to add value or weight to their existing contents. For instance, a recommender system on Amazon.com (www.amazon.com) suggests books to customers based on other books the customers have told Amazon they like. It also happens in some travel services. Travel.com is a travel recommender system that provides the information about hotel reservations, car rentals, airfares. The rating system of its website is driven by the users' assessment and recommendation.

UGC has the power of knowledge building, sharing, and recommending due to the collection of users' contribution. So far most of discussion and application of UGC focus on the online environment. However, when UGC refers to the users' locations, the integration with participatory sensing will bring more spatial issues and applications to the city environment.

2.2 Participatory Sensing

Participatory sensing offers a number of advantages over traditional static sensor networks, particularly in the urban scale. First, participatory sensing leverages existing mobile communication infrastructures, the deployment costs are quite low. Second, the mobile phone carriers provide ubiquitous spatiotemporal coverage. In addition, the ICT and GPS elements embedded in mobile devices support the location-based information. Therefore, using mobile phones as sensors not only affords economies of scale, but also facilitates the ubiquitous deployment. By including citizens in the sensing loop, it is possible to build or reveal the implicit information of city that supports the of citizen living or government management.

Several exciting participatory sensing applications have emerged in the recent decade. CarTel [14] is a mobile sensor computing system designed to collect, process, deliver, and visualize data collected from sensors embedded in mobile vehicles. The idea is used to design Google Maps Navigation service. Comparing with close-end GPS navigation system, Google Maps Navigation shows the significant feather that navigates drivers through the real-time traffic report. The real-time traffic report analysis is based on traffic users' collective feedback data to increase its accuracy and instantaneity. In terms of citizens as sensors [11], some participatory sensing applications engage the citizens' perception power to assess spatial issues. Streetscore [18] developed by MIT Media Lab is a scene understanding algorithm that can score city environmental issues. It reveals the perceived issue of a streetscape such as safe, lively, boring, depressing, wealthy, and beautiful by using training data from an online survey with contributions from more than one million participants. Other applications of participatory sensing include the collection and sharing of information about urban air [19], noise pollution [20], cyclist experiences [9], diets [21], or consumer pricing information in offline markets [8]. In short, participatory sensing engages citizens' perception and mobility to turn the complex urban context into measurable data.

By contributing recent convergence of greater access to ICT and GPS embedded mobile devices, vast numbers of citizens become able to create and share Volunteered Geographic Information (VGI) [22]. It generates large data related to the urban context that need to be efficiently compiled. Goodchild [12] emphasize scientific information visualization techniques as a way to handle large and complex data sets from participatory sensing and VGI location and time are crucial information in regard to data visualization of spatial issue. Recent work in geospatial visual analytics has focused on combining visualization, spatial data mining, and statistical methods to these ends [1, 17, 28]. For instance, Casewise Visual Assessment (CAVE) methodology used information visualization to present design options and analyze big data sets from public participation meetings held in urban and regional planning [2]. Currid and Williams applied GIS-based methods for identifying hot spots to large data sets comprised of georeferenced images [6]. In conclusion, large geospatial data generated from participatory or VGI benefit by geo-visualization methods. The visualized map-based information reveals the useful messages that feedback to citizens and authorities for decision making supports. It also enables the mass applications of LBS.

The following sections we will introduce our system that is developed for the spatial living quality assessment. In the end the experimental survey is also presented to demonstrate the performance of our system.

3   City Probe: The Participatory Sensing System

Taking inspiration from mobile network and the trend towards participatory sensing in data collecting and mapping, we propose a novel approach for the cooperative identification of spatial issues via citizens' perception. The system called City Probe consists of mobile phone APP and cloud platform that generates UGC data and compiles the visualized maps [23, 25].

3.1   Mobile-Based Interface

Citizens are the most powerful sensor for the environmental issues detection. The notion derived from Participatory Sensing [4], VGI [22], and Citizens as Sensors [11] drives us to develop the City Probe APP for citizens' perception collection. The perception means a citizen's cognition to the complex issue. In our paper, the complex issues are particularly related to the spatial and qualitative environmental context. They can be identified and quantified by citizens due to the power of human perception. The City Probe APP design the location-based photo taking and rating functions to extract the quantitative UGC information from citizens' perception.

The APP is compiled both to Android/IOS languages and allows full access from Google Play/Apple Store. The City Probe APP consists of three main functions including (1) City Probe, (2) Individual Map, (3) Crowd Map (Fig. 1).

1. City Probe
   The City Probe function is the most important part for the participatory sensing of citizens. When a citizen clicks this button, the APP will request him to select the preliminary issues we setup in advance. The issue setting is based on the principle of environmental complex that any artificial sensor is hard to detect or identify. For example, SAFETY issue is much more complex than the WEATHER issue. The weather can be consisted of several quantifiable parameters such as temperature, humidity, and air pressure etc. Besides, it can be measured by sensors. However, it is difficult to determine the safety state by sensors or other devices. Therefore, the qualitative issue like safety needs to depend on the human perception for comprehensive judgment.
   Once the citizen selects one of the qualitative issues, he needs to take a photo to identify the target environment. After shooting, the City Probe APP will enter the interactive rating screen for advance identification (Fig. 2 left). In the rating screen, the photo taken before is displayed on the top. The location of photo shooting is automatically detected and shown on the map. In the screen middle, the rating bar allow the citizen to grade the photo via scrolling the slider. The range of slider is from -10(negative) to $+10$(positive). The rating score represents how the citizen assess and quantify the issue. After the rating, the citizen can click the topic conform

button to finish this identification action. The collected data will be sent to the City Probe platform for archive and retrieved in the individual and crowd map function.

Fig. 1. The main functions of City Probe APP

2. Individual Map

The citizen who finished the identification activities can go back to the entrance screen and access his personal record by clicking the individual map button. The personal identification result will be visualized as the gradient color dots in the map. The red dots represent the positive rating scores. The darker red color means the higher positive rating score. The blue dots represent the negative rating scores and work on the same way.

The aim of individual map is to visualize the result of personal identification records. It can be regarded as a personal topology of the city. Through the individual map, the citizen can retrieve personal identified locations. When the citizen clicks one of the dots, the record including the issue, the rating score, and the photo will pop up for more detail retrieval. In addition, if the citizen identified multiple issues, he can use the topic filter function to select target single issue or multiple issues.

3. Crowd Map

The City Probe APP also provides the crowd map for collective results visualization (Fig. 2 right). The visualized results on the map are anonymous. It has the similar visualization type with the individual map but accumulates all the citizens' identification results together. The crowd map displays the collective identification results to reveal the pattern of special issue. Through the crowd map, all participatory citizens can observe the distribution of collective dots to understand the trend of special issue. When the citizen clicks one of the dots, the record including the issue, the rating score, and the photo will pop up for more detail retrieval. In addition, the single or multiple issues also can be selected or filtered via topic filter function.

Compared with the individual map, the crowd map is more like a UGC tool to quantify the spatial issues. The advance introduction will be discussed in the following section.

Fig. 2. Left: the main rating screen of City Probe APP for environmental identification; Right: the crowd map displays the collective identification results by gradient color dots. (Color figure online)

3.2   Spatial Information Visualization

Each UGC collected by City Probe App contains at least five data categories. The database fields include user ID, time, longitude and latitude, photo, and rating value. The geographic information (longitude and latitude) bound to each UGC data plays the critical role for data aggregation, dissemination, mapping, and analysis. It provides the opportunity to map diverse UGC data and visualize them in spatial way. The spatial distribution of UGC data in the map helps us to perceive the relationship between virtual data and the urban context. In addition, according to the rating value of each UGC data, we can manipulate the information visualization in diverse ways for advance analysis. However, in this paper we just focus on the discussion of collective data visualization, although we can extract individual UGC record according to the user ID. We believe the collective UGC is more powerful to reveal the trend and interest of citizens.

There are three kinds of collective visualization in our City Probe platform including (1) rating value visualization, (2) rating amount visualization, and (3) rating heat visualization. All records with longitude and latitude coordinate (in degrees, WGS84) are analyzed and visualized by CartoDB. CartoDB is a software-as-a-service (SaaS) cloud computing platform built on open source PostGIS and PostgreSQL. It enables users to utilize geographic information system (GIS) and geo-visualization mapping for data exploration and decision-making processes. The geo-visualization mapping provides geospatial data analysis through the use of interactive visualization; it also simplifies the display of raw data and facilitates the amateurs to understand the meaning of the data [10, 16]. Finally, the City Probe platform translates the quantitative data into color code and mark them as dots in the map.

1. Rating Value Visualization

   The rating value is derived from the users' identification score for the special issue. Users who participate in the identification not only locate the spots, but also quantify their perception into rating values. The span of rating value is from −10 to 10. Negative number represent that users disagree the issue, and vice versa. The grade of number means users' perception level. We use the rating value and color code to visualize the identified spot as a gradient dot in the map (Fig. 3). The red code represents the positive value and the gradient represents the grade. The higher positive rating value is shown as the darker blue color. The blue code represents the negative rating value and works in the same way. Through the visualized map, we can observe the distribution of users' interest of special issue.

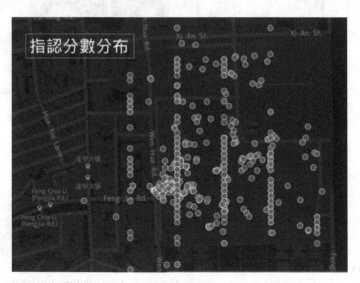

Fig. 3. Rating value map (Color figure online)

2. Rating Amount Visualization

   The rating amount is compiled from the users' identification amount for the special issue. However, if we just distribute all of the spot locations, the outcome will be similar with the rating value map but show less message. We use the geographical proximity value to decide the cluster of proximal data. It can cluster the geographical proximity UGC data to reveal the more observable map outcome (Fig. 4). The gathering amount of one cluster decides its visualized circle size. In addition, the geographical proximity value is adjustable to present different levels of data cluster.

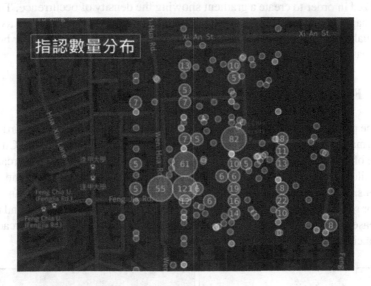

Fig. 4. Rating amount map

3. Rating Heat Visualization

Here the "heat" in the term refers to the concentration of the geographic entity within any given spot, not to be confused with heat mapping that refers to the mapping of

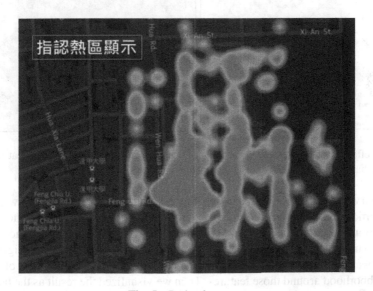

Fig. 5. Rating heat map

actual temperatures on the earth's surface. The rating heat map (Fig. 5) uses statistical analysis in order to define areas from high to low occurrence. Each point data is analyzed in order to create a gradient showing the density of occurrence. The rating heat map assist us to read the spatial pattern of issue. The resulting density surface is visualized using a gradient that allows the areas of highest density (or hot spots) to be easily identified.

4   The Filed Study for Special Issue

City Probe provides a tool for investigating the living quality in the city. In order to test the performance of City Probe, we conducted the survey implemented by the City Probe. The issue of this survey was addressed on the OCCUPANY of the arcade. Arcade is the typical building type built as a continuous pass-through corridor in the ground floor for pedestrians. Arcades in Taiwan are often occupied by car, motorcycle, and bicycle parking or some temporary commercial activities. Most of them are illegal and result in the decrease of living quality. Therefore, we try to take a survey about the arcade occupancy via citizens' identification and assessment.

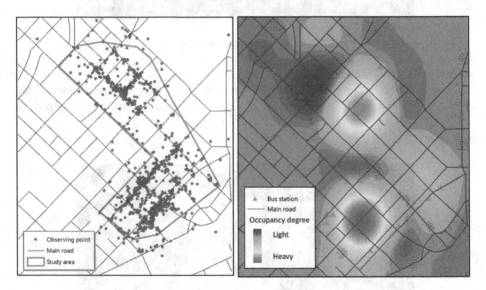

Fig. 6. Left: the total observing points reported from participants; Right: the heat map was visualized based on the collective data. (Color figure online)

The survey area was conducted in the central district of Taichung city, Taiwan. There are 52 participants who were asked to use City Probe APP in this survey. They needed to identify the occupied arcades and give them the rating score of occupancy degree. After the survey, 1453 UGC data were reported and marked on the map (Fig. 6 Left). The data were analyzed by kernel density method [26] to calculate the density of features in a neighborhood around those features. Then we visualized the result as the heat map.

Red area meant the heavy occupied area. In addition, for advance analysis the cause of occupancy, we overlaid the third party information provided by the city government. Here we added the bus station layer to our heat map (Fig. 6 Right). We found that the distribution of bus stations was hardly located in the red area. Most of them distributed around the blue areas that represented the light occupancy. The finding means occupied areas and bus stations may have spatially negative correlation. It may drive us to infer that the deployment of bus station can decrease the probability of arcade occupancy. Of course, our inference needs more sufficient evidences before we jump into conclusion; even so, City Probe still demonstrates the outstanding capability as an UGC tool.

5   Conclusion

City Probe provides the novel participatory sensing method to engage citizens' perception power for the identification and assessment of city. It functions as a crowdsourcing tool to survey qualitative issues and locate their spatial distributions. The design of rating function not only facilitates the citizens' participatory, but also engage their perception to assess the quality of environments. Though grading the score from -10 to $+10$(negative to positive of an issue), City Probe turns qualitative issues into measurable data. In other words, the UGC generated by City Probe creates the quantitative index of city issue; moreover, it carries the spatial characteristic for advanced mapping and visualization. The experiment of arcade survey verifies the value of City Probe in the spatial issue. By locating and assessing the OCCUPANCY, the pattern of occupied arcades is revealed and visualized on the map.

Compared with traditional top-down planning and management from authorities, City Probe provides an alternative bottom-up approach based on citizens' experience and interests. The crowd map visualized from City Probe UGC reveals the quantitative and statistic information that never exist before. Through the mapping of map-based visualization and the third party data, the geo-information-rich map delivers comprehensive feedbacks to participants or any interested party for advanced decision making supports. It may lead City Probe to become a powerful tool to engage citizens in the Urban Governance.

Acknowledgements. The financial support from Ministry of Science and Technology (MOST) including project "Brain Tagging System" (MOST 105-2221-E-035-070-) and project "Resilient Livable Smart City:" (MOST 105-2627-M-035-008-), is greatly acknowledged.

References

1. Andrienko, G., Andrienko, N., Demsar, U., Dransch, D., Dykes, J., Fabrikant, S.I., Tominski, C.: Space, time and visual analytics. Int. J. Geogr. Inf. Sci. **24**(10), 1577–1600 (2010)
2. Bailey, K., Brumm, J., Grossardt, T.: Towards structured public involvement in highway design: a comparative study of visualization methods and preference modeling using CAVE (Casewise Visual Evaluation). J. Geogr. Inf. Decis. Anal. **5**(1), 1–15 (2001)

3. Brabham, D.C.: Crowdsourcing as a model for problem solving: an introduction and cases. Convergence **14**(1), 75–90 (2008)
4. Burke, J.A., Estrin, D., Hansen, M., Parker, A., Ramanathan, N., Reddy, S., Srivastava, M.B.: Participatory sensing. In: Center for Embedded Network Sensing (2006)
5. Cha, M., Kwak, H., Rodriguez, P., Ahn, Y.Y., Moon, S.: I tube, you tube, everybody tubes: analyzing the world's largest user generated content video system. In: Proceedings of the 7th ACM SIGCOMM Conference on Internet Measurement, pp. 1–14. ACM (2007)
6. Currid, E., Williams, S.: Two cities, five industries: similarities and differences within and between cultural industries in New York and Los Angeles. J. Plann. Educ. Res. **29**(3), 322–335 (2010)
7. Daugherty, T., Eastin, M.S., Bright, L.: Exploring consumer motivations for creating user-generated content. J. Interact. Advertising **8**(2), 16–25 (2008)
8. Dong, Y.F., Kanhere, S., Chou, C.T., Bulusu, N.: Automatic collection of fuel prices from a network of mobile cameras. In: Nikoletseas, Sotiris E., Chlebus, Bogdan S., Johnson, David B., Krishnamachari, B. (eds.) DCOSS 2008. LNCS, vol. 5067, pp. 140–156. Springer, Heidelberg (2008). doi:10.1007/978-3-540-69170-9_10
9. Eisenman, S.B., Miluzzo, E., Lane, N.D., Peterson, R.A., Ahn, G.S., Campbell, A.T.: BikeNet: a mobile sensing system for cyclist experience mapping. ACM Trans. Sens. Netw. (TOSN) **6**(1), 6 (2009)
10. Gahegan, M., Wachowicz, M., Harrower, M., Rhyne, T.M.: The integration of geographic visualization with knowledge discovery in databases and geocomputation. Cartography Geogr. Inf. Sci. **28**(1), 29–44 (2001)
11. Goodchild, M.F.: Citizens as sensors: the world of volunteered geography. GeoJournal **69**(4), 211–221 (2007)
12. Goodchild, M.F., Glennon, J.A.: Crowdsourcing geographic information for disaster response: a research frontier. Int. J. Digit. Earth **3**(3), 231–241 (2010)
13. Haklay, M., Weber, P.: Openstreetmap: user-generated street maps. IEEE Pervasive Comput. **7**(4), 12–18 (2008)
14. Hull, B., Bychkovsky, V., Zhang, Y., Chen, K., Goraczko, M., Miu, A., Madden, S.: CarTel: a distributed mobile sensor computing system. In: Proceedings of the 4th International Conference on Embedded Networked Sensor Systems, pp. 125–138. ACM, October 2006
15. Livingstone, S.: The challenge of changing audiences: or, what is the audience researcher to do in the age of the Internet? Eur. J. Commun. **19**(1), 75–86 (2004)
16. MacEachren, A.M., Wachowicz, M., Edsall, R., Haug, D., Masters, R.: Constructing knowledge from multivariate spatiotemporal data: integrating geographical visualization with knowledge discovery in database methods. Int. J. Geogr. Inf. Sci. **13**(4), 311–334 (1999)
17. Mennis, J., Guo, D.: Spatial data mining and geographic knowledge discovery—an introduction. Comput. Environ. Urban Syst. **33**(6), 403–408 (2009)
18. Naik, N., Philipoom, J., Raskar, R., Hidalgo, C.: Streetscore-predicting the perceived safety of one million streetscapes. In: Proceedings of the IEEE Conference on Computer Vision and Pattern Recognition Workshops, pp. 779–785 (2014)
19. Paulos, E., Honicky, R.J., Goodman, E.: Sensing atmosphere. Hum.-Comput. Interact. Inst. 203 (2007)
20. Rana, R.K., Chou, C.T., Kanhere, S.S., Bulusu, N., Hu, W.: Ear-phone: an end-to-end participatory urban noise mapping system. In: Proceedings of the 9th ACM/IEEE International Conference on Information Processing in Sensor Networks, pp. 105–116. ACM, April 2010
21. Reddy, S., Parker, A., Hyman, J., Burke, J., Estrin, D., Hansen, M.: Image browsing, processing, and clustering for participatory sensing: lessons from a DietSense prototype. In: Proceedings of the 4th workshop on Embedded networked sensors, pp. 13–17. ACM, June 2007

22. Schade, S., Díaz, L., Ostermann, F., Spinsanti, L., Luraschi, G., Cox, S., De Longueville, B.: Citizen-based sensing of crisis events: sensor web enablement for volunteered geographic information. Appl. Geomatics **5**(1), 3–18 (2013)
23. Shen, Y.T., Shiu, Y.S., Lu, P.: City Probe: the crowdsourcing platform driven by citizen-based sensing for spatial identification and assessment. In: Luo, Y. (ed.) CDVE 2016. LNCS, vol. 9929, pp. 69–76. Springer, Cham (2016). doi:10.1007/978-3-319-46771-9_9
24. Sheth, A.: Citizen sensing, social signals, and enriching human experience. IEEE Internet Comput. **13**(4), 87 (2009)
25. Shiu, Y.S., Liu, Y.K., Lin, F.C., Shen, Y.T., Shih, C.Y., Lee, R.Y., Lei, T.C.: Mapping environmental perception with crowdsourced CityProbe mobile app and weights of evidence model. In: The International Symposium of Remote Sensing (2016)
26. Silverman, B.W.: Density Estimation for Statistics and Data Analysis, vol. 26. CRC Press, Boca Raton (1986)
27. Van Dijck, J.: Users like you? Theorizing agency in user-generated content. Media Cult. Soc. **31**(1), 41–58 (2009)
28. Virrantaus, K., Markkula, J., Garmash, A., Terziyan, V., Veijalainen, J., Katanosov, A., Tirri, H.: Developing GIS-supported location-based services. In: 2001. Proceedings of the Second International Conference on Web Information Systems Engineering, vol. 2, pp. 66–75. IEEE, December 2001

A Support System for Vitalizing Brainstorming with Related Images

Hidetsugu Suto(✉) and Shuichi Miyo

Muroran Institute of Technology, Hokkaido 050-8585, Japan
suto@sdlabo.net
http://www.sdlabo.net

Abstract. In this paper, a new supporting system for brainstorming is proposed, and the effects are discussed based on the results of experiments. Brainstorming is a method for encouraging ideas generation and obtaining useful ideas in order to achieve a particular goal. In a process of brainstorming, the participants are required to submit their ideas as much as they possible. However, generating huge volumes of new ideas is not easy for ordinary participants. Diversity of submitted ideas is another problem. When the participants are biased by conventional ideas, it is difficult for them to escape from the ideas and submit novel ones. The proposed system helps participants of brainstorming to generate new ideas by showing related images for them. The results of the experiment shows that participants of brainstorming can discuss more actively with the proposed system.

Keywords: Brainstorming · KJ-method · Idea creation method

1 Introduction

Several idea creation methods have been proposed to help generating novel and useful ideas. Brainstorming method is widely used in companies, educations, communities, etc. [1,2] because of the facile introduction.

KJ-method is one of the most popular method used in brainstormings [3]. In KJ-method, each idea submitted by the participants is written on a small card. By arranging the cards, participants can find relationships between submitted ideas during the discussion, and it helps them to submit more ideas and conclude the discussion.

Although KJ-method is a powerful tool, several weak points also have been pointed out. For instance, participants have to submit ideas as much as they can, but generating much new ideas is not easy for ordinal participants. In brainstormings, submitting novel ideas is required for the participants. However, it is also hard for ordinal participants because they tend to get effect from ideas which already submitted in the discussion.

In this paper, a new supporting system for brainstorming has been proposed in order to solve these problems. The proposed system shows participants some related images of important keyword used in the discussion. Participants can create novel ideas by referring the images.

© Springer International Publishing AG 2017
S. Yamamoto (Ed.): HIMI 2017, Part II, LNCS 10274, pp. 528–538, 2017.
DOI: 10.1007/978-3-319-58524-6_42

2   Related Works

Several methods for supporting brainstorming processes using digital devices have already proposed.

Miura et al. have proposed a system with a transmitted light table for supporting to conduct brainstormings [4]. By using the system, users can save processes and results of brainstormings easily. Aikawa et al. have proposed a system in which combined tablet devices are used [5]. With the system, users can conduct brainstormings anywhere together. There systems focus to support to conduct brainstormings, and supporting to generate new ideas is not the scopes.

Kang et al. have developed Category Camera for supporting to create new idea in brainstormings [6,7]. This mobile application was developed aimed to support fieldwork step of group works. The users can take photographs and put labels on them easily by using this mobile application. The labels help users to classify the photographs in discussion phases.

Matsuo et al. have developed a supporting system for idea generation [8]. First, a user input a topic word and a keyword which he/she thinks important for the topic. Then the system shows some words which relate to the topic word and the inputed keyword. Next, user selects several words from the shown words that he/she decides important for the topic, and then the topic word, the related words, and the selected words are connected together via a word which explains the relationships. In this way, the users can marshal relationships between ideas and the topic.

In comparison with these previous systems, the system proposed in this paper aims more instinctive ways. The proposed system represents some related images of submitted idea for users in order to help them to generate diverse and novel ideas.

3   Outline of the Proposed System

The aims of the proposed system is to solve the following two problems during brainstormings:

- It is not easy to submit many ideas in a limited time.
- It is difficult to submit novel ideas when we are influenced by preconceived ideas and images.

The proposed system shows the users related images of the important keywords used in ideas submitted in discussions. Figure 1 shows the outline of the proposed system.

(1) Participants submit their idea by using their own smartphones. The submitted ideas are stored in the DB on the Internet.
(2) Characteristic words are extracted from the submitted ideas.
(3) Related words of the extracted words are generated by using an external service.

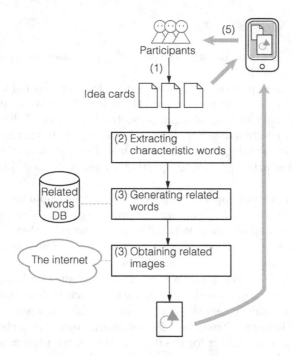

Fig. 1. Outline of the proposed system

(4) Related images are obtained by retrieving the related words as the retrieval
keywords on the Internet.

(5) Pairs of idea and related images are presented for the participants.

The system shows hints of discussions as images instead of words. Hence, the
users can get the hints instinctually without interrupting thinkings, and they
can focus on the topics.

The system has another remarkable point in step (3) and (4) in Fig. 1. The
extracting characteristic words are not used for obtaining related image directly.
Related words of the characteristic words are generating first, and then the
related images are obtained by using these related words as keywords. Because
of this mechanism, obtaining unpredictable images is expected. These unpredictable images can help to vitalize discussions, and also help to escape form
stagnating discussions.

4   Experiments

Experiments have been conducted in order to investigate the effects of related
images on discussions. Numbers of utterances in brainstormings were measured
to evaluate the activation levels.

The participants were 8 undergraduate students of engineering course in a
Japanese national university. 4 of them were 3rd grade and the others were 4th

grade. The participants were divided into 2 groups, Group A and Group B. They were asked to conduct brainstormings under two conditions, with related images and without related images.

In this experiments, kizAPI [9] was used for generating related words, and Bing search API [10] was used for obtaining related images.

4.1 Process of Experiments

A preliminary experiment was conducted beforehand. The purposes of the preliminary experiment are checking the participants' skill of brainstorming and accustoming the participants to the system. In the preliminary experiment, each group was asked to conduct a brainstorming with the proposed system without showing related images for 5 min. The topic was decided as "ways to continue diet" by considering the difficulty.

During the preliminary experiment, the number of submitted ideas was counted. As a result, the both of the group submitted the same number of ideas, 11. Thus it can be assumed that the two groups have the same level of skills of brainstorming.

The flow of the experiments is shown below:

1. Instructions of the proposed system and the experiments
2. Tutorial and exercise of the system
3. Break (3 min)
4. Brainstorming with topic 1 (10 min)
5. Break (3 min)
6. Brainstorming with topic 2 (10 min)

The following two topics were used in the experiments.

Topic 1. Ways to reduce smoking while walking
Topic 2. Ways to vitalize a life on Monday

Table 1 shows the combinations of topics and conditions. In order to reduce the effect of oder, Group A conducted under condition 1 first, meanwhile Group B conducted under condition 2 first.

Table 1. Conditions of the experiments (Condition 1: with related images, Condition 2: without related images

	Group A	Group B
Topic 1	Condition 1	Condition 2
Topic 2	Condition 2	Condition 1

Table 2. The number of submitted ideas (Condition 1: with related images, Condition 2: without related images

	Condition 1	Condition 2
Group A	14	14
Group B	14	9

4.2   Results and Discussions

Number of Ideas. Table 2 shows the number of ideas submitted during the experiment under each condition.

As we can see from the table, there is no difference between the number of utterances under condition 1 and under condition 2 for group A. Group A conducted brainstorming under condition 1 (with related images) first, and then conducted under condition 2 (without related images). Thus, the adjustment to the task might effect on the results. Meanwhile, Group B, they conducted brainstorming under condition 2 first. As a result, they submitted about 1.5 times more number of ideas under condition 1 than under condition 2. The fact also supports the assumption of the effects of adjustment.

The difference of difficulty of the topics also could effect on the results. For the topic 1, both of the group tended to submit common-sense ideas. On the other hand, both of the group could submit diverse ideas for the topic 2. Group A discussed topic 2 under condition 2. The facts could affect on the results.

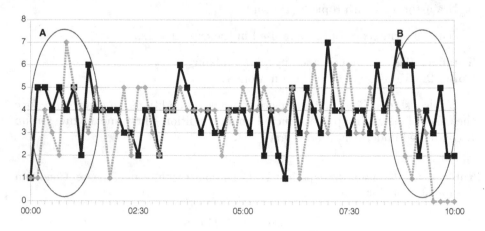

Fig. 2. Number of utterances during discussions

Flow of Discussions. Table 3 shows all of the utterances of group A for each 10 seconds under each condition. The left side shows the utterances under condition

Table 3. Utterances list

Time	Number of utterance	ID	Condition 1 (with related images)	Number of utterance	ID	Condition 2 (with out related images)
0:00~0:10	1	I001	月曜日を明るくするにはっていう文字から探するに月曜日がなくなったらさ、明るいもクソもないっぱい街に配置する「複数人の笑い声」(0:00)	1	N061	じゃあこの、歩きタバコは危ないっていう施設を奴らに持たせることが必要だから小学生たちをいっぱい街に配置する「複数人の笑い声」(0:09)
0:10~0:20	5	I002	月曜日なくす！？(0:12~0:13)	1	N062	なるほどね、配置するのね(0:18)
		I003	進め制やな「1人の笑い声」(0:14)			
		I004	日曜日の次が火曜日だ(0:15)			
		I005	そうそうそう(0:17)			
		I006	書いとけ書いとけ(0:17)			
0:20~0:30	5	I007	一発目からとぶな~「複数人の笑い声」(0:20)	4	N063	そう(0:20)
		I008	日曜日はない！(0:23)		N064	まぁまぁね(0:21)
		I009	日曜日じゃない日曜日の次は月曜日だ(0:23~0:25)		N065	本当に危ないのをわからせていく(0:23)
		I010	日曜日は休みだから、休みだからいけない(0:24~0:25)		N066	やっぱこう、ふらってやった時に子供がいたら、あぶねっておぶねってなってくると思うんだよね(0:25)
		I011	違うでしょ、なんで月曜が憂鬱かというとそっから五日間がくるから憂鬱なわけであって(0:26)			
0:30~0:40	4	I012	てことは今の日曜日がなくなってさ(0:32)	3	N067	とりあえず子供には偶発を負ってもらうと。仕方ない(0:31)
		I013	でもそれ4日になったら火曜日が憂鬱になるよ(0:35)		N068	小学生みたいな何かを(0:35)
		I014	じゃあ火曜日を休みにしよう(0:37)		N069	このぐらいの、なんセンチの何か(0:38)
		I015	え、じゃあ火曜日が今度なくなったら、まぁ6に3日になってる(0:38)			
0:40~0:50	5	I016	なんかもう短げれば憂鬱じゃないんじゃない？(0:41)	2	N010	普通にあれじゃないの？罰金とかかんか札幌とかやってるとこるはやっている(0:42)
		I017	以下ループで全部祝日だけに(0:43)		N011	まじ？(0:49)
		I018	え、じゃあれじゃない？曜日の感覚をなくして、毎日の朝くじ引きで今日は出勤ですみたいな「1人の笑い声」(0:45~0:50)			
		I019	なるほど~(0:49~0:50)			
		I020	それ面白いかもしれないきょうは出勤ですみたいな(0:50~0:54)			
0:50~1:00	4	I021	くじ引きで出勤日を決める(0:52)	7	N012	京都とか札幌もそうだっけな？(0:50)
		I022	どっかの国やってモー「1人の笑い声」(0:53~0:55)		N013	札幌は知らない、京都はそう(0:51)
		I023	くじ引きで出勤(0:57)		N014	京都はそうだよな(0:53)
		I024	くじ引きで出勤システム「1人の笑い声」(0:58)		N015	そう、罰金(0:54)
					N016	罰金はあるなぁ(0:55)
					N017	もっとなんかあれじゃない？治療みたいな(0:56)
					N018	体罰体罰(0:59)
1:00~1:10	5	I025	「1人の笑い笑い声」(0:59~1:04)	5	N019	体罰「笑いながら」(1:01)
		I026	どんだけ笑うの(1:00~1:02)		N020	増税増税(1:04)
		I027	すごいな~(1:02)		N021	体罰で取り締まる(1:05)
		I028	なんだよ？「笑いながら」(1:03)		N022	増税増税(1:07)
		I029	あ~もう~なんかもう一瞬たってくるこいつ「複数人の笑い声」(1:04)		N023	歩きタバコしなし、う~ん(1:08)
1:10~1:20	2	I030	や~もうさ、サッカー選手さ、こんな話すこ卒くない？曜日関係ないしょ(1:10)	4	N024	タバコの値段をあげれば(1:10)
		I031	ネタに走ってきた？ネタに走ってきたんじゃない「複数人の笑い声」(1:16~1:18)		N025	いや、そうタバコ自体を(1:13)
					N026	タバコをさ、無くせばいい(1:18)
					N027	輸入しません輸入しません(1:19)
1:20~1:30	6	I032	いや、マジどんどん書かないと、でない、出ないのさ(1:20)	3	N028	栽培しません(1:22)
		I033	朝ごはんが美味しいとかじゃダメなの？(1:23)		N029	書いて書いて書いて(1:23)
		I034	月曜日の朝だけ？(1:25)		N030	栽培しません「笑いながら」(1:25)
		I035	月曜日の朝！(1:26)			
		I036	月曜日の朝ごはんを気合をいれる(1:27)			
		I037	いいよ、いこいこいこいこ(1:28)			
1:30~1:40	4	I038	月曜日、朝組まない。愚痴まる(1:30)	5	N031	歩きタバコでなに(1:30)
		I039	あぁ、なるほど。良いんじゃない？(1:33)		N032	タバコを発売してもグキまずにすればいいんじゃない(1:32)
		I040	月曜日だけ、月曜日だけ朝から出勤(1:35)		N033	なるほどね(1:35)
		I041	そうそうそうそう(1:38)		N034	電子タバコでいい(1:36)
					N035	それはだってタバコを減らずには走っているからやっぱ歩きタバコってのにフォーカスしないと(1:37)
1:40~1:50	4	I042	月曜日が安くなるとかは？買い物行って物が安くなる(1:40)	4	N036	体罰で取り締まって！(1:42)
		I043	それ良いね(1:43)		N037	暮しのがいけない(1:43)
		I044	月曜日って明るいな~「複数人の笑い声」(1:45)		N038	ゆうこってなんやねん(1:44)
		I045	「複数人の笑い声」(1:47~1:49)		N039	つめたい、冷たい感じ？「複数人の笑い声」(1:46)
1:50~2:00	3	I046	それか月曜日以外を、全部暗くする方向で「複数人の笑い声」(1:51)	1	N040	痛い、熱たいか、火が効いかそれだからさやっぱ歩きタバコが減らしたい(1:54)
		I047	なるほど、逆にね？(1:55)			
		I048	もう日曜日も出勤したら良いんじゃね？(1:57)			
2:00~2:10	4	I049	土曜日を休みにして、会社日とそしたら日曜日が一番憂鬱じゃん？(2:00)	3	N041	あれじゃないいっぱつ自分の顔辺りにいっぱつタバコの火が(2:02)
		I050	まぁそうだね(2:04)		N042	タバコのあとが(2:07)
		I051	結局まぁ月曜日は明るい(2:06)		N043	歩きタバコしているやつに歩きタバコで反撃する的な(2:08)
		I052	明るいかって言われても5わかんないけど(2:08)			
2:10~2:20	3	I053	じゃあ数えてテーマに問題してみる？だけ憂鬱じゃないですみたいな感じで「1人の笑い声」(2:11~2:16)	5	N044	あぁ、それ(2:12)
		I054	憂鬱な前説で行ってきてるけど、(2:17)		N045	一回暗い目にあっても5う(2:13)
		I055	ゆうつじゃないもん別に(2:19~2:21)		N046	反射と(2:14)
					N047	空気海浄機みたいなものがあって(2:15)
					N048	危ない目に会われれば、身をもって体験してもらう(2:16)
2:20~2:30	3	I056	まぁでも、俺らは授業あるんだよな(2:22)	2	N049	ら~ん(2:22)
		I057	あれじゃない？なんか、月曜日だけ、頭の占い的なのを全体的によくするとか(2:24)		N050	あ、じゃあ歩きタバコに、歩きタバコで対応する(2:24)
		I058	あぁそれ良いかもしれない(2:29~2:31)			
2:30~2:40	2	I059	勝利するスローロリスくんの顔に見える「複数人の笑い声」(2:32)	5	N051	歩きタバコ目には目を(2:30)
		I060	なんつったけさっき？(2:41~2:42)		N052	反撃する(2:31)
					N053	そもそもなんで歩くでしょ？こいつ(2:32)
					N054	喫煙、喫煙所を増やすんだよ(2:35)

(continued)

Table 3. (continued)

Time	Number of utterance s	ID	Condition 1 (with related images)	Number of utterance s	ID	Condition 2 (with out related images)
					N055	あ、増やそ増やそ。喫煙所増やしたら(2:38)
2:40~2:50	4	I061	月曜日になんか良いことがあればいい(2:44)	5	N056	え、でもマルハンで歩き回っているのなんなの(2:40)
		I062	そうだ、朝起きないんだ(2:46)		N057	あいつらなんだろな(2:43)
		I063	そうだ、目覚ましテレビでパンチラ。どう？(2:47)		N058	てくてくてくしているから(2:45)
		I064	あぁ一起きるしかねぇ(2:49)		N059	あれはうちん、人間をやめている(2:47)
					N060	でもあそこはだってそどこでも喫煙していいってなってるから(2:49)
2:50~3:00	4	I065	おきるなぁ(2:51)	3	N061	だからと言ってさ、歩きタバコはちょっと違うじゃん(2:52)
		I066	月曜日だけ(2:53)		N062	まぁ小学生いないけど(2:52)
		I067	月曜日に朝からAV流せば良いんじゃない？(2:54)		N063	だからじゃん。マルハンも小学生を配置すれば「1人の笑い声」(2:58)
		I068	いやーAVはダメだってAVはいつでも見れちゃうから「1人の笑い声」(2:57)			
3:00~3:10	2	I069	ひっよ(3:05~3:06)	2	N064	確かにね、喫煙所配置してもね・・。増やしてってのもあれか・・・(3:03)
		I070	朝ごはんを食べる、豪華にする。豪華にする？(3:09)		N065	なんだろうねうーん。難しいなぁ(3:07)
3:10~3:20	4	I071	豪華やなあれ(3:13)	4	N066	ポイ捨てなんかとも同じ(3:11)
		I072	豪華やな一朝から何あんな食うのか(3:14)		N047	マナー違反だもんなの(3:13~3:14)
		I073	何あの貧みたいなやつ(3:18)		N068	前回をつけるってさっき言ってたしね(3:16)
		I074	え？片栗粉じゃね？多分(3:19)		N069	前回を誰が見ているか(3:18)
3:20~3:30	4	I075	片栗粉？片栗粉ってあんなリッチな入れ物に入ってるの？(3:20)	4	N070	警官を用ウに配置する「1人の笑い声」(3:21)
		I076	いや、あれじゃね(3:24~3:25)		N071	あれじゃあないの？その、歩きタバコを取り締まる人を(3:24)
		I077	薯粉なんじゃない確かに(3:26)		N072	そう、取り締まる人もね(3:27)
		I078	そーまぁ薯粉だけど(3:28)		N073	雇うのね(3:29)
3:30~3:40	6	I079	だから日曜日が楽しすぎるから高いんだ(3:30)	5	N074	いや、街にはホームレスいっぱいいるから(3:31)
		I080	そっか(3:32)		N075	あ、ホームレスを雇う(3:32)
		I081	うん(3:32)		N076	ホームレスを雇う(3:33)
		I082	日曜日つまんねぇなー(3:34)		N077	雇用じゃん。雇用が生まれたじゃんそこには「1人の笑い声」(3:34)
		I083	だから日曜日に出勤してる人は月曜日休みでき(3:35)		N078	やばいね(3:38)
		I084	そういうことか(3:39)			
3:40~3:50	5	I085	うん(3:40)	4	N079	てか歩きタバコって都会とかの方が多いの？(3:40)
		I086	波をつくるから高いんだ(3:40)		N080	いつが多いんだろうね(3:42)
		I087	楽なところを作るから豪華が来るわけで一大変にすれば良いん(3:42)		N081	いや、田舎って、そもそも歩きタバコして、うわってなるほど人がいない(3:44)
		I088	悩むね「複数人の笑い声」(3:47)		N082	うん、田舎じゃいても気づかない(3:46)
		I089	悩んで覚えて「1人の笑い声」(3:49)			
3:50~4:00	4	I090	現装るぞ(3:51)	4	N083	人語体を作らない。もっとこう、開散とさせる「1人の笑い声」(3:49)
		I091	明日火曜日だと自己暗示してるからこいつも(3:53)		N084	危なくないように(3:54)
		I092	あぁそういうことね(3:55)		N085	なるほどなぁ(3:55)
		I093	あ、かわいい「1人の笑い声」(3:56)		N086	歩きタバコを減らすこと自体にはつながっていない(3:57)
4:00~4:10	3	I094	あ！…いやこれわかんなかった。土日はペット没収される(4:00)	4	N088	減らずにはいいでしょう？(4:01)
		I095	土日をおいて月曜からペットに会えるか、現装るぞみたいな(4:05)		N089	歩かせないように歩く為には。歩かせないように(4:03)
		I096	ペットに会えんのに出勤するんやなー(4:09)		N090	路面をツルツルにする(4:06)
					N091	歩きタバコしたら歩きにくくすれば良い(4:09)
4:10~4:20	4	I097	土日できないことを作ればいいんじゃない？(4:11)	4	N092	右手使わないと歩けなくすれば良い(4:13)
		I098	土日できないことにルール(4:13~4:15)		N093	いや、人語みを配置したら良いんじゃない(4:15)
		I099	じゃあ土日に制限をかけよう(4:16)		N094	あ、人語みエージェント(4:18)
		I100	だから月曜日にしかできないことを作れば良いんじゃない？(4:18)		N095	人語みエージェント周りに配置したら、歩きながら捨てたら危ないからさ(4:19)
4:20~4:30	3	I101	土日制限をかけて、月曜日に解決する(4:22)	4	N096	なるほどね、人語みエージェントか(4:22)
		I102	月曜日って何やってる？(4:26)		N097	ゴミエージェント「複数人の笑い声」(4:25~4:26)
		I103	技術者管理(4:28~4:30)		N098	エージェントの話はちょっと止めて欲しいわね(4:27)
					N099	障害物は右の左にあるみたいな(4:28)
4:30~4:40	3	I104	月曜日に面白いことが、あるかなー(4:33)	2	N100	地型態らしゃ言えばいい。ガタガタ、お化け屋敷みたいにガタガタ(4:34)
		I105	あれだよ、設定6になるんだよ月曜日。スロットが(4:36)		N101	あぁーなんかもう東見出きさの感まるる「複数人の笑い声」(4:38)
		I106	あ、いいね。バジリスク全部6で(4:39)			
4:40~4:50	4	I107	明るくなるよ、それだ(4:41)	4	N182	まーだるまだだるまだだるる(4:44)
		I108	仕事しろよ…(4:44)		N183	なんだろうね(4:46)
		I109	仕事終わった焚なんやで。もうね一明るくなる(4:45)		N104	ラーんうん(4:47)
		I110	仕事終わった焚に楽しいことがある(4:49)		N185	歩かない、吸わない、減らすには？(4:48~4:51)
4:50~5:00	4	I111	あーじゃああねえ？ジャグラー全部設定6で(4:51)	3	N106	ラーん。減らすには？吸やせないじゃないもんな(4:53)
		I112	そう、月曜日に(4:53~4:55)		N107	喫煙所に椅子をつければ？(4:55)
		I113	すごいなー(4:57)		N108	普通に街中に椅子をおけば以(4:58)
		I114	パチンコ台の釘がバパパみたいな(4:58)			
5:00~5:10	4	I115	ゲーセンよっていっうくらいね(5:01)	5	N109	椅子も、椅子つければ？(5:00)
		I116	月曜日だけ24時間じゃなくなる(5:03)		N110	わかんないのなんだ(5:02)
		I117	大変なことになる、それどっかに影響でよ(5:05)		N111	子供ないの？(5:04)
		I118	いやだから家かえって、帰ったらその後時間がいっぱいあんのよ。次の日まで(5:08~5:10)		N112	いや、立ってない？なんか、イメージ的に(5:06)
					N113	いや、減らせなくない？実際だってさ目的地まで行く時にさ(5:08)
5:10~5:20	3	I119	したら火曜日に食い込むよ(5:14)	4	N114	ちょっと減るかな？って(5:13)
		I120	そうそうだから、そればいっぱいなんでも出来んのなんでも出来んの(5:16)		N115	何もそんな映像できないの歩いて吸って(5:15)
		I121	なんでもできんの？(5:19)		N116	俺らだってスマホいっじゃん歩きながら6(5:17)
					N117	うーんそういうことだわ(5:19)
5:20~5:30	6	I122	なんでもできて時間いっぱい(5:20)		N118	そういうことだよね多分、俺わかんないけど(5:20)
		I123	逆にあれじゃないの？月曜だけ午前にするとか(5:21)		N119	納得だ(5:21)
		I124	あの一仕事は午前、仕事は午前だけにするとか(5:23)		N120	目的地まで早くようにすれば良いんじゃない？一瞬で一瞬でヒューンと(5:23)
		I125	スロット行ったほうが良い(5:26)		N121	どこでもドアだなー(5:28)
		I126	楽しいね、ね(5:27)			

(continued)

Table 3. *(continued)*

Time	Number of utteranc	ID	Condition 1 (with related images)	Number of utteranc	ID	Condition 2 (with out related images)
	6	I127	なんか徐々に帰らしていけば良いんじゃない？日曜休みで月曜働いて(5:28)	6		
5:30~5:40	3	I128	うん、火曜もちょっとちょっと、ちょっとだけ緩めて。その代わり金曜もちょっと重くなるってこと？(5:34)	5	N122	帰りゃ良いんじゃない？「複数人の笑い声」(5:30)
		I129	うん(5:38~5:39)		N123	良いのかな？(5:33)
					N124	なんでも良いなんでも良い(5:34)
					N125	なんか非現実的なものでも良いって書いてあったから。買ってたから(5:35)
					N126	火が出ないタバコを出せば良い(5:39)
5:40~5:50	4	I130	らーん(5:41)	4	N127	危なくないタバコを作れば(5:43)
		I131	あんまりそこらへん考えすぎるとやばいから(5:42)		N128	タバコが危険じゃなかったらいいんだ(5:45)
		I132	その山を乗り越えたら大吉「1人の笑い声」(5:43)		N129	一瞬でなくなるタバコなら良いんじゃないの(5:48)
		I133	だれこいつ？(5:48~5:50)		N130	一瞬！ある、一瞬で吸い殻もなる？(5:49)
5:50~6:00	2	I134	スロット会もやばいな～まじで(5:55)	4	N131	一瞬で満足させられるタバコがあったら良い(5:52)
		I135	楽しいな～もう空いてねえな一仕事終わり(5:58)		N132	そうそうそう(5:55)
					N133	きづ、気づいたらあれ？(5:056)
					N134	でもあいつらロに父にかまれてないと落ち着かない(5:57)
6:00~6:10	1	I145	でも、悪いことじゃないんじゃない？月曜の仕事終わり、良いことがある(6:03)	4	N135	ガム食わせとけば良いじゃん(6:00)
					N136	みんなにガムを配れば(6:02)
					N137	街中でガムを配れば、それに一付随して(6:05~6:09)
					N138	ああ良いんじゃないの？(6:08)
6:10~6:20	5	I146	ご飯もおいしいってな。スロット勝って(6:10)	5	N139	ポケットティッシュみたいに配る？(6:10)
		I147	ふーん(6:14)		N140	タバコなくすキャンペーンつってガム渡しとけば(6:12)
		I148	肉がおいしいって(6:15)		N141	そういうことか、頭良いじゃん、俺らが日本変えられるかもしれない(6:13)
		I149	ふーん(6:17)		N142	街中でキャンペーン(6:18)
		I150	後は何あるかな(6:18~6:19)		N143	街中で、ガムを配る(6:19~6:21)
6:20~6:30	3	I151	なんだろ(6:22~6:23)	1	N144	タバコ吸ってる人のタバコ奪い取って、ほらこれ食えよって、ガム放り投げるの？なるほどね(6:26)
		I152	外食割引みたいな(6:26)			
		I153	なんかもう、すべてに割引してほしいよね月曜日だけ(6:27)			
6:30~6:40	5	I154	そうそうなんか月曜日だけ優遇されてても良いと思う(6:31)	3	N145	今度、タバコ落とした人からなんか音でもなるようにすれば？(6:33)
		I155	月曜日だけ価値(6:34)		N146	タバコ、吸ってる、人から(6:36)
		I156	サザエさんをやらない(6:36)		N147	吸ってる人から？(6:39)
		I157	やらない！(6:38)			
		I158	サザエさん見たら癒しくなるから「1人の笑い声」(6:39)			
6:40~6:50	4	I159	サザエさんとちびまる子ちゃんを夜にやらない(6:42)	6	N148	警報音見たいのなる感じ(6:40)
		I160	サザエさん(6:44)		N149	タバコの煙が白じゃなくて赤になるとか(6:42)
		I161	ふふみ、サザエさん何？(6:46)		N150	あぁ一なるほどな(6:45)
		I162	サザエさんの放送をやめる(6:48)		N151	あぁ一はぁ一あぁ一ありだ(6:46~6:48)
					N152	最初から、これやばいな。この人今いいって(6:48)
					N153	それもありだ。うん、いいね(6:49)
6:50~7:00	3	I163	サザエさん無くなるのかー(6:50)	4	N154	日本人目立つの嫌いだからね。奥ずかしがりやだからね(6:51)
		I164	ちびまる子ちゃんもなくしてほしい(6:52)		N155	ほら赤とか青とかに変わってったらあれって(6:53)
		I165	給料日が月曜日になったら？少なくとも給料日だけは月曜日だけ嬉しくなる(6:55)		N156	あぁ色も青ぽくなる(6:56)
					N157	なんかプールでおしっこしたらさ、そっから青色になっていくみたいなやつ(6:58)
7:00~7:10	7	I166	月曜日来るだけでお金もらえるようにしたら？(7:00)	3	N158	そんなんあったこともあるけど。(7:03)
		I167	土日の給料がさ(7:02)		N159	でもまぁそう嫌(7:05)
		I168	週給制にして、(7:03)		N160	外国の煙草入れてないからすぐ色染むもんな(7:08)
		I169	週給で月曜日は(7:05)			
		I170	週給制にして(7:08)			
		I171	月曜日に給料(7:08)			
		I172	それ良いね。アリだね(7:09)			
7:10~7:20	4	I173	それ良いじゃん(7:10)	6	N161	外国の煙草入れてないからすぐ色染むもんな(7:08)
		I174	なるほどね(7:12)		N162	開封しないからさ？(7:10)
		I175	毎週もらえてたら金ない日なんて無いね「1人の笑い声」(7:14)		N163	でも、日本人嫌がるよきっとそういうの(7:12)
		I176	日曜日影響になっちゃう「1人の笑い声」(7:18)		N164	うん(7:14)
					N165	目立つことが嫌いでたぶんたせない、目立たせない目立たせれば！いい(7:15)
					N166	いや、ヤンキーとか絶対喜ぶヤンキーとか赤いの(7:18)
7:20~7:30	4	I177	ログインボーナスほしい(7:25)	4	N167	カッケーって(7:21)
		I178	ログイン！？、ログインボーナス！？(7:26)		N168	俺黄色一みたいな「1人の笑い声」(7:22)
		I179	国に対する！？何もれ？(7:28)		N169	いやーそれ喫煙率をあげちゃうね確実にもう(7:24)
		I180	ちょっと書いてみて(7:30)		N170	タバコの形を変えちゃえばいいのか(7:28)
7:30~7:40	3	I181	国に対するログインボーナス(7:31)	6	N171	なんかめいで持てないように(7:30)
		I182	月曜日だけログインボーナス「1人の笑い声」(7:34)		N172	あぁ持ちにくいようにしよう。めっちゃめっちゃ重(7:31)
		I183	まいまいまいつまいしゅ毎週月曜日だけログインボーナス(7:38)		N173	重た重くする？(7:35)
					N174	めっちゃ重くすればいい(7:37)
					N175	あー(7:38)
					N176	歩きながらだと持ち辛い形みたいな(7:39)
7:40~7:50	4	I184	何もらえっかな。ほしいなー(7:43)	3	N177	良いんじゃない？(7:41)
		I185	魔法石が(7:46)		N178	ユニバーサルデザインの逆だよね(7:43~7:45)
		I186	魔法石ほしいな(7:47)		N179	タバコを、食べられるように(7:47)
		I187	オープかモンストだったら(7:49)			
7:50~8:00	4	I188	図書カードほしい(7:51)	3	N180	一本づつ売らないようにすればいいと思う(7:51)
		I189	図書カードほしい(7:53)		N181	んーあっ喫煙所でしか売らないと(7:54)
		I190	図書カードね(7:54)		N182	そう一本づつしか(7:57)

(continued)

Table 3. (continued)

Time	Number of utterance	ID	Condition 1 (with related images)	Number of utterance	ID	Condition 2 (with out related images)
	8	I191	いくらあっても、足りねぇ(7:55~7:57)	8		
8:00~8:10	3	I192	今予定でベッキーって書いてる「複数人の笑い声」(8:02)	5	N184	めっちゃおとなしい良いんじゃない?(8:00)
		I193	月曜日を(8:05~8:07)		N185	ああ出入り口にガードマンを配置して?(8:02)
		I194	ゲスの極みのボーカルに会える(8:08)		N186	まぁそれでも良いじゃないなんでも(8:04)
					N187	ふ〜ん(8:06)
					N188	まぁ聞いたいやつはそこでしか吸えないってことね(8:07~8:10)
8:10~8:20	6	I195	あ〜。いいねぇ(8:11)	3	N189	何分previ毎かみててね「複数人の笑い声」(8:14)
		I196	有名人くるとかは?(8:13)		N190	いや、そもそもなんか(8:17)
		I197	有名人が来るの?(8:14)		N191	あと2分2分(8:19)
		I198	月曜日だけ(8:15)			
		I199	したら有名人忙しくなるね。色んなとこ行かなきゃいけなくなる(8:16)			
		I200	何この、〜〜の巻「1人の笑い声」(8:19~8:21)			
8:20~8:30	4	I201	そいえば、そういえばさかい、(8:21~8:22)	3	N192	あんま意識しくなかった時間を(8:21~8:22)
		I202	声優じゃない?(8:25)		N193	なんだろうね(8:26)
		I203	波平?(8:27)		N194	ディズニーランドって挑戦?(8:27)
		I204	そうかもしんない、実写版の(8:28~8:30)			
8:30~8:40	5	I205	サザエさんね。結構、やめるってアリだな(8:33)	5	N195	きーつえんじょぶあるんじゃない?(8:30)
		I206	サザエさん見たらやな気持ちになる人いっぱいいるしょ(8:38)		N196	喫煙所ある(8:32)
		I207	うん(8:38)		N197	あるの?夢の国なのに?(8:34)
		I208	まぁ筋と(8:39)		N198	ユニバーサルスタジオジャパンには、あった(8:36)
		I209	月曜日ってなんか面白いテレビあるっけ?(8:40)		N199	確かにディズニーランドだったらやらんよな(8:39)
8:40~8:50	7	I210	月9(8:42)	4	N200	でしょ?なぜそれがやらないかというと(8:43)
		I211	月9って(8:43)		N201	目立つから(8:46)
		I212	俺別に見ない(8:44)		N202	小学生を配慮しているから(8:47)
		I213	月曜まで夜更かし(8:45)		N203	じゃあディズニーランド棚を日本中で出せば。じゃあ、(8:49)
		I214	ああ月曜まで夜更かし(8:47)			
		I215	もう火曜日になってるからさー(8:49~8:51)			
		I216	もうマツコデラックスに入れよ(8:50)			
8:50~9:00	6	I217	えそれ月曜からじゃないの?(8:52)	2	N204	まぁ、出し続けてみたらどうなるか考えよ(8:54)
		I218	なんだったっけ(8:53)		N205	そもそもやっぱ、挑戦すればいいんだよ(8:59)
		I219	月曜から夜更かしでしょ?(8:54)			
		I220	本物の名前知らない(8:56)			
		I221	俺も(8:57)			
		I222	たまぁに見てる(8:59)			
9:00~9:10	6	I223	きたきたきた、設定6設定6(9:00)	1	N206	歩きタバコでしょ、タバコを減らすにはじゃなくて、歩きタバコを減らすにはだから、歩かせなくする(9:04)
		I224	あぁちうスロット全6だジャグジャグジャグジャグ(9:01)			
		I225	ジャグ「笑いながら」(9:03)			
		I226	ヤーでも左のジャグラーはわかんねぇな(9:04)			
		I227	俺も、古すぎる(9:06)			
		I228	うわ、何ガッツポーズしてんだよブス!(9:07)			
9:10~9:20	2	I229	お前黙ってんじゃねぇそこら(9:00)	4	N207	恍惚させる(9:10)
		I230	やっぱ月曜日いらねぇね「1人の笑い声」(9:11~9:13)		N208	足を叩へ飛ばして「複数人の笑い声」(9:11)
					N209	歩きタバコをしている人間(9:14)
					N210	歩きタバコしている人ってでも周りは見えてるしな、歩きスマホと違って(9:17)
9:20~9:30	4	I231	月曜日、(9:22)	3	N211	うーん(9:21)
		I232	でも、学校だけあると筋と憂鬱じゃ無いよね(9:24)		N212	なんだろうね(9:22)
		I233	月曜日だけ試験なくしてほしいな(9:25)		N213	周り見えてないから危ない(9:23~9:25)
		I234	ああ、なるほど。いや、良いんじゃない?月曜日には試験やりませんて(9:27)			
9:30~9:40	3	I235	授業もやりません!(9:34)			
		I236	休みじゃねぇかよ(9:35)			
		I237	休みになれば良いんだよ、うん。全休全休(9:38)			
9:40~9:50	5	I238	全休で全休で(9:40)			
		I239	月曜日だけ全休(9:43)			
		I240	「複数人の大爆笑」(9:43~9:45)			
		I241	どこて!?(9:48)			
		I242	隣のせいだ(9:48)			
9:50~10:00	2	I243	だんだん俺たちの、これみ〜〜(9:58)			
		I244	だから月曜日の月9がこれになるんだよ(9:59)			
10:00~10:10	2	I245	あ、月9がエロい放送になる(10:02)			
		I246	そう。そっちによっていくんだよ。どんどん(10:04)			

1, and right side shows the utterances under condition 2. The columns labeled "Number of utterances" show number of utterances which brought out in the period. An ID number is put for each utterance.

Yellow highlighted columns show the ideas which might be inspired by related images provided by the system. For instance, I057: "Let all fortune information in morning television show make good luck" was submitted by refering an image of guide of palmistry. I070: "Have deluxe breakfast in each Monday" was submitted by refering an image of a huge hamburger. These idea could not be expected without the images.

The graph shown in Fig. 2 represents the transition of number of utterances of every ten seconds of group A. The solid line shows the number under condition 1 (with related images) and the dashed line shows the number under condition 2 (without related images).

Generally, lively discussion is hardly expected in the beginning of a discussion because the atmosphere is not activated yet. In accordance with the fact, the number of utterances was not stable in the beginning (from 00:00 to 01:30, Fig. 2-A) under condition 2 (average:3.33, SD:1.94). On the other hand, the number of utterances was stable in the same period under condition 1 (average:4.11, SD:1.63).

In the closing period (from 08:30 to 10:00, Fig. 2-B), the number of utterances was decreasing under condition 2 (average:1.90, SD:1.97) while active discussion was continuing by being inspired by related images under condition 1 (average:4.20, SD:1.87).

For the middle period (from 01:30 to 08:30), there are not significant difference between under condition 1 (average:3.79, SD:1.18) and under condition 2 (average:3.86, SD:1.20). Generally, lively discussions can be expected in middle period of discussions. Thus, they could keep active discussions despite with the supporting system.

5 Conclusion

In this paper, a supporting system for brainstorming has been proposed. The system aims to help users generating novel and divers ideas by showing related images of ideas submitted in discussions.

Experiments were conducted in order to investigate the effects of showing related images on generating new ideas. As a result, it has been found that discussions in beginning period and closing period are vitalized by related images.

Unfortunately, the differences are not shown statistically. Additional experiments under strict conditions should be scheduled as a future work. In addition, implementation of the system with user friendly interface is also required. The internal design and interface design have already completed [11], and the implementation is progressing.

Acknowledgement. This work was supported by Grants-in-Aid for Scientific Research from Japan Society for the Promotion of Science (NO. 26330376, 26350013, and 15K00486) Grants-in-Aid for research advancement from Muroran.

References

1. Takahashi, M.: The Bible of Creativity. JUSE Press Ltd., Tokyo (2002). (in Japanese)
2. Kunifuji, S.: A survey on creative thinking support systems and the issues for developing them. J. Jpn. Soc. AI **8–5**, 552–559 (1993). (in Japanese)
3. Kawakita, J.: The Original KJ Method. Kawakita Research Institute, Tokyo (1991). (Revised Edition)
4. Miura, M., Kunifuji, S.: A tabletop interface using controllable transparency glass for collaborative card-based creative activity. In: Lovrek, I., Howlett, R.J., Jain, L.C. (eds.) KES 2008. LNCS (LNAI), vol. 5178, pp. 855–862. Springer, Heidelberg (2008). doi:10.1007/978-3-540-85565-1_106
5. Aikawa, T., Go, H., Maeda, Y., Itou, J., Munemori, J.: G-Pad: ubiquitous creativity support system using multiple tablet gadgets, IPSJ SIG Technical report, vol. 2012-GN-83(20), Information Processing Society of Japan, pp. 1–6 (2012). (in Japanese)
6. Namgyu, K.A.N.G., Hidetsugu, S.U.T.O.: Patchanee PATITAD: role of design process based on expended ADT Model and TTS model. J. Integr. Des. Res. **13**(1), 107–116 (2014)
7. Suto, H., Patitad, P., Kang, N.: A collaboration support tool for multi-cultural design team based on extended ADT model. In: Yamamoto, S. (ed.) HCI 2014. LNCS, vol. 8521, pp. 548–557. Springer, Cham (2014). doi:10.1007/978-3-319-07731-4_54
8. Matsuo, H., Yamaoka, T.: Development of web-based application for analogical creativity support using linked open data. In: Proceedings of the 76th National Convention of IPSJ, Information Processing Society of Japan, pp. 611–612 (2014). (in Japanese)
9. http://kizasi.jp/tool/kizapi.html. Accessed 7 Feb 2017. (in Japanese)
10. https://datamarket.azure.com/dataset/bing/search. Accessed 7 Feb 2017
11. Miyo, S., Suto, H., Patitad, P.: Supporting system for brainstorming using information on SNS as wisdom of crowds. In: Proceedings of 43rd SICE Symposium on Intelligent Systems 2016, SICE, A5-4 (2015). (in Japanese)

Research on Information Architecture Design of Online Creative Space

Yajie Wang[✉], Yangshuo Zheng[✉], and Xing Fang[✉]

Wuhan University of Technology, Wuhan, China
411349548@qq.com, zhengyangshuo@163.com, 428037@qq.com

Abstract. The paper introduces the concept and feature set of online creative space and illustrates the development process of online creative space using three cases to seek design and building strategies for online creative community, with a view to facilitating the progress of urban information and intelligence, inspiring public perception, interaction and evolution on creative ideas and their diverse value, promoting productization and commercialization of creative design schemes and thus guiding future-oriented design innovation, technological innovation, cultural innovation and business innovation.

Keywords: Online creative space · Building strategies · Public collaborative innovation

1 Introduction

The evolution and innovation of information interaction have mirrored the flourishing of human advanced civilization in the context of information technology. The arrival of the Internet era has reshaped people's daily lives and behaviors. The user-centered innovation environment shows growing complexity when the separation between online communication and offline reality becomes increasingly prominent. In this context, the creative community becomes a bridge between social civilization, user needs and creative design, as well as a microcosm and symbol of an open innovation-oriented society. What role are the public playing today? As the coinage "prosumer" indicates, they become both producers and consumers. The building of the creative community is expected to break the boundaries between professions, disciplines, and display the charm of the knowledge-based economy with cross-boundary collaboration. In view of the wide scope of creative community, the paper will focus on online creative community, studying its concept and feature set, illustrating its development with three cases as set forth in Sects. 4, 5 and 6, and giving strategies for building online creative space in Sect. 7.

2 Concept of Online Creative Space

From the perspective of information science, the concept of online creative space should be traced to "information space", which means the place where information exists or occurs, or the set of information about a field. Compared with physical creative space,

© Springer International Publishing AG 2017
S. Yamamoto (Ed.): HIMI 2017, Part II, LNCS 10274, pp. 539–550, 2017.
DOI: 10.1007/978-3-319-58524-6_43

online creative space can be wide or narrow in scope and the key lies in rational design of the organization and structure of information so that users can better understand and use information.

With the advance of science and technology, the traditional process of cultural creation has been overturned by the creative modes of innovation for online information space based on cloud computing, ubiquitous technology and Internet of Things. At the same time, online creative space has gradually become a substantial complement to physical creative space, making the "makerspace" a new creative collaboration and display space that synthesizes the online and the offline, the virtual and the real.

Initially, American magazine Make defined "makerspace" as "a real physical place, an open lab, workspace or machine room with workshop and studio functions".

As the new industrial and technological revolution develops, makerspace has extended in meaning as a new open platform. The concept "mass innovation space" comes into being. It's a neologism with Chinese characteristics created by the Chinese Ministry of Science and Technology after surveying makerspaces and incubators in Beijing, Shenzhen, etc. and summarizing extensive experience in entrepreneurial support services. After a shift from "garage space" to "mass innovation space", maker movement and maker culture begin to thrive when "mass innovation space" plays a role in pushing for change in social production and lifestyle.

From a macro point of view, "mass innovation space" seems too narrow to cover all the forms of using platforms to share resources and provide innovation and entrepreneurial support services in today's society. The paper therefore uses "creative space" to grasp the concept in its broader sense, with its focus on online creative space, where creative thinking, creative interaction, creative practice and other links of creative ecology converge to achieve new social value and commercial value. As the number of users grows by leaps and bounds, many online creative spaces have fostered cross-zone, cross-regional and cross-media creative community ecosystems which have also brought considerable social and commercial value. The value and derivatives of creativity become easier to be exchanged and thus form a strong impetus to the process of social innovation.

3   Feature Set of Online Creative Space

The feature set of online creative space is divided into three parts, respectively education, interaction and management concerning innovation and entrepreneurship, as follows:

- Creative and innovative online education platform: Colleges and universities have accumulated methods, experience and modes in programs like "challenging courses", "open innovation", "maker marathon" and "entrepreneurial practice". All these educational resources can be systematically and intellectually integrated into one knowledge system. And when this system enters a more extensive online creative space for public education, it will influence more creative groups in the community and form a sustainable, iterative curriculum content production system.
- Creative interaction and exchange platform: Creative thinking and exchanges can be carried out on social hotspots, technological developments and interesting topics on

the scope of all the communities. Online interaction and discussion for hot topics may extend to offline lectures and workshops, thereby achieving better social innovation value.

- Creative project progress management platform: In the design and development process of a creative project, the creative team needs to have an information platform for efficient and convenient management of project progress from intellectual property protection research, to project development contract and agreement planning, and to market-oriented information media promotion.

Creative interaction and exchange platform and creative project progress management platform are the focus of the study of online creative space. In Sect. 4, development stages of online creative space will be presented through three cases and then strategies for building online creative space will be proposed. The analysis of the feature set of online creative space can hence contribute to a better understanding of the connotations and development stages of online creative space.

4   Online Creative Platform Based on the Exchange of Ideas

The idea exchange-based online creative platform is the initial stage of online creative space and the necessary supplement to physical creative platform. The users of this platform can express their opinions and exchange creative ideas on interesting topics and social events. Of such platforms Zhihu, Douban and Weibo are the popular ones in China.

Zhihu is known as an online Q & A platform. Its slogan "Share with the world your knowledge, experience and insights" shows that this platform will help users find answers and share knowledge. Click on one of the topics and the user can view all the answers to the question and write their own answer. The user can also give their comment to one of the answers. In this way, there will be more and more active users and topic hits. Zhihu is a typical representative of online creative platforms based on the exchange of ideas.

The exchange content of the platform is confined to the level of idea and the promotion is also limited to the level of discussion. In light of its limitations, this platform is only the initial stage of online creative space, but it acts as a bridge between the environment and the masses to a certain extent. From the standpoint of top-level design, the idea exchange-based online creative platform can help the public carry out more frequent information exchanges, so it can be regarded as an important research and practice carrier that centers on the public wisdom and turns it into a force that drives the city forward.

5   Extension of Online Creative Space

5.1   Ecosystem Model of Creative Communities

With an online creative community as a center, a creative space as a platform, creative associations as a talent pool, and creative practices as a value orientation, the ecosystem model of online creative communities (As show in Fig. 1) enables design of the smart creative products whose attributes can be iterated. The extension of an online creative community refers to combining creative association with creative practice organically. Since it is mainly made up of the creative class and emerging makers concerned, creative association is a "human-related" factor in an online creative community. Creative space, which consists of an offline physical space and network-based online space, is an environment and carrier of research on how to establish creative exchanges and collaborations. It is an "environment-based" factor in a creative community. Creative practice studies how to look for and incubate the huge value of creativity to social and urban development by means of information exchange, activity design, orientation interaction, collaboration and co-creation among creative groups.

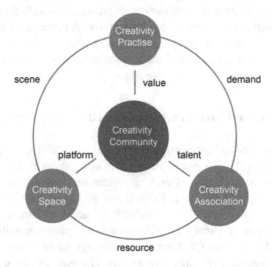

Fig. 1. Ecosystem of cc model

The design and construction of an online creative community will be specifically analyzed and discussed by Living Lab with the online creative community as a concrete carrier in the subsequent sections of this paper, to explore an effective method and path for online creative community construction.

5.2   The Concept of Living Lab

Living Lab is a new individual, enterprise and government-oriented ecosystem that facilitates social innovations through the collaboration and interaction between community, activity and cooperative work space, and a new R&D environment committed to training user-centered and future-oriented technological innovative patterns and innovation systems. In a manner of speaking, Living Lab is the most typical representative of mass collaborative innovation patterns. The value principles of Living Lab are as follows: user-centric, service-oriented, supportive of participation by diversified parties, continuous iteration, and real environment simulation.

5.3   Business Pattern Design for Online Creative Community JD Jian'erhuo

On November 14, 2015, ServiceDesign-Tsinghua analyzed the challenges and problems faced by "JD Jian'erhuo" (As shown in Fig. 2), and initiated co-design by teamwork based on the concept of Living Lab and the method of service design. The studio aimed to establish an extendable creative community for Jian'erhuo using social resources, and attempted to create a sustainable business pattern.

Fig. 2. JD Jian'erhuo web page

Run by JD Finance, JD Jian'erhuo gathers highly sophisticated creative hardware products from home and abroad, collects market feedbacks from ordinary users by winning praises from them, and implements crowdfunding for popular products or mass-produce them locally. Through mass praising, crowdfunding and vowing, JD Jian'erhuo is committed to establishing a social media platform perpendicular to the crowdfunding field.

The phrase "Jian'erhuo" comes from the cracked CD domain. The young people on fire for music and CD collection often call hard-won, expensive, rare, top-class or highly touted CD "Jian'erhuo". Product positioning on JD Jian'erhuo appears as that creative products are turned into real products and product value is realized. As can be seen, JD Jian'erhuo is a real online creative community and business platform.

From the perspective of Living Lab, JD Jian'erhuo can draw attention from four user groups: consumer, designer, insider and businessman, specifically including the masses that are enthusiastic about high technology, and intelligent, simple life; the makers that love life and artistic creation; the manufacturing plants and people that can provide highly-sophisticated technologies; the investors with a keen sense of smell.

Product positioning on JD Jian'erhuo mainly involves the following five parts: individual customization platform, enhancement of user's life quality, and crowdfunding market fore-end detector, platform for guidance on crowdfunding, efficient transformation and high-quality project incubation, attraction of attention from entrepreneurs and investors, and supply of a trade exchange platform for aspiring, strong-minded high-quality users to occupy the upper stream of the mass innovation ecosystem, which could help establish a foremost position where user demand leads the direction of market and industry.

The value of JD Jian'erhuo is reflected from four perspectives (As shown in Fig. 3). First, for ordinary users, it can help them find and investigate the information of creative products as early as possible; for manufacturers, it can help them find creative products' commercial value and achieve profitability; for makers, it can help them make direct communication with users and gain feedbacks from users, and obtain incubator-like entrepreneurial support; for JD, the complete creative ecosystem may be increasingly perfected as more creative products are developed.

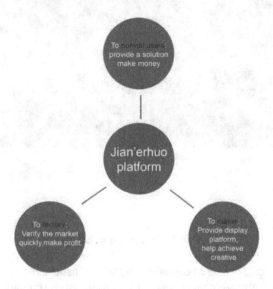

Fig. 3. Jian'erhuo structure platform

The "Creative Community & Service Design" Studio worked with the designers from JD Finance design team, Design Service Center and Tencent ISUX in establishing a Living Lab collaborative studio by the use of some design tools such as stakeholder, service blueprint, storyboard, character portrait and business model canvas. It also created goal-oriented business models, planned activity programs, and made planning for long-term creative community platform construction.

A day later, the studio offered the research achievements of design: in the future, "JD Jian'erhuo" will be further defined as a crowdfunding-oriented social media platform. Continuously integrated design, maker and supply chain resources can help JD retain its high-quality users, transform naive users into regular users, strengthen content operation, and optimize user experience to keep enhancing the attributes of creative community "JD Jian'erhuo". Besides, "JD Jian'erhuo" should pay more attention to the quality of community content, and enhance its social attributes, so that both professionals and green hands could get a sense of presence. Also, it should keep strengthening multi-dimensional interaction of information in the community.

To prepare for the "Creative Community & Service Design" Studio developed by "JD Jian'erhuo", the design team where I work has elaborately designed specific design tools. In practice, these design tools efficiently guided the overall process of studio design, and won praise from the designers. See the figure below for details (Fig. 4):

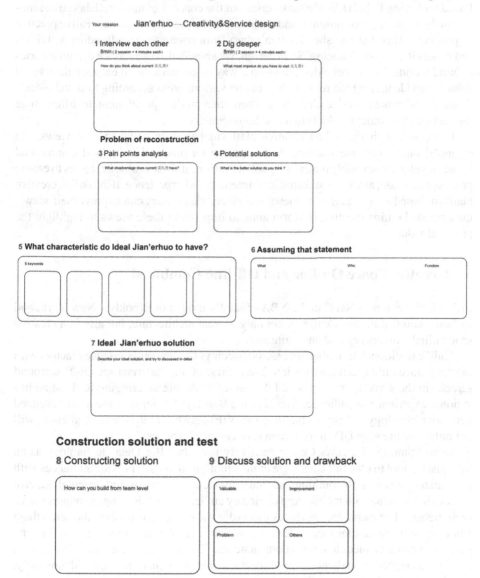

Fig. 4. Service design tools oriented to Jian'erhuo

JD Jian'erhuo is a representative of the extended online creative community and slightly different from a crowdfunding platform. In terms of positioning, JD Jian'erhuo is a social media platform perpendicular to the crowdfunding field. As an online creative platform, JD Jian'erhuo well combines "creative association" with "creative practice". As a collaborative human-centered user value-driven systematic research method, Living Lab is able to enhance innovation abilities in a research environment sustainably. Based on Living Lab, JD Jian'erhuo carries out the concept of mass collaborative innovation throughout the community and enables users to participate in the creative practice of products. This distinguishes JD Jian'erhuo from common crowdfunding activities, and makes it a way of financing. So in design, we should also use service design theories to build a bridge for stakeholders, develop a way of cooperation to enhance the overall value, keep identifying the relationship among various parts according to stakeholders' demand, and make a service blueprint to strengthen product positioning, to differentiate the service from other products to avoid homogeneity.

Compared with the online creative platform based on exchanges of views, the extended online creative platform focuses more on practical value and commercial value, develops sustainable business by collaboration, and uses value strategies to ensure process execution, as well as stakeholders' interests and experience. If the online creative platform based on exchanges of views is a place where users can express their views, the extended online creative platform aims to implement these views to highlight the practical value.

6   Creative Space On-line and Off-line Combined

In 2013, "New Jersey Nets" in the NBA officially moved to Brooklyn, New York, and its home court, Barclays Center, is not only a great architecture, but also is a creative space filled with energy and entertainment.

Unlike traditional basketball arenas, the Barclays Center combines many factors with most advanced high technologies into itself. First of all, the arena sets 360° surround screens in the wave-form entries and the center of the arena, bringing brilliant audiovisional experience to audiences. Besides, the Barclays Center uses the most advanced network technology of Cisco in building the WIFI network of the arena. Audiences will not only able to enjoy DIY information services of playbacks.

In addition, the Barclays Center creatively uses the "Big Data" technology as an information tool to take full advantage of information sources to provide audiences with customized services by building an interconnection between fundamental service devices in the arena with mobile App carried by audiences, considering the requirements of audiences. For example, audiences can order meals on their phones and fetch them from the auditorium after meals are ready, which saves the time of waiting in line and give them better chances to enjoy sports matches. Through designing in the direction of creative thoughts of audiences, new spectacle requirements are captured precisely, which makes customers fit in the environment better.

If the extension of on-line creative space is thought to show some practical values, business values, then the creative space on-line and off-line combined shows emotional values, which is at a high stage of on-line creative spaces. By a total control of aspects such as brand positioning, brand strategies, firm image designs, brand sales, product designs, space designs, it makes an upgrade of brand experience, and reaches emotional benefit points of customers by designing the brand emotionally and arousing sympathies. It leaves a good impression on customers in the scene through smooth comfortable experience, arouses emotions and thus obtains identifications.

7   Information Framework Designs of the On-line Creative Space

The on-line creative space changes itself into an intelligent information-interaction system by integrating information in the city and building connection between applicable information. The whole information framework of the on-line creative space mainly consists of four levels:

- Perception level: Acquire and collect information mainly, input through intelligent terminal devices operated by users, including information about nature, society, culture, economy, technology, etc..
- Network level: Transmit and deliver information mainly, achieve rapid barrier-free transmission of end-to-end information through connection of a number of nodes and base networks.
- Information level: Process information mainly. The core of information level is compiling all the information collected by the perception level, calculating and analyzing by corresponding models, and give valuable reference information by calling relevant results.
- Interaction level: Make information interacted mainly, where the on-line creative space and creative groups interact. Information can be accessed and uploaded through the interactive interface, and feedbacks are returned to users.

Specific strategies for building the creative space should take these four levels into consideration. A platform using the perception level as the base, the network level as the support, the information level as the link, and the interaction level as the media which provides users information communication methods and emotion expressions has a specific goal, has a spirit and aims to the future. On the one hand, it is because applications of all kinds of information technologies achieve functional goals; on the other hand, it concentrates on promoting the experience of users, and satisfying requirements of users which is viewed as a non-functional goal.

8   Strategies for Building the On-line Creative Space

8.1   Concept of Establishing Flat, Social, Trans-boundary, Sharing Services

A flat and acentric structure is suitable for the on-line creative space. Relatively loose and flat in the organization, without a uniform resource coordination structure, participators should be equal under the condition of programs and services, freely combinations are allowed in the fundamental regulated framework. With the concept of designing for service, find requirements of benefit relevant parties, depict service blueprints, emphasize on positioning products, and avoid homogeneity. Establish a kind of resource service which is integrated, visible, touchable, transparent and convenient, and a creative space on the service line which is direct, transparent and specific. Use the concept that people cooperate with creating, support enterprises, researching colleges and the government of joining programs altogether. Though the on-line creative space is a creative community ecological circle between time zones, territories and mediums, with the territorial advantages it is still an effective idea of strengthening abilities of creating independently. Complete the corresponding service system "Technology plus finance", increase the support of technology and finance to creative enterprises, in order to improve abilities of creating for systems. In the Sect. 4, on-line creative platforms like Zhihu, Douban which are based on communicating ideas are actually platforms which are flat and sociable. Furthermore, in the Sect. 5, crowd funding platforms like Jingdongjianerhuo or platforms in other types show the service concept of trans-boundary and sharing officially. Establishing the service concept which is flat, sociable, trans-boundary and sharing is an important first step in the process of building an on-line creative community.

8.2 Blend of Big Data

Big data, cloud computing and Internet of things have been the most popular tools of information technology and applications. In the process of designing to build an on-line creative space, heavy participations of public bring about a great number of big data about user information. If link, analyze and transform these big data resources, present human intelligence will definitely be extended. Establishing a big data information library can make management, analyze, iteration and application more specific, and the design plan of the on-line creative space more appropriate, accelerate the spread of various information functions and services, upgrade rapidly and complete incessantly space information functions and services. In the sixth chapter of this article, the reason that the technology experience museum of the Barclays Center earned such a success is a result of blending big data, cloud computing and Internet of things.

Under the method of on-line creative space designing based of the blend of big data, there will be more function settings of the on-line creative space, and construction plans of interactive, sharing and distributed applications of creative messages will be improved with the technology support. Predictably, resources of information, humanity and creativity of the on-line creative space in the future will be integrated and innovated more systematically in the view of applying big data.

8.3 Strategies Appropriate and Open

Open modules are not the more, the better. Open modules are products or service modules which are offered to customers by the on-line creative space. The threshold of opening is not the lower, the better. The threshold of opening is a regulation which allows entrepreneurs to enter when the on-line creative space offers module services. More the entrepreneurs, bigger the scale of the space platform, but the relation between the threshold of opening and performances of the space platform is not linear. When the threshold of opening is too high and does not reach the critical point stimulating Internet effects, the development will be limited.

9 Conclusion

In the design blueprint of the on-line creative space, with interactions of creative groups in the society, establishments of on-line creative communities will form environment and carriers for creation one by one, thus leading to build an intelligent city characterized by user creation, open creation, public creation and cooperative creation.

While satisfying the need of information communication, the on-line creative space should focus on practical values and business values, by searching a sustainable business mode through cooperative creation and using the concept of service designing, guarantee benefits and experience of every relevant party.

As a practical environment of building future cities, the on-line creative community should put the need of life and emotion sharing in the first place, create socially around customers, balance social environment, needs of customers and business modes by designing, and discover some original creative plans, products and designs.

The design goal of the on-line creative space should be increase the use efficiency of users as much as possible by promoting functional experience, emotional experience and value experience, meanwhile help users enjoy the process joyfully and the convenience and fluency of experience while using the system. In the promotion of overall socialization experience, user engagement mainly comes from stimulus of psychological experience and behavior experience of users, and it will last. The concept of establishing flat, sociable, trans-boundary and sharing service, blending the great number of big data resources brought by socialization of public management toward cities, making appropriate and open strategies and analyzing things like usage scenes and user behaviors help combine qualitative and quantitative researches and finally make design plans objective and scientific.

Acknowledgements. This paper was supported by the project from National social science fund of china "4D evaluation model research and application of information interaction design (16CG170)".

References

1. Wang, M.Z.: An Introduction to Industrial Design. Higher Education Press, Beijing (2007)
2. Kolko, J.: Reflections on the Interaction Design. Mechanical Industry Press, Beijing (2012)
3. Luo, S., Zhu, S.: Service Design. Mechanical Industry Press, Beijing (2011)
4. Liu, G.Z.: Design Methodology. Higher Education Press, Beijing (2011)
5. Jacobson, R.: Information Design. The MIT Press, Cambridge (2000)
6. Qiu, S.: Innovation and management - Innovation design based on brand strategy. Decoration, 04, 27–31 (2014)
7. Lockwood, T., Walton, T.: Building Design Strategy: Using Design to Achieve Key Business Objectives. Allworth Press, New York (2008)

8. Keruide, E.: Creative Cities. Citic Press, Beijing (2010)
9. Howe, J.: Crowdsourcing: Why the Power of the Crowd is Driving the Future of Business. Citic press, Beijing (2009)
10. Chen, J.: Service Product Design. Young Intellectual Culture, Taipei (2004)

Case Studies

Relationship Between Users' Operational Characteristics and User Interfaces: Study of the Multi-function Printer

Hiroko Akatsu[✉], Naotsune Hosono, Yasuyoshi Onoue,
Sachika Hitomi, and Hiroyuki Miki

Oki Electric Ind. Co., Ltd., 1-16-8 Chuou Warabi-shi, Saitama 335-8510, Japan
akatsu232@oki.com

Abstract. When the interface of a system targets various user groups, it will be designed on classifications ranging from novice to experienced based on the prospective users' experience, knowledge, and skill levels. Since mobile devices are increasingly used to remotely operate various systems nowadays, it is possible to develop and provide a selection of interfaces for them. A comfortable and highly satisfying usage experience can be provided by giving users by means to choose their own preferred interface from a variety which has been prepared.

In this study, we classified the users' operational preferences (operational characteristics) and considered the types of user, alongside several Multi-Function Printer (MFP) interface patterns in order to investigate the relationship between the two.

Keywords: User interface · Operational characteristic · Factor analysis · Multiple correspondence analysis · MFP

1 Introduction

Nowadays, remote operation of devices is increasing in popularity due to the rise of mobile terminals such as smartphones and tablet PCs.

When mobile terminals are used to interact with a system or device, it is no longer necessary for the user to operate the devices using the manufacturer's pre-made interface. Instead, they can use their own preferred interface for various devices/systems, by having it installed upon their mobile terminals.

Conventionally, interfaces for systems such as Automatic Teller Machines (ATM), Ticket Vending Machines, and Multi-Function Printers (MFP) for a variety of public users were designed to cater to novice users with little knowledge or skill regarding the operation.

However, when multiple interfaces are available to a mobile terminal as downloadable applications, they can provide a more comfortable and satisfying user experience by allowing the users to select not only one suitable to their own skill level, but also their personal interface preferences.

© Springer International Publishing AG 2017
S. Yamamoto (Ed.): HIMI 2017, Part II, LNCS 10274, pp. 553–561, 2017.
DOI: 10.1007/978-3-319-58524-6_44

The authors have been analyzing the relations between users' operational characteristics based on personalities, values and attitudes and their preferred interfaces [1].

Until now, it has been hard to say whether the user type and the interface are clearly related, since it seems that the favorable evaluation was more dependent on operational experience of the specific type of machines being controlled rather than actual pattern of the interface.

In other words, this study focused on multiple interface patterns when operating a Multi-Function Printer, in other words, we examined a variety of interfaces used to operate just one type of machine.

2   User Operational Characteristics and User Types

2.1   User Operational Characteristics

10 items from the Big Five reduced version [2], 12 items from the Value Orientation Scale [3] and 27 unpublished items from our prior research survey of experienced product users focusing on attitudes while using a device were selected for usage, based on the hypothesis shown in Fig. 1, in order to determine the experimental subjects operational preferences.

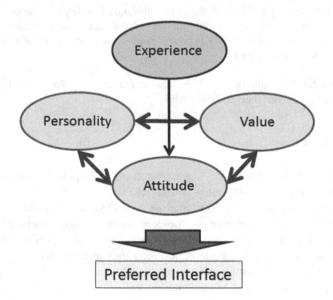

Fig. 1. Hypothetical model

Following two web surveys and exploratory factor analysis utilizing an eigenvalue of more than 1, maximum likelihood method and Promax rotation, 6 factors compried of 26 items were defined as "User Operation Characteristics", as shown in Table 1.

Table 1. Factor analysis results (operational characteristics)

Rationality	I am good at planning ahead
	I work (study) efficiently proceed with consideration of procedures/setup
	I advance while thinking things theoretically
	I am well-organized
	I like to find the laws and regularity of things
	I make effective use of a little idle time and waiting time
Novelty	I like new things
	I would like to know special features that are not familiar to everyone
	I am a curious person
	I tell people new operations and functions
	I take the initiative in advancing everything
	I am happy to be praised by people for mastering the equipment
Autonomy	I almost do initial setup
	I am not be troubled by registering/setting up the network
	I do not need the help of others to set up
Cooperativeness	I have the capacity to do well with others
	I like working hard with my colleagues
	I often listen to the other person's story and accept the feelings of the other party
	I am sociable
	I am generous with others
Experience harmony	I want to operate at my own pace without worrying about the surroundings
	I want to use something that fits my style
	I also find it helpful to have operation guidance on frequently used devices
Emotional	I am anxious all the time
	i am nervous all the time
	I feel secure about familiar words

Five User Classifications were defined. We then averaged each user's result based on the 26 user operational characteristics (Table 1), and found which of the User Classifications (Fig. 2) each average was closest to. The features of each user classification are as follows.

- User Type A: Follower
  Do not display rational thought, planning, theoretical thinking or easily accept new concepts. They can be unsociable or uncooperative.
- User Type B: Rational
  They think rationally, interested in new concepts, and attempt to solve problems independently.
- User Type C: Non-insistent
  Not especially focused/obsessive about things, and act moderately in operational characteristics factors.

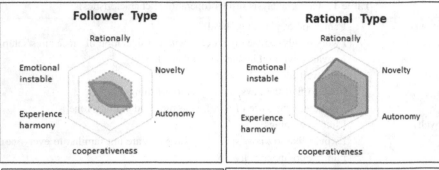

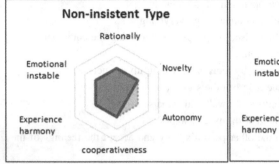
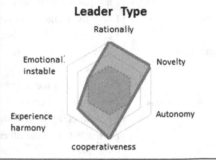

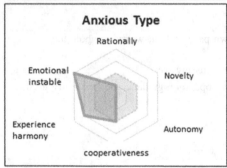

Fig. 2. User type

- User Type D: Leader
  Extremely rational, readily adapt to new concepts and cooperate well with others.
- User Type E: Anxious
  Display anxiety frequently. Dislike challenges and spontaneous actions. Struggle to use new equipment and utilize experience gained prior.

3 Experiment

3.1 Method

The six types of user interface patterns (UI patterns) in Fig. 3 were evaluated by the Marble method with Correspondence Analysis of Multivariate Analysis to figure out relationships between preference score points and user types.

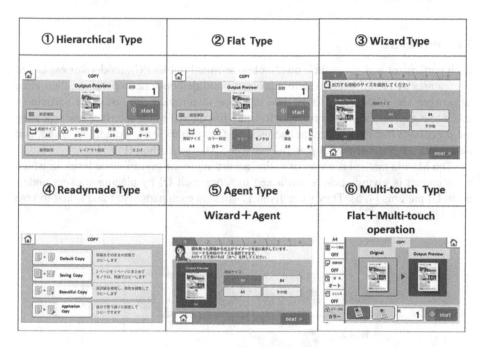

Fig. 3. UI patterns

3.2 Participants

41 participants took part in the experiment, consisting of both males and female between the ages of 20 to 59. The participants were drawn from two social groups; university students (in the 20's, 14 males, 10 females, average age 22.3 years old), and office workers (7 males, 10 females, average age 44.0 years old) who do not do administrative work in their regular jobs.

These social groups were chosen as neither having much prior experience using a MFP.

3.3 UI Patterns

Six different interfaces were prepared for evaluation (Fig. 3).

The first four interfaces were classified by basic structure (Hierarchical type, Flat type, Wizard type, and Readymade type), and two more structures (Agent type and Multi-touch type) were combined with suitable interfaces from the first four. Agent type was combined with the Wizard type, and Multi-touch type was combined with the Flat type interface.

3.4 Procedure

Each participant was given their own mobile terminal (tablet PC), moderator explained the features of the UI patterns with a projector and demonstrated operation, then three tasks were set. After trying to use one interface to complete the tasks, the participant asked to completed a questionnaire, before moving on to the next interface and repeating the process. When the participant had used all 6 interfaces, they were interviewed, and also asked to evaluate the UI patterns using the Marble method (Fig. 4).

The Marble method is a way of voting according to the performance level, in which a participant is giving stickers and asked to score each UI by placing stickers underneath UI patterns [4, 5]. They were given 17 stickers each participant and asked to vote each UI from 0 to 7.

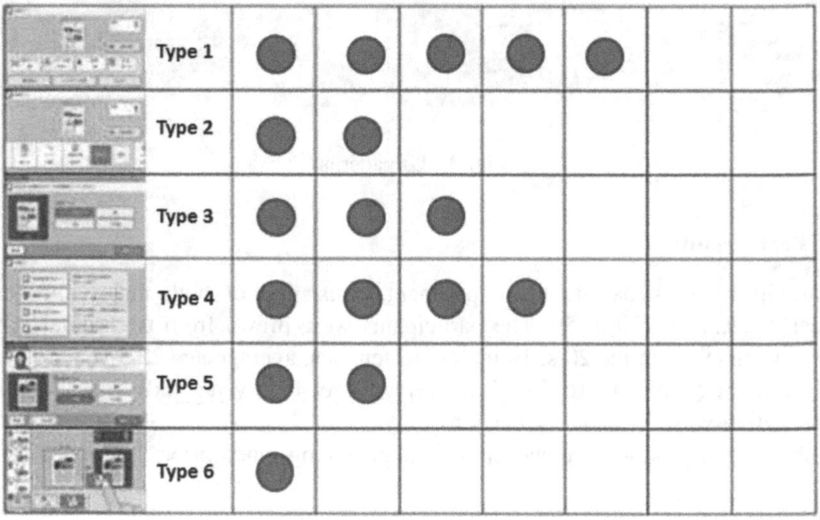

Fig. 4. Marble method

4 Results and Consideration

Analyzing participant types, there were 6 Follower users, 12 Rational users, 10 Non-insistent users, 9 Leader users, and 4 Anxious users.

In order to figure out the relationship between the user types and preferable UI patterns, obtained data were analyzed applying Marble method. The results are shown in Fig. 5. Table 2 was organized the plot of Fig. 5. The table shows the relationship between Users' Operational Characteristics and User Interfaces.

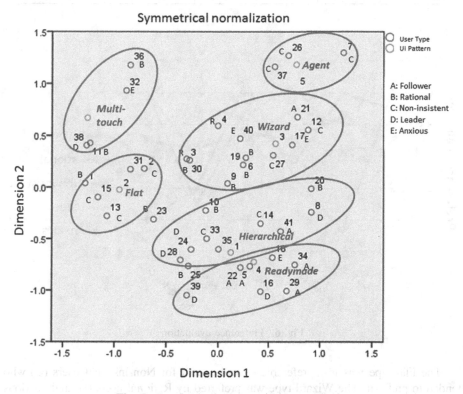

Fig. 5. Result plot by correspondence analysis

Furthermore, after each operation was completed, preference evaluation of each interface was conducted on a scale of one to seven (e.g., Very preference: 7 → Non preference at all: 1). The results are shown in Fig. 6.

The Hierarchical type of the UI patterns was preferred by Rational type users (B) and Leader users (D). The Agent type and the Wizard type were closely positioned, and this showed that the evaluation results are closely positioned because their structures are similar.

On the other hand, although the Flat type and the Multi-touch type are similar structures, it was concluded that they created a different impression when the operational methods were different.

Table 2. Relationship between users' operational characteristics and user interfaces by result plot.

	① Hierarchical	② Flat	③ Wizard	④ Readymade	⑤ Agent	⑥ Multi-touch
A: Follower				●		
B: Rational	●		●			
C: Non-insistent		●	●		●	●
D: Leader	●					
E: Anxious			●	●		

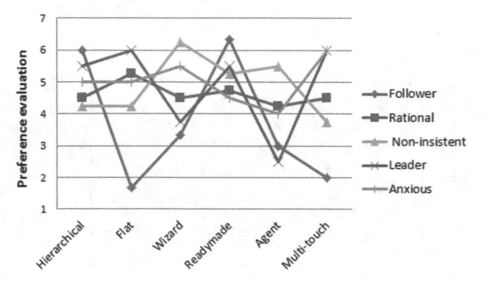

Fig. 6. Preference evaluation

The Flat type was less preferable overall except for Non-insistent users (C) who tended to prefer it. The Wizard type was preferred by Rational users (B) and Anxious users (E). The Readymade type was preferred by Follower users (A) and Anxious users (E). The Agent type was much preferred by Non-insistent users (C). The Multi-touch type was not preferred by any users.

The Hierarchical type was preferred by all users since it is the most familiar interface for MFP. At first the number of screen transitions of the hierarchical structure was expected to lead to a lower evaluation result, however it turned out when the menu composition is adequate, it was not considered a positive point.

The Readymade type was preferred by all users. It is considered that the reason for positive evaluation results is that when the preset menu is provided, the operation can be completed with just one touch. Without worrying about setting mistakes, and then the setting value can be changed easily according to users' intention.

The wizard type was preferred by all users. It was evaluated as easy to understand the settings due to the step-by-step procedure on one screen with one functional structure. However, the Agent type with voice assistant guidance was not at all preferred despite having the same structure as the Wizard type. Presumably, excessive information was troublesome for users. It will be necessary for the user to control the information with an ON/OFF switch with this type of interface.

The Multi-touch type is an interface combining the Flat type and drag operation, and it was supposed to be preferred by the students who use smartphones daily. However, the evaluation results of operation by dragging for a MFP was not preferred. It is considered that it is not suitable as an interface for a MFP.

From the results above, it can be said that there is a relational tendency towards the interface preference depending on user operational characteristics.

5 Conclusion

This research investigated the relationship between user types and interface patterns. As an experiment result, a general relevance was recognized with respect to the user types and the interfaces.

Young users use smartphones and other applications daily, and they are supposed to be accustomed to the Flat type or the Multi-touch type operations. However they did not prefer those UI patterns when equipped on a MFP. Considering the results, the next objects of evaluation for future study will need to be expanded for use with equipment other than a MFP.

References

1. Akatsu, H., et al.: Relationship between users' operational characteristics and user interfaces: a case study of MFP. In: UXSD Conference (2015)
2. Namikawa, T., et al.: Development of a short form of the Japanese big-five scale, and a test of its reliability and validity. Jpn. Psychol. Assoc. **83**(2), 91–99 (2012)
3. Sakai, K., et al.: Unidimensional-hierarchy in value-intention scale: an application of item response theory. Jpn. Assoc. Educ. Psychol. **46**(2), 153–162 (1998)
4. Inoue, H.: Theory and Method of Sensory Evaluation. JUSE Press, London (2012). ISBN 978-4-8171-9435-0
5. Hosono, N., et al.: Pictogram creation with sensory evaluation method based on multiplex sign languages. IARIA J. **8**(3), 233–244 (2015)

White Crane Dance-Transforming Woodcut Print and Folk Dance into Animation Art

Jia-Ming Day$^{(\boxtimes)}$, Su-Chu Hsu, and Chun-Chien Chen

Taipei National University of the Arts, Taipei, Taiwan
Jimmyday2010@gmail.com

Abstract. The new media art exhibitions integrated animation is gradually replacing the traditional "static" trend. For example, the cooperation of two palace museums of Taiwan and China unveiled. "The Dwelling in the Fuchun Mountains" combined with sound, light, and video technology to extend original work. By integrating the animation into the static art work, it will reflect the sense of time and dynamic feeling. The animation can make clearer annotation of life condition then, as well as join the situation sound to influence and persuade the audience. The topic of our research is to explain how we can use new technology to transform traditional contents into popular media format while preserving the originality of the art and culture. We found a process to integrate art, culture, woodcut print and folk dance with technology and animation, by using motion capture, 3d animation and photo retouch technology.

Keywords: Animation · Woodcut print · Folk dance · Motion capture

1 Introduction

Artist Chih-Hsin Lin spent over twenty years making his famous woodcut print entitled "Celebrating the Mazu Festival," [1] one of the most important religious celebrations in Taiwan and South China. It is to preserve the vanishing rural scenes and simple style of bygone days. With a total length of 408 feet (124 m), Lin's print is one of the longest woodcut prints by a solo artist. It has received much attention from international museums and academic research institutions (Fig. 1(a)). Lin's print used Chinese scrolls to expand the form of space and time of the screen factors, but also carefully arranged scenes of 70 folk dancing groups throughout the print, so that the overall structure shows a musical sense of rhythm. The content of the print becomes an important documentary for the people of Taiwan (Fig. 1(b)).

We took a small piece of the print subtitled "White Crane Dance" (Fig. 1(c)) to develop into animation. Two characters acted out a historical story as a Fairchild and a Crane. They are the only group that exists who can do White Crane Dance in Taiwan. We went to their temple to perform motion capture using a portable Kinect motion sensor to capture individual performer's choreography. Recording dramatic human performances of White Crane Dance derived animated content. The collected motion data was sent to a 3D program as animation frames. However, the Kinect sensor has a limitation of detection error, in comparison to the sync video, we were able to find missing or wrong motion data, then use traditional key frame to fix the problem caused

© Springer International Publishing AG 2017
S. Yamamoto (Ed.): HIMI 2017, Part II, LNCS 10274, pp. 562–571, 2017.
DOI: 10.1007/978-3-319-58524-6_45

Fig. 1. (a) Celebrating the Mazu festival exhibition at The Museum Fünf Kontinente München, Germany, 2009, (b) Lin with his woodcut print, (c) White Crane dance original print [1].

by Kinect sensor. Using thematic material from the original print, we manipulated the motion data to reconstruct the print as a set of animated 3D characters.

2   Goals

2.1   Complete Taiwan's First Digital Animation Featuring the White Crane Dance Art and Culture

Lin's print art has been recognized by the international art museum, and White Crane Dance as a vanishing folk dance. The above elements drew high attention in visual art. This study combined art style and culture content to build Taiwan's first White Crane Dance animation, to expose Taiwan's religious culture to the international community.

2.2   Integration of Folk Dance Themes, to Provide Opportunities for Learning and Appreciation

Integration of folk dance and animation is important for this study, it presented a joyful visual art but also provide the contents for learning and understanding folk dance. The animation will show the form and the state of the performing choreography in White Crane Dance, so that the people can appreciate the connotation of the cultural activities.

2.3   To Enhance the Development of Animation Systems, Build a New Application Model

The use of 3D animation system and capture system transformed the print style into animation art. It involves production planning, role modeling, action design and calculation and other complex steps. This study produced development process to enhance the production quality and efficiency. The content of this project can be used in the future design interactive display device and innovative application development.

3   Literature Research

3.1   Mazu Belief and Customs

UNESCO officially announced the Mazu belief and customs as the human intangible cultural heritage in August 2009. [2] Mazu belief is Taiwan and China's first world class heritage of faith and has a thousand years of history. Mazu is the goddess of merit, good deeds and love. [3] The Mazu temple is the main cultural venue. At current time, the Mazu culture is present in more than 20 countries, there are more than 5000 Mazu temples with more than 200 million believers. It became the most popular culture in Taiwan, residents celebrate it twice each year in formal temple fairs (Fig. 2). Farmers and fishermen temporarily suspend their work to sacrifice marine animals, venerate statues of Mazu and enjoy a variety of dances, including Mazu head flag, god of wealth, white crane dance, open drum, fighting spring cattle, eight-tone ancient band, car drum array, dragon array, Song Jiang array, seven fairies, twelve woman sister, clairvoyance and clairaudience, and other performances.

Fig. 2. Celebrating Mazu festival

3.2   White Crane Dance

Among the folk dance groups, White Crane Dance is an original display in Tainan, south of Taiwan. According to the elder's descriptions, the written materials and the relics, Bao-An Temple in Tainan wanted to escort Kong-Fu God in 1928. The people

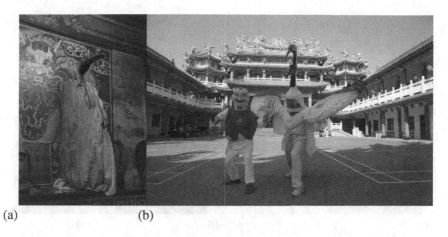

(a)   (b)

Fig. 3. (a) Statute of White Crane Master, (b) Dancers in front of Bao-An Temple

then got the god's message to protect him by displaying White Crane Master (Fig. 3(a)) as the battle front. [4] White Crane Dance became a significant temple activity of Bao-An Temple (Fig. 3(b)). The story describes a man wearing a mask of fairy, holding the red cloth fairy fan, make-up for Fairchild. Another man is put on the head of the crane disguised as a crane, left and right hands tied wings, you can open and close the wings, swing fly. Fairchild tease play crane, crane dances with the Fairchild's fan ups and downs, moving parts with both harmonious funny and dynamic rhythm.

3.3   Kinect Camera

In recent years, RGB-D (color and depth) cameras have a reasonable price (for example, Kinect camera), attracting the field of computer vision researchers with great attention. Shotten et al. [5] carried out real-time pose identification in depth images (Fig. 4(a)), using the depth image features and skeleton nodes provided by the Kinect camera. Plagemann et al. [6] used depth images for body part identification and localization (Fig. 4(b)). Although depth images obtained with Kinect cameras have attracted many researchers to develop body position recognition and location estimation applications, a few existing methods have been developed for the use of Kinect cameras for video surveillance and character positioning applications. For example, Luber et al. [7] set the Kinect camera in a common space and set it in a non-overlapping viewing angle range, using the RGB-D camera for character tracking as shown in Fig. 4(c). Park et al. [8] performed a 3D hand tracking technique from a front view image through a depth camera as shown in Fig. 4(d). Baum et al. [9] used the RGB-D bird's-eye view to track ground objects as shown in Fig. 4(e).

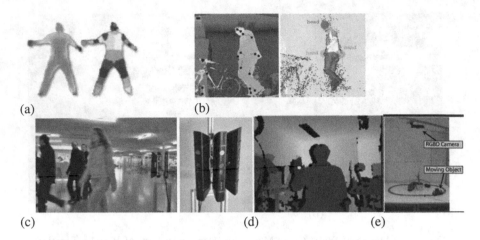

(a)   (b)

(c)   (d)   (e)

Fig. 4. (a) Real-time pose recognition [5] (b) real-time location and recognition of body parts [6], (c) non-overlapping viewing angle range character tracing [7], (d) 3D hand tracking techniques [8], and (e) simulated ground moving object detection [9].

4   Methods

From the time point of view, Mazu belief originated in the Song Dynasty. It reached Taiwan at about 1700 AD in Qing Dynasty. Lin's prints began in 1980, we used the Xbox Kinect for motion sensor launched in 2010. How can we link these time differences together? How to produce a new art form with technology? Our concept is to achieve cultural, artistic and technological integration; the core value of new media art is content-oriented art form of technology. Figure 5 shows our concept of art with technology.

Our method is to keep the brush style of original print into surface texture, deliberately removing the light shading on the three-dimensional model for the impact of light and dark. The resulting visual style of the 3D character animation still looks similar to the original prints. The dance action of the professional dancers cannot be seen when expanding the static part. With animation, viewers can see the folk dance action by motion capture sensor. The presentation of these movements will be an important document for the culture of art. Technology plays the role of integration, as the background of the control center to ensure the perfect front show. White Crane

Fig. 5. Concept of art with technology.

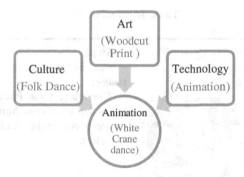

Fig. 6. Framework of White Crane dance

dance of animation art is completed in this framework (Fig. 6), it involves a lot of repetition and comparison.

From 2D image to trace shape and texture, we used Photoshop as image tool. Then we started to build 3D model by 3D Max, and it became the integrated center for texture and motion. Both texture and motion data were imported to 3D Max. Our motion data was taken by Kinect camera. The reason we choose Kinect camera because it is easy to carry and install fast, especially for dancers who do not want to enter the professional studio with equipment. As the Kinect camera can capture both motion data and video, we can fix the problem part by compare data and video of action. We used several steps to complete the idea of transforming woodcut print and folk dance into White Crane Dance animation (Table 1):

To evaluate the final result, we invited Chih-Hsin Lin to watch the animation and asked his satisfaction, in order to confirm the art style of continuity. Getting the artist's certification and support is important for this research. After watching the White Crane Dance animation, Lin was very satisfied with excitement that his art work became a new media art.

Table 1. Steps of making White Crane Dance animation

Step1
Scan the original woodcut print of White Crane Dance:

The White Crane Dance piece was taken from Lin's Celebrating Mazu festival. The image content is a fairchild and a crane facing each other.

Table 1. (*continued*)

Step2
Cut out characters from scanned image:
The image tools Photoshop was used to cut out characters from scanned images. Removed background to keep characters clear.

Step3
Restores full character image:
Two characters were separated, the crane has two parts missing, used the brush tool to repair the crane character.

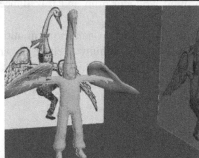

Step4
Build 3 D model of each character:
3D tool was used to build 3D model for each character, by using subdivision modeling technology to shape rough figure model.

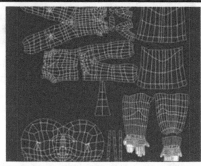

Step5
Making empty skin picture (UV texture map):
Each model can be unwrapped into an empty texture map, the empty texture map was used as skin picture for models.

Table 1. (*continued*)

Step6
Draw texture map for 3D model:
Back to image tool, using duplicate original texture to fill the empty map. The texture map was ready for character model.

Step7
Assign and compare:
Put the texture map back to model and compare difference with original printed images.

Step8
Make 3D skeleton:
Built Kinematic system for the model. With bone and skeleton, motion data can be applied to our characters.

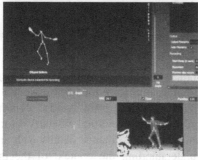

Step9
Using Kinect sensor to capture the action of each performer:
The folk dance group was captured, according to Kinect sensor limitation, we captured one performer each time, assisted with video recording for some blocked motion data.

Table 1. (*continued*)

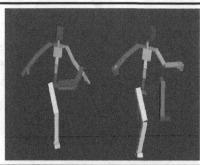	**Step10** **Fix captured motion data with key frame animation:** By compare to recorded sync video, we were able to find missed or wrong motion data, then used traditional key frame to fix the problem caused by Kinect sensor.
	**Step11** **Assign motion data to characters:** Applied motion data to 3d model, the motion data drove characters to perform folk dance.
	**Step12** **Rendering and compositing:** After rendered the final images frame by frame, we edited sequences with sound and output animation.

5 Conclusion

The study was carried out in accordance with the original plan. White Crane dance is a unique local cultural assets. With the use of digital animation media, we were able to give it a new look. Different from the original woodcut print "static" concept of exhibition, the new media art form "animation" interpreted cultural assets. Visitors can clearly watch the exhibit of the characters under the performance details with animation, so that viewers have an easier time understanding the context of the theme. Regardless of the academic research or the use of industry, this work can provide complete information to facilitate further value-added analysis and application.

Academic use of contents of this study can be analyzed and animated for in-depth local cultural studies. Industry can use the output of the text of this research content for mobile application value-added and development of cultural and creative goods, the establishment of local cultural brand.

Our artwork has two special achievements: (1) Save disappearing folk dance by injecting choreography into a woodcut print. (2) Transforming a landmark print work into animation and maintaining the original visual style. The result was accepted by SIGGRAPH2015 Dailies' program where we show our video work [10].

References

1. Chih-Shin, L.: Poseidon Mazu - Lin Chih-Shin Mazu woodcut prints, Taipei National Museum of History (2010)
2. UNESCO, Mazu belief and customs (2009). http://www.unesco.org/culture/ich/index.php?lg=en&pg=00011&RL=00227. Accessed 20 Feb 2013
3. Mao-Xian, L.: The mother of the Taiwanese - Mazu, Traditional Art Bimonthly, National Center for Traditional Arts, Taiwan, pp. 76, 33–36 (2008)
4. Huang, S.-H.: The study of Chu-A-Ka White Crane battle array in Tainan, National University of Tainan (2009)
5. Shotton, J., Fitzgibbon, A., Cook, M., Sharp, T., Finocchio, M., Moore, R., Kipman, A., Blake, A.: Real-time human pose recognition in parts from single depth images. In: IEEE CVPR (2011)
6. Plagemann, C., Ganapathi, V., Koller, D., Thrun, S.: Real-time identification and localization of body parts from depth images. In: IEEE ICRA (2010)
7. Park, S.S.: 3d hand tracking using Kalman filter in depth space. In: EURASIP JASP (2012)
8. Baum, M., Faion, F., Hanebeck, U.D.: Tracking ground moving extended objects using RGBD data. In: IEEE MFI (2012)
9. Luber, M., Spinello, L., O Arras, K.: People tracking in RGB-D data with on-line boosted target models. In: IEEE IROS (2011)
10. SIGGRAPH 2015-The 42nd International Conference and Exhibition. http://s2015.siggraph.org/attendees/dailies.html

Influence of "Feel Appetite" by Food Image

Shin'ichi Fukuzumi[1(✉)], Nobuyuki Watanabe[2], Keiko Kasamatsu[3],
Hiroaki Kiso[1], and Hideo Jingu[2]

[1] NEC Corporation, Kawasaki, Japan
s-fukuzumi@aj.jp.nec.com, h-kiso@ah.jp.nec.com
[2] Kanazwa Institute of Technology, Nonoichi, Japan
{n-watanabe,jinguh}@neptune.kanazawa-it.ac.jp
[3] Tokyo Metropolitan University, Hachioji, Japan
kasamatu@tmu.ac.jp

Abstract. In order to understand the structure of food image for "feeling appetite" when user sees the image, words related to "appetite" were extracted experimentally and clustered based on human information processing. Five scale evaluation for 33 items in four clusters, they are "feeling", "first impression", "estimation by vision", "image of the meal scene", were carried out. The result is obtained that "cool", "fresh", "healthy" are not influent to "appetite".

Keywords: Appetite · Food image · Subjective evaluation · Human information processing

1 Introduction

By product ordering duties at retail store like convenience store, a salesclerk with ordering authority orders while watching an order terminals. In case that kinds of products are foods, if a product image is an image feeling that a salesclerk would like to eat it, he/she would like to order this product positively. To do it like that, what should provider of photographs do for them? [1–3] There are many factors from the view point of information design, they are, layout of screen interface, character color and font, so on. As a part of fundamental research about information design of sizzle image, representation of appetite by food image are studied.

Appetite like sizzler is defined as "advertising photograph of food or drink which stimulates feel of desire for food or drink. Sense which appeal their daintiness and freshness to customers" by Japanese dictionary [4]. To consider appetite by food image displayed on an order terminal, the effect to which salesclerk's order is encouraged could expect.

The objective of this research is to extract evaluation items to assess appetite by food product image. To achieve this objective, two experiments were carried out. Experiment 1 tried to extract word sample to represent difference between images which feels appetite and images which not feel appetite. By using the samples extracted from this experiment, a list of evaluation items were developed by grouping same meaning words according to the descriptive evaluation method defined by JIS-Z9080 [5]. Experiment 2 was carried out

© Springer International Publishing AG 2017
S. Yamamoto (Ed.): HIMI 2017, Part II, LNCS 10274, pp. 572–580, 2017.
DOI: 10.1007/978-3-319-58524-6_46

by using these evaluation items and extracted items that evaluation results were different between two kinds of images, they were images which feels appetite and images which not feel appetite.

2 Experiment 1

Totally 33 graduate and undergraduate students were participated in this experiment. They are all normal and corrected normal vision.

22 images of food and drink which sold in general convenience store were used as stimulus images to show. Their breakdown were eleven kinds of food advertising pictures and food catalog pictures, respectively. The former defined images which feels appetite, the latter defined images which not feel appetite. Eleven kinds of foods were "Cheese hamburger", "Chinese rice bowl", "Iced coffee", "Meat doria", "Shrimp doria", "Japanese dumplings", "Spaghetti with meat sauce", "Melon bread", "Spaghetti with bacon and mushroom", "Cold noodle" and "Salad".

This experiment was carried out in the laboratory without windows. The environment condition such as illuminance in the laboratory was kept constantly. The participants evaluated independently. Choose one of eleven kinds of foods, both food advertising picture and catalog picture were shown to a participants. They were required to describe words that they hit on to sticky about the difference correspond catalog pictures to advertising picture. Time limit does not set. The experiment closed that the participants judged that they took out words up. During the experiment, experimenter waited outside of the experiment room.

3 Grouping Words

From the results, 350 words could be collected. The objective of this section is to make evaluation items to be able to assess appetite using word samples collected in the experiment 1. To achieve this, grouping used collected word samples was carried out according to the descriptive test method in JIS-Z9080 without considering difference of foods and gender of observers.

3.1 Method

The task of grouping was carried out through discussing six experimenters related to this research. Using sticky with evaluation words, grouping was performed every word which means the same contents.

3.2 Result

Finally, 37 groups were made by using 280 words shown in Table 1. During the discussion, the words do not related to appetite were not used in the analysis. They are about the way to take a photo (e.g. position of a camera, light condition, beauty) and so on.

Table 1. Result of grouping by same meanings

No.	Item	the number of sample	No.	Item	the number of sample
0	Reject	36	21	Juicy	4
1	Satisfaction	2	22	Cool	4
2	Young and vivacious	4	23	Fresh	6
3	Massive	11	24	Friendly	3
4	Clean	4	25	Grilled flavor	3
5	Invigorating	5	26	Healty	10
6	High-grade sense	14	27	Brilliant	10
7	Professional	4	28	Color	5
8	Good scent	6	29	Warm	27
9	Ingredient	9	30	Texture of foods	9
10	Three-dimensional feeling	7	31	Bright	2
11	Newly made	11	32	Yearning	1
12	Voluminous	8	33	Calm	1
13	Feeling of fashion	4	34	Elegant	1
14	Looks tasty	26	35	good materials	2
15	Easy to imagine at meals	14	36	good appearance	4
16	Glossy of the appearance	3	37	Image of time period for meal	5
17	Easy to whet my appetite	19		Position of camera	11
18	Hand made	14	Reject	Illuminant condition	9
19	Reality	9		Take a picture beautifully	4
20	Easy to imagine taste	9			

4   Experiment 2

The objective of this experiment is to verify that each item of evaluation word list made in Sect. 3 is suite for evaluating appetite by food image. To achieve this, evaluation items which are able to evaluate the difference between two images (they are images which feels appetite and images which not feel appetite) were tried to extract by evaluating these images using each item.

4.1   Experimental Method

Ten graduate and under graduate students who did not join the experiment 1 participated in this experiment. They are all normal and corrected normal vision. 33 evaluation items listed on Table 1 which were extracted based on 37 items obtained by Sect. 3 were used. Procedure of extraction is shown below.

Firstly, "yearning", "calm" and "elegant" were deleted from the evaluation items because the number of samples of each item is only one, respectively. Remained 34 items were classified into four groups, that is "sense", "first impression", "estimation by vision" and "beautiful", and "looks tasty", "satisfaction" and "friendly" were classified into

"delicious", "satisfaction" and "friendly" were classified into total evaluation. Lastly, about "good scent" and "grilled flavor" classified in "estimation by vision", the latter was deleted because meaning of these two words were similar. From these procedure, 33 items were listed shown in Table 2.

Table 2. Evaluation items using the experiment 2

Clusterng based on information processing in human	No.	Item	Clusterng based on information processing in human	No.	Item
Sense	1	Warm	Estimation by vision	16	Newly made
	2	Cool		17	Hand made
	3	Bright		18	Reality
First impression	4	Fresh		19	Massive
	5	Brilliant		20	Professional
	6	Invigoration		21	Clean
	7	Young and vivacious		22	Inrtedient
	8	Voluminous		23	Good scent
	9	Three-dimensional feeling		24	Juicy
	10	Color		25	Healty
	11	Feeling of fashion		26	Good materials
	12	Good appearance		27	Easy to imagine taste
	13	Glossy of appearance		28	Texture of foods
	14	Easy to whet my appetite	Image of meal scene	29	Image of time perood for meal
	15	High-grade sense		30	Easy to imagine at meal
			Total evaluation	31	Looks tasty
				32	satisfaction
				33	Friendly

The experimental environment was same as experiment 1. The evaluation item in Table 2 was lined up in turn, five step scale was located on the side of each item [6]. Evaluations were carried out by participant's own pace without time limit. The participant was required not to think too deeply and to judge by the intuition as much as possible. During the experiment, experimenter waited outside of the experiment room.

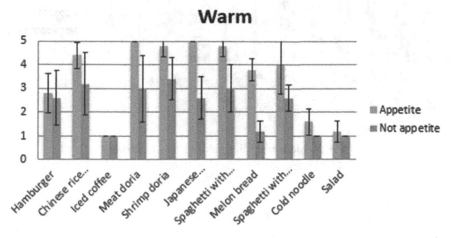

Fig. 1. Mean evaluation value of "warm"

4.2 Results and Discussions

From the results of evaluation data by using 33 items, average and standard deviations of evaluation data from 10 participants by each food image were calculated. Parts of results about "sense" were shown in Figs. 1 and 2, parts of results about "estimation by vision" were shown in Figs. 3, 4 and 5, and parts of results about "total evaluation" were shown in Figs. 6 and 7.

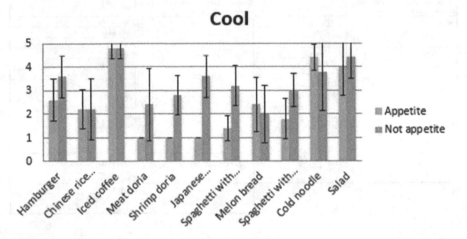

Fig. 2. Mean evaluation value of "cool"

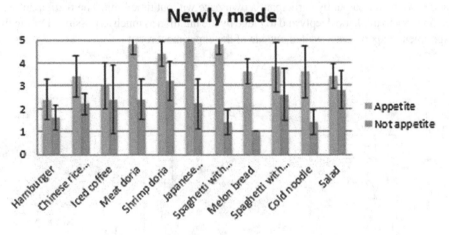

Fig. 3. Mean evaluation value of "newly made"

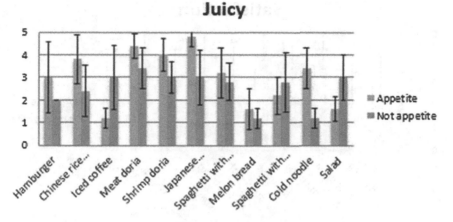

Fig. 4. Mean evaluation value of "juicy"

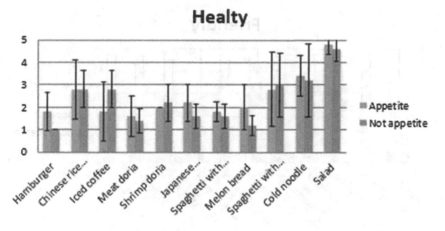

Fig. 5. Mean evaluation value of "healthy"

To extract items which shows the difference between images feel appetite (food advertising picture) and images not feel appetite (catalog pictures), t-test using average data between two conditions were carried out. From the results, two items ("warm", "bright") have significant difference, they were, (t(20) = 2.25, p < .05) and (t(20) = 4.12, p < .05), respectively.

There is no significant difference in all items in "cool" (t(20) = 1.67, ns). In "first impression", except "invigorating" (t(20) = 1.08, ns) and "young and vivacious" (t(20) = 1.08, ns), there are all significant difference. About "estimation by vision", nine items have significant difference (e.g. "newly made (t(20) = 5.37, p < .05), "hand made" (t(20) = 4.87, p < .05)).

About "total evaluation", all three items have significant difference ("looks tasty" (t(20) = 6.06, p < .05), "satisfaction" (t(20) = 4.38, p < .05), "friendly" (t(20) = 3.67, p < .05))

Satisfaction

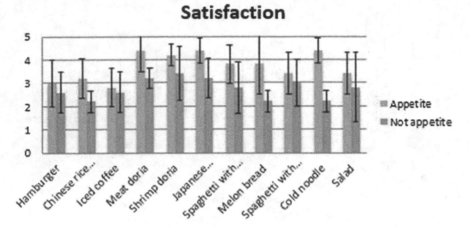

Fig. 6. Mean evaluation value of "satisfaction"

Friendly

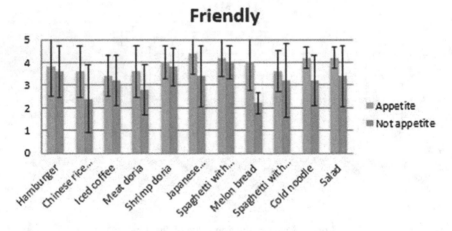

Fig. 7. Mean evaluation value of "friendly"

24 items which have significant difference between conditions got higher evaluation value for images feel appetite (food advertising picture) than images not feel appetite (catalog pictures). From this, these 24 evaluation items could evaluate "feel appetite".

Osgood [7, 8] described that there were three universal axes for evaluating things, they were "activity", "evaluation" and "potency". The rightest column in Table 3. Shows the results of applying these three words to evaluation items. From this, almost words were classified to "activity" or "evaluation". There was few "potency" because the objects of this time were related to food. So, the evaluation items obtained this research was validate from the view point of evaluating things.

Table 3. Mean evaluation value of "friendly"

Clusterng based on information processing in human	Old No.	New No	Evaluation item	
Sense	1	1	Warm	Evaluation
	3	2	Bright	Activity
First impression	4	3	Fresh	Evaluation or activity
	5	4	Brilliant	Activity
	8	5	Volumious	Potency
	9	6	Three-dimensional feelin	Potency
	10	7	Color	Activity
	11	8	Feeling of fashion	Evaluation
	12	9	Good appearance	Evaluation
	13	10	Glossy of appearance	Evaluation or activity
	14	11	Easy to whet my appetite	Evaluation
	15	12	High-grade scense	Evaluation
Estimation by vision	16	13	Newly made	Activity
	17	14	Hand made	Activity
	18	15	Reality	Evaluation
	19	16	Massive	Potency
	20	17	Professional	Evaluation
	22	18	Ingredient	Evaluation
	23	19	Good scent	Evaluation
	26	20	Good materials	Evaluation
	27	21	Easy to imagine taste	Evaluation
Total evaluation	31	22	Looks tasty	Evaluation
	32	23	Satisfaction	Evaluation
	33	24	Friendly	Evaluation

5 Conclusion

From the results obtained through the experiments, evaluation items for "feel appetite" could be narrowed down 24 items shown in Table 3. By using these items for evaluating food image, "feel appetite" is expected to evaluate.

To generalize these scale in the future, it is necessary to assess validity of these 24 items. As a concrete procedure, it is considered to verify the relationship between appetite by food image and score of 24 evaluation items through evaluation experiment using various food image not using this time experiments and to clarify the structure of "feel appetite" factors by extracting common factors between evaluation items using statistical methods. As there is a research to develop a method for representing "feel appetite" physically [3], quantification the relationship between physical value and psychological value of "feel appetite" could be expected.

This time, photography experience of participants and view point of photography were unknown. These factors are efficient for evaluation results, and angle of photography and background design are also efficient for evaluation results. So, experimental condition should be clarified.

To the future, an evaluation method of "feel appetite" could be established for verifying validity of evaluation items by trying additional experiment or additional analysis.

References

1. Arce–Lopera, C., Masuda, T., Kimura, A., Wada, Y., Okajima, K.: Luminance distribution modifies the perceived freshness of strawberries. i–Perception 3(5), 338–355 (2012)
2. Pneau, S., Brockoff, P., Escher, E., Nuessli, J.: A comprehensive approach to evaluate the freshness of strawberries and carrots. Postharvest Biol. Technol. 45(1), 20–29 (2007)
3. Wada, Y., Arce–Lopera, C., Masuda, T., Kimura, A., Dan, I., Goto, S., Tsuzuki, D., Okajima, K.: Influence of luminance distribution on the appetizingly fresh appearance of cabbage. Appetite 54(2), 363–368 (2010)
4. http://dictionary.goo.ne.jp/jn/257519/meaning/m0u/, 14 July 2016. (in Japanese)
5. JIS-Z9080: Sensory analysis-Methodology (2004). (in Japanese)
6. Osgood, C.E.: The nature and measurement of meaning. Psychol. Bull. 49(3), 197–237 (1952)
7. Osgood, C.E., Suci, F.J., Tannenbaum, P.H.: The Measurement of Meaning. University of Illinois Press, Urbana (1957). http://amzn.to/2jpxRBS
8. Osgood, C.E.: Semantic differential technique in the comparative study of cultures. Am. Anthopologist 66, 171–200 (1964)
9. Sakurai, K., et al.: Generation method of image with appetite, Technical report of IEICE, vol. 114(409), pp. 39–44 (2015). (in Japanese). SO9241-210: Human-centred design for interactive systems

A Study on Automatic Generation of Comic Strips from a Scenario

Shigeyoshi Iizuka[✉]

Faculty of Business Administration, Kanagawa University, Yokohama, Kanagawa, Japan
iizuka@kanagawa-u.ac.jp

Abstract. "Scenarios" used for requirements definition in interaction design are usually depicted through words, formed as sentences. Through this study, we are trying to simplify the expression of such scenarios using digital manga so that more and more people can produce comics based on these scenarios. For the study, a manga expert created comics from scenarios on a computer and studied the proposed production process. Based on the expert's observations and suggestions, we evaluated the feasibility of automatic generation of comics using digital manga scenarios, and in this paper, we are presenting the proposed automatic comic generation system.

Keywords: Manga · Digital cartoon · Scenario · Persona · Automatic generation · Automatic comic creation · Comics · Manga comics · Digital manga

1 Introduction

In recent years, more and more emphasis is being placed on "user experience" for the design of equipment and systems that interact with humans. It is a meaningful experience that users derive through use, consumption, possession etc., of the system/equipment and its growing significance indicates the motivation and emotional progress in the usage of products and services. User experience depicts the value provided by the system/equipment, which allows users to do what they really want with the system with "enjoyment," "interest," and "comfort." The "persona/scenario" method is extremely effective for realizing such a concept.

The persona or scenario-based methodology is followed for the analysis of user requirements in an upstream process of design to develop a product that a user would like to use. The advantage of using a persona to simulate user behavior is that all the members of the design and development team can provide inputs to help determine the target user, setting, timing, and purpose of their product as well the ways of using it. This approach helps the design team focus on the users' needs. Furthermore, it provides the designer insights into the users' actual experience of using a product or, say, a website. The scenario-based method does not involve long and text-heavy sentences. It relies more on tools such as storyboards with pictures or illustrations to visualize a user's behavior more intuitively and effectively.

To help the designers understand and communicate the scenario better, we conducted a trial in which a scenario was depicted through a comic strip. In this paper, we will

© Springer International Publishing AG 2017
S. Yamamoto (Ed.): HIMI 2017, Part II, LNCS 10274, pp. 581–590, 2017.
DOI: 10.1007/978-3-319-58524-6_47

demonstrate the impact of using digital manga by a manga expert to depict a scenario and evaluate the feasibility of automated creation of a comic strip based on the scenario. Based on the evaluation, we will propose the system that can be used for the automatic generation of a comic strip.

2 Past Effort

Efforts at cartooning of scenarios that have been carried out so far [1] are described in this section.

First, I tried cartooning a scenario created by students for renewal of a metal part processor's website.

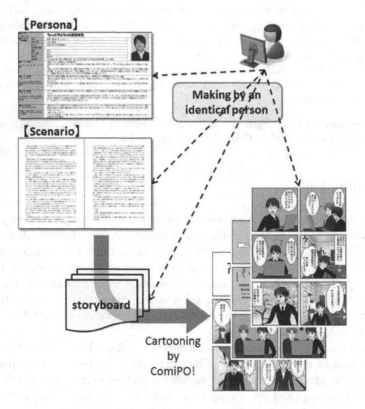

Fig. 1. Production process by student

It is thought that "expressing through a cartoon" affects the sensitivity of a person more than "expressing through sentences" does. Hence, I considered that the trial of "cartooning a scenario" was suitable to express the value the user appreciates by using the target design equipment or system, that is, the content equivalent to "value scenario" in the framework of the structured scenario method [2]. I made "value scenario" the subject of cartooning. Thus, "scenario" means "value scenario" in this trial. In addition, one who is not good at drawing a cartoon is not considered. Therefore, I thought that it is necessary to reduce the psychological burden at least a little bit. This trial used a digital cartooning tool "ComiPO! [3]". ComiPO! is a cartoon design tool involving 3-D characters. It has various presetting systems. I can illustrate various expressions and poses through transformations of the shape of the hand and slight adjustments of the inclination of the head by choosing the characters and basic parts from the presetting feature. The balloon, MANPU, and the effect line peculiar to a cartoon expression are also developed (Table 1).

Table 1. Three types of scenarios in the structured scenarios method

Classification of scenario	Content
Value scenario	The value and essential request for the user: the offer policy for business provider
Activity scenario	The user's activity: one scene of a Value scenario
Interactive scenario	Operation in detail to the target: one scene of an Activity scenario

Four kinds of scenario were created. A student cartooned all of those and verified the difference between the working hours. The production process is shown in the Fig. 1.

Furthermore, another student cartooned the two kinds of scenario, and the difference between the working hours was observed. The results showed that

- The relative volume of the scenario sentence may not always influence the hours spent in cartooning
- Even when a scenario was cartooned, there was a difference between the working hours spent by a person

3   The Trial Procedure

For the purpose of the trial, two sets of personas and scenarios (the number of characters in each of the two scenarios is about 900 characters, about 650 characters each) were provided to the manga expert. Because the trial aimed to automate the generation of comic strips, the production process and the output (manga) had to be in digital form.

Actual productions by the manga expert are shown in the Fig. 2.

And the process followed by the expert involved five steps, as illustrated in Fig. 3.

(1)   Understand the persona and scenario

Read through the content describing the given persona and scenario, understand them, and make note of the key aspects.

(2)   Design characters

Based on the description of the persona and the scenario, design suitable characters, their physical attributes such as hair style and body shapes as well as preferences in clothes, footwear etc. (Fig. 4).

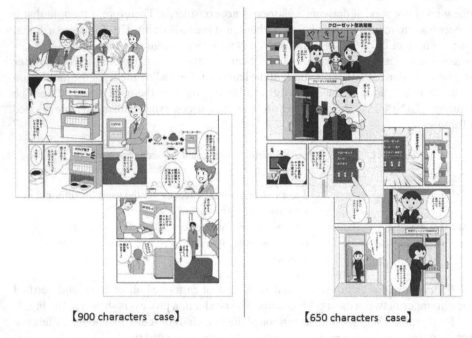

【900 characters case】   【650 characters case】

Fig. 2. Actual productions by manga expert

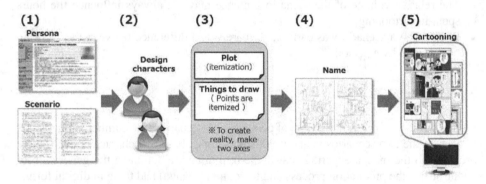

Fig. 3. Process flow from persona/scenario to cartoon

(3) Create a plot from the scenario

Typically, for the realistic creation of a plot from a scenario, the artist first creates two itemized lists – one for the key plot aspects and another for the essential points that need to be drawn. By plotting these lists across two axes, the artist creates a plot framework, as shown in Fig. 1.

Actual image which the manga expert created is shown in Fig. 5.

(4) Create names

Fig. 4. Actual image of characters design

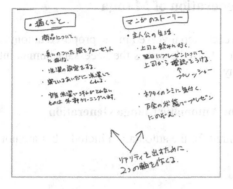

Fig. 5. Actual image of plot

A "name" is a sketch that depicts frame divisions, rough movements, and serifs (Fig. 6). As described in Steps 2 and 3, the characters and the plot should be small and abbreviated to ensure that the entire story development is visible. In this step, ensure that:

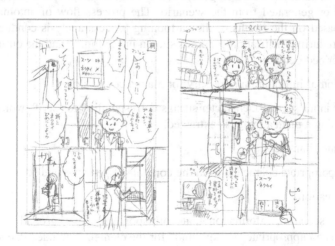

Fig. 6. Actual image of name

– Each name is created carefully because its function depends on the frame position

- As many pictures as possible are used for explanation instead of serifs (Don't explain using just serif)
- The drawings are simple and easy to understand

(5) Create a Cartoon

Use the appropriate software such as Adobe Animate CC on your computer to develop the manga.

4 Automated Generation of Manga

This chapter describes each step involved in the proposed automated manga generation system from a scenario. It also describes the necessary human intervention before the automation is underway.

4.1 Key Elements for Automatic Manga Generation

The key elements required for the automation include, but are not limited to:

- Characters
- Balloons
- Serif, Monologue
- Background
- Drawn Lettering
- Signs
- Effect Line

To build an automated cartoon generation system, each of these elements needs to be extracted or generated from the scenario. The process flow of automatic manga generation based on the results of the cartooning process analysis conducted by the manga expert during the trial procedure is shown in the Fig. 7, and the outline of each block is described below.

(1) Extraction of information necessary for manga conversion

From the input scenario, character strings corresponding to "serif" which is necessary for creating a manga image is extracted.

(2) Designing characters

Design appropriate characters from the contents of personas and scenarios.

(3) Scene creation

From the scenario, information that corresponds to "background" or makes it possible to set an appropriate "background" for the elements included in each frame is extracted and the corresponding compositions (scenes) are created.

(4) Addition of visual elements specific to manga

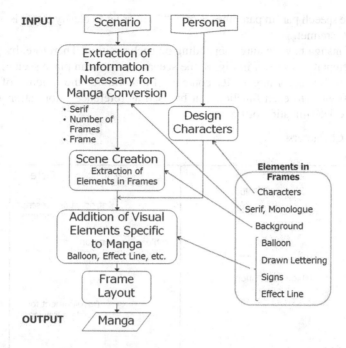

Fig. 7. Flow of automatic generation of manga

Based on the information extracted from the scenario, add balloons, effect lines, and other visual effects that characterize a typical manga and generate frame images.

(5) Framing the Layout

Adjust the size and shape of the completed frame and lay it out effectively, in a manner that facilitates the understanding of the order of reading and ensures sharpness on the page.

4.2 Semi-automatic Generation

The completely automatic generation system proposed in the previous section is still at the concept stage, while a semi-automatic generation system is now considered practical with necessary human intervention. In this section, we describe the requisite appropriate human intervention corresponding to each of the five steps of the automatic generation system described in the previous section.

The first pre-requisite is that the scenario writer should be aware of and well versed with steps such as tagging for manga creation, right from the beginning. Once the scenario is written, human intervention is required at each of the following stages:

(1) Extraction of information necessary for manga conversion

For extraction of serif character strings necessary for making manga images from the input scenario, the scenario writer should ensure that pre-conditions, for instance, enclosing the speech part in parentheses (e.g. " ") in order to clarify that it is a dialogue of characters, are met.

Strips of manga have features depending on each position. Therefore, by preparing a scenario template as shown in Fig. 8, the scenario writer can place scenario texts in appropriate places according to its contents. Furthermore, the amount of scenario sentences assigned to each function can be used as reference information for frame division (size determination of frames).

(2) Design Characters

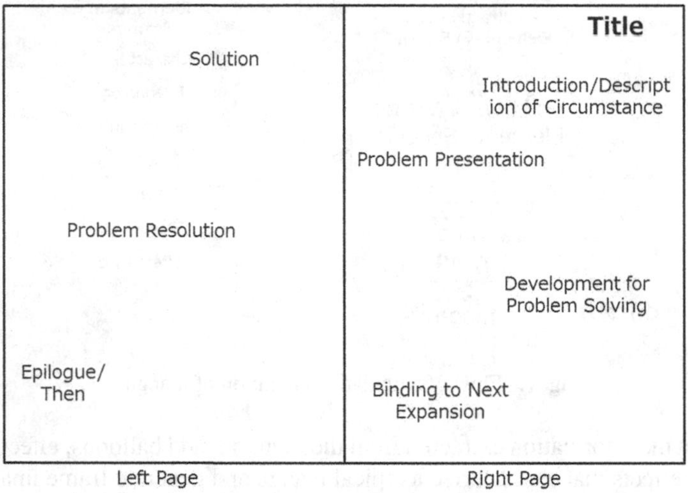

	Title
Solution	Introduction/Descript ion of Circumstance
	Problem Presentation
Problem Resolution	
	Development for Problem Solving
Epilogue/ Then	Binding to Next Expansion
Left Page	Right Page

Fig. 8. Frame function according to position (case of 2-page spread page)

There are also methods for creating characters with a combination of simple forms such as circles and triangles [4]. In an example of cartooning of the manga expert scenario shown in Sect. 3, character design was performed on the PC according to this method (Fig. 9). Therefore, it is considered that character design can be easily performed on a PC by combining such existing method with processing on computer and human hand.

(3) Scene Creation

As described in the previous section, information that corresponds to "background" or makes it possible to set "background" out of elements entering each frame are extracted from the scenario in this step. As shown in Fig. 10, the "background" constituting the manga's frame can be classified into "function" and "shape". Therefore, by utilizing this concept, it is thought that semi-automatic background generation becomes possible by having the scenario preparer give the tag meaning "function" and "shape" during the scenario as well.

(4) Addition of visual elements specific to manga

Fig. 9. Sample of character design using existing methods

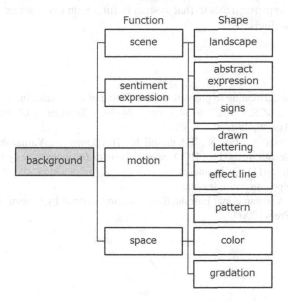

Fig. 10. Background components in manga

In this step as well, human intervention is required. For example, it is possible to generate a balloon of the size suitable for enclosing the dialogue, and write serif character strings in it by specifying the string size during scenario writing. Furthermore, human intervention at this stage can ensure appropriate positioning of the dialogue within the balloon. A symbolic line is used to represent movement in the frame or to express the feelings of the character. Therefore, because it contains human sensual elements, appropriate tagging by the scenario writer is necessary.

(5) Frame Layout

By utilizing the template focusing on "frame function" described in (1) of this section, automated frame division including frame number determination can be achieved. However, because it is difficult to automate changing the size and shape of completed frames or laying them in the right position, make the order of reading easier to understand, and make the page sharper, human intervention is necessary at this stage as well.

5   Conclusion

This paper describes the study conducted by a manga expert to evaluate the feasibility of automated cartoon generation using the scenario. However, the proposed automatic generation system poses various problems, as identified during the course of the study. Hence, a semi-automatic generation system was proposed.

Based on this study, a semi-automatic generation system can be evolved and by applying various improvements to that system in future, an even better and more effective system can be devised.

References

1. Iizuka, S.: A trial cartooning to promote understanding of a scenario. In: Yamamoto, S. (ed.) HIMI 2016. LNCS, vol. 9734, pp. 34–39. Springer, Cham (2016). doi: 10.1007/978-3-319-40349-6_4
2. Yanagida, K., Ueda, Y., Go, K., Takahashi, K., Hayakawa, S., Yamazaki, K.: Structured scenario-based design method for HCD. Special Issue of Japanese Society for the Science of Design, **18-2**(70) (2011). (in Japanese)
3. http://www.comipo.com/en/index.html
4. NHK: Even now you can draw! Introduction to 4-frame cartoon by Umezu. K (NHK Hobbies Calmly). NHK Press (2009)

How to Find a Recipe for Success of Popular Smart Phone Applications

Jun Ito[1]([envelope]), Shin'ichi Fukuzumi[2], Nobuyuki Watanabe[3], and Masao Ohmi[3]

[1] Measuring UX Lab., Yokohama, Japan
itojun@measuring-ux.com
[2] NEC Corporation, Kawasaki, Japan
s-fukuzumi@aj.jp.nec.com
[3] Kanazawa Institute of Technology, Kanazawa, Japan
n-watanabe@neptune.kanazawa-it.ac.jp, ohmi@his.kanazawa-it.ac.jp

Abstract. The number of smartphone appliances is increasing rapidly. However, it is divided into a popular application and an application not so popular. There must be some recipe for success in the application that is gaining popularity and continuously using by customers.

We investigate the recipe for success below 4 steps.

(1) Select multiple application categories and target applications to be surveyed
(2) Each group conducted interviews with users of target applications,
    Extract hypotheses of value and goodness by comparing multiple selected applications
(3) Perform questionnaire survey for users of target application and compare and verify hypotheses of value and goodness
(4) Perform comparative measurement using the physiological index while using the target application, and extract differences unconscious but feeling.

As a result of questionnaire survey, we can find popular application has value or strength and that is the reason people tend to use continuously.

As a result of physiological measurement, we can find some hint related to value or strength we find from questionnaire survey.

This result comes from half year workshop of Master's Program, so we can find more useful and practical knowledge can get from more deeply study.

Keywords: UX · Smartphone application · Value · Physiological measurement

1 Introduction

The number of smartphone appliances is increasing rapidly. When becoming a popular category, there are many applications of similar usage. Figure 1 shows the growth transition of number of available applications [1].

S. Yamamoto (Ed.): HIMI 2017, Part II, LNCS 10274, pp. 591–602, 2017.
DOI: 10.1007/978-3-319-58524-6_48

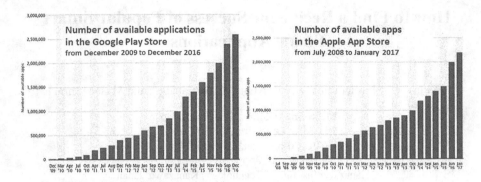

Fig. 1. Number of available apps in the Apple App Store and Google play [1]

[https://www.statista.com/statistics/263795/number-of-available-apps-in-the-apple-app-store/, Feb. 27th 2017]

[https://www.statista.com/markets/424/topic/538/mobile-internet-apps/, Feb. 27th 2017]

However, it is divided into a popular application and an application not so popular. There must be some recipe for success in the application that is gaining popularity and continuously using by customers.

2   Explore the Recipe for Success

To clarify recipe for success, applications could be made more popular by using these recipes.

The objective of this research is to find and clarify the recipe for success. To achieve this, we carried out a subjective evaluation and an objective evaluation. We assume the recipe for success has below 3 aspects, then we research using concrete examples. As a secret that users can keep using,

(a) user's sense of value (value)
(b) goodness in goal accomplishment (goodness)
(c) user's unconscious feeling factor.

2.1   Approach to Explore Recipe for Success

We adopted the approach which referred to human centered design and additionally physiological measurement, then we can define below 4 steps.

(1) Select multiple application categories and target applications to be surveyed
(2) Each group conducted interviews with users of target applications,
     Extract hypotheses of value and goodness by comparing multiple selected applications
(3) Perform questionnaire survey for users of target application and compare and verify hypotheses of value and goodness

(4) Perform comparative measurement using the physiological index while using the target application, and extract differences unconscious but feeling.

2.2 Selected Applications

We select 2 category 5 applications.

(1) calendar category:
    (1-1) preinstalled Google calendar [2]; major apps.
        [https://play.google.com/store/apps/details?
        id=com.google.android.calendar&hl=ja, Feb. 27th 2017]
    (1-2) Life Bear [2]; popular and customer likes this apps.
        [https://play.google.com/store/apps/details?id=jp.co.lifebear&hl=ja, Feb. 27th 2017]

The reason which selected this category is that customers use it frequently and basic feature and usage is almost same, so we expect each application's value is clear for customer (Fig. 2).

(2) News aggregation category;
    (2-1) Smart News [2]; very popular
        [https://play.google.com/store/apps/details?id=jp.gocro.smart-news.android&hl=ja, Feb. 27th 2017]
    (2-2) Yahoo! News [2]; Very popular
        [https://play.google.com/store/apps/details?
        id=jp.co.yahoo.android.news&hl=ja, Feb. 27th 2017]
    2-3) HACKA DOLL [2]; not so popular, but customer likes this apps.
        [https://play.google.com/store/apps/details?id=com.hackadoll&hl=ja, Feb. 27th 2017]

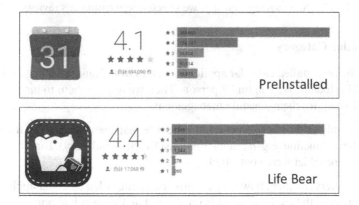

Fig. 2. Calendar apps we selected with customer's reviews.

The reason which selected this category is that customers use it frequently and most of customer use them separately. So, we expect customer notice each application's value and strength clear

3   Interviews with Users of Target Applications

To extract hypotheses which users evaluate the applications, we carried out interview investigation for application categories (Fig. 3).

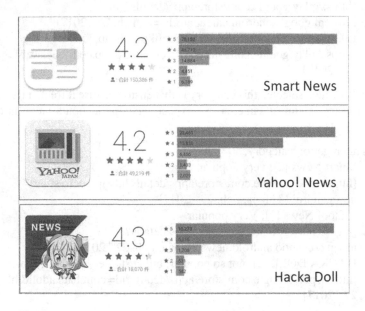

Fig. 3. News aggregation apps we selected with customer's reviews.

3.1   Calendar Category

We found the preinstalled calendar application users from Kanazawa Institute of Technology (KIT) student. We can find 7 person. Then we request them to install Life Bear and use it 1 week for their schedule management.

– They use only daily management and schedule management. During the use, they can use basic function (e.g. memorandum, list function and diary). But, share function among PC or tablet were controlled.

Then we interview them how they usually use preinstalled calendar application and ask comparison with Life Bear, what is good point and what is bad point.

3.2   News Aggregation Category

We select 7 students from KIT and ask below interview flow.

1. Which application do you use about news aggregation category?
2. Why you start to use the app's.
3. When you start to use the app's.
4. Why you select the app's.
5. What information you tend to read by the app's.
6. What is your favorite of the app's.
7. Are there some bad points or want to modify?
8. If you use multiple app's, why? And which one is better.

3.3 Hypotheses from Interview About Calendar Category

Major comment of the interview isbelow.

1. It's troublesome to learn how to use new calendar application.
2. Calendar application difficult to write what I want to write how we want to write, comparison with paper note
3. Life Bear's vertical scrolling operation is very good feeling.
4. Calendar application can write specific schedule quickly.

From those comments, we build a hypothesis, Value for calendar application is (1) simple and (2) useful functions.

3.4 Hypotheses from Interview About News Aggregation Category

We can find 3 applications have different characteristics.

- Smart News; User can get a wide variety of information.
  User can select many expendability is superior point.
- Yahoo News; User can easily use Yahoo! search function.
  User can get local area news they previously select.
- Hacka doll; User can easily select otaku culture & entertainment information.

  This application has convenient learning function.
  Hypotheses about value of this application is below.

- Reliability for an article
- Lightness of application
- Ease to dispose of information
- Ease to get the newest information
- Ease to read an article
- Ease to access deep information
- Ease to customize

4 Questionnaire Survey

4.1 Calendar Category

Questionnaire evaluation was carried out to calendar category. Question items were as follows:

1. Question about media using schedule management
2. Five scale evaluation of media which is the most use in schedule management
3. Free description about advantage and disadvantage of media which you use
4. Total evaluation of media used in schedule management

Detail items in Q2 were as follows:

1. You can write down your plan and memorandum much more
2. You can use like yourself
3. This media could be an opportunity for you to remind a written plan a few days before
4. You can check a plan and a schedule easily
5. You can use various way per your aim
6. You can write down your schedule easily as for any situation
7. A media design which you use is simple
8. You can manage a lot of schedule
9. You can use colors and graphic characters when you write down your schedule using this media

We distribute the questionnaire for the student of Kanazawa Institute of Technology. Then we receive from 135 students.

The results from this questionnaire evaluation were applied to principal component analysis. Figure 4 shows the result of this.

The result from principal component analysis with considering average of usability by total evaluation of application, Life Bear was found to be with usability and multifunction. The result of a notebook of a paper medium was usable though function was not many. A calendar application which installed originally evaluated as low usability and poor function. From these results, Life Bear is found to be more functional and usable than default calendar application.

4.2 News Aggregation Category

About News aggregation category, questionnaire valuation was also carried out during May 20 through 26, 2016. 164 graduate students and undergraduate students were joined in this evaluation. We made a questionnaire based on the result of interview. Items were shown in below.

1. Lower level
   - characteristics of participants
   - Gender, school year
   - About job hunting

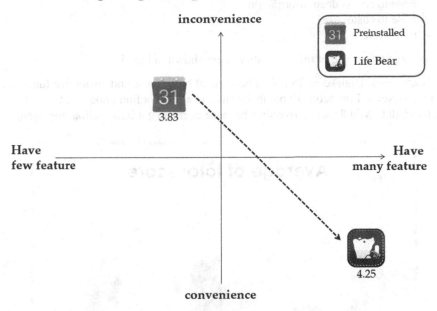

Fig. 4. Result of principal component analysis

- Aim of usage of this application
- Hobby
- Article in each application
- Width of area covering this application
- Area and category of articles often checked
2. Middle level
    - Function of application (interface)
    - Color
    - Sense of operation of the application
    - Size of image in an article
    - Impression for ad placement
    - Speed of loading
    - Ease of checking the distribution date of an article
    - Frequency of information
    - Sharing an article with SNS
    - Usability of default setting
3. Higher level
    - Value of application
    - Reliability for an article
    - Lightness of application
    - Ease to dispose of information
    - Ease to get the newest information

- Ease to read an article
- Ease to access deep information
- Ease to customize
- total score

Average total score of this evaluation were shown in Fig. 5.

- Smart News; High score 78 points because of easy to use and customize function.
- Yahoo News; Low score 72 points because user cannot find good point.
- Hacka doll; Middle score 76 points because user can get information they want.

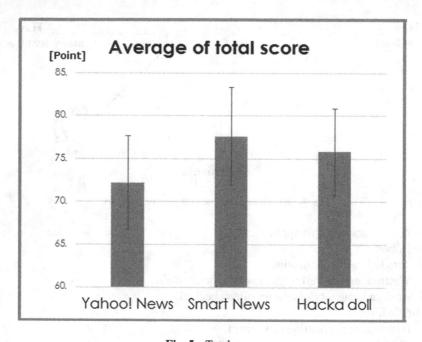

Fig. 5. Total score

From these results, we could find that total evaluation of Smart News was high because this application was popular for students during hunting job, articles dealt with this application were wide area, depth and reliable, and was superior for functions.

About Yahoo!! News, total evaluation was not so high because reliability was low, there was low depth and functionality was no good though articles dealt with this application were wide area and local.

About Hacka doll, total evaluation was high because articles of application itself met information which required by users. However, function about application was not regarded as important.

5   Physiological Measurement

The result shown above were subjective evaluation. To clarify human feeling objectively, physiological data during use applications were measured. For calendar category, oxyhemoglobin and ECG (Electrocardiogram) used by NIRS (Near InfraRed Sensor) and polygraph respectively were used as indices of human objective response and for News aggregation category, eye movement, pupil response and fixation time used by eye camera were measured.

5.1   Calendar Category

We prepared two tasks. One was a write down task and another was a search task. The former was that the task to write down schedules planed before. There were two activities in one event. e.g. back home, join a conference and presentation, go to Disney land and trip to Hokkaido. The latter was that the tasks to search the plans when and where to do. Answering three questions prepared before. Write down the contents to the paper during check application.

Before starting a task, participant wore electrodes of NIRS and had a rest for a few minutes. After the rest, participants started using an application for ten minutes. During this physiological data were measured. After measuring, participants had five minutes' rest. After the rest, participants started to use another application. During this, physiological data were also measured. Same procedure was applied to two tasks.

The results of these experiments which index was oxyhemoglobin were shown in Fig. 6. From these, we can found that there were no significant between two applications. This was similar results to interview analysis.

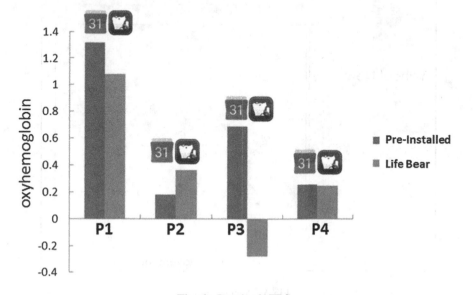

Fig. 6.   Result of NIRS

5.2   News Aggregation Category

About News aggregation category, during use of these application, eye movement, pupil response and fixation time used by eye camera were measured.

Analysis of eye movement for these applications were shown in Figs. 7, 8 and 9.

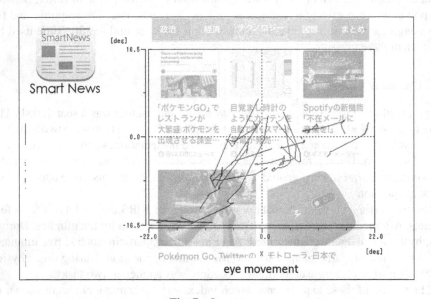

Fig. 7. Smart news

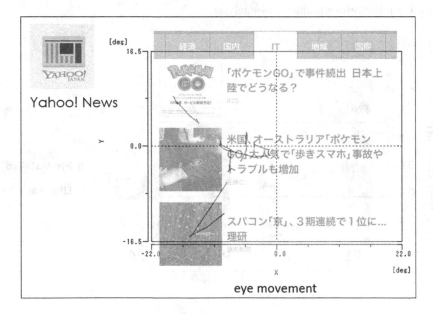

Fig. 8. Yahoo! news

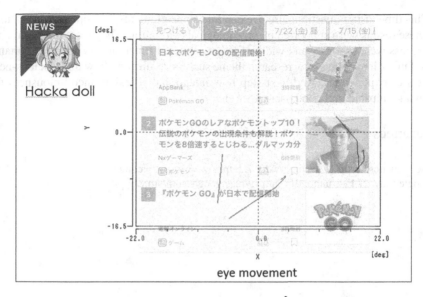

Fig. 9. Hacka doll

About Smart News, eyemark moved to wide area. The reason of this result was that there was not an united feeling for layout and thumbnail.

About Yahoo!! News, eyemark moved the left side to the center. It's because the influence of layout or thumbnail.

About Hacka doll, eyemark did not move. From the subjective evaluation result, Hacka doll has few functions. So, frequent of operation was very low.

The results from fixation point were shown in below.

- Smart News; Weak point; Layout is bad for reading news.
- Yahoo News; Strong point; Unified picture size lead easy to read news.
- Hacka doll; Strong point; User can get deeply interesting information.
  Weak point; User must wait for loading news contents.

This result represented not the condition of reading an article but the condition of searching target articles

As a conclusion of the experiment, the results from subjective evaluation and from objective evaluation were gotten adjustment.

6   Conclusion and Future Activity

In UX design, it is common to design values and goodness as design targets, but parts that you do not recognize unconsciously are not considered for design targets. The part that you feel unconsciously may actually effects the goodness or badness about user experience, for example, Kansei value when using, or the motivation to keep using it.

This time, using questionnaire, we can find some elements for popular applications and these results were supported by physiological evaluation. They were that the recipe for success were usability and width of target area, and function was not so important.

In future, it may be a new research theme such as confirming how unconscious-ness effect user experiences. And next step how intentionally design unconsciousness for achieving valuable and good user experience.

References

1. The Statistics Portal, 27 February 2017. https://www.statista.com/
2. Google Play, 27 February 2017. https://play.google.com/store/apps

Study on Indoor Light Environment and Appearance

Fuko Ohura[1](✉), Keiko Kasamatsu[1](✉), Takeo Ainoya[1], and Akio Tomita[2]

[1] Graduate School of System Design, Tokyo Metropolitan University, Hachioji, Japan
[2] Misawa Homes Institute of Research and Development Co., Ltd., Tokyo, Japan
fu.a7te@gmail.com, kasamatu@tmu.ac.jp

Abstract. In Japan, the proportion of diseases leading to visual disorders such as cataract increases with age, and about 73% of people with visual impairment are over 60 years old. While it is predicted that an aging society will proceed, it is expected that people needing low vision care will increase in the future. In the presence of education, medical care, social support and various forms of low vision care, the purpose of this research is to obtain knowledge to support people with low vision from the perspective of design taking advantage of the idea of ergonomics. In this study, we conducted two types of experiments to investigate the relationship between the appearance of objects and the light environment. First, we examined how the change in light affects visibility. As a result, it was suggested that <contrast of two sides> and <crease line of the wall (boundary line)> influenced visibility. Furthermore, in the irradiation situation with low visibility, the difference in the color of the wall was observed, so it turned out that the factor of reflectance also influences the visibility in the difference of appearance by the boundary line. Next, we conducted a waling experiment to investigate how people actually act in movement. In this study, the following was shown. The confirmation of boundaries such as "wall and floor" and "wall and wall" becomes important clue for space recognition when low vision person walks indoors. The visibility of the edge is also related to the illuminance of the space.

Keywords: Illumination · Appearance · Low vision · Design

1 Introduction

In Japan, the proportion of diseases leading to visual disorders such as cataract increases with age, and about 73% of people with visual impairment are over 60 years old [1]. While it is predicted that an aging society will proceed, it is expected that people needing low vision care will increase in the future. People with some visual impairment feel inconvenienced in their daily lives [2].

In the presence of education, medical care, social support and various forms of low vision care, the purpose of this research is to obtain knowledge to support people with low vision from the perspective of design taking advantage of the idea of ergonomics.

In this study, we conducted two types of experiments to investigate the relationship between the appearance of objects and the light environment. First, we examined how the change in light affects visibility. Next, we conducted a waling experiment to investigate how people actually act in movement.

© Springer International Publishing AG 2017
S. Yamamoto (Ed.): HIMI 2017, Part II, LNCS 10274, pp. 603–613, 2017.
DOI: 10.1007/978-3-319-58524-6_49

2 Experiment 1: Visibility by Combination of Different Illuminating Angles and Different Kinds of Walls

2.1 Purpose

Some people with low vision have difficulties in grasping the boundaries of the space such as "walls and floors" and "steps", so they are inconvenient in their lives [3]. In this experiment, we acquire knowledge to lead to care. Specifically, several types of paper assumed walls were illuminated with light, and the relationship between the light illumination angle and the visibility of the angle of the wall (the refracted portion) due to the change in color/irregularities of the wall was examined.

2.2 Method

Participants
There were 2 participants (female 47 years old, male 17 years old) participants. Both were sighted.

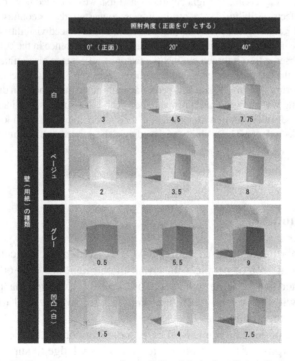

Fig. 1. Wall appearance at each condition (kind of wall, irradiation angle)

The Conditions on Wall and Irradiation Angle

Four types of paper, white, beige, gray, and white (concave-convex surface) were used assuming that the paper was folded at 90° as a wall. The walls are placed in a predetermined position, and light is irradiated to each wall at an angle of 0°, 20°, 40°. Figure 1 shows how the wall looks at each condition from the actual participant's position.

Procedure

Participants sit in front of 1 m from the fold of the wall. The order of presentation is white, beige, gray, white (concave-convex surface), and in order of 0°, 20°, 40°, such as white (0°), white (20°), white (40°), beige (0°), beige (20°).

Participants evaluate at 11 levels of 0 (completely unknown) to 10 (very clearly understood) about how to see the boundary of the refracted part of the wall. This evaluation value was regarded as visibility. The experimenter told participants to answer without taking too much time, and the participants answered at the irradiation of each condition. When the participants completed the entry, the next irradiation condition was presented.

2.3 Results

From the experimental results, the results shown in Table 1 were obtained. Numbers indicate the average value of the values (visibility) evaluated under that condition. For all four types of walls, the visibility is higher as the irradiation angle is larger.

Table 1. Visibility of boundary by wall type and irradiation angle

		Irradiation angle		
		0°	20°	40°
Wall type	White	3.0	4.5	7.8
	Beige	2.0	3.5	8.0
	Gray	0.5	5.5	9.0
	White (concave-convex surface)	1.5	4.0	7.5

2.4 Discussion

As can be seen from Fig. 1, as the irradiation angle shifts from the front to the lateral row as 0°, 20°, 40°, the contrast on the right and left of the wall (the difference in brightness) is large. For all four types of walls, the visibility is higher as the irradiation angle is larger. (Table 1) From these facts, when grasping the shape of the wall, the contrast of the surfaces of the two walls is largely concerned, and the larger the comparison, the higher the visibility. According to Table 1, the gray was very low visibility of 0.5 at 0° (front). However, it can be seen that the gray rises remarkably as the irradiation angle changes and exceeds the other walls.

Here we compare the three colors of white, beige and gray at 0° (front) (Fig. 2). The numbers in parentheses are visibility.

White (3.0)   Beige (2.0)   Gray (0.5)

Fig. 2. Boundary comparison at 0° (front) (Color figure online)

Comparing Fig. 2, gray appears almost one color on one side, white and beige have no contrast on the surfaces of the two walls, but the boundaries of the folds of the walls are whitish glowing. From this, it was thought that the corner portion gathers a lot of light, that light is reflected and it looks brighter.

Therefore, it examined how the reflectance differs depending on the color. As shown in Table 2, the reflectance is white, beige and gray in descending order. Therefore, it was thought that it influenced the value of visibility especially at 0° (front) of this experiment.

Table 2. Reflectance of color diffusion surface [4]

Color	Reflectance [%]		
	Bright	Average	Dark
Yellow	70	50	30
Beige	65	45	25
Brown	50	25	8
Red	35	20	10
Green	60	30	12
Blue	50	20	5
Gray	60	35	20
White	80	70	-
Black	-	4	-

It was suggested that contrast of two sides and boundary line influenced visibility. Furthermore, it was found that the differences in the appearance due to the boundary line showed a difference depending on the color of the wall in the irradiation situation with low visibility, so that the difference in the reflectance due to the color also affects the visibility.

3 Experiment 2: Walking Survey of Persons with Low Vision Indoors

3.1 Purpose

When low-vision people walk, what kind of things influence their spatial perception. In this experiment, we aimed to clarify how people with low vision perceive space by physiological index (objective observation) and hearing (subjective evaluation) by applying the result of Experiment 1.

3.2 Participants

There were two participants (A:male 68 years old, B:female 52 years old). Both were with low-vision.

3.3 Methods

In the complex of hospital and research, we carried out the task of walking a predetermined route. Participant A walked during the day and participant B walked before the evening for walking.

3.4 Procedure

First, we interviewed participants on diseases and characteristics. Next, we installed and prepared the gaze measuring device to the participants and moved on the walking survey. Participants walked along a predetermined route with their caregivers. During walking, we let participants utter how they look and notice.

At the same time, the walking situation was recorded using a video camera and voice recorder, and the illuminance of the place walked with a luminometer was measured.

Table 3. Participant characteristics

	Participant A	Participant B
Sex	Male	Female
Age	68	52
Disease name	Retinitis pigmentosa	Retinitis pigmentosa (Dominant inheritance)
Vision	-	0.02–0.04
Viewing angle	About 30°	About 5°
Walking training experience	No	Yes
Use of white cane	No use	Always use
Frequency of going out alone	2–3 times/week	Every day
Main destination	Near supermarket	Work places

Furthermore, the gaze of the participants was recorded using the gaze measuring device. After walking, we interviewed participants mainly about walking contents.

3.5 Results

Participant characteristics
Table 3 summarizes the characteristics related to the appearance and usual activities of participants obtained by hearing.

Illuminance measurement result in space
Figures 3 and 4 show the illuminance in walking survey of participant A and participant B, respectively. The measurement location on the horizontal axis in the figure is arranged in the order in which the participants passed from the left.

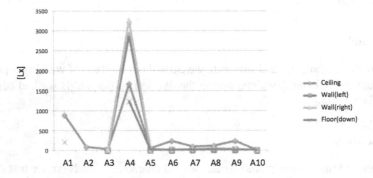

Fig. 3. The illuminance in walking of participant A

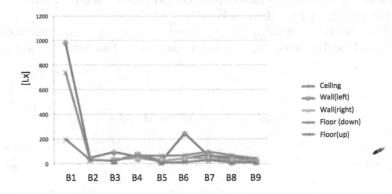

Fig. 4. The illuminance in walking of participant B

It can be seen that the illuminance of A4 (passage corridor) at participant A's walking is remarkably high. It can be seen that there is a large contrast between space and space like corridor - bridge corridor, bridge corridor - long corridor. In the case of participant A, the place with the lowest illuminance was A10. The illuminance here was lower than 10 lx, and the participants also gave a remark that "I can not see anything".

When Participant B walked, the change in illuminance was small compared to Participant A, and there were no places where it seemed to be dazzling. However, it was not dimly lit and dark, and it was not easy to walk.

Gaze analysis result Figures 5, 6, 7 and 8 show characteristic walking scenes and gaze trajectories. We extracted four characteristic scenes. "connecting corridor", "dark corridor", "long corridor - outward", "long corridor - return". We analyzed and compared the gaze trajectory and illuminance during walking in space. The features of each space extracted are as follows.

"connecting corridor": The left and right walls are glass-faced and the sunlight is plugged directly. The floor is white and glossy material.

"dark corridor": It is located between the hallway corridor and the long corridor and is dark because there is no lighting.

"long corridor - outward": Corridor of straight line. A row of illuminations is arranged on the ceiling. The deep side is a dead end and on the back side there is a glass wall. The floor is a gray carpet material and the left and right walls are white. There are no windows and dark blue doors are at approximately equal intervals.

"long corridor - return": Returning to "long corridor - outward". The back of the wall becomes a wall with a glass, and the dead end is on the back side.

In an environment with low illumination, the line of sight was easy to scatter, and it turned out that the scattering of the line of sight was noticeable immediately after moving from a particularly bright place to a dark place (Fig. 5). However, as the eyes adapt after a few seconds, the line of sight will be determined to some extent.

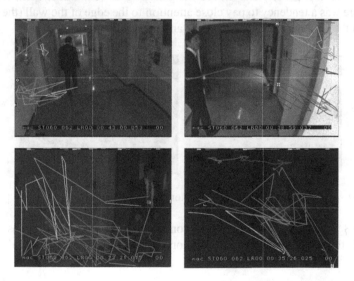

Fig. 5. A line of sight trajectory in a space with different illuminance

Particularly in a corridor with a particularly simple structure, participants have a tendency to pay close attention to the boundary between the wall and the floor on the side of walking. Also, when turning corners and dead ends, they were closely watching the front wall and the floor boundary (Fig. 6).

Fig. 6. Gaze trajectory confirming edge of space

As shown in Fig. 7, when posters are stretched on the wall or windows are lining up at regular intervals, participants moved the gaze to follow it. Also, when turning the corner, there was a tendency to pay close attention to the edge of the wall (the end part) rather than the boundary between the floor and the wall.

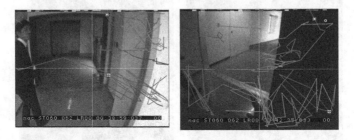

Fig. 7. Gaze trajectory of turning angle

Figure 8 shows a case where object confirmation during walking was observed, particularly those having confirmed the color and the texture of the material.

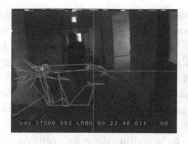

Fig. 8. The object confirmation

Hearing record on walking
We heard about the appearance of the wall and the color of a specific object several times by hearing while walking, and there was an opinion that "I am looking at the color by the reflection of light" among them. Regarding the door frame, the participants recognized that it is a metallic material from the reflection of light.

3.6 Discussion

Relationship between illuminance and eye movement
When comparing the illuminance measurement result and the line-of-sight trajectory analysis result, it was found that the gaze becomes easy to be scattered in an environment with low illuminance as shown in Fig. 5. Also, the scattering of the line of sight was noticeably observed immediately after moving from a particularly bright place to a dark place, but after a few seconds the line of sight became determined to some extent. From these facts, it can be indeicated that the absolute value (absolute viewpoint) in each space and the step (relative viewpoint) of the value existing between the space and space are necessary for the influence on the visibility by the illuminance.

In absolute terms, the illuminance in that space should be set simply. It is how to express the brightness of the illuminance and the appearance of the space. In this experiment, it was shown that the space where the illuminance is less than 10 is a dangerous value to walk, as participants were allowed to stop as they avoid collision like A10, B9.

In relative view, it is necessary to consider the difference in illuminance when moving from space to space. Participants said "Wow, dazzling" when a sudden illuminance change "low → high" was seen. When a sudden change in "high to low" of illuminance was observed, scattering of the line of sight was observed (Fig. 5). Therefore, from this survey, it was found that visibility became temporarily lowered and pedestrians feel discomfort if the difference in illuminance when moving from space to space is large.

Confirm edge of space when walking
From the gaze trajectory during walking recorded by the gaze measuring device, it turned out that the participants mainly confirmed the boundary of the space. There were scenes that confirm the boundary between the floor and the wall as in Fig. 6 and the scene to confirm the boundary between the walls as shown in Fig. 7.

Confirmation of the boundary between the floor and the wall occupied most of the gaze during walking. In a monotonous corridor of a single road, the participants mainly captured a certain position of the boundary between the floor and the wall. In scenes where there was a change in the spread of the space such as a parting road or a strike, the participants were looking around while following the boundary to explore its structure. Confirmation of the boundary of the wall was often seen in scenes where the dangers of collision are considered to be high, such as passing through corners and doors. Also in the corridor which is a monotonous structure it was confirmed. Therefore, confirmation of the boundary of the wall was thought to be mainly done for collision avoidance. In addition, it was thought that the perception of the spread of the space is supplemented by cognition based on the boundary between the floor and the wall.

Identification by reflected light
From the hearing results of the participants during walking, identification of the color/material of the object to be viewed was based on how to reflect the light and its extent. Furthermore, only the fire extinguisher was clearly recognized as red, while the navy color of the other door and the yellow color of the floor were recognized as a gray system. Three possibilities were considered regarding participants showing recognition of the color "fire extinguishers look red".

One is the possibility that red is recognized from other colors in color recognition and therefore it is a color that is easily recognizable even in the world seen by persons with low vision. Red is treated as a visible color that is easily perceived by sighted people, as it is also used for signs indicating danger and attention.

The second is the perception of color by matching between perceived information and memory. For example, a person judges that it is a vivid red color even if the post is seen in the dark. The color of the object (post) actually perceived through the eyes of the person is brown or nearly gray color, but from knowledge of the viewer's past experiences and memories, the object is recognized as red.

The third is correction of the color to be adjusted by the eye according to the state of the light surrounding the object. It is the same function as the so-called correction function of the camera, and is a function for making the actual color of the object more accurately recognized. The person with normal eyesight will compensate for changes in light due to weather, time of day, lighting conditions, etc. In addition to these, person with low vision may also be making corrections to their own appearance.

4   Conclusion and Future Works

In this research, we examined from the three viewpoints the relation between illuminance and eye movement, the edge confirmation of space, and identification by reflection light.

In the relationship between the illuminance and the movement of the line of sight, in a place where the illuminance is extremely low, the line of sight tends to be scattered and walking becomes difficult. Also, if there is a large difference in illuminance when moving from space to space, visibility is lowered or discomfort is felt.

In checking the edge of the space, it is important to confirm the boundary between the floor and the wall, the boundary of the wall according to the scene. it was found that the spread of the space was confirmed mainly at the boundary between the floor and the wall, and collision avoidance when turning through a corner or a door confirms the boundary (end) of the wall.

It was found that the color and material identification of the object being viewed was a clue as to how to reflect the light and its extent. Regarding cognition of red fire extinguishers, it is possible that three cognitive mechanisms, such as red coloring function, rubbing with memory, correction according to the state of light, are singular or mutually involved.

In the future research, we will explore the characteristics of the appearance of the low vision based on the findings on the appearance obtained in this research. We would like to conduct research aiming at extracting design elements that lead to QOL improvement while also incorporating approaches from a psychological point of view.

References

1. Ministry of Health, Labor and Welfare, Social & Aid Department, Disability Health and Welfare Department Planning Section: Results of actual survey on physical disabled children in 2006 (2008). (in Japanese)
2. Takahashi, H.: Actual of low vision care. To improve the quality of life for the visually impaired. Igaku-Shoin Ltd. (2006). (in Japanese)
3. Nakamura, Y.: The appearance of things and light, LISN, p. 118 (2004). (in Japanese)
4. Hirayama Takashi Architectural studies: 第 22 Interior Environmental Plan. Shokokusha Publishing Co. Ltd., Tokyo (1969). (in Japanese)

A Personal Relationship Analyzing Tool Based on Psychodrama Methodologies

Hidetsugu Suto$^{(\boxtimes)}$, Jun Maeda, and Patchanee Patitad

Graduate School of Engineer, Muroran Institute of Technology,
27 Mizumoto-cho, Muroran-shi, Hokkaido 050-8585, Japan
suto@sdlabo.net
http://www.sdlabo.net

Abstract. In modern societies, we need to face with various pressure that could lead us to mental illnesses. Human relationship is one of the well-known stressors despite it is a quite important for our daily life. To overcome cruel situations come from human relationship problems, sometimes we need any supporting systems. Psychodrama is one of the effective counseling methods which are used for solving several human relationship problems. The method has many advantages, on another front it has problems. The first, before conducting a Psychodrama event, we have to adjust our schedules. The second, some people do not want to talk about their human relationship problems for other people. These factors make difficult for us to conduct Psychodrama events easily. In this paper, a self psychotherapy tool is proposed as a approach for the problems. The proposed tool aims to produce similar results with original group therapy sessions of Psychodrama. To evaluate the proposed tool, an experiment was conducted. The results show that the tool can provide some hints for the users who had troubles in current human relationships and want to improve the situations.

Keywords: Psychodrama · Group therapy · Psychotherapy

1 Introduction

In modern societies, we cannot escape from various pressures that increase our mental burdens, and sometimes these incidents lead us to mental illnesses. Mental illness has negative effects on people both objective effects such as unemployment, social ostracism and reduce recovery orientation, and subjective psychological effects such as increased depression and reduced hopefulness and self-esteem [1].

Sometimes, we rely on advices from families and close friends to maintain mental health. In other words, many mental problems can be solved if sufferers can confide their troubles to get appropriate advices.

Human relationship is one of the well-known stressors despite it is quite important for our daily life [2]. Counseling with clinical psychologists is a way to relieve pressures and the stresses in human relationships. Counseling is a process

© Springer International Publishing AG 2017
S. Yamamoto (Ed.): HIMI 2017, Part II, LNCS 10274, pp. 614–622, 2017.
DOI: 10.1007/978-3-319-58524-6_50

of assisting persons who have any mental anguishes carried out by counselors through various number of service approaches [3].

Psychodrama is one of the effective counseling methods which are used for solving several human relationship problems. Psychodrama is a kind of group psychotherapy conducted with a director and the other members. Psychodrama has many advantages, on another front it has problems. The first, before conducting a Psychodrama event, the Participants have to adjust their schedules. The second, some people do not want to talk about their human relationship problems for other people. These factors make difficult for us to conduct Psychodrama events easily. In this paper, a self psychotherapy tool is proposed as a approach for the problems. The proposed tool is designed based on the basic idea of Psychodrama. It aims to produce similar results with original group therapy sessions of Psychodrama.

The outline of Psychodrama is introduced in Sect. 2. Next, the proposed tool is explained in Sect. 3. In Sect. 4, experiments conducted for showing the effects of the tool, and the results are described. Finally, the outcome of the proposed tool are discussed and concluded in Sects. 5 and 6.

2   Psychodrama

Psychodrama was developed by Jacob Moreno [4] in the early 1900s. The scope of the method is about the relationships with one or more people, e.g. members of a family, friends, acquaintances or colleagues, and with ourselves, or, the relationship between groups.

Psychodrama aims to make the clients (persons with some mental problems) understand their own human relationship problems deeply. Classical Psychodrama refers to a method of group psychotherapies in which clients are encouraged to continue and complete their actions through dramatization, role playing, and dramatic self-presentation. Both verbal and nonverbal communications are utilized in these activities. A number of scenes are enacted depicting, for example, memories of specific happenings in the past, unfinished situations, inner drama, fantasies, dreams, preparations for future risk-taking situations, or simply unrehearsed expressions of mental states in the here and now [5].

Because Psychodrama can help people to watch themselves and their situations from an outside perspective, Psychodrama sessions often can be a safe place for people to explore new solutions for difficulties or challenges [6]. Psychodrama shows potential for bringing about positive changes in participants. Through psychodrama, participants are often able to develop their use of language and perspective as they use action methods to explore past, present, or future occurrences [7].

Psychodrama sessions are often performed as weekly group therapy sessions, typically comprised of 8–12 members. Usually, sessions last between 90 min and 2 h. Each Psychodrama session focuses on a life situation of one individual, with group members taking on roles as needed [9].

To perform psychodrama session, these five roles are required:

Protagonist
A person who has a trouble in his/her human relationships and wants to solve it.
Auxilliary
A person who acts as significant person of the client.
Audience
A person who watches the drama. Sometimes, they become supporters.
Stage
A scene of the drama, e.g. living room in a house, class room in a school, etc.

A Psychodrama event is executed in three phases as follows:

Warm-Up Phase. The goals of the warm-up phase are building trusted relationships among the members, strengthen unity of the members, and relaxing the members. The director has to support the members to achieve the goals. Usually, all members introduce themselves followed by conducting small communication games.

Action Phase. After warm-up phase, a topic related human relationship problems is provided by the director. A participant who has troubles about the topic becomes the protagonist of the session. Then the director instructs the protagonist to recreate a scene in the past which causes the troubles in the protagonist's mind. auxilliary members will be chosen by the protagonist to play all the elements in the scene. The rest of the group members act as audiences. There are four techniques commonly used in action phase:

Role-reversal. The protagonist enacts the role of a significant person (auxilliary), while an auxilliary plays the roles as protagonist. With this technique, the protagonist can understand the other persons' role and get new perspectives on the underlying personal issues.
Mirroring. The protagonist become an observer while an auxilliary takes the place of the protagonist on the stage. This technique enables protagonists to be an observer of their issues and the scenes surrounding them.
Doubling. A group member acts the protagonist's behaviors and movements. He/she guesses the protagonist's feelings and thoughts, and expresses them aloud with emotion. This technique helps members to build empathies for the protagonist in the protagonist's actions.
Soliloquy. The protagonist walks around the stage with saying anything he/she noticed aloud. The physical activity, i.e. working, facilitates to express ideas and emotions intuitively.

Sharing Phase. After action phase, director changes the role as a therapist, and facilitate discussions about the drama. Sharing phase provides the members a time for discussing about the drama that took place in the action phase. Participants can exchange their experiences which are evoked from the drama [10].

3   Self Psychodrama Simulation Tool

In this paper, A self Psychodrama simulation tool is proposed based on the basic idea of actual Psychodrama. By using this tool, the users can visualize their human relationships, and they can gain experiences as same as from mirroring technique in action phase. The aim of this tool is to help the user to grasp their problems from different perspectives.

The proposed tool consists of a sheet which have two spaces to make association diagrams and stickers on which an eyes mark is printed. With the proposed tool, users can make association diagrams which represent a relationship among dominant peoples around them.

Example of a created association diagrams are shown in Fig. 1.

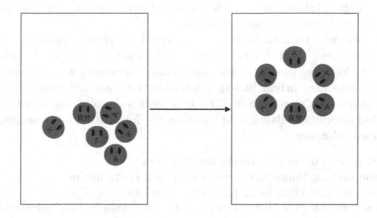

Fig. 1. Examples of created association diagrams (Color figure online)

The left side diagram stands for the current human relationships of the user. Meanwhile, the right side diagram stands for an ideal human relationship of the user, which the user though after making the current situation. The blue circles with eyes mark stand for the user and dominant persons of him/her. The distance between two circles stand for mental distance between the two persons. It represents a level of affinity with others which the user feels. Each direction of eyes indicates attitudes of the person.

A circle which stands for the user is printed in the middle of the space by turning the eyes up in advance. First, user writes initials of his/her dominant people on stickers one by one to distinguish individuals. Next, user makes an association diagram which represent his/her current human relationship by putting stickers on the left side of the sheet. Then, user makes an ideal association diagram of him/her on the right side of the sheet similarly.

4   Evaluation the Proposed Tool

To evaluate the proposed tool, an experiment has been conducted. In this experiment, the volunteers were asked to use the tool and fill out subjective questionnaires about usability of the tool. Detail of the experiment is described as follows:

- Date: December 21, 2016
- Time: 17:25–17:40
- Place: Muroran Institute of Technology, Hokkaido, JAPAN
- Volunteers: 119 Japanese students (19–21 years old)
- Evaluation method: subjective questionnaires

Because the tool is implemented for Japanese, all informations were given in Japanese. Figure 2 shows an image of sheet (A3 size) used for making association diagrams. Figure 3 shows an image of the questionnaire sheet. The questionnaire includes both of open and close questions.

Volunteers who thought to want to change the current human relationships and have made an ideal diagram were asked "what you can do for changing the relationships like this?" On the other hand, volunteers who did not feel to want to change the current human relationships were asked "why you do not want to change the relationships?" Besides, each volunteer was asked to name the created association diagram. In addition, the following closed questions were given for all volunteers:

1. Was it easy to make the association diagrams?
2. Did you find anythings in the current human relationships?
3. Can you get any hints for improving your relationships?
4. Do you think this tool helps you to understand your current relationships?
5. What can you know by making the association diagrams?

To evaluate the usability of the proposed tool, the first four questions adopt four ordinal level of measurement. The last question adopts nine nominal level of measurement; 1. ways to solve problems, 2. presence of your supporters, 3. presence of your important people, 4. relationships needed to change, 5. relationships which do not want to change, 6. I can do something, 7. I can do nothing, 8. I need help, 9. others (free description).

The step of the experiment is as follows:

Step 1. Fill out their personal data (such as gender, ages, have a trouble or not and need to change the relationship or not) in the left side area.
Step 2. Make an association diagram for the current relationships in the middle area.
Step 3. Consider the created diagram, then think whether they want to change the situation or not.
Step 4. Make another association diagram which represents an ideal relationships in the right side area of the sheet. Volunteers who did not feel to want to change the current relationships do not have to perform this step.
Step 5. Fill out the subjective questionnaires.

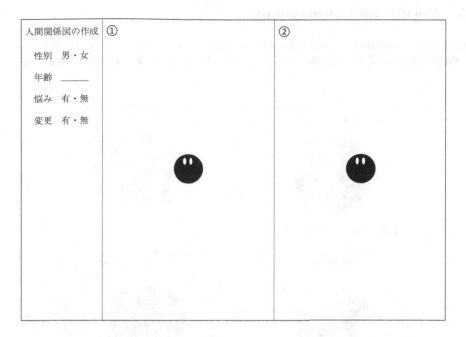

Fig. 2. The template of association diagram

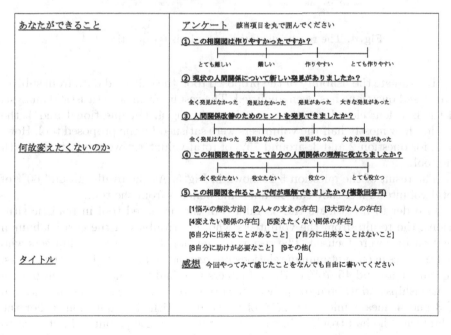

Fig. 3. The example of the subjective questionnaire

5   Results and Discussions

In the 119 volunteers, there were 42 volunteers who had troubles in their human relationships and 28 volunteers who wanted to change their current diagram.

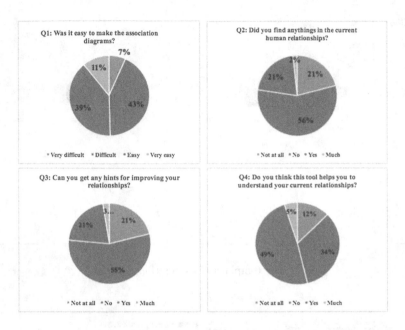

Fig. 4. The results of statistics analysis for question 1–4

To evaluate the usability of the proposed tool, the collected data from subjective closed questions has been analyzed. The results from the statistical analysis of the first four closed questions are shown in Fig. 4. For question 1 and 4, the results show mostly half the volunteers were satisfied by the proposed tool. However, for question 2 and 3, around 75% of total volunteers were unsatisfied with the tool.

The result of the question 5 is shown in Fig. 5. As the result, around 60% of total volunteers feel they can obtain some benefits from the tool.

In order to investigate the usefulness of the proposed tool in realistic situations, the results from the volunteers who had troubles in the current human relationships were focused. The results of question 1–5 from the volunteers who had troubles in current human relationships are shown in Fig. 6. From the results, we can see around 45–70% of the volunteers who had troubles in current human relationships and wanted to change the current diagram are satisfied in question 1, 3 and 4, meanwhile, only 25% of them are satisfied in question 2. For the volunteers who had troubles in current human relationships but did not want to change the current diagram, around half of them are satisfied in question 1, 2 and 4. However, only 18.2% of them are satisfied in question 3.

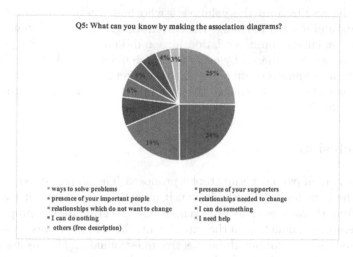

Fig. 5. The result of statistics analysis for question 5

Q1: Was it easy to make the association diagrams?		
	Satisfied	Unsatisfied
Trouble:Change (20人)	45%	55%
Trouble:Unchanging (22人)	45.5%	54.5%

Q2: Did you find anythings in the current human relationships?		
	Satisfied	Unsatisfied
Trouble:Change (20人)	25%	75%
Trouble:Unchanging (22人)	45.5	54.5%

Q3: Can you get any hints for improving your relationships?		
	Satisfied	Unsatisfied
Trouble:Change (20人)	50%	50%
Trouble:Unchanging (22人)	18.2%	81.8%

Q4: Do you think this tool helps you to understand your current relationships?		
	Satisfied	Unsatisfied
Trouble:Change (20人)	70%	30%
Trouble:Unchanging (22人)	54.5%	45.5%

Q5: What can you know by making the association diagrams?		
	Satisfied	Unsatisfied
Trouble:Change (20人)	84%	16%
Trouble:Unchanging (22人)	90%	10%

Fig. 6. The results of statistics analysis for question 1–5 from the volunteers who have a trouble in their human relationships

Then, the results from the volunteers who had troubles in current human relationships and wanted to change the current diagram, and the volunteers who had troubles in current human relationships and do not want to change the current diagram, were compared by using t-test (significant level: 0.05). The result shows there are significant difference of satisfaction level for question 3 between the volunteers who want to change the current diagram and the volunteers who do not want to change the current diagram.

6   Conclusion

In this paper, a self psychotherapy tool is proposed. The proposed tool is designed based on the basic idea of Psychodrama. It aims to produce similar results with original group therapy sessions of Psychodrama. To evaluate the proposed tool, a experiment was conducted. In the experiment, the volunteers were asked to use the proposed tool and fill out the subjective questionnaire. The results show the tool could provide some hints for the person who have a trouble in their mind and need to improve the relationships. As the results, we can say the proposed tool is a useful approach for self psychotherapy. For more handy using, an application which developed based on the idea of the proposed tool should be considered.

Acknowledgement. This work was supported by Grants-in-Aid for Scientific Research from Japan Society for the Promotion of Science (NO. 26330376, 26350013, and 15K00486).

References

1. Drapalski, A.L., Lucksted, A., Perrin, P.B., Aakre, J.M., Brown, C.H., DeForge, B.R.: A model of internalized stigma and its effects on people with mental illness. Psychiatr. Serv. **64**(3), 264–269 (2013)
2. Goldman, E.E.: Phychodrama-Experience and Process. Kango Publishing, Japan (2013)
3. Sulaiman, H., Kamaluddin Megat Daud, M.A.: The application of information technology among trainee counselors. Procedia Soc. Behav. Sci. **103**, 963–969 (2013)
4. Moreno, J.L.: Psychodrama, vol. 1. Beacon House, New York (1985)
5. Kellermann, P.F.: Outcome research in classical psychodrama. Small Group Behav. **18**(4), 459–469 (1987)
6. GoodTherapy. http://www.goodtherapy.org
7. Yehoshua, Chung, S.F.: A review of psychodrama and group process. Int. J. Soc. Work Hum. Serv. Pract. **1**(2), 105–114 (2013)
8. Anderson-Klontz, B.T., Dayton, T., Angerson-Klontz, L.S.: The use of psychodramatic techniques within solution-focused brief therapy: a theoretical and Technical Integration. Int. J. Action Method **2**, 113–120 (1999)
9. Clayton, G.M.: Enhancing Life and Relationship: A Role Training Manual. ICA Press, Caulfield (1992)
10. Dayton, T.: The Living Stage. Health Communications Inc, Deerfield Beach (2005)

The Effects of Group Size in the Furniture Assembly Task

Noriko Suzuki[1]([✉]), Mayuka Imashiro[2], Mamiko Sakata[2],
and Michiya Yamamoto[3]

[1] Faculty of Business Administration, Tezukayama University,
7-7-1 Tezukayama, Nara City, Nara 631-8501, Japan
nsuzuki@tezukayama-u.ac.jp
[2] Department of Culture and Information Science, Doshisha University,
1-3 Tatara Miyakodani, Kyotanabe, Kyoto 610-0394, Japan
[3] School of Science and Technology, Kwansei Gakuin University,
2-1, Gakuen, Sanda, Hyogo 669-1337, Japan

Abstract. Does the number of additional participants affect the physical performance or the psychological evaluation of participants on carrying out a task? This paper examines the effects of group size, either individuals, two-party or five-party, using the furniture assembly task. We use three behavioral indexes, i.e. degree of completion, time-to-completion, and duration of interaction with materials, in a physical performance evaluation. Furthermore, we use three psychological indexes, i.e., degrees of contribution, satisfaction, and familiarity, in a psychological evaluation. In duration of interaction with materials, time-to-completion, and degree of contribution, the members of two-person groups take longer or feel more individually significant than do the members of five-person groups. These results suggest that social loafing effects have emerged by increasing the number of participants. We expect these findings to help in designing relationality among people as well as between people and artifacts.

Keywords: Multiparty interaction · Effects of group size · Furniture assembly task · Social loafing · Social facilitation

1 Introduction

In our everyday life, the presence of others has the effect of improving the group performance of tasks, while it may also reduce an individual's performance. The former phenomenon is called social facilitation, and the latter is called social inhibition or social loafing [2,4,7].

This paper focuses on how group size affects the physical performance or psychological evaluation of the participants carrying out cooperative work in a group setting. In other words, we are interested in how different numbers of other participants facilitate or inhibit interaction during the task.

© Springer International Publishing AG 2017
S. Yamamoto (Ed.): HIMI 2017, Part II, LNCS 10274, pp. 623–632, 2017.
DOI: 10.1007/978-3-319-58524-6_51

A recent study on the group size effect pointed out that the difference in the number of participants, i.e., between five-person groups and ten-person groups, affected different aspects of group discussion [1]. On the other hand, a related study reported that groups perform better than individuals and that three-person groups showed better performance than two-, four- or five-person groups in a letters-to-numbers task [3]. However, few research works have analyzed both the physical performance and the psychological of the participants conducting collaborative physical tasks.

In this paper's task, people were instructed to assemble a piece of furniture, a bed-side table, consisting of six wooden boards and fifty-four screws and other hardware. We chose this task by referring to the TV-cart assembly task [5] and the large-structure assembly task [6]. Moreover, we analyzed the task using both behavioral and psychological indexes. To this end, we investigated whether the differences in group size in the furniture assembly task inhibit or facilitate the individual's involvement in the task.

Our research aim is to find a simple strategy of designing relationality among people from the viewpoint of the relationship between group size and the division of labor through the assembly task.

2   Method

2.1   Predictions

Physical performance. We predict that five-person groups will complete the task with shorter time than individuals or two-person groups because the members of five-person groups have many hands. On the other hand, the duration of interaction with materials in five-person groups will be shorter than that in individuals or two-person groups as a result of too many people being involved in the task.

Psychological evaluation. We predict that the members of five-person groups will feel lower degrees of contribution, satisfaction, and familiarity than the members of two-person groups because they will engage in the task for a shorter duration of interaction with the materials than the members of two-person groups.

2.2   Participants

A total of 54 graduate and undergraduate students (mean age: 20.778 years, SD: 1.449) participated in the experiment. They were randomly assigned to individuals, two-person or five-person groups. No participant was assigned a particular role in the task. Six individuals, nine two-person, and six five-person groups took part in the furniture assembly task.

2.3   Procedure

Each group was instructed to assemble the furniture as soon as possible (Fig. 1 (left)). They had to build a bed-side table, OLTEDAL of IKEA International Group, by using six boards and eight kinds of screws and other hardware, fifty-four parts totally, with an electric screwdriver according to graphical instructions (Fig. 1 (right)).

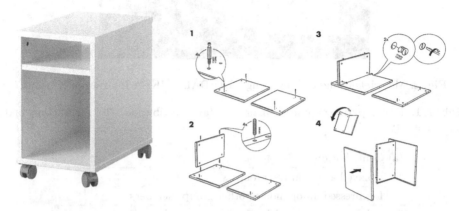

Fig. 1. Completed picture of a bed-side table and portion of instructions for the task of assembling furniture by using OLTEDAL of IKEA International Group

The characteristics of the task were: (a) it took thirty-minutes by a three-person group in a preliminary experiment, (b) it required the division of roles, i.e., carrying the boards, turning the screws with the screwdriver, checking the instructions, and (c) it was difficult to explain the graphical instructions without any caption text.

2.4   Materials

We prepared a bed-side table consisting of flat wooden boards as the target object of this furniture-assembly task. Figure 2 shows the experimental materials, consisting of 6 boards, 8 kinds of screws, fasteners, and castors (54 parts in total), an electric screwdriver, and an instruction sheet.

2.5   Parameters

Behavioral indexes. The experimenter calculated the following individuals or group performances as behavioral indexes.
1. **Degree of completion.** Whether participants were determined to succeed in building the bed-side table or gave up building it.
2. **TTC (Time-to-completion).** The amount of time required for the furniture assembly task to be completed.

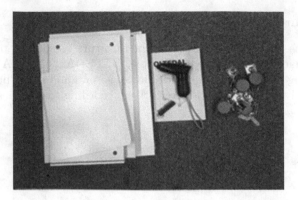

Fig. 2. Materials of the task by using OLTEDAL of IKEA International Group

Table 1. Post-experiment questionnaire on (a) contribution, (b) satisfaction and (c) familiarity

(a) Contribution	
1	I played a role in the group
2	I expressed an opinion to other group members
3	I shared opinions with other group members
4	I engaged actively in the task
(b) Satisfaction	
5	I was happy throughout the experiment
6	I felt a sense of accomplishment when the task was finished
(c) Familiarity	
7	I fit in well with other group members
8	I adapted to the group
9	I had a good time participating in this experiment
10	I spoke my opinions freely throughout the task
11	I interacted with other group members in a natural way
12	I agreed with other group members' opinions
13	I felt relaxed while engaged in the task
14	I cooperated with my group members throughout the task

3. **Duration of interaction with materials.** The amount of time duration of interaction with the materials, i.e., the boards, the screws, the
   screwdriver, and the instruction, per minute for an individual, one two-
   person group and one five-person group.

Psychological indexes. The experimenter examined the results of the following questions answered on a seven-point scale through a post-experiment
   questionnaire.

1. **Degree of contribution.** Four questions on the participant's degree of contribution to the task (Table 1(a)).
2. **Degree of satisfaction.** Two questions on the participant's degree of satisfaction with the task performance (Table 1(b)).
3. **Degree of familiarity.** Eight questions on the participant's degree of familiarity with other participants (Table 1(c)).

3 Results

3.1 Behavioral Indexes

Table 2 and Fig. 4(a) show the results of a chi-square test of the degree of completion for six individuals, nine two-person, and six five-person groups. As a result of a chi-square test, there were significant differences among individuals, two-person, and five-person groups ($\chi^2(2) = 8.986$, $p < 0.05$). The results of residual analysis suggest that five-person groups succeeded in building a bed-side table, although the individuals did not succeed.

Table 2. 2×3 contingency table for successful or unsuccessful groups among three group sizes

Group size		Successful groups	Unsuccessful groups
Individuals	Num. of groups	1	5
	Adjusted residuals	−2.7	2.7
Two-person	Num. of groups	6	3
	Adjusted residuals	0.4	−0.4
Five-person	Num. of groups	6	0
	Adjusted residuals	2.3	−2.3

Figure 4(b) shows the results of time-to-completion (TTC) for six individuals, nine two-person groups, and six five-person groups. As a result of ANOVA, there was a significant tendency in TTC among the three group sizes ($F(2) = 3.103$, $p = 0.07$). From multiple comparisons, there are significant tendencies between individuals and five-person groups ($p = 0.073$). It has been suggested that five-person groups had shorter time-to-completion than individuals.

Figure 4(c) shows the results of duration of interaction with materials for a individuals, a two-person group, and a five-person group. As a result of ANOVA, there was a significant difference among the three groups ($F(2) = 27.328$ $p = 0.002$). This result suggests that the members of the individuals and two-person groups took a longer time to interact with materials than did the five-person group. Figure 3 shows the distribution of the duration of interaction with materials throughout the task.

From these results, our predictions were partly supported.

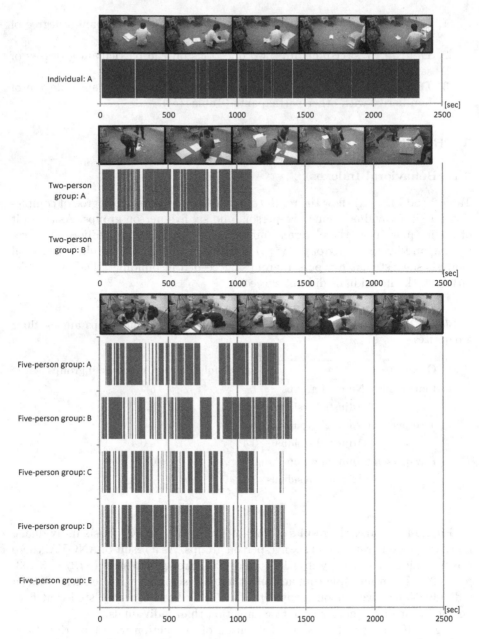

Fig. 3. Distribution of duration of interaction with materials: an individual (upper), a two-person group (middle), and a five-person group (lower)

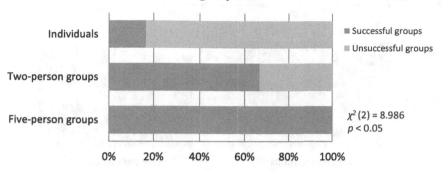

(a) Ratio of successful and unsuccessful groups among three group sizes

Individuals

■ Successful groups
■ Unsuccessful groups

Two-person groups

Five-person groups

$\chi^2(2) = 8.986$
$p < 0.05$

0%   20%   40%   60%   80%   100%

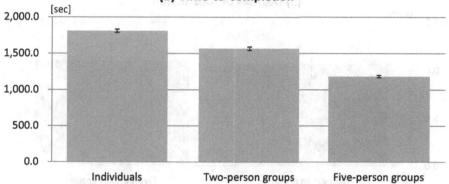

(b) Time-to-completion

[sec]

2,000.0

1,500.0

1,000.0

500.0

0.0

Individuals   Two-person groups   Five-person groups

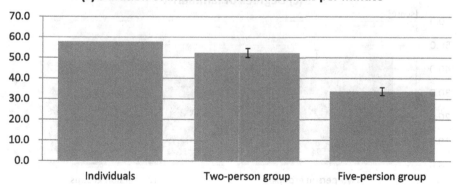

(c) Duration of interaction with materials per minute

70.0
60.0
50.0
40.0
30.0
20.0
10.0
0.0

Individuals   Two-person group   Five-persion group

Fig. 4. Results of behavioral indexes: (a) ratio of successful and unsuccessful groups among three group sizes, (b) time-to-completion, and (c) duration of interaction with materials per minute

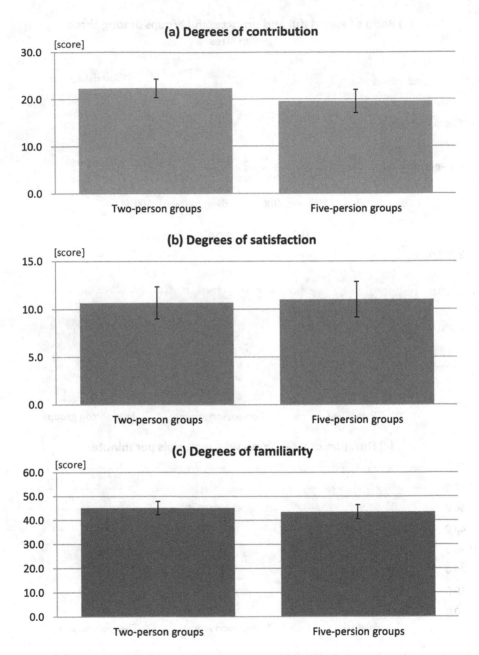

Fig. 5. Results of psychological indexes: (a) degrees of contribution, (b) degrees of satisfaction, and (c) degrees of familiarity

3.2 Psychological Indexes

Figure 5 show the results of the psychological indexes, i.e., the degrees of contribution (upper), satisfaction (middle), and familiarity (lower) for nine two-person groups and six five-person groups.

Figure 5(a) shows the results of degree of contribution. As a result of the unpaired t-test, a significant difference was found in the degree of contribution to the task between two-person and five-person groups ($t = 1.900$, $p = 0.064$). This result suggests that the members of two-person groups felt a greater need to contribute to the furniture assembly task than did the members of five-person groups.

Figure 5(b) shows the results of degree of satisfaction. As a result of the unpaired t-test, there was no significant difference in the degree of satisfaction with task performance between two-person and five-person groups ($t = -0.364$, $p = 0.718$).

Figure 5(c) shows the results of degree of familiarity. As a result of the unpaired t-test, there was no significant difference in the degree of familiarity with other participants between two-person and five-person groups ($t = 0.662$, $p = 0.512$).

From these results, our predictions were partly supported.

4   Conclusion

In this study, we examined the effect of group size among individuals, two-person, and five-person groups in the furniture assembly task. From the results of behavioral indexes, a individuals was apt to give up building a bed-side table. On the other hand, both two-person and five-person groups were apt to advance toward success. Moreover, individuals and two-person groups seemed to take a longer duration to interact with materials than did five-person groups. From the results of psychological indexes, the members of two-person groups seemed to feel they made a greater contribution to the furniture assembly task than did the members of five-person groups. Considering the effect of group size in the furniture assembly task, these results suggest that social loafing effects emerged by increasing the number of participants. In other words, our results can be understood as supporting the results from the studies of both Ingham et al. and Latane et al. [2,4].

As future work, we will analyze the behavioral indexes of more groups to test our predictions. In addition, the same experiment with other group sizes, i.e., three-person and four-person groups, should be conducted to gather findings on the most appropriate group size for the furniture assembly task. We expect these findings to help in designing relationality among people as well as between people and artifacts through the assembly task.

Acknowledgments. The findings of this study are based on the second author's graduation thesis. We thank 54 students of Doshisha University for their participation in the experiment. This work was supported by JSPS KAKENHI Grant Numbers JP16H03225 and JP15K00219.

References

1. Fay, N., Garrod, S., Carletta, J.: Group discussion as interactive dialogue or as serial monologue: the influence of group size. J. Psychol. Sci. **11**(6), 481–486 (2000)
2. Ingham, A.G., Levinger, G., Graves, J., Peckham, V.: The Ringelmann effect: studies of group size and group performance. J. Exp. Soc. Psychol. **10**, 371–384 (1974)
3. Laughlin, P.R., Hatch, E.C., Silver, J.S., Boh, L.: Groups perform better than the best individuals on letters-to-numbers problems: effects of group size. J. Pers. Soc. Psychol. **90**(4), 644–651 (2006)
4. Latane, B., Williams, K., Harkins, S.: Many hands make light the work: the causes and consequences of social loafing. J. Pers. Soc. Psychol. **37**, 822–832 (1979)
5. Lozano, S.C., Tversky, B.: Communicative gestures benefit communicators. In: Proceedings of CogSci 2004 (2004)
6. Suzuki, N., Umata, I., Kamiya, T., Ito, S., Iwasawa, S., Inoue, N., Toriyama, T., Kogure, K.: Nonverbal behaviors in cooperative work: a case study of successful and unsuccessful team. In: Proceedings of CogSci 2007, pp. 1527–1532 (2007)
7. Yamaguchi, S., Okamoto, K., Oka, T.: Effects of coactor's presence: social loafing and social facilitation. Jpn. Psychol. Res. **27**(4), 215–222 (1985)

Author Index

Printed in the United States
By Bookmasters